RACE and CRIME

Titles of Related Interest

Lawrence and Hemmens: *Juvenile Justice: A Text/Reader*
Stohr, Walsh, and Hemmens: *Corrections: A Text/Reader*
Spohn and Hemmens: *Courts: A Text/Reader*
Lilly, Cullen, and Ball: *Criminological Theory* (4th edition)
Wright, Tibbetts, and Daigle: *Criminals in the Making*
Walsh and Ellis: *Criminology: An Interdisciplinary Perspective*
Hagan: *Introduction to Criminology* (6th edition)
Crutchfield, Kubrin, Weiss, and Bridges: *Crime: Readings* (3rd edition)
Van Dijk: *The World of Crime*
Felson: *Crime and Everyday Life* (4th edition)
Hagan: *Crime Types and Criminals*
Hanser: *Community Corrections*
Mosher and Akins: *Drugs and Drug Policy*
Bachman and Schutt: *The Practice of Research in Criminology and Criminal Justice* (3rd edition)
Bachman and Schutt: *Fundamentals of Research in Criminology and Criminal Justice*
Loggio and Dowdall: *Adventures in Criminal Justice Research* (4th edition)
Gabbidon and Greene: *Race and Crime* (2nd edition)
Helfgott: *Criminal Behavior*
Bartol and Bartol: *Forensic Psychology* (2nd edition)
Banks: *Criminal Justice Ethics* (2nd edition)
Lippman: *Contemporary Criminal Law* (2nd edition)
Lippman: *Criminal Procedure*
Hemmens, Brody, and Spohn: *Criminal Courts*
Holmes and Holmes: *Profiling Violent Crime* (4th edition)
Holmes and Holmes: *Sex Crimes* (3rd edition)
Alvarez and Bachman: *Violence*
Howell: *Preventing and Reducing Juvenile Delinquency* (2nd edition)
Cox, Allan, Hanser, and Conrad: *Juvenile Justice* (6th edition)
Mahan and Griset: *Terrorism in Perspective* (2nd edition)
Martin: *Understanding Terrorism* (3rd edition)
Martin: *Essentials of Terrorism*

RACE and CRIME
A Text/Reader

Helen Taylor Greene
Texas Southern University
Shaun L. Gabbidon
Penn State Harrisburg

Los Angeles | London | New Delhi
Singapore | Washington DC

Los Angeles | London | New Delhi
Singapore | Washington DC

FOR INFORMATION:

SAGE Publications, Inc.
2455 Teller Road
Thousand Oaks, California 91320
E-mail: order@sagepub.com

SAGE Publications Ltd.
1 Oliver's Yard
55 City Road
London EC1Y 1SP
United Kingdom

SAGE Publications India Pvt. Ltd.
B 1/I 1 Mohan Cooperative Industrial Area
Mathura Road, New Delhi 110 044
India

SAGE Publications Asia-Pacific Pte. Ltd.
33 Pekin Street #02-01
Far East Square
Singapore 048763

Acquisitions Editor: Jerry Westby
Editorial Assistant: Erim Sarbuland
Production Editor: Catherine M. Chilton
Copy Editor: Jenifer Dill
Typesetter: C&M Digitals (P) Ltd.
Proofreader: Jennifer Gritt
Indexer: Molly Hall
Cover Designer: Gail Buschman
Marketing Manager: Erica DeLuca
Permissions: Karen Ehrmann and Sherri Gilbert

Printed in the United States of America

Library of Congress Cataloging-in-Publication Data

Race and crime : a text/reader / Helen Taylor Greene, Shaun L. Gabbidon.

p. cm.
Includes bibliographical references and index.

ISBN 978-1-4129-8907-7 (pbk.)

1. Crime and race—United States. 2. Criminal justice, Administration of—United States. 3. Discrimination in criminal justice administration—United States. 4. Minorities—United States. I. Greene, Helen Taylor, 1949-
II. Gabbidon, Shaun L., 1967-

HV6197.U5R325 2012
364.2′56—dc22
2010046788

This book is printed on acid-free paper.

11 12 13 14 15 10 9 8 7 6 5 4 3 2 1

Brief Contents

Detailed Contents

Section III. Theoretical Perspectives on Race and Crime 95

Readings 110

Section IV. Juvenile Justice 169

Foreword

You hold in your hands a book that we think is something new. It is billed as a "text/reader." What that means is that we have attempted to blend the two most commonly used types of books, the textbook and the reader, in a way that will appeal to both students and faculty.

Our experience as teachers and scholars has been that textbooks for the core classes in criminal justice and criminology (or any other social science discipline) leave many students and professors cold. The textbooks are huge, crammed with photographs, charts, highlighted material, and all sorts of pedagogical devices intended to increase student interest. Too often, though, these books end up creating a sort of sensory overload for students; they suffer from a focus on "bells and whistles," such as fancy graphics, at the expense of coverage of the most current research on the subject matter.

Readers, on the other hand, are typically comprised of recent and classic research articles on the subject matter. They generally suffer, however, from an absence of meaningful explanatory material. Articles are simply lined up and presented to the students, with little or no context or explanation. Students, particularly undergraduate students, are often confused and overwhelmed.

This text/reader represents our attempt to take the best of both the textbook and reader approaches. It is comprised of research articles on race and crime and is intended to serve either as a supplement to a core textbook or as a stand-alone text. The book includes a combination of previously published articles and textual material that introduces and provides some structure and context for the selected readings. The book is divided into a number of sections. The sections follow the typical content and structure of a textbook on the subject. Each section of the book has an overview of the topic that serves to introduce, explain, and provide context for the readings that follow. The readings are a selection of the best recent research that has appeared in academic journals, as well as some classic readings. The articles are edited as necessary. This variety of research and perspectives will provide students with an understanding of both the development of research and the current status of research on race and crime. This approach gives the student the opportunity to learn the basics (in the text portion of each section) and to read some of the most interesting research on the subject.

There is also a Preface and Introduction that explains the organization and content of the book and provides context for the articles that follow. This introductory chapter provides a framework for the text and articles that follow and introduces relevant themes, issues, and concepts. This will assist the student in understanding the articles.

Each section also includes a summary of the material covered and a selection of discussion questions. These summaries and discussion questions should facilitate student thought and class discussion of the material.

We acknowledge that this approach may be viewed by some as more challenging than the traditional textbook. To that we say, "Yes! It is!" But we believe that if we raise the bar, our students will rise to the challenge. Research shows that students and faculty often find textbooks boring to read. It is our belief that many criminology and criminal justice instructors would welcome the opportunity to teach without having to rely on a standard textbook that covers only the most basic information and that lacks both depth of coverage and an attention to current research. This book provides an alternative for instructors who want to get more out of the basic criminal justice courses or curriculum than one can get from a basic textbook that is aimed at the lowest common denominator and is filled with flashy but often useless features that merely serve to drive up the cost of the textbook. This book is intended for instructors who want to go beyond the ordinary, basic coverage provided in textbooks.

We also believe students will find this approach more interesting. They are given the opportunity to read current, cutting-edge research on the subject, while also being provided with background and context for this research. We hope that this unconventional approach will make learning and teaching more fun. Race and criminology are fascinating subjects, and they deserve to be presented in an interesting manner. We hope you will agree.

Craig Hemmens, JD, PhD
Department of Criminal Justice
Boise State University

We dedicate this book to Jerry Westby, our Acquisitions Editor at Sage Publications, Inc. His support of our scholarship has assisted us in realizing our vision of producing unique and meaningful contributions that will help transform the body of knowledge on race, ethnicity, and crime in the study of criminology and criminal justice.

Preface and Introduction

Race and crime continues to be a significant area of study in criminology and criminal justice. Some authors have suggested that "all roads in American criminology eventually lead to issues of race" (LaFree & Russell, 1993, p. 273). Thus, while scholars may want to avoid the controversy surrounding the race and crime debate, there are few areas of the discipline where it does not emerge. A cursory review of many of the leading and other journals in the discipline will find a strong contingent of articles pertaining to race. There are now journals and institutes in the discipline solely devoted to the study of race, ethnicity, and crime. Unfortunately, though, citizens and scholars alike have remained locked into misperceptions about race and crime (Covington, 2010; Mann, Zatz, & Rodriguez, 2006). For example, when we talk about street crime, many people assume we are talking about Blacks and Hispanics. Yet when we talk about corporate crime, the assumption is that we are talking about a White male offender. The reality is that all groups commit all types of crime, and such misperceptions lead to stereotypical views on crime. It is encouraging that in the last two decades, the discipline has moved toward a more open dialogue on race and crime. This can be seen by the fact that race and crime is a recognized specialty area within the discipline.

One of the strongest indicators that race and crime has become integrated as an area of study is the fact that many criminology departments now either require students to take a course in the area or offer the course as an elective. Consequently, within the discipline, there has emerged an assortment of texts and readers that focus on the topic.

This book is a text/reader that includes a combination of textual material and recent articles on race and crime. It is an alternative to traditional textbooks and readers used in the study of criminology and criminal justice. Unlike a textbook, a text/reader provides the reader with textual material and readings. The textual material serves as a foundation for understanding both historical and contemporary issues such as race as a social construct; the treatment of minorities and immigrants in American history; explanations of race and crime; disproportionate arrest, victimization, and confinement; racial profiling; wrongful convictions; and the "War on Drugs." The textual material also provides the reader with the requisite background necessary for understanding research presented in the selected edited readings. These readings include original and recent research published in leading criminology and criminal justice journals, such as *Crime & Delinquency, Criminology, Journal of Research in Crime and Delinquency, Justice Quarterly, Theoretical Criminology*, as well as others. The articles are authored by well known and emerging race and crime scholars.

The research articles were edited in several ways to improve their readability and reduce their length. At the beginning of each reading, a summary we prepared replaces the abstract that appeared in the original article. We retained most of the original content and references in each reading, but removed many of the authors' original notes. We varied the inclusion of text, tables, figures, and references from one reading to another. We also included reference citations from the originally published articles for those who want to read the articles in their entirety.

We are excited about introducing readers to this new format, which we believe has many benefits. First, it will increase students' knowledge of race and crime and its importance both nationally and internationally. Second, it will contribute to the development of students' knowledge of research methods and statistical analyses. Third, it will develop critical thinking skills by providing an opportunity for students to assess the strength and limitations of research methods and findings in the readings. Finally, it will provide the reader with enough information to continue to explore emerging race and crime topics they are interested in.

Ancillaries

We have developed high-quality ancillaries for instructors and students in order to enhance the use of this text/reader.

Instructor's Resource CD. This ancillary includes a variety of instructor's materials: PowerPoint slides, Web resources, and other helpful resources.

Student Study Site. The study site features useful resources for students, including Web exercises, references for further reading for each chapter, and more.

Acknowledgments

Many individuals assisted us in the completion of this book. First, we thank our editor, Jerry Westby, who continues to support our research endeavors and always shares his wealth of knowledge and expertise with us. Editorial assistants Nichole O'Grady and Erim Sarbuland, along with the editorial and productions team at Sage, were invaluable in guiding us through the writing format found in this publication. We also acknowledge the contributions of the authors of the original articles included here as edited readings. We appreciate their meaningful contributions to help transform the study of race and crime. We also thank Ms. Elycia Daniel for help in preparing the glossary of terms.

Several individuals assisted in the preparation of this publication. At Texas Southern University, Ms. Adrienne Moore, a doctoral student, assisted with reading, summarizing, and suggesting study questions for several of the edited readings. Ms. Heather Alaniz, a doctoral student, assisted with the edited reading by Western and Wildeman and helped identify study site materials. Professor Gabbidon thanks his graduate assistant at Penn State, Matthew Nelson, for his assistance. Professor Greene also thanks her son, Tamaa W. Patterson, for his assistance. SAGE Publications would like to thank the following reviewers: Tony Barringer, Florida Gulf Coast University; Isis Walton, Virginia State University; Peter Kratcoski, Kent State University; Lee Ross, University of Central Florida; Claire Renzetti, University of Dayton; Stephen Smith, Westfield State College; and Everette Penn, University of Houston.

Introduction to the Text

The study of race and crime has a long history. Even before the formal development of criminology/criminal justice, scholars were discussing the relationship between race and crime. In fact, Cesare Lombroso's well-known work was among the first to make the race and crime connection. Lombroso's *The Criminal Man* discussed the "ethnical" causes of crime in certain parts of India and Italy. Turning to America, he posited that Black women and American Indian women were "ideal type" examples of female criminals because they were manly looking. These sorts of comments became more pervasive in America as well. Early American scholarship on race and crime followed suit and also emphasized biological explanations (Gabbidon, 2010). Unfortunately, as with the existing research, many of the early criminology textbooks presented an unbalanced analysis of race and crime to students. This is despite the fact that there were ample historical sources to document racial oppression and to contextualize the brutal and criminal treatment of Black slaves and Native Americans.

It can be argued that the history of race and crime in America is actually a story of exploitation and violence by Whites not against them. For example, the brutal treatment of Native Americans and African Americans and later ethnic immigrants such as the Germans, Italians, Irish, Jews, Asians, and Latinos is omitted from most textbooks. As "White ethnic" groups assimilated into the populace, they, in turn, became part of the oppressive White population, continuing at times to engage in racial violence against other minority groups. For some Americans, regardless of race, crime has provided a way to ascend from the lower rungs of American society (i.e., from ghettoes to America's middle and upper classes).

The impact of historical misperceptions of minorities, especially those of Blacks as inferior, criminal, and less intelligent, is excluded from most early mainstream writings in criminology and criminal justice. Misperceptions about race, coupled with ongoing discrimination, segregation, and exclusion, shaped justice policies for more than a century. Some of these perceptions continue to exist today. Our review of the historical antecedents of race and crime in America has revealed that, over the past few centuries, although the level of crime in each group has varied over time, most racial/ethnic groups have committed the same kinds of offenses and have had similar offenses perpetrated against them by the dominant culture. This text reader gives students an opportunity to explore historical, contemporary, and emerging issues in the study of race and crime.

The Organization and Contents of the Book

This book includes eight sections that highlight topics found in most race and crime textbooks, readers, and edited volumes. Each section includes an overview of the topic covered, followed by contemporary race and crime issues, a summary, key terms, discussion questions, a list of relevant websites, and references. The textual portion is followed by selected readings to familiarize students with contemporary race and crime research. Each reading has questions at the end. The eight sections are as follows:

Section I: Overview of Race, Ethnicity, and Crime

Section II: Extent of Crime and Victimization

Section III: Theoretical Perspectives on Race and Crime

Section IV: Juvenile Justice

Section V: Policing

Section VI: Courts and Sentencing

Section VII: The Death Penalty

Section VIII: Corrections

Section I, Overview of Race, Ethnicity, and Crime, provides the reader with an overview of race and crime that includes a discussion of the concepts of race, ethnicity, prejudice, and discrimination. The experiences of Native Americans, African Americans, White ethnics, Latino Americans, and Asian Americans in American history are presented as well. The readings in the first section begin with one by Dickson-Gilmore and Woodiwiss (2008). In the article, they call for the reconsideration of the origins of American organized crime and argue that the crimes perpetrated against Native Americans should be considered the first wave of American organized crime. Gans (2005) then discusses the assimilation process that White ethnics went through before they were able to assimilate into mainstream White America. Webster (2007) discusses how discourse on crime excludes any substantive discussion of White ethnics and their crime-related issues.

In Section II, Extent of Crime and Victimization, a brief history of the development of crime and victimization data is presented that focuses on the two major sources of data, the Federal Bureau of Investigation's Uniform Crime Reports and the U.S. Bureau of the Census's National Crime Victimization Survey. It provides a discussion of the limitations of crime data for understanding race and crime and analyses of recent race, arrest, and victimization trends. The readings in this section familiarize readers with the research on three important topics: intimate partner homicide, the role of bystanders during violent victimizations, and co-offending and the age-crime curve. The selected readings present secondary analyses of official data to explore these topics. Campbell, Glass, Sharps, Kaughon, and Bloom (2007) use Supplemental Homicide Reports (SHR) to examine intimate-partner homicide. Hart and Miethe (2008) examine how bystanders either help or hurt nonfatal violent victimizations using data from the National Crime Victimization Survey. Stolzenberg and D'Alessio (2008) utilize data from the National Incident-Based Reporting System (NIBRS) to examine whether or not co-offending levels really vary by age.

Section III, Theoretical Perspectives on Race and Crime, gives the reader an introduction to the importance of theory in the study of race and crime. It provides a brief introduction to theories that have been applied to racial/ethnic groups and their involvement in crime. Several historical and contemporary biological and sociological theories are reviewed. The section includes edited readings that examine recent developments in theoretical explanations of race and crime. Eitle and Taylor (2008) explore whether the minority group threat theory is applicable to Hispanics. Another reading in the section, by Felson, Deane, and Armstrong (2008), investigates the utility of more general and specific theories (focused on violence) of crime to explain racial differences in offending. Kaufman, Rebellon, Thaxton, and Agnew (2008) provide a statement of how general strain theory can help explain racial differences in offending. The final article in the section reexamines Travis Hirschi's classic, *Causes of Delinquency* (1969). Unnever, Cullen, Mathers, McClure, and Allison (2009) note how Hirschi's original formulation of control theory underemphasized the role of racial discrimination in offending among African Americans. They further argue that there has long been a body of literature that argues for a connection between racial discrimination and offending.

Section IV, Juvenile Justice, provides an overview of the juvenile justice system and reviews race and juvenile justice, the problem of disproportionate minority confinement (DMC), juvenile involvement in crime and victimization, and race and delinquency prevention. The readings in this section present three interesting topics: an analysis of DMC progress during a recent decade, gender specific services for delinquent girls, and the role of race in school discipline. Davis and Sorensen (2010) present an historical analysis of DMC using arrest and placement data to see how much of the variance in placements is due to factors other than arrest. Kupchik (2009) examines school crime and responses in four high schools in two different states in order to examine how race, ethnicity, and class impact school discipline. Wolf, Graziano, and Hartney (2009) examine variations by race and ethnicity in a gender-specific program for females designed as an alternative to traditional probation.

Section V, Policing, gives the reader an overview of policing in America and presents an analysis of race and policing. Two contemporary race and policing issues are reviewed: public opinion and citizen satisfaction with police and racial profiling. The readings in this section present emerging issues in the study of race and policing. Gau, Mosher, and Pratt (2010) research the role of race in police use of Tasers in a state police agency. Stewart, Schreck, and Brunson (2008) explore how the "code of the streets" impacts violence and victimization in some urban areas and what can be done to improve police-citizen interactions. Taylor, Holleran, and Topalli (2009) examine race and police clearance of violent crime incidents other than homicides.

Section VI, Courts and Sentencing, provides the reader with an overview of how race matters in the court processes and also in sentencing. Sommers and Norton (2007) provide the results of an experiment that focused on whether a diverse sample of participants was more likely to remove jurors because of their race. Farrell, Ward, and Rousseau (2009) investigate the influence of a diverse workforce on reducing sentencing disparities. The section also includes an article by Johnson and Betsinger (2009) that focuses on whether the "Model Minority" perception impacts on the court outcomes of Asian Americans.

Section VII, The Death Penalty, includes an overview of race and the death penalty, significant death penalty cases, and contemporary issues related to race and the death penalty. Lee (2007) examines Hispanics and the death penalty to explore the nuances of their experience with capital punishment. Fleury-Steiner, Dunn, and Fleury-Steiner (2009) discuss how the media and legislators framed a high-profile crime by racial minorities to reenergize the death penalty in Delaware. Peffley and Hurwitz (2007) consider whether the opinions of Blacks and Whites on the death penalty are malleable.

The text reader concludes with Section VIII, Corrections. In this section, an overview of corrections, race and corrections in historical context, and two contemporary issues in race and corrections are reviewed: racial disparities in corrections and prisoner reentry. The first reading in this section, by Brewer and Heitzeg (2008), uses critical race theory to explore the racialization of crime and punishment, political economy, and the prison industrial complex in the so-called era of color-blind justice. Latessa and Lovins (2010) examine the role of offender risk assessment and explain why it is important in reducing imprisonment and recidivism. The final reading, by Western and Wildeman (2009), provides an analysis of how mass incarceration has impacted Black families.

How to Read a Research Article

As you travel through your criminal justice/criminology studies, you will soon learn that some of the best known or emerging explanations of crime and criminal behavior come from research articles in academic journals. This book has research articles throughout, but you may be asking yourself, "How do I read a research article?" It is our hope to answer this question with a quick summary of the key elements of any research article, followed by the questions you should be answering as you read through the assigned sections.

Every research article published in a social science journal will have the following elements: (1) introduction, (2) literature review, (3) methodology, (4) results, and (5) discussion/conclusion.

In the introduction, you will find an overview of the purpose of the research. Within the introduction, you will also find the hypothesis or hypotheses. A *hypothesis* is most easily defined as an educated statement or guess. In most hypotheses, the format followed is this: If *X, Y* will occur. For example, a simple hypothesis might be: "If the price of gas increases, more people will ride bikes." This is a testable statement that the researcher wants to address in his or her study. Usually, but not always, authors will state the hypothesis directly. Therefore, you must be aware of what the author is actually testing in the research project. If you are unable to find the hypothesis, ask yourself what is being tested or manipulated and what results are expected.

The next section of the research article is the literature review. At times, the literature review is separated from the text and organized into its own section; at other times, it is found within the introduction. In any case, the literature review is an examination of what other researchers have already produced in regard to the research question or hypothesis. For example, returning to the hypothesis on the relationship between gas prices and bike riding, we may find that five researchers have previously conducted studies on the increase of gas prices. In the literature review, I will discuss their findings and then discuss what my study will add to the existing research. The literature review may also be used as a platform of support for my hypothesis. For example, one researcher may have already determined that an increase in gas causes more people to rollerblade to work. I can use this study as evidence to support my hypothesis that increased gas prices will lead to more bike riding.

The methods used in the research design are found in the next section of the research article. In the methodology section you will find the following: who or what was studied, how many subjects were studied, the research tool (e.g., interview, survey, or observation), how long the subjects were studied, and how the data that was collected was processed. The methods section is usually very concise, with every step of the research project recorded. This is important because a major goal of the researcher is *reliability,* or whether the results will be the same if the research is done again.

The results section is an analysis of the researcher's findings. If the researcher conducted a quantitative study (using numbers or statistics to explain the research), you will find statistical tables and analyses that explain whether or not the researcher's hypothesis is supported. If the researcher conducted a qualitative study (non-numerical research for the purpose of theory construction), the results will usually be displayed as a theoretical analysis or interpretation of the research question.

Finally, the research article will conclude with a discussion and summary of the study. In the discussion, you will usually find the hypothesis restated, and perhaps a small discussion of why this is the hypothesis. You will also find a brief overview of the methodology and results. The discussion section will end with a discussion of the policy implications of the research and what future research is still needed.

Now that you know the key elements of a research article, let us examine a sample article from your text.

The Provision and Completion of Gender-Specific Services for Girls on Probation: Variations by Race and Ethnicity

By Angela M. Wolf, Juliette Graziano, and Christopher Hartneys

1. What is the thesis or main idea from this article?

The thesis or main idea is found in the introduction of this article. The thesis or main idea is that "although the services considered essential for effective girls' programming have been outlined, how well they have been incorporated into gender-responsive interventions remains largely unknown.... Without examining which services and program elements are beneficial for which groups for girls, our understanding of their effectiveness is severely limited" (p. 215). The authors are particularly concerned with "how probation officers utilize traditional and the RYSE [Reaffirming Young Sisters' Excellence] program services" and "the percentages of services completed by girls, with special attention given to race/ethnicity" (p. 218).

2. What is the hypothesis?

Wolf, Graziano, and Hartneys explore four hypotheses found in the methods section of the article. Hypothesis 1 states, "There will be no racial/ethnic group difference within the comparison group regarding services assigned, services completed, and the percentage of services completed" (p. 218). The other hypotheses examine racial/ethnic group differences within the RYSE group and between the RYSE group (Hypothesis 2 and 2a) and a comparison group (Hypothesis 3).

3. Is there any prior literature related to the hypothesis?

This article does not have a separate section titled "Literature Review." The authors present prior literature and research in the Introduction and under the headings Gender-Specific Programming, Services for Delinquent Girls, and RYSE Evaluation. The review of prior literature gives readers an overview of how gender-specific programs began, why they are important in addressing the specific needs of girls, and the importance of evaluating these programs to better understand racial and ethnic differences in program outcomes.

4. What methods are used to support the hypothesis?

The methodology in this article is described under the heading Research Design and Sample. It includes an experimental design and the use of secondary data collected for the RYSE evaluation conducted by the National Council on Crime and Delinquency (2001) and Le, Arifuku, and Nunez (2003). Girls in the juvenile justice system were randomly assigned to either an intervention (RYSE) or comparison group. The evaluation included 333 girls. Most were assigned to the RYSE group (249); the remainder (84) were in the comparison group.

5. Is this a qualitative study or a quantitative study?

Some researchers provide information about the type of study in the methods section. Wolf, Graziano, and Hartneys describe the sources of their data (e.g., State of California Board of Corrections Common Data Elements) although they don't discuss how they have analyzed the data. To determine whether or not a study is qualitative or quantitative, you must look at the results. The tables in the Results section indicate that it is a quantitative study. Descriptive statistics and analyses of variance (ANOVA) are reported in the results section.

6. What are the results and how does the author present the results?

The Discussion provides the reader with a summary of the results found in the study. The findings in this study indicate that "African American girls are having less success with traditional services than their White and API counterparts" (p. 222). The authors elaborate on differences in completion of traditional probation services, as well as RYSE services, by study participants. One positive finding is that the African American girls in the RYSE program successfully completed more traditional services than those in the comparison group. The researchers believe their findings provide preliminary support for the importance of analyzing racial and ethnic group differences in probation services to girls.

7. Do you believe that the author(s) provided a persuasive argument? Why or why not?

This answer is ultimately up to the reader, but, looking at this article, I believe that it is safe to assume that the readers will agree that the authors offer an interesting reanalysis of data on gender-specific programs. They also help readers understand why researchers should continue to explore and identify the characteristics of services that are most effective in diverting girls from the justice system. The fact that OJJDP requires gender-specific services and programs points to the importance of knowing the characteristics of probation programs that meet the needs of all girls. Another way to come to your own conclusion about whether or not author(s) provide a persuasive argument is to consider the strengths and limitations of their argument and/or study. You can revisit the hypotheses in this study and determine whether or not the researchers found support for each of them.

8. Who is the intended audience for this article?

A final question that will be useful for the reader deals with the intended audience. As you read the article, ask yourself, to whom does the author want to speak? After you read this article, you will see that Wolf, Graziano, and Hartney are writing not only for students but also for professors and justice practitioners, especially probation officers who work directly with delinquent girls and those who sponsor juvenile justice research. The target audience may most easily be identified if you ask yourself "Who will benefit from reading this article?"

9. What does the article add to your knowledge of the subject?

This answer is best left up to the reader, because the question is asking how the article improved your knowledge. One way to answer this question about this article is as follows: The article helps the reader to understand that gender-specific programs and services are important for delinquent girls, but it is also important that we determine which programs work and for whom. Until we better understand the characteristics of successful traditional and gender-specific probation programs and services, we don't meet the needs of delinquent girls. To meet their needs, we must also consider the race and ethnicity of the girls, which services work for them, and why.

10. What are the implications for research and justice policy that can be derived from this article?

Implications for justice policy are usually found in the conclusion or discussion sections of an article. In this article, implications for justice policy are presented in the Discussion and Future Directions sections. Even though these sections don't specifically identify implications for justice policy, they do emphasize the importance of not assuming girls are a homogeneous group. From this article, we can conclude that more research on services that effectively divert girls from the justice system will lead to juvenile justice policies that require such programs be made available. We can also conclude that as long as girls of color are overrepresented in the juvenile justice system, a better understanding of their needs and experiences will have implications for policy. OJJDP can be instrumental in funding research in both areas.

Now that we have gone through the elements of a research article, it is your turn to continue through your text, reading the various articles and answering the same questions. You may find that some articles are easier to follow than others, but do not be dissuaded. Remember that most research articles follow a similar format: introduction, literature review, methods, results, and discussion. If you have any problems, refer to this introduction for guidance.

References

Covington, J. (2010). *Crime and racial constructions: Cultural misinformation about African Americans in media academia.* Lanham, MD: Lexington Books.

LaFree, G., Russell, K. K. (1993). The argument for studying race and crime. *Journal of Criminal Justice Education, 4,* 273–289.

Mann, C. R., Zatz, M., & Rodriguez, N. (Eds.). (2006). *Images of color, images of crime.* Los Angeles: Roxbury.

Overview of Race, Ethnicity, and Crime

SECTION HIGHLIGHTS

- The Concepts of Race and Ethnicity
- Prejudice and Discrimination
- Race and Crime in American History
- Summary
- Edited Readings

The Concepts of Race and Ethnicity

There remains considerable debate about the concept of **race**. This is despite the fact that racial classifications are more than 5,000 years old. The earliest racial distinctions can be traced to India, but they were also found in China and Egypt and among Jews (Gossett, 1963). Francois Bernier is largely credited with first categorizing humans, but it was Carolus Linnaeus who invented the first system of categorizing plants and animals. The first racial categorization of humans is credited to German Johann Friedrich Blumenbach (1752–1840; see Photo 1.1). In his 1795 work, *On the Natural Variety of Mankind*, Blumenbach separated the human species into five races: Ethiopian (African or Negro), Mongolian (Asian), American (Native American), Malaysian (Pacific Islander), and Whites (Caucasian). Before long, Blumenbach's typology became the standard across Europe, with Europeans placing themselves at the top of the hierarchy and linking racial differences to biological factors (Feagin & Feagin, 2008).

This ideology led to vociferous debates about the origins of racial differences. For some time, the debates were quashed because it was generally agreed that the racial differences (skin color and other biological differences) were attributable to migratory patterns out of Africa. Such differences were believed to be insignificant. In more modern times, scholars have termed "race" a social construct or a classification scheme that is arbitrary and not based on biological differences. In fact, the U.S. Census Bureau uses the following qualifying statement regarding racial classifications: "The concept of race as used by the Census Bureau reflects self-identification by people according to the race or races with which they most closely identify. These categories are socio-political constructs and should not be interpreted as being scientific or anthropological in nature. Furthermore, the race categories include both racial and national-origin groups" (http://quickfacts.census.gov/qfd/meta/long_68184.htm). In contrast to the Census Bureau and those that believe race is a social construct, other scholars have argued that the increasing advances in genetics support the notion that race is a biological concept (Sesardic, 2010).

The term ***ethnicity*** comes from the Greek word *ethnos*, which means "nation." Generally, ethnic groups are defined by their similar genetic inheritances or by some identifiable traits visible among most members of a particular group. Ethnic groups are also generally held together by a common language, culture, group spirit (nationalism or group solidarity), or geography (most typically originate from the same region) (Marger, 1997). Therefore, in the case of race and ethnicity, most anthropologists generally see these terms as more culturally relevant than biologically relevant. Most scholars separate the American population into five groups (as do we): Native Americans, Whites, African Americans, Hispanic/Latino(a) Americans, and Asian Americans. We acknowledge that there are limitations to these categories. First, these categories do not take into account the ethnic variation within each group. For example, when we refer to "Latino Americans," there are a number of ethnic groups within this racial classification. This is true of other races as well. Another example is the category of African American/Black. There is also ethnic diversity within this category, with it often encompassing people from the Caribbean (e.g., Jamaica, Haiti, etc.), African countries, and other parts of the world. Because each of these groups has had a unique experience in America, it is, at times, presumptuous for researchers to take for granted that the experience of one African/Black American is representative of so many diverse groups. Nevertheless, although we are aware of the problems with these classifications, the research and data in the social sciences follow this taxonomy. Second, and relatedly, with the use of the multiracial category in the 2000 census, the lines between racial groups have become rather blurred, so population and crime data increasingly have considerable limits.

▲ **Photo 1.1** Johann Friedrich Blumenbach

Since the 2000 census, as has been their tradition, the U.S. Census Bureau has continued to provide population estimates. Nearly a decade later, in 2009, they released figures that revealed that the **minority** population topped 100 million. By this time, Hispanics/Latinos had become the largest minority group (15.4%; see Table 1.1), and Blacks had become the second largest (12.8%). Given the changing demographics of the United States, some have called for the discontinuance of the term *minority* (Texeira, 2005). In place of *minority*, which some believe is a "term of oppression," or a term that seeks to minimize the collective aspirations of a group, the term ***people of color*** has been suggested (Texeira, 2005). Whatever the term to be used, if current estimates are correct, it is clear that one day racial and ethnic groups now considered to be minorities will become nearly half the U.S. population (U.S. Census Bureau, 2004). In fact, current estimates are that Whites will represent only 50% of the population in 2050, with Hispanics representing nearly a quarter of the population and other racial and ethnic minorities comprising the remainder of the populace (U.S. Census Bureau, 2004).

Table 1.1 U.S. Racial/Ethnic Population Estimates, 2009

Racial/Ethnic Group	Percentage of Population
White persons	79.8
White persons not Hispanic	65.6
Persons of Hispanic or Latino origin	15.4
Black persons	12.8
Asian persons	4.5
American Indian and Alaska Native persons	1.0
Native Hawaiian and Other Pacific Islander	0.2
Persons reporting two or more races	1.7

NOTE: The percentages are based on a population estimate of 307,006,550.

Prejudice and Discrimination

Even with the growth in the minority population, **prejudice** and discrimination remain a central concern. Prejudice is when someone fosters a negative attitude toward a particular group. This is usually in the form of stereotypes that often result in people making negative generalizations about an entire group. Discrimination is considered the "unequal treatment of a person or persons based on group membership" (Healey, 2007, p. 20). As you can imagine, having prejudicial attitudes toward a particular group can lead to discriminatory actions in areas such as employment, housing, and the criminal justice system. Thus, determining whether racial prejudice and **racial discrimination** permeates the criminal justice system is critical to understanding the role of race in justice system outcomes.

Race and Crime in American History

Unquestionably, the American landscape has been shaped by the countless racial and ethnic groups that immigrated to the United States. Yet each group that arrived in America encountered stinging and pervasive resistance—often in the form of discrimination—from earlier arrivals. Notably, even Native Americans, who were living in America before Europeans arrived, were not immune to the discriminatory treatment of the foreigners who came to explore and exploit the land. In addition to discrimination, a large part of the initial American experience involved crime, violence, and doing what was necessary to survive. This section provides a discussion of the experiences of various racial and ethnic groups. In addition to racial and ethnic minorities, the section also reviews the process through which many **White ethnics** followed on the path to **assimilation**.

Native Americans

Prior to the arrival of Europeans in the Americas, people had existed on both continents for thousands of years. It is believed that they originated from eastern Asia. More specifically, it is believed that they have been in North America for the last 30,000 years, having crossed over from Asia into America on glaciers that, due to warming trends, later melted (Polk, 2006, pp. 3–4). Over time, they built complex societies throughout the Americas. Even so, on arrival in the Americas (South America and the West Indies), it is clear from their actions that Christopher Columbus and his followers viewed the native people (then referred to as "Indians," now referred to as "Native Americans" or "American Indians") as inferior (Clarke, 1992). The brutality that followed was painstakingly documented by firsthand observers of the massacres (De Las Casas, 1552/1993). Sale (1990) suggested that, prior to the arrival of Europeans, there were about 15 million Native Americans in North America. According to Healey (2003), nearly four centuries later, in 1890, only 250,000 remained. Today, there are nearly 4.5 million American Indians or Alaskan Natives in the United States. Nonetheless, considering the historical decimation of the Native American population, some criminologists have viewed their massacre as genocide (Barak, Flavin, & Leighton, 2010). Given this history, it is not a surprise that the relationship between Native Americans and the United States government is characterized by mistrust. Thus, while the Bureau of Indian Affairs (BIA) was established to handle matters related to this population, the agency had to deal with the competing aims of the federal government. On the one hand, the government created the agency to help Native Americans; on the other hand, the military had a policy of what might be considered genocidal extermination. Nearly 60 years after the creation of the BIA, the 1887 Dawes Act provided that individual families be provided with reservation lands. While well meaning, as Feagin and Feagin (2008) observed, "This new policy soon resulted in a large-scale land sale to Whites. Through means fair and foul, the remaining 140 million acres of Indian lands were further reduced to 50 million acres by the mid-1930s" (p. 144).

In the early part of the 20th century, the government tried to assimilate Native Americans by sending them to Indian boarding schools that were Christian-based and used to indoctrinate Native Americans with American culture. In the process, Native Americans were forced to abandon their native languages and customs. The attempt to assimilate Native Americans culminated during the 1920s with the passage of the Indian Citizenship Act of 1924, which granted all Native Americans citizenship. The end of this period saw Native Americans calling for new policies, one of which came in the form of the 1934 Indian Reorganization Act. The act, which essentially ended the Dawes Act, allowed Native Americans to "establish Indian civil and cultural rights, allow for semiautonomous tribal governments similar in legal status to counties and municipalities, and foster economic development on reservations" (Feagin & Feagin, 2008, p. 144). As with all legislation, there were problems. Most notably, Native Americans saw this act as giving too much power to the secretary of the interior. In addition, many Native Americans believed the act violated their sovereignty, or their right to govern themselves as provided by previously enacted treaties.

The second half of the 20th century spurred more attempts by Native Americans to rid themselves of governmental control. In the early 1950s, Congress enacted legislation called *termination*, which "call[ed] for an end to the reservation system and to the special relationships between the tribes and the federal government" (Healey, 2004, p. 134). This process also negated previous treaties, a policy that was vigorously opposed by Native Americans. In addition, based on the specifics of the policy, "tribes would no longer exist as legally recognized entities, and tribal lands and other resources would be placed in private hands" (Healey, 2004, p. 134). Because of this policy, many Native Americans moved to urban areas.

The decades following the enactment of the termination policy saw increasing opposition from Native Americans. After about 25 years, the policy was repealed. In 1975, the Indian Self-Determination and Education Assistance Act "increased aid to reservation schools and Native American students and increased the tribes' control over the administration of the reservations, from police forces to schools and road maintenance" (Healey, 2004, p. 136). This act provided much of the basis under which many tribes now operate. Recent federal legislation has allowed some tribes to open gambling facilities on reservations, which in 2000 generated more than $10 billion in revenues (Spilde, 2001). Other tribes have invested in other ways to generate revenue (e.g., tax-free cigarette sales). Native Americans' move toward self-determination also has resulted in suits against the federal government seeking reparations for past broken treaties. With 561 recognized tribes and a population of more than 4 million, Native Americans remain a notable presence in the United States.

African Americans

African Americans have also had a long and arduous relationship with the United States. With the Native American population nearly completely decimated because of the brutality, enslavement, and diseases that were brought to the Americas by the Spanish, Bartolomé de las Casas, a priest who accompanied Columbus on one of his voyages to America, sought a way to stem their extermination. De las Casas' idea centered not on ending the slave system, but instead on replacing the Native Americans with another labor force: Africans. As with the decimation of the Native American population, the slave trade involving Africans resulted in genocide that has been referred to as the "African holocaust" (Clarke, 1992).

It is believed that Africans arrived in the Americas in the early 1600s. Yet from their arrival in the 1600s up to the 1660s, Africans were not considered slaves. In fact, many of them fulfilled indentures and were fairly integrated into the life of the colony. After 1660, however, colonial legislation made it clear that Africans were to be considered slaves and were to serve as the primary labor force keeping the southern economy afloat. Southern slaveholders maintained the slave system through a combination of lawless brutality and legislative enactments that did not penalize brutality against slaves who rebelled against the slave system. An elaborate system of slave codes, or laws that pertained to slaves, dictated their lives from cradle to grave (Russell-Brown, 2009). In addition to the slave codes, Whites used psychology to keep the slave system intact. Claude Anderson (1994) wrote that "this process was designed to instill in Blacks strict discipline, a sense of inferiority, belief in the slave owners' superior power, acceptance of the owners' standards and a deep sense of a slave's helplessness and dependence" (p. 165). Moreover, Anderson noted that "the slave owners strove to cut Blacks off from their own history, culture, language and community, and to inculcate White society's value system" (p. 165).

Following the Emancipation Proclamation in 1863, which freed the slaves in the Confederate states, and the enactment of the Thirteenth Amendment in 1865, which ended slavery throughout the United States, many African Americans chose to remain in the South. Others had dreams of going north and starting anew. Unfortunately, southern landowners were unwilling to part so easily with their former free labor force. Therefore, following emancipation, they enacted the "**Black codes**." These codes were an assortment of laws that targeted poor Whites and African Americans. Some scholars have argued that the laws were specifically created so that a significant number of African Americans could be returned to plantation owners through the convict-lease system (Du Bois, 1901/2002; Myers, 1998; Oshinsky, 1996). The convict-lease system allowed states to lease convict labor to private landowners.

The Reconstruction Era (1865–1877) also brought the formal advent of hate groups (e.g., Klu Klux Klan). These groups terrorized African Americans and other citizens, who were the targets of their hatred. **Lynching** became the means used to intimidate and handle those who challenged the racist White power structure. These indiscriminate killings of African Americans (and some Native Americans and Spanish-speaking minorities), usually by hanging, were typically carried out to avenge some exaggerated crime committed by an African American or other "undesirable" minority against a White person (Zangrando, 1980). In most instances, the alleged crime of rape was used to justify these horrific actions. During the height of the era when lynchings were being carried out, the *Plessy v. Ferguson* (1896) "separate but equal" case was decided. The decision was significant in that it gave Whites legal support to enforce some of their ideas concerning White supremacy and the separation of the races. Furthermore, this decision allowed law enforcement officials to take action against African Americans who sought basic services that were reserved for Whites.

Ten years after the turn of the 20th century, African Americans were primarily southerners. Meier and Rudwick (1970) observed that "approximately three out of four lived in rural areas and nine out of ten lived in the South" (p. 213). The Great Migration, however, changed the landscape of the North and South. By the 1950s, "Negroes were mainly an urban population, almost three fourths of them being city-dwellers" (Meier & Rudwick, 1970, p. 213). During this era, African Americans crowded into northern cities in search of job opportunities; what they found, however, were overcrowded urban areas with assorted European immigrants either seeking similar opportunities or already established in the low-skill, low-wage jobs that African Americans had hoped to receive. African American women were able to secure employment in domestic service, where, unfortunately, White men often sexually assaulted them (Davis, 1981).

During the 1930s and 1940s, there was continued interest in the subject of crime among African Americans. By the early 1950s, African Americans and other ethnic groups were still struggling to survive in an increasingly segregated and hostile America. Some turned to crime, whereas others turned to social activism and joined the civil rights movement.

By the 1960s, according to figures from the Tuskegee Institute (Zangrando, 1980), lynchings were rare events; however, Whites had successfully used the practice to discourage any serious level of integration. Therefore, although Thurgood Marshall and his colleagues were successful in the landmark *Brown v. Board of Education* (1954) case, minority communities did not substantially change for decades. Because of "the White strategy of ghetto containment and tactical retreat before an advancing color line" (Massey & Denton, 1993, p. 45), substantial underclass communities were in existence by the 1970s. This bred a level of poverty and despair that fostered the continuation of the African American criminal classes and organized crime. The riots of the 1960s were a response to the long-standing troublesome conditions in some of these cities (National Advisory Commission on Civil Disorders, 1968).

When African Americans were finally able to take advantage of the opportunities forged by the civil rights movement and desegregation, many of them left inner-city areas. Unfortunately, many of those who left had brought an important level of stability to these communities. As a result of this exodus, these inner-city communities are now heavily comprised of those Wilson (1987) described as the "**truly disadvantaged**." They are heavily dependent on the underground economy for survival (see Venkatesh, 2006), which has likely contributed to the overrepresentation of African Americans throughout the U.S. criminal justice system.

Even with the many struggles encountered by African Americans and other Black ethnic groups, and the historical fixation on their criminality, they have contributed to every aspect of American life, from the tilling of the soil in the South and the factory work in the North that produced the wealth that made America what it is today to the innumerable scientific, musical, and artistic contributions that are now considered staples of American culture.

White Ethnics

During the early 1600s, while the slave trade in South America and the West Indies was going on, the British colonized parts of what would later become the American colonies. This led to many of the same kinds of conflicts with Native Americans that the Spanish had quelled elsewhere with unimaginable brutality. Although the British saw the colonies as somewhere they could send criminals and other undesirables, they also saw opportunity for monetary gain, so they encouraged emigration to the colonies. Some went freely, whereas others used indentures to get them to the New World. These arrangements allowed them to work for a period of time to pay for their travel expenses to the colonies. Once their indentures were completed, emigrants were free to pursue whatever opportunities they desired. In addition to British emigrants, Germans and Italians were among the first to immigrate to America.

Many began to arrive in the early 1600s, settling first in New Amsterdam (New York) and later in Pennsylvania (Sowell, 1981). Given this rich history of European emigration to the United States, we briefly review the process that many White ethnic groups followed on the path to full assimilation. It has been noted that, with some exceptions, many White ethnic immigrants had nearly identical experiences on their arrival in America (Feagin & Feagin, 2008). In fact, one could easily view the early experiences of most White ethnics as following a clear process.

Following the initial arrival of immigrants, who quickly started to consider themselves the new native population, there was generally a four step process toward assimilation. First, the established dominant racial and ethnic group (e.g., English, Scottish, etc.) noticed a large number of immigrants (e.g., Irish, Italian, Polish, etc.) settling into areas previously occupied mainly by the "native" population. The second stage of the process involved the new immigrants becoming despised by the dominant group. This led to the creation of stinging stereotypes and the perpetuation of deviant imagery of the new group. The third stage of the process related to the struggles that the immigrant group encountered. Often, because of the discriminatory treatment encountered by the new immigrants, they had difficulty surviving and might be forced to resort to criminal activities that culminated in their participation in organized crime or gang formation. Notably, after a generation of struggles to survive, the new immigrant moved toward the fourth stage: assimilation.

Milton Gordon (1964) described several phases of assimilation. Cultural assimilation is the first phase, in which the immigrant group abandons some of their cultural traditions to accept those of the dominant group. Structural assimilation is when immigrants begin to penetrate cliques and associations that were previously exclusive to the dominant group. The next phase is marital assimilation, in which the immigrant group has significant intermarriage with the dominant group. When the immigrant group starts to identify with the dominant group, they have moved to the identification phase of assimilation. The attitude-receptional phase represents the point in which the immigrant group is no longer stereotyped and the group assimilates into American life. The next phase is the behavior-receptional phase, which is when the immigrant group no longer encounters discrimination. Civic assimilation is the final phase. At this phase, there are no longer any value or power conflicts among the dominant group and the newest immigrant group. Notably, these phases of assimilation coincide with the general process that immigrant groups encountered as they became full-fledged Americans. Later, as new ethnic immigrants arrived, they followed the same process as previous European immigrants.

There are clear exceptions to this process. First, Native Americans were already here when Whites came and colonized them. Thus, given their unique cultural traditions, it was extremely hard for them to fully assimilate. Second, unlike White immigrants who came here looking for opportunities, as discussed earlier, Africans were brought to America forcibly. In addition, even after they were emancipated two centuries after becoming the primary labor force in the South, their search for prosperity was hampered by racism. It has been well-established that skin color prevented African Americans from assimilating into the mainstream of American life—something that White ethnics could easily overcome (Allen, 1994; Ignatiev, 1996). Two other groups that have had unique experiences in America are Latino and Asian Americans. A brief overview of their experiences is presented in the next two sections.

Latino Americans

Prior to the 2000 census, the term *Hispanic* was used to refer to persons from Mexico, Puerto Rico, Cuba, and Central and South America. Feagin and Feagin (2008) noted that the term *Latino* emerged because it "recognizes the complex Latin American origins of these groups. It is a Spanish language word and is preferred by many Spanish speaking Americans" (p. 206). Our review of their history focuses on the largest ethnic groups in the Latino category, with a brief overview of smaller Latino ethnic groups.

Mexicans

From 1500 to 1853, the Spanish ruled Mexico. For much of this period, Mexicans were exploited for their labor by the Spanish. Many Mexicans became Americans with the annexation of Texas. Following the Mexican-American War (1846–1848) and the Treaty of Guadalupe Hidalgo (1848), Mexicans had the option to stay in the United States or to return to Mexico. According to Feagin and Feagin (2008), although many stayed, others returned to Mexico.

Sowell (1981) wrote that Mexicans immigrated to America in three great waves. The first wave of Mexicans came to America by railroad—and ironically, over the years, railroads have become one of the largest employers of Mexicans. Specifically, they were employed "as construction workers, as watchmen, or as laborers maintaining the tracks. Many lived in boxcars or in shacks near the railroads—primitive settlements that were the beginning of many Mexican-American communities today" (Sowell, 1981, p. 249). Before World War I, other industries employing Mexicans were agriculture and mining. Mexican workers in America were paid considerably more than they were in Mexico. As a result, there was a steady flow of seasonal workers crossing the border to earn money to take back home to Mexico. Labor shortages caused by World War I resulted in formalized programs to encourage such practices. About 500,000 Mexicans came to America to work during this period (Tarver, Walker, & Wallace, 2002). Beginning in this period, Mexicans also were subject to negative stereotypes, such as being considered "dirty," "ignorant," and lacking standards of appropriate behavior (Sowell, 1981). But they were tolerated because of the dire need for their labor. With the arrival of the Great Depression, "fears of the unemployed created an anti-immigrant movement, and immigration laws were modified to deport the 'undesirables' and restrict the numbers of foreign-contract laborers" (Tarver et al., 2002, p. 54).

The second wave of Mexican immigrants came to the United States during World War II. Another war had resulted in another labor shortage, which produced the **Bracero Program,** which brought in thousands of agricultural workers to help with the labor shortage. *Bracero* is a Spanish term that was used to describe guest workers coming from Mexico to the United States. By the end of the Bracero Program in 1964, 5 million Mexican workers had been imported into this country (Tarver et al., 2002, p. 54).

The third wave of Mexican immigration is tied to the various immigration laws from the 1970s to the present, which have sought to protect, defend, or curtail Mexican immigration to the United States. One such law, the Immigration and Reform and Control Act of 1986, provided temporary residency for some illegal aliens. Furthermore, those who came to America before 1982 were provided with permanent resident status.

Another law aimed at Mexican illegal immigration is the Illegal Immigration Reform and Immigrant Responsibility Act of 1996. In addition to shoring up the borders in California and Texas, the act "increased the number of investigators monitoring workplace employment of aliens, passport fraud, and alien smuggling" (Tarver et al., 2002, p. 55). Today, the fears concerning illegal immigration continue with the recent passage of Arizona's Immigration Bill SB1070. Most notably, the bill requires immigrants to carry their alien registration information and provides law enforcement officials with the discretion to question those persons who they believe are illegal immigrants. Besides concerns about job competition and the strain on social services caused by the considerable illegal immigration, Americans have continued their fascination with the perceived connection between immigration and crime (Hickman & Suttorp, 2008; Higgins, Gabbidon, & Martin, 2010; Martinez, 2006; Martinez & Valenzuela, 2006; Stowell, 2007).

Puerto Ricans and Other Latino Groups

The island of Puerto Rico was colonized by the Spanish in the late 1400s. It was not until 1897 that Puerto Ricans gained their independence. However, the Spanish-American War resulted in America taking over the island in 1898. In the 1950s, Puerto Rico became a commonwealth of the United States, granting Puerto Ricans more independence in their governance. From 1945 to the 1970s, the high unemployment rate on the island resulted in one in three Puerto Ricans leaving the island (Feagin & Feagin, 2008). Significant numbers of Puerto Ricans headed to New York and other states, such as New Jersey and Delaware. Thus, there was significant Puerto Rican immigration to the United States, which resulted in an increase from 2,000 Puerto Ricans in New York in 1900 to 70,000 in 1940 and 887,000 by 1960 (Feagin & Feagin, 2008). Upon their arrival, as with other immigrants who headed to the "promised land," they were faced with high levels of unemployment and poverty. In fact, these dire circumstances resulted in what has been referred to as *circular migration.* That is, after the opportunities they were seeking did not materialize, Puerto Ricans would head home but then return because of the lack of opportunities in Puerto Rico. Mirroring the experience of other racial and ethnic groups, over time, Puerto Ricans were also saddled with negative stereotypes, such as "lazy," "submissive," "violent," and "criminal" (Feagin & Feagin, 2008). Moreover, because they cannot always "pass" as White, it has been difficult to assimilate like some other ethnic groups. As a result of their varying skin tones and backgrounds, they can be categorized as either White or Black.

Cubans have also been a force among the Latino American population. With much of their immigration coming after Fidel Castro's takeover of the government in 1959, they currently number about 1.5 million in the United States. Combined, South Americans from the Dominican Republic, El Salvador, and Colombia also represent another 2 million Latino Americans (Healey, 2006). Given these figures, it is no wonder that Latinos have become the largest minority group in the United States. In the process, they have surpassed African Americans, who have long held that title. They have also, however, suffered from some of the same crime-related concerns as other ethnic groups before them. On the whole, though, they have not experienced the same levels of crime and violence as African Americans (Martinez, 2002). This may reflect the fact that many Latinos have come to the United States specifically seeking opportunities for employment, with a willingness to take the most undesirable jobs in the labor market. For many, these jobs provide much more financial compensation than the available employment in the various Latin American countries from which a substantial portion of Latino immigrants originate. Nevertheless, some Latinos have drifted into gangs and other criminal activities as a way to survive in America. Unfortunately, their criminal activities have been exaggerated by the news media and Hollywood, which has resulted in continuing stereotypes (Martinez, Lee, & Nielsen, 2001).

Asian Americans

Asian Americans provide another interesting case study of ethnic group acculturation in America. Like Latinos, they belong to a number of ethnic groups, such as Chinese, Filipino, Korean, Japanese, and Vietnamese. We begin our review with a brief discussion of the Chinese American experience.

Chinese Americans

According to Daniels (1988), there were Chinese immigrants in America as early as the late 1700s. However, it was not until the California gold rush of the mid-1850s that any significant Chinese immigration to America took place. Between 1849 and 1882, nearly 300,000 Chinese came to America (Daniels, 1988). However, the **Chinese Exclusion Act** of 1882 limited immigration until the 1940s (Tarver et al., 2002). Most of the early Chinese immigrants were male (90%) and came to work in America temporarily. However, they came in significant enough numbers to represent nearly 10% of California's population between 1860 and 1880 (Daniels, 1988). Those who did stay were subjected to considerable violence due to anti-Chinese sentiment. Chinatowns had existed since the arrival of the Chinese in America; they embraced these areas because there they were free to maintain their own culture without fear of hostility—although some areas occupied exclusively by Chinese inhabitants were "shabby looking, vice-infested, and violence prone" (Sowell, 1981, p. 141).

The Chinese were quite successful as laborers as well as in independent businesses such as restaurants and laundries (Daniels, 1988; Sowell, 1981). Yet as with other immigrant groups, the Chinese were not immune from engaging in illegal activities. Daniels (1988) wrote that prostitution and gambling flourished in the communities of unmarried males that were created by the dearth of Asian women in America. In 1870, "More than 75% of the nearly 3,000 Chinese women workers in the United States identified themselves as prostitutes" (Perry, 2000, p. 104). Brothels and opium-smoking establishments became popular among both Asians and Whites. Regarding opium use among early Chinese immigrants, Mann (1993) suggested that 35% of the Chinese immigrants smoked opium regularly, which "led to the first national campaign against narcotics" (p. 59); the subsequent legislation was aimed at "excluding Chinese participation in American society" (p. 59). On the participation of the Chinese in these illegal activities, Daniels (1988) noted, "Since all of these activities were both lucrative and illegal, it seems clear that police and politicians in the White community were involved in sanctioning and profiting from them" (p. 22).

Eventually, following the pattern of other immigrants, Asian organized crime emerged, and secret societies such as "tongs" were formed. Describing these organizations, Perry (2000) indicated that such societies were originally created to assist Asian men in adjusting to America. But, as Perry noted, over time, many evolved into criminal organizations or developed links with Chinese triads. Consequently, the tongs came to dominate prostitution, along with gambling, drugs, and other vice crimes. So in addition to providing sexual outlets, they also created other opportunities for recreation and escapist behavior. Despite the profits reaped by Whites from the legal and illicit activities of the Chinese, heavy anti-Chinese sentiment persisted in California, which led to numerous negative campaigns against the population. Pointing to the roots of this negative sentiment, Sowell (1981) wrote, "The Chinese were both non-White and non-Christian, at a time when either trait alone was a serious handicap. They looked different, dressed differently, ate differently, and followed customs wholly unfamiliar to Americans" (pp. 136–137). By and large, the Chinese were generally relegated to the most menial and dirty occupations, such as mining, laying railroad tracks, and agricultural work. As a result of the Chinese Exclusion Act of 1882, unlike other ethnic minorities, the Chinese population decreased from the late 1880s through the mid-1940s. Since then, their numbers have increased, and they have remained the largest segment of the Asian American population.

Until the last 30 years of the 20th century, Japanese Americans represented the second-largest group among Asians in the United States. Several other Asian groups have now surpassed them in population (most notably, Filipinos). We review the Japanese American experience in the next section.

Japanese Americans

Like the Chinese before them, the Japanese arrived on North American shores as a result of labor needs, and the relatively small number of Japanese men who made it to America (about 2,200 by 1890) filled the continuing need for laborers on California farms (Daniels, 1988). Like the Chinese and other groups, some Japanese immigrants turned to illicit activities, such as prostitution and other petty crimes, to survive.

Over time, the number of Japanese in America began to increase. Feagin and Feagin (2008) wrote that "between the 1880s and . . . 1908, more than 150,000 Japanese entered (America); between 1909 and the 1920s, another 100,000 came" (p. 282). Mirroring the experience of the Chinese, anti-Japanese sentiment arose in the United States, culminating with the arrival of World War II. During World War II, negative sentiment toward the Japanese reached new heights; they were hated and mistrusted by many Americans. After the attack on Pearl Harbor, in December 1941, life for Japanese Americans changed. In February 1942, President Roosevelt issued Executive Order 9066 (Dinnerstein & Reimers, 1982). The order, which was upheld by the Supreme Court, required that all Japanese from the West Coast be rounded up and placed in camps called ***relocation centers***. In all, about 110,000 people were rounded up on 5 days' notice and were told they could take only what they could carry. The camps were nothing more than prison facilities with armed military police on patrol, watching for escapes.

Following the war, the Japanese population remained low in the United States due to immigration restrictions that were not lifted until the 1960s. At that time, Japanese Americans represented 52% of the Asian American population. However, over the next 20 years, the number of Japanese who immigrated to America declined. This trend was largely a result of the increased need for labor in Japan, which stunted the immigration of the Japanese to America (Takaki, 1989). Those Japanese who were already here or who came after stringent quotas were lifted in the 1960s would go on to become some of the most successful immigrants. Today, economic indicators related to income and unemployment levels all reveal a positive trend for Japanese Americans. Nonetheless, Japanese Americans "still face exclusion from certain positions in many business, entertainment, political, and civil service areas, regardless of abilities" (Feagin & Feagin, 2008, p. 293).

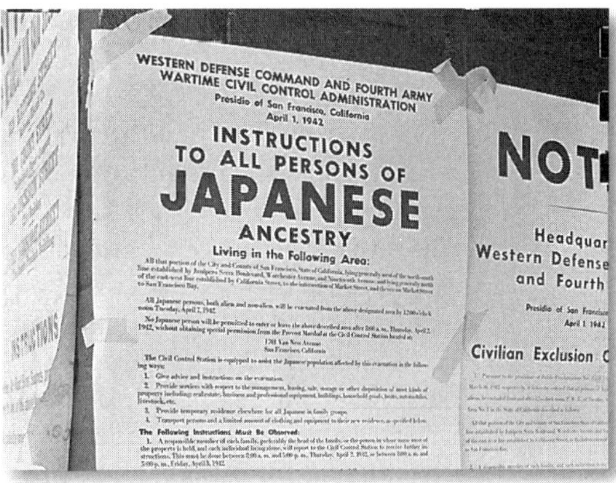

▲ **Photo 1.2** Posted Signs With Japanese American Exclusion Order

Two other Asian groups whose numbers have increased over the last few decades are Filipinos and Koreans. We provide brief overviews of their American experiences in the next section.

Filipinos and Koreans

Filipinos have been in the United States since the 1700s. But as you might expect, much of their most significant immigration to the United States occurred in the 19th and 20th centuries. Many headed to plantations in Hawaii due to labor shortages. Unfortunately, when they arrived in America, they encountered violent attacks from Whites. In California, they competed with White farm workers; besides receiving lower wages than their counterparts, they were the target of continuing violence. In fact, in 1929 and 1930, there were brutal riots that were brought on by anti-Filipino sentiment (Feagin & Feagin, 2008). During this same time period, the 1924 immigration law restricted the number of Filipinos that could enter the country to 50 (Kim, 2001). Since this early period, although their population has increased precipitously, they remain the targets of violence, and in post-9/11 America, some have been targeted as potential terrorists.

Like Filipino Americans, Korean Americans headed to Hawaii in the early part of the 20th century to fill labor shortages. Koreans also followed other Asian groups to California. In the case of Koreans, the place of choice was San Francisco. Limited by immigration restrictions, much of Korean immigration followed World War II. Not until 1965 were the stringent immigration restrictions lifted. This policy change coincided with more Koreans (mostly from South Korea) arriving in America. Looking for opportunities, Koreans headed to inner-city communities, where many of them opened small businesses. Unfortunately, the relations between Koreans and other urban residents were, at best, tenuous and, at worst, resentful—due mostly, as some have noted, to

Korean immigrants entering largely African American communities and "setting up shop." Therefore, besides feeling that they were mistreated by clerks in Korean establishments, some felt that such businesses should be owned by community members. This sentiment spilled over in the Los Angeles riot of 1992 (Kim, 1999). In 2007, Korean Americans again received negative attention because the perpetrator of the Virginia Tech massacre was an immigrant from South Korea.

The difference between Asians and ethnic groups who came to be classified as White is that, although they have attained high levels of achievement, Asians have never fully assimilated. This leaves them, as one author put it, "as perpetual outsiders" (Perry, 2000, p. 99). Like African Americans, Native Americans, and some Latinos, Asian Americans have maintained a distinct racial categorization. Gould (2000) suggested that physical characteristics unique to their race (e.g., skin color, facial characteristics, size) have barred them from full assimilation and acceptance in America.

In recent years, Asian Americans have been labeled the ***model minority*** because of their success in education. Some see their success as proof that all groups can succeed if they "put their best foot forward." Others see this label as problematic (Wu, 2002), noting that all Asians are not equally successful. For example, as Perry (2000) noted, "Koreans and Vietnamese consistently lag behind Chinese, Japanese, and Asian Indians on most indicators of socioeconomic status" (p. 100). Furthermore, the continuing discrimination in employment, income, and education are masked by such a label (Perry, 2000). Nevertheless, over the last century, Asian Americans have been a productive force in the United States.

Summary

- Since the categorization of races in the late 1700s, societies have, unfortunately, used this classification system to divide populations.
- In America, the notion of race was not of considerable use until the 1660s, when color was one of the deciding factors in the creation of the slave system. It was at this time in history that the category "White" began to take on increased importance.
- Our review of the historical antecedents of race and crime in America has revealed that, over the past few centuries, although the level of crime in each group has varied over time, most racial/ethnic groups have committed the same kinds of offenses and have had similar offenses perpetrated against them by the dominant culture.
- Initially, Whites criminally brutalized Native Americans and African Americans. As time went on, ethnic immigrants such as the Germans, Italians, Irish, Jews, Asians, and Latinos also were subjected to harsh treatment and sometimes violence. As "White ethnic" groups assimilated into the populace, they, in turn, became part of the oppressive White population, continuing at times to engage in racial violence against other minority groups.
- In short, the history of race and crime in America is a story of exploitation, violence, and in the case of most racial/ethnic groups, the common use of crime as a way to ascend from the lower rungs of American society. The next chapter examines official crime and victimization data for the various races.

KEY TERMS

assimilation

Black codes

Bracero Program

Chinese Exclusion Act

colonization

ethnicity

lynching

minority

model minority

people of color

prejudice

race

racial discrimination

relocation centers

truly disadvantaged

White ethnics

DISCUSSION QUESTIONS

1. Is there a better way to classify human beings besides using racial classifications?
2. How does racial discrimination in employment impact racial disparities in criminal justice?
3. Do you think Native Americans and African Americans are naturally more criminal than White Americans? Explain your reasoning.
4. Do you think the perception of Asians as the "model minority" influences their treatment by justice system officials?
5. Do you believe that whiteness still matters in succeeding in America?

WEB RESOURCES

U.S. Bureau of the Census: http://www.census.gov

Information on race data from the U.S. Census Bureau: http://www.census.gov/population/www/socdemo/race/racefactcb.html

American Anthropological Association website: "Race—Are we so different?" http://www.understandingrace.org/home.html

Bureau of Indian Affairs: http://www.bia.gov/

Information on Ellis Island: http://www.ellisisland.org/

READING

The article reexamines the origins of American organized crime. Once thought to be the cultural contribution of Italian and Sicilian immigrants, Dickson-Gilmore and Woodiwiss illustrate how the accepted notions about the origins of organized crime need to be reconsidered. They locate the beginnings of organized crime with the arrival of French, Dutch, and British colonists. During the **colonization** process, these groups exploited the natural resources and lands of Native Americans. In doing so, they systematically cheated them out of their goods and land. The authors' historical account detailing these practices provides compelling evidence that organized crime has a much longer history in America than previously acknowledged.

The History of Native Americans and the Misdirected Study of Organized Crime

Jane Dickson-Gilmore and Michael Woodiwiss

For more than half a century, countless newspaper and magazine articles, books, films, and television documentaries published and shown across the world have repeated the same perspective on American organised crime history as that of a leading criminological textbook. 'Organised crime', according to *Criminology*, edited by several of the leading lights of the discipline, 'had its origin in the great wave of immigrants from Southern Italy (especially from Sicily) to the United States between 1875 and 1920'. Their section on the problem then proceeds to give brief descriptions of the history of Sicily and the American effort to prohibit alcohol before stating that Sicilian families 'were so successful in their domination of organised crime that, especially after World War II, organised crime became virtually synonymous with the Sicilian Mafia'. The textbook then claims that 'organised crime had become an empire almost beyond the reach of government, with vast resources derived from a virtual monopoly on gambling and loan-sharking, drug trafficking, pornography' and other criminal activities.

An earlier version of this history of organised crime in America was expressed by Senator John McClellan of Arkansas in 1962, when he wrote the following on the origins of the Mafia: 'When Sicilians migrated to the United States in great numbers at the end of the last century . . . many of the new arrivals were members of or closely associated with the secret society'. McClellan was only expressing what had become the conventional wisdom on the origins of organised crime in America by the 1960s. When he made this statement, he was chairman of the influential Senate Permanent Subcommittee on Investigations and he went on to sponsor America's most significant organised crime control measures, including the Organised Crime Control Act of 1970.

Source: Dickson-Gilmore, J., & Woodiwiss, M. (2008). The history of Native Americans and the misdirected study of organized crime. *Global Crime, 9*, 66–83.

As we shall see, this 'foreign origins' version of the United States organised crime history emerged out of the xenophobic assumptions shared by America's leading historians of the late nineteenth and early twentieth centuries.

Although without substance, this distortion of the past matters. It reduces the problem of organised crime in America, and by extension the world, to a struggle between good guys in government versus bad guys in crime. The bad guys tend to be almost always portrayed as foreign, bureaucratically organised, almost completely in control of illegal markets, and constituting a threat to legitimate business. They are often said to be 'one step ahead' of the good guys. The only possible solution to this version of organised crime is to give the government good guys more power to get the bad guys. State and corporate criminal behaviour and public and private corruption are thus de-emphasised, and laws such as those prohibiting certain kinds of drugs are unquestioned. Such an understanding of organised crime history lies behind the passage not just of McClellan's Organised Crime Control Act but also of the United Nations Convention against Transnational Organised Crime and countless other organised crime control initiatives in many countries. This is particularly disturbing because, although these initiatives have clearly not controlled organised crime activities in the United States or anywhere else, they have been accepted almost everywhere with very little evaluation by policy makers or the mainstream media.

Tales about the Mafia, accompanied by assertions about its local, national, and global reach, have cast organised crime history into its own, mainly foreign compartment, far away from the 'master narrative' of American history. And yet, insofar as that master narrative is as much one of the noble immigrant as the history of organised crime is that of the ignoble newcomer, both chronicles share origins and important intersections. Both histories begin with the arrival of outsiders to a 'new world'. Those fortunate to have first claimed the right to initiate the identity of 'American', which subsequent generations would claim as their birthright, and which would be selectively granted or withheld from later waves of 'others', were all virtually perceived as posing some threat to the 'American way', by their novelty if not their culture. Within the 'master narrative' of the 'huddled masses' lay the basic ingredients of the chronicle of organised crime: the eternal immigrant, seeking a better life through embracing or perverting 'American values' of industry and profit. According to American organised crime folklore, the latter course was chosen by the Italian and Sicilian immigrants of the late nineteenth century, thus initiating the scourge of organised crime in the United States.

And yet the Italians and Sicilians were hardly the first immigrants to organise crime in America. As we shall see in the second section of this article, the first wave of outsiders, in north-eastern America at least, came in the form of French, Dutch, and British colonisers, and the locals they encountered were the Indian peoples of the Atlantic coast and the territories which would become New France, New Netherland, and New York. Notwithstanding the far later incipience of organised crime assigned by some commentators, there is much within the interactions between the natives and newcomers of the American north-east to suggest that it is in this much earlier historical juncture that the first instances of organised criminal activity in America are witnessed.

The 'Other' Among Us: Criminality and Complicity in the Colonisation of North-Eastern America

Conventional histories of organised crime in the United States link the rise of this phenomenon erroneously with successive waves of 'immigrant others', including primarily Jewish,

Irish, and Italian newcomers. And yet they were certainly not the first immigrants to arrive in north-eastern America, nor are they the first to be associated with the rise of illicit, exploitative criminal networks. Conspicuously absent in these histories are the activities of the predominantly French, Dutch, and British immigrants who arrived in the north-east as early as 1608, and who in many cases far more aptly reflect the stereotypical immigrant of conventional organised crime chronologies their descendents applied to later newcomers.

The colonisation of the American north-east has been characterised as a form of stealth corporatism, in which outsiders systematically exploited the fish, fur, timber, and territorial resources of the place and, by implication, those indigenous nations which held them. Colonial corporations, created in Europe, arrived on Atlantic shores to exploit whatever profit might be found in the 'new world'. Commonly endowed with 'monopolies' on any resources that were 'discovered', corporations such as the Company of New France, the New Netherland Company, and the Dutch East India Company competed to make whatever they could of those exclusionary rights. Expansion of empire was, in most contexts, a close, but secondary consideration which was largely at the mercy of the primary goals of trade and commerce which were required to support it. And as is the case today, so it was historically: the entrenchment of a so-called legitimate economy and the concomitant regulatory structure carried with it abundant opportunities for the development of illicit—and often far more profitable—counterparts. The emergence of these alternative economies came fast on the heels of the establishment of the state-sanctioned markets, and they flourished with the complicity of local government officials, members of the military, the traders and their aboriginal partners.

The exploitation of the local resource base in both the French and Dutch colonial contexts provides an apposite example to illustrate our argument. The French arrived shortly before the Dutch in the north-east and were the first to attempt to establish relations of trade and commerce with the aboriginal people residing in their midst. The Dutch were far more transparent and successful in their search for profit than were the French, though. In 1608, when Henry Hudson sailed down the river that would take his name, he did so as a representative of the Dutch East India Company and in the company of a number of traders and merchants. The latter were quick to initiate trade with local indigenous peoples on the Hudson River, along the Atlantic coast and inland. By 1614, the Dutch Van Tweenhuysen Company had erected a permanent post at Fort Nassau, and the corporate colonialism of north-eastern America had begun in earnest. Fort Nassau was soon abandoned due to flooding; the Dutch East Indian Company overtook the Tweenhuysen Company and built the more enduring Fort Orange by 1624.

The Dutch merchants at Fort Orange, although they dabbled briefly—and rather disastrously—in aboriginal politics, adopted a clear focus on trading and commerce with local Indians. The Indians, initially Mohicans but later primarily Mohawk Iroquois, seem to have been content with such a purely mercantile association, despite their general preference for more multi-faceted alliances. This relationship would not be altered significantly when the British defeated the New Netherlanders in 1664 and assumed control of their post at Fort Orange, which remained predominantly Dutch.

To the north, the French made much more of the idea of empire, but were also keenly interested in developing a prosperous trade in support of their new settlement. The French explorer Samuel de Champlain had established a fragile settlement at Québec in 1608, as one part of his mandate to 'manage the colony, to explore, to maintain alliances with the Indians and to forge new ones'. Managing the colony required paying for it, and alliances were largely matters of commerce and warfare pursued largely as a means of protecting trading partners and relations. Champlain entered the wilderness around the settlement, seeking alliances with the Iroquoian and Algonquin nations on its borders, working assiduously towards the trade that would sustain his colony.

Once exposed to the luxury of European goods brought by the trade, aboriginal nations were prepared to fight to retain access to them. Merchants and traders cared little with whom they traded, as long as they could obtain the raw resources (primarily furs, notably beaver) necessary to sustain their profits. Traders, many of whom were quite happy to venture deep into the frontier to ply their craft, were generally rough, violent men who had little regard for business ethics or 'compassionate capitalism'. They worked for, or were connected with, merchants located in trading centres and settlements, who shared their rather mercenary approach to doing business. As framed by Francis Jennings, 'a "good" trader was one who could cheat Indians without getting caught at it, and the trouble with "that sort of fellow was that he would cheat the merchant too, if he could. Merchants who, for the most part, remained at the centre—at the posts or settlements—relied upon a network of traders who fanned out from the centre to the peripheries of the surrounding aboriginal communities to obtain furs from Indian trading partners. At least some of those partners were silent, or unseen, as aboriginals holding territories closer to the posts quickly adopted roles as 'middlemen'. In this capacity, the Mohawk Iroquois especially excelled.

Travelling upriver from their settlements on the southern shore of the Saint Lawrence River near Montreal, Mohawk warriors would intercept shipments of furs on their way to the post at Montreal and purchase (at quite reduced prices) or steal furs from outer nation traders. The Mohawks would then deliver these furs to whomever would offer the best price; regrettably for New France, the presence of Dutch and, later, British traders at New York meant that there was always an alternative market, and often a more profitable one, within a day or two's journey from Montreal. The reality of competing markets gave rise early on to an 'illicit trade' between Montreal and Fort Orange/Albany, which was plied primarily by the Mohawks residing on the Saint Lawrence. That waterway, referred to as the trading 'superhighway' of the north, was intersected by the Richelieu River, which flowed south through Lake Champlain, into Lake George and down the Hudson River past Albany to New York. As this watershed, referred to as the 'Mahican channel', was largely controlled by Mohawk Iroquois, it provided a convenient access between competing, alternative markets for Mohawk middlemen.

The Montreal-Albany trade appears to have begun in earnest shortly after the English conquest of New York. It was made inevitable by the hard realities of the north-eastern colonial economics: Albany offered superior trade goods, most notably the coveted English stroud (woollen cloth or blanket), and were willing to pay higher prices, while Canada contained more and better peltries, for which lower prices and lesser quality goods were offered. An accommodation was presupposed by the desire of both Mohawks and French merchants and settlers for English goods, the greed of the traders and the complicity of everyone from Indian to intendant and Governor.

The French were the first to feel the ill effects of the underground trading economy. Losing profits and, just as dangerously, the Indian allies which generated and protected them, to the south, the French struggled to control the trade by a series of regulatory measures which rendered participation in the trade first, illegal and, that failing, unprofitable. The earliest of the controls resided in the system of granting trade monopolies, whereby a single company became the only legitimate recipient of peltries. Later, however, as this restriction proved inadequate to stay the tide of French furs south, the prohibitions became many and varied. Initially, these extraordinary measures focussed on the Indian trade and attempted to end the loss of beaver to Albany by reproducing in French mills the English strouds which the Mohawks appeared unwilling to live without. This policy failed and led to the importing of original strouds to Montreal, but this effort suffered from the same problems of expense already characterising the majority of French goods.

Because the greater part of the trade between Montreal and Albany was conducted via the 'Mahican channel', later controls were designed to impede as much as possible traffic on those pathways. These were equally ineffectual, owing in no small measure to the reality that those manning the controls were often also involved in the trade. There is evidence to indicate that French soldiers stationed at posts situated along the most common routes of the illicit trade refused to thwart the trade and may well have been actively involved, as were their British counterparts in New York. In an effort to compensate for this, other additional controls were created, but they were all of uniformly minimal effect; there were far too many key hands in the Montreal-Albany trading pot, and none of them were willing to come out empty. As a result, controls on the trade were largely fruitless, and business thrived. Documentary evidence suggests that, at one juncture in the history of the Montreal-Albany trade, as much as two-thirds of the peltries harvested in Canada per year were diverted to New York for considerable profit of those involved in the trade.

The extent to which the rich and powerful were complicit in the Montreal-Albany trade is evident in the records, which are especially illuminating regarding the impact of the trade on the ongoing battles between French and British to control the north-east. At the Seven Years' War, which would ultimately decide the contest that arose on the horizon, considerable ambivalence was apparent on the part of key colonial players. William Johnson, the British trader-turned-diplomat who was charged with managing Indian Affairs for the New York government prior to the outbreak of the war after 1756, was advised by an official that

> You cannot be) ignorant yt many in (ye Province,) and its Neighboring Traders, and ye Richest Men (in Albany) do not wish well to the Success of any Expedtn (against) Canada, & this from a view which a few Men of considerable estates & influence by their family relations have to their private advantage gained by a Trade with France, & which (for ye Common good) I hope I have effectualy Stopt, I must therfore tell you yt I am Suspicious yt all ye Difficulties I met with in ye War, arose chiefly from this Source; For it these men could have prevented ye Indians joining in ye War, & could have prevailed with them to declare for a Neutrality . . . without an open declaration of their Intentions were lay'd in ye way of every preparation that became necessary for ye Success of any Enterprise against Canada.

It is doubtful that this communication came as much surprise to Johnson, however, given his own connections to the trade. Johnson was related by marriage to the powerful DeLancey family of Albany, whose wealth was founded virtually entirely upon the Montreal-Albany trade network. When William Shirley, in his capacity as Governor of Massachusetts and Commander-in-Chief of the British Royal Forces, attempted to squelch the trade, which many viewed as a traitorous association, Johnson retaliated by convincing the Iroquois not to support Shirley's military aspirations, and the DeLanceys withheld funds for the same. The irony is not lost that the Saint Lawrence River and the Mohawk communities which dot its southern shores have been actively and openly implicated in the 'buttlegging' of contraband cigarettes and other commodities, both licit and illicit, through parts of the waterways which once defined the Montreal-Albany trade. Nor is it much surprising that, as the Montreal-Albany trade once carried the protection of the rich and powerful, the 'contraband corridor' through which modern Mohawks smuggled cigarettes had the complicity and support of the wealthy and powerful R. J. Reynolds

Company. There is thus a long tradition of well-organised, well-connected criminal enterprise in north-eastern America, and one that certainly predates the arrival of immigrants from Italy or Sicily.

Indeed, it seems likely that, if we wish to place blame for the rise of organised crime in America at the feet of immigrants, the most likely culprits are the French, Dutch, and British, who openly defrauded their aboriginal trading partners (who also seemed less than unwilling to exploit each other) and who together openly engaged in the illicit Montreal-Albany trade.

While the Montreal-Albany trade was probably the most conspicuous and well-organised illicit activity of the era, it is important to recognise that the interactions between native and newcomers in licit trade were also characterised by their own forms of lawlessness. To the degree that these practices worked to the benefit of the colonial empires and the economics that supported them, however, they were overlooked by officials, who were also willing to turn a blind eye to the degree to which these activities worked to the detriment of aboriginal communities. For example, in north-eastern America, no trader travelled without a good supply of liquor (brandy in New France, rum in New York), and any trade included a good dose of 'firewater'. To maximise profit, traders would regularly water down the liquor, but their Indian trading partners quickly caught on. Setting a match to the barrel or bottle became a standard part of any exchange—if the spirits ignited, the liquor was not watered and the trade was good; if it did not catch fire, the watery offering was likely to be rejected immediately. This was fraud, of course, but no official would have responded to it as such, largely because especially in New France, the official position of both Indian and non-Indian governments was opposed to the use of liquor in the trade—not that this official position translated into much effect in practice.

The situation in New France is a good example. For much of the history of the French regime in Canada, governance of the colony was subject to ongoing power struggles between the powerful Catholic Society of Jesus and their Jesuit missionaries, and colonial officials. The Jesuits, who spent much time in aboriginal communities, were well aware of the disastrous impact the brandy trade had on those communities and exerted pressure both on the Sovereign Council at Quebec and their own bishopric to stem the flow of liquor into aboriginal communities. In response, the colonial government, unwilling to press too strongly to control an essential aspect of the trade, sanctioned the sale of alcohol to the Indian people, but forbade those purchasing it to get drunk. For their part, Church condemned the sale of liquor to Indians and threatened with excommunication anyone caught defying this prohibition. Almost without exception, the controls amounted to nothing. Company and colonial officials turned a blind eye to the illicit trade in brandy, which Devine informs was merely 'winked at by the French officials'. Liquor always had been, and would continue to be, a central commodity of the trade, and therefore of the colonial enterprise in New France.

Traders brought impacts other than liquor and European technologies into communities, including fundamental shifts in their traditional economic, social and political structures. Epidemics and famines vastly exacerbated warfare over access to the trade, and participation in their colonial allies' conflicts effectively undermined traditional ways. Epidemics may perhaps be seen as the collateral damage of colonial corporatism, and most of the other consequences—warfare, famine, socioeconomic and political disruption—were a direct result of the practices that came to inform and underpin most legitimate capitalist—and non-legitimate—exchanges between aboriginal and non-aboriginal trading partners.

It is clear that there was much that was organised criminality in the early moments of contact and colonisation of North-eastern America; it is also apparent that this systematic abuse of power toward aboriginal people did not end with the fur trade. Indeed, in any comprehensive history of such activity America must acknowledge the systematic criminal activity against Native Americans by citizens of the newly created United States during the nineteenth century. Numerous government commissions appointed to investigate Indian affairs acknowledged that white crimes against Indians far outweighed Indian crimes against whites and that white crimes were both ruthless and systematic. Nineteenth and early twentieth century historians and school history textbooks until the 1960s reflected and perpetuated stereotypes of Native Americans. Francis Parkman, for example, a prominent representative of the first generation of American historians, characterised all Indians as 'rigid, inflexible, and unprogressive', a race that was inevitably and rightly doomed. He was followed by a succession of popular historians uniformly dismissing Indians as savages on their way to extinction due to racial deficiencies. These included the aforementioned Frederick Jackson Turner, Theodore Roosevelt, and Woodrow Wilson. Turner's thesis on the significance of America's frontier experience had made him one of the primary shapers of America's understanding of its past, not least through its influence on the narratives of Hollywood western films. Roosevelt and Wilson wrote influential survey histories before becoming the presidents who dominated national politics in the early twentieth century. All shared a belief in what became known as American exceptionalism, the idea that the United States offers hope for the democratic future of humanity due to the special historical circumstances of the spread of democracy across the North American continent. By accepting this belief in a universally benevolent exceptionalism, they had to ignore or downplay what Richard Hofstadter called the 'shame' of America, involving such aspects of Western development as 'riotous land speculation, vigilantism, the ruthless despoiling of the continent, the arrogance of American expansionism . . . even the near savagery, to which men were reduced on some portions of the frontier'.

These historians also ignored the impact of systematic criminality on America's native population, not least the wholesale corruption and fraud that followed the Dawes Allotment Act of 1887, which involved carving up the Indian Reservations into fee simple plots owned by individuals and families, in the same way that whites owned their land and in a way contrary to centuries of native tribal tradition. The allotment processes that followed allowed government officials and white land purchasers to cheat unsuspecting natives out of millions of acres of their land, helping to account for the reduction of Indian landholdings in the United States from 138 to 52 million acres. The main result of allotment, according to Cherokee rancher Richard-Martin, was 'to turn this illiterate people into the Shark like Jaws of the greedy grafter who are here in great numbers with the one Thought and that is gain'. Given the ignorance and bias of popular and academic history, the thought that native Americans might have been among the most significant victims of organised criminal activity would not have occurred to many Americans when they began to confront the problem of 'organised crime' at the end of the nineteenth century.

The descendents of the French, Dutch, and British immigrants, who may be understood as the first real perpetrators of organised crime in America, constructed and believed in revisionist histories which reified the colonial newcomers and cast native Americans as thwarters of progress and 'the American way'. It was but a small leap from there to see the efforts of native nations to move out of state-induced and reinforced poverty, largely through economic activities such as casinos, on-line gaming, and high-stakes bingos which remain associated with vice, as marginal, possibly criminal, activities. Generations of Americans, getting their knowledge of the past from Eurocentric textbooks and less than scholarly press accounts, would be kept ignorant of the fact that their pioneering forebears were involved in much activity that would qualify as organised crime in even the most restrictive definition. Indeed, some of the most prominent of early Americans may be seen as setting a precedent for well-organised, profit-motivated state lawlessness first involving and then victimising the Native Americans whose nations long predated that of the United States. It would prove to be a difficult precedent to break, as would the conceptualisations of organised crime which insulated influential elites and officials by characterising organized crime as essentially the province of the 'other'.

DISCUSSION QUESTIONS

1. What are your reactions to the argument made by Gilmore and Woodiwiss that organized crime began in the United States when the first wave of immigrants, primarily of French, Dutch, and British descent, arrived in the early 1600s? Do they make a compelling argument? Why or why not?
2. Why do you think criminologists studying organized crime have overlooked or dismissed the colonists' exploitation of Native Americans as a form of organized crime?
3. How does this article contribute to the understanding of organized crime not only in the United States, but also throughout the world?

❖

READING

Professor Gans' article provides a historical overview of how the American class structure has influenced the racial hierarchy in America. Beginning with an overview of how the lay public views race, he dissects the role that skin color plays in judgments about superiority and inferiority and also about who are the dangerous populations. Inevitably, those with dark skin color (African Americans and other Blacks) have been reduced to being both inferior and the most threatening population. He considers the way in which early White ethnic immigrants were able to use class mobility to rise out of their racially undesirable status. This, however, has not been the experience of African Americans. Because of discriminatory practices, they remain, in large part, unable to completely ascend the class ranks that provide the proven avenue for movement up the racial hierarchy.

Race as Class

Herbert J. Gans

Source: Gans, H. J. (2005). Race as class. *Contexts, 4*, 17–21.

Humans of all colors and shapes can make babies with each other. Consequently most biologists, who define races as subspecies that cannot interbreed, argue that scientifically there can be no human races. Nonetheless, lay people still see and distinguish between races. Thus, it is worth asking again why the lay notion of race continues to exist and to exert so much influence in human affairs.

Lay persons are not biologists, nor are they sociologists, who argue these days that race is a social construction arbitrary enough to be eliminated if "society" chose to do so. The laity operates with a very different definition of race. They see that humans vary, notably in skin color, the shape of the head, nose, and lips, and quality of hair, and they choose to define the variations as individual races.

More important, the lay public uses this definition of race to decide whether strangers (the so-called other) are to be treated as superior, inferior, or equal. Race is even more useful for deciding quickly whether strangers might be threatening and thus should be excluded. Whites often consider dark-skinned strangers threatening until they prove otherwise, and none more than African Americans.

Scholars believe the color differences in human skins can be traced to climatic adaptation. They argue that the high levels of melanin in dark skin originally protected people living outside in hot, sunny climates, notably in Africa and South Asia, from skin cancer. Conversely, in cold climates, the low amount of melanin in light skins enabled the early humans to soak up vitamin D from a sun often hidden behind clouds. These color differences were reinforced by millennia of inbreeding when humans lived in small groups that were geographically and socially isolated. This inbreeding also produced variations in head and nose shapes and other facial features so that Northern Europeans look different from people from the Mediterranean area, such as Italians and, long ago, Jews. Likewise, East African faces differ from West African ones, and Chinese faces from Japanese ones. (Presumably the inbreeding and isolation also produced the DNA patterns that geneticists refer to in the latest scientific revival and redefinition of race.)

Geographic and social isolation ended long ago, however, and human population movements, intermarriage, and other occasions for mixing are eroding physical differences in bodily features. Skin color stopped being adaptive too after people found ways to protect themselves from the sun and could get their vitamin D from the grocery or vitamin store. Even so, enough color variety persists to justify America's perception of white, yellow, red, brown, and black races.

Never mind for the moment that the skin of "whites," as well as [that of] many East Asians and Latinos, is actually pink; that Native Americans are not red; that most African Americans come in various shades of brown; and that really black skin is rare. Never mind either that color differences within each of these populations are as great as the differences between them and that, as DNA testing makes quite clear, most people are of racially mixed origins even if they do not know it. But remember that this color palette was invented by whites. Nonwhite people would probably divide the range of skin colors quite differently.

Advocates of racial equality use these contradictions to fight against racism. However, the general public also has other priorities. As long as people can roughly agree about who looks "white," "yellow," or "black" and find that their notion of race works for their purposes, they ignore its inaccuracies, inconsistencies, and other deficiencies.

Note, however, that only some facial and bodily features are selected for the lay definition of race. Some, like the color of women's nipples or the shape of toes (and male navels), cannot serve because they are kept covered. Most other visible ones, like height, weight, hairlines, ear lobes, finger or hand sizes—and even skin texture—vary too randomly and frequently to be useful for categorizing and ranking people or judging strangers. After all, your own child is apt to have the same stubby fingers as a child of another skin color or, what is equally important, a child from a very different income level.

Race, Class, and Status

In fact, the skin colors and facial features commonly used to define race are selected precisely because, when arranged hierarchically, they resemble the country's class-and-status hierarchy. Thus, whites are on top of the socioeconomic pecking order as they are on top of the racial one, while variously shaded nonwhites are below them in socioeconomic position (class) and prestige (status).

The darkest people are for the most part at the bottom of the class-status hierarchy. This is no accident, and Americans have therefore always used race as a marker or indicator of both class and status. Sometimes they also use it to enforce class position, to keep some people "in their place." Indeed, these uses are a major reason for its persistence.

Of course, race functions as more than a class marker, and the correlation between race and the socioeconomic pecking order is far from statistically perfect: All races can be found at every level of that order. Still, the race-class correlation is strong enough to utilize race for the general ranking of others. It also becomes more useful for ranking dark-skinned people as white poverty declines so much that whiteness becomes equivalent to being middle or upper class.

The relation between race and class is unmistakable. For example, the 1998–2000 median household income of non-Hispanic whites was $45,500; of Hispanics (currently seen by many as a race) as well as Native Americans, $32,000; and of African Americans, $29,000. The poverty rates for these same groups were 7.8 percent among whites, 23.1 among Hispanics, 23.9 among blacks, and 25.9 among Native Americans. (Asians' median income was $52,600—which does much to explain why we see them as a model minority.)

True, race is not the only indicator used as a clue to socioeconomic status. Others exist and are useful because they can also be applied to ranking co-racials. They include language (itself a rough indicator of education), dress, and various kinds of taste, from given names to cultural preferences, among others.

American English has no widely known working-class dialect like the English Cockney, although "Brooklynese" is a rough equivalent, as is "black vernacular." Most blue-collar people dress differently at work from white-collar, professional, and managerial workers. Although contemporary American leisure-time dress no longer signifies the wearers' class, middle-income Americans do not usually wear Armani suits or French haute couture, and the people who do can spot the knockoffs bought by the less affluent.

Actually, the cultural differences in language, dress, and so forth that were socially most noticeable are declining. Consequently, race could become yet more useful as a status marker, since it is so easily noticed and so hard to hide or change. And in a society that likes to see itself as classless, race comes in very handy as a substitute.

The Historical Background

Race became a marker of class and status almost with the first settling of the United States. The country's initial holders of cultural and political power were mostly WASPs (with a smattering of Dutch and Spanish in some parts of what later became the United States). They thus automatically assumed that their kind of whiteness marked the top of the class hierarchy. The bottom was assigned to the most powerless, who at first were Native Americans and slaves. However, even before the former had been virtually eradicated or pushed to the country's edges, the skin color and related facial features of the majority of colonial America's slaves had become the markers for the lowest class in the colonies.

Although dislike and fear of the dark are as old as the hills and found all over the world, the distinction between black and white skin became important in America only with slavery and was actually established only some decades after the first importation of black slaves. Originally, slave owners justified their enslavement of black Africans by their being heathens, not by their skin color.

In fact, early Southern plantation owners could have relied on white indentured servants to pick tobacco and cotton or purchased the white slaves that were available then, including the Slavs from whom the term *slave* is derived. They also had access to enslaved Native Americans. Blacks, however, were cheaper, more plentiful, more easily controlled, and physically more able to survive the intense heat and brutal working conditions of Southern plantations.

After slavery ended, blacks became farm laborers and sharecroppers, de facto indentured servants, really, and thus they remained at the bottom of the class hierarchy. When the pace of industrialization quickened, the country needed new sources of cheap labor. Northern industrialists, unable and unwilling to recruit southern African Americans, brought in very poor European immigrants, mostly peasants. Because these people were near the bottom of the class hierarchy, they were considered nonwhite and classified into races. Irish and Italian newcomers were sometimes even described as black (Italians as "guineas"), and the eastern and southern European immigrants were deemed "swarthy."

However, because skin color is socially constructed, it can also be reconstructed. Thus, when the descendants of the European immigrants began to move up economically and socially, their skins apparently began to look lighter to the whites who had come to America before them. When enough of these descendents became visibly middle class, their skin was seen as fully white. The biological skin color of the second and third generations had not changed, but it was socially blanched or whitened. The process probably began in earnest just before the Great Depression and resumed after World War II. As the cultural and other differences of the original European immigrants disappeared, their descendants became known as white ethnics.

This pattern is now repeating itself among the peoples of the post-1965 immigration. Many of the new immigrants came with money and higher education, and descriptions of their skin color have been shaped by their class position. Unlike the poor Chinese who were imported in the 19th century to build the West and who were hated and feared by whites as a "yellow horde," today's affluent Asian newcomers do not seem to look yellow. In fact, they are already sometimes thought of as honorary whites, and later in the 21st century they may well turn into a new set of white ethnics. Poor East and Southeast Asians may not be so privileged, however, although they are too few to be called a "yellow horde."

Hispanics are today's equivalent of a "swarthy" race. However, the children and grandchildren of immigrants among them will probably undergo "whitening" as they become middle class. Poor Mexicans, particularly in the Southwest, are less likely to be whitened, however. (Recently a WASP Harvard professor came close to describing these Mexican immigrants as a brown horde.)

Meanwhile, black Hispanics from Puerto Rico, the Dominican Republic, and other Caribbean countries may continue to be perceived, treated, and mistreated as if they were African American. One result of that mistreatment is their low median household income of $35,000, which was just $1,000 more than that of non-Hispanic blacks but $4,000 below that of so-called white Hispanics.

▲ **Photo 1.3** Not Quite White: Early 20th-Century Immigrants

Perhaps South Asians provide the best example of how race correlates with class and how it is affected by class position. Although the highly educated Indians and Sri Lankans who started coming to America after 1965 were often darker than African Americans, whites only noticed their economic success. They have rarely been seen as nonwhites, and are also often praised as a model minority.

Of course, even favorable color perceptions have not ended racial discrimination against newcomers, including model minorities and other affluent ones. When they become competitors for valued resources such as highly paid jobs, top schools, housing, and the like, they also become a threat to whites. California's Japanese-Americans still suffer from discrimination and prejudice four generations after their ancestors arrived here.

African-American Exceptionalism

The only population whose racial features are not automatically perceived differently with upward mobility are African Americans: Those who are affluent and well-educated remain as visibly black to whites as before. Although a significant number of African Americans have become middle class since the civil rights legislation of the 1960s, they still suffer from far harsher and more pervasive discrimination and segregation than nonwhite immigrants of equivalent class position. This not only keeps whites and blacks apart but prevents blacks from moving toward equality with whites. In their case, race is used both as a marker of class and, by keeping blacks "in their place," an enforcer of class position and a brake on upward mobility.

In the white South of the past, African Americans were lynched for being "uppity." Today, the enforcement of class position is less deadly but, for example, the glass ceiling for professional and managerial African Americans is set lower than for Asian Americans, and on-the-job harassment remains routine.

Why African-American upward economic mobility is either blocked or, if allowed, not followed by public blanching of skin color remains a mystery. Many explanations have been proposed for the white exceptionalism with which African Americans are treated. The most common is "racism," an almost innate prejudice against people of different skin color that takes both personal and institutional forms. But this does not tell us why such prejudice toward African Americans remains stronger than that toward other nonwhites.

A second explanation is the previously mentioned white antipathy to blackness, with an allegedly primeval fear of darkness extrapolated into a primordial fear of dark-skinned people. But according to this explanation, dark-skinned immigrants such as South Asians should be treated much like African Americans.

A better explanation might focus on "Negroid" features. African as well as Caribbean immigrants with such features—for example, West Indians and Haitians—seem to be treated somewhat better than African Americans. But this remains true only for new immigrants; their children are generally treated like African Americans.

Two additional explanations are class-related. For generations, a majority or plurality of all African Americans were poor, and about a quarter still remain so. In addition, African Americans continue to commit a proportionally greater share of the street crime, especially street drug sales—often because legitimate job opportunities are scarce. African Americans are apparently also more often arrested without cause. As one result, poor African Americans are more often considered undeserving than are other poor people, although in some parts of America, poor Hispanics, especially those who are black, are similarly stigmatized.

The second class-based explanation proposes that white exceptionalist treatment of African Americans is a continuing effect of slavery: They are still perceived as ex-slaves. Many hateful stereotypes with which today's African Americans are demonized have changed little from those used to dehumanize the slaves. (Black Hispanics seem to be equally demonized, but then they were also slaves, if not on the North American continent.) Although slavery ended officially in 1864, ever since the end of Reconstruction subtle efforts to discourage African-American upward mobility have not abated, although these efforts are today much less pervasive or effective than earlier.

Some African Americans are now millionaires, but the gap in wealth between average African Americans and whites is much greater than the gap between incomes. The African-American middle class continues to grow, but many of its members barely have a toehold in it, and some are only a few paychecks away from a return to poverty. And the African-American poor still face the most formidable obstacles to upward mobility. Close to a majority of working-age African-American men are jobless or out of the labor force. Many women, including single mothers, now work in the low-wage economy, but they must do without most of the support systems that help middle-class working mothers. Both federal and state governments have been punitive, even in recent Democratic administrations, and the

▲ **Photo 1.4** Mid-20th Century African American Youth

Republicans have cut back nearly every antipoverty program they cannot abolish.

Daily life in a white-dominated society reminds many African Americans that they are perceived as inferiors, and these reminders are louder and more relentless for the poor, especially young men. Regularly suspected of being criminals, they must constantly prove that they are worthy of equal access to the American Dream. For generations, African Americans have watched immigrants pass them in the class hierarchy, and those who are poor must continue to compete with current immigrants for the lowest-paying jobs. If unskilled African Americans reject such jobs or fail to act as deferentially as immigrants, they justify the white belief that they are less deserving than immigrants. Blacks' resentment of such treatment gives whites additional evidence of their unworthiness, thereby justifying another cycle of efforts to keep them from moving up in class and status.

Such practices raise the suspicion that the white political economy and white Americans may, with the help of nonwhites who are not black, use African Americans to anchor the American class structure with a permanently lower-class population. In effect, America, or those making decisions in its name, could be seeking, not necessarily consciously, to establish an undercaste that cannot move out and up. Such undercastes exist in other societies: the gypsies of Eastern Europe, India's untouchables, "indigenous people" and "aborigines" in yet other places. But these are far poorer countries than the United States.

Some Implications

The conventional wisdom and its accompanying morality treat racial prejudice, discrimination, and segregation as irrational social and individual evils that public policy can reduce but only changes in white behavior and values can eliminate. In fact, over the years, white prejudice as measured by attitude surveys has dramatically declined, far more dramatically than behavioral and institutional discrimination.

But what if discrimination and segregation are more than just a social evil? If they are used to keep African Americans down, then they also serve to eliminate or restrain competitors for valued or scarce resources, material and symbolic. Keeping African Americans from decent jobs and incomes as well as quality schools and housing makes more of these available to all the rest of the population. In that case, discrimination and segregation may decline significantly only if the rules of the competition change or if scarce resources, such as decent jobs, become plentiful enough to relax the competition, so that the African-American population can become as predominantly middle class as the white population. Then the stigmas, the stereotypes inherited from slavery, and the social and other arrangements that maintain segregation and discrimination could begin to lose their credibility. Perhaps "black" skin would eventually become as invisible as "yellow" skin is becoming.

The Multiracial Future

One trend that encourages upward mobility is the rapid increase in interracial marriage that began about a quarter century ago. As the children born to parents of different races also intermarry, more and more Americans will be multiracial, so that at some point far in the future the current quintet of skin colors will be irrelevant. About 40 percent of young Hispanics and two-thirds of young Asians now "marry out," but only about 10 percent of blacks now marry nonblacks—yet another instance of the exceptionalism that differentiates blacks.

Moreover, if race remains a class marker, new variations in skin color and in other visible bodily features will be taken to indicate class position. Thus, multiracials with "Negroid" characteristics could still find themselves disproportionately at the bottom of the class hierarchy. But what if at some point in the future everyone's skin color varied by only a few shades of brown? At that point, the dominant American classes might have to invent some new class markers.

If in some utopian future the class hierarchy disappears, people will probably stop judging differences in skin color and other features. Then lay Americans would probably agree with biologists that race does not exist. They might even insist that race does not need to exist.

Recommended Resources

David Brion Davis. *Challenging the Boundaries of Slavery* (Harvard University Press, 2001). A historical account of the relation between race and slavery.

Joe R. Feagin and Melvin P. Sikes. *Living with Racism: The Black Middleclass Experience* (Beacon, 1994). Documents continuing discrimination against middle- and upper-middle-class African Americans.

Barbara Jeanne Fields. "Slavery, Race and Ideology in the United States of America." *New Left Review* 181 (May/June 1990): 95–118. A provocative analysis of the relations between class and race.

Marvin Harris. "How Our Skins Got Their Color." in *Who We Are, Where We Came From, and Where We Are Going* (Harper Collins, 1989). An anthropologist explains the origins of different skin colors.

Jennifer Lee and Frank D. Bean. "Beyond Black and White: Remaking Race in America." *Contexts* (Summer 2003): 26–33. A concise analysis of changing perceptions and realities of race in America.

DISCUSSION QUESTIONS

1. What is your reaction to the idea that the general public uses race to decide how a person should be treated and whether or not they should be viewed as a threat? Do you agree with this idea? Why or why not?
2. How does the controversial history of race relations within the United States affect how people view race?
3. Discuss how the color of one's skin in the United States can directly impact how a person is treated even in today's world.

❖

READING

Webster discusses how White ethnicity is often overlooked in discourse on race and crime. He correctly asserts that much of the discourse on race and crime centers on racial and ethnic groups other than Whites. This is despite the fact that Whites, in both the United Kingdom and the United States, commit a large share of the criminal offenses. In shaping the debate about racial and ethnic minorities other than Whites, such groups are painted as the more criminal races. In short, they *are* the crime problem. The author turns the tables on the traditional race and crime debate by focusing on the racial and class hierarchy within the White race and how it racializes crime among certain segments within the White population. Noting that terms such as *White underclass* and *new immigrants* represent code words for the segment of the White population deemed troublesome and criminal, Webster discusses the nuances of this understudied aspect of race and crime.

Marginalized White Ethnicity, Race and Crime

Colin Webster

Source: Webster, C. (2008). Marginalized white ethnicity, race and crime. *Theoretical Criminology, 12*, 293–312.

Introduction

> The white English working class is now the only group of people that the chattering classes are happy to hear mocked and attacked.
>
> Julie Burchill (cited in Collins, 2004: 225)

Burchill's iconoclastic view of class relations in modern Britain can be read at a number of levels, not least its veracity and reductionism. Yet it is striking, that while sexist and particularly racist language has become taboo in official discourse, the language of class contempt has not (Sayer, 2005). Class contempt varies from the subtlest forms of aversion to visceral revulsion, disgust and sneering that serves to project all that is bad and immoral onto the other, while reciprocally enhancing and confirming the goodness, self-regard and status of one's own class. Class contempt 'through distance, denigration and disgust towards the disadvantaged white working class also serves darker and more disturbing purposes that racialize this group too (Skeggs, 2004: 118). Class distance is drawn from setting moral boundaries between different sorts of whiteness, especially through ascriptions of the body and appearance. The white working class is denigrated for their 'excessive artificial appearance' and behaviour, vulgarity, 'letting go' and moral irresponsibility. Designations such as 'white trash' or 'chav' perfectly encompass feelings of class contempt. Contempt can lead to the criminalization of the black and white working class, and the condoning of middle-class crime, and the whole effect is to reinforce and reproduce class hierarchy. At the same time it is important in making these and other claims, developed later, not to create simply inverted binaries of class and ethnic identity that posit the respectable as bad and demands for respect automatically valid (Sayer, 2005).

It is remarkable how white ethnicity and class retain their anonymity in discussions of ethnicity and crime—especially as self-report studies suggest that 'whites' disproportionately offend compared to other ethnic groups and obviously commit the vast bulk of crimes. After all, 85 per cent of offences involving children and young people were committed by those who classify their ethnicity as white, and 92 per cent of black young people and children are not subject to disposals in the youth justice system (House of Commons Home Affairs Committee, 2007). Similarly, recent studies have found white working-class boys living in disadvantaged areas are the lowest performing group of pupils in schools after the small population of Traveller children (Curtis, 2008). And of course, school failure is a strong predictor of delinquency, crime and antisocial behaviour.

In a sense these sorts of cultural, criminological and class issues make it all the more puzzling why white ethnicity has remained unaddressed in discussions of ethnicity, race and crime. The key problem seems to be a general difficulty in social science in conceiving whiteness or white ethnicity other than in terms of privilege, power and superiority over *other* ethnicities. Whiteness as an ethnicity appears as an empty signifier devoid of content or meaning *except* insofar as it racializes *other* 'visible minorities'. That is not to say that the racial persecution of some white groups goes unrecognized as the case of Jewish, Irish and Gypsies amply shows. It is, rather, that these examples are sometimes seen as distant, exceptional or atypical and there is a focus on the recent past and the present. When studies do uncover counter-intuitive forms of discrimination, for example, Mooney and Young's (1999) study of stop and search in North London, they tend to be ignored. This piece of research found that foot stops of Irish men were higher than for African-Caribbean and that African stops were lower than white English ones, because the police focus on groups that are disproportionately working class and/or male as well as visible ethnic groups. In a different mixed ethnic context, Waddington et al.'s (2004) observation study of stop and search arrived at not dissimilar conclusions, arguing that white urban lower-class men who were available to be stopped suffered disproportionate stop and search regardless of visible ethnicity.

As a final preamble for the discussion to follow, it is likely that ethnic and racial categories in the British context that are limited to 'Black', Asian', 'White', 'Other', and more recently, 'Mixed', hardly capture the increasingly complex demographic make-up of a society that has experienced recent large-scale immigration. Apart from the inability of these categories to capture diversity within them, descriptions of a white majority and ethnic minorities in some urban areas seem increasingly outmoded (Dorling and Thomas, 2007). Some of this immigration from 'white' EU countries, high levels of racist violence experienced by asylum seekers and the fact that many immigrants are exploited in unregulated jobs, trafficked or enslaved in the sex trade, all puts a new complexion on inter- and intra-ethnic group relations in European societies (Goodey, 2003; Melossi, 2003; Garner, 2004, 2007b; Stenson and Waddington, 2007).

These are some of the more obvious ways we can begin to think afresh about white ethnicities. The next section asks what constitutes 'whiteness' and white ethnicity, its peculiarities and how it can be said to exist as a distinct entity in its own right and in relation to other ethnicities. The following section discusses historical legacies of how marginalized white ethnicities have been represented in ways that give potency to the idea of their deviancy and criminality. The continuities and discontinuities of this legacy found in contemporary representations are explored, again drawing out the ways in which racialized 'white' groups such as the 'unfit', 'the antisocial', 'criminals', the poor, 'white trash' and the 'underclass' were and are elided around marginalized white ethnicity often associated with criminality (Webster, 2007). Classed, raced and gendered marginalized white ethnicity is spatialized as well through the creation of moral boundaries and disciplining within hierarchies of whiteness.

What Is White Ethnicity?

Ethnicity like class is relational, productive and active in social relationships rather than a mere fixed or passive descriptor or category. Whiteness conjures up other ethnicities while at the same time is often rendered invisible, 'normal', 'neutral'. It is an identity and a lifestyle, and a set of perspectives on social relationships, marked by varying degrees of self-awareness. Acquired in the course of collective and individual history, white ethnicity is about becoming, being and staying 'white', and its distinctiveness becomes realized in specific social and spatial locations. Certain locations are sought out, others are avoided, becoming one thing and not being something else (Ball, 2003). The relational and interdependent aspects of white ethnicity arise from it defining others as belonging to a different race or ethnicity and thus implicitly or explicitly defining itself as belonging to a race or ethnicity also. Changes in the situation, power or status of each group influence the position of the other (Scotson and Elias, 1994; Webster, 1997).

White ethnicity possesses peculiarities and powers that often mark it out from other ethnicities that can confer superiority or dominance even among whites who are themselves in positions of relative powerlessness. Garner's (2006, 2007a) survey on the uses and meaning of 'whiteness' shows how hierarchies of whiteness and class serve to reproduce social hierarchies by creating and maintaining internal borders between the more and less white. Another peculiarity is that white people frequently construct themselves as not possessing race or ethnicity even when they are beneficiaries of their whiteness, accrue 'white' privileges and racialize others. Like all ethnicities, whiteness is fluid and contingent rather than an essential or reified category. The focus here on marginalized white ethnicities encompasses the fact that whiteness has historically functioned as a racial supremacist identity—even when the main victims were 'white', that it is a normalizing, dominant and controlling ethnicity, and we cannot assume that whiteness operates on 'a level playing field' of inter-ethnic competition over scarce resources (Garner, 2007a: 9). Nevertheless, if whiteness is the norm by which measures and judgements about difference, deviance or criminality are made then we need to interrogate its nature and status critically rather than accept its 'normality' and 'invisibility' (Dyer, 1997). If whiteness has always been visible from the perspective of people of 'colour' creating a 'double consciousness' of always looking at and judging oneself through the eyes of others, then it needs to be rendered visible to whites too (Du Bois, [1903] 1996; Garner, 2007a). Indeed, some writers in the USA and increasingly Britain have argued that whiteness is excessively visible (and racialized too) and that there is a very high degree of 'colour-coding' of issues and in places to do with safety, fear of crime and the prospect of meeting violence (Webster, 1996, 1997, 2007).

Today increasingly, the emergence of linked academic, journalistic and popular discourses about whiteness are of significance for debates about ethnicity, race, crime and justice, and in particular for understanding the racialization and criminalization of marginalized white ethnicity. Debates cannot be left to dichotomous and gross over-simplifications of the 'threat' said to be posed by a de-industrialized white 'underclass' accused by liberals of harbouring endemic white racism and racist violence, and by conservatives of harbouring endemic amoral, family-breakdown-ridden, welfare-sponging and crime-prone behaviour, nor to the 'threat' that 'new' immigration and asylum are said to pose to stability, order and social cohesion (Garner, 2007a).

Emergence of Marginalized White Ethnicity: Immigrants, 'Abject Whites', 'White Trash' and Other 'Degenerates'

The emergence of 'whiteness' and white ethnicity as a focus of study is best exemplified in the United States with its long tradition of European immigration and codification of the idea that some whites are 'whiter' than others. The struggle of white working-class immigrant groups to be conferred white 'privileges' and membership of the 'white race' easily displaced their class interests (Allen, 1997). The example of Irish migrants is a case in point. For Irish-Americans their white-skin privileges were crucial to maintain their position against African-Americans, with whom they were aligned in the racial hierarchy of the time (Allen, 1994). As in Britain, where relatively recently 'Paddy-bashing' was only ever a stone's throw from 'Paki-bashing', so in the United States, nativist folk wisdom held that 'an Irishman was a "nigger", inside out' (Roediger, 2007: 133). Despite sharing neighbourhoods, poverty, criminalization and common experiences of racism with blacks, this denial of their 'whiteness' only resulted in their insisting all the more on their own whiteness and on white supremacy in opposition to blacks. The key was gaining better work, winning acceptance and political rights. 'White niggers' were white workers in arduous, unskilled manual work or subservient positions, and in part Irish-American whiteness took shape attempting to sever any racial connections to blacks and 'nigger work', i.e. the burden of doing unskilled work (Roediger, 2007). The role that labour competition and conflict was said to play in processes of becoming white among European immigrant groups has not gone unchallenged, and in any case labour competition was intense within each group—black and white (Ignatiev, 1995). Nevertheless, it was much easier for the Irish to defend jobs and rights as 'white' entitlements, that is, in racial terms instead of as Irish, ethnic or class ones, to gain access to better jobs. Between 1890 and 1945 eventual assimilation—best understood as 'whitening as a process'—saw how an initial status of 'inbetweenness' (neither securely white nor non-white) became 'fully white' (Roediger, 2007: 8).

In this sense, whiteness is nearly always salvageable in a way that black, Mexican, Asian and Native American ethnicity is not. Although denigrated and likened to blacks, marginalized white groups were, in law, white. Nevertheless a contingent white racialized hierarchy designated a number of white 'races', although in the end being white was not just about a certain range of phenotypes, but claims on culture and values (Garner, 2007a: 68). Other themes such as nativist fears about proximity to marginalized white groups were contradicted by complaints that these groups 'segregated themselves' on 'racial' grounds, and threatened 'white men's wages'. The greatest complaint, however, was of the fecundity of white working-class new migrants (Roediger, 2007). Of key importance here was the ways that the idea that 'white' was a racial identity became enshrined in the new racial science, and later the eugenics movement, from the mid- to the late 19th century (Webster, 2007). The new science produced complex schemas and typologies of subdivisions of whiteness, often associated with degeneration and criminality as well as racial superiority. In fact those who were phenotypically white were not equally incorporated into the dominant groups because they were disadvantaged by class and culture. The most intriguing case was the designation 'white trash', which has historical parallels with representations of some sections of the white working class in Britain (Webster, 2007; Wilson, 2007). Like the figure of the 'chav' in Britain today, the figure of 'white trash' represented pollution, excess and worklessness far from respectability.

A number of characteristics were attributed to the 19th-century working classes including fecundity and criminality as well as shared physical qualities so that the language of 'race' overlapped with that of class seen in tropes that fixed on the body and culture. Hartigan's tracing of the development of the phenomenon of 'white trash' from the mid-19th century onwards concluded that the 'objectifications of this group . . . arose from this moral categorization of those who will and will not work' (2005: 67)—poor whites and white trash respectively. The racial connotations of 'white trash' combined the following: natural habitat, blood lines to do with prolific sexuality, their designation as threat from below because weaker blood was multiplying faster than stronger, their moral incapacity to labour because of their racial status, all connected to anxieties about urbanization, crime and the migration of poor southern whites to northern cities. The main themes though were 'degeneration', debasement, worklessness and respectability— that later inform representation of lower-class whites throughout the 20th century. In some accounts they were upheld as a bulwark against black inferiority, in others as sacrificing the superiority of whites to the inferior race, yet in others as a contamination that could bring down the future of the white race (Hartigan, 2005: 69). In the southern version their origins were said to lie in British migration to the United States of paupers and convicts.

The particular problem that 'white trash' posed for racists, racial scientists and eugenicists was that they were both white and 'degenerate', in which the latter reflected not only a moral state but a phenotypical one of physical taints, stigmata and in some sense 'colour'. Turn-of-the-century eugenics and criminal family field studies—the 'Jukes' family, 'the tribe of Ishmael' and many others—perfectly embodied these concerns (Hartigan, 2005; Webster, 2007). Their image as incestuous, crime-ridden families associated with the range of social problems of urbanization profoundly impacted upon white middle-class audiences. Although these 'odd tribes' were constantly referred to by their supposed distinctive and telling physical appearance and behaviour, they were palpably white. The ways that eugenicists got around this was to argue that despite the fact these families were obviously white, poor whites were 'the worst of the race' through their hereditary (Hartigan, 2005: 88). Hereditary degeneration was seen in the physical markers of race—although emphasizing 'stature' and 'comportment' rather than skin colour—ensuring that class distinctions were encompassed by racial discourse. This also marked a shift from explanations about poor whites that had largely drawn on newly developing discourses on sexuality and criminality to the racial constitution of 'good' and 'bad' families, and the threats posed by the latter to the race posed by the breeding habits of poor whites and their sexuality. This shift in criminal family studies from class otherness to racial sameness had as its colloquy concerns over uncontrolled sexuality reconstituted as attention to hereditary and race.

Of course, criminology from its foundations in the 19th century had been mired in the racialization of white criminality, notably in the work of Lombroso whose main innovation was to equate the white European criminal with non-white races (see Webster, 2007). As Garland (1985) observed, criminological texts at the turn of the last century, in linking disparate themes and categories of the 'unfit', most commonly drew together criminality, degeneracy, the nation and 'the race' in an open appeal to the concerns about racial deterioration which were widespread in Edwardian Britain. This eugenicist 'population problem' contrasted the abundant fertility of the 'unfit' (criminals, alcoholics, imbeciles, etc.) with a lower birth rate of the better classes. The proposed solution was the forced sterilization of the lower classes, the physically and mentally 'unfit', the criminal, the degenerate among a panoply of individuals and populations considered socially undesirable. Differentiating whites into bio-social groups formed an important basis to subsequent attempts to distinguish the criminal from the noncriminal. In Britain, eugenicist discourse was always weaker than moral discourse about the marginalized white working class, particularly their pleasures and 'excess' and the blurring of these pleasures with criminality. The perceived problem in the early Victorian period, as it is now, was the working classes' prodigious consumption of alcohol, their lack of saving and a life lived day-to-day without care for what the future may bring (Wilson, 2007). Even Marx referred to the lower classes as 'social scum'.

Contemporary Representations of Marginalized White Ethnicity: The 'Social Scum' as 'White Niggers'

As Hartigan (2005) argues, the confidence with which people continue to be labelled white trash derives from a long tradition of social contempt, racial and class stereotyping sustained by ascriptions of naturalness, social difference and inferiority, far exceeding white supremacist or racist ideology's focus on non-whites. If anything, the mythic role of white trash and its reproduction through popular culture has greater salience today in post-industrial America. Instead of diminishing, contemporary representations of white trash have taken a different turn in that 'it is possible to read images of white trash as a carnivalesque aesthetic, a transgressive celebration of the *grotesque* body (with its illicit sexuality and propensity for cathartic emotions) that will not be restrained by (white) middle-class social decorums' (Hartigan, 2005: 121–2, emphasis in original). If those who use the term do so as a means of self-designation to transgress and resist designations of social contempt and tenuous economic standing, then this appears only to amplify inscriptions of social difference, even among members of the white working class (Hartigan, 2005: 122). Beyond self-designations, popular representations of white trash also take ironic forms. The American hip hop artist Eminem described himself as 'white trash' adopting the identity of 'wigger' (an oxymoronic 'white nigger', i.e., both white and lower working class, living in Detroit, described in another oxymoron as 'America's first Third World city') (cited in Taylor, 2005: 148). Eminem's ironic evocations of 'White America' neither romanticized blackness nor denied white privilege. They provided a trope on being white and poor in the richest country in the world. Clearly, and again, some people are 'whiter than others'.

In a British context, journalistic and popular representations—whether implicit or explicit—focus on consumption patterns, tastes and expression and where people live. Here are offered two contrasting tropes—one from *The Economist*, the other from a local newspaper—illustrative of our themes. In a generally sympathetic article, *The Economist* (26 October 2006) asked its readers to consider the plight of 'The forgotten underclass' and how white residents of a working-class neighbourhood in Dagenham in East London resented both white and multiethnic new arrivals to their neighbourhood, complaining that the new arrivals were more qualified and had better prospects than the people among whom they had settled.

Leaving aside the veracity of these claims for the moment, let's examine the *nomenclature* of these sorts of discussions. After identifying the aspirant and 'respectable' white working class who had left the area for the fringes of Essex, those left behind—the white underclass—are accorded and judged a social status *between* similarly disadvantaged visible minority ethnic groups and the 'respectable' white working class who have embraced mobility and opportunity. *The Economist* article implies or states that: first, poor whites lack aspirations themselves or for their children but are racist towards similarly positioned but more aspirant minority ethnic groups in their midst; second, that poor whites lack 'taste', i.e. appropriate consumer patterns and aspirations, particularly their 'choice' to live in council housing; third, that poor whites are disproportionately criminal compared to any other group; finally, that poor whites make poor choices and have bad judgement impairing their ability to take up opportunities of mobility, affluence and respectability.

Turning to an altogether different nomenclature that identifies and isolates the 'social scum' as an object of humour and ridicule, Hanley quotes a local newspaper:

> A Wood (local council estate) man found himself in hot water after asking his estranged partner to fill up his Pot Noodle. The 30-year-old admitted putting his hands around his partner's neck and pulling out her earring, causing a cut ear and lip and a scratched neck. Colin Doyle, defending, said that his client lived opposite the house where his partner lives with their two children, and he had gone over to ask for some hot water after his own home had been burgled, leaving him with no food. (2007: 10)

Hanley rightly comments on how the emblematic Pot Noodle—'the slag of all snacks'—is used 'as a fun insult by those who have grown tired of disguising their snobbery' (2007: 10). The quotation manages to juxtapose Pot Noodles, wife-beating, burglary and council estates in one overall 'joke'. As Hanley adds 'Poor taste, bad grammar, the betrayal of family history beyond that which is conveniently aspirational: all these traits are now deemed "council estate behaviour'" (2007: 10). The 'joke' does little to hide what is really going on here: contempt, fear and loathing of the white poor.

These tropes coalesce in the 'chav' phenomenon. The notion of respectability can be clearly observed as a racialized ascription here in the generation of class boundaries between respectable, poor whites and 'visible' minorities. These classifications offer potent and differing versions of whiteness based on entitlement and respectability (Garner, 2007a). For example, in Nayak's (2003) study of white youth subcultures in Newcastle, family and/or occupational histories based on 'hard work' were key signifiers of respectability among the 'Real Geordies' against the racialized and criminalized 'Charver Kids' with whom they compared themselves. And here a residue of earlier popular ideas that groups are criminal in their looks, including their 'racial' looks, survive today:

> If the postures of *Charver Kids* are 'ape-like' and pronounced, other body-reflexive practices such as smoking, spitting, swearing loudly and drinking alcohol from bottles and cans in public further served to authenticate their 'roughness'. . . . Like many minority ethnic groups before them, charvers were associated with street crime, disease, drugs, over-breeding (many came from large families) and the seedy underbelly of the 'black economy'. (Nayak, 2006: 823–4)

Here, poor whites are popularly identified and stigmatized as a 'race apart' by their *visible* comportment, body shape, dress and physical looks.

According to Hayward and Yar (2006) the popular reconfiguration of the underclass idea in the epithet 'chav' pathologizes class dispositions in relation to consumption rather than employment. In the wider public imagination the relationship between consumption and classification appears to shift from an explicit concern with 'race' and social marginality to one of 'class' and social marginality. Previous concerns about the underclass possessing a distinctive set of *cultural* pathological dispositions that inform behavioural patterns and choices—to be unemployed and give birth outside of marriage, have been joined by a shift that accords consumption a central role in the production of social distinctions and classifications of 'us' and 'them'. Popular discussion of the 'chav' focuses not on the inability to consume because of poverty, but on the excessive participation in aesthetically impoverished forms of consumption. Here stigmatization processes become analogous to, and substitute for, now 'discredited' racialization processes. The synonym 'chav' takes various popular forms including, '[C]ouncil [h]oused [a]nd [v]iolent', but it owes its origins to the Romany dialect word for small child ('chavo' or 'chavi')'. An altogether more sinister nomenclature describes the fecund, primitive, animalistic, 'sub-human' and criminal nature of the 'chav'. This symbolic marginalized white ethnicity has become a 'legitimate' target of displaced racism, and popular websites and commentary classify and judge 'chavs' according to their *appearance*—their 'tribal dress code' and ostentatious displays that liken them to 'pikeys'—and *location* and the consumer outlets they are said to frequent (see, for example, www.chavscum.co.uk, www.chavtowns.co.uk). Hayward and Yar conclude that

> the "chav" phenomenon partakes of a social process in which consumption, identity, marginality and social control converge; consumption practices now serve as the locus around which exclusion is configured and the excluded are classified, identified and subjected to (increasingly intense) regimes of management. (2006: 24)

The emphasis here on representations of 'excessive' consumption underestimates the continued salience of employment as a marker of class and respectability. Young people labelled as 'chavs' or 'charvas' affiliate on the basis of social class which directly affects and limits their subculture 'choice' as does their locality (McCulloch et al., 2006).

These themes are also heavily gendered. Skeggs' study of white working-class women in north-west England shows how respectability and the body are the most ubiquitous signifiers of class, and that respectability 'is usually the concern of those who are not seen to have it'; and is 'one of the key mechanisms by which people are othered and pathologized', something to 'desire, to prove and to achieve' in order to be valued and legitimated (1997: 1). The issue of being and appearing respectable pervaded the lives of the women she spoke to. Skeggs notes how these women, although inscribed and marked by their denigration as degenerate, attributed respectability and high moral standing to themselves. Here appearance was the signifier of conduct; to look was to be. Appearance worked as a sign of moral evaluation, of excessive sexuality just as modesty and propriety have been central to the formation of middle-class femininity.

White Racism? 'Respectability' and the Fearful Proximity of Poor Whites

Today, the 'problem' of the white working class is often posed in terms of their supposed endemic racism. Indeed, the few studies of white ethnicity available within debates about racism, crime and justice have focused exclusively on white identity as a source of support for the perpetration of racist violence (Webster, 1996, 2007; Sibbitt, 1997; Bowling, 1999; Ray et al., 2003, 2004; Ray and Smith, 2004). Less attention has been given to wider processes influencing the formation of white ethnicity and the relationship of white ethnicity to fear of crime and decline within neighbourhoods.

Seen as a 'disorganised, racist and sexist detritus' (Haylett, 2001: 358, cited in Garner, 2007a: 73), the white working-class poor are blamed for a 'decline' in the working-class, pathological masculinities, backwardness, degeneracy, crime, over-fecundity, fecklessness and above all are seen as an anachronistic remnant of an industrial culture blocking a full move to modernization and progress—just as they were accused of being in Victorian England (Wilson, 2007). This somewhat overwrought portrait has been interrogated by numerous studies of the lived realities of white working-class life both in the United States and Britain. Only some of the nuanced findings of these studies are rehearsed here drawing out some common themes and findings, again with a focus on marginalized white ethnicity. Hartigan's (1999, 2005) study of white enclaves in overwhelmingly black Detroit challenges academic and journalistic characterizations of white working-class communities as either the sole source of racism, or as the most stubbornly racist section of society. Instead, working-class whites are far more ambivalent about their class location and their relationships with whites and minorities from better and worse-off neighbourhoods. Whites made class as well as race distinctions about other poor whites living in their neighbourhood and whites were not simply in opposition to blacks. More often than not, issues of maintaining respectability overrode those of race. Similarly, Kefalas' (2003) comparable ethnographic study of a white working-class neighbourhood in Chicago's Southwest Side unpicks the construction of white racism in a 'white enclave' contiguous with Chicago's African-American West Side ghetto:

> Beltwayites' racism then can be seen as a byproduct of their efforts to fortify the cultural and moral boundaries

> between themselves and more stigmatized groups. Class-bound ideologies and boundaries make it difficult for garden [a local colloquialism for the area] dwellers to reconcile themselves to [the] existence of *white* teenage mothers, *white* drug addicts, *white* gangbangers, *white* single mothers, and poor *whites*. Whites are respectable, and respectability keeps people safe from the dangers posed by destructive social forces. (Kefalas, 2003: 155, emphases in original)

In a British context too the formation of white ethnicity at neighbourhood level sets itself not against visible ethnicity per se, but against *any* marginalized ethnicity including poor whites (Scotson and Elias, 1994). It is this proximity to *the poor* rather than visible ethnicity per se that so unsettles locals, leading to anxiety and fear—fear of crime and fear of 'falling' through downward mobility into the ranks of the poor. Spatial and social polarization occurs through prominent themes—'narratives of urban decline' and characterizations of 'respectability' contrasted with physical decay, disorder and nascent criminality. Watt, for example, concluded that the main preoccupation of white working-class council house tenants in Camden was to maintain respectability: 'The result was a permanent underlying urban anxiety about being *too close*, socially and spatially, to concentrated poverty' (2006: 788, emphasis in original).

What then of white working-class racism? Writing of the 1950s—a period which saw a second wave of white race riots against black areas—Burke (1994, cited in Collins, 2004: 185) argued that everyday white working-class racism did not seek justification in notions of biological inferiority, but in the fight for scarce resources around the body, the home and the marketplace. By the time Enoch Powell gave 'public' voice and vision to a certain sort of white working-class fear of being 'swamped' by 'immigrants' and 'foreigners' in Birmingham in 1968, the terms of a fully fledged racist white ethnicity had been laid. These misplaced fears grew from the more vulnerable, unskilled sectors of the white working class in a context of growing insecurity and nascent economic restructuring. Many others accepted the new multiracial environment in which they found themselves (Collins, 2004). Nevertheless, and especially in London's east end, the acute shortage of affordable housing and disruption of the white working class' intergenerational 'inheritance' of 'respectable' social housing, as well as its stigmatization, continues to make struggles over housing almost synonymous with inter-ethnic competition and conflict (Dench et al., 2006). The formation of 'confident', exclusive forms of racist white ethnicity in some neighbourhoods seems to occur when most areas of people's lives overlap a great deal at the local level—from work to family. Where residents tend to be dependent on family and local social networks for information about housing, jobs and leisure opportunities, they tend to exclude 'outsiders' more compared to people living in more 'open' neighbourhoods; that is, where most people have connections of different sorts outside it, their ties are spread more widely and are more able to pull in resources from other areas of their lives (Wallman, 1982, 1986).

As we have seen, the marginalization of white ethnicity is always mediated by notions of respectability. Marginalization and respectability are simultaneously formed by negatively assigning local poor, stigmatized or minority populations blame for perceived community decline and unwelcome social and economic change; bolstered, it is believed, by state immigration and welfare policy and local government multicultural policies. Garner (2007a) summarizes this trope as: respectability plus work leads to entitlement, and the white underclass, minority groups, migrant communities, asylum seekers, the unemployed and single mothers are accused of not paying their dues, and are perceived as feckless, fecund, hedonistic, excessive, queue-jumpers.

The Isolation and Segregation of the White Ghetto: 'People Living on Council Estates Aren't Like the Rest of Us'

The spatial confinement of marginalized white ethnicity to the habitus of the white council estate, the white rioting of these estates in 1991 and 1992 and their stigmatization as places of political and physical neglect, low incomes, high welfare dependency, poor job prospects and low educational attainment, mark the *prime* spatial location of marginalized white ethnicity (Power and Tunstall, 1997; Webster et al., 2004; MacDonald and Marsh, 2005; Stenson and Waddington, 2007). The much greater polarization and spatial concentration by social class rather than visible ethnicity in Britain compared to the United States greatly reinforces the marginalization and ghettoization of white ethnicity (Dorling et al., 2007; Thomas and Dorling, 2007). The objective trajectory and decline of social housing estates as white—or, in London, multiethnic ghettoes—is well known. What are less known are the subjective effects of this isolation and segregation. Seen as 'Little more than holding cages for the feral and the lazy' (Hanley, 2007: 140), white estates can be likened to the sorts of abandoned, isolated and segregated places usually attributed to black ghettoes in the USA.

The emergence and isolation of the white ghetto is vividly described by Hanley from her first-hand experience:

> To be working-class in Britain is also to have a *wall in the head*, and, since council housing has come to mean housing for the working class (and the non-working class), that wall exists unbroken throughout every estate in the land. . . . Your knowledge of what's out there, beyond the thick glass walls, is entirely reliant on what you can glean from the lives of the people you know, which usually means your own family members. If your family and friends all live on the same estate, that's a little wall built for you right there. . . . The world seems to stop on the edge of every estate. (2007: 149, emphasis added)

The ghettoization of the white working-class estates that she eloquently describes represents a novel reconfiguration of class reproduction through geographical entrapment—spatial segregation by class—where the internal wall coexists with external invisible barriers of class. Walled people are happily described as 'chav scum', estates as places of 'last resort' and as 'dumping grounds' for those who have no choice in where they live compared to the apparently abundant choices of everyone else. Their 'failure' is not only contagious but morally repugnant and, of course, people do not have to live on them, so those who do are accused of self-segregation (Hanley, 2007). Most of all they serve to give concrete spatial reality to the existence of marginalized whiteness in the eyes of everyone else and as irredeemably associated with dangerous and criminal places.

The Disciplining of Marginalized White Ethnicity

When asked what might be expected of daily life in 'lower-class Britain', the conservative American political scientist Charles Murray replied, 'based on observations and knowledge of the US underclass':

> The New Rabble will be characterised by high levels of criminality, child neglect and abuse and drug use . . . will exploit social benefit programmes . . . will not enter the legitimate labour force when economic times are good. . . . The children . . . unsocialised in the norms of considerate behaviour . . . the New Rabble will dominate, which will be

> enough to make life miserable for everyone else. (1994: 12)

There is little here that is new compared to the long-standing historical iconography of the disreputable white working class, their pleasures and the blurring of these with criminality (Wilson, 2007). What is perhaps more novel is the way that Murray presaged the transition from more relaxed to more puritan times. The tools and targets of moral censure may have changed—ASBOs and *people living on council estates*—but the sense of the contemporary poor as a recalcitrant drag on appeals to 'modernization' is palpable in popular and policy discourse (Hughes, 2007).

The same obsessions—with 'dysfunctional' families, lone mothers and absent fathers—found in 'moral underclass' discourses remain but are given a more benign twist in the notion of 'antisocial behaviour'. The 'progeny' of 'dysfunctional' families are to be met with an amalgam of authoritarian measures such as child curfews, antisocial behaviour orders and parenting orders, deployed in poor communities to regulate children and parents. The vindictiveness of local media provides dramatic illustrations of public humiliation of the targeted group—poor whites (Scraton, 2007). In May 2005 Tony Blair talked of antisocial behaviour as derived in irresponsible, undisciplined and improper parenting from 'generation to generation' (cited in Scraton, 2007: 145). This coded obsession with progeny and implicit concern with hereditary marks the group in terms of its deficient biological and/or cultural reproduction.

Much (rightly) has been made of the policing of black young men. Accounts of the policing of marginalized white ethnicities in some of the 'whitest' urban areas in Britain also deserve attention. One study of white young people in Edinburgh concluded that the police make distinctions about the respectable and unrespectable based on social class status—that do not always take account of serious and persistent offending—to construct a population of permanent suspects. This works in two ways: first, the lifestyles of lower-class young people make them more 'available' for policing and more likely to experience adversarial contact; second, police officers consistently elide moral status with affluence and are consistently more likely to pick on youngsters from less affluent backgrounds as individuals rather than on the basis of police targeting of deprived areas. Although less deferential in their manner to the police than more affluent young people, those who are less affluent tend to be 'baited' by the police. They are judged about their 'respectability' on the basis of their dress and physical appearance (typically 'charva' dress) and comportment, rendering an individual more suspect in the eyes of the police (McAra and McVie, 2005). Another study of police culture and nomenclature in Newcastle City Police revealed how the police reflected *in extremis* the contempt and fear of the wider white population towards poor whites living in certain areas (Young, 1991). 'Real criminals' were identified by their supposed genealogy—'racial' origins and places of residence—wherein certain working-class areas were deemed places that housed families of criminals. 'Real criminals' lived in the 'jungle' in and around the derogatorily termed 'African villages' where the residents were all said to be Bridewell regulars. Famous 'criminal' families were 'second generation gypsy horse thieves', illegitimate—socially and by birth—dirty and tattooed.

Conclusion and Discussion

'Whiteness' is most 'visible' and most likely to be racialized and criminalized in its marginalized or subordinate forms, Hegemonic white ethnicity—typical of powerful white elites—tends to retain only an implicit view of itself as 'white'. Whiteness is rarely evoked or mobilized as an ethnic resource or as a target of racialized discourses other than in situations of scarcity, competition or rapid social, economic and demographic change. It is here *in extremis* that white ethnicity comes to have salience, and form an identifiable shape, profile and presence.

Representations of marginalized white ethnicity, despite their claims to the contrary, give away the 'hidden injuries of class' (Sennett and Cobb, 1977). As Sayer (2005) argues, if class damages, then this implies that people themselves are damaged, often in ways that not only limit their potential but may in extreme cases lead to antisocial behaviour. This seems particularly the case concerning attitudes towards poor white working-class males (Haylett, 2001). If class inequalities generate shame, and sometimes rage, among the most disadvantaged, then their racialization (whether recognized or not) compounds the felt contempt and denigration.

Contemporary popular, political and policy discourses about the white working class have lost none of their historical legacy and potency to stereotype, stigmatize and blame social exclusion on the culture of this group rather than as something that is done to them (Skeggs, 2004: 86). The conditions of existence of marginalized white working-class ethnicity unleash a 'chain of signifiers': familial disorder and dysfunction, dangerous masculinities, dependency, fecund and excessive femininities, antisocial behaviour, moral and ecological decay and quick to resort to criminality, and all spatialized. Culture becomes segregated by territory and place, seen in the naming and shaming of 'sink estates' or 'the worst housing estates' (Haylett, 2001; Hanley, 2007). Most of all—strangely echoing Lombroso— the unifying theme is of the atavistic backwardness of the white working class as a burdensome barrier and break on the development of a modern, 'multicultural' nation—a role previously projected onto 'black youth'—and as a 'detritus of the Industrial Revolution' (Daley, 1994: 16, cited in Skeggs, 2004: 91). Political rhetoric now distinguishes between different sorts of whiteness: the respectable who can be incorporated into the nation and the non-respectable who cannot.

A key objection to many of the arguments presented here will be that some cultural and racial characteristics fix some groups and enable others to be mobile. For example, Skeggs (2004) makes the point that black working-class masculinity as it operates in popular culture is available to be appropriated by black or white in ways that black boys cannot easily perform being white, because they are always inscribed as black and cannot move between black and white in the same ways. The mobility of white attachment and inscription are not equally available to all. In this sense the couplet 'black male/criminal' is said to be always stronger and more deterministic than the couplet 'poor white/criminal'. The argument presented here suggests that this may not be the case.

Class contempt towards economically and socially marginalized 'white' groups reveal features of discourses and representations previously reserved for visible minorities. This moralistic targeting of the disadvantaged white working class—through tropes of moral culpability, laziness, aesthetically impoverished consumption and housing 'choices'—works as a displacement activity and 'legitimate' outlet for racist social opprobrium. The racist undertone risks accusations of racism circumvented because the targets are 'degenerate whites'. Race and ethnically based class contempt is shown, however, to have a long history both in Britain and the United States. Drawing distinctions between different sorts of 'whiteness' deemed inferior or superior according to attributions of 'degeneracy', 'respectability', antisocial behaviour, criminality, the body, appearance and hereditability, class contempt is shown to be social and racial. The use of derogatory designations by the white middle class and even by the white working class—'family dysfunction', 'white trash', 'chav underclass', 'living on a council estate'—denigrates and distances (mostly) poor whites to justify and reproduce social hierarchies. Feared and disciplined because of their supposed inherent criminality, racism and distance from respectability, resented as 'detritus' of deindustrialization and a burden on 'progress', blamed for their self-exclusion and 'self-segregation', there is, finally, avoidance of any serious critical engagement with what is done to marginalize white ethnicity.

References

Allen, T.W. (1994) *The Invention of the White Race. Volume One: Racial Oppression and Social Control.* London: Verso.

Allen, T.W. (1997) *The Invention of the White Race. Volume Two: The Origin of Racial Oppression in Anglo-America.* London: Verso.

Ball, S.J. (2003) *Class Strategies and the Education Market: The Middle Classes and Social Advantage.* London: Routledge.

Bowling, B. (1999) *Violent Racism: Victimisation, Policing and Social Context.* Oxford: Clarendon Press.

Burke, J. (1994) *Working Class Cultures in Britain (1890–1960).* London: Routledge.

Collins, M. (2004) *The Likes of Us: A Biography of the White Working Class.* London: Granta Books.

Curtis, P. (2008) '85% of Poorer White Boys Fall Short in GCSEs', *Guardian,* 1 February.

Daley, J. (1994) The Janet Daley column', *The Times,* London: 16.

Dench, G., K. Gavron and M. Young (2006) *The New East End: Kinship, Race and Conflict.* London: Profile Books.

Dorling, D. and B. Thomas (2007) *A Short Report on Plurality and the Cities of Britain.* London: Barrow Cadbury Trust.

Dorling, D., J. Rigby, B. Wheeler, D. Ballas, B. Thomas, E. Fahmy, D. Gordon and R. Lupton (2007) *Poverty, Wealth and Place in Britain, 1968 to 2005.* Bristol: Policy Press.

Du Bois, W.E.B. [1903] (1996) *The Souls of Black Folk.* New York: Penguin.

Dyer, R. (1997) *White.* London: Routledge.

Economist, The (2006) The Forgotten Underclass, 28 October, p. 34.

Garland, D. (1985) *Punishment and Welfare: A History of Penal Strategies.* Aldershot: Gower.

Garner, S. (2004) *Racism in the Irish Experience.* London: Pluto Press.

Garner, S. (2006) The Uses of Whiteness: What Sociologists Working on Europe Can Draw from US Research on Whiteness, *Sociology* 40(2): *257–75.*

Garner, S. (2007a) *Whiteness: An Introduction.* London: Routledge.

Garner, S. (2007b) 'The European Union and the Racialization of Immigration, 1985–2006', *Race/ Ethnicity* 1(1): 61–87.

Garner, S. (2007c) 'Atlantic Crossing: Whiteness as a Transatlantic Experience', *Atlantic Studies* 4(1): 117–32.

Goodey, J. (2003) 'Migration, Crime and Victimhood: Responses to Sex Trafficking in the EU', *Punishment & Society* 5(4): 415–31.

Hanley, L. (2007) *Estates: An Intimate History.* London: Granta Books.

Hartigan, J. (1999) *Racial Situations: Class Predicaments of Whiteness in Detroit.* Princeton: Princeton University Press.

Hartigan, J. (2005) *Odd Tribes: Toward a Cultural Analysis of White People.* London: Duke University Press.

Haylett, C. (2001) 'Illegitimate Subjects? Abject Whites, Neoliberal Modernisation and Middle Class Multiculturalism', *Environment and Planning D: Society and Space* 19: 351–70.

Hayward, K. and M. Yar (2006) The "Chav" Phenomenon: Consumption, Media and the Construction of a New Underclass', *Crime, Media, Culture* 2(1): 9–28.

House of Commons Home Affairs Committee (2007) *Young Black People and the Criminal Justice System, Volume 1.* London: The Stationery Office.

Hughes, G. (2007) *The Politics of Crime and Community.* Basingstoke: Palgrave.

Ignatiev, N. (1995) *How the Irish Became White.* London: Routledge.

Kefalas, M. (2003) *Working-Class Heroes: Protecting Home, Community, and Nation in a Chicago Neighborhood.* Berkeley: University of California Press.

MacDonald, R. and J. Marsh (2005) *Disconnected Youth? Growing Up in Poor Britain.* Basingstoke, UK: Palgrave.

McAra, L. and S. McVie (2005) 'The Usual Suspects? Street-Life, Young People and the Police', *Criminal Justice* 5(1): 5–36.

McCulloch, K., A. Stewart and N. Lovegreen (2006) '"We Just Hang Out Together": Youth Cultures and Social Class', *Journal of Youth Studies* 9(5): *539–56.*

Melossi, D. (2003) '"In a Peaceful Life": Migration and the Crime of Modernity in Europe/Italy', *Punishment & Society* 5(4): 371–97.

Mooney, J. and J. Young (1999) *Social Exclusion and Criminal Justice: Ethnic Minorities and Stop and Search in North London.* Middlesex, UK: Centre of Criminology, Middlesex University.

Murray, C. (1994) 'The New Victorians . . . and the New Rabble', *The Sunday Times,* 29 May, p. 12.

Nayak, A. (2003) 'Ivory Lives: Economic Restructuring and the Making of Whiteness in a Post-Industrial Youth Community', *European Journal of Cultural Studies* 6(3): 305–25.

Nayak, A. (2006) 'Displaced Masculinities: Chavs, Youth and Class in the Post-Industrial City', *Sociology* 40(5): 813–31.

Power, A. and R. Tunstall (1997) *Dangerous Disorder: Riots and Violent Disturbances in Thirteen Areas of Britain, 1991–92.* York: Joseph Rowntree Foundation.

Ray, L. and D. Smith (2004) 'Racist Offending, Policing and Community Conflict', *Sociology* 38(4): 681–99.

Ray, L., D. Smith and L. Wastell (2003) 'Understanding Racist Violence', in B. Stanko (ed.) *The Meanings of Violence,* pp. 112–29. London: Routledge.

Ray, L., D. Smith and L. Wastell (2004) 'Shame, Rage and Racist Violence', *British Journal of Criminology* 44(3): 350–68.

Roediger, D.R. (2007) *The Wages of Whiteness: Race and the Making of the American Working Class* (new edn). London: Verso.

Sayer, A. (2005) *The Moral Significance of Class.* Cambridge: Cambridge University Press.

Scotson, J.L. and N. Elias (1994) *The Established and the Outsiders.* London: SAGE.

Scraton, P. (2007) *Power, Conflict and Criminalisation.* London: Routledge.

Sennett, R. and J. Cobb (1977) *Hidden Injuries of Class.* Cambridge: Cambridge University Press.

Sibbitt, R. (1997) *The Perpetrators of Racial Harassment and Violence.* Research Study 176. London: Home Office.

Skeggs, B. (1997) *Formations of Class & Gender.* London: SAGE.

Skeggs, B. (2004) *Class, Self, Culture.* London: Routledge.

Stenson, K. and P.A.J. Waddington (2007) 'Macpherson, Police Stops and Institutionalised Racism', in M. Rowe (ed.) *Policing Beyond Macpherson: Issues in Policing, Race and Society,* pp. 128–47. Cullompton: Willan.

Taylor, G. (2005) *Buying Whiteness: Race, Culture, and Identity from Columbus to Hip-Hop.* Basingstoke, UK: Palgrave.

Thomas, B. and D. Dorling (2007) *Identity in Britain: A Cradle-to-Grave Atlas.* Bristol: Policy Press.

Waddington, P.A.J., K. Stenson and D. Don (2004) 'In Proportion: Race, and Police Stop and Search', *British Journal of Criminology* 44(6): 889–914.

Wallman, S. (1982) *Living in South London: Perspectives on Battersea 1871–1981.* London: Gower.

Wallman, S. (1986) 'Ethnicity and the Boundary Process in Context', in J. Rex and D. Mason (eds) *Theories of Race and Ethnic Relations,* pp. 226–45. Cambridge: Cambridge University Press.

Watt, P. (2006) 'Respectability, Roughness and "Race": Neighbourhood Place Images and the Making of Working-Class Social Distinctions in London', *International Journal of Urban and Regional Research* 30(4): 776–97.

Webster, C. (1996) 'Local Heroes: Violent Racism, Spacism and Localism among White and Asian Young People', *Youth & Policy* 53(Summer): 15–27.

Webster, C. (1997) 'The Construction of British "Asian" Criminality', *International Journal of the Sociology of Law* 25(1): 65–86.

Webster, C. (2007) *Understanding Race and Crime.* Maidenhead, UK: Open University Press.

Webster, C., D. Simpson, R. MacDonald, A. Abbas, M. Cieslik and T. Shildrick (2004) *Poor Transitions: Young Adults and Social Exclusion.* Bristol: Policy Press.

Wilson, B. (2007) *Decency & Disorder: The Age of Cant 1789–1837.* London: Faber & Faber.

Young, M. (1991) *An Inside Job: Policing and Police Culture in Britain.* Oxford: Oxford University Press.

DISCUSSION QUESTIONS

1. Does Webster make a strong argument about why different white ethnicities should be discussed when examining issues of race, ethnicity, and crime? Explain why or why not.
2. How do the experiences described by Webster differ or relate to forms of racism that have been committed against working-class minorities?
3. Discuss Webster's assertion that the racism and classism acts committed against white working-class ethnicities have led to the criminalization of such groups in a similar way to the criminalization of visible working-class minorities. Why is this an important assertion?

Extent of Crime and Victimization

SECTION HIGHLIGHTS

- Sources of Crime and Victimization Statistics
- Limitations of Crime, Arrest, and Victimization Statistics
- Race and the Extent of Crime and Victimization
- Summary
- Edited Readings

Sources of Crime and Victimization Statistics

The collection of crime data began in the 19th century in an effort to understand the nature and extent of criminality as well as the changes in each (Robinson, 1911). Between 1829 and 1905, 25 states required the collection of judicial statistics. Prisoner statistics collected by prison officials and sheriffs began in the 1800s as well. In 1850, the U.S. Bureau of the Census began collecting crime-related data, including characteristics of prisoners (Maltz, 1977). It is unclear whether or not lynching and lynchers were included in official crime statistics. In the late 1800s and 1900s, lynching data was collected and reported by the *Chicago Tribune*, the Tuskegee Institute, and the National Association for the Advancement of Colored People.

In the 1920s, the International Association of Chiefs of Police (IACP) established a committee to explore the issue of collecting national crime statistics in the United States, which was completed in 1929. Shortly thereafter, in 1930, Congress authorized the United States Attorney General to collect crime data. The Federal Bureau of Investigation was designated as the clearinghouse for crime data collected by police agencies (Federal Bureau of Investigation [FBI], 1995). Throughout the 20th century, the FBI's **Uniform Crime Reports** (UCR), titled *Crime in the United States,* were the major source of information on crimes reported and persons arrested by the police. Since its inception the UCR has been revised several times, and it continues to be the primary source of information on the crime-related statistics that are released annually. A year after President George H. W. Bush signed the Hate Crime Statistics Act, the FBI developed the National Hate Crime Data Collection Program, and they have published *Hate Crime Statistics* annually since 1992. In addition to the UCR, the FBI's **National Incident-Based Reporting System** (NIBRS) was designed to enhance the quantity and quality of crime data collected by the police. The NIBRS data contain more information than the UCR, but not all states participate in the program. Statistics on missing and unidentified persons and data on law enforcement officers killed and assaulted are prepared by the FBI as well. The FBI also publishes reports on topics such as terrorism, white-collar crime, violent crime, law enforcement, and homicide offenders and victims (FBI, 2010).

The UCR provides data on four violent crimes against persons, including murder (and non-negligent manslaughter), forcible rape, robbery, and aggravated assault, and four serious property crimes, including larceny-theft, burglary, arson, and motor-vehicle theft. Historically, these crimes were referred to as *Part I Crimes* and the *Crime Index.* Information on more than 20 other types of crimes, including other assaults, fraud, vandalism, drug abuse violations, prostitution and other sex offenses, gambling, driving under the influence, and several status offenses crimes, are also reported. The UCR arrest data provide information on the race, gender, and age of arrestees.

The other major source of data, the **National Crime Victimization Survey** (NCVS), began in 1973 and is the major source of information about criminal victimization. It was implemented as an alternative to the UCR partly due to concerns about the amount of crime that went unreported, often referred to as the *dark figure of crime.* The NCVS is funded by the Department of Justice (DOJ)—**Bureau of Justice Statistics** (BJS) and is compiled by the U.S. Bureau of the Census. The NCVS collects information each year about the extent and characteristics of victims of violent crimes (excluding homicide) and property crimes (including theft, motor vehicle theft, and household burglary), and it provides detailed estimates about the likelihood of victimizations by race and ethnicity of victims over the age of 12. Participants self-report victimization incidents and provide information about the offenders, such as whether or not they are related to the offender, whether or not alcohol or drugs were involved, and whether or not the offender belonged to a gang. There have been several redesigns of the NCVS, and the BJS is currently considering other changes. Secondary analyses of NCVS data are available online through the National Archive of Criminal Justice Data, which is housed at the University of Michigan (www.icpsr.umich.edu).

There are numerous other sources of crime-related statistics, and many are available online (see Table 2.1). The BJS is the primary statistical agency in the DOJ. At its website, the BJS provides access to data and numerous online data analysis tools (http://bjs.ojp.usdoj.gov/). For example, users can examine homicide trends and victim characteristics in a specific state or multiple states that include not only the number of homicide victims and their ages, races, and genders, but also their race and gender combined. The sources of the data are the FBI's UCR and Supplementary Homicide Reports (SHR).

Table 2.1 Sources of Crime and Victimization Statistics

Source	Sponsor	Inception	Methodology	Scope	Race Included	Online Analysis	Website
Behavioral Risk Factor Surveillance System (BRFSS)	CDC	1984	Annual survey		Yes	Yes 2005 only	Yes
Crime in the United States (UCRs)	FBI	1930	Crimes reported to the police	• Crimes reported • Crimes cleared • Persons arrested • Law enforcement personnel	Yes	Available at the BSJ website	Yes
Indicators of School Crime and Safety	BJS National Center for Education Statistics (NCES) Institute of Education Sciences (IES) Both in DOE	1997	Annual survey	• Compendium of information on school crime and student safety from varying sources	Yes	No	Yes
National Crime Victimization Survey (NCVS)	Bureau of Justice Statistics (BJS)	1972	Interviews	• Victims • Offenders • Offenses	Yes	No	Yes
Sourcebook of Criminal Justice Statistics	BJS	1973	Compendium of statistics	• Criminal justice system • Public attitudes • Arrests • Judicial processing • Prisoners	Yes	No	Yes

(Continued)

Table 2.1 (Continued)

Source	Sponsor	Inception	Methodology	Scope	Race Included	Online Analysis	Website
Law Enforcement Management and Administrative Statistics (LEMAS)	BJS	1987	Surveys of police agencies	• Personnel expenditures • Operations • Equipment	Yes	No	Yes
National Incident-Based Reporting System (NIBRS)	FBI	1988	Crime incidents	• Victims • Offenders • Offenses • Circumstances	Yes	Available from the Criminal Justice Archive of Criminal Justice Data	Yes
Hate Crime Statistics	FBI	1991	Crimes reported to the police	• Victims • Offender motivation • Location	Yes	Yes	Yes
Statistical Briefing Book	OJJDP	1998	Juvenile delinquency	• Juvenile offenders • Victims • Juvenile justice system	Yes	Yes	Yes
Supplemental Homicide Reports (SHR)	FBI	1980	Homicides reported to the FBI	• Characteristics of homicide incidents	Yes	No	No
Homicide Trends	BJS	2001	Secondary data analysis	• Trends	Yes	Yes BJS	Yes

Numerous reports and fact sheets on juvenile delinquency and juvenile justice are available from The Office of Juvenile Justice and Delinquency Prevention (OJJDP). OJJDP has an online *Statistical Briefing Book* with data analysis tools and access to national data sets. Information on the juvenile population, juvenile crime, victimization, and youth in the juvenile justice system is readily available, though it is not always the most recent information. OJJDP also provides information on Disproportionate Minority Contact (DMC) in the juvenile justice system.

The **Centers for Disease Control and Prevention** (CDC) provides statistical and other information on topics such as youth violence, school violence, **intimate partner violence**, elder maltreatment, and their prevention. Violence was first recognized as a public health issue in the 1979 U.S. Surgeon General's Report titled *Healthy People.*

The objectives for ***Healthy People 2020*** include decreasing the number of youth and young adults involved in criminal activity (Centers for Disease Control [CDC], 2010).

Many state and local justice agencies also provide crime statistics on their websites. For example, statistics are available on some police department websites, and most state-level law enforcement agencies compile annual reports with crime statistics. Data on offenders are available at state correctional agency websites, and information on sex offenders returning to the community is online as well. Even though crime statistics are readily available today, they have limitations that are described in the next section.

Limitations of Crime, Arrest, and Victimization Statistics

Despite redesigns and other improvements, the UCR and NCVS (the foci in this section) both have methodological limitations that impact their reliability. A common criticism of crime statistics is that they are unreliable because they cannot tell us how much crime takes place, how many persons were arrested, or how many crime victims there are. The NCVS is limited by the respondents' age, recall, and truthfulness. Other limitations include the following:

- How race and ethnicity are defined
- Reporting and recording methods
- Use of estimates of the population, reported crimes, arrests, and victimizations in calculations

Efforts to understand race, ethnicity, and crime are limited by (1) how the terms are defined in sources of data, (2) how each is determined during the collection of data, and (3) cultural differences within racial and ethnic groups that are overlooked. Georges-Abeyie (1989) was one of the first scholars to emphasize that racial groups are not homogeneous but rather are comprised of individuals and subgroups with varying norms and values. Thus, crime and victimization among subgroups of Blacks vary. For example, crimes committed by Blacks born in the United States and those committed by Blacks with different heritages (such as Jamaican American, Nigerian American, etc.) are indistinguishable within the Black/African American category. This is also true for Latinos, American Indians, and Asian Americans that have different cultural or subcultural identities.

Racial categories in federal statistics are guided by Directive No. 15, issued by the Office of Federal Statistical Policy and Standards in 1977. Despite expanded categories and improvements in federal statistical policies, racial categories in crime and victimization statistics are still problematic because there are inconsistencies from one source to another. For example, Hispanics are classified as an ethnic group in some federal statistics, but the category is completely omitted from arrest statistics. A Hispanic ethnic category first appeared in to the UCR between 1980 and 1985, even though the Hispanic/Latino identity (such as Cuban, Mexican, Puerto Rican, etc.) was not reported. Today, Hispanics/Latinos are included in the White category in the UCR. The NCVS has included racial categories (Blacks, Whites, Others) since its inception in 1973. The "Other" category was used for American Indians and Asians. A Hispanic category was added in 1977.

Another limitation of crime and **victimization data** is that reporting and recording methods vary from place to place and from time to time. There are many reasons why citizens are reluctant to report crimes to the police. Some view incidents as private and want them kept out of the public eye. For example, a family may not want others to know that a father or brother sexually assaulted a daughter or sister. A wife might not want to report an aggravated assault by her husband. Others don't interact with police, even when there is a serious crime committed, because of poor police–community relations. More recently, illegal immigrants are probably unlikely to involve justice professionals when crimes and victimizations occur. When an official report is prepared by a police officer and sent to the FBI, there are varying definitions of offenses, and when multiple crimes occur, only the most serious gets recorded by the UCR program.

Using estimates is the last limitation of crime and victimization data. Estimates are flawed because we can't capture the exact number of persons, crimes, arrests, and victimizations. Related to the problem of estimation is the problem of constructing rates based on inaccurate estimates. In spite of these limitations, crime and victimization data do give us useful information on reported crimes, arrests, and victimizations that permit trend analyses and the identification of crime and victimizations patterns. The next section examines recent trends in arrests and victimizations by race and ethnicity.

Race and the Extent of Crime and Victimization

One of the most challenging issues in the study of race and crime is the disproportionate representation of minorities, especially African Americans and Latinos, in the criminal and juvenile justice systems. The UCR data provide information on persons arrested, including age, race, and gender, and detailed information on the race of homicide offenders and victims. One pattern that has held over time, regardless of racial categories, is that the majority of persons arrested are adult males arrested for property offenses. Fewer persons are arrested for violent crimes against persons, such as murder, rape, robbery, and aggravated assault. Another pattern that has held over time is the disproportionate number of Blacks arrested for two of the most violent crimes against a person: homicide and robbery. In 2008, they comprised 50% of persons arrested for murder, and 56.7% of persons arrested for robbery.

According to the 2000 through 2008 UCR, about 69% of the (estimated number of) persons arrested were White and 28% were Black (FBI, 2001, 2003, 2004, 2005a, 2009a). In 2008, Blacks represented 39% of persons arrested for violent personal crimes and 30% of those arrested for serious property crimes. The percentages of Blacks arrested for property crimes in 2008 included 34.2% for burglary, 31.4% for larceny, 38.1% for motor vehicle theft, and 21.7% for arson. Blacks were not disproportionately arrested for only two offenses, driving under the influence (10%) and liquor law violations (11.5%) (FBI, 2009a).

Reported murder and nonnegligent manslaughters have fluctuated during the 2000s, increasing from 2000 to 2003, decreasing in 2004, increasing in 2005 and 2006, and decreasing again in 2007 and 2008. Reported murders were substantially lower in the 2000s than in the 1990s; murders peaked in 1993 at 24,326. In 2008, of the estimated 1,382,012 violent crimes reported, 16,272 were murders or nonnegligent manslaughters. In December 2008, Fox and Swatt released a report based on a trend analysis of reported homicide victims and offenders for the years 1976 through 2007 that focused on young Black male offenders and victims. Three important conclusions of their analysis were as follows:

1. Between 2002 and 2007, the number of young Black male homicide perpetrators grew by 43%, and 47% were gun killings.
2. After some decline during the previous decade, the percentage of homicides with a gun has increased since 2000 for young White and Black offenders of all ages.
3. The recent surge in homicide among young Black males clearly falls far short of the extraordinarily high levels witnessed during the crack-related street gang wars of the late 1980s and early 1990s.

Fox and Swatt's (2008) data indicate that offenders between the ages of 18 and 34 represented a 19.5% percent change and juveniles (under 18) represented an 18.3% percent change between 2000 and 2007. However, the percentage changes mask the fact that adult Black males commit more homicides than do younger offenders. It is easy to lose sight of the fact that during the past 20 years there has been a substantial decrease in persons arrested for murder even though the percentage of Black arrestees has not changed very much. In 2008, an estimated 9,859 persons were arrested for murder, a substantial decrease from 1988 (16,090) and 1998 (12,318).

Arrests for serious violent and property crimes are important and indicative of how some devalue and disrespect both the lives and property of others. A fixation on murder and other violent crimes and arrestees causes us to ignore other types of crimes that occur, such as larceny-theft, other assaults, drug abuse violations, and driving under the influence. For example, in 2001, there were 1,039,086 drug abuse violation arrests, 64.2% White and 34.5% Black. In 2008, more persons were arrested for drug abuse violations (1,299,708) than any other offense; 34.8% were Black and 63.8% were White. Even though the percentages didn't change very much, the actual estimated number of arrests by race in 2008 is up considerably compared to 2000 (FBI, 2001, 2009a).

Another fact that is often overlooked is that disproportionality in arrests exists for the other racial categories as well. Whites were disproportionality arrested for arson (75.8%), alcohol-related offenses including driving under the influence (87.3%), liquor law violations (84.4%), drunkenness (82.5%), and vandalism (75.3%). The estimated number of arrests of American Indians/Alaskan Natives (1.3%) and Asians/Pacific Islanders (1.1%) is much lower than Whites and Blacks. Like Whites, American Indians/Alaskan Natives are overrepresented in two alcohol related offenses (liquor laws and drunkenness), as well as disorderly conduct, vagrancy, other assaults, and vandalism. Asians/Pacific Islanders are overrepresented in arrests for prostitution, gambling, and running away (FBI, 2009a). As mentioned previously, since Latinos/Hispanics are classified as White in the UCR, we can't rely on the data to understand the arrests of either Whites or Latinos.

Like lynchings in the past, **hate crime** statistics do not receive a great deal of attention in the study of criminology and criminal justice today. Even within the study of race and crime, hate crimes are often overlooked. Hate and bias crimes refer to offenses committed against individuals because of their race, religion, ethnicity, sexual orientation, or disability.

Hate crime is more likely than street crime to involve crimes against the person rather than crimes against property (Perry, 2002). Hate crime statistics provide information about offenders, victims, incidents, and both bias motivation and types of bias (FBI, 2004). These crimes are more likely to be interracial and committed by younger offenders. While Whites are more likely to be bias crime offenders, Blacks are more likely to be victims. In 2004, the number of single-bias incidents reported was 7,649, compared to 7,783 reported incidents in 2008 (FBI, 2004, 2009b). In 2008, of the 7,783 reported incidents, 51.3% were racially motivated. Most of the racial bias crimes reported were due to the offender's anti-Black bias (FBI, 2009b). Racial bias crimes are more frequent than those committed because of religious, sexual orientation, and other categories of bias included in the statistics. Within the single-bias category, 51.3% were racially motivated, 19.5% were due to religious bias, 16.7% were due to sexual-orientation bias, and 11.5% were motivated by disability bias (FBI, 2009b). Of the 4,704 offenses among single-bias hate crime incidents, 72.6% were motivated by anti-Black bias and 17.3% by anti-White bias. Sixty one percent of known offenders were White and 20.2% were Black. Like other sources of data, the hate crime statistics have several limitations, the most serious of which is that not all agencies record and report such incidents. The characteristics of victims of crimes reported in the NCVS are discussed in the next section.

Race and Victimization

The NCVS is the major source of information on victims of nonfatal violent and property crimes in the United States. The NCVS includes 135,000 persons and 76,000 households in its survey to estimate victimizations. Information is collected from victims age 12 or older on crimes both reported and not reported to the police (Bureau of Justice Statistics [BJS], 2010). As previously stated, the NCVS includes information about the race and Hispanic origin of victims, which permits comparative analyses. The race category includes Whites, Blacks, other races, and a new category: individuals of two or more races. The Hispanic origin category includes the choices of Hispanic and Non-Hispanic. In addition to its annual reports, the NCVS periodically publishes reports on trends and analyses of victimization within racial groups. Recent special reports include *American Indians and Crime: A BJS Statistical Profile, 1992–2002* (Perry, 2004); *Black Victims of Violent Crime* (Harrell, 2007); and *Asian, Native Hawaiian, and Pacific Island Victims of Crime, 2009* (Harrell, 2009).

In the past, comparisons between the NCVS and the UCR were discouraged—in spite of the fact that similar patterns and trends occurred in both. Today, the similar findings in both datasets are accepted, as the following statement by Rand (2009) indicates:

> NCVS year-to-year findings between 2007 and 2008 are consistent with the preliminary findings from the Federal Bureau of Investigation's (FBI) Uniform Crime Reporting (UCR) program. NCVS findings show a nominal, but not statistically significant, decline in the number of violent crimes and a significant decline in the number of property crimes. Findings from the UCR program show small declines in the numbers of violent (−2.5%) and property (−1.6%) crimes. Because both programs measure an overlapping but not an

identical set of offenses and use different methodologies, exact congruity between NCVS and UCR estimates is not to be expected. (p. 1)

In 2008, more than 21 million violent and property crime victimizations were reported, a decrease from 2007. Victimizations were close to their lowest levels in 30 years and continued a decline that began in 1999. Rates of violent victimizations (per 1,000 persons age 12 or older) were highest for the racial group "two or more races" (51.6) followed by Blacks (25.9), Whites (18.1), and Hispanics (16.4) (Rand, 2009). The violent victimization of those in the "two or more races" category is surprising. Even though they represent about 1% of the total population in the United States, their violent crime rate is much higher than that for other races and Hispanics (Rand, 2009). Harrell (2009) reported that between 2002 and 2006, the violent **victimization rate** for Asians was much lower than for other non-Asians, about 11 per 1,000 persons over the age of 12.

In 2008, an estimated 16,319,180 property crime victimizations occurred, a decrease of about 8% compared to 2007 (17,508,530). The property crime rate of 135 victimizations per 1,000 households in 2008 was lower than the rate of 147 per 1,000 households in 2007. A breakdown by race and ethnicity for property crimes is not included in the most recent reports. In 2008, victims only reported about 47% of violent crimes and 40% of property crimes to the police. The property crime victimization rate (134.7 per 1,000) was higher than violent crime victimization rate (19.3 per 1,000). Even though we can't say for sure, it is unlikely that violent crimes would outnumber property crimes if we could uncover more of them. The fact that the property crime victimization patterns have existed for decades and appear in both data sets is somewhat reassuring. However, that doesn't mean that we can diminish the significance of violent crimes, especially those for which Blacks are disproportionately arrested and victimized, including murder and robbery.

The NCVS, UCR, and the UCR Supplementary Homicide Reports provide information on the race of homicide victims and offenders. According Zawitz (2003), homicide rates have declined considerably over time, and males are the most likely victims and offenders. In 2008, the majority of murder victims (6,838) were White, 4,934 were males and 1,903 females. Even though there were more White murder victims overall, there were more Black male murder victims (5,752) and fewer Black female murder victims (1,028) in 2008. White females are more likely to be victims of intimate homicides (see Figure 2.1). Between 1975 and 2005, the offender was an intimate partner of the victim in 11% of homicides. There has been a decline in intimate homicides for each race and gender (BJS, 2010). The BJS website provides information on circumstances of homicides that indicates that White homicide victimizations are more likely to occur in the workplace (84.6%) and in sex related (66.9%) circumstances, while Blacks are more often victims in drug related (61.6) and argument (49.3%) circumstances (Fox & Zawitz, 2007).

At this time, the NCVS does not include hate crime victimizations, though the NIBRS does. According to the Hate Crime Statistics Program, the victim of a hate crime can be an individual, business, institution, or society as a whole. Law enforcement agencies reported 9,691 victims of hate crimes in 2008. As stated previously, most hate crime victims in single-bias incidents were targeted because of their race, not their religion or sexual orientation. While the majority of these victims were Black, there were also White,

Figure 2.1 Homicides of Intimates by Gender and Race of Victim, 1976–2005

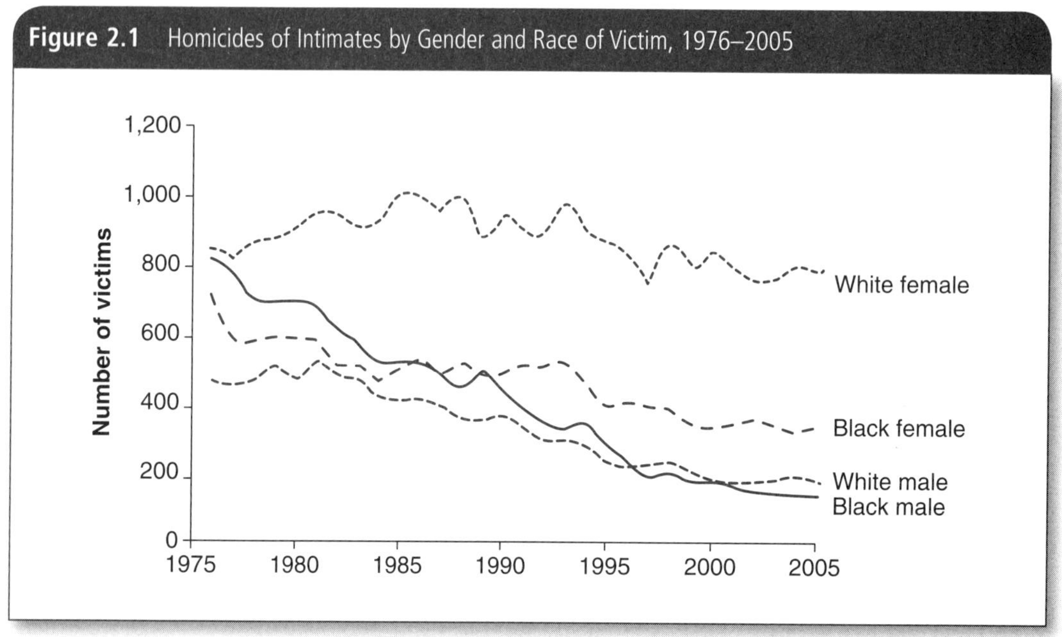

Asian/Pacific Islander, and American Indian/Alaskan Native victims, as well as victims who were of multiple races. Victims were involved in offenses against both persons and property, including intimidation (2,704), destruction/damage/vandalism (2,970), and simple assaults (1,776) (see Table 2.2).

Table 2.2 Hate Crime Incidents, Offenses, Victims, and Known Offenders by Bias Motivation, 2008

Bias Motivation	Incidents	Offenses	Victims[a]	Known Offenders[b]
Total	7,783	9,168	9,691	6,927
Single-bias incidents	7,780	9,160	9,683	6,921
Race:	3,992	4,704	4,934	3,723
Anti-White	716	812	829	811
Anti-Black	2,876	3,413	3,596	2,596
Anti-American Indian/Alaskan Native	54	59	63	61
Anti-Asian/Pacific Islander	137	162	170	140
Anti-multiple races, group	209	258	276	115

Bias Motivation	Incidents	Offenses	Victims[a]	Known Offenders[b]
Religion:	1,519	1,606	1,732	632
Anti-Jewish	1,013	1,055	1,145	353
Anti-Catholic	75	75	89	35
Anti-Protestant	56	60	62	34
Anti-Islamic	105	123	130	85
Anti-other religion	191	212	222	90
Anti-multiple religions, group	65	67	70	33
Anti-atheism/agnosticism/etc.	14	14	14	2
Sexual orientation:	1,297	1,617	1,706	1,460
Anti-male homosexual	776	948	981	921
Anti-female homosexual	154	194	198	156
Anti-homosexual	307	415	466	336
Anti-heterosexual	33	33	34	25
Anti-bisexual	27	27	27	22
Ethnicity/national origin:	894	1,148	1,226	1,034
Anti-Hispanic	561	735	792	711
Anti-other ethnicity/national origin	333	413	434	323
Disability:	78	85	85	72
Anti-physical	22	28	28	26
Anti-mental	56	57	57	46
Multiple-bias incidents[c]	3	8	8	6

a. The term *victim* may refer to a person, business, institution, or society as a whole.

b. The term *known offender* does not imply that the identity of the suspect is known, but only that an attribute of the suspect has been identified, which distinguishes him/her from an unknown offender.

c. In a *multiple-bias incident*, two conditions must be met: (a) more than one offense type must occur in the incident and (b) at least two offense types must be motivated by different biases.

Summary

- There are several sources of crime statistics that provide information on the race and ethnicity of persons arrested and victims of crime.
- The UCR and NCVS data have several limitations, which include how they categorize race and ethnicity.
- The UCR and NCVS report similar patterns and trends despite using different methodologies.
- The BJS provides tools for online data analysis that include racial categories.
- Analyses of crimes reported, persons arrested, and victimizations indicate that property crimes occur more often than violent crimes.
- Blacks are overrepresented in arrests and victimizations for both violent and property crimes, even though more Whites are arrested.
- In 2008, more persons were arrested for drug abuse violations than for either violent or property crimes.
- Persons that self-identified themselves as more than one race in the 2008 NCVS were more likely to be victims of violent crimes than any other racial or ethnic category.
- Blacks are overrepresented as victims and Whites as offenders in reported hate crimes.

KEY TERMS

arrest rates

Bureau of Justice Statistics

Centers for Disease Control and Prevention

crime rates

crime statistics

hate crimes

Healthy People 2020

intimate partner violence

National Crime Victimization Survey

National Incident-Based Reporting System

self-report studies

Supplemental Homicide Reports

Uniform Crime Reports

victimization data

victimization rates

DISCUSSION QUESTIONS

1. Describe the similarities and differences between the UCR and the NCVS.
2. What are the limitations of how race and ethnicity are determined in the UCR and the NCVS?
3. If Whites are arrested and victimized more than Blacks, why is so much attention devoted to Black arrestees and victims?

4. Why are hate crime statistics important to understanding race, crime, and victimization?
5. Are statistics about race and crime misleading?

WEB RESOURCES

Bureau of Justice Statistics: www.bjs.ojp.usdoj.gov

Center for Disease Control and Prevention: www.cdc.gov

Federal Bureau of Investigation: www.fbi.gov

Interuniversity Consortium for Political and Social Science Research: http://www.icpsr.umich.edu

READING

There have been dramatic changes in responses to intimate partner (IP) homicide during the past 30 years, including changes in laws, training for justice professionals, the creation of shelters for victims, and batterer intervention programs. Campbell, Glass, Sharps, Laughon, and Bloom (2007) present a review of IP homicide research from the past 10 years. They also examine the FBI's **Supplemental Homicide Reports** (SHR) to understand IP homicide offenders and victims. Even though IP homicide is decreasing, women are still more likely to be killed by an intimate partner than are men. The authors present IP homicide risk factors identified in the research, including prior battering, stalking, use of a gun, and nonfatal strangulations. The article concludes with a discussion of the limitations of previous research and suggested directions for future IP homicide research, policy, and practice.

Intimate Partner Homicide

Review and Implications of Research and Policy

Jacquelyn C. Campbell, Nancy Glass, Phyllis W. Sharps, Kathryn Laughon, and Tina Bloom

Women in the United States are murdered by intimate partners (married and nonmarried) or former partners approximately 9 times more often than by a stranger (Bureau of Justice Statistics, 2004). Using data from the Supplemental Homicide Reports (SHR), approximately 30% of murdered American women (42% of those with a known perpetrator) are killed by an intimate partner (e.g., husband, ex-husband, or boyfriend), compared to 5.5% of men killed by an intimate partner (Fox, 2005). When hand counts or medical record reviews correct for misclassifications in the SHR (Langford, Isaac, & Kabat, 1998; Websdale, 1999), the percentage of women killed by an intimate or ex-intimate partner increases to 40% to 50% (Campbell et al., 2003a; Campbell et al., 2003b; Frye, Hosein, Waltermaurer, Blaney, & Wilt, 2005). According to a statewide analysis in Massachusetts, the SHR misclassifies as many as 13% of intimate partner (IP) homicides of women as nonintimate partners (Langford et al., 1998), primarily because there is no category in the SHR for the ex-boyfriend/girlfriend relationship of perpetrator and victim, which accounts for about 20% of the IP homicides of women (Campbell et al., 2003a). Another recent analysis of the data on homicide of women found that husbands and intimates (boyfriends and ex-boyfriends) actually perpetrated 51% of the cases (Brock, 2003). This means that research based on the SHR alone, however sophisticated analytically, will give an incomplete picture of IP homicide.

SOURCE: Campbell, J. C., Glass, N., Sharps, P. W., Laughon, K., & Bloom, T. (2007). Intimate partner homicide: Review and implications of research and policy. *Trauma, Violence, & Abuse, 8*(3), 246–269.

Research on IP homicide during the past 30 years has demonstrated that the majority of IP homicides (65%–70% of cases where the female partner is killed, 75% of cases where the male partner is killed) are preceded by intimate partner violence (IPV) against the female partner (e.g., Campbell, 1992; Campbell et al., 2003b; Morton, Runyan, Moracco, & Butts, 1998), making IPV the most important risk factor for IP homicide. It is important to note that IP homicide has been decreasing during the past 30 years; however, this decline is nearly twice the rate for husbands and ex-husbands as wives and ex-wives (Puzone, Saltzman, Kresnow, Thompson, & Mercy, 2000). Although the proportions of IP homicides of men have dropped steadily since 1976, in the late 1990s, the overall proportion of IP homicides of women actually started to increase with only a recent stabilization (Fox & Zawitz, 2004).

This review presents the research related to IP homicide during the past 10 years with implications for the health care, advocacy, and criminal justice systems. The review is organized according to risk and protective factors for IP homicide supported by research with an introductory section addressing the change in rates of IP homicide with a review of the research that addresses the variables related to that change. Furthermore, updated research on lethality risk assessment related to IP homicide is presented. Critique of individual studies are mentioned as reviewed, with an overall critique of the studies in the field, gaps in knowledge, and recommendations for policy and future research presented at the end.

Decreasing Rates of IP Homicide

During the past three decades, there has been a dramatic transformation in the response to IPV across all sectors of society, including the criminal justice system, social services, health care, and public opinion (Klein, Campbell, Soler, & Ghcz, 1997; Renzetti, Edleson, & Bergen, 2001). Enhancement of the response in the criminal justice system includes a change in law enforcement response to domestic violence calls, policies of mandatory arrest and prosecution, training for law enforcement and judges on the dynamics of domestic violence, increased penalties, and domestic violence courts. In social services and advocacy, the past 30 years have seen the creation of domestic violence hotlines and emergency shelters for battered women and their children across the United States, establishment of support groups for IPV survivors and batterer intervention programs, implementation of advocacy programs in family and criminal courts, and intervention programs in virtually every community. In a more recent development, child welfare programs are beginning to take domestic violence into account and colocating domestic violence advocates at child welfare offices to advocate for services to battered mothers as an integral component of child safety. In health care settings, emergency departments, primary care, and prenatal settings increasingly screen for domestic violence, and many hospitals have on-site advocacy and counseling programs for victims of domestic violence (Campbell, 1998). Public opinion and awareness of domestic violence as a crime, not a private family matter, has also increased the demand for services and policies to address the complexity of IPV (Klein et al., 1997). In a recent study of cases of IP homicide, the majority of victims or perpetrators (up to 83% of the cases) or both had contact with criminal justice, victim assistance, and/or health care agencies in the year prior to the homicide (Sharps, Koziol-McLain, et al., 2001). At least partly as a result of the improvements in domestic violence laws and resources, especially arrest policy improvement for unmarried couples, the incidence of IP homicide has dramatically decreased since the mid-1970s (Dugan, Nagin, & Rosenfeld, 2003b).

As indicated previously, the largest decreases in IP homicide have been for male victims. Consequently, the proportion of male homicides by female intimate partners has decreased and the proportion of femicides (murder of women) by male intimate partners has increased. From 1976 to 1996, the percentage of IP homicides with female victims increased from 54% to 70% (Fox & Zawitz, 2004; National Institute of Justice [NIJ], 1997; Zawitz, 1994), so that now there are approximately four to five women killed by an intimate partner for every one male killed by an intimate partner. The states having the most comprehensive domestic violence laws and resources reported the largest decreases in rates of IP homicide of men (Browne, Williams, & Dutton, 1998). Because the vast majority of IP homicides of men are preceded by domestic violence against the woman (Campbell, 1992; Moracco, Runyan, & Butts, 1998), the improvements in legal sanctions and shelter resources has resulted in women being more able to seek and secure safety from IPV rather than kill an abusive partner (Browne et al., 1998; Dugan, Nagin, & Rosenfeld, 2003a; Rosenfeld, 1997).

The decrease in IP homicide is 9% for White females, in contrast to a 49% decrease for African American females, a 56% decrease for White males, and 81% for Black males (Fox & Zawitz, 2004; NIJ, 1997; Zawitz, 1994). The differential rates of decline by racial groups tracked have not been addressed in published research, except for Dugan et al. (2003a, 2003b) who found differential effects of contextual variables in affecting the homicide rates for different racial groups. For instance, for African American women, increasing levels of education are linked to increased rates of IP homicide, whereas for White women higher levels of education are associated with decreases in homicide. This paradoxical result is perhaps because for White women, increasing level of education has resulted in gender parity, whereas for African Americans it has resulted in women being more highly educated than African American men, contributing to gender status inconsistency that has been found to be associated with IPV (Vest, Catlin, Chen, & Brownson, 2002).

Also important in the decrease for male and female IP homicides from a contextual viewpoint are women's resources (e.g., earnings, education) and status, availability of divorce, and lower marriage rates (Dugan, Nagin, & Rosenfeld, 1999; M. N. Smith & Brewer, 1990). However, a later analysis of the SHR by Dugan et al. (2003a) found that the declines attributable to these factors were different for different groups of victims, with marriage being protective for White couples. And even though there has been a decrease in murders of married women by their husbands, there has been an increase in murders of nonmarried women by their boyfriends (Fox & Zawitz, 2004; Rosenfeld, 1997), especially for White girlfriends.

A third factor, at least in some locales, such as New York City, has been a decrease in the availability of handguns (NIJ, 1997; Wilt, Illman, & Brodyfield, 1995). In a sophisticated analysis of SHR data over time in terms of the effects of laws related to removing guns from batterers, Vigdor and Mercy (2006) demonstrated that laws stipulating actual removal (in addition to prohibiting possession and/or purchase) with restraining or protective orders were the most effective in decreasing IP homicide. In the states where purchase restrictions were in place in addition to protective order information being entered into the state database in a timely manner, and possession prohibition, there was a decrease in overall IP homicide of 10% and IP femicide and firearm femicide of 12% to 13%.

Risk Factors Associated With IP Homicide and Femicide

Battering

The most important risk factor of IP homicide identified to date is IPV against the female partner, with approximately 67% to 75% of

IP homicides with a reported history of IPV against the female partner, no matter which partner is killed (Bailey et al., 1997; Campbell, 1992; Campbell et al., 2003b; McFarlane et al., 1999; Mercy & Saltzman, 1989; Moracco et al., 1998; Pataki, 1998; Websdale, 1999). Two studies in different U.S. jurisdictions (Dayton, Ohio, and the state of North Carolina) documented that IP homicides of men by women were characterized by a documented history of IPV of the female perpetrator by the male partner or ex-partner homicide victim in as many as 75% of the cases (Campbell, 1992; Hall-Smith, Moracco, & Butts, 1998; Moracco et al., 1998). It has long been noted that female-perpetrated IP homicide is often characterized by immediate self-defense by the woman, when the male partner is the first to show a weapon or strike a blow and is subsequently killed by his victim (Block & Christakos, 1995; Browne et al., 1998; Campbell, 1992; Crawford & Gartner, 1992; Jurik & Winn, 1990; P. H. Smith, Moracco, & Butts, 1998; Websdale, 1999; Wolfgang, 1958). In the 11-city study Risk Factors for Intimate Partner Femicide, 72% of the IP femicides were preceded by IPV by the male partner before he killed his female partner (Campbell et al., 2003b).

Stalking

Stalking is defined here as repeated occasions of visual or physical proximity, nonconsensual communication, or verbal, written, or implied threats that would cause a reasonable person fear (Tjaden & Thoennes, 1998). Stalking by current or former intimate partners may be an even more common risk factor of IP homicide than IPV, and women almost exclusively experience this form of IPV. However, stalking has not been measured in most IP homicide studies so that the extent of the association has not been established. McFarlane et al. (1999) reported that stalking and harassment occurred in 70% to 90% of 200 actual and attempted femicides in 11 U.S. cities. The strongest association was the combination of estrangement and prior IPV. Yet stalking also occurred in the majority of femicides in intact marriages and relationships where there was no history of IPV. The forms of stalking with the strongest association with IP femicide were following her to work or school, destruction of her property, and leaving threatening messages on answering machines (Campbell et al., 2003b).

Estrangement

A consistent association across many studies has been found between IP homicide involving husbands and wives and a history of estrangement (Dawson & Gartner, 1998; Websdale, 1999; Wilson & Daly, 1993; Wilson, Johnson, & Daly, 1995). The estrangement may take the form of physical leaving or starting legal separation procedures. It has been theorized that male partners are threatened by loss of control over the relationship when women announce their decision to separate, and some men will stop at nothing to regain control, including femicide. Although it is clear that the period after separation is a time of increased risk of violence, this danger has not been compared with the risk of staying in an abusive relationship. It has also been difficult to calculate whether or not separation increases risk in unmarried couples because the proportion of separated to intact couples is not known.

In spite of the importance of estrangement as a risk factor for IP homicide, it is important to remember the increased risk is immediate, not long term. Wilson and Daly (1993; Wilson et al., 1995) found that the first 3 months after separation was the time of most risk, and the 11-city study measured estrangement in the prior year only. The majority of abused women eventually leave their partners (e.g., Campbell, Rose, Kub, & Nedd, 1998; Campbell & Soeken, 1999b), but only a small proportion end up being killed; and if killed, this usually happens in the first year after separation.

Demographic Characteristics Associated With IP Homicides

Like perpetrators of other homicides, male perpetrators of IP homicides in the United States are disproportionately poor, young, a member of an ethnic minority group, have a history of other violence, and have a history of substance abuse (Weiner, Zahn, Sagi, & Merton, 1990). Often young ethnic minority males are poorly educated, unemployed, or underemployed in comparison with their female partners (Bowman, 1993; Jaynes & Williams, 1989; NIJ, 1997; M. N. Smith & Brewer, 1990). As a result, a small percentage may resort to violence and eventually murder as a means of exerting power and control to elevate or equalize their status in their intimate relationships

Immigration status may also increase the risk for IP femicide for women. Frye et al. (2005) found that the strongest risk factors for being a victim of IP femicide in New York City, in contrast to female victims of murders by other perpetrators, was living in a private residence, having children younger than age 18 years, and being foreign born.

Guns

Guns are the agents of homicide in the majority of IP homicides, with the percentages varying according to gender and marital status (Fox & Zawitz, 2004). Ex-husbands and ex-wives are the most frequently killed with guns (87% and 78%, respectively), with husbands and wives at 70% and 68%, and boyfriends (46%) and girlfriends (57%) least often killed with guns in 1990 through 2002 SHR data.

Retrospective and case control studies have associated the use of guns with IP homicide (Browne et al., 1998; Campbell, 1995b). Access to and availability of firearms in the United States greatly increases the risk of homicide in general, and the risk of IP homicide (Kellerman, Rivara, & Rushforth, 1993). Bailey et al. (1997) reanalyzed the results of two population-based case-control studies and found that prior IPV and access to a gun in the home were strongly associated with femicide in the home. In a study of 134 homicides of American Indian, Hispanic, and non-Hispanic White women in New Mexico, researchers also found that firearms were nearly 2 times more likely to be used in "domestic" (intimate partner) femicides than other femicides (Arbuckle et al., 1996).

In a related study, 542 female victims of serious IPV who have accessed formal systems (either criminal justice, health care, or social services) in New York City and Los Angeles were queried about partner gun ownership (Webster et al., 2007). Of those who had obtained an order of protection and knew whether their abuser owned a firearm, 82 (15%) reported that their abuser owned a firearm. Although state law either allowed or mandated judges issuing orders of protection for IPV victims to require abusers to surrender their firearms, only 21 victims (26%) reported that judges used this authority. Only 10 victims (12%) reported that the abuser either surrendered all of his firearms or had them seized. Direct orders from judges to have an abuser disarmed increased the likelihood that all firearms would be removed.

Alcohol and Drug Use

It is generally difficult to identify perpetrator's substance abuse at the time of the homicide with certainty unless they have committed suicide or have volunteered samples at the time of the homicide and blood alcohol and other toxin levels are thus available. There may also be differential risk depending on the substance used (drugs vs. alcohol), general substance abuse versus intoxication at the time of the IP homicide, whether the victim or perpetrator or both were substance abusers, and gender of the victim and perpetrator. Males are more likely to be chronic alcohol abusers when victims than when perpetrators, and males whether victims or perpetrators are more likely to chronically abuse alcohol than are females in either category (Block & Christakos, 1995; Campbell, 1992; P. H. Smith et al., 1998). Furthermore, alcohol use is not uniquely associated with IP homicide for women as victims. Wilt, Illman, and Brodyfield (1995) and Moracco et al. (1998) found alcohol use in as many women killed by intimate partners as killed by others. Persuasive evidence about drug abuse was found in two large data sets (Chicago and North Carolina) where significantly less drug abuse was found in cases of IP homicide than other homicides (Block & Christakos, 1995; Moracco et al., 1998).

Mental Illness

Although further research is needed [to] explicate the link between mental illness and IP homicide, an analysis of 540 IP homicides across the United States found that 13% of perpetrators (11% of males, 15% of females) had a history of mental illness, compared to 3% (not reported by gender) of nonfamily murderers (Zawitz, 1994).

In other data, approximately one third of the 200 male perpetrators in the 11-city study of attempted femicides and femicides were described as being in poor (vs. fair, good, or excellent) mental health (Sharps, Koziol-McLain, et al., 2001). Forty-six percent of the male perpetrators had had at least one contact with a mental health professional, as compared to 29% of the victims of attempted or actual femicides; 33% had had some contact with an alcohol or drug treatment program, as compared to 25% of attempted or actual femicides. In the comparative analysis, perpetrator mental health was a significant predictor of homicide on the bivariate level but not in multivariate analysis.

Few other studies have found mental illness to be a significant risk factor for IP homicides; however, few have been able to use adequate operationalization. The 11-city study (Campbell et al., 2003b) used proxy informants to judge mental health of the perpetrators of femicide and the female partner to assess mental health in the attempted femicide cases. These are hardly precise measures of mental illness.

Differential Risk by Gender: Homicide-Suicide, Forced Sex, and Abuse During Pregnancy

Homicide-suicides represent a significant proportion, 27% to 32%, of IP femicides. This pattern is almost never seen when women kill a male intimate, only for 0.1% of such cases in Chicago and North Carolina (Block & Christakos, 1995; Moracco et al., 1998). There is some speculation that the proportion of IP femicides that are femicide-suicides is increasing; however, the data is difficult to track over time nationally because suicide following the femicide is not data routinely recorded for the SHR. The Centers for Disease Control and Prevention has begun a pilot data-linking project in a limited number of states that will link medical examiner (ME) and homicide data to allow better study of these incidents. When examining all homicide-suicides in the United States, at least 74% involve intimate partners (Violence Policy Center, 2006).

IP homicide-suicides follow different patterns than other IP homicides. In this type of homicide, Whites are disproportionately represented (Buteau, Lesage, & Kiely, 1993; Stack, 1997; Websdale, 1999). Buteau et al. (1993) in Canada and U.S. researchers (e.g., Morton et al., 1998; Stack, 1997) have divided homicide-suicides into "mercy killings" or "suicide pacts" that involve older couples afflicted by physical illness or other serious problems on the one hand, and the more common case of intimate partner involuntary (on the part of the victim) homicide followed by suicide of the perpetrator, on the other. In the much larger category of involuntary homicide-suicides involving younger perpetrators and victims (accounting for 90% of such cases in North Carolina), risk factors for perpetrators included being male, jealousy, current or past depression, a long-standing relationship with the victim, a history of physical abuse or separation/reunion episodes, personality disorder, and alcohol abuse (Buteau et al., 1993; Morton et al., 1998). Separation was a factor in 45% of the North Carolina homicide-suicides (Morton et al., 1998).

In the analysis of the 32% of femicides that were femicide-suicides in the 11-city femicide study, perpetrator threats of suicide and perpetrator history of poor mental health were unique predictors of this form of femicide (Koziol-McLain et al., 2006), along with the shared risk factors of prior IPV, estrangement, a stepchild in the home as the IPV femicides without suicide. It was also noted that the perpetrators of IP femicide-suicide were slightly more likely to be married and White than IP femicide perpetrators who did not commit suicide, although unemployment was the strongest demographic risk factor for both groups. The scenario was more typically an abusive man distraught because his wife had left him (usually because of the IPV), who had never been arrested for domestic violence, but was more likely to have been seen in the health or mental health system because of depression or threats of suicide in the year prior to the incident.

Descriptive evidence and bivariate case control analysis from the 11-city study showed associations of forced sex and abuse during pregnancy with IP femicide (Campbell, 1986; Campbell & Soeken, 1999a; Campbell, Soeken, McFarlane, & Parker, 1998; McFarlane, Campbell, Sharps, & Watson, 2002). Particularly violent and dangerous men may be those who also force their partners into sex and beat them during pregnancy. In addition, jealous and controlling men may suspect or have evidence that the unborn child is not their biological progeny and therefore may kill their partners out of male sexual competitiveness (Daly, Wiseman, & Wilson, 1997). This theory was supported by evidence linking an increased risk of IP femicide with the presence of stepchildren (nonbiological child of the abusive partner) in the home in data from Canada and Chicago (Daly et al., 1997) and also in data from Houston, Texas (Brewer & Paulsen, 1999). The importance of the presence of a stepchild in the home as an important risk factor was also found in the 11-city IP femicide study (Campbell et al., 2003b). However, the evidence can also be explained through a power and control framework, which also predicts extreme jealousy among abusive men.

Nonfatal strangulation. There is little research on strangulation, and even less examining strangulation in the context of IPV and/or femicide. There are no national prevalence rates for strangulation in any context; however, several recent studies suggest that it is a common form of violence against women and is associated with more severe abuse and risk of lethal violence. In the Chicago Women's Health Risk Study (CWHRS; Block et al., 2000) of 457 women who were seeking care in a medical setting for any reason and who had experienced IPV within the past year, almost one half (47.3%) reported strangulation by the abuser within the past year, and more (57.6%) had "ever" experienced strangulation. Nonfatal strangulation was reported in 43% ($n = 89$) of the cases prior to the murder among the femicides in the 11-city study (Glass et al., in press). Sixty-eight percent of women presenting to domestic violence advocacy programs ($n = 62$) reported strangulation by the abuser (Wilbur et al., 2001). In Chicago, one study of all women killed by an intimate partner during a 2-year period found that nearly one fourth were killed by strangulation (Block et al., 2000).

Nonfatal strangulation is a risk factor for lethal violence in several studies. Prior nonfatal strangulation was associated with greater than sevenfold odds (OR = 7.48, 95% confidence interval [CI] = 4.53–12.35) of femicide in comparison to abused women in the 11-city study (10% reported episodes of being "choked" (Glass et al., in press). Although

Block et al. (2000) did not find that experience of actual or attempted strangulation was an increased risk factor for IP femicide, they did find that strangulation during a specific incident increased the odds of that incident being fatal. These results underscore the need to screen specifically for nonfatal strangulation when assessing abused women.

Pregnancy-associated femicide. A *pregnancy-associated death* is defined as death occurring during or within 1 year of pregnancy (Chang, Berg, Saltzman, & Herndon, 2005). A pregnancy-associated death in which homicide is determined to be the manner of death is labeled a *pregnancy-associated homicide.* Pregnancy-associated homicide has emerged as a leading cause of maternal mortality (Dannenberg et al., 1995; Dietz, Rochat, Thompson, Berg, & Griffin, 1998; Krulewitch, Pierre-Louis, de Leon-Gomez, Guy, & Green, 2001; Krulewitch, Roberts, & Thompson, 2003; McFarlane et al., 2002; Parsons & Harper, 1999). Two studies concluded that pregnant and recently pregnant women are at 2 to 3 times the risk of homicide compared to nonpregnant women (Krulewitch et al., 2003; McFarlane et al., 2002).

Studies at the city and state levels have found that homicide is the, or one of the, leading causes of maternal mortality, responsible for up to 20% of maternal deaths (Horon & Cheng, 2001; Krulewitch et al, 2001). In a national analysis, homicide was the second leading cause of injury-related maternal mortality (1.7 per 100,000 deaths) after automobile accidents (Chang et al., 2005). That study examined the vital records and ME records between 1991 and 1999 and found that nearly 9% of pregnancy-associated deaths nationwide were the result of homicide (Chang et al., 2005). The methods used in this study most likely resulted in an undercount of cases, however, for two reasons. The researchers relied on the SHR for data on homicide, which omits femicides committed by ex-boyfriends. In addition, ascertainment of pregnancy, especially early pregnancy and early pregnancy loss, is imperfect when using vital records, and thus pregnancies are likely undercounted as well (Chang et al., 2005). Ascertainment of pregnancy-associated homicide is difficult, however. Although there are check-off boxes on standard death certificates that prompt the ME to indicate if a deceased woman was pregnant at the time of death or had been pregnant within the past year, that information is often not known to the examiner, and thus the information is missing or marked as "unknown."

African American women and young women are at substantially greater risk of pregnancy-associated homicide compared to White women. African American women have 3 to 7 times the risk of White women (Chang et al., 2005; McFarlane et al., 2002), which may be a result of increased unemployment among African American men rather than a true racial difference. Krulewitch et al. (2003) found that pregnant homicide victims were 3.3 times more likely to be adolescents compared to nonpregnant women.

Neglected Areas in IP Homicide Research

There are two particularly noteworthy areas of neglected research in the area of IP homicide. First is same-sex IP homicides, and the second is attempted homicides.

Same-Sex IP Homicide

IP homicide in same-sex relationships has seldom been studied. Data from the SHR estimates that 6.2% of the total murder rate for men in this country is male same-sex couple IP homicides in comparison to 0.5% female same-sex partner homicides from 1981 to 1998. Thus, the male proportion is 12 times the female rate. However, we have been unable to find any systematic study of male same-sex partner homicides, and there has been only one study of female same-sex partner IP homicides (Glass, Koziol-McLain, Campbell, & Block, 2004). In that subsample analysis of five femicides and four attempted femicides by female partners, the primary characteristics of prior IPV, estrangement, jealousy, and substance abuse were notable prior to the lethal or near-lethal event. The dynamics were thus similar to heterosexual couples; however, because of the small sample, definitive conclusions cannot be drawn.

Near-Fatal IP Violence

IPV is the most common cause of nonfatal injuries to young women in the United States (Grisso et al., 1991; Kyriacou et al., 1999). The best available evidence from the national IP femicide study (Campbell et al., 2003b) and from gun injury data indicate that there are approximately nine near-lethal (gunshot or stab wound to head, neck, or torso; choking or immersion in water to the point of unconsciousness; severe head injuries with a blunt object weapon) incidents for every IP homicide.

Findings from a national population-based study indicated that 41.5% of the estimated 4.9 million IP sexual and physical assaults perpetrated against women annually result in an injury to the woman. About 28% of the injured women will seek care in a health care setting (Tjaden & Thoennes, 2000). Of those who sought health care, 16.7% needed at least overnight hospitalization, and 17% said they had a head or spinal cord injury or a knife wound. An analysis of National Victim Survey data from 1992 to 1996 shows a 51% injury rate from IPV for women with 7% treated in the emergency department (ED), 3% treated in an outpatient setting, and < 1% hospitalized (Greenfeld, Rand, & Craven, 1998). Of those treated in the ED, 21% were injured by a weapon (1.1% firearms) and 25% were diagnosed with a head injury, stab wound, or internal injury.

Without intervention, the violence in these cases is likely to continue to escalate with potentially fatal outcomes (Crowell & Burgess, 1996). In the national femicide study (Campbell et al., 2003b), we found very few (< 10%) of the survivors of a near-lethal IP incident had been referred to domestic violence services even though they spent considerable time in EDs and hospital settings, including trauma and rehabilitation centers.

The risk factors for IP near-lethal IP violent incidents against women were substantially the same as for femicide (including approximately 75% prior IPV). Meaningful differences did exist, however. Among the survivors of the near-lethal incidents, minority ethnicity (African American and Hispanic) of the perpetrator was a significant risk factor whereas perpetrator unemployment was not. Also, college education was protective. Prior choking (attempted strangulation), forced sex, and threats to harm the children were stronger risk factors (OR = 2.9, 3.4, and 10.5, respectively) for the near-lethal cases compared to the femicide cases. This last difference may be due to more complete data (fewer "don't know" answers) for near-lethal survivors who were actually interviewed compared to data obtained from the proxy informants for the femicide group.

In the national femicide study (Campbell et al., 2003b), it was difficult to identify and locate victims of lethal IPV (who might not all be present in police and hospital data), and thus the sample was less representative than that of the actual femicide cases. Specifically, the near-lethal sample was skewed toward poor, mostly minority women who lacked the resources to move after the incident. By involving these survivors, however, we were able to obtain information directly from the women and thus had less missing data and more confidence in the validity of the findings. This is an important but understudied group of IPV victims, and further research is needed to address the needs of these women and to better identify risk factors for this severe form of partner violence.

Assessing Lethality in Violent Intimate Relationships

The Danger Assessment (DA) is a clinical research instrument that was designed to assist battered women in assessing their danger of being murdered by their intimate partner as well as using lethal violence against a male intimate partner. This instrument was first developed in conjunction with a wide variety of experts on IPV, including battered women, advocates, and representatives of the criminal justice system (Campbell, 1986). The original DA items were selected based on existing retrospective studies of IP homicide or serious injury (Berk, Berk, Loseke, & Rauma, 1983; Browne, 1987; Campbell, 1981; Fagan, Stewart, & Hansen, 1983).

To measure the severity and frequency of battering, women are asked to mark approximate dates of abusive incidents on a calendar, and to rank the severity of the incident on a 1 to 5 (1 = *slap, pushing, no injuries and/or lasting pain* through 5 = *use of weapon, wounds from weapon*) scale. The use of the calendar in this and other contexts has been shown to improve the accuracy of women's recall and reduces women's tendency to minimize the IPV she has experienced (Campbell, 1986, 1995a; Ferraro & Johnson, 1983). The second portion of the DA consists of 20 dichotomous (yes/no) items consisting of risk factors for IP homicide. (Five items were added to the original 15-item scale based on findings from the 11-city IP femicide study; Campbell et al., 2003b.)

There are two ways of scoring the DA. Users can simply count the number of responses endorsed, with a higher number indicating that more of the risk factors for femicide are present in the relationship.

In summary, the DA is meant to be a collaborative exercise between a domestic violence advocate, health care professional, and/or criminal justice practitioner and the abused woman herself. It is meant to give the woman and the practitioner information about her risk of femicide as the basis for safety planning as an adjunct to her own perception of risk and the clinical wisdom of the practitioner (Goodman et al., 2000; Heckert & Gondolf, 2004; Pinard & Pagani, 2000; Weisz, Tolman, & Saunders, 2000). Although there are several other risk assessment instruments that have been introduced to assess risk of IPV reassault, the risk factors for IP homicide, although overlapping, are not exactly the same (Campbell, 2005b). The DA is the only such instrument designed for determining risk of IP lethality only, although DV-MOSAIC is a threat assessment computerized system with validity support that encompasses risk of homicide (Campbell et al., 2005; De Becker & Associates, 2000).

Limitations of Current Research

Data Sources

Although the SHR offer a rich database for homicide research over time, it is limited in several important ways that have particular ramifications for the knowledge base in IP homicide. First, the perpetrator categories exclude ex-boyfriend/ex-girlfriend, a category that accounts for about 20% of IP homicides against women (Campbell et al., 2003b) and an unknown proportion of IP homicides of males. In addition, there are many other possibilities for misclassification. Another limitation is the inability to determine which homicides are followed by suicides and which homicides involve pregnant or recently pregnant women. These issues will be addressed by the linking of the homicide and ME data projects currently being launched by the Centers for Disease Control and Prevention. Another issue with homicide studies based on the SHR is how to treat missing data, primarily in cases where the homicide has not been solved and the perpetrator is unknown. Although various correction factors have been proposed, it is not known how well the perpetrator categories apply to IP homicides, and studies vary as to how they treat this variable.

Another approach to the study of IP homicide to the SHR is using records from individual police departments. Generally, this approach has been used with either one city over time (e.g., Block & Christakos, 1995) or several large cities (e.g., Campbell et al., 2003b) to give a sufficient sample size for analysis. The obvious limitation there is the omission of rural and suburban cases, which means that the risk factor summary given here may misspecify the strength and nature of risk in nonurban settings, although homicides are rarer in those locales. One notable exception to this limitation is the statewide analysis in North Carolina conducted by Runyan and colleagues (Moracco et al., 1998; Morton et al., 1998). More such statewide analyses are needed.

Police homicide files do have limitations. The completeness of the information varies tremendously, depending on the extent of the investigation necessary to resolve the case. In homicide-suicide cases, therefore, the files often have little information because the perpetrator is immediately identified and no trial is necessary. Homicide-suicide represents a large proportion of IP femicides, and therefore this dearth of information is particularly problematic. Another issue is that the files are usually not available for analysis until the case has come to trial, which means that there is often considerable delay before research can be conducted. Finally, some of the records from the investigation are in the prosecutor's files, not the police files which generally end at the point when a perpetrator is charged and arrested, although the investigation continues.

An alternative to police homicide files as a starting point is ME files. Those databases are missing information related to prior criminality of the perpetrator and victim (such as prior domestic violence charges) and the circumstances of the actual murder. However, ongoing surveillance using ME databases such as the New York City femicide database started by Susan Wilt (Frye et al., 2005) is possible from this source and gives rich information.

Inconsistent Comparison Groups

Different research groups have taken different approaches to analyzing IP homicides. Frye et al.'s (2005) analysis also illustrates an additional issue in IP homicide research, the most useful comparison group. Frye et al. compared IP femicides with other murders of women, whereas Dobash et al. (2004) compared IP femicide perpetrators with other male homicide perpetrators, while other analyses have compared IP homicide in general with other homicides. The issue with the final approach is that gender of the victim changes the dynamics of IP homicide, as shown in the comparison of the Dobash et al. and Frye et al. findings. Others have compared male and female victims whereas Campbell et al. (2003b) compared victims of IP femicide with other battered women. Each approach has strengths and limitations that need to be taken into account when interpreting results.

Incomplete Data on the Event

A challenge inherent to IP homicide research is to find a source of information to "speak for" the victim, especially in terms of identification of risk factors specific to the relationship that occur prior to the actual event that are not necessarily in the police homicide files or other records. Two studies have developed creative strategies to address this. Runyan and colleagues (Moracco et al., 1998; Morton et al., 1998) interviewed the investigating police or sheriff's officers. Campbell et al. (2003b) interviewed a family member or close friend of the victim as a "proxy" informant. Both of these approaches have limitations in terms of the validity and completeness of the information but still go far beyond the police homicide files and SHR.

Conclusions and Discussion

In conclusion, IP femicide and attempted femicide continues to be a major threat to women's safety and health. Abuse against women is the major risk factor for IPV femicide. The other most important risk factors that significantly elevate danger over prior abuse are estrangement, perpetrator gun ownership, perpetrator unemployment, a highly controlling abuser, threats to kill, threats with a weapon or use of a weapon, forced sex, violence during pregnancy, attempted strangulation, a stepchild in the home (her biological child, not his), and the perpetrator avoiding arrest for domestic violence. The woman having a separate domicile ("a place of her own") is protective against IP femicide. Near-lethal IPV is also an important issue, particularly for health care professionals as these severely injured women are usually treated in the health care system and need intensive and proactive individualized safety planning. The DA can be used as the basis for safety planning so that women have a realistic appraisal of their level of risk.

In the 11-city IP femicide study, the majority of victims or perpetrators (up to 83% of the cases) or both had contact with criminal justice, victim assistance, and/or health care agencies in the year prior to the homicide (Sharps, Koziol-McLain, et al., 2001). This indicates opportunities for prevention by identification of women at risk and appropriate intervention. One of the key areas for intervention is related to guns because guns are the most frequent weapon used in IP homicide. More consistent application of current policies that support removal of guns from the home through training of police officers, judges, and magistrates and strengthening of those policies is also needed. Specifically, in homes where there is a history of or prior arrest for domestic violence or active protective orders, policy should mandate that gun ownership is prohibited, and the removal of the guns should be enforced as indicated under the federal Violence Against Women Act (VAWA) and according to individual state laws where they exist. All too often the policies related to enforcement of gun removal are overlooked or not strictly enforced. Frattaroli and Vernick (2006) demonstrated that there is a myriad of different state statutes applying to gun access restrictions for domestic violence perpetrators. Frattaroli and Teret (2006) in Maryland and Seave (2006) in California showed that implementation of the laws that do exist is often the issue, presenting further challenges in conducting such research. However, Vigdor and Mercy (2006) were able to demonstrate a significant decrease (10%) in IP homicide overall (and 13% of IP femicide) in SHR-recorded homicides in states where gun removal was mandated with orders of protection along with efficient background checks and prohibition of possession.

References

Arbuckle, J., Olson, L., Howard, M., Brillman, J., Ancti, C., & Sklar, D. (1996). Safe at home? Domestic violence and other homicides among women in Mexico. *Annals of Emergency Medicine, 27*(2), 210–215.

Bailey, J. E., Kellermann, A. L., Somes, G. W., Banton, J. G., Rivara, F. P., & Rushford, N. P. (1997). Risk factors for violent death of women in the home. *Archives of Internal Medicine, 157*, 777–782.

Berk, R. A., Berk, S., Loseke, D. R., & Rauma, D. (1983). Mutual combat and other family violence myths. In D. Finkelhor, R. J. Gelles, G. T. Hotaling, & M. A. Straus (Eds.), *The dark side of families* (pp. 197–212). Beverly Hills, CA: Sage.

Block, C. R., & Christakos, A. (1995). Intimate partner homicide in Chicago over 29 years. *Crime & Delinquency, 41*(4), 496–526.

Block, C. R., Devitt, C. O., Fonda, D., Fugate, M., Marting, C., McFarlane, J., et al. (2000). *The Chicago Women's Health Study: Risk of serious injury or death in intimate violence: A collaborative research project.* Washington, DC: U.S. Department of Justice, National Institute of Justice.

Bowman, P. J. (1993). The impact of economic marginality among African American husbands and fathers. In H. McAdoo (Ed.), *Family ethnicity: Strength in diversity* (pp. 120–140). Newbury Park, CA: Sage.

Brewer, V. E., & Paulsen, D. J. (1999). A comparison of US and Canadian findings on uxorcide risk for women with children sired by previous partners. *Homicide Studies 3*(4), 317–332.

*Brock, K. (2003). *When men murder women: An analysis of 2001 homicide data.* Washington, DC: Violence Policy Center Publications.

Browne, A. (1987). *Battered women who kill.* New York: Free Press.

Browne, A., Williams, K. R., & Dutton, D. C. (1998). Homicide between intimate partners. In M. D. Smith & M. Zahn (Eds.), *Homicide: A sourcebook of social research* (pp. 149–164). Thousand Oaks, CA: Sage.

Bureau of Justice Statistics. (2004). *Homicide trends in the United States.* Washington, DC: U.S. Department of Justice, Office of Justice Programs.

Buteau, J., Lesage, A. D., & Kiely, M. C. (1993). Homicide followed by suicide: A Quebec case series, 1988–1990. *Canadian Journal of Psychiatry, 38*(8), 552–556.

Campbell, J. C. (1981). Misogyny and homicide of women. *Advances in Nursing Science, 3*(2), 67–85.

Campbell, J. C. (1986). Nursing assessment of risk of homicide for battered women. *Advances in Nursing Science, 8*(4), 36–51.

Campbell, J. C. (1992). "If I can't have you, no one can": Power and control in homicide of female partners. In J. Radford & D. E. H. Russell (Eds.), *Femicide: The politics of woman killing* (pp. 99–113). New York: Twayne.

Campbell, J. C. (1995a). *Assessing dangerousness.* Newbury Park, CA: Sage.

Campbell, J. C. (1995b). Prediction of homicide of and by battered women. In J. C. Campbell (Ed.), *Assessing the risk of dangerousness: Potential for further violence of sexual offenders, batterers, and child abusers* (pp. 96–113). Thousand Oaks, CA: Sage.

Campbell, J. C. (1998). *Empowering survivors of abuse: Health care for battered women and their children.* Thousand Oaks, CA: Sage.

Campbell, J. C. (2005b). Lethality assessment approaches: Reflections on their use and ways forward. *Violence Against Women, 11,* 1206–1213.

Campbell, J. C., O'Sullivan, C., Roehl, J., & Webster, D. W. (2005). *Intimate Partner Violence Risk Assessment Validation Study: The RAVE Study. Final report to the National Institute of Justice* (NCJ 209731–209732). Available at http://www.ncjrs.org/pdffiles1/nij/grants/209731.pdf

Campbell, J. C., Rose, L. E., Kub, J., & Nedd, D. (1998). Voices of strength and resistance: A contextual and longitudinal analysis of women's responses to battering. *Journal of Interpersonal Violence, 13,* 743–762.

Campbell, J. C., & Soeken, K. (1999a). Forced sex and intimate partner violence: Effects on women's health. *Violence Against Women 5*(9), 1017–1035.

Campbell, J., & Soeken, K. (1999b). Women's responses to battering over time: An analysis of change. *Journal of Interpersonal Violence, 14*(1), 21–40.

Campbell, J. C., Soeken, K., McFarlane, J., & Parker, B. (1998). Risk factors for femicide among pregnant and nonpregnant battered women. In J. C. Campbell (Ed.), *Empowering survivors of abuse: Health care for battered women and their children* (pp. 90–97). Thousand Oaks, CA: Sage.

Campbell, J. C., Webster, D., Koziol-McLain, J., Block, C. R., Campbell, D. W., Curry, M. A., et al. (2003a). Assessing risk factors for intimate partner homicide. *National Institute of Justice Journal, 250,* 14–19.

Campbell, J. C., Webster, D., Koziol-McLain, J., Block, C. R., Campbell, D. W., Curry, M. A., et al. (2003b). Risk factors for femicide in abusive relationships: Results from a multisite case control study. *American Journal of Public Health, 93*(7), 1089–1097.

Chang, J., Berg, C. J., Saltzman, L. E., & Herndon, J. (2005). Homicide: A leading cause of injury deaths among pregnant and postpartum women in the United States, 1991–1999. *American Journal of Public Health, 95*(3), 471–477.

Crawford, M., & Gartner, R. (1992). *Woman killing: Intimate femicide in Ontario: 1974–1990.* Ontario, Canada: Women We Honor Action Committee.

Crowell, N. A., & Burgess, A. W. (1996). *Understanding violence against women.* Washington, DC: National Research Council.

Daly, M., Wiseman, K. A., & Wilson, M. (1997). Women with children sired by previous partners incur excess risk of uxoricide. *Homicide Studies, 1*(1), 61–71.

Dannenberg, A. L., Carter, D. M., Lawson, H. W., Ashton, D. M., Dorfman, S. F., & Graham, E. H. (1995). Homicide and other injuries as causes of maternal death in New York City, 1987 through 1991. *American Journal of Obstetrics and Gynecology, 172*(5), 1557–1564.

Dawson, R., & Gartner, R. (1998). Differences in the characteristics of intimate femicides: The role of relationship state and relationship status. *Homicide Studies, 2,* 378–399.

De Becker, G., & Associates. (2000). *Domestic violence method (DV MOSAIC).* Available at http://www.mosaicsystem.com/dv.htm

Dietz, P. M., Rochat, R. W., Thompson, B. L., Berg, C. J., & Griffin, G. W. (1998). Differences in the risk of homicide and other fatal injuries between postpartum women and other women of childbearing age. *American Journal of Public Health, 88*(4), 641–643.

Dobash, R. E., Dobash, R. P., Cavanagh, K., & Lewis, R. (2004). Not an ordinary killer—Just an ordinary guy. When men murder an intimate woman partner. *Violence Against Women, 10,* 577–605.

Dugan, L., Nagin, D., & Rosenfeld, R. (1999). Explaining the decline in intimate partner homicide: The effects of changing domesticity, women's status, and domestic violence resources. *Homicide Studies, 3,* 187–214.

Dugan, L., Nagin, D., & Rosenfeld, R. (2003a). Do domestic violence services save lives? *National Institute of Justice Journal, 250,* 20–25.

Dugan, L., Nagin, D., & Rosenfeld, R. (2003b). Exposure reduction or retaliation? The effects of domestic violence resources on intimate-partner homicide. *Law & Society Review, 37,* 169–198.

Dutton, D. G., & Kropp, P. R. (2000). A review of domestic violence risk instruments. *Trauma, Violence, & Abuse 1*(2), 171–181.

Fagan, J., Stewart, D. E., & Hansen, K. (1983). Violent men or violent husbands? Background factors and situational correlates. In R. J. Gelles, G. Hotaling, M. A. Straus, & D. Finkelhor (Eds.), *The dark side of families* (pp. 49–68). Beverly Hills, CA: Sage.

Ferraro, K. J., & Johnson, J. M. (1983). How women experience battering: The process of victimization. *Social Problems, 30,* 325–339.

Fox, J. A. (2005). *Uniform crime reports [United States]: Supplementary homicide reports, 1976–2002* [Computer file] (ICPSR ed.). Ann Arbor, MI: Inter-university Consortium for Political and Social Research.

Fox, J. A., & Zawitz, M. W. (2004). *Homicide trends in the US.* Washington, DC: Bureau of Justice Statistics. Available at www.ojp.usdoj/bjs/

Frattaroli, S., & Teret, S. (2006). Understanding and informing policy implementation: A case study of the domestic violence provisions of the Maryland Gun Violence Act. *Evaluation Review, 30,* 347–360.

Frattaroli, S., & Vernick, J. (2006). Separating batterers and guns: A review and analysis of gun removal laws in 50 states. *Evaluation Review, 30,* 296–313.

Frye, V., Hosein, V., Waltermaurer, E., Blaney, S., & Wilt, S. (2005). Femicide in New York City, 1990 to 1999. *Homicide Studies, 9,* 204–228.

Glass, N. E., Koziol-McLain, J., Campbell, J. C., & Block, C. R. (2004). Female-perpetrated femicide and attempted femicide. *Violence Against Women 10,* 606–625.

Glass, N., Laughon, K., Campbell, J. C., Block, R. B., Hanson, G., & Sharps, P. S. (in press). Strangulation is an important risk factor for attempted and completed femicides. *Journal of Emergency Medicine.*

Goodman, L., Dutton, M. A., & Bennett, L. (2000). Predicting repeat abuse among arrested batterers: Use of the Danger Assessment Scale in the criminal justice system. *Journal of Interpersonal Violence, 10,* 63–74.

Greenfeld, L. A., Rand, M. R., & Craven, D. (1998). *Violence by intimates: Analysis of data on crimes by current or former spouses, boyfriends, or girlfriends.* Washington, DC: U.S. Department of Justice.

Grisso, J. A., Wishner, A. R., Schwarz, D. F., Weene, B. A., Holmes, J. H., & Sutton, R. L. (1991). A population-based study of injuries in inner-city women. *Journal of Epidemiology, 134,* 59–68.

Hall-Smith, P., Moracco, K. E., & Butts, J. (1998). Partner homicide in context. *Homicide Studies, 2*(4), 400–421.

Heckert, D. A., & Gondolf, E. W. (2004). Battered women's perceptions of risk versus risk factors and instruments in predicting repeat reassault. *Journal of Interpersonal Violence, 19*(7), 778–800.

Horon, I. L., & Cheng, D. (2001). Enhanced surveillance for pregnancy-associated mortality—Maryland, 1993–1998. *Journal of the American Medical Association, 285,* 1455–1459.

Jaynes, G. D., & Williams, R. M. (1989). *A common destiny: Blacks and American society.* Washington, DC: National Academy Press.

Jurik, N. C., & Winn, R. (1990). Gender and homicide: A comparison of men and women who kill. *Violence and Victims, 5,* 227–242.

Kellerman, A. L., Rivara, F. P., & Rushforth, N. B. (1993). Gun ownership as a risk factor for homicide in the home. *New England Journal of Medicine, 329,* 1084–1091.

*Klein, E., Campbell, J., Soler, E., & Ghez, M. (1997). *Ending domestic violence: Changing public perceptions.* Thousand Oaks, CA: Sage.

Koziol-McLain, J., Webster, D., McFarlane, J., Block, C. R., Curry, M. A., Ulrich, Y., et al. (2006). Risk factors for femicide-suicide in abusive relationships: Results from a multi-site case control study. *Violence and Victims, 21,* 3–21.

Krulewitch, C. J., Pierre-Louis, M. L., de Leon-Gomez, R., Guy, R., & Green, R. (2001). Hidden from view: Violent deaths among pregnant women in the District of Columbia, 1988–1996. *Journal of Midwifery and Women's Health, 46*(1), 4–10.

Krulewitch, C. J., Roberts, D. W., & Thompson, L. S. (2003). Adolescent pregnancy and homicide: Findings for the Maryland Office of the Chief Medical Examiner, 1994–1998. *Child Maltreatment, 8*(2), 122–128.

Kyriacou, D. N., Anglin, D., Taliaferro, E., Stone, S., Tubb, T., Linden, J. A., et al. (1999). Risk factors for injury to women from domestic violence against women [see comments]. *New England Journal of Medicine, 341,* 1892–1898.

Langford, L., Isaac, N. E., & Kabat, S. (1998). Homicides related to intimate partner violence in Massachusetts. *Homicide Studies, 2*(4), 353–377.

McFarlane, J., Campbell, J. C., Sharps, P. W., & Watson, K. (2002). Abuse during pregnancy and femicide: Urgent implications for women's health. *Obstetrics & Gynecology, 100*(1), 27–36.

McFarlane, J., Campbell, J. C., Wilt, S., Sachs, C., Ulrich, Y., & Xu, X. (1999). Stalking and intimate partner femicide. *Homicide Studies, 3*(4), 300–316.

Mercy, J. A., & Saltzman, L. E. (1989). Fatal violence among spouses in the United States 1976–8. *American Journal of Public Health, 79,* 595–599.

Moracco, K. E., Runyan, C. W., & Butts, J. (1998). Femicide in North Carolina. *Homicide Studies, 2,* 422–446.

Morton, E., Runyan, C. W., Moracco, K. E., & Butts, J. (1998). Partner homicide victims: A population based study in North Carolina, 1988–1992. *Violence and Victims, 13*(2), 91–106.

National Institute of Justice. (1997). *A study of homicide in eight US cities: An NIJ intramural research project.* Washington, DC: U.S. Department of Justice.

Parsons, L. H., & Harper, M. A. (1999). Violent maternal deaths in North Carolina. *Obstetrics & Gynecology, 94*(6), 990–993.

Pataki, G. (1998). *Intimate partner homicides in New York State.* Albany: State of New York.

Pinard, G. F., & Pagani, L. (Eds.). (2000). *Clinical assessment of dangerousness: Empirical contributions.* New York: Cambridge University Press.

Puzone, C. A., Saltzman, L. E., Kresnow, M.-J., Thompson, M. P., & Mercy, J. A. (2000). National trends in intimate partner homicide: United States, 1976–1995. *Violence Against Women, 6*(4), 409–426.

Renzetti, C. M., Edleson, J. L., & Bergen, R. K. (2001). *Source-book on violence against women.* Thousand Oaks, CA: Sage.

Rosenfeld, R. (1997). Changing relationships between men and women. A note on the decline of intimate partner homicide. *Homicide Studies, 1*(1), 72–83.

Seave, P. L. (2006). Disarming batterers through restraining orders: The promise and the reality in California. *Evaluation Review, 30*(3), 245–265.

Sharps, P. W., Koziol-McLain, J., Campbell, J. C., McFarlane, J., Sachs, C. J., & Xu, X. (2001). Health care provider's missed opportunities for preventing femicide. *Preventive Medicine, 33,* 373–380.

Smith, M. N., & Brewer, V. E. (1990). Female status and the "gender gap" in US homicide victimization. *Violence Against Women, 1*(4), 339–350.

Smith, P. H., Moracco, K. E., & Butts, J. (1998). Partner homicide in context: A population based perspective. *Homicide Studies, 2,* 400–421.

Stack, S. (1997). Homicide followed by suicide: An analysis of Chicago data. *Criminology, 35*(3), 435–453.

Tjaden, P., & Thoennes, N. (1998, April). *Stalking in America: Findings from the National Violence Against Women Survey* (Research in Brief from National Institute of Justice/ Centers for Disease Control and Prevention). Washington, DC: U.S. Department of Justice.

Tjaden, P., & Thoennes, N. (2000). *Full report of the prevalence, incidence, and consequences of violence against women* (NCJ 183781). Washington, DC: U.S. Department of Justice, Office of Justice Programs.

Vest, J. R., Catlin, T. K., Chen, J. J., & Brownson, R. C. (2002). Multistate analysis of factors associated with intimate partner violence. *American Journal of Preventive Medicine, 22*(3), 156–164.

Vigdor, E. R., & Mercy, J. A. (2006). Do laws restricting access to firearms by domestic violence offenders prevent intimate partner homicide? *Evaluation Review, 30,* 313–346.

Violence Policy Center. (2006). *American roulette: Homicide-suicide in the United States.* Washington, DC: Author.

Websdale, N. (1999). *Understanding domestic homicide.* Boston: Northeastern University Press.

Webster, D. W., Frattaroli, S., Vernick, J., Sullivan, C., Roehl, J., & Campbell, J. (2007). *Victims' reports of criminal justice system actions to remove firearms from abusive intimate partners: An exploratory study.* Unpublished manuscript.

Weiner, N. A., Zahn, M. A., Sagi, R. J., & Merton, R. K (1990). *Violence: Patterns, causes, public policy.* Belmont, CA: Wadsworth.

Weisz, A., Tolman, R., & Saunders, D. G. (2000). Assessing the risk of severe domestic violence. *Journal of Interpersonal Violence, 15*(1), 75–90.

Wilbur, L., Higley, M., Hatfield, J., Surprenant, Z., Taliaferro, E., & Smith, D. J., et al. (2001). Survey results of women who have been strangled while in an abusive relationship. *Journal of Emergency Medicine, 21*(3), 297–302.

Wilson, M., & Daly, M. (1993). Spousal homicide risk and estrangement. *Violence and Victims, 8*(1), 3–15.

Wilson, M., Johnson, H., & Daly, M. (1995). Lethal and nonlethal violence against wives. *Canadian Journal of Criminology, 37,* 331–362.

Wilt, S. A., Illman, S. M., & Brodyfield, M. (1995). *Female homicide victims in New York City.* New York: New York City Department of Health.

Wolfgang, M. E. (1958). *Patterns in criminal homicide.* Philadelphia: University of Pennsylvania Press.

Zawitz, M. W. (1994). *Violence between intimates.* Washington, DC: Bureau of Justice Statistics.

DISCUSSION QUESTIONS

1. Describe 1976 to 1996 trends in intimate partner homicides.
2. What are the most important risk factors for female IPV victims?
3. What are some possible explanations for the differences in IPV for African American and White females and males?
4. Explain the implication of the authors' study for IPV policy and research in the future.

READING

The role of third parties or bystanders in violent victimizations has received very little attention in the research literature. The authors use 1994 to 2004 National Crime Victimization Survey data to identify violent crime situations with bystanders present and how they either help or hurt nonfatal victimization. The authors found that bystander involvement in violent victimizations varies with situational circumstances. For example, bystanders are more likely to be found in public rather than private places. In public places, they are more likely to witness physical assaults. They are more helpful in sexual assault situations when there is no dangerous weapon involved. Bystanders seem to worsen robbery attacks by non-strangers that occur in evening hours. The authors conclude the article with a discussion of the limitations of their research and suggestions for future research on the role of bystanders in violent crime events.

Exploring Bystander Presence and Intervention in Nonfatal Violent Victimization

When Does Helping Really Help?

Timothy C. Hart and Terance D. Miethe

Although much has been written about the victims and offenders of violent crime, an important but relatively neglected situational factor in these offenses involves the presence and role of third parties or bystanders. Bystanders are the social audience in many crime events, and their actions and reactions may affect both the risks of the onset of violence and its ultimate consequences to the victim. As potential witnesses and guardians that may provide direct assistance to victims, bystanders serve as a visible deterrent to crime, and their intervention may help the victim thwart a violent attack in progress. Through poorly executed helping behavior or by serving as public audience for "saving face" or maintaining a masculine identity, however, the presence of bystanders may also escalate the gravity of potential conflict situations. It is these contrasting roles of third parties as impeding and escalating violent situations that contribute to their unique position as correlates of individuals' risks of criminal victimization.

Using data from the National Crime Victimization Survey (NCVS), the current study explores the situational context of bystander intervention in violent crimes. Conjunctive analyses of case configurations are conducted to identify the most dominant situational contexts in which a bystander is present in violent crimes

Source: Hart, T. C., & Miethe, T. D. (2008). Exploring bystander presence and intervention in nonfatal violent victimization: When does helping really help? *Violence and Victims, 23*(5), 637–652.

and the relative prevalence of helping and hurting responses within them. Results and the modeling approach used in this study are then discussed in terms of their implications for future research on the normative and deviant reactions to crime by third parties and its victims.

Literature Review

Contrary to their popular image as secluded private acts, most violent crimes are committed in the presence of a social audience. For example, data from the National Crime Victimization Survey (NCVS) in the 1990s suggest that bystanders are present in about two-thirds of violent victimizations. Bystanders are present in about 70% of assaults, 52% of robberies, and 29% of the rapes or sexual assaults in these national data (Planty, 2002). According to NCVS data, an estimated 6.4 million violent crimes are witnessed by third parties each year.

When witnessing a criminal act or any other potentially dangerous situation, bystanders have several choices. They can ignore the situation and do nothing, offer indirect intervention by summoning the police or other people for help, or directly intervene to assist the victim in thwarting the attack. Previous research on helping behavior suggests that bystander inactivity is the predominant response in a variety of potentially dangerous situations. Field experiments and observational studies reveal that helping behavior is often the exceptional case when people are seriously injured in accidents, have excessive bleeding, or are involved in an intense verbal altercation with another party (see, for review; Fischer, Greitemeyer, Pollozek, & Frey, 2006; Howard & Crano, 1974; Latane & Darley, 1970; Smithson, Amato, & Pearce, 1983). Even when helping involves little direct costs to the bystander, most people do not typically offer assistance to another. The passage of "Good Samaritan" laws and the public designation of people who help others in selfless acts of bravery as heroes is also indirect evidence of the relative infrequency of helping behavior in contemporary American society.

NCVS data do not provide a direct measure of bystander inaction. Instead, victims are asked survey questions about whether third-party involvement "helped or worsened" the situation. Among offenses in which the actions of the third party were known, nearly half the victims reported that the bystander neither helped nor worsened the situation (Planty, 2002). Consistent with general studies of helping behavior, these results also suggest that inactivity is the typical reaction of bystanders who witness violent crimes.

When bystanders intervene in criminal offenses, their behavior is judged far more likely to help than hurt (see Planty, 2002). This ratio of helping/hurting is highest among aggravated assaults (3.5:1) and lowest in cases of rape and sexual assault (2.2:1). The predominant way in which bystanders help is through the "prevention of injury or further injury" to the victim. Bystanders are judged as worsening the situation primarily by "making the offender angrier." Third parties may worsen the situation by overreacting or saying something foolish that escalates the violence. Alternatively, offenders may inflict greater injury to victims in front of third parties as an immediate public forum for maintaining or reaffirming one's masculine identity as a "tough guy" (see Goffman, 1959; Lofland, 1969; Miethe & Deibert, 2007). It is within these public situations that the presence of bystanders may hurt more than help.

Normative Rules and the Situational Context of Bystander Intervention

Norms are shared evaluations of what is appropriate and inappropriate behavior in a particular social context. Sociologists and criminologists have long used normative explanations for a wide range of conventional and criminal behaviors.

Normative rules of appropriate behavior are found in virtually all aspects of everyday life (e.g., rules of fair play in sports, driving behavior, manners, and etiquette). When applied to criminal behavior, normative theories have been used to explain the onset of criminal behavior and its social, spatial, and temporal distribution (see Miethe & Deibert, 2007). For example, a normative "code of the street" is said to exist within particular segments of society where violence is an expected response to threats to one's "rep" and other anger-provoking stimuli (see Anderson, 1999; Miethe & Regoeczi, 2004). Normative rules and rituals also underlie the behavior of victims and offenders in other types of criminal activity (see Luckenbill, 1977; Miethe & Deibert, 2007).

Similar to other aspects of social life, various normative rules also exist in the area of helping behavior. These norms of helping behavior offer an explanation for the overall level of bystander intervention and the particular social contexts in which it is facilitated and constrained.

One immediate normative constraint on bystander intervention is the widely held adage of "minding one's own business." This norm against meddling is well entrenched in everyday life and may serve as an important heuristic for decision making under conditions of uncertainty. In particular, most bystanders, by definition, are outsiders who are not fully aware of the nature or gravity of an ongoing dispute among the victims and offenders. Otherwise rational thought by these outside observers may also be temporarily suspended by the immediate ambiguity of these dangerous situations. Under these conditions, the normative script of "minding one's own business" may lead most bystanders to avoid getting involved in the criminal transaction.

Although norms of avoidance may explain the low rate of helping behavior in interpersonal disputes, several situational factors may serve to decrease the ambiguity surrounding criminal offenses and lead to differential likelihoods of bystander responses. These situational factors include the type of criminal activity, presence of a weapon, location of the crime, time of occurrence, and victim-offender relationship. Both the presence of bystanders and their likely response to observed criminal behavior may be strongly influenced by the particular combination of situational factors underlying violent offenses.

The Current Study

The role of bystanders in violent victimization has been widely recognized in crime prevention and as a major structural feature of crime events (see Banyard, Plante, & Moynihan, 2004; Felson, 2002; Kennedy & Forde, 1999; Sacco & Kennedy, 2002; Schwartz, DeKeseredy, Tait, & Alvi, 2001). The correlates of bystander intervention have also been investigated in previous research. Previous studies, however, have not systematically examined the situational context of third-party intervention because their analyses are based on exploring bivariate relationships and estimating "main effect" models. By ignoring the interrelations among variables that define the situational context, the analytical approach used in previous studies may dramatically misrepresent how particular situational factors influence the likelihood and consequence of bystander intervention.

Using NCVS data from 1995 through 2004, the current study identifies the most dominant situational contexts in which bystanders are present in violent crimes and their relative prevalence of helping and hurting responses within them. These situational contexts are defined by the conjunctive distribution of all possible combinations of the following situational factors: type of violent crime, presence of a dangerous weapon, location of the offense, time of occurrence, and victim-offender relationship. The nature of these dominant situational contexts in which bystanders are present, the relative prevalence of their helping and hurting responses within them, and the implications of these findings are the primary questions underlying the current study.

Methods

Data for this study derive from the National Crime Victimization Surveys (NCVS) that were conducted from 1995 through 2004. Our analysis focuses on the characteristics of violent crime that were reported during this timeframe and where a bystander was present (n = 19,204). A subset of these data that represent victimizations where a bystander was reportedly present and either helped or worsened the situation are used for the conjunctive analysis (n = 12,404). The measurement of the primary variables and the analytical strategy underlying this research are summarized next.

Measurement of Variables. The primary variables in the current study involve measures of bystander involvement and the situational context of violent victimizations. Measures of these concepts were derived from survey questions about the circumstances surrounding criminal victimizations that were identified during NCVS interviews.

Bystander's Presence and Intervention Outcome. Our measures of bystander presence and the effectiveness of their actions in violent situations are based on the victim's account of the crime event. Based on the questions used in the NCVS interview, bystanders are defined as "any person or group of persons other than the victim or offender who was present during the victimization, and who is at least 12 years of age" (see NCVS, 2003). Under this definition, the term bystander includes people who may serve a variety of different roles (e.g., eyewitnesses, instigators, interlopers, other household members, fellow victims in the incident, police officers). In our analysis, the presence of a bystander is dummy coded (1 = present; 0 = absent). Measures of the number of bystanders and their specific roles are not available in the NCVS data.

The perceived effectiveness of bystander intervention is measured by the victim's assessment of whether the bystander helped or worsened the incident. The categories of "neither helped nor worsened" and "both helped and hurt" are also possible responses to this NCVS question. For our analysis of the situational contexts of bystander intervention, this variable is recoded as a ratio representing the relative prevalence of helping/hurting reactions. Higher ratio values indicate situational contexts that are more conducive to effective bystander intervention. In contrast, lower ratios represent situations of bystander intervention that have greater risks of adverse consequences for the victim.

The Situational Context. The situational context for bystander intervention is measured in this study by the conjunctive distribution of the categories within each of the following situational factors: type of crime (i.e., 1 = rape/sexual assaults, 2 = personal robberies, 3 = physical assaults); weapon present in incident (0 = no, 1 = yes); location of offense (0 = public place, 1 = home/private); time of occurrence (0 = daytime, 1 = nighttime); and victim-offender relationship (0 = non-stranger, 1 = stranger).

When these variables are considered simultaneously, they represent 48 distinct situational contexts. This total number of situational contexts is found by multiplying together the number of categories within each variable (i.e., 3 [crimes] × 2 [weapons] × 2 [locations] × 2 [time of day] × 2 [victim-offender relationship] = 48 combinations).

To minimize attention to situational contexts that are rarely found among violent crimes, a minimum frequency rule of 10 cases ($n \geq 10$) is used for inclusion in this study. When the prevalence of victims in a particular situational context exceeds this minimum frequency, we will use the term dominant to represent these situations. Minimum frequency rules have also been used in other studies of conjunctive interrelationships among sets of variables (see Miethe & Regoeczi, 2004; Ragin, 1987). By restricting our analysis to these dominant situations, the current study focuses on empirical identification of the most predominant situations of bystander intervention and its relative effectiveness within them.

Analytical Approach

The current study involves a conjunctive analysis of the nature of the dominant situational contexts for bystander intervention in violent crimes. This approach is similar to qualitative comparative analysis 5 in that we seek to identify the most common combinations of situational attributes that underlie criminal incidents in which bystanders are present and offer effective intervention within them.

The current study involves a conjunctive analysis of the nature of the dominant situational contexts for bystander intervention in violent crimes. This approach is similar to qualitative comparative analysis 5 in that we seek to identify the most common combinations of situational attributes that underlie criminal incidents in which bystanders are present and offer effective intervention within them.

For purposes of identifying normative and deviant patterns of bystander intervention in violent offenses, the current study uses the mean and standard deviation to derive empirical boundaries of normative responses within this NCVS sample. In particular, normative situational contexts for the presence of a bystander and beneficial intervention are those that fall within 1 standard deviation of the average values for all situations combined (i.e., x? ± 1 SD). Deviant situational contexts for bystander involvement, in contrast, are those situations that fall either above (i.e., they are more helpful than average) or below the overall mean (i.e., they are less helpful than average). This approach allows a rank-ordering of situational attributes that underlie criminal incidents and, in turn, enables us to interpret situations where a bystander is more helpful in the context of the prevalence of the situation.

 Results

Univariate and bivariate analyses were performed to assess the general characteristics of violent victimizations in this NCVS sample. The observed results of these analyses are consistent with the findings in other research using NCVS data for earlier time periods (see Planty, 2002). A bystander was present in nearly two-thirds (65%) of the violent victimizations in these NCVS data. Their presence was most common in cases of physical assaults (68%) and less likely in robberies (49%) and sexual assaults (28%). The actions of bystanders were most frequently judged by victims as "neither helping nor hurting" (48%), followed by "helping" (37%), "hurting" (10%), and "both helping and hurting" (3%). Respondents were unable to assess the impact of the bystander in 3% of the cases.

Among the situational variables, physical assaults accounted for the vast majority of these violent victimizations (92%). Of the remaining violent victimizations, robberies (6%) were slightly more common than rapes and sexual assaults (2%). A dangerous weapon was present in about one-fifth (21%) of all violent victimizations. A sizable minority (32%) of violent offenses occurred within the home and other private locations. About two-in-five violent crimes in which a bystander was present occurred during evening hours. Nearly half (45%) of attacks in the presence of bystanders involved victims and offenders who were strangers.

Dominant Situational Contexts for the Presence of a Bystander

Of the 48 possible combinations of situational factors that define the situational context for violent crime, violent victimizations were empirically observed in all of them. Seven of these profiles contained fewer than 10 victimizations and were excluded from the analysis under this minimum frequency criterion.

The likelihood of bystander presence varies dramatically across different situational contexts for violent crime. For example, 83% of the stranger assaults in public places at night that do not involve a dangerous weapon are committed in the presence of bystanders. In contrast, a bystander is present in only 14% of the weaponless nonstranger rapes or sexual assaults that occur in private locations during the daytime.

An examination of the exceptional or deviant contexts in which bystander's presence is relatively more and less common than the statistical average reveals the distinct role of specific situational factors. Both the type of crime and its physical locations are clearly discriminating factors in these situations. In particular, the highest rates of bystander presence are found in situations of physical assaults in public places, whereas the lowest rates almost always involve sexual assaults in private locations. None of the other situational variables exhibit consistent pattern of "main effects" across these different contexts of high and low bystander presence. Instead, their association with the likelihood of bystander presence is highly contextual, depending on the particular combination of other factors that define the situational context.

Dominant Contexts for the Most and Least Effective Intervention

A bystander offered assistance in 37 different situational contexts that contained at least 10 victimizations. Situations with the highest ratios of helping were most often sexual assaults without a dangerous weapon. The remaining contexts in which helping exceeds its normative average involved stranger robberies in public places. For both sex offenses and robberies, daytime hours and attacks by strangers are also common elements in most of the situational contexts that elicit the greatest helping responses. The highest ratio of helping behavior occurred in situations of nighttime sexual assaults by strangers in the home and without dangerous weapons. Although this situation is a rare context for bystander witnesses ($n = 21$), their assistance was 10 times more likely to be perceived as helping than as worsening these incidents. Most situations with the least effective helping involve nonstranger robberies within the home. Nighttime hours and the absence of dangerous weapons are other situational factors in most of these least helpful situations.

Situational contexts within the normative range of helping are best characterized by instances of physical assaults that occur in a wide variety of circumstances. Aggravated assaults (i.e., physical assaults with weapons) among strangers often have helping ratios in the upper segment of the normative range, whereas simple assaults (i.e., physical assaults without dangerous weapons) are often in the lower half of this normative range. Other situational factors exhibit less uniform patterns across this normative range of helping/hurting ratios.

Discussion and Conclusions

The current study explores the situational contexts of bystander intervention in violent crime. Bystanders are most commonly found in situations of physical assaults in public places, and they are rarely witnesses of sexual assaults and rapes in private locations. When bystanders are present, they neither help nor hurt in the typical violent crime; however, bystanders are far more likely to help than hurt in situations of sexual assaults without a dangerous weapon. They are more likely to worsen violent attacks in situations of robberies by nonstrangers in evening hours. These results, their limitations, and implications for future research are discussed next.

Explanations for the Observed Results

Our conjunctive analysis of case configurations in violent crimes indicates that the opportunity for bystander intervention and its consequences vary dramatically across different situational contexts. As a definitional property of these locations, the higher observed prevalence of bystander presence in public places and the lower likelihood of witnesses in private places require little additional explanation. The patterns of situational variability in the relative ratios of helping and hurting responses of third parties, however, may be attributed to a variety of theoretical explanations.

Normative explanations have been used to understand helping behavior and its situational constraints and facilitators in a variety of contexts. It is also the dominant explanation for the observed results in this study. In particular, norms of minding one's own business are pervasive in contemporary American society, and the fact that most bystanders neither help nor hurt may be indicative of this wider context of apathy.

When bystanders intervene in violent crime, their response may also be dictated by normative expectations. For example, situations of above-average helping behavior are often sexual assaults by strangers without dangerous weapons. The cumulative impact of norms of chivalry (because most sexual assaults involve female victims), less ambiguity in interpreting the situation as a crime (because of the sexual attack by a stranger), and the relatively lower risks of physical injury to the bystander (because a dangerous weapon is not present) may serve as visual situational cues that increase the likelihood of beneficial intervention. In contrast, situations in which bystanders are less helpful than the normative average are often robberies by nonstrangers that occur within the home. The bystander's violation of the norms of privacy and meddling in affairs of known parties in private settings may explain why the actions of bystanders are more commonly interpreted by victims as worsening rather than helping in these situations.

A normative explanation may also account for the situational contexts of extreme forms of helping ratios that fall outside the normative thresholds of within 1 standard deviation of the statistical mean. In particular, these social contexts of helping behavior were shown to be exceptional or "deviant" circumstances, both in terms of their relative rarity as contexts for violent crime in general and for offenses that occur in the presence of a bystander. Within these rare contexts for violent crime, it may be the novelty of the particular criminal incident and a particular combination of other situational factors (e.g., age, race, gender of the participants) that result in the extreme forms of helping and hurting within these situations. Although numerically less prevalent than other contexts for bystander intervention, these types of deviant contexts of extreme forms of helping or apathy often serve as the basis for both media attention and public policy on the role of third parties in crime prevention.

The present study uses conjunctive analysis because we assume that this is the proper specification of the interrelationships among situational factors that define the social context for bystander intervention. An alternative specification, however, is a "main effects" model that assumes that the effects of any particular situational factor are constant across levels of the other variables. When a "main effects" regression model is used for predicting the helping/hurting ratio, only the type of crime exhibited a significant main effect. In particular, when compared to sexual assaults as the reference category, both physical assaults and robberies were related to significantly lower ratios of helping/hurting. None of the other situational factors (i.e., weapon use, location, time of day, victim-offender relationship) were significantly associated with this outcome variable under this regression model.

Although a more parsimonious specification of the functional form of the relationship among a set of variables, the limitations of a "main effect" model for studying situational contexts can be illustrated by several observations. First, the effect of type of crime on the helping ratio is not consistent across contexts. For example, there are clearly situations in which robbery is linked with higher helping ratios than most situations involving rapes, but the main effect model ignores these differences. Similar circumstances are found for comparisons of helping ratios in situations of rape versus physical assaults, but these differences are also blurred in this alternative model. Second, although the "main effects" model suggests that other situational factors are largely ignorable because their effects are not statistically significant, a close examination of these variables suggests that their effects may be rather dramatic, depending on the particular combination of other situational factors associated with them. It is because of the formal recognition of the conjunctive effects of variables as defining the situational context for violent crimes that we question the utility of a "main effects" modeling approach and instead use a conjunctive analysis in this study. For each variable in this analysis, it is their conjunctive impact with other situational factors that best represents whether a bystander's response will be viewed as relatively more likely to help or hurt.

Limitations of the Current Study

As a basis for studying bystander intervention in violent crimes, the NCVS data used in the present study have several limitations that restrict our substantive conclusions. For example, these data do not include violent crimes that are deterred by the mere presence of third parties. The measure of bystander intervention also does not provide sufficient information on the number of bystanders, their particular roles, the type of assistance offered (e.g., physical intervention or indirect aid by summoning help) or whether the response "neither helped nor hurt" is inclusive of all cases in which bystanders did not offer any assistance at all. Some of what may be driving the differences in bystander helpfulness within the different situational contexts is the particular role of the bystander and/or number of bystanders present. It is possible that there are systematic differences associated with the type and/or number of bystanders by these situational contexts, but the data used in the current study cannot address these issues.

Although limitations of the sample and measures restrict our inferences about the prevalence of bystander intervention in violent crimes, these problems do not limit our conclusions about the dominant contexts in which a bystander helps or hurts in criminal offenses that are attempted or completed. For this type of research question, the national scope of these data collection, the large number of victimizations included in them, and their wide availability for secondary analysis contribute to the NCVS data's unique value for studying third-party involvement in violent victimizations. Even with its limitations, there are no other comparable data for studying the situational contexts for bystander intervention than NCVS data.

Implications for Future Research

Most previous criminological research has recognized the importance of the situational context for understanding crime events. The typical analytical approach used in this research, however, rarely is designed to assess this situational context because the unit of analysis is the individual victim or offense. As an alternative to conventional methods for discrete multivariate analysis, consistent with the research of others (see Miethe & Regoeczi, 2004; LaFree & Birkbeck, 1991), we use a conjunctive analysis of case configurations to identify the most dominant social contexts for violent crimes and bystander intervention within them.

Similar to qualitative comparative analysis, we think this type of conjunctive analysis would be useful for studying various aspects of criminal behavior and victimization. For example, studies of situational crime prevention often focus on the "main effects" of particular characteristics rather than assessing whether the effectiveness of a particular intervention (e.g., neighborhood watch) is relatively more or less likely in different situational contexts (see Elliot et al., 1996; Piquero & Tibbetts, 1996). Similarly, studies of the prevalence and effectiveness of self-protective actions by victims in criminal victimizations are also easily amenable to this type of conjunctive analysis of situational factors (see Kleck & DeLone, 1993; Kleck & McElrath, 1991; Tark & Kleck, 2004). We hope this application of conjunctive analysis to studying bystander intervention and its effectiveness serves as a model for further study of crime and victimization in these other substantive areas.

The results and implications of the current study can be briefly summarized. Bystander intervention and its consequences are not uniform across different situational contexts. Depending on the particular combination of situational factors, some contexts are more conducive to the presence of bystanders. Some situational contexts are also associated with relatively high levels of helping responses, whereas other situations are linked to lower ratios of helping and more damaging consequences to the victims. By applying conjunctive analysis in future studies of crime and victimization, the results of the current research and its analytical approach may offer an alternative method for studying the situational context of criminal acts and the role of bystanders, victims, and offenders within these social contexts.

References

Anderson, E. (1999). *Code of the street: Decency, violence, and the moral life of the inner city.* New York: W. W. Norton.

Banyard, V. L., Plante, E., & Moynihan, M. M. (2004). Bystander education: Bringing a broader community perspective to sexual violence prevention. *Journal of Community Psychology, 32,* 61–79.

Elliott, D. S., William, J. W., Huizinga, D., Sampson, R. J., Elliott, A., & Rankin, B. (1996). The effects of neighborhood disadvantage on adolescent development. *Journal of Research in Crime and Delinquency, 33,* 389–426.

Felson, M. (2002). *Crime and everyday life.* Thousand Oaks, CA: Sage.

Fischer, P., Greitemeyer, T., Pollozek, F., & Frey, D. (2006). The unresponsive bystander: Are bystanders more responsive in dangerous situations? *European Journal of Social Psychology, 36,* 267–278.

Goffman, E. (1959). *The presentation of self in everyday life.* New York: Doubleday Anchor Books.

Howard, W., & Crano, W. D. (1974). Effects of sex, conservation location, and size of observer group on bystander intervention in high risk situations. *Sociometry, 37,* 491–507.

Kennedy, L. W., & Forde, D. R. (1999). *When push comes to shove: A routine conflict approach to violence.* Albany: State University of New York Press.

Kleck, G., & DeLone, M. A. (1993). Victim resistance and offender weapon effects in robbery. *Journal of Quantitative Criminology, 9*(1), 55–81.

Kleck, G., & McElrath, K. (1991). Effects of weaponry on human violence. *Social Forces, 69*(3), 669–692.

LaFree, G., & Birkbeck, C. (1991). The neglected situation: A cross-national study of the situational characteristics of crime. *Criminology, 29,* 73–98.

Latane, B., & Darley, J. M. (1970). *The unresponsive bystander: Why doesn't he help?* New York: Appleton-Century-Crofts.

Lofland, J. (1969). *Deviance and identity.* Englewood Cliffs, NJ: Prentice Hall.

Luckenbill, D. F. (1977). Criminal homicide as a situated transaction. *Social Problems, 25,*176–186.

Miethe, T. D., & Deibert, G. R. (2007). *Fight time: The normative rules and routines of interpersonal violence.* Long Grove, IL: Waveland Press.

Miethe, T. D., & Rogoeczi, W. C. (2004). *Rethinking homicide: Exploring the structure and process underlying deadly situations.* New York: Cambridge University Press.

National Crime Victimization Survey. (2003). *National Crime Victimization Survey Interviewing Manual for Field Representatives.* NCVS-550. Washington,

D.C. Retrieved April 4, 2007, from http://www.ojp.usdoj.gov/bjs/pub/pdf/manual.pdf

Planty, M. (2002). *Third-party involvement in violent crime, 1993-1999.* Washington, DC: U.S. Department of Justice.

Piquero, A., & Tibbetts, S. (1996). Specifying the direct and indirect effects of low self-control and situational factors in offenders' decision making: Toward a more complete model of rational offending. *Justice Quarterly, 13*(3), 481–510.

Ragin, C. (1987). *The comparative method.* Berkeley: The University of California Press.

Sacco, V. F., & Kennedy, L. W. (2002). *The criminal event: Perspectives in space and time.* Belmont, CA: Wadsworth/Thomson Learning.

Schwartz, M. D., DeKeseredy, W. S., Tait, D., & Alvi, S. (2001). Male peer support and a feminist routine activities theory: Understanding sexual assault on the college campus. *Justice Quarterly, 18,* 623–649.

Smithson, M., Amato, P., & Pierce, P. (1983). *Dimensions of helping behavior.* Oxford: Pergamon.

Tark, J., & Kleck, G. (2004). Resisting crime: The effects of victim action on the outcomes of crimes. *Criminology, 42*(4), 861–909.

DISCUSSION QUESTIONS

1. Explain the normative and situational factors that influence a bystander's decision on whether or not to intervene in a violent criminal transaction. Do you think the bystander's race matters?
2. Describe the methodology used by the authors to identify the situations in which bystanders are present and their helping and hurting responses in violent crimes.
3. According to the authors, what are the situational contexts that elicit helping or hurting responses by bystanders?
4. What are some of the limitations of the National Crime Victimization Survey (NCVS) for studying bystander intervention in violent crimes?

READING

The *age-crime curve* refers to the relationship between age and involvement in crime. Scholars agree that crime ascends during adolescence and peaks and falls sometime thereafter. Prior research has found considerable support for this phenomenon, and some conclude that it is due primarily to the tendency of youth to commit crime either with one or two others or in a group The authors of this article present the companion crime hypothesis (i.e., involvement with others in committing crime) and examine whether or not co-offending occurs across age-groups and types of offenses. Instead of using self-report surveys, data from seven states participating in the FBI's National Incident-Based Reporting System (NIBRS) are used to explore how age, solo-offending, and co-offending

---

Source: Stolzenberg, L., and D'Alessio, S. J. (2008). Co-offending and the age-crime curve. *Journal of Research in Crime and Delinquency, 45,* 65–86.

are related. Their findings indicate that both juveniles and adults engage in more solo-offending than co-offending. They conclude that regardless of sex, race, and offense type, co-offending is not a good explanation for offenses committed by juveniles.

Co-offending and the Age-Crime Curve

Lisa Stolzenberg and Stewart J. D'Alessio

Since the 1800s, the form of the association between age and crime has been observed to be curvilinear (Quetelet, 1831). When age is plotted by crime rates, the slope of the relationship ascends rapidly during adolescence, peaks in early adulthood and then falls thereafter. Although the age-crime curve is well documented and is regarded as "one of the brute facts of criminology" (Hirschi and Gottfredson 1983:552), the causal mechanisms underlying this relationship remain in dispute. While theory pertaining to the effect of age on crime is broad and diverse, two fairly divergent perspectives can be distinguished in the literature. This classification inevitably simplifies some substantive theoretical issues, but it identifies the essential differences between the two positions.

One prominent view asserts that a single immutable factor underlies the full range of measures of illegal behavior (Hirschi and Gottfredson 1983). The propensity position maintains that the cause of crime hinges on a single enduring trait of the individual rather than on particular circumstances that change over the individual's life course. This persisting or latent trait is labeled "self-control," and is conceived as the tendency to avoid acts whose long-term negative ramifications exceed their momentary advantages (Gottfredson and Hirschi 1990). The antisocial trait of low self-control is shaped early in childhood by inadequate child-rearing practices and remains with an individual throughout his or her life course. Evidence of this immutable trait is evinced by an individual's tendency to engage in criminal activity and other impulsive, risk-taking behaviors such as smoking or promiscuous sexual behavior with little regard for the future consequences of his or her actions. The key aspect for the occurrence of a given crime is the interaction between an individual's level of self-control and the opportunity for such a crime to occur.

A second and probably more commonly adduced explanation for the inverted U-shaped relationship between age and crime is that conceptually distinct causal factors underlie different measures of offending over an individual's life course (Brandt 2006; Greenberg 1983). This perspective focuses on differences in the social experiences and circumstances of individuals, as well as on dissimilarities in relevant personal and social resources that are related to criminality and that vary systematically over the life course. Changes in criminal behavior patterns are speculated to transpire as a person progresses from childhood through old age with him or her experiencing a variety of major life-altering experiences such as full-time employment, military service, marriage, parenthood, and entering college. These transitional experiences facilitate desistance from crime because of increased exposure to social capital.

Greenberg (1977, 1983), for example, emphasized the role of economic factors in explicating the age-crime curve. Because juveniles are excluded from the labor market or restricted to part-time jobs that are poorly compensated, they have insufficient funds from legitimate sources to finance their desired level of social activities. Juveniles are thus motivated to commit crimes so as to actualize their perceived social needs. The lack of parental supervision at home engendered from the absence of working parents also makes juveniles less susceptible to the constraints of informal social control. When juveniles become adults, full-time employment helps to placate these sources of criminogenic frustration while simultaneously enhancing informal social control (but see Cullen, Williams, and Wright [1997] for a different view). While Greenberg (1977, 1983) focuses his attention on changes in employment status others report that military service, marriage, and cohabitation have salience in determining criminal trajectories (see Benson 2001 for a comprehensive review of this literature).

Drawing from this literature, Warr (2002) has articulated the thesis that the curvilinear relationship between age and crime is rooted in the social nature of juvenile delinquency. According to what is commonly referred to as the companion crime hypothesis, the age distribution of crime is theorized to stem from age-related changes in peer relations. The basic premise is that individuals undergo a dramatic change in their exposure to delinquent peers during adolescence, and that this enhanced exposure to delinquent peers acts to amplify group participation in illegal behavior (Clinard 1957; Eynon and Reckless 1961; Haynie 2002; Heimer 1997; Heimer and Matsueda 1994; Kreager 2004; Matsueda 1982; Parker and Auerhahn 1998; Reckless 1967; Shaw and McKay 1969; Warr 2002).

The amplification in group offending during adolescence is not only grounded in the premise that criminally inclined companions are more readily available to juveniles, but also in the theoretical proposition that "the gang is an important contributing factor, facilitating the commission of crime and greatly extending its spread and range" (Thrasher 1936:265). It has been argued for example that companions furnish the motivation and/or means to facilitate cooperation in illegal activities (Warr 2002). It has also been asserted that criminal companions help to mollify an individual's fear of punishment and thereby amplify the likelihood of co-offending behavior (Cloward and Ohlin 1960; Short and Strodtbeck 1965).

As individuals age, however, the bonds with criminally inclined peers are weakened or severed entirely by other life-course transitions. The weakening or severing of these peer relationships is theorized to effectuate a reduction [of] criminal offending, especially co-offending, that begins to manifest itself in early adulthood and that continues into old age. Although technically considered a life-course perspective, the companion crime hypothesis is different from other life-course theories in that life transitions are presumed to engender desistance from crime not by increasing social bonds but rather by weakening ties with friends and accomplices (Warr 1998, 2002).

To date the companion crime hypothesis has only been evaluated using self-report data. The principal strategy adopted in these research endeavors is to correlate a measure of delinquent peer association with participation in illegal activities. If the coefficient for the delinquent peer association variable is positive and consequential, it is then adduced as evidence in support of the companion crime hypothesis. Conversely, if the magnitude of the coefficient is not substantive, it is taken as proof against the theory. The vast majority of self-report studies have evinced a strong, positive association between an individual's associations with delinquent peers and his or her reporting of illegal behaviors (see Warr, 2002, for a comprehensive review). Evidence has also been unearthed of a curvilinear age distribution of peer influence. Using data drawn from the National Youth Survey, Warr (1993) found that the curvilinear relationship between age and delinquency vanished for most criminal offenses once a measure of exposure to delinquent peers was included in the analysis. The strong and consistent relationship between an individual's association with delinquent peers and his or her self-reported delinquency, coupled with evidence that juveniles are more apt than adults to commit crime in groups, has been adduced as evidence in support of the companion crime hypothesis (Warr 1996, 2002).

However, while prior studies appear to furnish unambiguous results, their continued reliance on survey data remains problematic. As Warr (2002:120) points out, "Nearly all research on peer influence and delinquency, for example, has relied on survey methods; yet those methods are inherently limited for such purposes." One concern is that while peer influence and group offending are "far from being mutually exclusive" (Warr 2002:8) co-offending has rarely been measured in these studies. It has simply been assumed by researchers that the more an individual associates with delinquent peers, the greater his or her likelihood of perpetrating illegal acts with others. It is not that peer pressure has no influence on solo-offending patterns; rather, the expectation is that peer pressure has a "*greater*" effect on co-offending crime because these types of offenses cannot transpire without accomplices. Thus, changes in peer pressure that are theorized to occur naturally over the life course, with peer pressure playing a more salient role in the gestation of crime during adolescence, make co-offending much more prevalent among juveniles than adults. The greater prevalence of co-offending among juveniles, engendered to a large extent from the influence of criminally inclined peers, in turn explains why crime levels peak during adolescence and then begin to decline in early adulthood following graduation from high school.

There is also a possibility that retrospective reports regarding an individual's criminal behavior may be subject to response bias. With the utilization of self-report surveys, it is highly probable that errors manifest themselves in the reporting of an individual's partaking in illegal activities, and that these errors most likely stem from a respondent's hesitancy in reporting socially unacceptable behavior. This problem is further compounded by the possibility that certain types of individuals may be less willing to be forthcoming in their participation in illegal activities. For example, if older respondents report fewer criminal offenses than younger individuals, it may be because they are more likely than younger individuals to give socially acceptable answers to sensitive questions. Such a bias would naturally aggravate differences in criminal activity between juveniles and adults.

There also remains the question as to whether delinquent peer associations are the cause or the effect of delinquent behavior (Tittle and Grasmick 1998). The causal relationship between peer influence and delinquency may not be unidirectional as assumed in many studies, but rather reciprocal. That is, if peer influence and delinquent behavior are related, the causal influence could run in the opposite direction: delinquent behavior could affect peer associations. The problem is that most of the research on the companion crime hypothesis is predicated on the assumption that the temporal sequencing between peer associations and delinquent behavior provides a sufficient basis for making inferences about causal order.

Yet, while the companion crime hypothesis is consistent with existing evidence notwithstanding any potential methodological problems with survey data, the key assertion that the age-crime curve stems from differences in the proclivity of different age groups to co-offend has not been tested adequately. Further research is necessary before a defensible position can be reached on whether the companion crime hypothesis has any empirical merit. It is important to recognize that the analysis of survey data is not the only way to gain insight into the validity of the companion crime hypothesis. Another way is to probe the relationship between age and co-offending directly. Somewhat surprisingly, no published study to our knowledge has examined the relationship between age and co-offending for a large number of offenses across a wide range of age categories. This is a critical oversight because if changes in co-offending patterns are salient in explaining the age-crime curve, then the curvilinear relationship between age and crime should be attenuated or should disappear entirely once co-offending is distinguished from solo-offending.

In the current study, we use data drawn from the FBI's National Incident-Based Reporting System (NIBRS) to explore the relations between age, solo-offending, and co-offending. The NIBRS data are well suited for our intentions because these data can be used to ascertain whether an individual arrested for a particular offense perpetrated his or her crime with others. The ability to differentiate solo-offending from co-offending by age is important because it affords us the opportunity to discern whether age differences in the propensity to co-offend account for the curvilinear relationship between age and crime. Recall that a central aspect of the companion crime hypothesis involves the premise that the proportion of co-offending to solo-offending is higher among juveniles than adults because of the enhanced salience of peer pressure during adolescence, and that this difference accounts for the age-crime curve. Thus, if co-offending behavior is noteworthy in accounting for the rapid onset of illegal behavior in adolescence and its sharp decline shortly thereafter as postulated by the companion crime hypothesis, then one should naturally expect that once co-offending is differentiated from solo-offending the curvilinear relationship between age and crime should be attenuated or disappear entirely. The ability to distinguish solo- from co-offending crimes was heretofore not feasible with the Uniform Crime Reports (UCR) (Inciardi 1978). Our data also afford us the opportunity to determine whether any relationship between age and co-offending is conditioned by an offender's sex, race, or by offense type.

 Data

The data used in this study were obtained from the following states for 2002: Delaware, Idaho, Iowa, South Carolina, Tennessee, Virginia, and West Virginia. These seven states were selected because 100% of their law enforcement agencies reported to NIBRS in 2002. NIBRS was designed to "enhance the quantity, quality, and timeliness of crime statistical data collected by the law enforcement community and to improve the methodology used for compiling, analyzing, auditing, and publishing the collected crime data" (Federal Bureau of Investigation 2000:1). The implementation of NIBRS has been slow, however. In 1982, the Bureau of Justice Statistics (BJS) and the FBI sponsored a study of the UCR program, which began in 1929, with the objective of revising it to meet law enforcement needs into the 21st century. A 5-year redesign effort to provide more comprehensive and detailed crime statistics resulted in NIBRS. Currently under the UCR program, law enforcement authorities aggregate the number of incidents by offense type monthly and report these totals to the FBI. In contrast, with incident-based reporting agencies provide an individual record for each crime reported.

The Summary UCR Program collects offense information on the eight Part I crimes of homicide, forcible rape, robbery, aggravated assault, burglary, larceny-theft, motor vehicle theft, and arson. It provides limited information about offenses, victims, and offenders, and includes reported arrests for 21 additional crime categories. Under NIBRS, law enforcement authorities provide information to the FBI on each criminal incident involving 46 specific offenses, including the eight Part I crimes, that occur in their jurisdiction. Details about each incident include information about victim and offender demographics, victim and/or offender relationship, time and place of occurrence, weapon use, and victim injuries. Arrest information on the 46 offenses plus 11 lesser offenses is also provided in NIBRS. As with UCR, participation in NIBRS is voluntary on the part of law enforcement agencies. Both the guidelines and the specifications used in the development of NIBRS can be found in the *Blueprint for the Future of the Uniform Crime Reporting Program* (Abt Associates 1985).

As of December 2003, a total of 5,271 law enforcement agencies in 23 states contributed NIBRS data to the FBI. The data submitted by these agencies represent 16% of the U.S. population and 20% of all law enforcement agencies. Seven states have 100% of their law enforcement agencies reporting NIBRS data (Delaware, Idaho, Iowa, South Carolina, Tennessee, Virginia, and West Virginia). An additional 11 states have more than 50% of their population covered by NIBRS, while in five states the coverage by NIBRS represents fewer than half of their total population. NIBRS is a valuable tool in the study of crime because it is capable of producing more detailed, accurate, and meaningful data than that generated by the UCR.

We standardized the age-specific arrest data by age-specific populations in each of these states. Although a potential problem exists in reference to whether offenders who escape detection are somehow demographically different than those who are caught by police, most research suggests that such an issue is not of serious consequence at least in regards to the age of the offender. As Allan and Steffensmeier (1989:112) point out, "the body of research comparing the UCR index arrest rates with age-specific offending rates estimated from surveys and self-reports has found close agreement."

Findings

The tendency of age to vary in an inverted-U pattern with level of crime is readily apparent from inspecting Figure 2.2. The amount of crime perpetrated by individuals rises during adolescence, peaks sharply by the age of 18, at about 7,300 criminal arrests per 100,000 population, and then drops precipitously thereafter. This finding mirrors previous research (Hirschi and Gottfredson 1983), but the question of import is whether co-offending explains this curvilinear relationship. If co-offending is salient in influencing the rapid rise in criminal activity during the early teens and for the sharp decline in criminal activity after the age of 18, then the curvilinear relationship between age and crime should be attenuated or disappear entirely when co-offending is distinguished from solo offending.

Figure 2.3 shows solo-offending and co-offending levels by age. A visual inspection of this figure reveals that when co-offending is differentiated from solo offending there still remains a clearly visible inverted U-shaped association between age and solo-offending and between age and co-offending. Two conclusions can be deduced from this graph. First, it has generally been assumed that co-offending rather than solo-offending is the dominate form of offending among juveniles. However, the data depicted in Figure 2.3 are incongruous with this position because solo offending is clearly the dominate form of offending for all age groups including juveniles. The concordance of the two age-crime curves suggests that juveniles are more apt to engage in illegal activities in groups simply because they have a greater proclivity to partake in crime generally (i.e., solo offend). The amount of co-offending is greater among juveniles because willing accomplices are more readily available to them. The age distribution of criminal behavior and the social nature of crime thus appear to be independent and not linked causally. Furthermore, because solo offending is the dominate form of offending for all ages, even for individuals younger than 10 years of age, it seems unlikely that co-offending plays a salient role in the initiation or onset of delinquent behavior as has often been assumed (Eynon and Reckless 1961; Reiss 1986; Reiss and Farrington 1991; Warr 2002).

Figure 2.2 Relationship Between Offender's Age and Arrest Rate

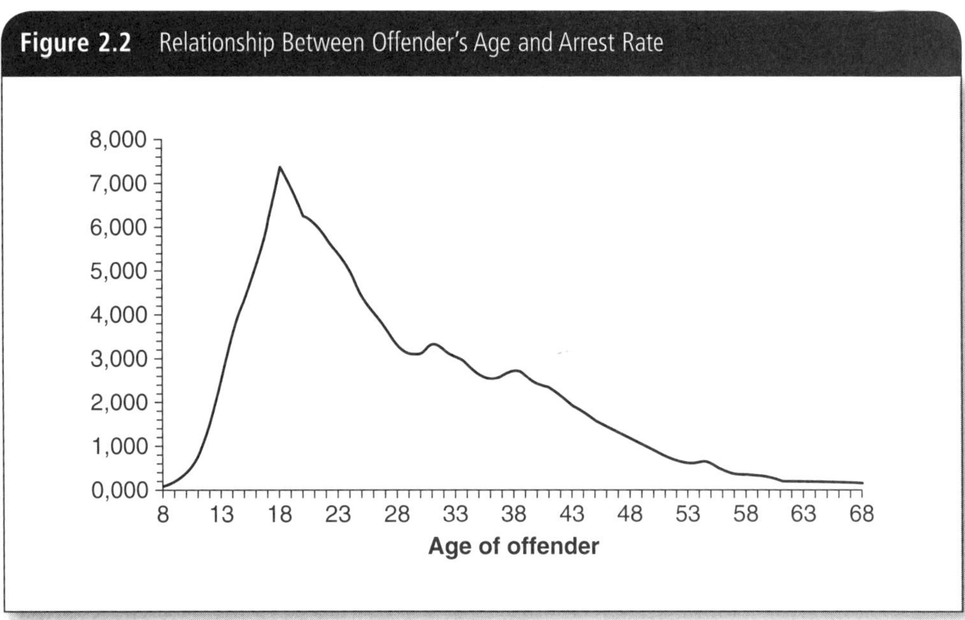

NOTE: Arrest rate is per 100,000 age-specific population. Ages 00–08 are excluded from the figure because they account for an insufficient number of cases.

Figure 2.3 Relationship Between Offender's Age and Solo- and Co-offending Arrest Rates

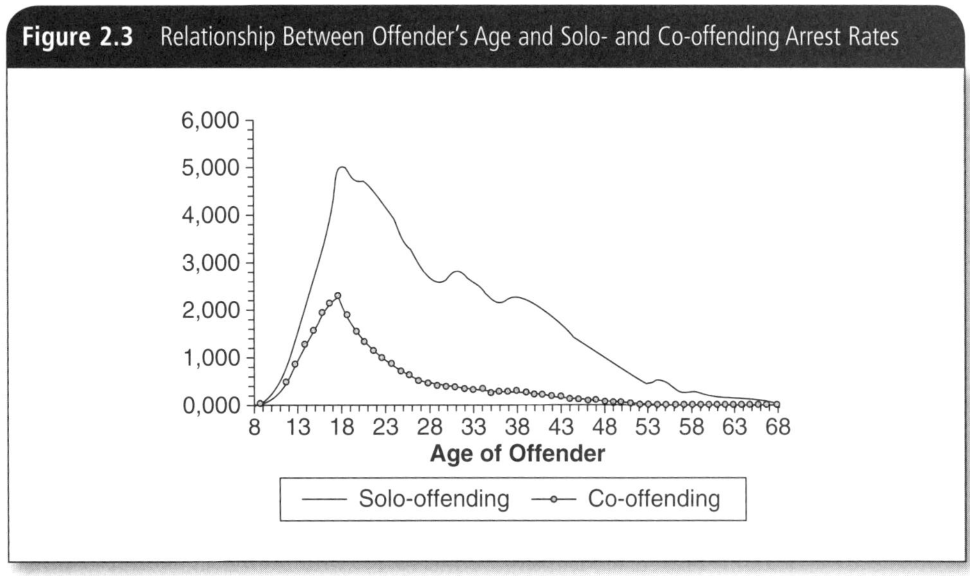

NOTE: Arrest rate is per 100,000 age-specific population. Ages 00–08 are excluded from the figure because they account for an insufficient number of cases.

The data shown in Figure 2.3 also invoke skepticism regarding the companion crime hypothesis. Although this hypothesis argues that the relationship between age and co-offending is at least partly responsible for the age-crime curve, our analysis finds no credible evidence for this view. The curvilinear relationship between age and crime cannot be attributed solely or even in large measure to differential co-offending patterns by age. This conclusion is further buttressed by the more rapid rise in solo offending observed during adolescence. As previously discussed, because co-offending crimes necessitate one or more accomplices, the logical inference drawn is that peer pressure acts to amplify co-offending to a greater degree than solo offending. Consequently, if peer pressure is a salient causal factor in predicting criminal activity one would expect that co-offending crimes are not only the dominate form of criminal activity among juveniles, but that the rise in co-offending that is speculated to transpire during adolescence would be much steeper than for solo offending. However, as shown in Figure 2.3, the rate of growth in solo-offending is about 68% faster than the rate of growth in co-offending between the ages of 8 and 18.

In addition, while both solo- and co-offending drop sharply after the age of 18, the decline in co-offending is much more precipitous. Between the ages of 18 to 23 solo-offending crime falls by about 14%, whereas co-offending crime decreases by about 55%. Such a finding also adds credence to the view that co-offending is driven by opportunity considerations. It appears that the severing of peer relationships that occurs about the age of 18 because of high school graduation and other life-course transitions that transpire about this time affect co-offending behavior to a much greater extent than solo-offending behavior, but this severing of relations, at least as it relates to co-offending, is still incapable of explaining the curvilinear relationship between age and crime.

Does the relationship between age and co-offending hold independently of sex, race, and offense type? The answer is a qualified yes. Solo offending tends to be the dominate form of offending for nearly all ages notwithstanding an offender's sex, race, or offense type. Age-crime curves are fairly similar for males and females, Whites and Blacks, and for violent and property offenses. Only for property offenses does co-offending have any salience in early adolescence. Co-offending tends to be the dominate form of offending for property crimes to the age of 12. The peak age of crime for males, females, Whites and Blacks is approximately 18. The peak age for violent and property offenders is also 18.

Supplemental Analysis

Although there is close agreement between the arrest rates for index crimes and age-specific offending rates derived from surveys and self-reports (Allan and Steffensmeier 1989), we still felt it prudent to discern whether our findings would remain robust when analyzing offender age data derived from crime victims and/or witnesses. We used crimes reported to police where offenders could be identified by victims and/or witnesses. These confrontational types of crimes allow for the estimation of the approximate age of the offender(s) and the number of offenders involved in a given crime. Although the determination of an offender's age is probably difficult for a crime victim to ascertain during the commission of a criminal offense, the identification of an offender's age, sex, and racial characteristics by victims is deemed to be fairly accurate (Hindelang 1981).

Our results using data reported to the police by the victim or other witnesses to the crime mirror our findings using the arrest data (see Figure 2.4). Although there is much greater instability in the age-crime curve due to the ages of offenders being "estimated" by crime victim(s), the Figure 2.4 still shows that criminal activity rises in adolescence, peaks shortly thereafter, and then declines thereafter. In addition, as shown with the arrest data, solo offending is

Figure 2.4 Relationship Between Offender's Age and Solo- and Co-offending Crime Rates

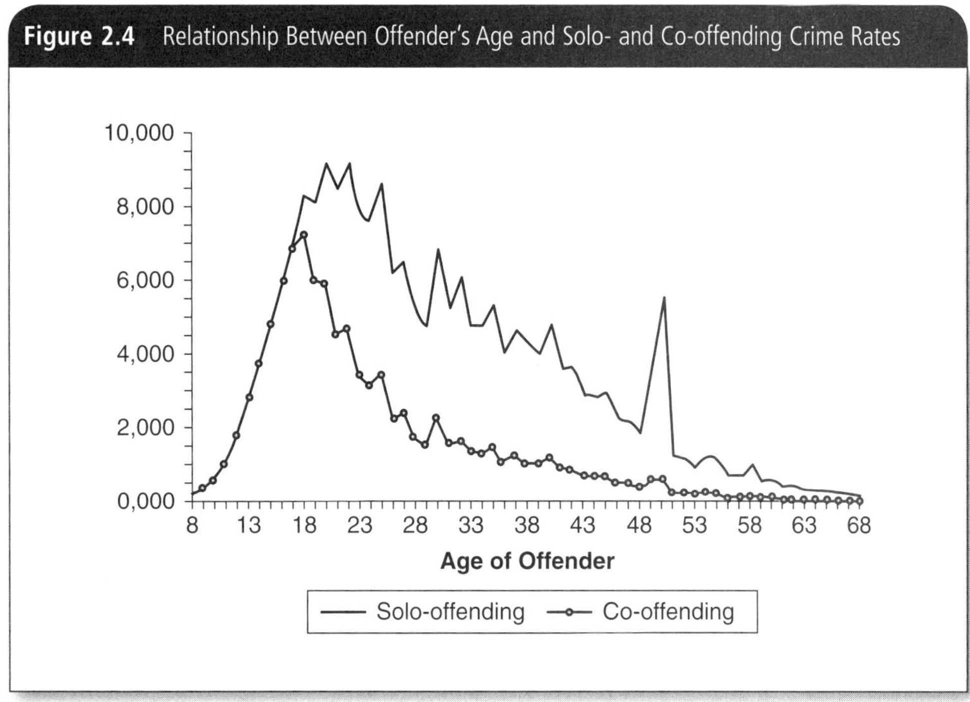

NOTE: Crime rate is per 100,000 age-specific population. Ages 00–08 are excluded from the figure because they account for an insufficient number of cases. The large spikes in solo- and co-offending at ages 49 and 50 appear to be due to a coding error in the NIBRS 2002 dataset.

clearly the dominate form of offending for reported offenses. The relationship between age and co-offending and the relationship between age and solo offending are also observed to be invariant in reference to sex and race using data obtained from crime victims.

To summarize, although co-offending has been linked to the age-crime curve in theoretical arguments, our analysis finds no credible evidence for the assertion that the difference in co-offending patterns between juveniles and adults explains why participation in illegal activities climbs in adolescence, peaks in early adulthood, and then declines steadily thereafter.

Our analyses also show that the age-crime curves for solo offending and for co-offending are not conditioned by sex, race, or by offense type. Furthermore, the group nature of juvenile offending appears to be overstated. While co-offending has been considered the primary form of offending among juveniles, our analysis reveals that solo offending rather than co-offending is the dominate form of criminal activity among juveniles. Solo offending is also the principal form of offending for adults, males, females, Whites, Blacks, violent offenders, and property offenders. Because of the breadth of the data and the consistency of our results, it is exceedingly difficult to dismiss our findings as a minor anomaly.

Conclusion

The curvilinear relationship between age and crime is one of the most enduring findings reported in the literature. Using a variety of data sets and different methodologies, criminal activity is reported to climb rapidly in adolescence, peak in early adulthood, and then descend thereafter. This pattern remains net the conditioning effects of a wide variety of demographic factors (Hirschi and Gottfredson 1983). Although the age-crime curve is regarded to be substantial and consistent, explanations for this association continue to be debated. One perspective maintains that the age-crime curve stems primarily from age-related changes in co-offending patterns, which in turn account for the curvilinear relationship between age and crime. Social scientists interested in testing the validity of what has become known as the companion crime hypothesis have only analyzed data drawn from self-report surveys. Although changes in co-offending patterns by age are theorized to be the underlying casual mechanism responsible for the age-crime curve, actual co-offending behavior has not been measured in these studies. Researchers have simply used surrogate measures of co-offending. However, such measures are not necessarily synonymous with co-offending despite the often seeming logical parallel.

The present study endeavored to furnish an innovative test of the companion crime hypothesis by investigating whether co-offending patterns influence the curvilinear relationship between age and crime. The nature of our data permitted us to undertake a different type of study than usually possible, thereby shedding new light on the conclusions reached in prior research that relied on surrogate measures of co-offending. What do these data tell us about the relationship between age and crime, and what do they say about the adequacy of companion crime hypothesis in explaining the age-crime curve? The form of the relationship between age and crime is curvilinear: When age is plotted by crime levels, the slope of the relationship ascends sharply during adolescence, peaks at the age of 18, and then declines steadily thereafter. However, while a curvilinear relationship is readily apparent, we are still unable to evince empirical support for the companion crime hypothesis. Because the age-crime curve endures after solo-offending is distinguished from co-offending the contention that the curvilinear relationship between age and crime is due chiefly to differences in co-offending patterns by age is not affirmed.

The relationship between age and crime, notwithstanding whether it is co-offending or solo offending, is also invariant across sex, race, and offense type. The data also indicate that solo offending is the primary form of offending among all ages including juveniles. This is an interesting finding and contravenes nearly all previous research. It has been widely accepted that "solo-offending is relatively uncommon at young ages and does not become the modal category until the late teens or early twenties" (Reiss 1986:145). However, because we find that solo offending is the dominate form of offending for all ages, even for children younger than 10 years of age, it does not appear that co-offending plays a role in the initiation or onset of delinquent behavior.

The data do not permit us to specify the precise casual mechanisms responsible for the curvilinear relationship between age and crime. The age-crime curve is not only stable for solo- and co-offending, but the relationship between age and solo offending and age and co-offending failed to be conditioned by sex, race, or by offense type. Such findings furnish evidence in support of the propensity thesis. It should also be noted that the findings reported here do not suggest that the life course perspective is wrong, only that the companion crime hypothesis is at odds with the data. Furthermore, despite being considered a life-course perspective, the companion crime hypothesis does differ markedly from other life-course perspectives in that life transitions are speculated to reduce crime not by increasing social bonds but rather by dissolving relations with friends and accomplices (Warr 2002:195). Thus, although the null effect of co-offending in explaining the curvilinear relationship between age and crime tends to cast doubt on the validity of the companion crime hypothesis, it is still entirely plausible that the gradual accumulation of social bonds that transpires over the life course produces a subtle movement away from criminal offending. In addition, contextual factors may play an influential role in explaining the age-crime curve (Lizotte et al. 1994). Clearly, a firmer grasp of the factors associated with the age-crime curve is sorely needed. We leave the burdensome task of identifying these causal factors to others.

Although by no means conclusive, we have gained further insight into the age-crime curve by using data that afforded us the unique opportunity to differentiate co-offending from solo offending by age. By moving beyond the domain of self-report data and including co-offending information by age, we provide a new type of data that challenges the common belief that juvenile offending is synonymous with group offending. Our analysis also shows that the companion crime hypothesis is not useful in explaining the age-crime curve because this curve cannot be attributed solely, or even in large measure, to differential co-offending patterns among various age groupings. We emphasize, however, that the current study is only preliminary. We are fully mindful of the limitations of the data, but we feel that our study furnishes a starting point for future empirical research in this area. Until further analyses are conducted, however, it would be premature to accept our findings and conclusions without question. Future investigations need to more clearly delineate the causal mechanisms responsible for the curvilinear relationship between age and crime. Many have already begun to answer this call, often taking either the propensity or the life-course perspective in attempting to identify the causal mechanisms responsible for the age-crime curve. Much more theoretical and empirical work remains to be done, however. We hope that this study not only stimulates more empirical research in this important area, but that it also encourages theoretical work for a fuller and richer understanding of the robust association between age and crime.

References

Abt Associates. (1985). *Blueprint for the Future of the Uniform Crime Reporting Program.* Washington, DC: Bureau of Justice Statistics.

Allan, Emilie Andersen and Darrell J. Steffensmeier. 1989. "Youth, Underemployment, and Property Crime: Differential Effects of Job Availability and Job Quality on Juvenile and Young Adult Arrest Rates." *American Sociological Review* 54:107–123.

Benson, Michael L. 2001. *Crime and the Life Course: An Introduction.* Los Angeles: Roxbury.

Brandt, David. 2006. *Delinquency, Development and Social Policy.* New Haven, CT: Yale University Press.

Clinard, Marshall B. 1957. *Sociology of Deviant Behavior.* New York: Rinehart and Company.

Cloward, Richard A. and Lloyde E. Ohlin. 1960. *Delinquency and Opportunity.* New York: Free Press.

Cullen, Francis T., Nicolas Williams, and John Paul Wright. 1997. "Work Conditions and Juvenile Delinquency: Is Youth Employment Criminogenic?" *Criminal Justice Policy Review* 8:119–143.

Eynon, Thomas G. and Walter C. Reckless. 1961. "Companionship at Delinquency Onset." *British Journal of Criminology* 2:162–70.

Federal Bureau of Investigation. 2000. *National Incident–Based Reporting System, Volume 1: Data Collection Guidelines.* Washington, DC: Government Printing Office.

Gottfredson, Michael R. and Travis Hirschi. 1990. *A General Theory of Crime.* Palo Alto, CA: Stanford University Press.

Greenberg, David F. 1977. "Delinquency and the Age Structure of Society." *Contemporary Crisis* 1:189–223.

Greenberg, David F. 1983. "Crime and Age." Pp. 30–35 in *Encyclopedia of Crime and Justice.* Vol. 1, edited by Stanford H. Kadish. New York: Macmillan.

Haynie, Dana L. 2002. "Friendship Networks and Delinquency: The Relative Nature of Peer Delinquency." *Journal of Quantitative Criminology* 18:99–134.

Heimer, Karen. 1997. "Socioeconomic Status, Subcultural Definitions, and Violent Delinquency." Social Forces 75:799–833.

Heimer, Karen, and Ross L. Matsueda. 1994. "Role-Taking, Role Commitment, and Delinquency: A Theory of Differential Social Control." *American Sociological Review* 59:365–390.

Hindelang, Michael J. 1981. "Variation in Sex-Race-Age-Specific Rates of Offending." *American Sociological Review* 46:461–74.

Hirschi, Travis and Michael R. Gottfredson. 1983. "Age and the Explanation of Crime." *American Journal of Sociology* 89:552–84.

Inciardi, James A. 1978. "The Uniform Crime Reports: Some Considerations on Their Shortcomings and Utility." *Public Data Use* 6:3–16.

Kreager, Derek A. 2004. "Strangers in the Halls: Isolation and Delinquency in School Networks." *Social Forces* 83:351–390.

Lizotte, Alan J., Terence P. Thornberry, Marvin D. Krohn, Deborah Chard-Wierschem, and David McDowall. 1994. "Neighborhood context and delinquency: A Longitudinal Analysis." Pp. 217–227 in *Cross-National Longitudinal Research on Human Development and Criminal Behavior*, edited by H. J. Kerner and E. Weitekamp. Dordrecht, The Netherlands: Kluwer.

Matsueda, Ross L. 1982. "Testing Control Theory and Differential Association: A Causal Modeling Approach." *American Sociological Review* 47: 489–504.

Parker, Robert Nash and Kathleen Auerhahn. 1998. "Alcohol, Drugs and Violence." *Annual Review of Sociology* 24:291–311.

Quetelet, Adolphe. 1831. *Research on the Propensity to Crime of Different Ages.* Brussels: Hayez.

Reiss, Albert J., Jr. 1986. "Co-Offender Influences on Criminal Careers." Pp. 121–60 in *Criminal Careers and Career Criminals*, Vol. 2, edited by Alfred Blumstein, Jacqueline Cohen, Jeffery A. Roth, and Christy A. Visher. Washington, DC: National Academy Press.

Reiss, Albert J., Jr., and David P. Farrington. 1991. "Advancing Knowledge about Co–Offending: Results from a Prospective Longitudinal Survey of London Males." *Journal of Criminal Law and Criminology* 82:360–95.

Reckless, Walter. 1967. *The Crime Problem.* New York: Appleton-Century-Crofts.

Shaw, Clifford R., and Henry D. McKay. 1969. *Juvenile Delinquency and Urban Areas.* Chicago: University of Chicago Press.

Short, James F., and Fred Strodtbeck. 1965. *Group Process and Gang Delinquency.* Chicago: University of Chicago Press.

Thrasher, Frederic M. 1936. *The Gang*, 2d ed. Chicago: University of Chicago Press.

Tittle, Charles R., and Harold G. Grasmick. 1998. "Criminal Behavior and Age: A Test of Three Provocative Hypotheses." *Journal of Criminal Law and Criminology* 88:309–42.

Warr, Mark. 1993. "Age, Peers, and Delinquency." *Criminology* 31:17–40.

Warr, Mark. 1996. "Organization and Instigation in Delinquent Groups." *Criminology* 34:11–37.

Warr, Mark. 1998. "Life-Course Transitions and Desistance from Crime." *Criminology* 36:183–216.

Warr, Mark. 2002. *Companions in Crime: The Social Aspects of Criminal Conduct.* Cambridge, UK: Cambridge University Press.

DISCUSSION QUESTIONS

1. Why do the authors believe that differentiating between solo-offending and co-offending is important?
2. Explain why the methodology of the National Incident Based Reporting System (NIBRS) improves our ability to understand the relationship between age and crime.
3. What does this study tell us about age, race, and co-offending?
4. What are some of the limitations of the NIBRS?

Theoretical Perspectives on Race and Crime

SECTION HIGHLIGHTS

- What Is Theory?
- Biological Theories on Race and Crime
- Sociological Theories on Race and Crime
- Summary
- Edited Readings

What Is Theory?

According to Bohm (2001), "A **theory** is an explanation" (p. 1). Some theory can be found in practically everything we do. When it comes to explaining crime, just about everyone has an opinion. All of these insights, however, might not qualify as *scientific* theory. Curran and Renzetti (2001) stated that a scientific theory is "a set of interconnected statements or propositions that explain how two or more events or factors are related to one another" (p. 2). Furthermore, scientific theories are usually logically sound and empirically testable. They also help us "expand our knowledge of the world around us and suggest systematic solutions to problems we repeatedly confront" (p. 2).

Many of the theories reviewed in this chapter fit some of the criteria posed by Curran and Renzetti, whereas others do not—but in our view, they all provide useful insights into race and crime. This section provides a brief introduction to theories that have been applied to racial/ethnic groups and their involvement in crime. For example, we review biological approaches that look to physical features or genetic inheritance to explain crime. We also review sociological theories that have their foundations in the American social structure, social processes, or culture. We begin with a review of biological theories and how they have been applied to explain crime committed by racial/ethnic groups.

Biological Theories on Race and Crime

The linking of biology and crime has its roots in Europe and dates back to the 1840s when Spanish physician Soler made reference to the concept of the born criminal (Reid, 1957). Europe was also where phrenology, the study of the external shape of the head, was first popularized (Vold, Bernard, & Snipes, 1998). Darwin's *The Origin of the Species* (1859) and *Descent of Man* (1871) were also influential in this era. Once the ideas became accepted, **Cesare Lombroso**, a doctor in the Italian Army in the 19th century and the so-called father of criminology, began studying army personnel from the southern portions of Italy and wrote of them being inferior and having a host of negative characteristics. Continuing this theme, Lombroso (1876/1911) made the importance of race in explaining crime clear in his first major work, *The Criminal Man*. Specifically, he attributed some crime to ethnicity and also referred specifically to Africans, Orientals, and American Indians as being especially criminal. His works were widely hailed and were soon translated into English. By the time Lombroso's works were translated into English, the notion of biological determinism had already taken hold on American shores.

Although biological notions were vigorously challenged here and abroad, such ideas dominated the late 19th- and early 20th-century literature and gave rise to the racist eugenics movement. However, as noted in Section I, with increasing immigration to the United States, these ideas were also applied to the unwelcome new arrivals. Noting the overrepresentation of African Americans and some immigrants in the crime statistics, observers continued to look to racial and ethnic diversity to explain these differences (see Hooton, 1939). Further, with the development and acceptance of intelligent tests, another linkage was developed: intelligence and crime (Gould, 1996). Much of the early literature suggested that criminals were of low intelligence or feebleminded. This line of thinking was based on the early work of Richard Dugdale's 19th-century Jukes study, which chronicled the genealogy of a family that had experienced generations of immorality and criminality. Before long, the connection between **IQ**, race, and crime was being made. However, because of a critical review of numerous studies on IQ and crime by Edwin Sutherland (1931), as well as Simon Tulchin's (1939) classic *Intelligence and Crime*, intelligence-based theories disappeared from the criminological literature until the 1970s. In 1977, two prominent criminologists conducted a review of the literature on intelligence and crime and noted that "there can be no doubt that IQ is related to delinquency within race categories" (Hirschi & Hindelang, 1977, p. 575). From their research, they concluded that students with low intelligence had difficulty in school and, as a result, were more likely to engage in delinquency—ergo, given that Blacks have traditionally scored lower on IQ tests, they are likely to commit more crimes (see, more recently, Herrnstein & Murray, 1994).

Numerous shortcomings have been noted with the intelligence, race, and crime approach, however. First, there still remain questions as to what IQ tests really measure. There have always been questions of cultural and class biases with IQ tests. An additional concern relates to this question: If a lack of intelligence is associated with crime, then what explains the fact that persons with high IQs commit white-collar and political crime (Lanier & Henry, 1998)? Finally, there is also some uncertainty about whether differences in IQ are genetic or related to one's environment (Onwudiwe & Lynch, 2000; Vold et al., 1998).

Today, biological approaches take into account both biological factors and environmental considerations. Because of this integration of biological and environmental factors, theorists now refer to this approach as *biosocial criminology*. It is noteworthy that within the biosocial approach some of the current biosocial-oriented theorists either directly or indirectly point to a race and crime linkage (Wright, 2009). Opponents of the biosocial approach have countered with an array of sociological perspectives.

Sociological Theories on Race and Crime

Sociological explanations for crime in general have existed for nearly two centuries. Beginning with the early work of the cartographic school, led by Adolphe Quetelet, who is believed to have produced the first scientific work on crime (see Quetelet, 1833/1984), this approach looked to sociological factors to explain criminality (i.e., age, social class, poverty, education level, etc.). Several decades after the publication of Quetelet's (1833/1984) work, as noted earlier, biological notions related to crime were being espoused across Europe and in America. Numerous American scholars, however, challenged the biological approach using sociological analyses of crime problems.

▲ **Photo 3.1** W. E. B. Du Bois

In the late 1890s, Philadelphia officials sought out **W. E. B. Du Bois** (see Photo 3.1) to conduct a study of the city's notorious Seventh Ward. To better understand the state of Blacks in the city, Du Bois (1899/1996) conducted a comprehensive review of the ward, outlining the conditions in the area and also pointing to several possible explanations for crime among African Americans. Du Bois felt that the mass migration from the South to the North produced problems of adjustment for African Americans, who were previously familiar only with southern life.

Du Bois' ideas were in line with the concept of social disorganization, which we will discuss later. Like Quetelet earlier, to explain criminality in the Seventh Ward, Du Bois pointed to issues related to age, unemployment, and poverty. Du Bois, however, added the sociological variable of discrimination, noting that Blacks were arrested for less cause than Whites, served longer sentences for similar crimes, and were subject to employment discrimination (Gabbidon, 2007; Taylor Greene & Gabbidon, 2000).

Social Disorganization

Northern cities, such as Chicago, were experiencing the same social problems as Philadelphia as a result of population booms caused by the mass immigration of racial and ethnic groups outlined in Section I. With unparalleled philanthropic support from numerous foundations (Blumer, 1984), by the 1920s, the University of Chicago had put together a formidable cadre of scholars to investigate the social ills plaguing the city. Together, these scholars combined their ideas to formulate what is now known as the Chicago School.

The leaders of the school were Robert Park and Ernest Burgess. They viewed the city as an environment that functioned much like other ecological environments: It was formed based on the principles of invasion, dominance, and succession. In short, one group moves in and battles the previous group until they dominate the area, after which, to continue the cycle, it is likely that another group will invade the area and pursue dominance. This ecological approach was believed to explain the conflict that occurred in emerging cities across the United States. Moreover, it was Burgess (1925) who had earlier conducted a study that produced the notion that a town or city tends to "expand radially from its central business district—on the map" (p. 5). From this, he and Park produced their now famous map of Chicago (see Figure 3.1). The map divided the city into several concentric circles or "zones," as described by Park and Burgess. Of the numerous zones, Zone 2 is of the most significance to the theory. This area was referred to as "the zone in transition" or "the slums," (p.148), which, according to the theory, is where most of the crime should take place. As predicted by the theory, the farther one moves away from this zone, the more crime decreases (Shaw & McKay, 1942/1969).

In the tradition of Quetelet's (1833/1984) work, two University of Chicago researchers, Clifford Shaw and Henry D. McKay, tested the theory by examining juvenile delinquency. To do so, they made use of 20 different types of maps that charted different characteristics of Chicago's residents and delinquent youth. For example, there were maps that outlined neighborhood characteristics such as population fluctuations, percentage of families on welfare, monthly rents, percent foreign-born and Negro, and the distribution of male delinquents (Shaw & McKay, 1942/1969). Their results were striking. As postulated by the theory, over several decades and with several changes in ethnic groups, Zone 2 had the most delinquency. Describing this dramatic finding, Shaw and McKay (1942/1969) wrote the following:

> The proportions of Germans, Irish, English-Scotch, and Scandinavians in the foreign-born population in 8 inner-city areas underwent, between 1884 and 1930, a decided decline (90.1 to 12.2 per cent); while the proportion of Italians, Poles, and Slavs increased . . . the 8 areas maintained, throughout these decades, approximately the same rates of delinquents relative to other areas. (pp. 150–151)

In the end, the scholars concluded that the crime in these areas was caused by social disorganization. Social disorganization refers to areas characterized by the following conditions: (a) fluctuating populations, (b) significant numbers of families on welfare, (c) families renting, (d) several ethnic groups in one area, (e) high truancy rates, (f) high infant mortality rates, (g) high levels of unemployment, (h) large numbers of condemned buildings, and (i) a higher percentage of foreign-born and Negro heads of families (Sampson & Groves, 1989; Shaw & McKay, 1942/1969).

Figure 3.1 Zone Map of Male Delinquents in Chicago 1925-1933

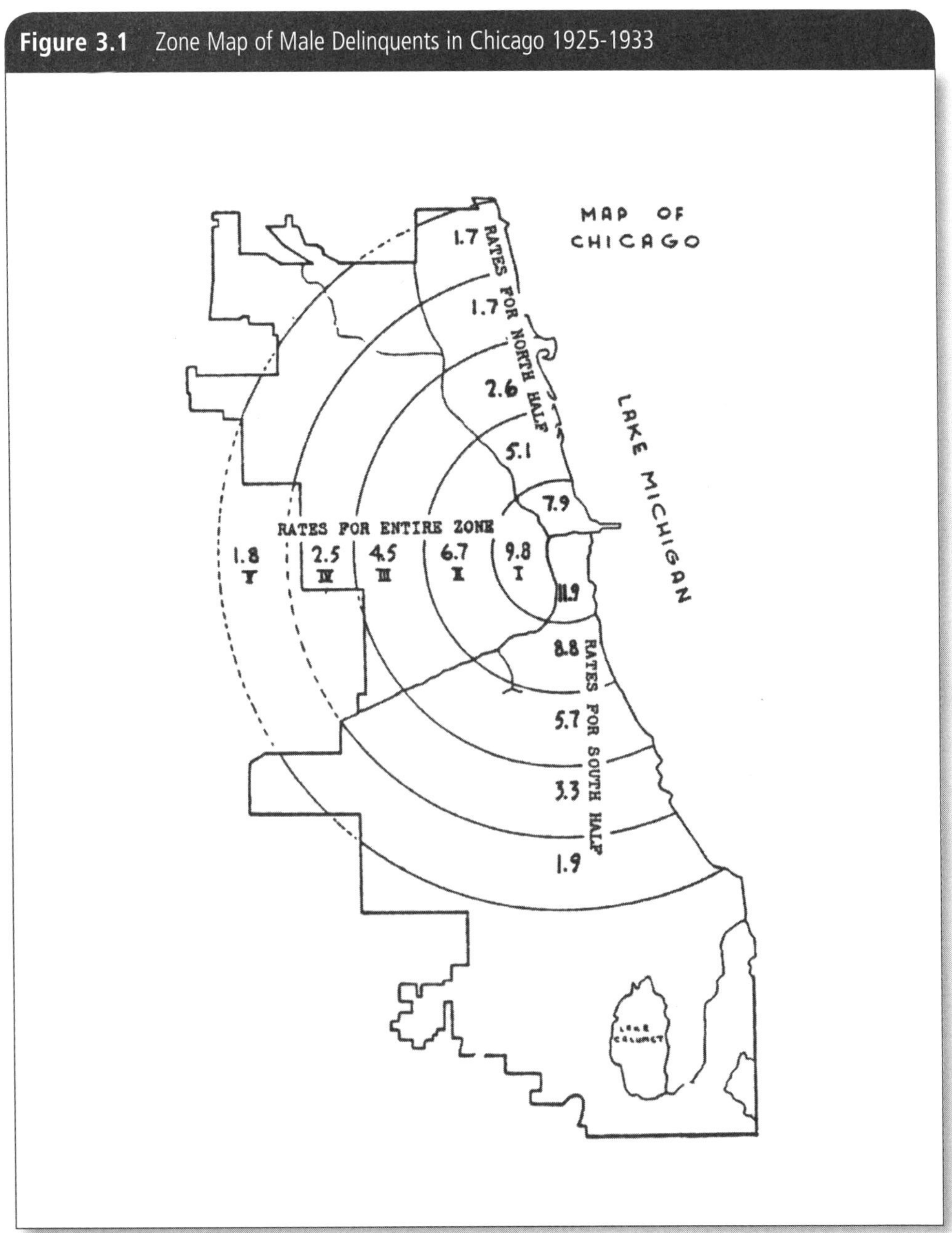

Contemporary Social Disorganization Theory

Since these early articles, scholars have continued to explore the viability of social disorganization to explain crime, particularly in urban areas. Sampson (1987) found a connection between Black male joblessness, economic deprivation, and violent crime.

This connection was an indirect one mediated by family disruption (i.e., female-headed households). Building on this research and the important research of William Julius Wilson (1987), Sampson and Wilson (1995) posited a theory targeted at explaining race and crime with structural and cultural constructs:

> [Our] basic thesis is that macro social patterns of residential inequality give rise to the social isolation and ecological concentration of the truly disadvantaged, which in turn leads to structural barriers and cultural adaptations that undermine social organization and hence the control of crime. This thesis is grounded in what is actually an old idea in criminology that has been overlooked in the race and crime debate—the importance of communities. (p. 38)

The theory, which is referred to as the racial invariance thesis, draws heavily on two of W. Wilson's (1987) concepts from *The Truly Disadvantaged.* The first, concentration effects, speaks to the fact that Whites and Blacks live in considerably different areas. In his research, Wilson found that many African Americans live in areas where there are significant concentrations of poverty. Once neighborhoods reach this point, working-class and middle-class African Americans abandon these areas.

This removes important "**social buffers**" (role models) who show neighborhood kids that there are successful people who go to work, day in and day out. When all the social buffers have abandoned a community, Wilson (1987) suggested that the remaining individuals are in a state of *social isolation*, which he defined as "the lack of contact or of sustained interaction with individuals and institutions that represent mainstream society" (p. 60). The notion of social isolation adds the cultural component to the theory. By not being exposed to mainstream individuals and institutions, socially isolated people tend to develop their own norms within these isolated areas. In a series of articles, Lauren Krivo and Ruth Peterson of Ohio State University tested some of the ideas of Wilson (1987) and Sampson and Wilson (1995) and found considerable support for them (see Krivo & Peterson, 1996, 2000; Peterson & Krivo, 1993, 2005). Returning to the perspective, Sampson and Bean (2006) called for a revision of the theory to account for concentrated immigration and culture, both of which have profound implications for communities. Notably, scholars have also successfully applied the theory to nonurban areas and with populations such as Native Americans (Bachman, 1991; Lanier & Huff-Corzine, 2006) and Latinos (Martinez, 2003; Lee & Martinez, 2002; Velez, 2006).

Mass Incarceration and Social Disorganization

In the late 1990s, Todd Clear and Dina Rose articulated an expansion of **social disorganization** theory. Contrary to the punitive approach being heralded at the time, Rose and Clear (1998) posited that the overuse of prison sentences, or what has been referred to as mass incarceration, actually exasperated social disorganization in the most depressed communities. According to their thesis, this happens for three reasons. First, mass incarceration removes large numbers of laborers from the communities, which impacts on the socioeconomic nature of the communities. Second, because mass incarceration results in people leaving for prison and then being released from prisons, it increases the mobility in certain communities. Finally, mass incarceration increases the heterogeneity of communities because offenders who spend time in correctional institutions learn new antisocial behaviors that they bring back to their communities (for a recent articulation of the perspective, see Clear, 2007; see also Western, 2006). Using data from Florida, they found considerable support for their theory (Clear, Rose, & Ryder, 2001; Clear, Rose, Waring, & Scully, 2003).

Collective Efficacy

More than a decade ago, Sampson, Raudenbush, and Earls (1997) sought to determine why urban communities differ in their levels of crime. From their research, they concluded that crime was related to the amount of collective efficacy found in a particular community. They defined ***collective efficacy*** as "social cohesion among neighbors combined with their willingness to intervene on the behalf of the common good" (p. 918). In short, in the communities where residents do not retreat behind their locked doors and actively look out for one another, there is a diminished likelihood that they will have many of the ills found in similar urban areas. Since their work, other scholars have found some support for collective efficacy among African Americans (Simons, Gordon Simons, Burt, Brody, & Cutrona, 2005) and Native Americans (Abril, 2007). Other research has suggested that the impact of collective efficacy is not as significant in communities as are more official strategies such as community policing (Xu, Fiedler, & Flaming, 2005).

All in all, there has been considerable support for social disorganization theory. There have, however, been several persistent criticisms of the theory. The most often cited weakness of the social disorganization perspective is the so-called ecological fallacy. This refers to the fact that the perspective is usually tested at the aggregate level, but researchers still use the data to make assertions about individuals. The theory also does not explain how certain groups, such as Asian and Jewish communities, maintained low levels of crime and delinquency even though they lived in areas that might be categorized as socially disorganized (Lanier & Henry, 1998). Moreover, although there were high levels of delinquency in the study areas, the theory does not explain why, in general, most juveniles in these areas do not become delinquent.

▲ **Photo 3.2** Robert K. Merton

Strain/Anomie Theory

The 1938 publication of Robert K. Merton's (see Photo 3.2) "Social Structure and Anomie" produced what is likely one of the most cited theories in criminology: strain or anomie theory (Lilly, Cullen, & Ball, 2001). The theory was influenced by the classic work of Emile Durkheim, who first made use of the word *anomie* in a criminological sense. According to Akers (2000), "Durkheim (1951[1897]) used the term anomie to refer to a state of normlessness or lack of social regulation in modern society as one condition that promotes higher rates of suicide" (p. 143). Merton's (1938) work showed that in every society, there are "culturally defined goals, purposes, and interest" (p. 672). He also suggested that there are generally "acceptable modes of achieving these goals" (p. 673). Turning to American society, Merton recognized that "the extreme emphasis upon the accumulation of wealth as a symbol of success in our own society mitigates against the completely effective control of the institutionally regulated modes of acquiring a fortune" (p. 675). In short, in pursuit of the "American Dream," some people turn to alternative means to secure this cultural goal. When applying the theory to race and crime, Merton recognized the special case of African Americans:

> Certain elements of the Negro population have assimilated the dominant caste's values of pecuniary success and advancement, but they also recognize that social ascent is at present restricted to their own caste almost exclusively. The pressures upon the Negro which would otherwise derive from the structural inconsistencies we have noticed are hence not identical to those upon lower class Whites. (p. 680)

Merton (1938) understood that the strain experienced by African Americans was unlike any other in American society. Basically, no matter how much they sought to achieve the American Dream, they could never legitimately reach the status of Whites, so they maintained lower aspirations and were resigned to achieving a lower level of success and advancement. Such a situation likely contributed to a strain that resulted in some African Americans turning to crime.

Cernkovich, Giordano, and Rudolph (2000) tested whether African Americans still subscribed to the American Dream and whether this was related to their involvement in criminal behavior. Making use of longitudinal data involving African Americans and Whites from private households and an institutional sample (both from Toledo, Ohio), the authors found the following:

> African Americans maintain a very strong commitment to the American dream. Blacks report higher levels of commitment to economic success goals than do their White counterparts and indicate that they are prepared to work harder and sacrifice more to realize them. Even though the young Black adults in our study report low incomes and are more likely to be unemployed than are Whites, they continue to maintain a very strong commitment to the American dream. (Cernkovich et al., 2000, pp. 158–159)

Their study, which also partially tested social control theory, found support for **strain theory**, but only in the case of Whites. That is, many of the variables used to test strain theory "were significant correlates of crime among . . . Whites in our sample but not among African Americans" (Cernkovich et al., 2000, p. 161), a finding that the authors could not explain; curiously, the authors implied that the African American participants might not have been forthright with their answers—something that likely applied to all participants.

McCluskey (2002) also applied strain theory to Latinos. Using survey data from Denver and Rochester, she sought to determine whether strain theory was applicable to all ethnic groups. However, even when she took into account various aspects of Latino culture (e.g., family involvement, acculturation, and religiousness), her results indicated that "the adequacy of traditional strain theory in explaining Latino delinquency is relatively weak" (McCluskey, 2002, p. 198). Because strain was not applicable to all ethnic groups, she suggested that the creation of culturally specific models might be necessary.

Most of the criticisms of strain theory have been leveled at Merton's original formulation of the theory. Bohm (2001), for example, noted that anomie theories have a middle-class bias: They presume that lower class individuals commit crimes in an effort to reach middle-class status. As was seen by some of the research reviewed, this is not always the case. Another persistent criticism is that the theories do not explain white-collar and government crimes. Given that people at this level have already achieved middle-class status, why, then, do they engage in crime? Even in its various incarnations, the theory is generally silent on this issue. Because of the shortcomings of strain/anomie theory, Agnew (1992) developed a revised version of the theory.

General Strain Theory

Robert Agnew (1992) renewed interest in strain theory by expanding Merton's original formulation. He incorporated the premise that the removal (or loss) of positive stimuli or the introduction of negative stimuli into an environment can cause a strain such that, as with blocked opportunities, the removal or loss of positive stimuli from an individual can result in criminal behavior. As for the removal of positively valued stimuli, Agnew (1992) specifically pointed to the following conditions: "loss of a boyfriend/girlfriend, the death of or serious illness of a friend, moving to a new school district, the divorce/separation of one's parents, suspension from school, and the presence of a variety of adverse conditions at work" (p. 57). Turning to the presentation of negative stimuli, Agnew pointed to the following: child abuse and neglect, criminal victimization, physical punishment, negative relations with parents, negative relations with peers, adverse or negative school experience, stressful life events, verbal threats and insults, physical pain, unpleasant odors, disgusting scenes, noise, heat, air, pollution, personal space violations, and high density.

Building on these ideas, Jang and Johnson (2003) used the National Survey of Black Americans (comprising a sample of 2,107 African American adults) to test whether Agnew's theory held true for African Americans. In addition to testing core tenets of Agnew's work, they sought to determine whether African American religiosity, an area where research has consistently shown more commitment by African Americans than by other ethnic groups, has any impact in helping them cope when strain occurs. In contrast to the earlier research of Cernkovich et al. (2000), these authors found support for Agnew's modified version of strain theory, noting the following regarding the role of religiosity:

> We find that individuals who are religiously committed are less likely than those who are not to engage in deviant coping in reaction to personal problems because their religiosity buffers the effects of negative emotions on deviance as well as directly and indirectly (via outerdirected emotions) affects their coping strategies. (Jang & Johnson, 2003, p. 98)

Studies by Simons, Chen, Stewart, and Brody (2003), Eitle and Turner (2003), and Rocque (2008) also found some support for **general strain theory**. In the Simons et al. (2003) research study, the authors found that experiencing discrimination was a significant predictor of delinquency. Eitle and Turner's (2003) work revealed that disparities in crime commission were largely attributable to African Americans' increased exposure to stressors. Most recently, Jang and Johnson (2005) found additional support for their earlier research on the benefit of religiosity when coping with strain (see also Jang & Lyons, 2006).

The Code of the Street

A recent subcultural theory approach that has some connections to several of the approaches previously reviewed is the "code of the street" (Anderson, 1994, 1999). Based on his research in Philadelphia, Elijah Anderson, an urban ethnographer, published a highly acclaimed article, "The Code of the Street," which focused on interpersonal violence in an impoverished Philadelphia neighborhood and how residents in the area adopted the **code of the streets** to survive. Anderson (1994) believed that, "at the heart of the code is the issue of respect—loosely defined as being treated 'right,' or granted deference one deserves" (p. 82). In such an environment, something that has little meaning to one person might be interpreted as dissing by someone else and result in a confrontation that could lead to violence. Being able to defend oneself is also an important part of the code. Within such depressed neighborhoods, Anderson suggested that there are "decent" and "street" families. Decent families "tend to accept mainstream values more fully and attempt to instill them in their children" (pp. 82–83). Such families are also strict and teach their children to respect authority and act in a moral way. In addition, they are not seriously tied to the code.

In contrast, Anderson (1994) described "street families," who loosely supervise their children and in many cases are unable to cope with them. Unlike the decent families, "They believe in the code and judge themselves and others according to its values" (p. 83). Subsequently, their lives "are marked by disorganization" (p. 83). In such families, children learn early on that they must fend for themselves. This produces a cycle in which they also become vested in the code and take to the streets to prove their "manhood," which involves securing pretty women, being able to defend themselves, and being able to support themselves by any means necessary.

In recent years, there has been some support found for Anderson's ideas when focusing on Blacks (Baumer, Horney, Felson, & Lauritsen, 2003; Brezina, Agnew, Cullen, & Wright, 2004; Chilton, 2004; Stewart & Simons, 2006, 2010; Stewart, Simons, & Conger, 2002), Hispanics (Lopez, Roosa, Tein, & Dinh, 2004), and more recently, young Black women (Brunson & Stewart, 2006; Jones, 2010). Other recent studies have also noted the role of rap music in the perpetuation of the code of the streets (Kubrin, 2005). In contrast to these positive findings, Stewart, Schreck, and Simons (2006) recently found limited support for the perspective. In line with the theory, they postulated that those who adhered to the code of the streets would reduce one's likelihood of being victimized. However, their research revealed the opposite: Adherents to the code of the streets reported *higher* levels of victimization (see also McGee, 1999; McGee, Barber, Joseph, Dudley, & Howell, 2005; Stewart, Schreck, & Brunson, 2008).

Besides the need for nationwide replications of the theory, there have been other concerns expressed about the viability of Anderson's ideas. Commenting on one of the life histories presented in Anderson's work, J. Miller (2001) wrote that, based on the way Anderson described the person's prison experience, it could be that the prison, not the streets, is the more powerful contributor to the development of the code of the streets. Wacquant (2002) provided a more expansive critique of Anderson's work, pointing to the "loose and over expansive definition of the code of the streets" (p. 1491). Another point of concern for Wacquant was that "there is considerable confusion as to the origins and vectors of the code of the streets" (p. 1491). In general, a common shortcoming of subcultural theories is that they ignore criminality in the middle and upper classes (Hagan, 2002). An additional criticism of subcultural theories is that, in most instances, they speak only to male criminality (Lilly et al., 2001).

One of the most popular theories used to explain racial differences in offending is **conflict theory**. Our discussion of that theory is presented next.

Conflict Theory

Conflict theory likely represents the most popular theoretical framework used to explain race and crime. The theory, which has seeds in many of those previously discussed, has some of its origins in Germany. Specifically, the works of German scholars Karl Marx, George Simmel, and Max Weber have been credited with providing the impetus for the theory. According to Lilly et al. (2001), "Theories that focus attention on struggles between individuals and/or groups in terms of power differentials fall into the general category of *conflict theory*" (p. 126; italics original). In short, when applying conflict theory to race and crime, one would look to whether the enforcement of laws and the distribution of punishment are done in a discriminatory manner. Although social class and gender also would be important to investigate, the way in which the White power structure administers justice would be of central concern to conflict theorists.

An early observer of race and crime, W. E. B. Du Bois studied under Weber and produced one of the earliest works to incorporate a conflict analysis (Gabbidon, 1999, 2007; Taylor Greene & Gabbidon, 2000). In 1901, Du Bois published an article on the convict-lease system that spoke to the conflict perspective and traced the history of the system. Immediately after the passage of the Thirteenth Amendment, states began leasing convicts out to private landowners, who no longer had the free labor of African American slaves. Du Bois wrote about how states strategically enacted "Black codes" to snare Blacks into the criminal justice system so they could be returned to the labor force, which helped maintain the power and privileged status of southern plantation owners. Du Bois (1901/2002) also rebutted the biological theorists of his day by noting that crime among Blacks was not normal and was a symptom of the dire social conditions they encountered.

By this time, as reviewed earlier, Du Bois had already made significant statements on crime, pointing to discrimination, segregation, lynching, and the attitudes of the courts as explanations for African American criminality (Gabbidon, 2007; Taylor Greene & Gabbidon, 2000). Other prominent scholars found considerable support for Du Bois' ideas (Myrdal, 1944; Sellin, 1928, 1935; Work, 1900, 1913). In each case, the authors wrote of the discrimination and economic conditions that were contributing to African American involvement in the criminal justice system—matters that directly speak to conflict theory.

Hawkins (1987) further expanded the conflict model by examining it in terms of race, crime, and punishment. He emphasized the need to consider race discrimination in conflict theory. According to Hawkins, other considerations usually lacking in conflict theory at that time included victim characteristics, region, and accounting for race-appropriate behaviors. Whereas the first two characteristics are self-explanatory, for the latter, Hawkins noted that anomalies found in some studies do not take into account behaviors that are generally committed by one race, which, when committed by another, result in a punishment that seems out of line.

Finally, Hawkins (1987) also suggested that too often conflict theorists do not consider the power threat approach of Blalock (1967). The approach, which some have called a "power threat version of conflict theory" (Ellis & Walsh, 2000, pp. 384–385), argues that once a majority population sees a minority group encroaching on spheres traditionally reserved for majority group members, they respond in a number of ways, including additional social control (Hawkins, 1987). This usually comes in the form of increased investments in police forces. According to past and recent scholarship, there is support for the power threat thesis (see D'Alessio, Eitle, & Stolzenberg, 2005; Jackson, 1989; King, 2007; Sharp, 2006).

Along with Hawkins' (1987) concern about the oversimplification of the theory, a few other shortcomings have been noted with conflict theory. Bohm (2001) noted that the perspective does not take into account individual differences. That is, not all people who are oppressed or discriminated against will respond the same way. Also, some have suggested that, in some of its forms, the theory is not testable. A perspective related to conflict theory that has been applied to race and crime is the **colonial model**.

The Colonial Model

The colonial model has its foundations in the work of psychiatrist and activist Frantz Fanon (Tatum, 1994). Although Fanon used the model to examine the relations between Blacks and Whites in colonial settings, Blauner (1969) and Staples (1975), leaning heavily on intellectuals of the Black power movement such as Stokely Carmichael and Charles Hamilton, were among the first to substantively apply the theory to crime. Applying the perspective to the conditions of African Americans, Blauner (1969) provided the following definition of *colonialism:*

> Colonialism traditionally refers to the establishment of domination over a geographically external political unit, most of them inhabited by people of a different race and culture, where this domination is political and economic, and the colony exists subordinated and dependent on the mother country. Typically the colonizers exploit the land, the raw materials, the labor, and other resources of the colonized nation; in addition a formal recognition is given to the difference in power, autonomy, and political status, and various agencies are set up to maintain this subordination. (p. 395)

Blauner (1972) also generally applied the model to Native Americans. In the work *Gringo Justice,* Mirande (1987) reviewed the historical treatment of Mexican Americans by the criminal justice system and formulated a theory of "gringo justice," integrating the colonial model and conflict theory. Although African Americans were not colonized in the sense that Native Americans or Mexican Americans were, according to Tatum (1994), internal colonialism, which is "when foreign control of a state or territory is eliminated and the control and exploitation of subordinate groups passes to the dominant group within the newly created society" (p. 41), produces many of the same characteristics as the more traditional colonization process. Such characteristics include "a caste system based in racism, cultural imposition, cultural disintegration and recreation and members of the colonized being governed by representatives of the dominant power" (p. 41). Such characteristics within a society leave the colonized with feelings of alienation, which result in either crime and delinquency or the desire to assimilate or protest.

All articulations of the theory note the important role that agents of the criminal justice system (or "internal military agents," as they are called by Staples, 1975) play in maintaining order in a colonial society. In the words of Blauner (1969),

> The police are the most crucial institution maintaining the colonized status of Black Americans. . . . Police are key agents in the power equation as well as the drama of dehumanization. In the final analysis they do the dirty work for the larger system by restricting the striking back of Black rebels to skirmishes inside the ghetto, thus deflecting energies and attacks from the communities and institutions of the larger power structure. (pp. 404–405)

R. Austin (1983) was one of the first to empirically test the theory. Using violence rates before and after the decolonization of the Caribbean island of St. Vincent, he sought to determine whether crime rates declined following the removal of British colonial rule. Although he did find that crime rates declined after the end of colonial rule, this did not hold true when he examined data related to murder and manslaughter. Here, Austin noted that the increasing availability of guns might have played a role in this finding.

Nearly a decade ago, Tatum (2000) provided one of the more comprehensive tests of the theory. She formulated several propositions related to the model, including the connections among race, class, and oppression; how race and class are associated with the availability of social support; and issues related to alienation. Relying on survey data from African American, Mexican American, and White juniors and seniors at two high schools in a major southwestern urban area, she found limited support for the model.

The colonial model has applicability for racial groups who have been subjected to colonization (most notably Native Americans, African Americans, and Mexican Americans). There have been mixed results when the theory has been tested, and there need to be more direct tests of it. Tatum (1994) also noted several additional concerns with regard to the theory. First, as reflected in other structural models, she noted that two people can be exposed to the same oppression yet respond differently; in such instances, the model does not account for the different adaptations. Second, as with conflict theory, the model is difficult to test. Another weakness of the model is that it does not adequately address class issues.

Criminologist Agozino (2003) also considered colonialism in his groundbreaking work *Counter-Colonial Criminology: A Critique of Imperialist Reason.* In the work, he argued that "criminology is concentrated in former colonizing countries, and virtually absent in the former colonized countries, because criminology is a social science that served colonialism more directly than many other social sciences" (p. 1). More specifically, Agozino focused on the following:

> How imperialism used criminological knowledge and how it can be seen as a criminological project—imprisonment with or without walls, a widening of the net of incarceration, and how the close kinship between the two fields of knowledge and power, criminology and imperialism, served both. (p. 6)

Agozino (2003) also highlighted that the discipline of criminology originated "at the height of European colonialism" (p. 6). As a product of these origins, he noted that "criminology is dominated by scholars in former colonial centres of authority," which has led to what he considers "theoretical underdevelopment through the concealment of the bloody legacy of colonialist criminology" (p. 6). Although on the surface his ideas might seem controversial, it is clear that Agozino's work provides a critical new direction for race and crime theorists.

In general, however, the impact of colonialism on countries around the globe has been neglected too long by criminologists. Notably, scholars have begun to revisit the role of colonialism in crime and justice (see Bosworth & Flavin, 2007; Gabbidon, 2010; Saleh-Hanna, 2008).

Summary

- Theories represent an explanation. Nearly all facets of society operate based on some underlying theoretical premise. Criminological theories try to help researchers explain current or predict future offending.
- For more than 100 years scholars have linked race and crime and sought to create theoretical explanations for racial disparities in offending. The theories have run the gamut from biological to sociological.
- Cesare Lombroso was one of the first theorists to connect biology, race/ethnicity, and crime in his work, *The Criminal Man.*
- In the beginning, scholars turned to the biology of African Americans, Native Americans, and Asian Americans to answer the question of why some groups commit more crimes than others. However, over the years, this has changed. The decline in popularity of the biological approach gave rise to the sociological approach. Beginning with scholars such as Du Bois, the sociological approach continues to be a mainstay of those interested in studying race and crime.
- Among the most popular theories used to contextualize race and crime is social disorganization. Theorists believe that the findings from the pioneering research of Shaw and Mckay and more recent researchers such as Robert Sampson reveals that urban crime is a product of place not of person. That is, where you live plays more of a role in your criminality then who you are (race/ethnicity).

- Strain and general strain theory both speak to the challenges faced by minorities in American society as well as in their personal lives. The original strain theory centered on the economic challenges faced by minorities, whereas general strain theory discusses the many societal stressors that can contribute to offending among all racial and ethnic groups.
- With the development of Anderson's code of the street, subcultural theory researchers now have a better understanding of how residents navigate inner-city communities. Respect is at the core of the code.
- Conflict theory represents one of the more popular theoretical frameworks when studying race and crime. According to the theory, the power differential in society between Whites and racial and ethnic minorities is considered critical to understanding why minorities are overrepresented in the criminal justice system. In addition, scholars are beginning to reexamine the role of colonization in race, crime, and justice.
- When one reviews the plethora of theories on criminal behavior, it seems safe to say that, although the research methodologies have become more sophisticated, many of the same ideas presented about race and crime 100 years ago remain popular today.

KEY TERMS

Cesare Lombroso

code of the streets

collective efficacy

colonial model

conflict theory

general strain theory

IQ

Social buffers

social disorganization

strain theory

theory

W. E. B. Du Bois

DISCUSSION QUESTIONS

1. Discuss the characteristics of theory as outlined by Curren and Renzetti.
2. Explain how IQ has been linked to the race and crime discourse.
3. Compare and contrast how strain theory and general strain theory differ in their explanations of racial differences in offending.
4. Do you think racism contributes to offending among racial and ethnic minorities? If so, explain the relationship.
5. Explain how two versions of social disorganization explain offending in communities.

WEB RESOURCES

IQ Test: http://www.iqtest.com/

READING

This article examines whether the rising number of Latinos in America are emerging as the new "threat."It draws on minority group threat theory, which argues that when the number of racial/ethnic minorities increases in society the majority population becomes threatened and takes action to stem the progress. Action on the part of the majority population typically comes in the form of more social control measures such as new laws and increased police enforcement. In this article, the authors take advantage of the diversity of the Miami-Dade area to determine whether minority group threat theory can be applied to the fear of Latinos and Blacks.

Are Hispanics the New "Threat"?

Minority Group Threat and Fear of Crime in Miami-Dade County

David Eitle and John Taylor

Introduction

Public opinion surveys have consistently revealed that crime is one of the top concerns for Americans. This concern over crime and its consequences has spawned a plethora of research inquiries, including a substantial body of research that has investigated the determinants of the emotional component of our concern over crime, the "fear of crime." Despite the voluminous nature of this research, it can be argued that past inquiries have generated more questions than answers (Garofalo, 1981), particularly when attempting to determine the antecedents of fear of crime. Yet there is growing evidence that fear of crime, regardless of its determinants, is associated with an array of adverse consequences, including a fractured sense of community, restricted behavior, anxiety, distress, and distrust of others, and overall reduction in the quality of life that people experience (Box et al., 1988; Garofalo, 1981; Skogan, 1986). What makes fear of crime such a compelling issue for many social scientists is that such fear appears to be only loosely associated with actual risk of being a victim of crime (Ferraro, 1996).There is not consistent evidence supporting an association between prior criminal victimization and fear of crime (Rountree, 1998).

While the processes that generate fear of crime are clearly complex, one factor that plays a salient role in understanding anxiety about crime is race and ethnicity. There are (at least) two dimensions of interest that have emerged from this research perspective: (a) the perceived criminal threat posed by Blacks and/or other ethnic minority groups for individuals and (b) differences in the fear of crime experienced by white individuals vs. Blacks and other

Authors' Note: This study was supported by Grant RO1DA13292 to R. Jay Turner from the National Institute on Drug Abuse, Bethesda, Maryland, and a Scholarship and Creativity Grant from Montana State University to David Eitle.

Source: Eitle, D., & Taylor, J. (2008). Are Hispanics the new "threat"? Minority group threat and fear of crime in Miami-Dade County. *Social Science Research, 37,* 1102–1115. © Elsevier.

ethnic minorities. With regards to the first dimension, Chiricos, McEntire, and Gertz suggest that "the typification of crime as a Black male threat has reached iconic proportions" (2001, p. 322). While somewhat limited in nature, research examining an association between the racial composition of place and fear of crime has been largely supportive of a link, with respondents reporting greater fear of crime when residing in places with relatively higher proportions of Black residents (e.g., Liska et al., 1982; Taylor and Covington, 1993) or when respondents perceive that they reside in communities with relatively high proportions of Black residents (Chiricos et al., 1997). With regards to the second dimension, several studies have found that nonwhite respondents are more fearful of crime than white respondents (e.g., Chiricos et al., 1997; Houts and Kassab, 1997; Thompson et al., 1992). Additionally, there exists some evidence that the associations between various risk factors and fear of crime are moderated by race (Chiricos et al., 1997).

While such studies represent an important foundation for making sense out of the entangled interrelationship between race and fear of crime, there are additional questions that have yet to be broached. Two interrelated questions that this paper seeks to examine concern the role of Latinos/Hispanics,[1] both as respondents and as a "threatening" group. Few studies have examined both micro and macro-level influences on Hispanic respondent's fear of crime, and only one published study to date has examined the potential role of the relative size of the Latino population as a measure of minority crime threat (Chiricos et al., 2001). There are, however, a number of compelling reasons for expanding our scope of inquiry into the fear of crime by including Latinos/Hispanics, both as individuals who experience fear and as a potential threatening group. First, recent Census results (Grieco and Cassidy, 2001) demonstrate that Hispanics/Latinos now outnumber Blacks in the United States. Indeed, non-Hispanic whites will constitute only 50% of the population by 2050 (Frey, 1999) and the Census Bureau predicts that Latinos will eventually surpass non-Hispanic whites in population (United States Bureau of the Census, 1999). Furthermore, public opinion polls suggest that non-Hispanic whites perceive Hispanic immigration as a major social problem, and their concerns include the fear of immigrant crime (Cooper, 2000; Lane and Meeker, 2000, 2003). Finally, Peterson and Krivo (2005), among others, have noted that Latino/Hispanic groups have been relatively neglected in criminological research. Given these persuasive reasons, the present study is organized to address the following two questions:

1. What is the role of racial and ethnic composition at the neighborhood level in shaping fear of crime? Is the relative size of the Latino population related to fear of crime?

2. What is the role of respondent race and ethnicity in shaping fear of crime? What (if any) are the important intersections between the race/ethnicity of the respondent and the racial/ethnic composition of the neighborhood that produce variation in fear of crime?

Using both 2000 Census and survey data from respondents in Miami-Dade County, we extend prior research by considering the role of Hispanic ethnicity, both as a potential threatening group and as a potential moderating socio-demographic characteristic that conditions associations between both community and individual level predictors of fear of crime.

---

[1]In previous work, many scholars have used the terms *Latino/a* and *Hispanic* interchangeably. While we will also employ this method, we do distinguish Cuban-American from non-Cuban Hispanic respondents in our analyses.

Background

One major issue that has been the subject of debate among scholars concerns how the fear of crime is conceptualized and measured. Indeed, a number of scholars have suggested that a major source of the inconsistency of findings regarding the predictors of fear of crime is due to the failure to consider its multidimensional nature (Ferraro, 1995; Ferraro and LaGrange, 1987; Rountree, 1998; Ward and Stafford, 1983). One notion that has gained momentum is the idea that there exist two important dimensions: the cognitive component, which captures the respondent's evaluation of one's safety or the risk of criminal victimization; and the emotional dimension, which captures the respondent's actual fear of being victimized. There is considerable evidence that perceived risk mediates the relationship between several antecedents and fear of crime (Chiricos et al., 1997; Ferraro, 1995; Liska et al., 1982; Rountree, 1998; but see also Rader, 2004) and that perceived risk and fear may have different predictors (Ferraro, 1995; LaGrange and Ferraro, 1989; LaGrange et al., 1992; Rountree and Land, 1996). Gender and age characteristics in particular have demonstrated different patterns of association with perceived risk and fear, with females and the elderly reporting greater fear, but similar levels of perceived risk than their counterparts (e.g., Ferraro and LaGrange, 1987; Rountree and Land, 1996).

Research examining the predictors of fear of crime has generally explored the issue at either the individual or the community/structural level, with only a few recent studies simultaneously examining predictors of individual-level variation in fear of crime at *both* the micro- and macro-level (e.g., Rountree, 1998; Rountree and Land, 1996; Wilcox et al., 2003). Of the research that has examined community (or larger jurisdictions) antecedents of fear of crime, most studies have been predicated on the insights of one of two structural explanations: racial threat theory or social disorganization theory.

Minority Group Threat Theory and Fear of Crime

The central theoretical basis for examining whether neighborhood racial composition is a determinant of individual fear of crime is racial or minority group threat theory. This thesis traditionally has been employed to explain how dominant groups use state apparatuses, including the criminal law, to control subordinate groups who threaten their interests (Blalock, 1967). This hypothesis asserts that social control measures directed against Blacks intensify as the Black population grows larger in size. Several studies, inspired by the minority group threat thesis, have found that the relative size of the Black population is predictive of the mobilization of punitive and law enforcement responses, including such factors as police use of deadly force (Chamlin, 1989), police force size (Jacobs, 1979; Jackson and Carroll, 1981; Greenberg et al., 1985), arrest rates (Brown and Warner, 1992; Liska and Chamlin, 1984), incarceration rates (Myers, 1990; Tittle and Curran, 1988), and executions (Phillips, 1986). Other scholars have used the racial threat thesis to explain informal punitive actions including lynchings (Corzine et al., 1983), hate crimes (Green et al., 1998), and interracial killings (Jacobs and Wood, 1999).

While the racial (or minority) threat thesis has been conceptualized as multidimensional (Eitle et al., 2003), one conceptualization emphasizes the *criminal threat* of Blacks and other minorities in understanding the actions of the state against minorities (Liska and Chamlin, 1984). One core proposition of the racial threat thesis then is that "aggregate measures of punitiveness will vary with aggregate measures of racial composition because the presence of Blacks creates a fear of crime that helps to mobilize punitive resources" (Chiricos et al., 2001, p. 323). Thus, at the individual level, the racial threat thesis implies a positive relationship between perceived risk and proximity to racial/ethnic minorities (Chiricos et al., 2001).

Of the studies that have examined the association between the relative size of the minority population and fear of crime/perceived risk of victimization, most have found support for the minority threat thesis (Liska et al., 1982; Covington and Taylor, 1991; Taylor and Covington, 1993; Thompson et al., 1992; Ward et al., 1986). The relative size of the minority population varies with the fear of crime reported by respondents. Further, three other studies have found support for a relationship between *perceived* racial composition and fear of crime (Chiricos et al., 2001; Moeller, 1989; Skogan, 1995). While the measurement of fear of crime has been the subject of considerable discussion and debate (Dubow et al., 1979; Ferraro, 1995; Ferraro and LaGrange, 1987; Gabriel and Creve, 2003; Rountree, 1998; Rountree and Land, 1996), the research that has explored the relationship between racial composition and either emotional-based measures capturing fear of crime (Moeller, 1989; Skogan, 1995; Thompson et al., 1992) or indicators of safety or victimization risk (Chiricos et al., 2001; Covington and Taylor, 1991: Liska et al., 1982: Taylor and Covington, 1993; Ward et al., 1986) have revealed that both indicators of perceived risk of crime are associated with the relative size of the minority population.

Few studies in this vein, however, have considered the potential fear producing effects of the relative size of the Latino population. In fact, most prior studies examining the role of racial and ethnic composition in understanding fear of crime have either failed to include Hispanics as a potential threatening group or have combined Blacks with Hispanics as a pan-ethnic measure of minority group threat. While there is some evidence that whites view all minority groups as threatening (e.g., Stein et al., 1998), there are compelling reasons for distinguishing between Blacks and Hispanics as separate threatening groups. First, some evidence exists that whites are less hostile towards Hispanics than Blacks (Link and Oldendick, 1996). If whites see Hispanics with less hostility, it is possible that whites would also perceive Hispanics as less of a threat. Second, we have very little insight into whether Hispanics perceive Blacks as a threatening group—almost all prior research has examined the threat of Blacks to whites' political and economic power. Third, prior research has examined only Blacks as the threatening group because African Americans have tended to be the largest minority population in urban centers. Has the nature of the threat changed, however, with Hispanics now surpassing Blacks in number in the United States and in many metro areas? In particular, the question of whether Hispanics are seen as a distinct threat relative to Blacks may be particularly salient in cities where Hispanics constitute a large minority, or even a majority, of residents.

Despite these reasons, we are aware of only one study that has examined the possible effects of the Hispanic population, and that study examined the respondent's *perception* of the size of the Hispanic population, not a measure of the actual size of the Hispanic population (Chiricos et al., 2001). Further, that study also examined perceived risk of criminal victimization, rather than fear of crime (the focus of the present study). Hence, no published study has examined the role of the relative size of the Hispanic population, independent of the percentage of Black residents, either objectively or perceived, on respondent fear of crime.

Social Disorganization Theory and Fear of Crime

While racial threat theory has been proffered by a number of studies as a macro-level explanation for understanding fear of crime, arguably the most often utilized theoretical framework for explaining fear of crime/perceived risk is social disorganization theory (Shaw and McKay, 1942). While there are a couple of variants on the original model (see Markowitz et al., 2001), social disorganization theory emphasizes the role that urbanization, industrialization, and (traditionally) immigration plays in producing neighborhoods that are unable to come together to collectively solve their problems, including crime. Population instability, concentrated disadvantage, and racial heterogeneity serve to reduce neighborhood cohesion, which provides the context (i.e., the socially disorganized community) for the problems of disorder, incivilities, crime, and fear of crime to emerge. There is also some evidence that the core structural aspects of social disorganization produce a feedback loop with fear of crime—population instability and heterogeneity produce more fear of crime, which in turn produces greater population turnover and greater subsequent heterogeneity (Liska and Bellair, 1995; Markowitz et al., 2001). There is also considerable evidence that social disorganization variables are strong predictors of fear of crime (Lewis and Maxfield, 1980; Lewis and Salem, 1986; Markowitz et al., 2001; McGarrell et al., 1997; Skogan, 1990; Taylor and Hale, 1986), even stronger than indicators of crime itself (Rountree, 1998. p. 342; see also Taylor and Hale, 1986). Clearly a comprehensive examination of the contextual determinants of fear of crime should incorporate structural indicators of both racial threat and social disorganization theory.

Individual Level Explanations for Fear of Crime

At the individual level, there are two predominant models that have been advanced to explain variation in fear of crime. The first, the victimization model, posits a relatively direct basis for experiencing fear of crime: people who have been victimized by crime, either directly or vicariously, experience higher levels of fear as a result of their victimization. While most of the research has supported the victimization model (Bursik and Grasmick, 1993; Taylor, 1995; Skogan, 1990), there are some scholars who argue that the strength of the association between victimization and fear of crime may be weaker than expected (Liska et al., 1988; McGarrell et al., 1997).

The second model, the vulnerability hypothesis, is a bit more nuanced. This model proposes that personal characteristics are a contributory factor in people's fear of crime. Some people such as females and the elderly see themselves to be physically vulnerable to attack and thus (perceive) that they are unable to resist an attack on them or their property. Others, such as the impoverished, perceive themselves as being socially vulnerable. They are unable to take the necessary actions to reduce their likelihood of victimization because of a lack of resources. Both theses have garnered empirical support. There is a large body of evidence demonstrating that gender, income, and age are predictive of fear of crime (Baldassare, 1986; Braungart et al., 1980; Cook et al., 1978; Clarke and Lewis, 1982; Fattah and Sacco, 1989; Ferraro, 1995; Hill et al., 1985; Pain, 2000; Rountree, 1998; Warr, 1984; Whitley and Prince, 2005; Will and McGrath, 1995; but see also Ferraro and LaGrange, 1987; Rountree and Land, 1996). The results, however, have been far from unequivocal, leading scholars to begin exploring the conditions and factors that may mediate or moderate the associations between these predictors and fear of crime.

One important variable that may predict vulnerability is the race/ethnicity of the respondent. While some evidence exists that Black respondents experience greater levels of fear of crime than whites (Braungart et al., 1980; Covington and Taylor, 1991; Garolfalo, 1977; Parker et al., 1993; Skogan and Maxfield, 1981), few studies have examined the association between Hispanics and fear of crime. In one study, Parker et al. (1993) examined differences in fear of crime among a sample of 2235 Black and Hispanic New York City respondents. They found that Hispanics reported higher levels of fear of crime than Blacks. There are also reasons to expect that Hispanics would experience higher levels of fear of crime than either whites or Blacks. Walker et al. (2007, p. 115) report that a 2001 Bureau of Justice Statistics report found that Hispanics were less likely to initiate contact with the police than either whites or Blacks (see also Skogan, 2005; Walker, 1997). Indeed, Davis and Erez (1998) found that immigrants were less willing to report crimes to the police because of a number of factors: language barriers, cultural beliefs (e.g., reporting a rape brings shame to the family), and ignorance and apprehension of the American criminal justice system, including fears based on their (or others in their neighborhoods) immigration status (Walker et al., 2007). Further, Menjivar and Bejarano (2004) found that some Hispanic immigrants may be particularly fearful of retaliation if they contact the police. To the extent that Hispanic immigrants are more hesitant or unwilling to call the police (relative to whites and Blacks), the perceived lack of police protection may exacerbate fears of crime and victimization.

While most studies have employed explanations of variability in fear of crime based largely on whether the focus of the inquiry was on contextual or individual factors, some recent studies that have examined both micro- and macro-level influences on fear of crime have employed a different theoretical framework. Rountree (1998) posited that multilevel explorations of the factors associated with fear of crime can be derived from a general opportunity or routine activities framework (Felson, 1998; see also Miethe and Meier, 1990). Rountree argued that a combination of personal experiences (e.g., prior criminal victimization) and characteristics (being female and/or elderly), lifestyle differences, and cues derived from their social environment (crime rates, social disorganization cues, lack of social integration) generate differential levels of fear of crime. In this regard, fear of crime is theorized to be a relatively rational response to the threat of/or vulnerability to crime. Moreover, Rountree has suggested prior characterizations in which some individuals exhibit "irrational" fear of crime are amiss, because scholars have failed to consider lifestyle and contextual factors simultaneously with individual characteristics, like gender or age. While Rountree does not explicitly incorporate a racial threat argument into her work, she does find that the racial composition of the community conditions the association between gender and fear of crime, finding that the gender "effect does not hold in non-White communities where the vulnerability to violent victimization of young men appears particularly heightened" (1998, p. 365). However, Rountree did not specifically differentiate between Blacks and Hispanics in her analyses of community racial composition's role as a moderating variable.

Of the limited number of studies that have examined both micro and macro-level predictors of fear of crime/risk perceptions simultaneously (e.g., Rountree, 1998; Rountree and Land, 1996; Wilcox et al., 2003), one study is particularly salient to our present inquiry. Chiricos et al. (2001) is the only study we are aware of that differentiated between Blacks and Hispanics, both as a threatening group and as threatened respondents. They found that both Hispanic and white respondents believed that they were more at risk of crime victimization (not fear of crime) when they lived in neighborhoods with relatively large numbers of Blacks or Hispanics. That study, however, included only one contextual indicator, the city crime rate, and investigated the respondent's *perception* of the percentage of Blacks and Hispanics in a neighborhood. Hence, no published study has examined the role of objective measures of the Black and Hispanic composition of neighborhoods, in the context of other neighborhood factors (including social disorganization-based measures), as determinants of the fear of crime.

Date and Methods

Research Site

For a number of reasons, Miami-Dade County represents a provocative location for testing the core hypotheses of this research. First, Miami-Dade County is very large; it is larger than 16 states and the District of Columbia, and is the largest metropolitan area in the Southeastern United States. Second, it is as ethnically diverse a population as can be found in urban America, particularly with regards to a burgeoning Hispanic population. Approximately 45% of Dade County residents were foreign born during the 1990s (Fernandez et al., 1999) and up to 51.4% by 2000, giving Miami-Dade County the highest percentage of foreign born residents of any major U.S. city and the highest in the world, according to the United Nations Development Program (2004). According to the 2000 Census, over 57% of the population in Miami-Dade County is Hispanic, yet there were few Hispanics (approximately 5.3% of the population) residing in the county as late as 1960. Clearly, Miami has undergone, and continues to undergo, a radical transformation in terms of its racial and ethnic composition. Like other metropolitan areas undergoing such dynamic changes, Miami-Dade County suffers from a number of social problems, including being ranked as the 2nd most dangerous metropolitan area in the United States, according to official crime reports (Morgan, 2006).

A recent public opinion survey sponsored by the Knight Foundation (Princeton Survey Research Associates, 2002) included questions regarding fear of crime, social trust (distrust), and race relations in Miami-Dade County. While the researchers reported that the majority of respondents reported feeling *very* or *somewhat* safe from crime in their homes and neighborhoods, only 33% reported feeling secure when they were downtown at night. Overall, African Americans reported the lowest levels of feeling safe in their home/neighborhoods, followed by Hispanics and non-Hispanic whites. Furthermore, 64% of respondents reported social distrust—that you cannot be too careful in dealing with people, with African Americans reporting the highest levels of distrust. According to the Knight Foundation report, this level of distrust is considerably higher than the national average (44%) in like studies. Finally, approximately 6 out of 10 respondents reported that the tension between different racial and ethnic groups was a problem in the community. Overall, this report reaffirms the attractiveness of Miami-Dade County as a research setting to examine the role of ethnicity and race in explaining fear of crime in a racially and ethnically diverse urban area.

There are other factors that also make Miami-Dade County somewhat unique as a multiethnic metropolitan area. Martinez et al. (2004) suggested that the stark differences in their findings linking structural conditions, including ethnicity and immigration, and drug violence across the cities of Miami and San Diego were largely due to the differential experiences of Cubans in Miami compared to Mexicans in San Diego. They argued that Cubans (in Miami) have been advantaged relative to Mexicans (in cities such as San Diego) because of the differences in resources that the initial Cuban immigrants possessed, the differences in federal government assistance for Cuban immigrants, and the resulting social capital differences derived from such advantages (Martinez et al., 2004, p. 153). Indeed, there is some evidence that second generation Cuban Americans compare favorably to the average American in income levels (Boswell, 2002, p. 21). On the other hand, Cubans who reside in Miami have been found to be of lower socioeconomic status than Cubans who reside elsewhere in the United States, primarily due to the limited resources of first generation immigrants (Boswell, 2002). Further, Cuban Americans represent only half of the Hispanics living in the greater Miami area, with large communities of Central and South American immigrants also residing in the County. Overall, the distinctiveness of Miami-Dade County must be considered when considering how the findings of the present study would apply to other multiethnic cities.

Data

The purpose of the larger study, from which the present study was derived, was to identify a representative sample of physically disabled Miami-Dade County community residents, and a comparison sample of non-disabled study participants who were matched on age, gender, ethnicity, and area of residence. We use data collected in the first of two waves (initially consisting of 1986 individuals, of whom 900 were self-identified or identified by someone who resided with the respondent as disabled). In order to identify a random sample of the disabled, stratified equally by four racial/ethnic groups (Cuban, other Hispanic, African American, and non-Hispanic whites), a complex sampling design was employed. Further details of the sampling design are described comprehensively elsewhere (Turner et al., 2006). The interview success rate was 82%, and 1467 respondents provided complete answers to all of the questions measuring the variables of interest for the current study and are included in the present analyses. Since the research design was not structured to draw a random sample of Miami-Dade County residents, the results gleaned from our ensuring analyses should be regarded as exploratory in nature.

Measures

Fear of crime. Fear of crime is a 10 item scale (α = .97) based on the work of Ferraro and LaGrange (1987). As mentioned previously, this measure captures the emotional component of being a potential crime victim. Examples of these items include "How afraid are you of being physically attacked?" and "How afraid are you of being conned or cheated out of your money?" The response categories for these questions were "very afraid", "moderately afraid", "mildly afraid", and "not at all afraid". Responses were coded such that higher values indicate a greater fear of crime. Because of evidence of hetereoskedasticity, wc transformed this measure by taking its natural log.

Individual Level Variables

We consider both individual and contextual level predictors of the dependent variable in this study. Sociodemographic characteristics in the analyses include age, gender (female = 1), socioeconomic status, and race/ethnicity. Ethnicity is based on respondents' self-report and includes four categories: White, non-Hispanic, Black, Cuban Americans, and Other Hispanics. Socioeconomic status is estimated using a composite score based on household income level, occupational category (Hollingshead, 1965), and educational attainment. Scores on the three status dimensions were standardized, summed, and divided by the number of status dimensions for which data were available.

In addition to the sociodemographic characteristics, we include other characteristics and experiences that have been found to be salient predictors of fear of crime. Twelve items assessing level of physical impairment measured daily activity limitations. All respondents were asked how much difficulty, if any, they had doing tasks ranging from "turning faucets on and off" and "lifting ten pounds" to more strenuous activities such as "lifting heavy objects" or "running." Physical limitations may be associated with perceived vulnerability. Prior criminal victimization is also considered; our measure captures the respondent's experience with four different criminal events: rape, assault, robbery, and physical attacks, with scores ranging from 0 to 4 on this measure. We also include a measure of vicarious victimization, which assessed whether or not the respondent witnessed one or more of four different criminal events. These events include robbery, rape, homicide, and physical attacks. Three hundred and thirty eight respondents (43%) reported that they had witnessed one or more of these events. Prior research has found that both direct and vicarious victimization may be predictive of fear of crime (Mesch, 2000). Further, vicarious victimization may be a proxy for the perception a respondent has regarding the amount of serious crime in their neighborhood.

We also include reports of crime as a measure. This captures information that the respondent has received about violent events that he or she did not witness, namely hearing about a rape, murder, or non-lethal shooting of someone the respondent knew. This three item measure sums the number of affirmative responses, ranging from 0–3. As is the case with vicarious victimization, we suggest that reports of crime may be a proxy for the respondent's perception about the amount of serious crime in their community.

Contextual Level Variables

At the neighborhood (measured at the Census tract) level, the following contextual variables are considered: racial composition, a disadvantage index, comprised of three measures (poverty rate, unemployment rate, and percent of female headed households), and residential stability. Two measures of racial composition are considered—percentage of black and percentage of Hispanic residents. Consistent with racial threat theory, we expect that the greater the percentage of black and/or Hispanic residents in a neighborhood, the greater the fear of crime. This relationship may be conditioned though by the race of the respondent. The other contextual measures have each been employed in past studies as antecedents of a community's degree of social (dis)organization. We consider three interrelated variables to capture neighborhood disadvantage. The poverty rate is calculated as the percentage of households below the poverty rate. The unemployment rate is calculated as the percentage of unemployed men and women, divided by the total civilian workforce (100 times). The measure percent female-headed households is calculated by dividing the number of female-headed households by the total number of households in the neighborhood. A principal components analysis revealed that these three measures produce high factor loadings, suggesting redundancy. Thus, *z*-score transformations of each of the three measures are summed to form an overall disadvantage index (see also Land et al., 1990). Finally, residential stability is defined as the percentage of residents who have lived in their current household for 5 years or longer. Residential instability has been a core factor in the development of socially disorganized communities.

However, to include vicarious experiences and getting reports about crime from others, we find that some differences do emerge, and in the directions one would expect. Relative to all other groups, African Americans do report having the most vicarious victimization experiences and receiving the most reports about crime from others. While Blacks may report the greatest exposure to crime, they still were found to have significantly lower levels of fear of crime compared to both of the Hispanic groups. Additionally, the average number of reports of crime experienced by non-Hispanic whites is higher than Cuban Americans, which again, is somewhat at odds with the fact that whites have significantly lower levels of fear of crime than Cuban Americans.

While there may be some discordance between the individual level factors and mean levels of fear of crime among the different groups, such differences may be due to the differences in the neighborhoods in which the respondents reside. The last four rows of Table 3.1 present the neighborhood level factors included in the analysis. The most important distinction to take note of is likely the differences in the percentage of Blacks that live in the respondent's respective neighborhoods. While Black respondents report living in neighborhoods that are almost half African American, the other groups live in communities that have relatively few Black residents. This is not surprising given the level of Black isolation in major American cities, but it is an important

Table 3.1 Descriptive Statistics for Variables Used in Analysis (*N* = 1467; 166 Census tracts)

Variable	Mean	Standard Deviation	Minimum	Maximum
Dependent variable				
Fear of crime (original metric)	9.66	10.59	0	30
Fear of crime (natural log)	1.68	1.30	0	3.43
Demographic characteristics				
Socioeconomic status	.04	.99	−2.72	2.70
Age	55.25	17.23	18	93
Gender (female = 1)	.52		0	1
Marital status (married = 1)	.50		0	1
Physical limitations	7.85	10.02	0	40
Unemployed	.50		0	1
Race/ethnicity				
Cuban American	.27		0	1
African American	.27		0	1
Other Hispanics	.25		0	1
White Non-Hispanics	.21		0	1
Victimization/exposure				
Personal victimization	.23	.51	0	4
Vicarious victimization	.43	.88	0	4
Reports of crime	.46	.76	0	3
Neighborhood factors				
% African American	20.77	28.25	0	96.65
% Hispanic	52.32	27.47	1.34	95.25
Residential stability	50.11	12.38	4.99	74.17
Disadvantage index	−.27	3.04	−4.60	9.40

Table 3.2 Descriptive Statistics for Select Variables by Race/Ethnicity (N = 1467)

Variable	Whites (n = 304)	Blacks (n = 402)	Cubans (n = 391)	Other Hispanics (n = 370)	Scheffé or Adjusted Wald Test[a]
Dependent variable					
Fear of crime (natural log)	1.28 (1.13)	1.51 (1.27)	2.08 (1.29)	1.77 (1.34)	WC;WO;CO;CB;OB
Demographic factors					
Socioeconomic status	.65 (.85)	−.16(.89)	−.20 (1.02)	−.003	WB;WC;WO;CO
Age	60.19 (17.07)	56.51 (16.05)	57.09 (16.98)	47.88 (16.60)	WO;CO;WB;OB
Gender	48%	55%	52%	51%	WB
Marital status	55%	42%	55%	51%	WB;OB;CB
Physical limitations	7.96 (9.57)	10.32 (11.26)	7.55 (9.79)	5.39 (8.48)	WO;CO;WB;CB;OB
Unemployed	48%	58%	55%	38%	WO;WB;CO;CB
Victimization/exposure					
Personal victimization	.24 (.53)	.22 (53)	.21 (.46)	.26 (.54)	
Vicarious victimization	.41 (.89)	.68 (1.09)	.26 (.66)	.37 (.77)	WB;CB;OB
Reports of crime	.48 (.72)	.75 (.93)	.24 (.52)	.37 (.70)	WC;WB;CB;OB
Neighborhood factors	(n = 96)	(n = 54)	(n = 94)	(n = 98)	
% African American	12.28 (19.23)	46.37 (30.98)	15.34 (25.38)	16.15 (23.48)	WB;CB;OB
% Hispanic	51.75 (23.95)	31.67 (21.45)	61.57 (27.05)	59.58 (25.85)	WB;CB;OB
Residential stability	49.05 (12.74)	53.76 (10.91)	51.46 (12.37)	48.96 (13.34)	
Disadvantage index	−1.22 (2.44)	1.52 (3.46)	−.61 (2.80)	−.42 (2.86)	WB;CB;OB

NOTE: Standard deviations in parentheses.

a. Significant differences in means or proportions are indicated by the following abbreviations: WO (Whites vs. Other Hispanics); WB (Whites vs. Blacks); WC (Whites vs. Cuban Americans); BC (Blacks vs. Cuban Americans); BO (Blacks vs. Other Hispanics); and CO (Cuban Americans vs. Other Hispanics).

contrast to consider when interpreting the results of the upcoming multivariate analyses. It is also important to note that the other three groups report residing (on average) in communities that are ethnically diverse, with Hispanics representing a majority of residents for whites, Cuban Americans, and other Hispanics alike. Thus, the data presented document high levels of Black segregation and high levels of Hispanic integration with their peers. Finally, the neighborhoods that white respondents reside in are the least disadvantaged, with African Americans residing in communities that have significantly greater disadvantages than any of the other groups.

In order to address the simultaneous contributions of individual and neighborhood factors in explaining variation in fear of crime, we turn our attention to the multivariate models. Of the demographic characteristics presented in the baseline model, a relatively expected pattern of associations is found. Socioeconomic status is inversely associated with fear of crime, while gender (being female) and experiencing physical limitations both are associated with greater fear of crime. Somewhat unanticipated is the finding that being married is associated with greater fear of crime, although this may reflect concern for family members as victims (indirectly or directly) of crime. Age was not found to be a significant predictor of the dependent variable, further contributing to the controversy regarding whether or not age is positively associated with fear of crime. Finally, being unemployed was found to be a consistent predictor of lower fear of crime. While this may be somewhat surprising, the association between unemployment and physical limitations (.44) suggests that this finding may be an artifact of the large percentage of physically limited people in the sample, especially when one considers that employment status fails to reach statistical significance in any of the regression models that exclude the physically disabled.

Once we include ethnicity and race into the equation, we find that as expected, being a minority (versus White non-Hispanic) is a significant predictor of the dependent variable. Indeed, the effect of socioeconomic status appears to be mediated entirely through the ethnicity or race of the respondent. The magnitude of the other coefficients is not greatly altered by the introduction of ethnicity/race into the model. Likewise, the inclusion of each of the victimization/exposure measures also contributes to the explanatory power of the model. Having a personal experience with crime, witnessing crimes, or even getting reports about crimes from others are each significantly associated with fear of crime, in the expected direction. Moreover, previous victimization accounts for much of the Black/White disparity in fear of crime.

Consistent with expectations, residential stability reduces the level of fear reported. The measure of community disadvantage is not found to be a significant predictor of the dependent variable. When we consider each of the minority group threat indicators, we discover that percent African American actually serves to reduce fear of crime, contrary to the predictions of traditional racial threat theory. Consistent with our core hypothesis however, we find that living in neighborhoods with a greater percentage of Hispanic residents appears to translate into greater fear of crime for its respondents. The estimates presented include both measures of racial composition. These results suggest that some of the effect of percent African American is mediated by the inclusion of percent Hispanics, to the point that percent African American is no longer statistically significant, but regression diagnostics suggest that there is redundancy in the two measures. This is not surprising given the great degree of segregation in this city, where only Blacks are exposed to communities with a large number of Black residents, while the other groups are exposed to varying degrees of Hispanic residents. Because of the severe racial isolation of Blacks in Miami, it is likely that few white non-Hispanics and Hispanics live in communities in which Blacks would reach the proportions where their presence would be translated into a "threat." Likewise, the very low percentage of African Americans residing in ethnically diverse neighborhoods is shown here to be a protective factor for fear of crime

Overall, the results demonstrate that both individual and neighborhood factors contribute to explaining variation in fear of crime. It is also obvious that of the factors considered, the individual factors have greater explanatory power than the contextual level factors, which reinforces the previously reported finding that approximately 7.6% of the variation in the dependent variable could be explained by contextual factors.

In order to further clarify the importance of ethnicity and race in understanding variation in fear of crime, we have included analyses in which separate models are estimated for each of the four ethnic/racial groups. We also have included the results of tests of the equality of regression coefficients across the subgroup models (Paternoster et al., 1998). While there are a number of compelling contrasts, one fascinating difference can be found in examining the importance of personal victimizations as a predictor of crime. Personal victimization is only a significant predictor of fear of crime among white non-Hispanics and other Hispanics, and the effect (for both Whites and non-Cuban Hispanics) is significantly different from the coefficient estimated in the Blacks-only model. Conjecturally, it may be that the expectations of being a victim in Black America are such that the actual victimization experience does not have a significant effect on the level of fear of crime experienced by Black respondents. Reports of crime differ in the magnitude of the effect on fear of crime. Such reports have a greater influence on White non-Hispanics and African Americans than Hispanic respondents.

Of the neighborhood factors, only one coefficient reaches statistical significance—percent Hispanic residents for the white, non-Hispanics and Cuban-American sub-samples, respectively. However, the test of equality of coefficients fails to reach statistical significance, meaning that the magnitude of the coefficient for two groups is not significantly different than the other group's coefficients. While it may be somewhat surprising to find that percent Hispanic is positively associated with fear of crime among Cuban Americans, a couple of caveats need be considered. First, the contextual measure, percent Hispanic residents, is a blunt measure that does not distinguish between Cuban Americans and other Hispanic groups. It is possible that Cuban Americans report higher levels of fear of crime in these communities, not because they reside with a high percentage of other Cuban Americans, but rather they reside with a high percentage of other Hispanic groups, whom the respondents may fear. Second, an inspection of the *R*s across models reveals that the amount of variation accounted for in the non-Hispanic white equation is much greater than in the African American and Cuban-American models (and to a lesser extent the non-Cuban Hispanics). This suggests that the risk and protective factors considered here, including percentage Hispanic, are of greater salience for predicting of fear of crime for whites in Miami than other groups. Third, this finding is consistent with the results of Rountree's (1998) study in which they found that the perceived percentage of Hispanic residents predicted fear of crime among Hispanic residents. This provocative finding merits future attention, where research can explore whether fear of violent crime is associated with the percentage of Hispanic residents generally, or whether such fear is specific to Hispanic residents from different backgrounds than the respondent.

We also estimated models that included each of the racial composition measures separately (not reported), and found that percent African American is inversely related to fear of crime in the Whites-only sample (although the coefficient was not found to be significantly different from the other subgroup coefficients). Largely, these results both reinforce and clarify the findings reported using the overall sample.

In addition to the analyses reported, we also consider the possibility that predictors of the fear of specific crimes may have differential effects, consistent with recent research (e.g., Ferraro, 1995; Rountree, 1998). We re-ran the models, substituting the dependent variable with two, more specific measures (decomposed from the overall measure): violent crimes and property crimes (results available upon request from authors). Contrary to some of the recent studies, we failed to uncover significant differences in the associations between the predictors for the violent versus property fear of crime measure.

Discussion and Conclusions

Twenty-first century urban America is experiencing a dramatic transformation in its racial and ethnic composition. With Hispanics already outnumbering African Americans in the United States, an answer to the question of whether non-Hispanic Whites will perceive of Hispanics as the 'threatening' population is clearly emerging. There is considerable evidence that White Americans are fearful of the largely Hispanic immigration to the United States and there is additional evidence that whites perceive of immigrants as a criminal threat. This analysis extends prior research by asking whether ethnicity matters in explaining variation in fear of crime in Miami where Hispanics comprise the majority of residents.

The results of our study provide qualified support for our core hypotheses. First, ethnic background is clearly an important determinant of individual variation in fear of crime, even after controlling for several different factors, including socio-demographic factors, experiences and exposure to crime, and psychosocial resources. While this finding is consistent with other research suggesting minorities experience greater levels of fear of crime than non-Hispanic whites, there is an obvious need for further inquiry into the sources of this difference, beyond such factors as victimization and exposure differences. Second, we find that consistent with our expectations, the relative size of the Hispanic population in a neighborhood is a significant contextual predictor of fear of crime, supporting the hypothesis derived from minority group threat theory. We did fail to find, however, that the relative size of the Black population was a significant positive predictor of fear of crime. Indeed, we found evidence that for white non-Hispanics, percent African American was inversely associated with fear of crime. We suggest that this peculiar finding is due to the extreme segregation of Blacks in Miami-Dade County. The lack of racial heterogeneity in the typical Miami neighborhood, coupled with the extensive ethnic heterogeneity of many neighborhoods, appears instrumental in explaining these findings. The index of dissimilarity, a commonly used measure of segregation, is calculated as 69 (out of 100), according to 2000 Census data, indicating that Blacks are highly segregated in Miami-Dade County. According to one study, Miami ranked 89th out of the 100 largest Metropolitan Statistical Areas in the United States in terms of Black-white integration (Quinn and Pawasarat, 2003). In short, Blacks are not seen as threatening because they are isolated from non-Hispanic whites and Hispanics alike, whereas non-Hispanic whites in Miami-Dade are likely to live in neighborhoods with some ethnic diversity. To the extent that Miami-Dade represents ethnically diverse metro areas where the Hispanic population is the largest minority group, Hispanics do appear to be the "new" threatening population, especially for non-Hispanic whites. Our findings reinforce the importance of decomposing racial threat measures into African American and (at the least) Hispanic populations in cities that have sizable populations of both. In separate analyses (not reported), we found that an oft-used measure of racial threat, percent minority residents, *failed* to reach statistical significance in the estimated model. Such a blunt measure of threatening groups may be obsolete, given the dynamic changes in the racial and ethnic composition of many American cities.

While we believe our findings are provocative, there are important caveats that warrant emphasis. First, the sampling strategy of the overarching research project was designed to identify a stratified random sample of disabled persons, and then match them with non-disabled neighbors in close proximity. Hence, the sample is skewed towards people with disabilities and may not be representative of the general population in Miami-Dade County. In fact, the median age of our sample is approximately 55 years of age, significantly older than the median age in the county (36 years of age). We did employ two approaches to minimize such concerns: a) we included a measure of physical limitation to statistically control for the influence of disability in the models estimated; and b) we ran additional analyses in which those identified as disabled were dropped from the analysis. The results of those analyses suggest that the pattern of findings revealed in the reported analyses is largely replicated by the non-disabled subgroup analysis. Nonetheless, the reader should consider this limitation when assessing the results of our analysis. Our study is best viewed as exploratory in nature.

Second, we were unable to provide official crime rate data at the census tract level, primarily because of the number of different law enforcement jurisdictions that exist in Miami-Dade County, including two large urban police departments. We do include, however, two measures that are arguably more salient predictors of one's perception of the neighborhood crime rate—vicarious victimization and reports of crime—that most prior studies of fear of crime have not incorporated. We suggest that future research should strive to include race and ethnic-specific crime rates to more accurately gauge the extent to which the fear of ethnic minorities is driven by aggregate crime rates.

If Miami is a social laboratory as many have described it, then our research suggests that the trend towards increasing ethnic diversity in many urban American centers will be accompanied by fear, distrust, and anguish by white non-Hispanics. While we did not explicitly test the merits of an alternative thesis to the minority group threat thesis explored in this paper, our results do suggest that the contact hypothesis of Allport (1954) and others may not extend into the realm of fear of racial and ethnic minorities. Contrary to the core notion of the contact hypothesis, that large populations of out-groups leads to interracial (and interethnic) contact, which ultimately produces less hostility and competition among diverse groups, our findings suggest that white fear of crime is greater in communities with a greater number of out-group (i.e., Hispanic) members. While speculative, one reason our finding may be contrary to the contact hypothesis is the obvious language and cultural barriers that may obfuscate efforts to achieve inter-group contact in Miami. According to the most recent Census, almost 60% of Miami-Dade County residents spoke Spanish as their first language, indicating a potential barrier to improving inter-group relations between Hispanics and non-Hispanic whites. Clearly, further research is needed to develop a more comprehensive understanding of what factors contribute to fear of crime among residents in ethnically heterogeneous neighborhoods, including such factors as bilingualism. But if our findings have merit, they reiterate the challenge of integrating urban dwellers in a rapidly changing world.

References

Allport, C., 1954. *The Nature of Prejudice.* Addison-Wesley Publishing Company, Cambridge.

Baldassare, M., 1986. The elderly and fear of crime. *Sociology and Social Research* 70, 218–221.

Blalock, H.M., 1967. *Toward a Theory of Minority Group Relations.* Wiley and Sons, New York.

Boswell, T.D., 2002. *A Demographic Profile of Cuban Americans.* Cuban American National Council, Inc., Miami.

Box, S., Hale, C., Anders, G., 1988. Explaining fear of crime. *British Journal of Criminology* 28, 340–356.

Braungart, M.M., Braumgart, R.G., Hoyer, W.J., 1980. Age, sex, and social factors in fear of crime. *Sociological Focus* 13, 55–66.

Brown, CM., Warner, B.D., 1992. Immigrants, urban politics, and policing in 1990. *American Sociological Review* 57, 293–305.

Bursik Jr., R.J., Grasmick, H.G., 1993. *Neighborhoods and Crime: The Dimensions of Effective Community Control.* Lexington Books, New York.

Chamlin, M.B., 1989. Conflict theory and police killings. *Deviant Behavior 10,* 353–368.

Chiricos, T., Hogan, M., Gertz, M., 1997. Racial composition of neighborhood and fear of crime. *Criminology* 35, 107–129.

Chiricos, T., McEntire, R., Gertz, M., 2001. Perceived racial and ethnic composition of neighborhood and perceived risk of crime. *Social Problems* 48, 322–340.

Clarke, A.H., Lewis, M.J., 1982. Fear of crime among the elderly. *British Journal of Criminology* 22, 49–62.

Cook, F.L, Skogan, W.G., Cook, T.D., Antunes, G., 1978. Criminal victimization of the elderly: the physical and economic consequences. *The Gerontologist* 18, 338–349.

Cooper, M., 2000. Arizona: the new border war. *Nation* 271, 20–24.

Corzine, J., Creech, J., Corzine, L., 1983. Black concentration and lynchings in the South: testing Blalock's power-threat hypothesis. *Social Forces* 61,774–796.

Covington, J., Taylor, R.B., 1991. Fear of crime in urban residential neighborhoods: implications of between- and within-neighborhood sources for current models. *The Sociological Quarterly* 32, 231–249.

Davis, R.C., Erez, E., 1998. *Immigrant Populations as Victims: Toward a Multicultural Criminal Justice System* (NCJ167571). U.S. Department of Justice, Office of Justice Programs, National Institute of Justice, Washington, DC.

Dubow, F., McCabe, E., Kaplan, G., 1979. *Reactions to Crime: A Critical Review of the Literature.* National Institute of Law Enforcement and Criminal Justice, U.S. Government Printing Office, Washington, DC.

Eitle, D., D'Alessio, S.J., Stolzenberg, L., 2003. Racial threat and social control: a test of the political, economic, and threat of Black crime hypotheses. *Social Forces* 81, 557–576.

Fattah, E.A., Sacco, V.F., 1989. *Crime and Victimization of the Elderly.* Springer-Verlag, New York.

Felson, M., 1998. *Crime and Everyday Life,* Second ed. Pine Forge Press, Thousand Oaks, CA.

Ferraro, K.F., 1995. *Fear of Crime: Interpreting Victim Risk.* State University of New York, New York.

Ferraro, K.F., 1996. Women's fear of victimization: shadow of sexual assault? *Social Forces* 75, 667–690.

Ferraro, K.F., LaGrange, R., 1987. The Measurement of fear of crime. *Sociological Inquiry* 57, 70–101.

Frey, W.H., 1999. *The New American Reality.* Russell Sage Foundation, New York.

Gabriel, U., Greve, W., 2003. The psychology of fear of crime. Conceptual and methodological perspectives. *British Journal of Criminology* 43, 594–608.

Garolfalo, J., 1977. *Public Opinion about Crime: The Attitudes of Victims and Non-Victims in Selected Cities.* National Criminal Justice Statistics and Information Service, LEAA, United States Department of Justice. Government Printing Office, Washington, DC.

Garolfalo, J., 1981. The fear of crime: causes and consequences. *The Journal of Criminal Law and Criminology* 72, 839–857.

Greenberg, D.F., Kessler, R.C., Loftin, C., 1985. Social inequality and crime control. *Journal of Criminal Law and Criminology* 76, 684–704.

Green, D.P., Strolovitch, D.Z., Wong, J.S., 1998. Defended neighborhoods, integration, and racially motivated crime. *American Journal of Sociology* 104, 372–403.

Grieco, E.M., Cassidy, R.C., 2001. *Overview of Race and Hispanic Origin: Census 2000 Brief.* United States Census Bureau, Washington, DC.

Hill, G.D., Howell, F.M., Driver, E.T., 1985. Gender, fear, and protective handgun ownership. *Criminology* 23, 541–552.

Houts, S., Kassab, C., 1997. Rotter's social learning theory and fear of crime: differences by race and ethnicity. *Social Science Quarterly* 78,122–136.

Jackson, P.I., Carroll, L., 1981. Race and the war on crime: the sociopolitical determinants of municipal police expenditures. *American Sociological Review* 46, 290–305.

Jacobs, D., 1979. Inequality and police strength: conflict theory and coercive control in metropolitan areas. *American Sociological Review* 44, 913–925.

Jacobs, D., Wood, K., 1999. Interracial conflict and interracial homicide: do political and economic rivalries explain white killings of Blacks or Black killings of whites? *American Journal of Sociology* 105, 157–190.

LaGrange, R.L., Ferraro, K.F., 1989. Assessing age and gender differences in perceived risk and fear of crime. *Criminology* 27, 697–719.

LaGrange, R.L., Ferraro, K.F., Supancic, M., 1992. Perceived risk and fear of crime: role of social and physical incivilities. *Journal of Research in Crime and Delinquency* 29, 311–334.

Land, K.C., McCall, P.L., Cohen, L.E., 1990. Structural covariates of homicide rates: are there any invariances across time and social space? *American Journal of Sociology* 95, 922–963.

Lane, J., Meeker, J.W., 2000. Subcultural diversity and the fear of crime and gangs. *Crime & Delinquency* 46, 497–521.

Lane, J., Meeker, J.W., 2003. Ethnicity, information sources, and fear of crime. *Deviant Behavior* 24, 1–26.

Lewis, D.A., Maxfield, M.G., 1980. Fear in the neighborhoods: an investigation of the impact of crime. *Journal of Research in Crime and Delinquency* 17, 160–189.

Lewis, D.A., Salem, G., 1986. *Fear of Crime: Incivility and the Production of a Social Problem.* Transaction, New Brunswick, NJ.

Liska, A.E., Bellair, P.E., 1995. Violent-crime rates and racial composition: convergence over time. *American Journal of Sociology* 101, 578–610.

Liska, A.E., Chamlin, M.B., 1984. Social structure and crime control among macrosocial units. *American Journal of Sociology* 90, 383–395.

Link, M.W., Oldendick, R.W., 1996. Social construction and white attitudes toward equal opportunity and multiculturalism. *Journal of Politics* 58, 149–168.

Liska, A.E., Lawrence, J.J., Sanchirico, A., 1982. Fear of crime as social fact. *Social Forces* 60, 760–770.

Liska, A.E., Sanchirico, A., Reed, M.D., 1988. Fear of crime and constrained behavior specifying and estimating a reciprocal effects model. *Social Forces* 66, 827–837.

Markowitz, F.E., Bellair, P.E., Liska, A.E., Liu, J., 2001. Extending social disorganization theory: modeling the relationships between cohesion, disorder, and fear. *Criminology* 39, 293–320.

Martinez Jr., R., Lee, M.T., Nielsen, A.L., 2004. Segmented assimilation, local context, and determinants of drug violence in Miami and San Diego: does ethnicity and immigration matter? *International Migration Review* 38, 131–157.

McGarrell, E.F., Giacomazzi, A., Thurman, Q.C., 1997. Neighborhood disorder, integration, and fear of crime. *Justice Quarterly* 14, 479–500.

Menjivar, C., Bejarano, C.L., 2004. Latino immigrants' perceptions of crime and police authorities in the United States: a case study from the Phoenix Metropolitan area. *Ethnic and Racial Studies* 27,120–148.

Mesch, G.S., 2000. Perceptions of risk, lifestyle activities, and fear of crime. *Deviant Behavior* 21, 47–62.

Miethe, T.D., Meier, R.F., 1990. *Crime and Its Social Context.* State University of New York Press, Albany.

Moeller, G.L., 1989. Fear of criminal victimization: the effect of neighborhood racial composition. *Sociological Inquiry* 59, 208–221.

Morgan, K.O. (Ed.), 2006. *City Crime Rankings: Crime in Metropolitan America*, thirteenth ed. Morgan Quitno Corporation, Lawrence, KS.

Myers, MA, 1990. Black threat and incarceration in postbellum Georgia. *Social Forces* 69, 373–393.

Pain, R.H., 2000. Place, social relations, and the fear of crime: a review. *Progress in Human Geography* 24, 365–387.

Parker, K.D., McMorris, B.J., Smith, E., Murty, K.S., 1993. Fear of crime and the likelihood of victimization: a bi-ethnic comparison. *Journal of Social Psychology* 133, 723–732.

Paternoster, R., Brame, R., Mazerolle, P., Piquero, A., 1998. Using the correct statistical test for the equality of regression coefficients. *Criminology* 36, 859–866.

Peterson, R.D., Krivo, L.K., 2005. Macrostructural analyses of race, ethnicity, and violent crime: recent lessons and new directions for research. *Annual Review of Sociology* 31, 331–356.

Phillips, C.D., 1986. Exploring relations among forms of social control: the lynching and execution of Blacks in North Carolina, 1889-1918. *Law and Society Review* 21, 361–374.

Princeton Survey Research Associates, 2002. John S. and James L. Knight Foundation Community Indicators Project. An Update of Public Opinion on Local Issues in Miami-Dade County, Fla. Available at: http://www.knightfdn.org/indicators/2002/mia/mia_miamidade-co_report_2002.pdf

Quinn, L.M., Pawasarat, J., 2003. Racial integration in Urban America: A block level analysis of African American and white housing patterns. Employment and Training Institute, School of Continuing Education, University of Milwaukee. Available at: http://www.uwm.edu/Dept/ETI/integration/integration.htm

Rader, N., 2004. The threat of victimization: a theoretical reconceptualization of fear of crime. *Sociological Spectrum* 24, 689–704.

Rountree, P.W., 1998. A reexamination of the crime-fear linkage. *Journal of Research in Crime and Delinquency* 35, 341–373.

Rountree, P.W., Land, K.C, 1996. Burglary victimization, perceptions of crime risk, and routine activities: a multilevel analysis across Seattle neighborhoods and census tracts. *Journal of Research in Crime and Delinquency* 33, 147–180.

Shaw, C.R., McKay, H.D., 1942. *Juvenile Delinquency and Urban Areas*. University Press, Chicago.

Skogan, W.G., 1986. Fear of Crime and Neighborhood Change. In: Reiss, A.J., Tonry, M. (Eds.), *Communities and Crime*. University of Chicago Press, Chicago, pp. 203–229.

Skogan, W.G., 1990. *Disorder and Decline*. Free Press, New York.

Skogan, W.G., 1995. Crime and the racial fears of white Americans. *The Annals of the American Academy of Social Science* 539, 59–71.

Skogan, W.G., 2005. Citizen satisfaction with police encounters. *Police Quarterly* 8, 298–321.

Skogan, W.G., Maxfield, M., 1981. *Coping with Crime: Individual and neighborhood reactions*. Sage, Beverly Hills, CA.

Stein, R.M., Post, S.S., Rinden, A.L., 1998. Reconciling context and contact effects on racial attitudes. *Political Research Quarterly* 53, 285–303.

Taylor, R.B., 1995. The impact of crime on communities. *The Annals of the American Academy of Political and Social Science* 539, 28–45.

Taylor, R.B., Covington, J., 1993. Community structural change and fear of crime. *Social Problems* 40, 374–395.

Taylor, R.B., Hale, M., 1986. Testing alternative models of fear of crime. *The Journal of Criminal Law and Criminology* 77,151–189.

Thompson, C.Y., Bankston, W.B., St. Pierre, R.L, 1992. Parity and disparity among three measures of crime: a research note. *Deviant Behavior* 13, 373–389.

Tittle, C.R., Curran, D.A., 1988. Contingencies for dispositional disparities in juvenile justice. *Social Forces* 67, 23–58.

Turner, R.J., Lloyd, D.A., Taylor, J., 2006. Physical disability and mental health: an epidemiology of psychiatric and substance disorders. *Rehabilitation Psychology* 51, 214–223.

United States Bureau of the Census, 1999. *Statistical abstract of the United States: 1999*. Government Printing Office, Washington. DC.

Walker, S., 1997. Complaints against the police: a focus group study of citizen perceptions, goals, and expectations. *Criminal Justice Review* 22, 207–225.

Walker, S., Spohn, C., DeLone, M., 2007. *The Color of Justice: Race, Ethnicity, and Crime in America*, fourth ed. Thomson, Belmont, CA.

Ward, M., Stafford, M., 1983. Fear of victimization: a look at the proximate causes. *Social Forces* 61, 1033–1043.

Ward, R.A., LaGory, M., Sherman, S.R., 1986. Fear of crime among the elderly as person/environment interaction. *The Sociological Quarterly* 27, 327–341.

Warr, M., 1984. Fear of victimization: why are women and the elderly more afraid? *Social Science Quarterly* 65, 681–702.

Whitley, R., Prince, M., 2005. Fear of crime, mobility, and mental health in inner-city London, UK. *Social Science and Medicine* 61, 1678–1688.

Wilcox, P., Quisenberry, N., Jones, S., 2003. The built environment and community crime risk interpretation. *Journal of Research in Crime and Delinquency* 40, 322–345.

Will, J.A., McCrath, J.H., 1995. Crime, neighborhood perceptions, and the underclass: the relationship between fear of crime and class position. *Journal of Criminal Justice* 23, 163–176.

DISCUSSION QUESTIONS

1. Why, in your opinion, does race play a role in the "fear of crime" concept?
2. Did the location in which the authors conducted this survey possibly affect their results? Why or why not?
3. What criminological theory discussed in this article best explains peoples' varying levels with respect to fear of crime? Explain.

READING

Felson, Deane, and Armstrong tackle the question of what type of theory is best suited to explain racial differences in offending. The authors make use of the heavily used National Longitudinal Study of Adolescent Health (AddHealth) dataset to determine if there are racial differences in offending by offense. They attempt to determine whether a specific type of theory is necessary to understand racial differences in offending. So for example, if Blacks are only more likely than other groups to commit violent offenses, then maybe researchers should be constructing a theory of violent offending—not using a more general theory of offending to explain racial disparities that only exist for violent offenses.

Do Theories of Crime or Violence Explain Race Differences in Delinquency?

Richard B. Felson, Glenn Deane, and David P. Armstrong

Introduction

Arrest data and data from victimization surveys suggest that African Americans have higher crime rates than White Americans (e.g., Bureau of Justice Statistics, 1995; Hawkins et al., 2000; see Sampson and Lauritsen, 1994). While race differences can ultimately be attributed to racism and the historic oppression of African Americans (e.g., Hawkins, 1995; McCord, 1997; Sampson and Wilson, 1995), the more proximate causal process is unclear. In fact, we argue that it is not even clear what racial patterns in offending require explanation.

In this research, we use data from the National Longitudinal Study of Adolescent Health (hereafter AddHealth) to examine racial patterns in violence and delinquency (Udry, 1998). We attempt to determine whether Blacks and Whites differ in their tendency to engage in violence or in their tendency to engage in serious delinquency, violent or not. AddHealth is particularly useful for examining racial patterns because it is based on a large national sample, it over-samples African Americans, and it uses a method that yields higher frequencies of self-reported delinquency (Harris et al., 2003). As a result, this research is more likely than past research to reveal the extent to which race effects are mediated and moderated by other demographic variables.

We use a method of theory testing that focuses on establishing the dependent variable rather than the introduction of mediating variables (although we do that as well). We argue that it is theoretically important to determine whether there are race differences in violent offenses or any type of serious offenses. If race is associated with violence but not other types of crimes, then one must look to theories of

Source: Felson, R. B., Deane, G., & Armstrong, D. P. (2008). Do theories of crime or violence explain race differences in delinquency? *Social Science Research*, 37, 624–641.

violence, not crime, for an explanation. On the other hand, if race is associated with all types of crime, or serious crime, then theories of crime and norm violation are likely to provide the explanation. Our goal, therefore, is to examine what group of theories is likely to explain race differences.

Our methods also differ from the methods used in earlier studies. First, we rely upon a statistical method that yields a true measure of specialization and that allows us to determine exactly what types of offenses vary by race (Deane et al., 2005). This method is well-suited to the analysis of criminal behavior, since most offenders commit a variety of offenses, and offenses cannot easily be rank ordered. The versatility of many offenders, however, does not preclude the possibility that predictors might be different for different types of criminal behaviors (Nagin and Paternoster, 1993; Horney et al., 1995).

Discriminant Prediction

Some theories attempt to explain why people engage in deviance, while others attempt to explain why they engage in aggression. The task is complicated by the fact that deviance and aggression are overlapping domains; some aggressive behavior violates norms (and is therefore deviant behavior) and some deviant behavior involves intentional harm-doing (or aggression). For example, spanking children involves violence but not deviance, the use of illegal drugs involves deviance but not aggression, and violent crime involves both deviance and aggression (see Felson et al., 1994). The pattern of offending is therefore important in determining what type of theory is most useful for explaining the behavior. If an offender engages in violence but not other deviant behavior then a theory of aggression is necessary to understand the behavior. If an offender engages in criminal behavior generally, then a theory of deviance is needed to understand the behavior.

Stinchcombe (1968) emphasizes the importance of proper conceptualization of the dependent variable in his classic work on theory construction. He uses delinquency as an example, pointing out that different kinds of action that concern the police may turn out to have different causes:

> Natural variables that create administrative problems are not the same variables that have a unique set of causes. Sometimes applied researchers formulate this by saying that a natural variable "has multiple causes." From the scientific point of view, this means that the applied researcher is trying to explain the wrong thing. (p. 41)

Gottfredson and Hirschi (1990) provide the most well-known example of using offense patterns as evidence for theoretical claims (see also Felson, 2002). They argue that the tendency of offenders to engage in a variety of criminal offenses (as well as other impulsive behavior) supports their theory of self-control and argues against theories of aggression to explain violent crime. Another example is Zimring and Hawkins's (1997) analyses and discussion of evidence showing that homicide rates but not other crime are relatively high in the United States. Their work suggests that crime theories are not useful for explaining this international pattern. Finally, Felson (1996) reviews evidence showing that children exposed to media violence engage in antisocial behavior generally, not just violent behavior, casting doubt on the idea that the children are modeling the violence they observed.

We argue that scholars interested in race differences may be trying to explain the wrong phenomenon. Criminological theories attempt to explain race differences in criminal behavior (or deviance) while research often examines race differences in violence (e.g., Sampson and Wilson, 1995; McNulty and Bellair, 2003a).

This strategy is not problematic if violent behavior is viewed as an indicator of crime or serious crime. However, if there are race differences in violence but not other serious crime, a theory of violence is required.

We believe that an understanding of race differences in offense patterns is necessary before theoretical progress on this important issue is possible. It is important to establish what facts require explanation, before attempting to explain them. In statistical language, it is necessary to determine the appropriate dependent variable before examining potential mediating variables. Moreover, since different theories imply different racial patterns, such an analysis provides a test of those theoretical explanations. This method of theory testing might be called "discriminant prediction" (see Felson, 2002). A theoretical explanation is *not* supported if: (1) race is only related to certain types of criminal offending when the theory predicts it should be related to all offending; or (2) race is related to all types of offending when the theory predicts it should be related to only some types of offending. More generally, a theory is not supported if evidence fails to confirm its predictions that either (1) X affects all Ys or (2) X affects Y_1, but not Y_2 or Y_n. The difference between discriminant prediction and discriminant validity is that the former refers to the validity of a theory while the latter refers to the validity of measurement.

This research described below uses this method to test theories of crime and theories of aggression as explanations for race differences. Crime theories (e.g., strain, control, and social disorganization theories) predict that African Americans are more likely to commit a variety of offenses, not specialize in a particular type of crime. They would not have much difficulty explaining why race differences are stronger for more serious offenses than minor offenses, but they would have trouble explaining differences in violent offenses alone. On the other hand, theories of violence (i.e., the frustration-aggression approach; the subculture of violence thesis and the code of the streets) can explain race differences in violence, but they cannot explain race differences in general offending.

Note, however, that these theories of crime and violence are all middle-range theories. General theories of human behavior that emphasize incentives and costs (i.e., social learning theory and the rational choice perspective) could conceivably explain any offense patterns. In addition, the routine activity approach can accommodate different offense patterns, if opportunities for deviance and aggression are different. However, it would be necessary for these theories to suggest a theoretical mechanism to account for the offense patterns observed.

We first describe the empirical literature on race and offense patterns and consider the role of social-demographic factors as mediators and moderators of race effects. We then examine race differences in specific offenses in order to determine whether there are race differences in all offending, serious offending, or violent offending. Finally, in the discussion, we consider the implications of the research literature for specific theories of crime and aggression.

Prior Research on Race and Offense Patterns

Prior research suggests that race differences in offending vary depending on the type of offense. Thus, the Uniform Crime Statistics reveals stronger race differences in arrests for violent crime than property crime or drug abuse violations (see Zimring and Hawkins, 1997). Further, both arrest data and data from the National Crime Victimization Survey show stronger race differences in offending for robbery than assault, and for aggravated assault compared to simple assault (Bureau of Justice Statistics, 1997). In federal prisons, black inmates have higher rates of violence than white inmates but lower rates of drug violations (Harer and Steffensmeier, 1996). On the other hand, self-report data obtained from 12 year olds participating in the 1997 National

Longitudinal Survey of Youth reveal that non-whites have higher rates of property crime, lower rates of drug use, and similar rates of assault (Hawkins et al., 2000).

It may be that the race patterns observed in the UCR reflect the seriousness of the offense rather the presence of violence. While violent crime is generally perceived as more serious than property crime (Rossi et al., 1974), violence and seriousness are conceptually distinct. Thus, property crimes vary in their seriousness, as reflected in the different penalties for grand larceny, petty larceny, burglary, and shoplifting. Drug violations also vary in their seriousness: we punish offenders more severely for selling drugs than using drugs and we evaluate it more severely (Rossi et al., 1974). Finally, injurious violence is considered more serious than violence in which the offender causes no injury and armed violence is considered more serious than violence in which the offender is unarmed.

An analysis of UCR tables supports the idea that race differences are stronger for serious offenses. The correlation between percentage black offenders and the seriousness of 29 crime categories, using a ranking based on Federal sentencing recommendations, is .36 ($p = .025$; one-tailed test). However, it is impossible to disentangle the effects of violence and seriousness in the UCR data, i.e., to determine whether race differences are stronger for violent offenses or serious offenses, or both.

Hindelang et al. (1981) provide some evidence that addresses this issue in their analyses of self-reported delinquency among adolescents in Seattle in 1978. Their analyses of black/white ratios for different offenses provided mixed evidence: Blacks were more likely than Whites to engage in violence and some more serious forms of theft, but not most property or drug crimes. However, they did not control for socioeconomic status and other demographic characteristics associated with race. Thus, it is not clear from their data whether race has net effects.

In general, the literature is unclear about whether Blacks are more likely than Whites to commit serious crimes or violent crimes. To address this issue it is necessary to examine race differences in serious and minor violent crime and serious and minor non-violent crime. In addition, our method allows us to examine specialization by controlling for any race differences in the general tendency to offend. The traditional method in which specific offenses are examined separately confounds the tendency to commit particular offenses with the tendency to offend generally.

The Role of Other Demographic Factors

Race effects are to some extent mediated by other social-demographic factors. Black youth are more likely than white youth to be raised in single parent impoverished families, and to live in impoverished, urban neighborhoods. All of these are well-known risk factors for delinquency. However, research on the net effects of race, controlling for these variables, is somewhat limited. One problem with UCR data and victimization surveys is that they have limited information on the demographic characteristics of offenders. Surveys of youth based on self-reports have much more extensive information on offenders, but these studies find that violence and crime are either unrelated or only weakly related to race and other demographic factors (e.g., Elliot, 1994; Markowitz and Felson, 1998; Bridges and Weis, 1989; Farrington et al., 2003; McLeod et al., 1994; Paschall et al., 1996). For example, McNulty and Bellair (2003a) find a small relationship between race and involvement in fights at, or on the way, to school. The relationship is no longer statistically significant in their longitudinal analysis when demographic variables, a lagged measure of fighting, and other measures are controlled. In a longitudinal analysis of AddHealth data, McNulty and Bellair (2003b) found that neighborhood disadvantage and other variables mediated effects of race on change in serious violence over a two-year period. Note, however, that the inclusion of lagged variables limits the size of race effects (see also Kaufman, 2005).

It may be that most self-report surveys tap less serious forms of violence and crime, since more serious offenses are relatively rare. As indicated above, the effects of race and other social-demographic variables are probably stronger for serious offenses (Elliot and Ageton, 1980; Loftin, 1991; Bureau of Justice Statistics, 1995). One approach to this problem is to survey high-risk populations. For example, Farrington et al. (2003) over-sample delinquent boys in the Pittsburgh Youth Study. They find a race difference in self-reported violence, with controls for other demographic factors, although that difference is much smaller than the race difference in the level of violence reported to the police.

Rowe et al. (1994) argue, and provide evidence, that the effects of race and other demographic factors are additive. Others have reported a variety of statistical interactions (e.g., McLeod et al., 1994; Deater-Deckard et al., 1998; Paschall et al., 1996). The theoretical basis for predicting statistical interactions, however, is weak. Perhaps multiple disadvantages are most likely to lead to crime when they occur in combination. In other words, adolescents who are exposed to one risk factor—and thus have a predisposition to commit crime—are particularly likely to offend if they are exposed to some other risk factor. For example, one might expect that black adolescents from impoverished families or neighborhoods are particularly likely to experience discrimination. Paschall et al. (1996) found support for the multiple disadvantage interaction pattern based on their study of young adults in a largely urban county. Race was more strongly related to violence for respondents of lower economic status. On the other hand, Farrington et al. (2003) found an interaction in the opposite direction: socioeconomic status was more highly related to violence for whites than blacks. Statistical interactions between race and socioeconomic status have also been examined in aggregate level research on homicide rates. These studies tend to show that economic deprivation has stronger effects on homicide rates for whites than for blacks, but the evidence is mixed, and at least one study reports a statistical interaction in the opposite direction (e.g., Loftin, 1991; Ousey, 1999; Messner and Sampson, 1991; Lafree and Drass, 1996; Harer and Steffensmeier, 1992).

It is not clear whether to expect statistical interactions between race and residence in urban or disadvantaged neighborhoods. A neighborhood's social disorganization might have similar effects regardless of the characteristics of its residents. However, Wilson's (1987) thesis about the de-industrialization of northern cities implies that the increase in crime in African American communities is largely an urban phenomenon (see also Short, 1997). Anderson's discussion of the code of the streets focuses on black youth living in impoverished, urban neighborhoods where the threat of violence is strongest. His argument suggests that African American youth who experience the greatest threat of violence should have the highest violence rates. He therefore implies statistical interactions between race and urban residence, and between race and neighborhood disadvantage. However, there is no strong theoretical reason to expect that race effects are stronger in disadvantaged or urban neighborhoods.

Nor is it clear whether to expect statistical interactions between race and gender. Elliot (1994) found no gender differences in race effects using self-reports of serious violence from the National Youth Survey. Hindelang et al. (1981), using victimization data from the National Crime Survey, also found additive effects of race and gender on assault but stronger race effects for males on robbery offending. Hindelang et al. (1981) study of the Seattle data found stronger race differences in violence among girls than boys. In addition, research on spousal violence shows that black women are more likely than black men to kill their spouse, while the reverse is true for whites (Daly and Wilson, 1988).

Finally, it is not clear whether one should expect a statistical interaction between race and age. A strain perspective (e.g., Agnew, 1987; Messner and Rosenfeld, 1994) might imply that race differences should be stronger for older adolescents than younger adolescents since economic and other opportunities are likely to be more salient.

Methodology

We first describe the data and measurement, and then provide an extended discussion of our incident-based approach to data analysis. The extended discussion is necessary because of the novelty of this method.

The AddHealth study

AddHealth is a large longitudinal data set based on a nationally representative sample of adolescents in Grades 7 to 12 (Harris et al., 2003). The data are useful in examining race effects for several reasons. First, previous survey research typically relies on more local, and less representative samples. The use of a national sample allows us to determine to what extent race differences are an urban phenomenon. Second, because the sample is so large, research can examine more serious, but less frequent offenses. Using incident-based analyses that allow us to examine the commission of specific offenses, we can determine exactly what offenses vary by race. Third, AddHealth's use of computers for eliciting more sensitive information yields higher frequencies of self-reported crime than the usual methods (Turner et al., 1998). Underreporting may be a problem in examining race differences using survey research.[2] Fourth, unlike most youth surveys examining race, AddHealth surveys girls as well as boys. This feature enables us to examine whether race effects are conditioned by gender. Fifth, AddHealth provides independent information on ethnic background and race, enabling us to disentangle their effects. Past research has typically ignored violent crime among Latino groups, a large and growing segment of the population (Martinez and Lee, 1999). Finally, the sample includes a large number of African Americans (including a special sample of middle-class blacks). This sampling method provides more reliable estimates of race effects and increases our power to detect interactions.

AddHealth is a complex survey sample that includes regional stratification, a cluster sample design using schools as primary sampling units (PSUs), and over-samples of special populations. Our analyses are based on the in-home sample that includes the core ($N = 12{,}105$) and several special samples. One of the special samples includes 1038 Black adolescents from well-educated families, i.e., at least one parent has a college degree. The special samples combined with the core sample (which includes 2400 Blacks) yield a combined sample (after listwise deletion) of 15,430.[3]

All students who completed an in-school questionnaire, plus those who did not complete a questionnaire but who were listed on a school roster, were eligible for selection into the study

[2]Evidence suggests that African Americans are less likely than whites to self-report violent or serious crime (Bridges and Weis, 1989; Hindelang et al., 1981). Perhaps some black respondents fear that reporting criminal behavior will encourage stereotyping and prejudice.

[3]We account for AddHealth's complex survey design in our statistical analyses via a strategy similar to that recommended by Korn and Graubard (1991). Stratification and special sample weights are accounted for by including the variables (e.g., region, race, education, etc.) used in defining these aspects of the survey design in the right hand side of the regression equation (see Korn and Graubard's "E analyses"), while AddHealth's cluster design is explicitly accounted for in the GEE methodology we employ (described in the Section 5.3).

sample. The respondents attended 144 schools in 80 school districts.[4] Students and their parents (usually mothers) were interviewed at home between April and December, 1995.

Measurement

We examine the prevalence of nine types of criminal behaviors: armed violence; unarmed violence; group violence; seriously injuring someone; armed robbery; selling drugs; using drugs; serious property crime; and minor property crime (see Appendix A). Our selection is motivated by our interest in distinguishing violent crimes from other crimes and serious crimes from minor crimes. We recognize that there is some ambiguity about which offenses are more serious than others. We consider alternative classifications and examine their effects in the results section.

We used multiple items when they were available (five of our nine categories). We code the behavior as 1 if the respondent gave an affirmative response on any of the items. Note that the items for armed violence and drug use are based on life-time incidence while the other items are based on the last twelve months. While items that are not time-bound result in higher prevalence rates, it is unlikely that they affect the relative size of our coefficients. It is possible that behavior categories based on single items have more measurement error than those categories based on multiple items, but we shall see that some of the strongest effects are observed for the single item categories. The distributions of the categories are shown in Table 3.3.

Table 3.3 Distributions of Criminal Offenses

Criminal Behavior	Number of Respondents Reporting Behavior[a]	Response Percentage[b]	Incidence Percentage[c]
Armed violence	923.73	6.00	2.82
Unarmed violence	6307.52	40.87	19.21
Group violence	3099.90	20.09	9.44
Cause serious injury	2863.16	18.56	8.72
Armed robbery	611.32	3.96	1.86
Sell drugs	1160.14	7.52	3.53
Use drugs	4729.42	30.65	14.40
Serious properly crime	2299.92	14.91	7.00
Minor property crime	5581.31	36.17	17.00
No criminal offense	5256.58	34.07	16.01
	$n^* = 32{,}835$		100.00

a. Fractional counts result from application of sample weights.

b. Response percentages based on number of respondents ($n = 15{,}430$).

c. Incidence percentages based on number of respondents reporting behavior ($n^* = 32{,}835$).

[4]Some districts included high schools and their feeder middle schools.

AddHealth allows respondents to choose multiple racial identifications, but also asks respondents "if you had to choose only one race, what race would you choose?" We used responses to this question to code race. Ethnicity is measured separately from race since Latinos and Blacks are not mutually exclusive groups. In addition, it is important to distinguish between different Latino groups (see Martinez and Lee, 1999). For example, Martinez (1996) finds that Latinos have a lower homicide rate than Anglos in Miami but a higher rate in El Paso, reflecting substantial differences in homicide rates between Cuban and Mexican Americans. Accordingly, we code respondents as Mexican/Mexican American, Cuban, Puerto Rican, Central American, Other Hispanic, or Non-Hispanic.

Other demographic predictors are age, gender, and place of residence. Place of residence is a dichotomy reflecting whether the adolescent is an urban resident or not. We use Add Health's constructed variable which is based on the 1990 census definition of urban area except that it does not include places outside urbanized areas of 2500 or more people. Information on whether or not the respondent is living in a single-parent (either female- or male-headed) family is obtained from the parents' questionnaire. We use two measures of socioeconomic status: parents' education and whether the family was on public assistance. Both measures were derived from the parents' questionnaire. Parents' education is based on the *highest* educational attainment of a parent. Our use of the public assistance indicator is consistent with evidence that criminal violence may be more an effect of poverty than a linear function of socioeconomic status (Brownfield, 1986). Such an argument is implied in the notion of concentration effects (Wilson, 1987).

Our final explanatory variable is a neighborhood concentrated disadvantage index. AddHealth provides selected contextual measures from the 1990 Census for the tract group in which respondents' reside. Following Sampson et al. (1997), we create a standardized component measure of neighborhood concentrated disadvantage based on the proportion in the tract who are younger than age eighteen, receiving public assistance, unemployed, living in poverty, African American, and living in female-headed households. Some scholars might question the inclusion of the age and race components in this measure. However, in alternative analyses (not presented), we omitted the age and race components and achieved similar results.

Discussion

This research suggests that black adolescents are more likely than white adolescents to engage in violent crime but not property or drug crime. In fact, blacks are *less* likely to use illegal drugs, when demographic variables are controlled. For African American youth: crime is not the problem.

Some of our evidence is consistent with evidence from earlier studies, but we control for social demographic variables and use a large, nationally representative, sample. Most importantly, we show for the first time that race differences in violence among youth are not due to race differences in the tendency to commit more serious crime. Effects are no stronger for serious delinquency than for minor delinquency, i.e., they are no stronger for selling drugs than for using drugs, for injurious violence than for other violence, or for serious property crime than for minor property crime.

Race differences in violence are mediated to some extent by demographic factors. Controls for family structure, urban residence, and socioeconomic status reduce the size of race effects on violent crime. In other words, black adolescents are more likely to engage in violent crime than white adolescents because they are more likely to reside in urban areas, their parents are more likely to be poor and uneducated, and their families are more likely to be headed by a single parent. However, demographic variables only partially explained why black adolescents are more likely than white adolescents to engage in violent crime. The race difference in violence that remains when demographic factors are controlled is substantial.

The race difference in armed violence is particularly strong. A black adolescent is more than twice as likely to commit violence with a weapon than a white adolescent, controlling for demographic variables. Unfortunately, we cannot determine with our item whether this difference involves firearms or other weapons. While the literature focuses on firearms (e.g., Blumstein, 1995), an examination of assault data from the National Crime Victimization Survey (not presented) shows that, during an assault, black offenders are more likely than white offenders to use other weapons as well as firearms.[5]

We do not find evidence that race combines with other forms of disadvantage to produce particularly high rates of violent crime. The results are not consistent with the idea that youth who are predisposed to engage in crime because they experience one risk factor are particularly likely to offend if they experience some other risk factor. Our analysis of statistical interactions is more consistent with the argument that race effects on violence are stronger for adolescents who would otherwise be at lower risk of violence: girls and adolescents from educated and intact families. This pattern is consistent with much, but not all, of the prior research cited earlier.

It is interesting to note that socioeconomic status, like race, is associated with violence but not other crime. Adolescents from lower status families are more likely to engage in most forms of violent crime but they are no more likely to engage in drug or property crime. In fact, adolescents with educated parents are *more* likely to engage in drug-related and minor property offenses. In addition, adolescents whose parents receive public assistance are particularly likely to engage in armed violence. Thus, poverty *and* race are most strongly related to armed violence.

We also examined crime patterns for Hispanic adolescents, a neglected topic in the literature. The extensive race/ethnicity questions and the large sample size of AddHealth allowed us to examine delinquency among a variety of Hispanic groups, and disentangle race from ethnic effects. This has not been done before. The results show that most Hispanic groups have similar crime rates as Anglos, suggesting that violence is not associated with machismo Hispanic culture. Puerto Ricans are a notable exception: they are more likely to commit a variety of crimes than Anglos. Their rates of unarmed violence and armed robbery are particularly high, suggesting some violence specialization.[6] However, the pattern is not as clear as it is for African Americans, as they are also more likely to commit minor property offenses. At any rate, our results suggest that it is important to distinguish different Hispanic groups when studying crime and delinquency. Unfortunately, most crime surveys group all Hispanics into the same category.

Measurement error is always an important issue in research that relies on self-reports. The evidence cited earlier suggests that computer assisted method used in AddHealth yields higher rates of reporting of deviant behavior than self-administered questionnaires. In addition, the race differences we observe have been observed with arrest and victimization data, although those studies lack adequate controls and do not disentangle effects on violence from effects on serious crime. Finally, it is difficult to imagine how measurement error could account for either the violence differential or the statistical interactions. It seems unlikely, for example, that African Americans over-report violent

[5]The analyses are based on 16,672 assaults from a pooled sample (1993-1998).

[6]We also examined statistical interactions between Puerto Rican background and the other demographic variables. None were statistically significant.

behavior but not other criminal behavior, and that this bias is particularly strong for girls and adolescents from intact or middle-class families. However, it may be that, because of measurement error, this survey is not sensitive enough to detect differences in non-violent crime but that these differences are not as strong as race differences in violence.

Our study is also limited by the fact that it is based on a school sample. Serious delinquents are under-sampled because some of them have dropped out of school. In addition, Blacks and Hispanics are more likely to drop out of school than non-Hispanic Whites (Hauser et al., 2000). Note, however, that race differences in violence are just as strong at younger ages before adolescents are likely to leave school. Another potential limitation is our reliance on a self-report survey. Minor forms of delinquency are likely to have a stronger influence on results from self-report surveys than serious forms of delinquency because they are much more frequent. It is not clear how these sampling biases would affect our results. Perhaps we would have found some race differences in serious non-violent delinquency if the category focused on the most serious property and drug offenses. It would still be necessary to explain why the race difference in violence is so much greater.

Implications for Specific Theories

Our main goal in this research was to describe racial patterns of adolescent offending and to determine whether theories of crime or violence could explain them. Our results suggest that neither strain theory nor control theories, nor the social disorganization approach can explain the *net* effects of race that we observed since they imply race differences in a variety of offenses, not just violent offenses (e.g., Agnew, 1987; Hirschi, 1969; Gottfredson and Hirschi, 1990; Sampson and Wilson, 1995). Strain, control, and social disorganization could have indirect effects, however. For example, it may be that a subculture of violence develops in a social disorganized neighborhood. But then one must explain why only attitudes toward violence are affected. Should not a subculture of delinquency or an "oppositional culture" also develop in these neighborhoods and lead to more criminal behavior generally (e.g., Rose and McClain, 1998)? Note also that our results say nothing about the general validity of these theories. For example, control theories may very well explain individual differences or the effects of growing up in single-parent families or social disorganized neighborhoods. Our purpose was only to examine whether crime or violence theories can explain the race differences in offending that remain when other demographic variables are controlled.

Our results point to theoretical explanations that focus on violence. For example, frustration-aggression theories could possibly explain race differences in violence but then one must interpret most violence by African Americans as displaced aggression, since most of it is directed at other blacks. Studies of violent disputes, however, suggest that offenders typically target their adversaries, not innocent third parties (Luckenbill, 1977; Tedeschi and Felson, 1994). In addition, frustration-aggression approaches cannot easily account for our finding that race differences in armed robbery—generally recognized as instrumental violence—are just as strong as race differences in assault. Finally, prior research suggests that blacks are no more likely than whites to engage in verbal aggression (e.g., Steadman and Felson, 1984; Atkin et al., 2002; Harris, 1992). A frustration-aggression argument implies that blacks should be more likely to engage in all types of expressive aggression, not just its relatively rare physical manifestation. In general, frustration-aggression approaches are not supported by the test of discriminant predictions.

The contagion process implied in Anderson's (1999) "code of the streets" might help explain race differences in violence. Structural or historical factors may have led to high crime rates in African American communities, providing a starting mechanism. For example, the association between race and poverty, urban residence, and single parent households may have led initially to group differences in violence and other crime. Violence may then have spread in these communities because of residential segregation and because violence is more contagious than other crime. The contagiousness is due to an "adversary effect:" the threat of violence leads adversaries to use violence to protect themselves and to retaliate when attacked. A competitive or adversarial process, implied in Anderson's code of the streets, produces more contagion than peer support or sub-cultural beliefs do alone. Adversary effects also lead to an arms race and therefore help explain the strong race differences in armed violence.

The fact that we did not find evidence that race effects are stronger in urban areas might be viewed as contrary to the idea of adversary effects implied in Anderson's approach. Note, however, that our measure of urban residence is based on population density not location in an "inner city" or residential segregation. Future research should examine whether violence is particularly likely to spread in segregated African American communities.

A competitive contagion process, however, cannot explain strong race differences in committing robbery or sexual assault, race differences in the use of physical punishment by parents, or race differences in violence observed in colleges and prisons (e.g., Bureau of Justice Statistics, 1997; Gil, 1970; Volkwein et al., 1995; Harer and Steffensmeier, 1996). These patterns imply some degree of internalization of norms and attitudes conducive to violence among African Americans. They imply a type of contagion produced by differential association or a subculture of violence (e.g., Wolfgang and Ferracuti, 1967). While research on race differences in attitudes toward violence yields mixed results, attitudes regarding violence are complex and contingent on circumstances, and measuring them is difficult (see, e.g., Blumenthal et al., 1972; Rossi et al., 1974; Erlanger, 1974; Luckenbill and Doyle, 1989; Markowitz and Felson, 1998; Wolfgang et al., 1985; Cao et al., 1997).

More general theories of human behavior—social learning and rational choice—can explain race differences, but they must posit some process that produces differences in violence alone. In fact, the contagion and subcultural arguments just described are based on rational choice and social learning perspectives. Our point is that it is necessary to examine variation in the social learning of violence, not crime. Finally, the routine activities approach (e.g., Felson, 1994) could account for differences in effects on violent and non-violent crime if the opportunities to commit these crimes vary by race. Violent crime is different from other crimes in that it requires personal contact between offender and victim and poses a greater risk of reprisal for potential guardians who intervene. Perhaps, Black communities are more likely than White communities to bring potential offenders and victims into contact in places where potential guardians are afraid to intervene. On the other hand, the evidence showing race differences in violence in prisons and universities is difficult for the routine activities theory to explain.

With the exception of poverty, violent crime may be the most important issue in the study of race in American society. Yet, perhaps because of the sensitivity of this issue, the research literature is limited. Our research suggests that there are race differences in violence, not crime generally, net of other social-demographic factors, and that we need to consider theories of violence rather than theories of crime in order to understand these patterns. Blacks and Whites in American society differ in their use of physical forms of aggression, not in their tendency to break rules or in their intention to do harm. We have not yet found the house, but we think we know what street it is on.

Appendix A

Armed Violence (1 item): "Have you ever used a weapon in a fight?"

Unarmed Violence (2 items): "In the past 12 months, how often did you get into a serious physical fight?"

"During the past 12 months, how often did you get into a physical fight?"

Group Violence (1 item): "In the past 12 months, how often did you take in a fight where a group of your friends was against another group?"

Cause Serious Injury (1 item): "In the past 12 months, how often did you hurt someone badly enough to need bandages or care from a doctor or nurse?"

Armed Robbery (1 item): "In the past 12 months, how often did you use or threaten to use a weapon to get something from someone?"

Sell Drugs (1 item): "In the past 12 months, how often did you sell marijuana or other drugs?"

Use Drugs (4 items): "During your life, how many times have you used cocaine?"

"How old were you when you tried marijuana for the first time? If you never tried marijuana, enter '0.'"

"How old were you when you tried inhalants, such as glue or solvents, for the first time? If you never tried inhalants such as these, enter '0.'"

"How old were you when you first tried any other type of drug, such as LSD, PCP, ecstasy, mushrooms, speed, ice, heroin, or pills without a doctor's prescription? If you never tried any other type of illegal drug, enter '0.'"

Serious Property Crime (3 items): "In the past 12 months, how often did you go into a house or building to steal something?"

"In the past 12 months, how often did you steal something worth more than $50?"

"In the past 12 months, how often did you drive a car without its owner's permission?

Minor Property Crime (4 items): "In the past 12 months, how often did you paint graffiti or signs on someone else's property or in a public place?"

"In the past 12 months, how often did you deliberately damage property that did not belong to you?"

"In the past 12 months, how often did you take something from a store without paying for it?"

"In the past 12 months, how often did you steal something worth less than $50?"

References

Agnew, Robert, 1987. On testing structural strain theories. Journal of Research in Crime and Delinquency 24, 281–286.

Anderson, Elijah, 1999. Code of the Street. W.W. Norton & Company, New York.

Atkin, Charles K., Smith, Sandi W., Roberto, Anthony J., Fediuk, Thomas, Wagner, Thomas, 2002. Correlates of verbally aggressive communication in adolescents. Journal of Applied Communication Research 30, 251–268.

Blumenthal, Monica, Kahn, Robert L., Andrews, Frank M., Head, Kendra B., 1972. Justifying Violence. Attitudes of American Men. Institute for Social Research, Ann Arbor, MI.

Blumstein, Alfred, 1995. Youth violence, guns and the illicit-drug industry. Journal of Criminal Law and Criminology 86, 10–36.

Bridges, George S., Weis, Joseph G., 1989. Measuring violent behavior: effects of study design on reported correlates of violence. In: Neil Alan, Weiner, Wolfgang, Marvin E. (Eds.), Violent Crime, Violent *Criminals.* Sage, Beverly Hills, CA, pp. 14–35.

Brownfield, David, 1986. Social class and violent behavior. Criminology 24, 421–437.

Bureau of Justice Statistics, 1997. Criminal Victimization in the United States—1994. Washington, DC: U.S. Government Printing Office.

Bureau of Justice Statistics, 1995. Sourcebook of Criminal Justice Statistics, 1994. Washington, DC: U.S. Department of Justice.

Cao, Liqun, Anthony Adams., Vickie J. Jensen, 1997. A Test of the Black Subculture of Violence Thesis: A Research Note. Criminology 35, 367–379.

Daly, Martin, Wilson, Margo, 1988. Homicide. Aldine de Gruyter, Hawthorne, NY.

Deane, Glenn D., Armstrong, David P., Felson, Richard B., 2005. An examination of offense specialization using marginal logit models. Criminology 43, 955–988.

Deater-Deckard, Kirby, Dodge, Kenneth A., Bates, John E., Pettit, Gregory S., 1998. Multiple risk factors in the development of externalizing behavior problems: group and individual differences. Development and Psychopathology 10, 469–493.

Elliot, Delbert S., 1994, 1993. Presidential address: serious violent offenders: onset, developmental course, and termination. Criminology 32, 1–23.

Elliot, Delbert S., Ageton, Suzanne S., 1980. Reconciling race and class differences in self-reported and official estimates of delinquency. American Sociological Review 45, 95–110.

Erlanger, Howard S., 1974. The empirical status of the subculture of violence thesis. Social Problems 22, 280–291.

Farrington, David P., Loeber, Rolf, Magda, Stouthamer-Loeber, 2003. How can the relationship between race and violence be explained? In: Hawkins, Darnell F. (Ed.), Violent Crime: Assessing Race and Ethnic Differences. Cambridge University Press, New York, pp. 213–237.

Felson, Marcus, 1994. Crime and Everyday Life. Pine Forge Press, Thousand Oaks, CA.

Felson, Richard B., 1996. Mass media effects on violent behavior. Annual Review of Sociology 22, 103–128.

Felson, Richard B., 2002. Violence and Gender Reexamined. American Psychological Association, Wash., D.C.

Felson, Richard B., Liska, Allen E., South, Scott J., McNulty, Thomas J., 1994. The subculture of violence and delinquency: individual vs. school context effects. Social Forces 73, 155–174.

Gil, David, 1970. Violence Against Children: Physical Child Abuse in the United States. Harvard University Press, Cambridge, MA.

Gottfredson, Michael, Hirschi, Travis, 1990. A General Theory of Crime. Stanford University Press, Stanford, CA.

Harer, Miles D., Steffensmeier, Darrell J., 1992. The differing effects of economic inequality on black and white rates of violence. Social Forces 70, 1035–1054.

Harer, Miles D., Steffensmeier, Darrell J., 1996. Race and prison violence. Criminology 34, 323–355.

Harris, Kathleen Mullan, Francesca Florey, Joyce Tabor, Peter S. Bearman, Jo Jones, J. Richard Udry, 2003. The National Longitudinal Study of Adolescent Health: Research Design [WWW document]. URL: <http://www.cpc.unc.edu/projects/addhealth/design>.

Harris, Mary B., 1992. Sex, race, and experiences of aggression. Aggressive Behavior 18, 201–217.

Hauser, R.M., Simmons, S.J., Pager, D.I, 2000. High School Dropout, Race-Ethnicity and Social Background from the 1970s to the 1990s. Center for Ecology and Demography Working Paper No, 2000-12, University of Wisconsin-Madison.

Hawkins, Darnell F, 1995. Ed. Ethnicity, Race and Crime: Perspectives across Time and Place. Albany, NY: SUNY Press.

Hawkins, Darnell F., Laub, John H., Lauritsen, Janel L., Cotghern, Lynn, 2000. Race, Ethnicity and Serious and Violent Juvenile Offending. Juvenile Justice Bulletin. Dept of Justice, Washington: US.

Hindelang, Michael, Travis, Hirschi, Joseph, Weis, 1981. Measuring Delinquency. Sage, Beverly Hills, CA.

Hirschi, Travis, 1969. Causes of Delinquency. University of California Press, Berkeley, CA.

Horney, Julie D., Osgood, Wayne, Marshall, Ineke H., 1995. Criminal careers in the short-term: intra-individual variability in crime and its relation to local life circumstances. American Sociological Review 60, 655–673.

Kaufman, Joanne M., 2005. Explaining the race-ethnicity violence relationship: neighborhood context and social psychological processes. Justice Quarterly 22, 224–251.

Lafree, Gary, Drass, Kriss A., 1996. Variables affecting arrest rates of black and whites, 1957 to 1990. American Sociological Review 61, 614–634.

Loftin, Colin, 1991. Socioeconomic Status and Race. Memorandum prepared for the Panel on Understanding and Control of Violent Behavior established by the Committee on Law and Justice a Subcommittee of the Commission on Behavioral and Social Sciences and Education a Division of the National Research Council, Washington DC.

Luckenbill, David F., 1977. Criminal homicide as a situated transaction. Social Problems 25, 176–186.

Luckenbill, David F., Doyle, Daniel P., 1989. Structural position and violence: developing a cultural explanation. Criminology 27, 801–818.

Markowitz, Fred, Felson, Richard B., 1998. Social-demographic differences in attitudes and violence. Criminology 36, 117–138.

Martinez Jr., Ramiro, 1996. Latinos and lethal violence: the impact of poverty and inequality. Social Problems 43, 131–146.

Martinez, Ramiro, Lee, Matthew T., 1999. Extending ethnicity in homicide research: the case of Latinos. In: Smith, Dwayne M., Zahn, Margaret A. (Eds.), Homicide: A Sourcebook of Social Research. Sage, Thousand Oaks, CA, pp. 211–220.

McCord, Joan, 1997. Violence and Childhood in the Inner City. Cambridge University Press, Cambridge, MA.

McLeod, Jane D., Kruttschnitt, Candace, Dornfeld, Maude, 1994. Does parenting explain the effects of structural conditions on children's antisocial behavior? A comparison of blacks and whites. Social Forces 73, 575–604.

McNulty, Thomas L., Bellair, Paul E., 2003a. Explaining racial and ethnic differences in adolescent violence: structural disadvantage, family well-being, and social capital. Justice Quarterly 20, 1–31.

McNulty, Thomas L., Bellair, Paul E., 2003b. Explaining racial and ethnic differences in serious adolescent violent behavior. Criminology 41, 709–748.

Messner, Steve F., Rosenfeld, Richard, 1994. Crime and the American Dream. Wadsworth Publishing Company, Belmont, CA.

Messner, Steve F., Sampson, Robert J., 1991. The sex ratio, family disruption, and rates of violent crime: the paradox of demographic structure. Social Forces 69, 693–713.

Nagin, Daniel S., Paternoster, Raymond, 1993. Enduring individual differences and rational choice theories of crime. Law and Society Review 27, 467–496.

Ousey, Graham C, 1999. Homicide, structural factors, and the racial invariance assumption. Criminology 37, 405–426.

Paschall, Mallie J., Ennett, Susan T., Flewelling, Robert L., 1996. Relationships among family characteristics and violent behavior by black and white male adolescents. Journal of Youth and Adolescence 25, 177–197.

Rose, Harold M., McClain, Paula D., 1998. Race, place, and risk revisited: a perspective on the emergence of a new structural paradigm. Homicide Studies 2, 101–129.

Rossi, Peter, Waite, Emily, Bose, Christine E., Berk, Richard E., 1974. The seriousness of crime: normative structure and individual differences. American Sociological Review 39, 224–237.

Rowe, David C, Vazsonyi, Alexander T., Flannery, Daniel J., 1994. No more than skin deep: ethnic and racial similarity in developmental processes. Psychological Review 101, 396–413.

Sampson, Robert, Lauritsen, Janet, 1994. Violent victimization and offending: individual-, situational-, and community-level risk factors in understanding and preventing violence. In: Reiss, Albert J., Roth, Jeffrey A. (Eds.), Social Influence, vol. 3. National Academy Press, Washington, DC, pp. 1–115.

Sampson, Robert J., Raudenbush, Stephen W., Felton, Earls, 1997. Neighborhoods and violent crime: a multilevel study of collective efficacy. Science 277, 918–924.

Sampson, Robert J., Wilson, William J., 1995. Toward a theory of race, crime, and urban inequality. In: Hagan, John, Peterson, R.D. (Eds.), Crime and Inequality. Stanford University Press, Stanford, CA.

Short, James, 1997. Poverty, Ethnicity, and Violent Crime. Boulder, CO, Westview.

Steadman, Henry, Felson, Richard B., 1984. Self-reports of violence: ex-mental patients, ex-offenders, and the general population. Criminology 22, 321–342.

Stinchcombe, Arthur L., 1968. Constructing Social Theories. University of Chicago Press, Chicago.

Tedeschi, James T., Felson, Richard B., 1994. Violence, Aggression, and Coercive Actions. American Psychological Association, Washington, DC.

Turner, Charles F., Ku, Leighton, Rogers, Susan M., Lindberg, Laura D., Pleck, Joseph H., Sonenstein, Freya L., 1998. Adolescent sexual behavior, drug use, and violence: increased reporting with computer survey technology. Science 280, 867–873.

Udry, J.R, 1998. The National Longitudinal Study of Adolescent Health (AddHealth), Waves I & II, 1994-1996 [machine-readable data file and documentation]. Chapel Hill, NC: Carolina Population Center, University of North Carolina at Chapel Hill.

Volkwein, Fredericks J., Szelest, Bruce P., Lizotte, Allen J., 1995. The relationship of campus crime to campus and student characteristics. Research in Higher Education 36, 647–670.

Wilson, William J., 1987. The Truly Disadvantaged: The Inner City, the Underclass, and Public Policy. University of Chicago Press, Chicago, IL.

Wolfgang, Marvin E., Robert M. Figlio, Paul E. Tracey, Simon I. Singer, 1985. The National Survey of Crime Severity. Washington D.C.: U.S. Department of Justice, Bureau of Justice Statistics.

Wolfgang, Marvin E., Ferracuti, Franco, 1967. The Subculture of Violence. Tavistock, London.

Zimring, Franklin, Hawkins, Gordon, 1997. Crime is not the Problem: Lethal Violence in America. Oxford University Press, New York.

DISCUSSION QUESTIONS

1. According to the authors, what type of theoretical explanations best explain race differences in offending when controlling for other demographic variables, such as gender and race?
2. Discuss how the limitations of this study could possibly affect the conclusions reached by the authors?
3. Do you think that the authors make a convincing argument for the need to distinguish between different Hispanic groups when studying crime and delinquency? If so, how can this obscure the results of previous studies conducted examining this relationship?

READING

In the early 1990s, building on Robert Merton's classic strain theory, Robert Agnew proposed his general strain theory—or the notion that there are more than economic strains that matter in influencing criminal offending. He suggested offending occurs because of the failure to achieve positively valued outcomes, the removal of positively valued outcomes, and the introduction of negative or noxious stimuli. By the early 2000s Agnew had refined his theory and included racial discrimination as a potential stressor that contributes to offending among African Americans. In this article, Kaufman and his collaborators (including Agnew) flesh out exactly how general strain theory can be used to better understand racial differences in criminal offending.

A General Strain Theory of Racial Differences in Criminal Offending

Joanne M. Kaufman, Cesar J. Rebellon, Sherod Thaxton, and Robert Agnew

Source: Kaufman, J. M., Rebellon, C. J., Thaxton, S., & Agnew, R. (2008). A general strain theory of racial differences in criminal offending. *The Australian and New Zealand Journal of Criminology, 41*(3), 421–437. Reprinted with permission of the authors.

Since the publication of Agnew's (1992) foundational paper on General Strain Theory (GST), GST has garnered much empirical support (see Agnew, 2006 for review). Scholars have further built on Agnew's foundation by applying GST's insights to several key correlates of crime including age, sex, community, school and the family (e.g., see Agnew, 2006, for review). Although a few recent empirical pieces have highlighted how greater exposure to certain types of serious strains may aid in explaining racial differences in criminal offending (Eitle & Turner, 2003; Kaufman, 2005; Simons, Chen, Stewart, & Brody, 2003), researchers have yet to fully extend GST to examine these differences.

While race is a social construct (Duster, 2003; Hawkins, 1996), scholars have long recognised its impact in various areas including poverty (DeNavas-Walt, Proctor, & Smith, 2007), discrimination (Feagin, 1991), mental health (Massey, 2004; Willie, Kramer, & Brown, 1974), educational attainment (Epps, 1995), family structure (Cherlin, 1992) and interpersonal victimisation (US Department of Justice, 2006). Criminologists, however, have constructed relatively little theory to explain racial differences in crime, and the major theories that address this topic are at the macro level. Although some recent researchers have explored contextual and multilevel models to empirically explain racial differences in offending (McNulty & Bellair, 2003a, 2003b; Sampson, Morenoff, & Raudenbush, 2005), these models have been driven by macro theorising with consideration of social capital and social control oriented processes at the individual level. We believe that individual level motivational processes contribute to a fuller explanation of the race–crime relationship and require explicit theorising.

In this article, we first assess racial differences in offending in the United States by reviewing the primary criminological data sources. Although our focus is on the United States, we believe that these ideas have implications for group differences in other contexts with racially diverse and indigenous populations, such as Australia and New Zealand. Because existing literature concerning racial differences in offending in the United States focuses almost exclusively on African Americans, we similarly limit our own focus. Second, we briefly discuss prior accounts of the race–crime relationship and how GST complements these theories. Third, we argue that African Americans experience more and qualitatively different types of strain than Whites, particularly those types of strain most conducive to crime, and that African Americans are more likely to cope with strain through crime.

Are There Racial Differences in Offending?

Three primary data sources in the US provide information on race and crime: arrest, victimisation and self-report data. African Americans have been disproportionately represented among arrestees in the US criminal justice system since the mid-19th century (Du Bois, 1899, 1904; Hawkins, 1995). Comprising close to 13% of the US population in 2006, African Americans accounted for 28% of all offence arrests and 39.3% of violent crime arrests, including 50.9% of homicide arrests and 56.3% of robbery arrests (US Department of Justice, 2007). Though discrimination may account for a portion of African American arrest statistics (see Walker, Spohn, & DeLone, 2000), criminologists generally argue that racial differences in arrests cannot be explained solely by discrimination (e.g., Hawkins, Laub, & Lauritsen, 1998; Hindelang, 1978; Sampson & Lauritsen, 1997).

The most recent National Crime Victimization Survey data indicate that victims perceived 25.3% of single offenders and 33.9% of offenders in multiple offender victimisations to be African American (US Department of Justice, 2006). Similar to arrest statistics, the percentage varied depending upon the crime, with offenders perceived as black in 47.7% of the robberies and 22% of the assaults (US Department of Justice, 2006). Although victims of crime may be incorrect in the assessment of race due to the stressful circumstances of the incident and the common stereotypes of offenders as people of colour, victimisation data parallel arrest data with African Americans being disproportionately represented as offenders.

While early self-report surveys did not reveal a significant relationship between race and crime (e.g., Elliott & Voss, 1974; Williams & Gold, 1972), more recent self-report studies demonstrate that African American and Hispanic youths are disproportionately prone to engage in serious violence (Kelley, Huizinga, Thornberry, & Loeber, 1997; Snyder & Sickmund, 2006). Given these three key data sources, criminologists should not ignore the evidence of racial differences in offending in the United States, particularly for crimes of interpersonal violence (Hawkins et al., 1998). There is also evidence of a similar relationship of disproportionate offending and victimisation among Black and indigenous populations in many advanced democracies such as Canada, New Zealand and Australia (Broadhurst, 1997; Doone, 2000; Tonry, 1997). This recognition does not negate the existence of discrimination at all levels of the criminal justice system, but it does support the utility of exploring theoretical explanations for racial disparities in offending.

How Have Prior Theories Explained Racial Differences?

Prior attempts to explain racial differences in offending have been primarily at the macro level and typically involve variants of either social disorganisation theory or subcultural violence theories. Social disorganisation research focuses on how structural barriers (e.g., poverty, residential mobility, single-parent households) impede social networks and the social control of crime, suggesting that African Americans engage in more crime than Whites because they are more likely to live in neighbourhoods with those characteristics (Sampson & Wilson, 1995). Recent researchers have expanded on this theory to consider contextual and multi-level processes whereby structural community measures and individual-level measures (demographic, social capital, social control) affect levels of individual violence (McNulty & Bellair, 2003a, 2003b; Sampson, Morenoff, & Raudenbush, 2005). While social disorganisation theory and the recent multi-level modelling strategies account for a significant portion of the racial differences in offending, they do not offer a complete explanation.

According to subcultural violence theories (e.g., Anderson, 1999; Wolfgang & Ferracuti, 1967), many urban Americans have embraced a system of values conducive to violence under certain circumstances, particularly overt challenges to individuals' reputations. Thus, the race–crime relationship stems from African Americans' disproportionate exposure to beliefs and values that condone violence in the pursuit of status maintenance. The evidence concerning subcultural theories is mixed (e.g., Cao, Adams, & Jensen, 1997; Felson, Liska, South, & McNulty, 1994). Recent researchers have considered how the structure of communities (from social disorganisation theory) may impact neighbourhood cultural processes that influence violence (see Anderson, 1999; Kubrin & Weitzer, 2003).

While we recognise the merits of the above theoretical research traditions, two factors may render them incomplete explanations of racial differences in offending. First, social disorganisation theory (and multi-level variants) does not provide adequate discussion of those motivational processes that may increase crime. Following Agnew (1999), we believe that complete explanations of crime in general, and of the race-crime relationship in particular, require a treatment of both those forces that serve to control *and* promote crime. Second, dominant explanations of racial differences in offending have only begun to link macro-level considerations to the individual level of analysis and have focused primarily on social control processes (e.g., McNulty & Bellair, 2003a, 2003b; Sampson et al., 2005). We believe, however, that the full influence of community-level variables can be best understood by explicitly examining their effects on multiple aspects of the lives of a community's individual residents (see Kaufman, 2005). Below, we discuss the ways in which GST may be able to address the above issues.

Can GST Help Explain Racial Differences in Offending?

General Strain Theory

GST is most clearly distinguished from competing crime theories by its assertion that negative experiences and relationships motivate and promote criminal behaviour. While control theorists would argue that African Americans are more prone to engage in violent crime because their bond to society is weaker than Whites (e.g., Hirschi, 1969), learning theorists would argue that African Americans are disproportionately prone to form positive relationships with violent peers (e.g., Akers, 1998). A GST explanation of racial differences in offending instead implies that African Americans experience disproportionate strain in the social environment and/or have fewer resources for coping with strain in conventional ways.

Agnew (1992) argues that crime may result from a broad range of strains: those resulting from an actual or anticipated (1) failure to achieve positively valued outcomes, (2) removal of positively valued outcomes and (3) imposition of negative or noxious stimuli. Agnew contends that each of these strains may result in negative emotions that trigger criminal behaviour aimed at lowering or eliminating strain. Strain, however, does not inevitably result in crime. Rather, the impact of strain is conditioned by a number of variables, including whether the strain is attributed to others, the extent of an individual's legitimate coping resources, the level of conventional social support and an individual's predisposition toward crime. Specifically, Agnew argues that individuals who attribute their strain to others are more likely to experience anger and react with crime. Likewise, those who possess significant cognitive, emotional and social coping resources may be better able to cope with strain in a noncriminal manner. Agnew further argues that individuals who are restrained by a high degree of social control (see Hirschi, 1969) or who do not associate with delinquent peers (see Akers, 1998) will be less prone to cope with strain through crime.

While preliminary tests indicate that many of the types of strain listed by Agnew are related to crime, more recent empirical tests highlight the fact that strain and anger have a strong impact on violence (see Agnew, 2006; Mazerolle & Piquero, 1997; Mazerolle, Burton, Cullen, Evans, & Payne, 2000). Given the promise of recent empirical research concerning GST, we believe GST merits investigation as an account of racial differences in offending.

Do African Americans Experience More/Different Strains?

Two major ways in which GST would explain higher levels of violence among African Americans is by arguing that African Americans experience more and qualitatively different types of strains than Whites, particularly those types of strain most conducive to crime. Agnew (2001) recently clarified GST by pointing out that strains are most conducive to crime when they are perceived as unjust (e.g., discrimination), seen as high in magnitude (e.g., excessive discipline, criminal victimisation), associated with low social control (e.g., erratic parental supervision of children) and create incentive or pressure to engage in criminal coping (e.g., work in the secondary labour market). We thus focus on areas of strains that reflect those four characteristics and are relevant to the study of race and crime: economic strain, family strain, educational strain, criminal victimisation, discrimination and community strain.

Economic Strain

African Americans are more likely than Whites to be poor, unemployed and employed in jobs in the secondary labour market (Conley, 2001; DeNavas-Walt, Proctor, & Smith, 2007; Gittleman & Wolff, 2004; Sullivan, 1989; US Department of Labor, 2008). While the relationship between economic strain and crime is complex (see Cernkovich, Giordano, & Rudolph, 2000; Tittle & Meier, 1990), some evidence suggests that severe poverty and chronic unemployment contribute to crime (Colvin, 2000; Massey, 1990). The same is true of work in the secondary labour market, with such work being characterised by low pay, few benefits, unsteady employment and poor working conditions, including low autonomy, high demands and coercive forms of control (Bausman & Goe, 2004; Colvin, 2000; Crutchfield, 1989). The greater economic strain experienced by African Americans may increase the likelihood of striking out at others or engaging in income-generating crime like robbery, the crime with the highest levels of disproportionate offending by African Americans (US Department of Justice, 2006, 2007).

It is important to note, however, that economic strain may be more likely to lead to crime in some conditions than others. Drawing on Agnew (1999), economic strain may be most conducive to crime when individuals are surrounded by advantaged others who are visible and perceived as similar. This is more likely under certain conditions, such as when high levels of inequality exist between and within neighbourhoods, and when economic returns to education vary greatly across individuals and groups (see Agnew, 1999, p. 135). Economic strain is more likely to be seen as unjust under such conditions and is therefore more likely to generate crime.

In addition, a GST account of racial differences in offending suggests that criminologists follow the lead of family researchers, who employ more sophisticated measures of economic strain than do most criminologists. In particular, while most criminological research measures economic strain using one- or two-item scales tapping primarily a family's overall income at one time point, family researchers employ more precise and dynamic measures of economic hardship including per capita family income, debt-to-asset ratio, demotion and job changes over the course of a given period (see Agnew, 2001; Conley, 1999; Oliver & Shapiro, 1995). Such measures may more precisely gauge those economic hardships most associated with dissatisfaction.

Family Strain

Though the family context is generally associated with control theories, GST has much to say about the family's impact on crime. Many types of parental strain (e.g., residence in high-poverty communities, economic hardship, work in the secondary labour market, divorce) increase the likelihood of poor parenting practices, such as harsh and inconsistent discipline (Agnew et al., 2000; Patterson & Forgatch, 1990; Patterson, Reid, & Dishion, 1992). These parenting practices, in turn, contribute to strain in children. Such strain leads directly to juvenile crime, or indirectly leads to crime by weakening the bonds between parents and children (Agnew et al., 2000; McLoyd, 1990; Patterson, 1982).

There is some evidence that African American parents display lower levels of warmth and use more inconsistent discipline with their children than White families (Pinderhughes, Nix, Foster, & Jones, 2001).

However, once researchers control for the neighbourhood context (levels of poverty, residential stability, public services, social networks and levels of danger), these racial differences in parenting practices disappear (Pinderhughes et al., 2001). This research demonstrates that what many researchers have assumed to be racial differences between family practices are really neighbourhood context differences. Since African Americans are much more likely to live in disadvantaged neighbourhoods (Sampson & Wilson, 1995), they are differentially exposed to various strains that may produce poorer parenting styles. While the extended family networks of many African American families may ameliorate some of these problems, these networks may also impede these families climbing out of poverty and leaving bad neighbourhoods (Cherlin, 1992). Thus, a GST explanation of racial differences in offending suggests that African American parents experience disproportionate strain that may impact their parenting. Such strained parents are likely to increase the probability of children experiencing various forms of strain, thus increasing the chances of delinquency.

Educational Strain

The educational context is another key area for examining African Americans' greater exposure to strain and qualitatively distinct types of strain. In the US schooling system, African Americans may experience a variety of problems including poor grades, unfair discipline, negative relations with teachers and interpersonal problems with other students. In mixed race schools, race may serve as a characteristic that determines whether an individual will be placed in a high or low educational track independent of the individual's academic ability (Irvine & York, 1993). Numerous scholars suggest that low tracks often provide qualitatively inferior curricula to students of disadvantaged or minority backgrounds (Epps, 1995; Oakes, 1985). If African American students perceive that their placement in lower tracks is unjust, that experience itself will likely serve as a strain (Agnew, 2001). Further, the often poorer quality education in those lower tracks mixed with teachers' lower expectations may additionally strain these students. Some teachers expect African American and lower class students to perform worse academically (Cooper & Moore, 1995), and teachers of a different race are significantly more likely than African American teachers to rate African American students as exhibiting problem behaviours (Zimmerman, Khoury, Vega, Gil, & Warheit, 1995). These teacher expectations likely impact interactions with African American students and contribute to further negative relations with both teachers and peers that may increase in magnitude over time.

African Americans are also more likely than Whites to attend racially segregated schools, especially in central cities and rural areas (Bankston III & Caldas, 1996; Kozol, 1991). Ample research demonstrates that schools with a large percentage of minority students have lower levels of achievement (Bankston III & Caldas, 1996), fewer resources for academics and therefore fewer quality teachers (Anyon, 1997; Kozol, 1991). In fact, Whites in primarily minority schools also do worse than their counterparts in majority White schools (Bankston III & Caldas, 1996). Thus, African Americans appear to experience more educational strain than their White counterparts and different types of educational strain that Whites never have the misfortune to experience. While these higher levels of educational strain are partly due to lower socioeconomic status, the experiences of educational strain and bad schools further engender the continuation of lower socioeconomic status among African Americans including work in the secondary labour market and the other economic strains outlined above.

Criminal Victimisation

In addition to economic, family and educational strains, African Americans are more likely than Whites to experience noxious stimuli like criminal victimisation. African Americans are victimised at a rate 37.3% higher than Whites for violent crimes (US Department of Justice, 2006) and account for 49.5% of murder and non-negligent manslaughter victims (US Department of Justice, 2007). In particular, African American youths between the ages of 12–19 are among the most vulnerable to serious violent crime (e.g., murder, rape, robbery etc.) with a victimisation rate 48% higher than White youth aged 12–19 (US Department of Justice, 2006), and 58% of African American murder victims are below the age of 30 (US Department of Justice, 2007). African American households are burglarised at a rate 22.4% higher than White households (US Department of Justice, 2006). These high levels of African American victimisation occur in both the nation's inner cities and in suburbia (Logan & Stults, 1999). Moreover, aside from experiencing more personal victimisation than Whites, African Americans are also more likely to experience vicarious strain via the victimisation of close friends and relatives. Youths who witness violence, particularly violence perpetrated against their friends or family, are at higher risk of victimising others (Attar, Guerra, & Tolan, 1994).

Since victimisation is among the most serious type of negative experience, it is highly likely to induce strain (Agnew, 2001; Brezina, 1998). It is also one of the types of strain most likely to engender a desire for retaliation and revenge, which offenders commonly report as the leading reasons for their own acts of violence (Agnew, 1990; Dawkins, 1997). While other research supports the strong association between victimisation and crime (e.g., Esbensen & Huizinga, 1991; Lauritsen, Sampson, & Laub, 1991), GST suggests that high rates of victimisation among African Americans can explain a portion of their disproportionate representation among violent offenders. Eitle and Turner (2003) and Kaufman (2005), using regional and national self-report data (respectively), provide evidence in support of this argument.

Discrimination

In addition to experiencing quantitatively more strain than Whites, African Americans may experience qualitatively unique forms of strain. While 36% of Whites reported experiencing at least one discriminatory event in their lifetime, 70% of African Americans reported such an experience (Forman, Williams, & Jackson, 1997). However, African Americans are not only more likely to experience discrimination, but are likely to experience it across a wide variety of situations including walking down the street, buying a house or car, seeking a job, eating at a restaurant, attending university and navigating many other everyday situations (Ayres & Siegelman, 1995; Farrell & Jones, 1988; Feagin, 1991; Forman et al., 1997; Kirschenman & Neckerman, 1991; Yinger, 1995). Often, these forms of discriminatory behaviour begin with children as young as age 3 (Van Ausdale & Feagin, 1996) and persist long after achieving middle-class status (Feagin, 1991). Agnew (2001) suggests that prejudice and discrimination may be among those strains most conducive to crime-provoking negative emotions, and research has linked aggregate discrimination at the macro level to homicide rates (Messner, 1989) and racial segregation to high rates of Black-on-Black crime (Messner & South, 1986; Shihadeh & Flynn, 1996). At the micro level, Simons et al. (2003) found that experiences of discrimination are positively associated with delinquency among African American youth.

African Americans also experience discrimination on the part of police officers and other law enforcement officials who are charged with protecting the social order (Miller, 1996). Parker, Onyekwuluje, and Murty (1995) found that African Americans living in high crime neighbourhoods in large cities have frequent contact with police but also have less favourable impressions of the police. African American college students often believe that police officers arbitrarily and disproportionately stop them on campus (Anderson, 1990). In addition, African Americans are more likely to be arrested if the victim of a given crime is White and case evidence is weak (Petersilia, 1983). Even African American children of prominent middle-class doctors and lawyers are disproportionately subject to police detention or arrest, net of delinquent behaviour (Miller, 1996). Further, African Americans are shot and killed by police much more frequently than Whites (Walker, Spohn, & DeLone, 2000).

Community Strain

Aside from their greater probability of experiencing strain at the individual level, African Americans are disproportionately prone to live in urban neighbourhoods characterised by high concentrations of economic disadvantage and high rates of violence (e.g., Krivo & Peterson, 1996; Massey, 1990; Shihadeh & Flynn, 1996). At present, the social disorganisation perspective dominates explanations of the relationships among urbanisation, concentrated economic disadvantage and community crime rates (e.g., Sampson & Wilson, 1995). However, recent empirical research suggests that indicators of social disorganisation (low participation in informal organisations and weak social network structures) do not explain the entire relationship between urbanisation and community crime rates (Veysey & Messner, 1999). GST may therefore offer several important insights that can supplement social disorganisation theory to better explain racial differences in offending at the macro level.

For example, GST suggests that urbanisation and concentrated disadvantage may be associated with a number of strains above and beyond those that result from economic strain at the individual level of analysis, such as strain resulting from the interaction of individuals who may already be angry as a result of their own personal economic and social situations. When two individuals already have a 'short fuse' as a result of individual-level strains, Agnew (1999) suggests that their interaction is likely to serve as a further strain for both parties, thereby amplifying the probability that even the slightest conflict will escalate. Luckenbill (1977), in fact, suggests that violence is often not the result of one motivated perpetrator's behaviour so much as it is the result of a motivated perpetrator interacting with a determined 'victim' whose resistance yields an escalation of conflict. To the degree that strain is responsible for the escalation of such conflict, GST predicts that African Americans, who are disproportionately prone to live in areas of concentrated disadvantage, will be disproportionately prone to engage in interpersonal violence.

In addition, GST suggests that concentrated populations of African Americans may evoke greater discriminatory treatment than do individual African Americans. Such treatment, particularly when attributed to specific others who act with intent, increases collective strain. Massey (1990) suggests that this may occur for African Americans more than for other ethnic groups in a self-fulfilling cycle of prejudice. Specifically, while Whites may benefit economically from discriminatory residential segregation, the resulting concentrations of African American poverty may serve to reinforce White beliefs about racial pathology among minority groups, in turn promoting further prejudice and discrimination (Massey, 1990). Moreover, research suggests that income inequality is associated with violent crime, particularly when the inequality is linked to race (e.g., Blau & Blau, 1982). GST provides a coherent framework in which these findings can be integrated, and suggests that future research test the degree to which negative emotions mediate the association between urban inequality and violent crime at the macro level.

Though less work has examined the effects of discriminatory community strain on African Americans in nonurban contexts, GST suggests that they too may experience disproportionate strain at the community level. In particular, African Americans may feel unwelcome in certain suburban neighbourhoods or may experience overt discrimination that prevents them from moving into certain neighbourhoods (Massey & Denton, 1988). Those African Americans who are able to move to the suburbs still experience higher levels of residential segregation than other ethnic groups (Massey & Denton, 1988). Researchers have yet to examine directly the implications of such findings for crime among suburban African Americans. Thus, in addition to supplementing a social disorganisation account of the race–crime relationship in inner cities, GST suggests avenues of research concerning race and crime in other geographic regions.

Are There Racial Differences in Reactions to Strain?

While the above discussion delineated the manner in which African Americans may experience disproportionate amounts of strain in the social environment, GST makes further predictions concerning racial differences in offending. GST argues that African Americans are more likely to react to a given strain with crime than Whites because they are more likely to experience such strain as stressful or upsetting and are more likely to view it as unjust.

Currently, only limited research examines emotional experience and expression among Africans Americans. To cite one example, Armstead, Lawler, Gorden, Cross, and Gibbons (1989) measured the blood pressure, anger experience and anger expression of African American college students after viewing videos showing anger-provoking nonracist situations, racist situations involving African Americans and neutral situations. Although respondents reported significant anger experience for both the nonracist anger-provoking situation and the racist situation, respondents' blood pressure increased significantly only after viewing the portrayals of racism.

Research also suggests that African Americans experience a greater sense of overall alienation than do other racial/ethnic groups in the United States even when they experience personal economic success (Bobo & Hutchings, 1996; Cose, 1993). Bobo and Hutchings (1996), in fact, find that African Americans' alienation *increases* as their socioeconomic status increases and that African Americans feel more threatened than other racial/ethnic groups by interracial competition for socioeconomic resources. While increases in socioeconomic status are likely to protect Whites from many negative experiences, African Americans often do not see those benefits, such that well-off African Americans still experience discrimination and are at higher risk of victimisation than comparable Whites (Feagin, 1991; Logan & Stults, 1999). Such experiences and the resultant negative emotions may be exacerbated when young African Americans perceive a given instance of deprivation to be based on discriminatory, prejudiced or otherwise unjust circumstances (Brown, 1998). In sum, limited research suggests that African Americans, perhaps by virtue of their traditional marginalisation, experience more *subjective* strain than members of other groups when confronted with the same objective stimuli, and may be more likely to react with anger.

Cognitive Attributions

Agnew (1992) suggests that the link between strain and crime depends, in part, on how an individual chooses to interpret strain. If a young male loses a job and believes the loss to be the just result of his own behaviour, such strain may not contribute to a criminal response. However, if he believes the lost job to be the unjust result of racial discrimination, he may become more motivated to cheat a system or society that he perceives to be inequitable. In addition, an individual's cognitive attributions may direct the valence of general emotional arousal such that the same generalised arousal could produce either anger or amusement, depending on the behaviour of a subject's peers (Schachter & Singer, 1962). Similarly, Bernard (1990) suggests that the unique position of disadvantaged inner city African Americans promotes arousal that they will likely attribute to aggressive anger (also see Anderson, 1999). Thus, GST predicts that African Americans, more often than Whites, attribute failures and negative life experiences to unjust situational factors.

Coping Resources and Social Support

Agnew (1992) also claims that social support and coping resources, such as problem-solving skills, self-esteem, and self-efficacy, condition the impact of strain on crime. According to GST, criminal behaviour results from a high ratio of strain to coping resources, rather than from strain alone. While African Americans report higher levels of self-esteem and self-efficacy than their White peers (Tashakkori & Thompson, 1991), the disadvantaged status of many African Americans may provide them with fewer resources for coping with strain in legitimate ways. For example, research suggests that parents of low socioeconomic status are less likely to promote self-directed problem-solving ability in their children (see Gecas, 1979), and that individuals of low education and income are less likely to possess good stress management skills (Pearlin & Schooler, 1978). Thus, while African American youth are strengthened by higher levels of self-esteem and self-efficacy, they may be hindered by insufficient problem-solving and stress management skills.

In addition to experiencing fewer personal resources for handling strain, African Americans may experience less social support in their families. For example, though 58% of African American youths lived in two-parent homes in 1970, a mere 38% lived in two-parent homes by 1990 (O'Hare, Pollard, Mann, & Kent, 1991). While African Americans have traditionally relied on extended families for social support to a greater degree than Whites (Cherlin, 1992), even those networks have been strained by the changing economic conditions in many cities in the United States from the 1970s onward that have produced pockets of concentrated, disadvantaged African Americans with little access to jobs and services and with higher rates of female-headed households (Massey, 1990; Wilson, 1978, 1987). To the degree that urban African American youth grow up in single-parent families (see Sampson, 1987) or lack extended family in the inner city (see Wilson, 1987), they may experience diminished social support networks with which to handle strain via noncriminal means.

Beliefs and Values Conducive to Crime

GST suggests that strain is most likely to promote crime/violence among groups that hold values conducive to crime and violence, such as those embodied in the 'code of the street' (Anderson, 1999). Likewise, GST suggests that strain at the macro level may account for the origin of these values. Several researchers, for example, argue that many African American males find it difficult to achieve a masculine identity through legitimate channels. This is especially true of males in poor, inner-city communities where decent work is exceedingly scarce. As a consequence, such males may attempt to achieve a masculine identity through illegitimate channels, like aggression (Anderson, 1999; Sampson & Wilson, 1995; Staples, 1982; Wilson, 1996). Following Agnew (1992), we suggest that strain is particularly conducive to crime among individuals who value physical toughness and associate with others who reinforce such values.

Conclusions

Racial differences in offending have been widely documented but seldom explained. While most explanations focus on social control processes at the macro level (e.g., Sampson & Wilson, 1995) and have begun to link the macro and micro contexts (e.g., Sampson et al., 2005), empirical research has yet to find that such theories account for the entire race–crime relationship. GST, however, suggests an additional and complementary explanation that highlights the importance of emotional and motivational social psychological processes. GST argues that African Americans experience more and qualitatively unique types of strain than Whites, thus engendering more negative emotions. Further, it suggests that African Americans are especially prone to cope with those emotions through crime under certain conditions.

In particular, we argue that African Americans may experience a variety of disproportionate economic strains, but that only certain of these strains are likely to be associated with crime. We suggest that economic strain may impede consistent and effective parenting, and that family problems not only decrease social control but also increase juvenile strain. In addition, we suggest that African Americans are more likely than Whites to have negative educational experiences, experience criminal victimisation, experience discrimination and suffer from community strain. Finally, we propose that African Americans may not only experience greater objective strain than Whites, but also react to the same objective strain with greater negative emotion. In particular, we point to conditions (low social support, inadequate problem-solving skills) under which African Americans might be disproportionately prone to cope with strain via criminal behaviour. We argue that GST has much to say about racial differences in offending and fills an important theoretical gap in the current literature. Finally, each of these contributions can guide future empirical research concerning racial differences in offending.

While this article offers important theoretical insight into explaining racial differences in offending, our focus has been limited to African American and White comparisons in the US context (similar to most literature on race and crime in the United States). Other scholars, however, have considered some of these issues for other races and ethnicity in the US context (see Kaufman, 2005; McNulty & Bellair, 2003a, 2003b), and this is an important area for future theoretical development and empirical research. There is also good reason to believe that many of these insights may be extended to racial differences in offending in other countries. Researchers have noted that some minority groups, especially Black and indigenous peoples, are overrepresented as crime victims and offenders in the criminal justice systems of many advanced democracies including Canada, England, France, the Netherlands, Australia and New Zealand (Broadhurst, 1997; Doone, 2000; Tonry, 1997). In particular, these issues are likely relevant for studies of the Aboriginal and Torres Strait Islander peoples of Australia and the Maori of New Zealand. Future research should explore extending the application of strain to racial differences in offending in other countries and contexts with a sensitivity toward important historical, cultural, and governmental differences.

References

Agnew, R. (1990). Origins of delinquent events: An examination of offender accounts. *Journal of Research in Crime and Delinquency, 27,* 267–294.

Agnew, R. (1992). Foundation for a general strain theory of crime and delinquency. *Criminology,* 30, 47–87.

Agnew, R. (1999). A general strain theory of community differences in crime rates. *Journal of Research in Crime and Delinquency, 36,* 123–155.

Agnew, R. (2001). Building on the foundation of general strain theory. Journal of *Research in* Crime and Delinquency, 38, 319-361.

Agnew, R. (2006). General strain theory: Current status and directions for further research. In F.T. Cullen, J.P. Wright, & K.R. Blevins (Eds.), *Taking stock: The status of criminological theory, advances in criminological theory* (Vol. 15, pp. 101–123). New Brunswick, NJ: Transaction Publishers.

Agnew, R., Rebellon, C.J., & Thaxton, S. (2000). A general strain theory approach to families and delinquency. In G.L. Fox and M.L. Benson (Eds.), *Families, crime and criminal justice: Contemporary perspectives in family research* (Vol. 2) (pp. 113–138). New York, NY: JAI.

Akers, R.L. (1998). *Social learning and social structure: A general theory of crime and deviance.* Boston, MA: Northeastern University Press.

Anderson, E. (1990). *Streetwise: Race, class, and change in an urban community.* Chicago: University of Chicago Press.

Anderson, E. (1999). *Code of the street.* New York: W.W. Norton and Company.

Anyon, J. (1997). *Ghetto schooling: A political economy of urban educational reform.* New York: Teachers College Press.

Armstead, C.A., Lawler, K.A., Gorden, G., Cross, J., & Gibbons, J. (1989). Relationship of racial stressors to blood pressure responses and anger expression in Black college students. *Health Psychology, 8,* 541–556.

Attar, B.K., Guerra, N.G., & Tolan, P.H. (1994). Neighborhood disadvantage, stressful life events, and adjustment in urban elementary-school children. *Journal of Clinical Child Psychology, 23,* 391–400.

Ayres, I., & Siegelman, P. (1995). Race and gender discrimination in bargaining for a new car. *American Economic Review, 85,* 304–321.

Bankston III, C., & Caldas, S.J. (1996). Majority African American schools and social injustice. *Social Forces, 75,* 535–555.

Bausman, K., & Goe, R.W (2004). An examination of the link between employment volatility and the spatial distribution of property crime rates. *American Journal of Economics and Sociology, 63,* 665–695.

Bernard, T.J. (1990). Angry aggression among the truly disadvantaged. *Criminology, 28,* 73–96.

Blau, J., & Blau, P. (1982). The cost of inequality: Metropolitan structure and violent crime. *American Sociological Review, 47,* 114–129.

Bobo, L., & Hutchings, V.L (1996). Perceptions of racial group competition. *American Sociological Review, 61,* 951–972.

Brezina, T. (1998). Adolescent maltreatment and delinquency: The question of intervening processes. *Journal of Research in Crime and Delinquency,* 35, 71–99.

Broadhurst, R. (1997). Aborigines and crime in Australia. In M. Tonry (Ed.). *Ethnicity, crime, and immigration: Comparative and cross-national perspectives* (pp. 407–468). Chicago: University of Chicago Press.

Brown, W.B. (1998). African American gang members and their families in a segregated society. *Juvenile and Family Court Journal, 49,* 1–14.

Cao, L., Adams, A., & Jensen, V.J. (1997). A test of the Black subculture of violence thesis: A research note. *Criminology, 35,* 367–379.

Cernkovich, S.A., Giordano, P.C., & Rudolph, J.L. (2000). Race, crime, and the American dream. *Journal of Research in Crime and Delinquency, 37,* 131–170.

Cherlin, A.J. (1992). *Marriage, divorce, remarriage.* Cambridge, MA: Harvard University Press.

Colvin, M. (2000). *Crime and coercion: An integrated theory of chronic criminality.* New York, NY: St. Martin's Press.

Conley, D. (1999). *Being Black, living in the red: Race, wealth, and social policy in America.* Berkeley, CA: University of California Press.

Conley, D. (2001). Decomposing the Black-White wealth gap: The role for parental resources, inheritance, and investment dynamics. *Sociological Inquiry, 71,* 39–66.

Cooper, H., & Moore, C.J. (1995). Teenage motherhood, mother-only households, and teacher expectations. *The Journal of Experimental Education, 63,* 231–248.

Cose, E. (1993). *The rage of a privileged class.* New York: Harper-Collins.

Crutchfield, R.D. (1989). Labor stratification and violent crime. *Social Forces, 68,* 489–512.

Dawkins, N. (1997). 'Striking back': An empirical test of the impact of victimization on violent crime. Paper presented at the annual meeting of the American Society of Criminology, November, San Diego, CA.

DeNavas-Walt, C., Proctor, B.D., &. Smith, J., U.S. Census Bureau. (2007). Current Population Reports, Series P60–233, *Income, poverty and health insurance coverage in the United States: 2006.* U.S. Government Printing Office, Washington, DC.

Doone, P. (2000). *Report on combating and preventing Maori crime.* Crime Prevention Unit, New Zealand Ministry of Justice. Retrieved September 3, 2008, from: http://www.justice.govt.nz/pubs/reports/2000/doone_rpt/index. html

Du Bois, W.E.B. (1899). *The Philadelphia Negro: A Social Study.* New York, NY: Benjamin Blom.

Du Bois, W.E.B. (1968). *Some notes on Negro crime, particularly in Georgia.* Atlanta, GA: Atlanta University. (Original work published 1904)

Duster, T. (2003). Buried alive: The concept of race in science. In A.H. Goodman, D. Heath, and M.S. Lindee (Eds.), *Generic nature/culture: Anthropology and science beyond the two-culture divide* (pp. 258–277). Berkeley, CA: University of California Press.

Eitle, D., & Turner, R.J. (2003). Stress exposure, race, and young adult male crime. *The Sociological Quarterly, 44,* 243–269.

Elliott, D.S., & Voss, H. (1974). *Delinquency and Dropout.* Lexington, MA: D.C. Health.

Epps, E.G. (1995). Race, class, and educational opportunity. *Sociological Forum, 10,* 593–608.

Esbensen, F., & Huizinga, D. (1991). Juvenile victimization and delinquency. *Youth and Society, 23,* 202–228.

Farrell, W.C., & Jones, C.K. (1988). Recent racial incidents in higher education. *The Urban Review,* 20, 211–226.

Feagin, J.R. (1991). The continuing significance of race: Antiblack discrimination in public places. *American Sociological Review, 56,* 101–116.

Felson, R.B., Liska, A.E., South, S.J., & McNulty, T.L (1994). The subculture of violence and delinquency: Individual vs. school context effects. *Social Forces, 73,* 155–173.

Forman, T.A., Williams, D.R., & Jackson, J.S. (1997). Race, place, and discrimination. *Perspectives on Social Problems, 9,* 231–261.

Gecas, V. (1979). The influence of social class on socialization. In W.R. Burr, R. Hill, F.I. Nye, & I.L. Reiss (Eds.), *Contemporary Theories about the Family* (Vol. 1, pp. 365–404). New York: Free Press.

Gittleman, M., & Wolff, E.N. (2004). Racial differences in patterns of wealth accumulation. *Journal of Human Resources, 39,* 193–227.

Hawkins, D.F. (1995). *Ethnicity, race, and crime: Perspectives across time and place.* Albany, NY: SUNY Press.

Hawkins, D.F. (1996). *Ethnicity, race, class, and adolescent violence.* Paper No. 006 from the Center for the Study and Prevention of Violence, University of Colorado, Boulder.

Hawkins, D.E, Laub, J.H., & Lauritsen, J.L. (1998). Race, ethnicity, and serious juvenile offending. In R. Loeber & D.P. Farrington (Eds.), *Serious and violent juvenile offenders* (pp. 30–46). Thousand Oaks, CA: Sage.

Hindelang, M.J. (1978). Race and involvement in common law personal crimes. American *Sociological Review,* 43, 775–805.

Hirschi, T. (1969). The *causes of delinquency.* Berkley, CA: University of California.

Irvine, J., & York, D.E. (1993). Teacher perspectives. In S.W. Rothstein (Ed.), *Handbook of* schooling in urban America (pp. 161–173). Westport, CT: Greenwood Press.

Kaufman, J.M. (2005). Explaining the race/ethnicity–violence relationship: Neighborhood context and social psychological processes. *Justice Quarterly,* 22, 224–251.

Kelley, B.T, Huizinga, D., Thornberry, T.P., & Loeber, R. (1997). Epidemiology of serious violence. *Juvenile Justice Bulletin,* Office of Juvenile Justice and Delinquency Prevention, June 1–11.

Kirschenman, J., & Neckerman, K. (1991). We'd love to hire them, but. In C. Jencks & P.E. Peterson (Eds.), *The urban underclass* (pp. 203–232). Washington, DC: Brookings Institution.

Kozol, J. (1991). *Savage inequalities: Children in America's schools.* New York: Harper Perennial.

Krivo, L.J., & Peterson, R.D. (1996). Extremely disadvantaged neighborhoods and urban crime. *Social Forces, 75,* 619–650.

Kubrin, C.E., & Weitzer, R. (2003). Retaliatory homicide: Concentrated disadvantage and neighborhood culture. *Social Problems, 50,* 157–180.

Lauritsen, J.L., Sampson, R.J., & Laub, J.H. (1991). The link between offending and victimization among adolescents. *Criminology, 29,* 265–292.

Logan, J.R., & Stults, B.J. (1999). Racial differences in exposure to crime: The city and suburbs of Cleveland in 1990. *Criminology, 37,* 251–276.

Luckenbill, D.F. (1977). Homicide as a situated transaction. *Social Problems,* 25, 176–186.

Massey, D.S. (1990). American apartheid: Segregation and the making of the underclass. *American Journal of Sociology, 96,* 329–357.

Massey, D.S. (2004). Segregation and stratification: A biosocial perspective. *Du Bois Review, 1,* 7–25.

Massey, D.S., & Denton, N.A. (1988). Suburbanization and segregation in U.S. metropolitan areas. *American Journal of Sociology, 94,* 592–626.

Mazerolle, P., Burton, Jr., V.S., Cullen, F.T., Evans, T.D., & Payne, G.L. (2000). Strain, anger, and delinquency adaptations. *Journal of Criminal Justice, 28,* 89–101.

Mazerolle, P., & Piquero, A. (1997). Violent responses to strain. *Violence and Victims, 12, 323–* 343.

McLoyd, V.C. (1990). The impact of economic hardship on Black families and children. *Child Development, 61,* 311–346.

McNulty, T.L., & Bellair, P.E. (2003a). Explaining racial and ethnic differences in adolescent violence: Structural disadvantage, family well-being, and social capital. *Justice Quarterly, 20,* 1–27.

McNulty, T.L., & Bellair, P.E. (2003b). Explaining racial and ethnic differences in serious adolescent violent behavior. *Criminology, 41,* 709–748.

Messner, S.F (1989). Economic discrimination and societal homicide rates: Further evidence on the cost of inequality. *American Sociological Review, 54,* 597–611.

Messner, S.F, & South, S.J. (1986). Economic deprivation, opportunity structure, and robbery victimization: Intra- and inter-racial patterns. *Social Forces,* 64, 975–991.

Miller, J.G. (1996). *Search and destroy. African American males in the criminal justice system.* New York: Cambridge University Press.

Oakes, J. (1985). *Keeping track: How schools structure inequality.* New Haven, CT: Yale University.

O'Hare, W.P, Pollard, K.M., Mann, T.L, & Kent, M.M. (1991). African Americans in the 1990s. *Population Bulletin, 46.1.* Washington, DC: Population Reference Bureau, Inc.

Oliver, M.L., & Shapiro, T.M. (1995). *Black wealth/ White wealth: A new perspective on racial inequality.* New York: Routledge.

Parker, K.D., Onyekwuluje, A.B., & Murty, K.S. (1995). African Americans' attitudes toward the local police. *Journal of Black Studies,* 25, 396–409.

Patterson, G.R. (1982). *Coercive family practices.* Eugene, OR: Castalia Press.

Patterson, G.R., & Forgatch, M.S. (1990). Initiation and maintenance of process disrupting single-mother families. In G.R. Patterson (Ed.), *Depression and aggression in family interaction* (pp. 209–246). Hillsdale, NJ: Lawrence Erlbaum Associates.

Patterson, G.R., Reid, J.B., & Dishion, T.J. (1992). *Antisocial boys.* Eugene, OR: Castalia Press.

Pearlin, L.I., & Schooler, C. (1978). The structure of coping. *Journal of Health and Social Behavior, 19,* 2–21.

Petersilia, J. (1983). *Racial disparities in the criminal justice system.* Santa Monica, CA: Rand.

Pinderhughes, E.E., Nix, R., Foster, E.M., & Jones, D. (2001). Parenting in context. *Journal of Marriage and Family, 63,* 941–953.

Sampson, R.J. (1987). Urban black violence. *American Journal of Sociology,* 93, 348–382.

Sampson, R.J., & Lauritsen, J.L. (1997). Racial and ethnic disparities in crime and criminal justice in the United States. In M. Tonry (Ed.), *Ethnicity, crime, and immigration: Comparative and cross-national perspectives* (pp. 311–374). Chicago: University of Chicago Press.

Sampson, R.J., & Wilson, W.J. (1995). Toward a theory of race, crime, and urban inequality. In J. Hagan & R. Peterson (Eds.), *Crime and inequality* (pp. 37-54). Stanford, CA: Stanford University Press.

Sampson, R.J., Morenoff, J.D., & Raudenbush, S. (2005). Social anatomy of racial and ethnic disparities in violence. *American Journal of Public Health, 95,* 224–232.

Schachter, S., & Singer, J.E. (1962). Cognitive, social, and physiological determinants of emotional state. *Psychological Review, 69,* 379–399.

Shihadeh, E.S., & Flynn, N. (1996). Segregation and crime. *Social Forces, 74,* 1325–1352.

Simons, R.L., Chen, Y., Stewart, E.A., & Brody, G.H. (2003). Incidents of discrimination and risk for delinquency: A longitudinal test of strain theory with an African American sample. *Justice Quarterly, 20,* 827–854.

Snyder, H., & Sickmund, M. (2006). *Juvenile offenders and victims: 2006 national report.* Washington, DC: US Department of Justice, Office of Justice Programs, Office of Juvenile Justice and Delinquency Prevention.

Staples, R. (1982). *Black masculinity: The Black male's role in American society.* San Francisco: Black Scholar Press.

Sullivan, M.L. (1989). *'Getting paid': Youth crime and work in the inner city.* Ithaca, NY: Cornell University Press.

Tashakkori, A., &. Thompson, V.D. (1991). Race differences in self-perception and locus of control during adolescence and early adulthood: Methodological implications. *Genetic, Social, and General Psychology Monographs, 117,*133–152.

Tittle, C.R., & Meier, R.F. (1990). Specifying the SES/ delinquency relationship. *Criminology, 28,* 271–299.

Tonry, M. (1997). Ethnicity, crime, and immigration. In M. Tonry (Ed.), *Ethnicity, crime, and immigration: Comparative and cross-national perspectives* (pp. 1–29). Chicago: University of Chicago Press.

U.S. Department of Justice. (2006). *Criminal victimization in the United States 2005: Statistical tables.* NCJ-215244. Retrieved August 1, 2008, from: http://www.ojp.usdoj.gov/bjs/pub/pdf/cvus05.pdf

U.S. Department of Justice. (2007). *Crime in the United States, 2006.* Federal Bureau of Investigation. Retrieved August 1, 2008, from: http://www.fbi.gov/ucr/cius2006/arrests/index.html

U.S. Department of Labor. (2008). *Employment & Earnings,* April 2008, Vol 55, No. 4. Bureau of Labor Statistics. Retrieved August 4, 2008, from: http://www.bls.gov/opub/ee/empearn200804.pdf

Van Ausdale, D., & Feagin, J.R. (1996). Using racial and ethnic concepts: The critical case of very young children. *American Sociological Review, 61,* 779–793.

Veysey, B.M., &. Messner, S.F. (1999). Further testing of social disorganization theory. *Journal of Research in Crime and Delinquency, 36,* 156–174.

Walker, S., Spohn, C., DeLone, M. (2000). *The color of justice: Race, ethnicity, and crime in America* (2nd ed.). Belmont, CA: Wadsworth.

Williams, J.R., & Gold, M. (1972). From delinquent behavior to official delinquency. *Social Problems, 20,* 209–229.

Willie, C.V., Kramer, B.M., & Brown, B.S. (Eds.). (1974). *Racism and mental health.* Pittsburgh, PA: University of Pittsburgh Press.

Wilson, W.J. (1978). *The declining significance of race.* Chicago: University of Chicago.

Wilson, W.J. (1987). *The truly disadvantaged.* Chicago: University of Chicago.

Wilson, W.J. (1996). *When work disappears.* New York: Knopf.

Wolfgang, M.E., & Ferracuti, F. (1967). *The subculture of violence.* New York: Tavistock.

Yinger, J. (1995). *Closed doors, opportunities lost: The continuing costs of housing discrimination.* New York, NY: Russell Sage Foundation.

Zimmerman, R.S., Khoury, E.L., Vega, W.A., Gil, A.G., & Warheit, G.J. (1995). Teacher and parent perceptions of behavior problems among a sample of African American, Hispanic, and Non-Hispanic White students. *American Journal of Community Psychology, 23,* 181–197.

DISCUSSION QUESTIONS

1. According to the authors, what factors are considered critical in general strain theory that are not discussed in previous criminological theories, such as social disorganization theory?

2. Based on the arguments made by the authors, do you believe that general strain theory provides the best explanation for racial differences in offending? Why or why not?

3. Agnew (1992) argued that strain causes a person to feel negative emotions, which in turn can result in that person turning to crime in order to alleviate the strain. Taking into account the general strain theory framework, what type of programs could be put in place to reduce strain and negative emotions or to both reduce or prevent offending?

READING

In this article, Unnever and his colleagues revisit the classic research of Travis Hirschi. In doing so, they uncover findings that tell another story than the one told in *Causes of Delinquency* (1969). The authors suggest that Hirschi overlooked important findings related to race. In fact, they found that perceived discrimination was a predictor of delinquency. Going further, the authors argue that racial animus has long been present in the criminological literature as a potential correlate of crime. However, early minority theorists such as W. E. B. Du Bois who spoke of such connections received little attention from criminological theorists then or now. Nonetheless, the authors provide an argument for the discipline to consider the role of racial discrimination in offending among African Americans.

Racial Discrimination and Hirschi's Criminological Classic

A Chapter in the Sociology of Knowledge

James D. Unnever, Francis T. Cullen, Scott A. Mathers, Timothy E. McClure, and Marisa C. Allison

Not long ago, we were rummaging around in the Richmond Youth Project data set—kindly supplied by Travis Hirschi—that was used as the basis of Hirschi's (1969) criminological classic, *Causes of Delinquency*. We approached this adventure with no clear agenda, but we were aware that these data contained extensive measures of the "lived reality" of African Americans, including perceived racial discrimination. Because we were familiar with recent theory and research suggesting that these perceptions comprised a criminogenic risk factor, we wondered whether this also was true empirically for African American youths in the Richmond Youth Project data. Much like archaeologists digging into the past, we thus embarked on an expedition exploring this site of historic theoretical development in criminology.

Here we tell the story of what we discovered. This tale is framed within the sociology of knowledge. As Cole (1975) notes, science was once understood as an enterprise in which knowledge was produced in a steady march toward the unraveling of objective truth. Kuhn's (1962) *The Structure of Scientific Revolutions* challenged this view of steady scientific progress, arguing instead that science is marked by a succession of paradigms that rule until their collapse and replacement. Whether Kuhn's theory accurately describes the development of science, let alone the development of social sciences, such as criminology, is open to dispute (see, e.g., Lakatos & Musgrave, 1970). Regardless, his challenge to the traditional perspective opened up a floodgate of interest in documenting how the growth of knowledge is affected not only by the internal

Source: Unnever, J. D., Cullen, F. T., Mathers, S. A., McClure, T. E., & Allison, M. C. (2009). Racial discrimination and Hirschi's criminological classic: A chapter in the sociology of knowledge. *Justice Quarterly, 26,* 377–409.

dynamics of a field's ideas but also by the social organization of a discipline and by the intersection of biography with the prevailing social context (Cole, 1975; see, e.g., Gouldner, 1970; Lilly, Cullen, & Ball, 2006). In the end, a field's development is not ineluctable but socially constructed by the choices that scholars make. Topics are studied and advanced or are ignored and languish on the research vine; turning points are made or not made (see, e.g., Cullen, 2005; Laub, 2004).

Our story, then, is about a criminological road that was not taken—a turning point that might have been but, because it did not occur, impoverished our understanding of crime. There are four parts to this chapter in the sociology of knowledge. First, we revisit *Causes of Delinquency.* Using the Richmond Youth Project data, and by closely reproducing Hirschi's original analysis (albeit with multivariate techniques), we show that perceived racial discrimination is a robust predictor of delinquency. Based on more recent studies using rigorous research designs, we suggest that this finding is not idiosyncratic or due to the cross-sectional nature of Hirschi's data. It is a real effect that was not identified.

Second, this finding leads us to probe why Hirschi did not discover this relationship in his data. Importantly—and we want to be very clear on this point—we argue that unlike theorists whose racial bias shaped their science (Bruinius, 2006; Gould, 1981), Hirschi's blind spot with regard to discrimination was *not* tied to any racial animus. In fact, in *Causes of Delinquency,* he considered the possibility that racial discrimination might be criminogenic. However, this analysis, and his selection of some survey items from the Richmond Youth Project but not others, was guided by his effort to falsify Cloward and Ohlin's (1960) version of strain theory and to show the empirical vitality of his social bond theory. This narrow theoretical agenda thus limited the content of his analysis and made further probing of his data ostensibly theoretically irrelevant.

Third, we contend that Hirschi's omission was consequential for criminology. It is speculative, of course, to contemplate "what might have been" had Hirschi trumpeted in 1969 the finding that perceived racial discrimination places African American youth at risk for engaging in crime. Still, the late 1960s and early 1970s comprised a social context in which this message might well have fallen on receptive ears and inspired an important research agenda. Further, had Hirschi given this finding focused attention—as opposed to arguing that the causes of crime are general and not race specific—others would likely have paid attention. Over the past four decades, Hirschi has exerted a remarkable influence on criminological thinking and in defining research questions. During this period, he has been one of the most cited scholars in criminology (Cohn & Farrington, 2007; Cohn, Farrington, & Wright, 1998; Laub, 2002). His theoretical ideas are a staple of crime theory texts (see, e.g., Akers & Sellers, 2004; Cao, 2003; Lilly et al., 2006) and have generated a wealth of empirical investigations (Gottfredson, 2006; Kempf, 1993; Kubrin, Stucky, & Krohn, 2009; Pratt & Cullen, 2000). In recent years, Hirschi's self-control theory—a perspective introduced in 1990 with Michael Gottfredson—has earned much attention (Gottfredson, 2006; Pratt & Cullen, 2000; see also Taylor, 2001). But the ascendancy of this version of control theory has not undermined the continued vitality of social bond theory, which Hirschi set forth in 1969 in *Causes of Delinquency* (see, e.g., Sampson & Laub, 1993). Indeed, this book's enduring influence has earned it the status of a criminological classic.

Fourth and perhaps most important, we note that beyond Hirschi and "what might have been," criminologists collectively ignored the possible criminogenic effects of racial discrimination until very recently. Hirschi was hardly alone in his limited interest in racial discrimination as a cause of delinquency; a generation of criminologists shares this stunning oversight. Indeed, despite residing in a discipline that investigates the impact of race in other areas and whose professional ideology is progressive if not "politically correct," criminologists—including those who reanalyzed the Richmond Youth Project data—strangely ignored this topic in the decades following the publication of *Causes of Delinquency.* As Agnew (2006a, p. 74) observes, although "discrimination based on race . . . is quite common in the United States," scholars have "not devoted much attention to the effects of discrimination on individual offending." In the discussion section, we return to this problem, commenting on how interest in the impact of racial discrimination on offending was likely deflected by strategic approaches to theory testing and by the social composition of the field of criminology that led to the "lived reality" of African Americans being ignored. The broader point, of course, is that the impact of perceived racial discrimination should receive more systematic investigation in the time ahead.

In short, there are factors that shape how individual scholars develop, test, and modify criminological theory—factors that often remain unknown to authors and their contemporaries. Within a sociology of knowledge framework, we thus undertake to illuminate the trajectory of one strand of theoretical development that, within control theory and criminology more generally, was knifed off and remained latent until recently. Toward this end, in the pages immediately below and as a prelude to presenting a reanalysis of Hirschi's data set, we first revisit his efforts to falsify strain theory and assess how this shaped his conclusions on racial discrimination. We then review how we were drawn to this project and how recent developments in criminology have guided our efforts.

Revisiting *Causes of Delinquency*

Attacking Strain Theory

A second line of inquiry, however, was more compelling. Hirschi (1969, pp. 172–173) showed that high aspirations were invariably related to lower levels of delinquency and, notably, that low aspirations were a source of misconduct. This finding was contrary to strain theory's prediction that delinquency would occur only when high aspirations or success goals were present (albeit when they were blocked). Hirschi suggested that aspirations were a source of commitment that tied youngsters to the conventional order. Their presence prevented crime, whereas their absence fostered crime.

Examining Racial Discrimination

It was within this theoretical context that Hirschi subsequently addressed the issue of the potential effects of racial discrimination. In *Delinquency and Opportunity,* Cloward and Ohlin (1960, p. 113) argued that delinquency was more likely when youths experienced "unjust deprivation." A process of alienation would set in because "unjust deprivation can play a significant role in the withdrawal of attributions of legitimacy from official norms" (p. 117). Minority youths were particularly likely to develop unjust sentiments because they suffer "from discrimination" (p. 118). Indeed, "an increase in the visibility of external barriers to the advancement of Negroes heightens their sense of discrimination and justified withdrawal of attributions of legitimacy from conventional rules of conduct" (p. 121). Thus, those who blamed the system, rather than themselves, for their failure were more likely to respond criminally.

In this context, Hirschi was interested not in racial discrimination per se but rather in falsifying the causal claims that Cloward and Ohlin, as the chief representatives of strain theory, made about racial discrimination. Equipped with this constrained theoretical prism, *he did not search the Richmond Youth Project for all measures of discrimination and conduct a systematic assessment of the issue.*

Recall that the Richmond Youth Project data were collected in the mid-1960s, a period of tumultuous and contentious racial relations in the USA. The research team for this study—of which Hirschi was a part—was not blind to the volatile nature of race relations in the 1960s. Indeed, they included nearly the same number of questions related to race relations as they devoted to measuring parenting. In fact, they assigned an entire section, Part III, to race relations, which was titled "Human Relations." These survey items make the Richmond data set a rich source for examining whether perceived racial discrimination is related to adolescent offending.

Regardless, in his efforts to falsify strain theory, Hirschi (1969, p. 184) limited his analysis to test Cloward and Ohlin's thesis linking delinquency to unjust deprivation/blame the system. His strategy was to start by measuring whether African American youths perceived racial discrimination as an external barrier. They were asked, "Do you think that any of the following things will keep you from getting the kind of job you want to have eventually?" Racial discrimination was one option that could be answered "yes, maybe, or no." The youths also were asked about other potential obstacles to their success, which included "am not smart enough." Again, the responses were "yes, maybe, or no." Hirschi reasoned that if strain theory was correct, the highest rates of delinquency would be found among those who answered "yes" to racial discrimination and "no" to the item "am not smart enough." That is, the "Negro boy convinced of his own competence and convinced that racial discrimination will prevent him from attaining his goals is, according to this [strain] hypothesis, a prime candidate for delinquency" (1969, p. 184). When the cross-tabulated responses to these questions were examined (1969, p. 184, Table 69), Hirschi concluded that "the general thrust of this test is not, however, in a direction favorable to the Cloward-Ohlin hypothesis" (p. 184). This was another nail in the strain theory coffin.

It is noteworthy that Hirschi did not deny that African American youths experienced racial bias. He noted, for example, that the racial gap in delinquency was higher for official statistics than for self-reports. Among other conditions, this was due in part to the fact that police "patrol more heavily in Negro areas" and are prone to overestimate the extent to which African Americans commit crimes (1969, pp. 78-79). Still, although acknowledging that there are reasons for the differential official processing of youths by race, Hirschi (1969, p. 79) asserted that "there is no reason to believe that the causes of crime among Negroes are different from those among whites."

In short, for Hirschi, the causes of crime are *general* and not *race-specific.* Hirschi thus presented data showing that the racial gap in delinquency between African Americans and whites was substantially explained when controls were introduced for "academic achievement" (1969, p. 80). "It follows," Hirschi boldly continued, *"that we need not study Negro boys to determine the causes of their delinquency"* (1969, p. 80, emphasis added). In reaching this firm conclusion, he sought to foreclose any investigations that examined how experience with racial injustice—a factor fundamental in the lives of African Americans—might be implicated in the criminality of black youths.

Digging Into the Past: An Expedition in Criminological Archaeology

Our reanalysis of Hirschi's data was due to serendipity and context. Initially, one of us secured the data set from Professor Hirschi for use in a graduate seminar. There was no intent to illuminate Hirschi's "omission" or to write this article. Once the data were in our hands, however, we were sensitized—apparently unlike previous researchers over the years—to recognize "ignored survey items" because of our ongoing scholarly interest in deep racial divisions in perceived injustice. As we began to dig into the data further, we were influenced by a small and recent literature that had taken up the issue of the potential criminogenic effects of racial discrimination. This scholarly context—partly theoretical, partly empirical—guided our subsequent archaeology of the data from the Richmond Youth Project.

Revitalizing Strain Theory

Asserting that strain is not a risk factor and that all causes of crime are general as did Hirschi diverts attention away from the racial experiences of youths. As we have argued, however, applying a strain theory paradigm to race and delinquency inevitably shines a light on the issue of racial discrimination. Indeed, in his efforts to revitalize the strain tradition through his general strain theory (GST), Agnew (2006b) has called for research to investigate whether racial discrimination is a noxious stimulus that pressures African Americans to offend. He observes that "discrimination based on ascribed characteristics" is among the "strains that are seldom examined in the literature" (p. 103). In fact, Agnew considers racial discrimination as a strain that is *highly* likely to cause crime because: it (1) is high in magnitude, (2) is perceived as unjust, (3) is associated with low control, and (4) creates pressure to engage in criminal coping.

Notably, GST does not ignore the importance of social bonds. GST posits that those with weak social bonds will be particularly susceptible to cope with strain through offending. In this context, GST would hypothesize that African American adolescents who have experienced racial discrimination and have weak social bonds are the ones most at risk for engaging in delinquency. As Agnew (2006a, p, 100) argues, those low in social bonds are more likely to offend because they "have little to lose" if detected breaking the law and are less likely to have relationships with others who "will teach them coping skills or provide them with social support." We explore this possibility in the current study.

Recent Research

As we initiated our exploration of the Richmond Youth Project data set, we wished to learn if it contained a "hidden treasure"—evidence that perceived racial discrimination was criminogenic—that Hirschi or subsequent scholars might have uncovered. If so, then in and of itself, this fact is important historically to the field of criminology. Still, as was true with Hirschi's original study reported in *Causes of Delinquency*, we knew that the Richmond data had limitations. Thus, our reanalysis could be questioned for limited generalizability (the Project was conducted in one location in the 1960s) and for being based on cross-sectional data. Accordingly, we believed that faith in our findings would be enhanced if it could be shown that they converge with existing research—that is, if it could be demonstrated that the relationships we report generalize across time, places, and methodologies. This appears to be the case.

Based on an analysis of a longitudinal data set consisting of African American families residing in Georgia and Iowa, researchers have marshaled compelling evidence that perceived racial discrimination predicts higher rates of offending among African American youths (Brody et al, 2006; Gibbons, Gerrard, Cleveland, Wills, & Brody, 2004; Simons, Chen, Stewart, & Brody, 2003; Simons et al., 2006; Stewart, Schreck, & Simons, 2006a, 2006b). Scholars have reproduced these findings using other longitudinal data sets (see, e.g., McCord & Ensminger, 2003), lending credence to the conclusion that perceived racial discrimination is a cause and not a consequence of offending. Further, over the past 30 years, other disciplines have documented the potential deleterious effects of racial discrimination on African Americans over a wide range of outcomes, including diminished mental health, stress, high blood pressure, cognitive processing, substance abuse, depression, and hypertension (for reviews of this literature, see Clark, Anderson, Clark, & Williams, 1999; Williams, Neighbors, & Jackson, 2003).

In sum, this body of research suggests that the connection between perceived racial discrimination and misconduct was an empirical fact waiting to be uncovered and studied in detail.

As we suggest, Hirschi's *Causes of Delinquency* offered an important missed opportunity to inspire interest in this issue. This claim rests on the assumption that this empirical finding showing the criminogenic effects of perceived racial discrimination was, in fact, latent within his data and could have been discovered. We turn to this matter shortly.

Research Strategy

We first explore whether personal experiences with racial discrimination—a negative relationship and unjust form of a noxious stimuli—are related to African American offending (Agnew, 2006a, 2006b). We find that African American youths are more likely to offend if they perceive that they have been treated badly because of their race. To assess the robustness of this association, we test whether perceived racial discrimination predicts delinquency after controlling for the different dimensions of control theory. In conducting this investigation, we try to show fidelity to Hirschi's original analysis. Thus, rather than construct a single, overarching scale of each social bond (as is common practice today), we include a variety of measures of commitment, involvement, attachment, and belief in our analyses. In *Causes of Delinquency,* Hirschi (1969) probed the impact of social bonds through numerous measures that he cross-tabulated (one or two at a time) with delinquency. In our study, we have incorporated those variables that were most central to his analysis. This has resulted in a detailed roster of measures, but this approach has the advantage of remaining faithful to Hirschi's investigation. Consistent with GST, we also examine whether the effects of perceived racial discrimination varies by the strength of a youth's social bonds. Further, because the Richmond Youth Project contains alternative measures of perceived discrimination, we reproduce our main analysis with four other dimensions of discrimination. Of particular relevance, we investigate whether African American youths who believed that they attended a racially hostile school were more likely to commit delinquency.

Methods

Sample

The Richmond Youth Project is a cross-sectional self-report survey of 4075 high school students residing in the Richmond, California area that was conducted in 1965. A complete description of the survey, the methodology used to collect the data, and the codebook can be found in *Causes of Delinquency* (Hirschi, 1969). As is standard in the research literature on this topic, we analyze only the African Americans students. Those who reported that they were not African American were omitted from our analyses. There were 1440 African American adolescents included in the survey. In contrast to Hirschi's (1969) sample that was limited to boys, our analysis includes females as well.

Discussion: A Chapter in the Sociology of Knowledge

A Criminological Blind Spot

Hirschi (1969) should be credited for using the Richmond Youth Project data to address Cloward and Ohlin's (1960) claim that delinquency is fostered by the unjust deprivation stemming from racial discrimination. In rejecting this proposition, however, he failed to probe fully whether the different dimensions of racial discrimination might be criminogenic. If he had—as our analysis reveals—he would likely have found that perceived discrimination placed African American youths at risk for crime. Although the effect of perceived discrimination in the data is not huge, it nonetheless rivals, if not surpasses, the influence of other measures of social bonds (and of delinquent peers). Accordingly, Hirschi might have championed not only his social bond perspective as a general theory but also the importance of considering a challenge unique to minority youths: experiences with racial animus.

Again, this missed opportunity is understandable in that Hirschi did not place the discrimination items on the survey and was using the available data for selective theoretical purposes. In fact, in a more recent replication of his earlier study (conducted in Fayetteville, Arkansas), Hirschi and his team of researchers did not retain the discrimination items included in the Richmond Youth Project on the updated survey instrument. Regardless, it is consequential that Hirschi did not mine his data set more fully, for he might well have sensitized a generation of criminologists to the deleterious effects of perceived racial discrimination. Hirschi, however, is not alone in this oversight. Over the years, a number of scholars have reanalyzed the Richmond Youth Project data without calling attention to the finding on discrimination we discovered (see, e.g., Costello & Vowell, 1999; Matsueda, 1982; Matsueda & Heimer, 1987).

But there is an even larger conundrum to this chapter in the sociology of knowledge: why this blind spot regarding the criminogenic effects of perceived racial discrimination extended to virtually all criminologists and thus far beyond Hirschi and the single data set of the Richmond Youth Project. This omission is all the more puzzling when one considers the voluminous literature examining racial bias in arrest, sentencing, imprisonment, and crime policy (see, e.g., Gabbidon, 2007; Kennedy, 1997; Mauer, 1999; Miller, 1996; Mitchell, 2005; Tonry, 1995). Further, with regard to crime causation, macro-level researchers have explored how racial inequality, whose effects are often attributed to feelings of unjust deprivation (Blau & Blau, 1982), is a source of crime rates across communities (Pratt & Cullen, 2005). Although limited, scholars have even examined how social bonds affect delinquency for African Americans and whites (for a summary, see Felson, Deane, & Armstrong, 2008; Gabbidon, 2007). Nonetheless, with the exception of Simon et al.'s recent research agenda and those by a few other scholars, individual-level studies conducted by criminologists have rarely included measures of perceived racial discrimination in their multivariate models—an omission that has occurred across decades marked by the civil rights movement and unprecedented discourse about race in the halls of academia.

Three factors likely contributed to the reluctance of scholars to explore whether racial discrimination is a criminogenic risk factor for African Americans. First, following Hirschi's approach, criminologists set about the task of testing existing individual-level theories against one another. However, as general theories, the main criminological perspectives, especially control and differential association/social learning theories, did not accord race a central causal role (see Gabbidon, 2007). Experiences unique to African Americans thus received little theoretical attention. In self-report study after self-report study, race therefore reverted to a background factor, a variable "controlled" for in multivariate analyses.

It is noteworthy that both control theories and differential association/social learning theories trace their origins to the Chicago School of criminology, in particular to the "mixed model" of Shaw and McKay (see Finestone, 1976; Kornhauser, 1978). In this paradigm, establishing a general theory in which the causes of crime traversed ethnic and racial groups was politically progressive. The challenge was to show that no ethnic or racial group's biology or culture was inherently criminogenic. By demonstrating empirically that crime is linked to community organization, not to specific groups of people, Shaw and McKay could argue that crime's causes were general, social, and changeable (e.g., through the Chicago Area Project).

Further, theories that might have called attention to racial discrimination—those authored by conflict or radical criminologists—focused more on the discriminatory application of law (Piquero & Brame, 2008). When considering crime causation, they were more interested in calling attention to the crimes of the powerful (e.g., corporate criminals) or offered causal propositions that did not detail the mechanisms (e.g., perceived discrimination) through which structures of inequality moved individuals (e.g., African Americans) to break the law.

Second, there was the very practical matter that testing theories at the individual-level had increasingly become a matter of secondary analyses of large cross-sectional and longitudinal data sets. At the macro-level, measures of racial inequality are readily available; by contrast, most extant secondary data sets that use self-report data to test theories do not contain systematic measures of racial discrimination. It is difficult to study the effects of racial discrimination when researchers failed to consider it worthy enough to include in the surveys they design.

Third, it is likely that the relatively small number of African American scholars in the discipline shaped the field's theorizing. With only few exceptions (e.g., Anderson, 1999; Wilson, 1987), these scholars' contributions have remained at the edge of criminology (Gabbidon, 2007; Greene & Gabbidon, 2000). By contrast, the extensive infusion of women into criminology has led not only to the study of gender but also to the formulation of gender-specific theories of crime (e.g., Chesney-Lind, 1989; see also Miller & Mullins, 2006).

Again, it is not that white criminologists are insensitive to racial inequalities. But, although speculative on our part, it would appear that they tend to approach the study of race as an "outsider" rather than as an "insider" (Merton, 1972). As outsiders, they are concerned about race, yet they inadvertently tend to see its consequences from a "white," albeit a politically liberal, perspective. Thus, for these researchers, the focus is largely on white oppression of African Americans, especially through discriminatory practices in the criminal justice system. However, because they are not insiders—that is, they are not African American—they do not naturally focus on the "lived reality" of what it is like to be African American in this society (for a contrast, see Anderson, 1999). A fundamental fact African Americans continue to face is that, during the course of a day, their race may become salient and they may experience racial animus. Only a field dominated by white scholars could leave the potential consequences of this lived reality unstudied for so many years.

Racial Animus as a Continuing Lived Reality

Writing in his classic *The Philadelphia Negro,* originally published in 1899, W. E. B. Du Bois (1973) focused on the "contact of the races." Although reluctant to attribute most African American crime to racial animus, Du Bois felt that it was a factor that clearly could "encourage" black criminality (Greene & Gabbidon, 2000, pp. 28–29). Du Bois (1973, p. 351) thus cautioned that the "connection of crime and prejudice is . . . subtle and dangerous; it is the atmosphere of rebellion and discontent that unrewarded merit and reasonable but unsatisfied ambition make." Du Bois observed that prejudice creates a "social environment of excuse, listless despair, careless indulgence and lack of inspiration to work [that] is the growing force that turns black boys and girls into gamblers, prostitutes and rascals" (p. 351). He then concluded:

> How long can a city say to a part of its citizens, "It is useless to work; it is fruitless to deserve well of men; education will gain you nothing but disappointment and humiliation?" How long can a city teach its black children that the road to success is to have a white face? How long can a city do this and escape the inevitable penalty? (1973, p. 351)

It is remarkable that, with only a limited number of exceptions, criminologists have ignored the possibility—identified by Du Bois—that African Americans' experiences with racial bias may have criminogenic effects (Agnew, 2006a). This neglect is "remarkable" because of the continuing salience of racial animus in the USA. To be sure, advances in civil rights have diminished the most visible forms of legal and socially approved forms of racial mistreatment legitimated in the Jim Crow era. Still, researchers have documented the continued existence of racism (see, e.g., Feagin, 2000; Feagin & O'Brien, 2003). Particularly prevalent is a new form of "racial resentment "—sometimes called "symbolic racism"—in which whites express anger toward African Americans for receiving preferential treatment and failing to "help themselves" in a supposedly color-blind society (see, e.g., Bobo, 1997; Kinder & Sanders, 1996; Sears & Henry, 2003). Similarly, Bobo, Kluegel, and Smith (1997, p, 16) identify "laissez-fair racism," which "involves the persistent negative stereotyping of African Americans, a tendency to blame blacks themselves for the black-white gap in socioeconomic standing, and resistance to meaningful policy efforts to ameliorate U.S. racist social conditions and institutions."

It may be hyperbole to claim, as does Hacker (1995 [book cover]), that the USA remains "two nations, black and white, separate, hostile, unequal." Even so, despite sharing many common values, African Americans and whites diverge in their evaluation of the American experience. As Sniderman and Piazza (1993) show, whites generally do not often think about race. "They neither suffer from the problem of racial inequality, nor see themselves responsible for it" (1993, p. 154). For many African Americans, however, race is part of their "lived experience"—an inescapable social fact that looms over their everyday lives (Feagin & Sikes, 1994, p. 15). For example, there is ample evidence that perceptions of discrimination among African Americans are widespread (Bell, 1992; Cose, 1993; McCall, 1994). A 2006 survey reveals that many African American youths (aged 18–29) report experiencing different forms of discrimination, including being unfairly stopped by the police (51%), being denied a job that they were qualified for (28%), being physically threatened or attacked because of their race (26%), "people acting as if they are afraid of you" (21%), and "people acting if they think you are not smart" (14%). About two-thirds of the sample (65%) felt that racial discrimination was a "big problem facing black men today" (The Henry J. Kaiser Family Foundation, 2007, see also Unnever, 2008). Research also shows that compared to whites, African Americans of all ages are more likely to see the criminal justice system as unjust (Buckler, Unnever, & Cullen, 2007; Hagan & Albonetti, 1982; Hagan, Shedd, & Payne, 2005; Henderson, Cullen, Cao, Browning & Kopache, 1997; Johnson, 2008; Unnever, 2008).

More broadly, whereas whites generally trumpet America as an equitable society, African Americans do not share this view. Most whites believe that "blacks no longer face barriers to achieving economic parity with whites," viewing "limits to equality a matter of the American past" (Kluegel & Smith, 1986, p. 200). Or, as Schuman, Steeh, Bobo, and Krysan (1997, p. 275) note in their assessment of perspectives on the "causes of black disadvantage," African Americans "emphasize continuing discrimination; whites stress low motivation on the part of blacks." Not surprisingly, whites are far less likely to support government programs aimed at advancing equal opportunity. In fact, with regard to such policies, Kinder and Sanders (1996, p. 27) conclude that "differences between blacks and whites are extraordinary"—that this is a "divide without peer" (see also Tuch, Sigelman, & Martin, 1997).

Scholars are free to debate the extent to which this version of the American dilemma is accurate. Regardless, the belief among many African Americans that they face racial resentments and inequality is a social reality—a lived reality—that is potentially consequential. Indeed, as our study has revealed, it appears that perceived racial discrimination is implicated in the delinquency of African American adolescents. As a result, it is a potential risk factor for crime that should be systematically explored in future research.

References

Agnew, R. (2006a). *Pressured into crime: An overview of general strain theory.* Los Angeles: Roxbury.

Agnew, R. (2006b). General strain theory: Current status and directions for future research. In F. T. Cullen, J. P. Wright & K. R. Blevins (Eds.), *Taking stock: The status of criminological theory-Advances in criminological theory* (Vol. 15, pp. 101–123). New Brunswick, NJ: Transaction.

Akers, R. L., & Sellers, C. S. (2004). *Criminological theories: Introduction, evaluation, and application* (4th ed.). Los Angeles: Roxbury.

Anderson, E. (1999). *Code of the street: Decency, violence, and the moral life of the inner city.* New York: Norton.

Bell, D. (1992). *Faces at the bottom of the well: The permanence of racism.* New York: Basic Books.

Blau, J. R., & Blau, P. M. (1982). The cost of inequality: Metropolitan structure and violent crime. *American Sociological Review, 47,* 114–129.

Bobo. L. (1997). Race, public opinion, and the social sphere. *Public Opinion Quarterly, 61,* 1–15.

Bobo, L., Kluegel, J. F., & Smith, R. A. (1997). Laissez-faire racism: The crystallization of a kinder, gentler, antiblack ideology. In S. A. Tuch & J. K. Martin (Eds.), *Racial attitudes in the 1990s: Continuity and change* (pp. 15-42). Westport, CT: Praeger.

Brody, G. H., Chen, Y.-F., Murry, V. M., Ge, X., Simons, R. L., Gibbons, F. X., et al. (2006). Perceived discrimination and the adjustment of African American youths: A five-year longitudinal analysis with contextual moderation effects. *Child Development, 77,* 1170–1189.

Bruinius, H. (2006). *Better for all the world: The secret history of forced sterilization and America's quest for racial purity.* New York: Alfred A. Knopf.

Buckler, K., Unnever, J. D., & Cullen, F. T. (2008). Perceptions of injustice revisited: A test of Hagan et al.'s comparative conflict theory. *Journal of Crime and Justice, 31,* 35–57.

Cao, L. (2003). *Major criminological theories: Concepts and measurements.* Belmont: Wadsworth.

Chesney-Lind, M. (1989). Girls' crime and woman's place: Toward a feminist model of female delinquency. *Crime and Delinquency, 35,* 5–29.

Clark, R., Anderson, N. B., Clark, V. R., & Williams, D. R. (1999). Racism as a stressor for African Americans: A biopsychosocial model. *American Psychologist, 54,* 805–816.

Cloward, R. A., & Ohlin, L. E. (1960). *Delinquency and opportunity: A theory of delinquent gangs.* New York: Free Press.

Cohn, E. G., & Farrington, D. P. (2007). Changes in scholarly influence in major American criminology and criminal justice journals between 1986 and 2000. *Journal of Criminal Justice Education, 18,* 6–34.

Cohn, E. G., Farrington, D. P., & Wright, R. A. (1998). *Evaluating criminology and criminal justice.* Westport, CT: Greenwood Press.

Cole, S. (1975). The growth of scientific knowledge: Theories of deviance as a case study. In L. A. Coser (Ed.), *The idea of social structure: Papers in honor of Robert K. Merton* (pp. 175–220). New York: Harcourt Brace Jovanovich.

Cose, E. (1993). *The rage of the privileged class.* New York: HarperCollins.

Costello, B. J., & Vowell, P. R. (1999). Testing control theory and differential association: A reanalysis of the Richmond Youth Project data. *Criminology, 37,* 815–842.

Cullen, F. T. (2005). The twelve people who saved rehabilitation: How the science of criminology made a difference The American Society of Criminology 2004 presidential address. *Criminology, 43,* 1–42.

Du Bois, W. E. B. (1973 [1899]). *The Philadelphia Negro.* Millwood, NY: Kraus-Thomson Organization.

Feagin, J. R. (2000). *Racist America: Roots, cultural realities, and future reparations.* New York: Routledge.

Feagin, J. R., & O'Brien, E. (2003). White *men on race: Power, privilege, and the shaping of cultural consciousness.* Boston: Beacon Press.

Feagin, J. R., & Sikes, M. P. (1994). *Living with racism: The black middle-class experience.* Boston: Beacon Press.

Felson, R. B., Deane, G., & Armstrong, D. P. (2008). Do theories of crime or violence explain race differences in delinquency? *Social Science Research, 37,* 624–641.

Finestone, H. (1976). The delinquent and society: The Shaw and McKay tradition. In J. F. Short, Jr. (Ed.), *Delinquency, crime, and society* (pp. 23–49). Chicago: University of Chicago Press.

Gabbidon, S. (2007). *Criminological perspectives on race and crime.* New York: Routledge.

Gibbons, F. X., Gerrard, M., Cleveland, M. J., Wills, T. A., & Brody, G. (2004). Perceived discrimination and substance use in African American parents and their children: A panel study. *Journal of Personality and Social Psychology, 86,* 517–529.

Gottfredson, M. R. (2006). The empirical status of control theory in criminology. In F. T. Cullen, J. P. Wright & K. R. Blevins (Eds.), *Taking stock: The status of criminological theory–Advances in criminological theory* (Vol. 15, pp. 77–100). New Brunswick, NJ: Transaction.

Gottfredson, M. R., & Hirschi, T. (1990). *A general theory of crime.* Stanford: Stanford University Press.

Gould, S. J. (1981). *The mismeasure of man.* New York: W. W. Norton.

Gouldner, A. W. (1970). *The coming crisis of western sociology.* New York: Avon Books.

Greene, H. T., & Gabbidon, S. (2000). *African American criminological thought.* Albany: State University of New York Press.

Hacker, A. (1995). *Two nations: Black and white, separate, hostile, unequal.* New York: Charles Scribner's Sons.

Hagan, J., & Albonetti, C. (1982). Race, class, and the perception of criminal injustice in America. *American Journal of Sociology, 88,* 329–355.

Hagan, J., Shedd, C., & Payne, M. R. (2005). Race, ethnicity, and youth perceptions of criminal injustice. *American Sociological Review, 70,* 381–407.

Henderson, M. L., Cullen, F. T., Cao, L, Browning, S. L, & Kopache, R. (1997). The impact of race on perceptions of criminal injustice. *Journal of Criminal Justice,* 25, 447–462.

The Henry J. Kaiser Family Foundation. (2007). *Survey Snapshot: Views and Experiences of young black men: Findings from the Washington Post/Kaiser Family Foundation/Harvard University African American Men Survey.* Retrieved January 8, 2008, from http://www.kff.org/kaiserpolls/upload/7535.pdf

Hirschi, T. (1969). Causes *of delinquency.* Berkeley: University of California Press.

Johnson, D. (2008). Racial prejudice, perceived injustice, and the black-white gap in punitive attitudes. *Journal of Criminal Justice, 36,* 198–206.

Kempf, K. L. (1993). The empirical status of Hirschi's control theory. In F. Adler & W. S. Laufer (Eds.), New *directions in criminological theory: Advances in criminological theory* (Vol. 4, pp. 143–185). New Brunswick, NJ: Transaction.

Kennedy, R. (1997). *Race, crime, and the law.* New York: Vintage Books.

Kinder, D. R., & Sanders, L. M. (1996). *Divided by color: Racial politics and democratic ideals.* Chicago: University of Chicago Press.

Kluegel, J. R., & Smith, E. R. (1986). *Beliefs about inequality: Americans' views of what is and what ought to be.* New York: Aldine de Gruyter.

Kornhauser, R. R. (1978). *Social sources of delinquency: An appraisal of analytic models.* Chicago: University of Chicago Press.

Kubrin, C. E., Stucky, T. D., & Krohn, M. D. (2009). *Researching theories of crime and deviance.* New York: Oxford University Press.

Kuhn, T. S. (1962). *The structure of scientific revolutions.* Chicago: University of Chicago Press.

Lakatos, I., & Musgrave, A. (Eds.). (1970). *Criticism and the growth of knowledge.* London: Cambridge University Press.

Laub, J. H. (2002). Introduction: The life and work of Travis Hirschi. In J. H. Laub (Ed.), *The craft of criminology: Selected papers* (pp. vii-xlix). New Brunswick, NJ: Transaction.

Laub, J. H. (2004). The life course of criminology in the United States: The American Society of Criminology 2003 presidential address. *Criminology, 42,* 1–26.

Lilly, J. R., Cullen, F. T., & Ball, R. A. (2006). *Criminological theory: Context and consequences* (4th ed.). Thousand Oaks: Sage.

Matsueda, R. L. (1982). Testing control theory and differential association: A causal modeling approach. *American Sociological Review, 47,* 489 504.

Matsueda, R. L., & Heimer, K. (1987). Race, family structure, and delinquency: A test of differential association and control theories. *American Sociological Review, 52,* 826 840.

Mauer, M. (1999). *Race to incarcerate.* New York: New Press.

McCall, N. (1994). *Makes me wanna holler: A young black man in America.* New York: Random House.

McCord, J., & Ensminger, M. E. (2003). Racial discrimination and violence: A longitudinal perspective. In D. F. Hawkins (Ed.), *Violent crime: Assessing race and ethnic differences* (pp. 319–330). New York: Cambridge University Press.

Merton, R. K. (1972). Insiders and outsiders: A chapter in the sociology of knowledge. *American Journal of Sociology, 78,* 9-47.

Miller, J. G. (1996). *Search and destroy: African American males in the criminal justice system.* New York: Cambridge University Press.

Miller, J., & Mullins, C. W. (2006). The status of feminist theories in criminology. In F. T. Cullen, J. P. Wright, & K. R. Blevins (Eds.), *Taking stock: The status of criminological theory-Advances in criminological theory* (Vol. 15, pp. 217 249). New Brunswick, NJ: Transaction.

Mitchell, O. (2005). A meta-analysis of race and sentencing research: Explaining the inconsistencies. *Journal of Quantitative Criminology, 21,* 439–466.

Piquero, A. R., & Brame, R. (2008). Assessing the race-crime and ethnicity-crime relationship in a sample of serious adolescent delinquents. *Crime and Delinquency,* 54, 390–422.

Pratt, T. C, a Cullen, F. T. (2000). The empirical status of Gottfredson and Hirschi's general theory of crime: A meta-analysis. *Criminology, 38,* 931–964.

Pratt, T. C., & Cullen, F. T. (2005). Assessing macro-level predictors and theories of crime: A meta-analysis. In M. Tonry (Ed.), *Crime and justice: A review of research* (Vol. 32, pp. 373–450). Chicago: University of Chicago Press.

Sampson, R. J., & Laub, J. H. (1993). *Crime in the making: Pathways and turning points through life.* Cambridge, MA: Harvard University Press.

Schuman, H., Steeh, C., Bobo, L., & Krysan, M. (1997). *Racial attitudes in America: Trends and interpretations.* Cambridge, MA: Harvard University Press.

Sears, D. O., & Henry, P. J. (2003). The origins of symbolic racism. *Journal of Personality and Social Psychology, 85,* 259–275.

Simons, R. L., Chen, Y.-F., Stewart, E. A., & Brody, G. H. (2003). Incidents of discrimination and risk for delinquency: A longitudinal test of strain theory with an African American sample. Justice *Quarterly, 20,* 27–854.

Simons, R. L., Simons, L. G., Burt, C. H., Drummund, H., Stewart, E., Brody, G. H., et al. (2006). Supportive parenting moderates the effect of discrimination upon anger, hostile view of relationships, and violence among African American boys. *Journal of Health and Social Behavior, 47,* 373–389.

*Sniderman, P. M., & Piazza, T. (1993). *The scar of race.* Cambridge, MA: Belknap Press.

*Stewart, E. A., Schreck, C. J., & Simons, R. L. (2006a). "I ain't gonna let no one disrespect me": Does the code of the street reduce or increase violent victimization among African American adolescents? *Journal of Research in Crime and Delinquency, 43,* 427–458.

Stewart, E. A., Schreck, C. J., & Simons, R. L. (2006b). Structure and culture in African American adolescent violence: A partial test of the "code of the streets" thesis. *Justice Quarterly, 23,* 1–33.

Taylor, C. (2001). The relationship between social and self-control: Tracing Hirschi's criminological career. *Theoretical Criminology, 3,* 369–388.

Tonry, M. (1995). *Malign neglect: Race, crime, and punishment in America.* New York: Oxford University Press.

Tuch, S. A., Sigelman, L., & Martin, J. K. (1997). Fifty years after Myrdal: Blacks' racial policy attitudes in the 1990s. In S. A. Tuch & J. K. Martin (Eds.), *Racial attitudes in the 1990s: Continuity and change* (pp. 226–237). Westport, CT: Praeger.

Unnever, J. D. (2008). Two worlds far apart: Black-white differences in beliefs about why African American men are disproportionately imprisoned. *Criminology, 85,* 511–538.

Williams, D. R., Neighbors, H. W., & Jackson, J. S. (2003). Racial/ethnic discrimination and health: Findings from community studies. *American Journal of Public Health, 93,* 200–208.

Wilson, W. J. (1987). The *truly disadvantaged: The inner city, the underclass, and public policy.* Chicago: University of Chicago Press.

DISCUSSION QUESTIONS

1. What type of impact, if any, do you think the time in which the data were collected and analyzed by Hirschi had on his decision not to further explore the effect of race on crime?
2. How do the findings of this article encourage or discourage criminologists to further explore the affect that racial discrimination has on crime?
3. Discuss how the results of this study highlight the notion that a key aspect of any science, including criminology, should include the replication of findings in order to ensure the validity of a finding?

Juvenile Justice

SECTION HIGHLIGHTS

- Overview of the Juvenile Justice System
- Race and Juvenile Justice
- Race, Crime, and Victimization
- Race and Juvenile Delinquency Prevention
- Summary
- Edited Readings

Overview of the Juvenile Justice System

The phrase ***juvenile justice system*** refers to the agencies and processes responsible for the prevention and control of delinquency. Minimally, it includes police agencies, courts, and correctional facilities that are involved with juvenile delinquents and other youth that are in need of supervision. The juvenile justice system today is very different from that of earlier periods in American history when delinquents were treated the same as adult criminals. In fact, juvenile (and family) courts and juvenile facilities didn't exist prior to the 1800s. During the colonial era, families and communities were primarily responsible for both the socialization and control of American youth. Over time, industrialization, immigration, and urbanization during earlier time periods contributed to the breakdown in families, communities, and social control. It was during the 1800s that youth in trouble began to be placed in institutions as an alternative to placement in adult prisons. By the turn of the 20th century, the first **juvenile court** opened in Cook County (Chicago), Illinois. At that time, the juvenile court was informal and primarily concerned with rehabilitation. At the end of the 20th century and during the 2000s, thousands of delinquent youth were transferred to adult courts and sentenced to adult correctional facilities, reminiscent of the more punitive responses to juvenile delinquency that existed centuries ago.

The jurisdiction of the juvenile court includes not only delinquent youth but also status offenders and those who are dependent, neglected, and abused. More recently, teen (youth) courts and juvenile drug courts have emerged in some jurisdictions. **Intake** (referral), **adjudication** (hearing), and **disposition** (sentencing) are key decision points in the juvenile justice process. Juveniles are often diverted from the process by police, probation officers, and judges depending on their delinquent history and the nature of the offense. In most states today, the word *juveniles* refers to youth who are under the age of 18. Juveniles can be transferred (waived) to criminal court if they commit certain offenses or if the juvenile court judges or prosecutor recommends transfer. The age at which juveniles can be waived to criminal court ranges from 13 (in IL, MS, WY) to 17 (in RI).

There are similarities and differences between the juvenile and criminal justice systems. Some similarities include procedural safeguards, pretrial detention, the right to an appeal (in some states), the use of probation, and discretionary decision making. Differences between the two systems include terminology, the level of parental involvement in the juvenile system, and that juveniles do not have a constitutional right to a jury trial (Siegel, 2002). Another difference is that unlike adults, juveniles can be apprehended for running away, curfew violations, underage drinking, and other offenses due solely to their status as children or adolescents.

For most of the 20th century, many believed that juvenile courts were acting in the best interest of the child, while others pointed to the lack of procedural safeguards (prior to the 1960s) and increases in juvenile crime, especially among minority youth, as evidence of the courts' failure (Empey, Stafford, & Hay, 1999; Feld, 1999). By the 1980s, in response to (1) an increase in juvenile crime and (2) youth involvement in drug distribution and gangs, a more punitive approach to juvenile delinquency emerged. Differential treatment of Black and other minority youth that began in the 1800s has culminated in what is known as **disproportionate minority confinement and contact (DMC)** today. This means that the representation of a racial group in confinement exceeds their representation in the general population.

Race and Juvenile Justice

When the movement to salvage youth began in the 1800s, Black youth were treated differently. What Ward (2001) referred to as "historical racial inequality" in juvenile justice included a difference in ideas about Black childhood and the importance of Black children's development. Separation of the races was the norm in America throughout its history and especially prior to the Civil War, in the early 1800s. Many urban areas were full of poor and neglected youth in need of moral development, education, and training for work that concerned citizens, often referred to as **child savers**, were trying to help. While the intentions of the founders of some of the earliest facilities for delinquents, known as *houses of refuge*, were admirable, there still was prejudice against immigrants, Blacks, and girls. For some, placing White and Black children together was thought to be degrading (Mennel, 1973). The New York and Boston **houses of refuge** admitted Blacks, although they were segregated, and the city of Philadelphia opened a separate house for colored juvenile delinquents, as they were referred to at the time (Frey, 1981). Black youth were more likely to be sent to adult jails and prisons than to juvenile facilities such as houses of refuge and juvenile **reformatories**

(Young, 1993). In 1873, the first separate reformatories for "colored boys" opened in Baltimore (Ward, 2001; Young, 1993). It was not until the early 1900s that other reformatories opened for colored girls and boys due to the efforts of **Black child savers**.

Platt (1969) provided a detailed description of the individuals and organizations known as child savers that coalesced to safeguard youth, develop separate juvenile facilities, and create the first juvenile court in Cook County (Chicago), Illinois. Less is known about the lack of concern for colored or Negro children among the white child savers of the time (Ward 2001). Feld (1999) argued that, from its inception, one of the most important functions of the juvenile court was to control ethnic and racial minorities. Black child savers, educated women of a higher social class, emerged in response to the unfair and prejudicial handling of Black youth. The Federation of Colored Women's Clubs was at the forefront of the Black child savers and, in spite of barriers, was instrumental in creating the first reformatories for female and male Negro juveniles (Neverdon-Morton, 1989). In the 20th century, their efforts to improve the treatment of Black youth were strengthened by other individuals and organizations, including White child savers (Ward, 2001).

Although we know quite a bit about the development of juvenile courts, little information is available about the treatment of Black and minority youth in these courts prior to the 1980s. Feld (1999) posited that in postindustrial American cities today, juvenile courts function to maintain social control of minority youths, predominantly young Black males (p. 5). In spite of legislative changes, research, and prevention efforts, Black youth continue to be disproportionately arrested, waived to adult court, and sentenced to secure confinement for both violent and nonviolent crimes. According to Sickmund (2009), the following is true:

> A comparison of the rate at which cases involving different groups of youth proceed from one decision point to the next as they go through the court system shows the unique contributions made by each decision point to the overall disparity in the system. The rate at which black youth were referred to juvenile court for a delinquency offense was about 140% greater than the rate for white youth. The rate at which referred cases were petitioned for formal processing was 18% greater for black youth than for white youth. The rate at which petitioned cases were adjudicated was about 9% less for black youth than for white youth. The rate at which petitioned cases were waived to criminal court was 10% greater for black youth than the rate for white youth. The rate at which youth in adjudicated cases were ordered to residential placement was 24% greater for black youth than for white youth, but the rate at which they were ordered to probation was 10% less for black youth than for white youth. (p. 2)

DMC exists in most states, is greater for African Americans than Hispanics, and is often greater in states with smaller minority populations (Leiber, 2002). There are several explanations for why the proportion of juvenile minorities (especially African Americans, Native Americans, and Hispanics) at several stages in juvenile justice is greater than their proportion of the general population. First, DMC is thought to be a direct result of the involvement of Black and other minority youth in crime, especially serious violent and property crime. Second, there is differential treatment of minority youth for similar behaviors. For example,

Bell (2010), of the W. Haywood Burns Institute, noted that racial disparities in detention decisions can be reduced by taking the individual's level of risk into consideration. Often, Black youth of low and medium risk are placed in detention for failure to appear in court and for aggravated battery charges that result from fights at school.

The **Office of Juvenile Justice and Delinquency Prevention (OJJDP)** has worked with States for two decades "to ensure equal and fair treatment for every youth in the juvenile justice system, regardless of race and ethnicity" (Office of Juvenile Justice and Delinquency Prevention [OJJDP], 2009, p. 1). In 1988, amendments to the Juvenile Justice and Delinquency Prevention Act (JJDP Act) required states receiving funding to address DMC and in 1992 tied 25% of grant funding to compliance efforts. OJJDP has developed a DMC Reduction Model that includes five phases: identification, assessment, intervention, evaluation, and monitoring. Table 4.1 provides a summary of states' DMC-reduction activities. One problem related to unraveling DMC is the lack of disaggregated data. This is a problem with many of the statistics available at the state and local levels as well. Race and trends in juvenile crimes, arrests, victimization, and confinement are discussed next.

Table 4.1 Summary of States' DMC-Reduction Activities

Activity	# of States	States
Have full-time, state-level DMC coordinators	23	AK, AR, FL, GA, IA, IL, IN, KY, MD, MI, MO, MS, NC, NE, NM, OH, OK, SD, TN, TX, WA, WV, WY
Have part-time or other state-level staff designated as DMC coordinators	31	AL, AS, AZ, CA, CO, CT, DC, DE, GU, HI, ID, KS, LA, MA, ME, MN, MP, MT, ND, NH, NJ, NV, NY, OH, PA, RI, SC, VA, VI, VT, WI
Have DMC subcommittees under their state advisory groups	37	AK, AR, AZ, CA, CO, CT, DE, HI, IA, ID, IL, IN, KY, LA, MA, MI, MN, MO, MS, MT, NC, NE, NH, NM, NY, OH, OK, OR, PA, SC, SD, TN, UT, VA, VT, WI, WV
Have data for six or more (out of nine) contact points in their juvenile justice systems	39	AK, AL, AR, AZ, CA, CO, CT, DE, FL, GA, HI, IN, IA, KY, LA, ME, MD, MO, MT, NC, ND, NE, NJ, NM, NV, OH, OK, OR, PA, SC, SD, TN, TX, UT, VT, VA, WA, WV, WI
Have data for all nine contact points in their juvenile justice systems	22	AK, AL, AR, AZ, CA, CO, FL, IN, IA, MT, NC, NE, NM, ND, NV, OH, OK, SC, UT, VT, WA, WV
Update data annually (more frequently than OJJDP's minimum requirement of every 3 years)	30	AK, AL, CA, CO, FL, GA, IA, ID, IN, KS, LA, MD, MN, MT, ND, NE, NM, NY, OH, OK, OR, PA, RI, SC, TN, TX, UT, VA, VT, WI
Have invested in targeted local DMC-reduction sites	34	AK, AR, AZ, CA, FL, IA, ID, IL, IN, KS, KY, LA, MD, MI, MN, MO, MT, NC, NE, NH, NJ, NM, NV, NY, OH, OK, OR, PA, SC, SD, TN, VA, WA, WI

Activity	# of States	States
Have funded alternatives to detention and/or Burns Institute approach	25	AR, AZ, DC, DE, GA, IL, IN, KS, KY, LA, MA, MD, MN, MO, MT, NJ, ND, NM, OH, OR, SC, TN, VA, WA, WI
Use objective risk assessment instruments	19	AK, AZ, FL, GA, IA, KS, KY, MO, NC, ND, NM, OH, OK, OR, SC, TN, UT, VA, WV
Have done significant work with American Indians	6	AK, ID, MT, ND, SD, WA
Have implemented cultural competency training and/or organizational cultural competency assessment	15	AZ, CO, GA, IA, ID, KS, MT, NC, ND, NE, NV, PA, SC, UT, VA
Have state laws intended and/or expected to positively impact DMC	12	CO, IN, KS, MO, MT, NJ, NM, NV, SD, VA, WA, WV

Race, Juvenile Crime, and Victimization

Even though the majority of persons arrested and incarcerated are adults, juvenile involvement in crime, especially violent crime, is a continuing concern. DiLulio's (1996) prediction about superpredators and Fox and Swatt's (2008) more recent report on Black youth involvement in juvenile homicides between 1976 and 2007 paint a dire picture of Black youth involved in crime and Black victims. As discussed in Section II, the FBI's Uniform Crime Reports (UCR), National Incident Based Reporting System (NIBRS), and Hate Crime Statistics, the Bureau of Justice Statistics' (BJS) National Crime Victimization Survey (NCVS), and the Centers for Disease Control provide data on crime and victimization that include information on juveniles. Other sources of juvenile data include self-report studies such as the Monitoring the Future Survey, the National Adolescent Survey, the National Survey on Drug Use, and the Youth Risk Behavior Surveillance System; juvenile court statistics; and data on youth in residential confinement. The Statistical Briefing Book (SBB), available at the OJJDP website, is the best source of statistics on juveniles because it contains statistics and other information on nearly every aspect of juvenile justice. It also has FAQs (frequently asked questions/answers), data analysis tools, and links to other data sets.

Even though there are numerous sources of information, those sources do have limitations specific to understanding race, juvenile crime, and victimization. As mentioned in Section II, the UCR and NCVS rely on estimates. Some of the data is not disaggregated by race or age or gender. Even though the NCVS includes both race and ethnicity, it only includes that information for persons over the age of 12.

Juvenile justice data (juvenile court and confinement) are informative, but dated. For example, a recent compilation titled *Juvenile Offenders and Victims: 2006 National Report* includes data for 2003 and earlier. The most recent juvenile court data is for data collected in 2005 (Sickmund, 2009). Despite these limitations, the available data are helpful in understanding trends and patterns.

Juvenile arrests have fluctuated over time. Juvenile arrest rates declined between 1980 and 1984, increased after 1984 until 1987, and then decreased again until 1989 (Feld, 1999).

Although juvenile arrests increased in the early 1990s, they have leveled off since then. In 1995, juveniles comprised 19% (147,000) of violent crime index (VCI) arrests and 35% (737,400) of property crime index (PCI) arrests (Snyder, 1997). Stated another way, less than one half of 1% of all people aged 10 to 17 were arrested for VCI offenses. According to the UCR, in 2001, an estimated 1.5 million juveniles were arrested (Federal Bureau of Investigation [FBI], 2001). In 2002, the number of persons arrested increased 0.5% for the first time in several years to 1,624,192 (FBI, 2002). In 2006, an estimated 1,626,523 juveniles were arrested, a slight increase over 2005 (FBI, 2006). In 2008, of the 10,662,206 arrests, 1,616,672 were juveniles under 18. The number of arrests of juveniles decreased 2.8% in 2008 when compared with 2007 (FBI, 2009a). White youth represented 66.4% of arrests, Black youth 30.9%, American Indian or Alaskan Native 1.2%, and Asian or Pacific Islander 1.5%. Black youth were disproportionately arrested for all violent and property crimes recognized as the most serious crimes (see Table 4.2). Even though there are fewer Black youths than Black adults arrested, and a downward trend in juvenile arrests overall, juvenile involvement in serious violent and property crimes is challenging.

The majority of juvenile arrestees are males, although the number of female arrestees has increased in recent years. For example, in 1980, only 20% of juveniles arrested were female (Snyder & Sickmund, 2008); in 2006, 29% were female (Office of Juvenile Justice and Delinquency Prevention [OJJDP], 2008). In 2008, 18.5% were female (FBI, 2009). Most juveniles arrested for Part I (Crime Index) violent and property crimes, regardless of age, race, and gender, are arrested for larceny-theft. In 2006, juveniles under the age of 15 were responsible for 29% of arrests, including 58% of persons arrested for arson, 47% for sex offenses (other than rape and prostitution), and 41% of juvenile arrests for vandalism. Some juveniles arrested belong to gangs, although we cannot determine this from UCR arrest data as currently reported. Youth gang members are involved in a disproportionate amount of serious and violent crime.

The NCVS includes reported violent victimizations (rape, sexual assault, robbery, aggravated assault, and simple assault) and property victimizations (attempted and completed theft, household burglary, and motor vehicle theft). According to the NCVS (Bureau of Justice Statistics [BJS], 2005), youth between the ages of 12 and 15 had high rates of violent crime victimizations between 2002 and 2003 (48.1, meaning that 48.1 out of every 1,000 youth age 12 or older were victims) and 2004 and 2005 (46.9), and there was a slight decrease (–2.5%) in victimization rates. In the 16- to 19-year-old category, violent victimizations fell from 55.6 to 45.09 between 2002 and 2003 and 2004 and 2005, a 19% decrease (Catalano, 2006). In 2008, 12 to 15 year olds (42.2) and 16 to 19 year olds (37.0) had higher victimization rates than older adults, and 12 to 15 year olds had the highest victimization rates for assaults. In 2008, the rate of violent victimization for youths 12 through 15 was 42.2, and it was 37.0 for youths 16 through 19 (BJS, 2009). According to Snyder and Sickmund (2008), other important facts about juvenile victimizations include the following:

- Violent victimization is related to individual, family, and community characteristics (p. 30).
- A youth's risk of being a violent crime victim is most likely due to family and community characteristics, not race (p. 30).
- Juveniles are as likely to be victims of suicide as they are to be victims of homicide (p. 25).

Table 4.2 2008 Arrests of Juveniles Under 18

Offense Charged	Arrests Under 18					Percent Distribution				
	Total	White	Black	American Indian or Alaskan Native	Asian or Pacific Islander	Total	White	Black	American Indian or Alaskan Native	Asian or Pacific Islander
TOTAL	1,616,672	1,073,970	498,970	19,154	24,578	100.0	66.4	30.9	1.2	1.5
Murder and nonnegligent manslaughter	970	387	567	5	11	100.0	39.9	58.5	0.5	1.1
Forcible rape	2,487	1,539	912	20	16	100.0	61.9	36.7	0.8	0.6
Robbery	27,476	8,590	18,465	96	325	100.0	31.3	67.2	0.3	1.2
Aggravated assault	42,779	23,844	18,061	406	468	100.0	55.7	42.2	0.9	1.1
Burglary	64,198	40,436	22,545	538	679	100.0	63.0	35.1	0.8	1.1
Larceny-theft	250,281	164,660	78,212	2,972	4,437	100.0	65.8	31.2	1.2	1.8
Motor vehicle theft	19,002	9,936	8,564	239	263	100.0	52.3	45.1	1.3	1.4
Arson	4,989	3,857	1,001	52	79	100.0	77.3	20.1	1.0	1.6
Violent crime	73,712	34,360	38,005	527	820	100.0	46.6	51.6	0.7	1.1
Property crime	338,470	218,889	110,322	3,801	5,458	100.0	64.7	32.6	1.1	1.6
Other assaults	176,903	103,993	69,110	1,749	2,051	100.0	58.8	39.1	1.0	1.2
Forgery and counterfeiting	1,993	1,325	626	16	26	100.0	66.5	31.4	0.8	1.3

(Continued)

Table 4.2 (Continued)

Offense Charged	Arrests Under 18					Percent Distribution				
	Total	White	Black	American Indian or Alaskan Native	Asian or Pacific Islander	Total	White	Black	American Indian or Alaskan Native	Asian or Pacific Islander
Embezzlement	987	596	369	8	14	100.0	60.4	37.4	0.8	1.4
Stolen property; buying, receiving, possessing	16,020	8,734	6,993	132	161	100.0	54.5	43.7	0.8	1.0
Vandalism	82,064	64,547	15,424	985	1,108	100.0	78.7	18.8	1.2	1.4
Weapons; carrying, possessing, etc.	30,701	18,536	11,583	225	357	100.0	60.4	37.7	0.7	1.2
Prostitution and commercialized vice	1,156	459	662	17	18	100.0	39.7	57.3	1.5	1.6
Sex offenses (except forcible rape and prostitution)	10,965	7,755	2,990	84	136	100.0	70.7	27.3	0.8	1.2
Drug abuse violations	137,495	97,257	37,806	1,146	1,286	100.0	70.7	27.5	0.8	0.9
Gambling	1,295	68	1,213	0	14	100.0	5.3	93.7	0.0	1.1
Offenses against the family and children	4,343	3,136	1,126	63	18	100.0	72.2	25.9	1.5	0.4

Offense Charged	Arrests Under 18					Percent Distribution				
	Total	White	Black	American Indian or Alaskan Native	Asian or Pacific Islander	Total	White	Black	American Indian or Alaskan Native	Asian or Pacific Islander
Liquor laws	100,204	90,378	5,761	2,906	1,159	100.0	90.2	5.7	2.9	1.2
Drunkenness	11,905	10,555	989	277	84	100.0	88.7	8.3	2.3	0.7
Disorderly conduct	144,470	82,714	59,206	1,419	1,131	100.0	57.3	41.0	1.0	0.8
Vagrancy	3,097	2,429	645	7	16	100.0	78.4	20.8	0.2	0.5
All other offenses (except traffic)	275,281	192,550	74,523	3,033	5,175	100.0	69.9	27.1	1.1	1.9
Suspicion	210	105	104	0	1	100.0	50.0	49.5	0.0	0.5
Curfew and loitering law violations	103,992	65,661	36,223	828	1,280	100.0	63.1	34.8	0.8	1.2
Runaways	83,827	55,400	22,749	1,631	4,047	100.0	66.1	27.1	1.9	4.8

As previously mentioned, there are other sources of data on juvenile delinquents as well. Unlike the UCR and the NCVS, some sources—including the Monitoring the Future Series (MFS) and the **National Youth Risk Behavior Survey** (NYRBS)—focus specifically on youth self-reports of their involvement in various behaviors, including drug use. Discrepancies by race in self-report studies and official statistics are often reported (Davis & Sorenson, 2010).

Delinquency Prevention

The federal government has provided billions of dollars to state and local governments to assist them in their efforts to prevent crime (Sherman, 1997). Yet the amount spent on prevention programs pales in comparison to what is spent on the punishment and placement of youth in secure confinement. During the 2000s, numerous delinquency programs have emerged, many of them targeting minority youth and funded by OJJDP. According to Taylor Greene and Penn (2005), the pendulum might be shifting from punishment to prevention in juvenile justice due, at least in part, to the high cost of "get tough" policies that do not necessarily work. Howell (2003) identified several juvenile justice programs and strategies that do not work, including drug abuse resistance education, zero-tolerance policies, shock incarceration, and incarceration of juveniles in adult prisons.

The Center for the Study and Prevention of Violence (CSPV) has been identifying and evaluating violence prevention efforts since 1996. It selects "Blueprint Model Programs" based on several criteria for effectiveness, including evidence of a deterrent effect with a strong research design, sustained effect, and replication elsewhere (CSPV, 2008). "Promising Programs" are required to meet only the first criteria. Currently, there are 11 Blueprint Model Programs and 17 Promising Programs. The Blueprint Model Programs include Big Brothers Big Sisters of America (mentoring), Multisystemic Therapy, Olweus Bullying Prevention Program, Project Towards No Drug Abuse, and Life Skills Training (CSPV, 2008). What we don't know is what programs work best for minority youth, especially Blacks. Are any of these strategies effective for minority youth?

Taylor Greene and Penn (2005) noted that identifying programs that work for minority youth is difficult. First, just because programs like the Blueprint Models, for example, have proved effectiveness based on their deterrent effects, research design, effects, and replication does not necessarily mean that they work for minority youth. If we could determine that more than 50% of the study samples of effective programs were minority youths, then we could believe that they are effective with these youth. One Blueprint Model Program that probably works with minority youth is the Boys & Girls Clubs of America mentoring program because this organization has traditionally serviced minorities in communities with concentrated effects of social disorganization and poverty.

Understanding the relationship between violence and victimization is also important to developing effective prevention programs for minority youth. Youths who witness violence in their homes and in their communities are more vulnerable to involvement in delinquency. For some, the behavior is viewed as acceptable, and for others, it is required to have what E. Anderson (1999) described as *juice* or status. McGee (2003) and McGee and Baker (2002) found that direct victimization as a measure of exposure to violence was a predictor of problem behaviors. Victimization was linked to both internalizing and externalizing behaviors. McGee (2003) suggested that violence prevention programs must take into consideration the specific needs of students exposed to danger and the importance of developing problem- and emotion-focused coping strategies. Programs that emphasize resilience also are important.

Summary

- Ever since the development of separate facilities and courts for youth, Black and other minority youth have been discriminated against.
- The shift from rehabilitation to punishment as the primary goal of the juvenile courts has negatively impacted minority youth.
- Recent efforts by the Office of Juvenile Justice and Delinquency Prevention to address DMC have slowly impacted the problem, although much more needs to be done in most states.
- Even though the majority of persons arrested and incarcerated are adults, juvenile involvement in crime, especially violent crime, is a continuing concern.
- Regardless of race, most youth are arrested for larceny-thefts, a trend that has lasted for decades.
- Victimization rates for youths 12 to 15 are higher than for all other age groups, although we don't know how victimizations by race, gender, and Hispanic origin vary within age groups.
- Identifying delinquency prevention programs that work for minority youth is important.
- The relationship between violence and victimization should be considered in developing prevention programs for youth.

KEY TERMS

adjudication

Black child savers

best practices

child Savers

disposition

disproportionate minority confinement and contact

gender-specific programs

houses of refuge

intake

juvenile court

juvenile justice system

National Youth Risk Behavior Survey

Office of Juvenile Justice and Delinquency Prevention (OJJDP)

OJJDP Statistical Briefing Book

reformatories

DISCUSSION QUESTIONS

1. Is there any relationship between the historical segregation in juvenile justice in earlier centuries and the disproportionate minority confinement that exists today?
2. Do you think that juveniles who commit serious violent and property crimes under the age of 15 should be waived to adult courts?
3. Why are males more likely than females to be delinquent?
4. What prevention strategies do you think are most successful?

WEB RESOURCES

OJJDP In Focus: Disproportionate Minority Contact
http://www.ncjrs.gov/pdffiles1/ojjdp/228306.pdf

OJJDP Statistical Briefing Book: http://www.ojjdp.ncjrs.gov/ojstatbb/default.asp

Building Blocks for Youth: http://www.buildingblocksforyouth.org

W. Hayward Burns Institute: www.burnsinstitute.org

READING

States that receive Federal Formula Grants from the OJJDP are required to address DMC in several ways, including identifying causes and implementing corrective strategies. Davis and Sorensen use data on incarcerated juveniles found in OJJDPs *Census of Juveniles in Residential Placement* (CJRP) and FBI UCR arrest data to determine whether or not juvenile justice systems in the United States have been successful in reducing DMC. They also seek to determine how much juvenile incarceration can be accounted for by juvenile arrests. The proportion that can't be accounted for by arrests points to other causes. They found that when controlling for arrest rates, the Black-White ratio for juvenile placements decreased between 1997 and 2006. Another important finding is that cases that allow more discretion, such as drug and public order offenses, have higher levels of disproportionality that are not explained by arrest.

Disproportionate Minority Confinement of Juveniles

A National Examination of Black-White Disparity in Placements, 1997–2006

Jaya Davis and Jon R. Sorensen

The issue of disproportionate minority confinement (DMC) in the juvenile justice system had been a growing concern since the 1960s. When the deinstitutionalization movement swept the nation in the 1970s, Whites accounted for 75% of the reduction in incarcerated status offenders; when incarceration rates began to rise again during the early 1980s, minority youth bore 93% of the increase (Krisberg, Schwartz, Fishman, Gutman, & Joe, 1987). The first legislative reference to DMC came with the June 1986 testimony of Ira Schwartz of the Center for the Study of Youth Policy before the House Subcommittee on Human Resources. Schwartz (1986) stated that minority youth accounted for more than half of juveniles in custody despite research showing that they did not disproportionately commit crimes. Explanations for the overrepresentation of minorities in the justice system have traditionally focused on minorities' level of differential involvement in crime or selection bias by the justice system. Either explanation may have deserved further investigation; however, because of the rhetoric of advocates such as Schwartz, the legislative lens focused on selection bias—specifically, the inequitable use of confinement (Leiber, 2002).

Two years later at the 1988 conference of the National Coalition of State Juvenile Justice Advisory Groups, the national policy and advocacy body concentrated on DMC. That same year, an amendment to the Juvenile Justice and Delinquency Prevention Act was authorized requiring states to study and address efforts to reduce overrepresentation of minority youths

Source: Davis, J., & Sorensen, J. R. (2010). Disproportionate minority confinement of juveniles: A national examination of Black-White disparity in placements, 1997–2006. *Crime & Delinquency, 20*(10), 1–25. First published in *Crime & Delinquency OnlineFirst* March 4, 2010 (DOI: 10.1177/0011128709359653).

if the portion of minority youth detained or confined exceeded the proportion of such groups in the general population (Feyerherm, 1995). Beginning in fiscal year 1994, the Office of Juvenile Justice and Delinquency Prevention (OJJDP) included, as a requirement for a state to receive Federal Formula Grants, the determination of whether DMC existed in its juvenile justice system, the identification of its causes, and the development and implementation of corrective strategies (Hsia, 1999). In response to the DMC mandate, researchers undertook serious investigation of the issue, and states began to document DMC results and progress, in the way of internal investigations and reports filed with the OJJDP in the mid- to late 1990s (Leiber, 2002).

Subsequent to the mandates, an explosion in DMC research was seen in the 1990s, which raised a question of whether the increase was "a chance convergence of research and policy interests" (Feyerherm, 1995, p, 15) that would eventually dissipate or actually culminate in improvement of the juvenile justice system. City-, county-, and state-level assessments continued throughout the ensuing years with varying results (Leiber, 2002; Pope, Lovell, & Hsia, 2002). These studies inspected different stages of processing and locations, employed various methods, and included legal and extralegal factors (e.g., seriousness of crime and criminal history, for the former; single-parent-headed households and average income of neighborhood, for the latter) that may have affected minority overrepresentation (Huizinga et al., 2007). After briefly reviewing the existing literature, we examined the combined extent to which research, initiatives, mandates, and policies may have affected levels of DMC in state juvenile justice systems across the nation during the past decade.

Prior Studies

Feyerherm (1995) summarized the complexity of studying disproportionate minority contact in the juvenile justice system. He stated that complying with the OJJDP mandate and producing change could not "be met by the simple elimination of a type of treatment or confinement, nor one that for which success (compliance) [could] be measured in a simple counting operation" (p. 6). Subsequently, the production of a large body of literature has resulted in mixed outcomes. Examinations of each stage of juvenile justice processing produced results indicating no evidence of racial disparity (Barrett, Katslyannis, & Zhang, 2006), results finding disparity at one stage and no race effect at another (DeJong & Jackson, 1998), and consistent discrimination throughout the system (Bishop & Frazier, 1996; Conley, 1994; Leiber, 2002).

One of the main findings from this body of research is that racial disparities that were present later in the system often resulted from decisions made during the early stages of case processing. As expected, researchers found that legal factors significantly influenced secure detention and referral decisions; that is, juveniles with more extensive prior offense histories and those charged with more serious crimes, those involving weapons, and drug offenses received less favorable decisions (DeJong & Jackson, 1998; Wordes, Bynum, & Corley, 1994). Independent of offense seriousness and other legal matters, race affected the likelihood of detention (DeJong & Jackson, 1998; Wordes et al., 1994; Wu, Cernkovich, & Dunn, 1997) and differential processing of minority youth (Bishop & Frazier, 1996; Leiber, 2002). Huizinga et al. (2007) studied self-reported delinquency data in three cities from 1985 through 1988 and official contact/arrest/referral data for the juvenile justice system to uncover the magnitude of racial effects on juvenile justice decision making, after controls were added. They found that DMC at the initial stages of juvenile justice decision making could not "be fully explained by level of involvement in delinquency nor by delinquency level and risk factors combined" (p. 42).

Another major finding from this body of research is that small racial differences in decision making may accrue throughout the process. Researchers have well documented this cumulative effect wherein racial disparities build up as a result of decisions made at various stages during case processing. Detained juveniles, for instance, were twice as likely to be adjudicated delinquent in comparison to youths who were not detained before adjudication (Wu et al., 1997). Bishop and Frazier (1996) found that because of a cumulative effect of many case processing decisions, minorities made up 29% of cases referred to delinquency intake but 44% of incarcerated or transferred youth.

In addition to individual studies, analyses of previous work have been undertaken to summarize the empirical research on minority representation in the juvenile justice system. Pope and Feyerherm (1995) reviewed publications regarding minority youth in the juvenile justice system from 1969 through 1989. They found racial effects generally present at some stages of processing but not others, although bias could occur at any stage of case processing. They also noted that when it did exist, racial disparity tended to accumulate as youths were processed through the system. No relationship was found between rigor of methodology or data quality and disparity, although controlling for legal and extralegal factors tended to reduce observed level of disparity. Pope et al. (2002) conducted a review of research literature from 1989 through 2001. They concluded that race effects continued to be evident in the juvenile processing system. However, compared to prior research, the latter studies tended to use complex statistical designs and were more likely to result in mixed findings.

Leiber (2002) reviewed state assessment studies to determine the extent of racial disparities when relevant legal and extralegal factors were taken into consideration. The report examined studies from 43 states where data were collected in the mid- to late 1990s. Leiber found that at the identification stage, minority youth overrepresentation was evident in every state reviewed, existed at all decision-making points, and was greater in states with smaller minority populations. African American youths were the most disproportionately represented minority group. The assessment reports that attempted to determine the reasons for the overrepresentation were more difficult to compare because the states' assessment procedures and levels of methodological sophistication varied substantially. However, Leiber found "overwhelming evidence to support the presence of race effects in juvenile justice decision making" (p. 13), with 32 states unable to account for racial disproportionality by minority youths' differential involvement in crime.

An effort was undertaken herein to review current state DMC assessments since Leiber's work (2002). The 13 states identified in the studies represent all regions of the United States and include diverse demographic characteristics, particularly with regard to minority populations. The results from these studies are mixed. The outcomes indicate that DMC was present for many states and at various decision points; however, no state showed consistent DMC for any minority group throughout all decision-making points. For minorities, higher odds of being negatively affected at any particular stage of processing in the juvenile justice system were evident in some studies, but this seemed to be the exception instead of the rule. However, owing to the attrition of studies in analyzing stages throughout the decision-making process, it is difficult to say for certain if it occurred and to what extent DMC arose during various stages of case processing across studies and cumulatively within studies.

From the state-level studies, it is difficult to make generalizations about the level of DMC over the course of time in the United States because these studies were jurisdiction specific and relied on cross-sectional designs. They employed vastly different analytic techniques and varied in their degree of methodological sophistication while relying on samples from various locales and including a variety of decision points and control variables. Without standardization, it is difficult to determine whether any perceived changes occurring in DMC over time were simply due to measurement artifact or actual differences in justice system processing.

By reviewing prior studies, one can easily get mired in their details and lose sight of the larger picture. Although each is important in identifying and assessing DMC and evaluating the effectiveness of reduction strategies at the jurisdictional level, the focus of the current research is broader in scope. It has been more than a decade since the announcement of the OJJDP mandate for states to reduce DMC in their juvenile justice systems. The purpose of the current study was to determine the extent to which U.S. juvenile justice systems have been successful overall in reducing DMC—specifically, disproportionate African American placement—since the implementation of the OJJDP initiative.

Considering a National Systemic Measure of Racial Disproportionality

Blumstein (1982) pioneered the methodology used to disentangle the expected portion from the unexpected portion of the total overrepresentation of adult African Americans in U.S. prisons vis-à-vis Whites relative to their representation in the population. He proposed that if no discriminatory practices existed in the criminal justice system after arrest, then the racial distribution of prisoners incarcerated for a particular crime type would equal the racial distribution of persons arrested for that crime type. By comparing crime-specific race ratios at arrest to the distribution of prisoners by crime of conviction in prison, he was able to estimate the expected racial distribution of incarcerated prisoners. Any differences between the estimated racial distribution (based on arrest) and actual racial distribution of incarcerated prisoners had to be accounted for by factors other than differences in Black-White arrest rates, one of which could be bias in the justice system.

Blumstein (1982) noted that, compared to their representation in the population, African Americans were overrepresented in the prison system relative to Whites by a ratio of nearly 7:1. He found that 80% of the disproportionality witnessed in incarceration during 1974 was accounted for by differential arrest rates and was thus expected. Although Blumstein noted that the remaining 20% of the original disproportionality (not accounted for by differential arrest rates) could be partially due to differences in criminal record or seriousness of the crimes within offense categories, he acknowledged that some portion was undoubtedly due to bias in the processing of cases by the justice system. In a later study, Blumstein (1993) found that a similar portion of the disproportionality in incarceration rates in 1991 was expected, given Black-White arrest differentials. But he noted that the surge in the sentencing of drug offenders to prison (a nearly fourfold increase) was having much more of an impact on disproportionality in the latter study as compared to the earlier one. The percentage of disproportionality in incarceration rates explained by Black-White arrest differentials increased from 76% to nearly 94% when those incarcerated for drug offenses were removed from the equation using the 1991 data set.

Blumstein's work spurred other efforts to gauge the level of racial disproportionality in adult incarceration rates.

Blumstein's methodology has never been applied to an analysis of racial disproportionality in incarceration in the juvenile justice system; yet, its applicability to the current research strategy is clear. The analytic method for the current study is one that provides a national systemic measure capable of discerning incarceration trends across the United States. It roughly partitions variance in confinement by race into that which is accounted for by differences in group arrest rates and that which remains unaccounted for by arrest rates and therefore conceivably results from improper factors working within the juvenile justice system. Because the analysis of data spans several years with varying levels of initially observed disproportionality, the adjusted ratios are employed to provide a summary measure of disproportionality in the Black:White ratio of institutional juvenile placements, after controlling for race-specific arrest rates across the studied period.

Method

Data Sources

The OJJDP provided the necessary data on incarcerated juveniles. The OJJDP has administered the Census of Juveniles in Residential Placement (CJRP) on a biennial basis since 1997 when it replaced the former Children in Custody Census, conducted since the early 1970s. Whereas the Children in Custody Census collected only aggregate data on juveniles held in facilities, the CJRP collects individual-level information regarding the juvenile's gender, date of birth, race, placement authority, most serious offense charged, court adjudication status, date of admission, and security status. The CJRP requests data from 4,000 public and private residential facilities on each youth assigned to a bed on the last Wednesday of October. From these data, race of juveniles was disaggregated to find the actual number of Black and White juveniles in secure confinement by offense of adjudication (Sickmund, Sladky, Kang, & Puzzanchera, 2008).

Race and offense figures for arrests were collected through the Federal Bureau of Investigation from the Uniform Crime Reports (UCR), Crime in the United States series (Federal Bureau of Investigation, 2005). We used these figures to calculate the expected racial distribution of incarcerated juveniles by crime type. UCR data on ethnicity were invalid because of underreporting. Because *Hispanic* is an ethnic designation instead of a race, most Hispanic arrestees were classified as White (Snyder, 2006). To maintain consistency with racial arrest designations, Hispanics in the CJRP placement data set were combined in the White racial category.

Relying on arrest rates to calculate expected incarceration rates does not take into consideration the potential for bias at the point of contact with the justice system. National self-report surveys have called into question official statistics' portrayal of the extent of criminal involvement by Black youth vis-à-vis White youth. Results from the National Youth Risk Behavior Surveillance System, Monitoring the Future, and the National Longitudinal Survey of Youth have indicated small or nonexistent racial disparities in overall self-reported delinquent behavior (Campaign for Youth Justice, 2008; Morenoff, 2005). Huizinga et al. (2007) found that although self-reported delinquency was somewhat higher for minorities in comparison to Whites, the contact/arrest/referral frequency was disproportionately higher for minorities. Specifically, African American reported delinquency was 1.1 to 1.5 times higher than that of Whites, but the contact/arrest/referral rate was 1.5 to 3.4 times as high.

Research comparing official sources and victim accounts yields conclusions opposite those based on self-reports. Hindelang (1978) compared UCR arrest statistics with the victimization results of the National Crime Survey (a predecessor to the National Crime Victimization Survey) to uncover differences between race of arrestees and race of perpetrators as reported by victims. He found a high degree of correspondence in the race of perpetrators between the two sources. Although he noted some discrepancies in race identification between the sources for the crimes of rape and assault, most of the disproportionality in arrests was accounted for by racial differences in crime involvement. A recent analysis of National Crime Victimization Survey data found Black involvement in serious violent crime to be 4.6 times higher than that of Whites, close to their arrest rates, which were 4.9 times higher (Lynch, 2002). D'Alessio and Stolzenberg (2003) used the National Incident-Based Reporting System to investigate offender's race in relation to probability of arrest where the victim was able to identify the offender's race. For offenses of forcible rape, robbery, aggravated assault, and simple assault, the authors found "little empirical evidence of systematic racial bias against blacks" (p. 1392) and considered their findings to "refute the argument that racial bias in policing [was] affecting the arrest rate for blacks" (p. 1393).

Different explanations have been offered in an attempt to reconcile discrepancies in findings between research relying on self-report and victimization surveys. Some studies suggested that these differences result from African Americans' underreporting their involvement in criminal activity on self-report surveys (Kirk, 2006; Thornberry & Krohn, 2003). Others suggested that differences lie primarily in the aggregation of offender and offense types. In examining self-reported arrests and official arrest records among a sample of serious adolescent offenders, Piquero and Brame (2008) found little evidence of racial differences between the reporting sources. Monitoring the Future results show that whereas White youth were more likely to report involvement in more common delinquency, such as committing petty theft, breaking into buildings, and damaging property, Black youth had higher self-reported rates of crimes against persons and more serious forms of offending (Morenoff, 2005).

The purpose of this article is not to debate the accuracy and validity of one data source over another. It remains clear that discrepancies among sources exist. Yet, arrest statistics provide the only national longitudinal data source measuring the types of serious crimes necessary for calculating expected racial differences in incarceration rates. Nevertheless, in relying on arrest data, this study is limited in its ability to detect selection bias resulting from changes in law enforcement practices over the past decade. As examined herein, Black-White disproportionality in juvenile placements should be viewed as a cumulative measure of the level of systemic bias resulting from decisions made after juveniles have been taken into custody.

Case processing from arrest to final decision can take several months. As with previous studies, the UCR data from a year before the CJRP data were used to allow for a 1-year lag period between arrest and placement (Austin & Allen, 2000; Sorensen et al., 2003). For example, arrest data from 2002 were used to estimate placement data for 2003. Although CJRP data are available for 1997, 1999, 2001, 2003, and 2006, national arrest data coverage for 1996 is incomplete. Florida, a substantial contributor of juvenile arrests, did not report arrest statistics through the UCR. Florida's 1996 juvenile arrests by offense were, however, available via the Florida Department of Law Enforcement (n.d.).

In some instances, categories of offenses for incarcerated juveniles in the CJRP are broader than categories for juvenile arrests in the UCR. Where possible, we directly matched UCR categories to incarceration offenses by CJRP definitions. In cases where the CJRP did not include an offense category outlined in the UCR, we included UCR categories under the CJRP offense categories that were the closest definitional match. Some categories of incarcerated juveniles had to be excluded from the analysis because their institutional categorization (e.g., technical violators) did not allow a match with the UCR arrest database. In all, 86.3% of the incarcerated juveniles had offense types that were identified in the UCR data and, as such, could be used in the calculation of disproportionality.

Measures

The formula presented by Blumstein (1982) served as the basis for the analytical procedures performed herein.

We began the following analysis of juvenile disproportionality with a look at the unadjusted levels of racial disproportionality by comparing Black:White ratios of placement using baseline population data for 1997, 1999, 2001, 2003, and 2006. Then we applied Blumstein's analytic method (1982) to the most recent year in which the CJRP was available (2006), providing intense scrutiny of how the approach breaks racial disproportionality into its two major components—that which was explained by differences in arrests versus that which was not (unexplained). We subsequently made the same calculations so that we could examine each year in the CJRP data series in a longitudinal analysis. In relation to the longitudinal analysis, we calculated adjusted ratios (controlling for rates of arrests) as the most refined measure of changes in the level of DMC over time. Finally, we disaggregated crime-specific racial differentials in incarceration rates, then longitudinally compared the level of disproportionality explained by arrest.

Results

Table 4.3 combines population and placement data to present placement rates per 100,000 by race and the corresponding unadjusted Black:White ratios. The first column includes data for both races (Blacks and Whites combined). What is immediately apparent is that over the decade (1997 to 2006), total placement rates fell, as did rates for both Whites and Blacks. There are several ways to interpret the rates of incarceration for Blacks relative to Whites. One way is to simply calculate the percentage decline in incarceration rates for each group over the decade. On this measure Blacks fared better, with a nearly 30% decrease in placement rates from 1997 to 2006, compared to the 25% decrease in placement rates for Whites during the same period. The final column provides another way of looking at the relative rates, providing the Black:White ratios for each year. There again the pattern shows one of Black placements decreasing relative to White placements throughout the decade for all but the last census, dropping from nearly 3.7:1 in 1997 to 3.1:1 in 2003. Note that the slight upturn in 2006 was not due to an increase in Black placements but rather a marginally larger decrease in White placements from 2003 to 2006 than that experienced by Blacks during the same period.

The figures in Table 4.3 suggest a decline in Black-White racial disproportionality in juvenile placement rates in the United States over the past decade. One positive aspect of the table

Table 4.3 Black-White Placement Rates in U.S. Juvenile Institutions

	Total[a]	White	Black	Black:White
1997	197	137	502	3.66:1.00
1999	194	138	474	3.43:1.00
2001	174	124	415	3.35:1.00
2003	157	115	355	3.09:1.00
2006	146	103	350	3.40:1.00

NOTE: Placement rates are juveniles per population of 100,000. Age range was set from 10 through 17 years. Placement data are from institutions responding to the Census of Juveniles in Residential Placement.

a. Based on White and Black statistics only.

is that the figures have been standardized by the size of the population at risk; that is, the rates of placement per 100,000 are presented rather than raw numbers. These rates are still considered unadjusted because they do not take the groups' rates of arrest for particular crimes into consideration. The presumed target when such raw figures are presented is a ratio of 1:1, wherein Blacks are placed at a rate commensurate with their representation in the population. This would be an inappropriate baseline if Black juveniles' rate of arrest for serious and violent crimes was higher than that of White youth. What is needed then is a more realistic baseline measure to use as an estimate of what one should expect each racial group's rate of placement to be so that the actual figures can be matched against those expectations. Without such information, it is simply not possible to discern the portion of the ratio of disproportionality that is unaccounted for and possibly unwarranted versus that which is expected given differences in arrest.

For the current analysis, it is important to have a measure of the groups' arrest rates over the course of the time series because trends by race could otherwise act as potential confounds when we attempt to measure the influence of DMC initiatives on placement trends during the past decade. Arrest rates for young Black males peaked in the early to mid-1990s just before the beginning of the data series analyzed herein and advent of the DMC movement across the United States (Snyder & Sickmund, 2006). Afterward, arrests—particularly for violent crimes such as murder, robbery, and aggravated assault—declined to prepeak levels. As such, one should expect substantial decreases in Black juvenile placement rates owing to decreases in arrests since that time. What appears to be positive system responses to DMC initiatives could be broader social, political, and economic factors or even systemic factors operating contemporaneously that have driven down crime and subsequent arrest rates for Blacks more than Whites, hence lowering their incarceration rates independent of the OJJDP DMC initiative. Although Whites experienced a decrease in arrest rates during this same period, their initial rates of arrest were lower, the mix of offenses was less severe, and consequently, their likelihood of ending up in placement for such offenses was lower. The only way to determine whether racial disproportionality in placement may have been influenced by systemic responses resulting from the DMC movement (rather than from changing rates of arrest) is to examine placement data in conjunction with the relative changes in the level of arrest and the mixture of offenses for which Blacks were arrested vis-à-vis Whites during that period.

Table 4.4 provides the figures used in estimating the Black percentage of juvenile placements for 2006 based on their group arrest rates assuming no postarrest discrimination. The expected percentage of Black juveniles in placement by most serious offense (R_j) was determined by multiplying the percentage of Black arrestees for each offense (B_j) by the percentage of juveniles placed for a particular crime type (F_j). For example, because Blacks made up 68.7% of juveniles arrested for robbery and because 7.1% of juveniles in placement were serving time for robbery, it was expected that 4.9% of all juvenile placements would be Black juveniles placed for robbery offenses: $4.9 = (.687 \times .071) \times 100$. The expected percentage of all Black juvenile placements (R) is the sum of the expected percentage of Black juveniles placed for each offense, as shown in Equation 2. For 2006, the expected percentage of Blacks in juvenile placements was 34.1%. Assuming no postarrest discrimination, the actual percentage of Black juveniles in placement should be the same.

However, as shown in Table 4.5, the actual percentage of Black juveniles in placement was 42.1% (Q). By introducing the figures above into Equation 1, we can calculate the ratio of Black-White racial disproportionality in juvenile placement explained by

Table 4.4 Estimation of Black Percentage in Juvenile Placement, Assuming No Postarrest Discrimination—2006

	Arrests			Juveniles in Placement	
	White + Black	Black	Black (B_j)	Offense Distribution (F_j)	Expected Black (R_j)
Crime Type	*n*	*n*	%	%	%
Homicide	896	499	55.7	0.6	0.3
Sexual assault	14,563	4,195	28.8	8.9	2.7
Robbery	21,085	14,487	68.7	7.1	4.9
Aggravated assault	43,893	18,942	43.2	8.8	3.8
Simple assault	177,170	71,486	40.3	10.6	4.3
Burglary	55,950	17,663	31.6	12.8	4.0
Theft	211,161	61,407	29.1	6.9	2.0
Auto theft	26,741	11,943	44.7	6.2	2.8
Arson	5,651	1,076	19.0	0.9	0.2
Other property	99,783	24,979	25.0	5.9	1.5
Drug	137,283	41,076	29.9	10.6	3.2
Public order	488,708	81,391	16.7	13.0	2.2
Status	178,298	55,588	31.2	7.7	2.4
Total	1,461,182	404,732			$R = 34.1$

arrest, $X = 100[34.1(100 - 42.1)/(100 - 34.1)42.1]$, $X = 71.2\%$. Likewise, it is possible to calculate that portion of Black-White racial disproportionality in juvenile placement in 2006 that is not accounted for by arrest, $(1 - X) = 28.8\%$. These same figures were then calculated for the earlier years in the series, obtaining the following levels of explained disproportionality: 1997, 68.3%; 1999, 64.0%; 2001, 63.8%; and 2003, 68.1%.

Table 4.5 illustrates crime-specific measures of racial disproportionality in placements. As the percentage of expected disproportionality nears 100% (X_j), parity is approached in placement rates between the races for particular offense types based on arrest rates. For some offense types, X_j exceeds 100%, as is the case in 2006 for homicides, sexual assaults, and auto thefts, indicating reverse racial disproportionality. For homicides, it appears that Whites were

Table 4.5 Percentages of Blacks Among Juvenile Placements and Arrests by Crime Type—2006

	Juveniles in Placement				
	White + Black	Black	Black (Q_j)	Arrests Expected Black[a] (R_j)	Explained by Arrest (X_j)
Crime Type	*n*	*n*	%	%	%
Homicide	248	110	44.4	55.7	157.7
Sexual assault	4,112	1,174	28.6	28.8	101.6
Robbery	3,300	2,321	0.3	68.7	92.6
Aggravated assault	4,049	1,952	48.2	43.2	81.6
Simple assault	4,842	2,166	44.7	40.3	83.6
Burglary	5,894	2,254	38.2	31.6	74.5
Theft	3,178	1,324	41.7	29.1	57.4
Auto theft	2,816	1,174	41.7	44.7	112.9
Arson	407	119	29.2	19.0	56.9
Other property	2,716	968	35.6	25.0	60.3
Drug	4,882	2,119	43.4	29.9	55.7
Public order	6,005	2,393	39.9	16.7	30.2
Status	3,817	1,392	36.5	31.2	78.9
Total	46,266	19,466	$Q = 42.1$	$R = 34.1$	$X = 71.2$

a. The actual Black percentage of placements equals the expected Black percentage in placement if there is no postarrest discrimination.

more likely to be placed in juvenile institutions vis-à-vis Blacks given their relative arrest rates. Rather than from reverse discrimination, this could likely result from a host of factors, such as the greater likelihood of charging Black juveniles in, or transferring them to, adult court for homicide. These differences could also stem from different circumstances surrounding Black versus White homicides. For instance, whereas Black youths were more likely to be arrested in cases involving multiple perpetrators (wherein charges may have been later reduced for those who were less culpable), White juveniles were more likely to have been lone offenders and therefore held fully accountable for their offenses. Overall, the violent crime types had the highest percentage of Black-White disproportionality in placement accounted for by arrests (all above 80%), whereas certain property crimes, drugs, and public order crimes had much lower percentages of Black-White disproportionality in placement accounted for by arrests.

Overall there appears to have been one major shift in explained disproportionality by crime category during the decade examined (1997–2006). The level of explained disproportionality for property offenses dropped precipitously from 2001 (where it was over 90%) to 2003 (just over 60%) and remained near that level in 2006. Although violent offenses experienced a slight dip in the middle of the series and a rise at the end, the overall level of disproportionality accounted for by arrests among violent offenses was consistently high, around 80%. Juxtaposed, placements for drugs and status/public order offenses fell below the overall explained level of disproportionality for juvenile placements throughout the series. Consistent with prior adult studies (Austin & Allen, 2000; Blumstein, 1982; Sorensen et al., 2003), drug placements had the least amount of disproportionality accounted for by arrest rates (with the exception of 2006), although the upturn at the end of the series provides a glimmer of hope. Because only juveniles can be charged with status offenses, this category could not be compared to similar adult studies. Interestingly, this category, when combined with public order offenses, can be described as the least harmful to others; however, next to drug offenses, it had the highest percentage of unexpected disproportionality. Therefore, it appears that the categories of crime with the greatest amount of potential discretion also had the highest percentage of Black-White disproportionality in residential placement not accounted for by arrests.

The final analysis looks at the interpretation of the overall level of disproportionality not accounted for by arrests across the time series. The most appropriate interpretation for this longitudinal data given various starting points in the observed Black:White placement ratios over time is the adjusted ratio—that is, the percentage of disproportionality in placements that remains unaccounted for after that expected by arrest is applied to the initial unadjusted Black:White ratio. With the figures for 1997 from Table 4.3, the calculation shows the adjusted ratio to be $1.84 = [(1 - .683) \times 3.66] + .683$. What this means is that in 1997, the initial 3.66:1.00 disproportionate Black:White ratio of juvenile placements decreased to 1.84:1.00 after controlling for the groups' differential rates of arrest.

Across the United States, there was, on average, a reduction of nearly one fifth in the disproportionate Black:White ratio of juvenile placements, controlling for the groups' rate of arrests during 1997 to 2006. The drop therefore cannot be attributed directly to Blacks' lower rates of arrest relative to Whites or even the mix of the crimes for which they were arrested, nor can it be indirectly due to political, economic, social, or system-level factors aimed at lowering Blacks' crime rates before arrest. Rather, the factors influencing the reduction of Black–White disproportionality occurred postarrest in the juvenile justice system, indicating a systemwide reduction in the level of DMC across the nation during the previous decade.

Discussion

At midyear 2007, adult African American males were incarcerated at a rate 6 times that of White males—4,618 versus 773 per 100,000. The Bureau of Justice Statistics estimated that 33% of all Black males born in 2001 will spend some time in prison during their lifetime, compared to 6% of White males (Bonczar, 2003). Time spent in prison entails a host of obvious and subtle, immediate and long-term, personal, psychological, and financial burdens to the individual, family, neighborhood, and society. The prison cycle is intergenerational, and the pathway to prison often begins at the juvenile institution, wherein Blacks are overrepresented at a margin of more than 3 to 1 when considering their representation in the population.

Using arrest rates to calculate expected placement rates among racial groups, this study roughly separated the observed disproportionality in Black:White placement ratios into that which could be expected given their rates of arrest and that which was unaccounted for by arrests. Some portion of the latter was presumed to result from biased case processing in the juvenile justice system following arrest. Remember that some portion of the DMC unaccounted for by arrests could have resulted from factors other than discriminatory processing by the system, such as Blacks' lengthier records of prior arrests or their commission of more serious offense types within the broader offense categories captured herein. Although the rate of unexplained disproportionality was found to be far less than the unadjusted ratios based on population figures in the denominator, the adjusted ratios still show that Blacks were placed at rates nearly 70% higher than those of Whites after controlling for arrest since 2003. Although the evidence suggests that the DMC initiative may be making headway, this level of disproportionality is still unacceptable.

The results show a decrease in the disproportionate Black:White ratio of juvenile placements, controlling for the groups' rate of arrests from the baseline in 1997, which indicates partial support for the effectiveness of the federal DMC initiative. However, other possible explanations for this reduction are not completely ruled out by the research design. Because of vague language employed in the Juvenile Justice and Delinquency Prevention Act amendment, there were no clear provisions for steps required of states in reducing racial disparities, no oversight of reduction efforts, and no assurance of accurate collection of data or regular monitoring, evaluation, and reporting (Bilchik, 2007). As a result, the level of implementation and commitment to reducing DMC varied greatly by jurisdiction. With the broad stroke employed in this research design, the current study was not able to determine the extent to which improvements to legal defense systems, investments in alternatives to incarceration, and other local initiatives not spurred by the OJJDP mandate contributed to the national reduction in DMC.

Another limitation to the current study was its inability to separate Hispanic from White arrests. Including Hispanics in the White racial category is less than optimal. Recent research has shown that Hispanics offend at a slightly higher rate than do Whites (Felson, Deane, & Armstrong, 2008). Leiber (2002) found that Hispanics have been subjected to confinement for their offenses at intermediate levels in comparison to those of White and Black juveniles. These findings suggest that including Hispanics in the White racial category in the current study likely increased the White arrest and placement rates and, most important, biased the adjusted Black:White ratios downward from what it would have been if Hispanics had been analyzed separately.

A further limitation was that some of the most serious juvenile offenders were no longer controlled by the juvenile justice system but had been waived or transferred to the adult corrections system. The primary goal of judicial waiver is the ability to impose more severe sanctions for serious juvenile offenders than are available in the juvenile system (Fritsch, Caeti, & Hemmens, 1996). Although only a small percentage of juveniles are waived or transferred to the adult system each year, race has been found to influence such decisions (Fagan, Forst, & Vivona, 1987). Furthermore, because Blacks have higher rates of arrest for the most serious crimes, which are typically dealt with in adult courts, Blacks are disproportionately handled in adult courts. Thus, failing to include in the current study those juveniles sentenced to adult institutions likely had a downwardly biasing impact on the level of Black-White racial disproportionality observed.

Consistent with previous studies, the crime-specific analyses in the current study show that cases that allow the greatest degree of discretion in processing, such as those involving drugs and public order offenses, result in the highest level of disproportionality unaccounted for by arrest. Further assessment of how these low-level, low-visibility, high-discretion cases are treated at point of contact through case processing in particular jurisdictions is one of the primary policy implications suggested by the current research findings. Without attaining near levels of parity in these sorts of cases, an appearance of fairness in the system is difficult to achieve. However, these cases are the same sort in which the resources of the family and the community may be confounding the effects of race. In these cases, children from more affluent families and neighborhoods that have the resources available for treatment or community alternatives may be able to avoid placement, whereas for those from poorer families and neighborhoods (variables highly correlated with race), juvenile placements may be serving more of a social welfare function.

Finally, the analyses presented herein show that eliminating postarrest bias in the justice system will not completely eradicate DMC. Only when Black youths' arrest rate for serious crimes of violence has been reduced to a level on par with White youths' can one expect their rates of placements to be similar. In this regard, preventive efforts aimed at reducing Black delinquency are also important in solving the problem of disproportionately higher rates of placement and incarceration of Blacks in the United States.

References

Austin, R. L., & Allen, M. D. (2000). Racial disparity in arrest rates as an explanation of racial disparity in commitment to Pennsylvania's prisons. *Journal of Research in Crime and Delinquency, 37,* 200–220.

Barrett, D. E., Katslyannis, A., & Zhang, D. (2006). Predictors of offense severity, prosecution, incarceration and repeat violations for adolescent male and female offenders. *Journal of Child and Family Studies, 15,* 709–719.

Bilchik, S. (2007, December 5). *The Juvenile Justice and Delinquency Prevention Act: Protecting our children and our communities* [Testimony]. Washington, DC: U.S. Senate Judiciary Committee.

Bishop, D., & Frazier, C. (1996). Race effects in juvenile justice decision-making: Findings of a statewide analysis. *Journal of Criminal Law and Criminology, 86,* 392–413.

Blumstein, A. (1982). On the racial disproportionality of the United States' prison populations. *Journal of Criminal Law & Criminology, 73,* 1259–1281.

Blumstein, A. (1993). Racial disproportionality of U.S. prison population revisited. *University of Colorado Law Review, 64,* 743–760.

Bonczar, T. P. (2003, August). *Prevalence of imprisonment in the U. S. population, 1974–2001* (NCJ No, 19976). Washington, DC: U.S. Department of Justice.

Campaign for Youth Justice. (2008). *Critical condition: African American youth in the justice system.* Retrieved March 10, 2009, from http://www.campaign4youthjustice.org/documents/AfricanAmericanBrief.pdf

Conley, D. J. (1994). Adding color to a Black and White picture: Using qualitative data to explain racial disproportionality in the juvenile justice system. *Journal of Research in Crime and Delinquency, 31,* 135–148.

D'Alessio, S. J., & Stolzenberg, L. (2003). Race and the probability of arrest. *Social Forces, 81,* 1381–1397.

DeJong, C., & Jackson, K. C. (1998). Putting race into context: Race, juvenile justice processing, and urbanization. *Justice Quarterly, 15,* 487–504.

Fagan, J., Forst, M., & Vivona, T. (1987). Racial determinants of the judicial transfer decision: Prosecuting violent youth in criminal court. *Crime & Delinquency, 33,* 259–286.

Federal Bureau of Investigation. (2005). *Crime in the United States.* Washington, DC: U.S. Government Printing Office.

Felson, R., Deane, G., & Armstrong, D. P. (2008). Do theories of crime or violence explain race differences in delinquency? *Social Science Research, 37,* 624–641.

Feyerherm, W. H. (1995). The DMC initiative: The convergence of policy and research themes. In K. K. Leonard, C. E. Pope, & W. H. Feyerherm (Eds.),

Minorities in juvenile justice (pp. 1–15). Thousand Oaks, CA: Sage.

Florida Department of Law Enforcement. (n.d.). *1996 crime in Florida report.* Retrieved March 24, 2008, from http://www.fdle.state.fl.us/Crime_Statistics/1996/arrests.asp

Fritsch, E. J., Caeti, T. J., & Hemmens, C. (1996). Spare the needle but not the punishment: The incarceration of waived youth in Texas prisons. *Crime & Delinquency, 42,* 593–609.

Hindelang, M. J. (1978). Race and involvement in common-law personal crimes. *American Sociological Review, 43,* 93–109.

Hsia, H. (1999). *OJJDP Formula Grants Program* (No. FS 99122). Washington, DC: U.S. Department of Justice, Office of Justice Programs, Office of Juvenile Justice and Delinquency Prevention.

Huizinga, D., Thornberry, T., Knight, K., Lovegrove, P., Loeber, R., Hill, K., et al. (2007). *Disproportionate minority contact in the juvenile justice system: A study of differential minority arrest/referral to court in three cities* (NCJRS Document No. 219743). Rockville, MD: National Criminal Justice Reference Service.

Kirk, D. S. (2006). Examining the divergence across self-report and official data sources on inferences about the adolescent life-course of crime. *Journal of Quantitative Criminology, 22,* 107–129.

Krisberg, B., Schwartz, I., Fishman, G., Gutman, E., & Joe, K. (1987). The incarceration of minority youth. *Crime and Delinquency, 33,* 173–205.

Leiber, M. J. (2002). Disproportionate minority confinement (DMC) of youth: An analysis of state and federal efforts to address the issue. *Crime & Delinquency, 48,* 3–45.

Lynch, J. P. (2002). *Trends in juvenile violent offending: An analysis of victim survey data* (NCJ No. 191052). Washington, DC: U.S. Department of Justice, Office of Justice Programs, Office of Juvenile Justice and Delinquency Prevention.

Morenoff, J. D. (2005). Racial and ethnic disparities in crime and delinquency in the United States. In M. Rutter & M. Tienda (Eds.), *Ethnicity and causal mechanisms* (pp. 139–173). Cambridge, UK: Cambridge University Press.

Piquero, A. R., & Brame, R. W. (2008). Assessing the race–crime and ethnicity–crime relationship in a sample of serious adolescent delinquents. *Crime & Delinquency, 54,* 390–422.

Pope, C. E., & Feyerherm, W. (1995). *Minorities in the juvenile justice system: Research summary* (No. NCJ 145849). Washington, DC: U.S. Department of Justice, Office of Juvenile Justice and Delinquency Prevention.

Pope, C. E., Lovell, R., & Hsia, H. M. (2002). *Disproportionate minority confinement: A review of the research literature from 1989 through 2001* (No. NCJ 198428). Washington, DC: U.S. Department of Justice, Office of Juvenile Justice and Delinquency Prevention.

Schwartz, I. (1986, June 19). *Testimony before the House Subcommittee on Human Resources.* Washington, DC: Government Printing Office.

Sickmund, M., Sladky, T. J., Kang, W., & Puzzanchera, C. (2008). *Easy access to the census of juveniles in residential placement.* Washington, DC: U.S. Department of Justice, Office of Justice Programs, Office of Juvenile Justice and Delinquency Prevention. Available at http://ojjdp.ncjrs.gov/ojstatbb/ezacjrp (last accessed January 5, 2010)

Snyder, H. (2006). *Juvenile arrests 2004.* Washington, DC: U.S. Department of Justice, Office of Justice Programs, Office of Juvenile Justice and Delinquency Prevention.

Snyder, H., & Sickmund, M. (2006). *Juvenile offenders and victims: 2006 national report* (No. NCJ 212906). Washington, DC: U.S. Department of Justice, Office of Justice Programs, Office of Juvenile Justice and Delinquency Prevention.

Sorensen, J., Hope, R., & Stemen, D. (2003). Racial disproportionality in state prison admissions: Can regional variation be explained by differential arrest rates? *Journal of Criminal Justice, 31,* 73–84.

Thornberry, T. P., & Krohn, M. D. (2003). Comparison of self-report and official data for measuring crime. In J. Pepper & C. Petrie (Eds.), *Measurement problems in criminal justice research: Workshop summary* (pp. 43–94). Washington, DC: National Academic Press.

Wordes, M., Bynum, T. S., & Corley, C. J. (1994). Locking up youth: The impact of race on detention decisions. *Journal of Research in Crime and Delinquency, 31,* 149–165.

Wu, B., Cernkovich, S., & Dunn, C. S. (1997). Assessing the effects of race and class on juvenile justice processing in Ohio. *Journal of Criminal Justice, 25,* 265–277.

DISCUSSION QUESTIONS

1. Briefly summarize the findings from previous studies of disproportionate minority confinement (DMC) of juveniles.
2. Why do the authors believe the methodology of the current study is helpful for understanding DMC?
3. What do the authors mean when they state that the categories of crime with the potential for the most discretion also have high percentages of Black-White disproportionality in residential placement not accounted for by arrests?
4. What are some limitations of this study?

READING

School discipline is more punitive today than in the past, and many rely on police officers, zero-tolerance policies, and technology to control students and crime. Research shows that racial/ethnic minorities and lower-income youth are more likely to be punished when crime occurs in school. Kupchik uses ethnographic data from four public high schools to examine whether or not schools that vary by race, class, and place are similar in how they manage crime. The findings indicate that even though the schools have similar policies and approaches, youth of color and lower-income youth have higher suspension rates than more advantaged youth. The article concludes with a discussion of the implications of a crime control strategy in schools for students and schools.

Things Are Tough All Over

Race, Ethnicity, Class and School Discipline

Aaron Kupchik

Schools across the USA have dramatically altered how they perceive and respond to school crime in recent decades, with increasing police presence in schools and more punitive responses to student misbehaviors (see Casella, 2001; Skiba and Noam, 2002; Noguera, 2003a; Reyes, 2006; Simon, 2007; Hirschfield, 2008). It is now common in public high schools to find police officers, armed security guards, surveillance cameras, zero-tolerance

Source: Kupchik, A. (2009). Things are tough all over: Race, ethnicity, class and school discipline. *Punishment & Society, 11*, 291–317.

policies and random searches with drug-sniffing dogs. For example, this last strategy, drug-sniffing dogs, was used in 58.6 percent of public high schools in the 2003–4 school year (Dinkes et al., 2006).

The introduction of police officers (often called School Resource Officers, or SROs) to schools has been widespread. The number of SROs nationwide seems to have grown dramatically in recent years, fueled by federal funding such as a Bill Clinton sponsored program known as COPS: Community Oriented Policing. Indeed, as of 2007 the National Association of School Resource Officers boasts over 9000 members (though this is likely a conservative estimate since it represents dues-paying members rather than an actual count of SROs). Additionally, a recent national survey found that 60 percent of high school teachers reported having armed police in their schools (Public Agenda, 2004). Though a few evaluations find that students and school staff members within schools served by SROs claim to feel safer because a SRO is present daily (Finn and McDevitt, 2000; Schuiteman, 2001), others are more critical of SRO programs. These critics argue that a police presence in school can lead to increased arrests for behaviors like fighting that, in years past, would have led to only in-school punishment, and they discuss how police in schools facilitate a 'school-to-prison pipeline' (Skiba et al., 2000; Casella, 2001; Noguera, 2003b; Wald and Losen, 2003; Simon, 2007; Hirschfield, 2008).

A second particularly important and controversial trend is the introduction of zero-tolerance policies. These policies were spurred by the 1994 Safe Schools Act, which mandates that in order for a school to receive federal money, it must have written policies detailing: 'a) its internal procedures, b) clear conditions under which exclusion will be imposed, and c) close cooperation with police and juvenile justice agencies' (Simon, 2007: 218). In response, many schools have created rules under the zero-tolerance umbrella, whereby students who commit certain categorical acts, such as possessing weapons, alcohol or drugs, are suspended or expelled, regardless of the severity of the act (Skiba, 2000; Reyes, 2006; Simon, 2007). By limiting school administrators' discretion to divert some students from punishment and by highlighting certain behaviors as being qualitatively beyond a threshold of what schools will allow, these policies have led to increased punishments for students (Rimer, 2004; Reyes, 2006). Indeed, national data from the Federal Department of Education show a clear increase in suspension rates from 1974 to 1998 (Schiraldi and Ziedenberg, 2001).

In this article I use data from participant observation and interviews in public high schools to explore how contemporary school discipline takes shape across schools with varying demographics: across schools attended by mostly middle-class white students and schools attended by mostly lower-income racial/ethnic minority students. As I discuss below, much prior work on the sociology of education would lead us to expect that these school safety policies would operate very differently across the two types of schools, in ways likely to exacerbate the status and life opportunity gaps between the two student bodies. Though I find some support for this thesis, the data also show that in some ways, both groups of students have a similar, negative experience. Practices that were once reserved primarily for schools hosting poor students and students of color (Devine, 1996; Ferguson, 2000) are now implemented in mostly white middle-class schools as well. As a result, the contemporary focus on policing and punishment subjects both white middle-class students and lower-income students of color to more similar modes of control than one would expect. The similarities across schools suggest that a status reproduction approach to understanding differences across schools fails to capture how the contemporary focus on discipline in US public schools affects *all* students.

Cultural Reproduction

Scholars have often and consistently noted the important socialization function of schools, and how this function maintains class and power distinctions. The historian David Tyack (1974), for example, illustrates how 19th-century and early 20th-century schools were a mechanism for Americanizing immigrant and rural children, and teaching them the skills necessary for factory labor (see also Rothstein, 1984). Others have applied and further developed this idea by considering how contemporary schools perpetuate social inequalities, particularly economic stratification, through training into class-divided labor market roles (Cicourel and Kitsuse, 1963; Bowles and Gintis, 1976; Willis, 1977; Apple, 1979; see also Illich, 1971; Rist, 1973; Oakes, 1985).

In *Reproduction in education*, Bourdieu and Passeron (1990) extend this line of thought to consider cultural reproduction more broadly. They argue that schools reinforce an arbitrary distribution of cultural capital, both through the content of what students learn and through the dissemination of titles and degrees; but since school achievement is viewed as a legitimate marker of ability, this uneven distribution of capital is legitimized by educational systems. In this way, schools maintain existing social inequalities while making these inequalities appear to be a matter of competition and ability (see also Apple, 1979; Gee, 1996).

This literature shows how students' experiences and training are distributed unequally according to their class, race, gender or other status characteristics. Empirical research on school discipline clearly supports this view. In particular, several studies demonstrate that the consequences of school punishments fall disproportionately on racial/ethnic minority youth and lower-income youth, as each group is far more likely to be suspended or expelled than white or middle-class youth, respectively (e.g., Wu et al., 1982; Skiba et al., 2000; Raffaele Mendez and Knoff, 2003; Eitle and Eitle, 2004). With regard to race and ethnicity, the few studies to investigate why minorities are disproportionately punished have focused on perceptions of threat; they find that teachers and administrators tend to perceive African American and Latino/a youth as louder (Morris, 2007), more disruptive or disrespectful (McCarthy and Hoge, 1987; Ferguson, 2000; Morris, 2005), or more challenging of teachers' authority than white students (Vavrus and Cole, 2002), and therefore they may be quicker to punish these students or refer them to administrators for punishment (see also Eckert, 1989). With regard to social class, prior research suggests that educators' biases lead them to assume worse school performance and greater misbehavior among lower-income youth (Chambliss, 1973; Rist, 1973). Moreover, lower-income youth are more likely to violate the middle-class behavioral norms that educators expect to see (Cohen, 1955; Ferguson, 2000), and they are less likely than middle-class youth to manipulate learning environments to their advantage (Lareau, 2003), each of which makes them more vulnerable to being singled out for school punishment than middle-class youth.

Thus, social class and race have distinct and complex effects on school environments, and each has repeatedly been found to have an independent effect on the likelihood of punishment for any individual student. One would therefore predict substantial variation among different schools' approaches to discipline in ways that correspond to schools' student demographics. Based on cultural reproduction theory, one might also predict that these differences in approaches to discipline across schools would mirror, legitimate and exacerbate students' status and power inequalities, thereby socializing students into very different future roles. When considering the independent effect of both race and social class in shaping adults' experiences with the carceral state, and particularly the overwhelmingly disproportionate rate at which lower-class African Americans are sentenced to prison (e.g., Western, 2006), it makes sense to predict that schools' disciplinary practices mirror these experiences with state punishment. One would predict that schools with mostly lower-income youth and youth of color prepare students to live under close watch by the State by subjecting them to frequent police surveillance and harsh punishments for misbehaviors; in contrast, one would expect that schools with mostly wealthier, white students teach skills that empower them to avoid, manage and control such risks, or to use these elements of control to their social, professional and economic advantage. This hypothesis is captured by Lyons and Drew (2006: 5; see also Hirschfield, 2008) in their study of school punishments: 'Zero tolerance approaches to conflict and ongoing struggles over identity teach us to reproduce the social stratifications in school culture that are predicated on race, class, and gender subordination.'

Widespread Shifts: Governing Through Crime

Though the idea of cultural reproduction and the above evidence on who gets punished in schools are essential for understanding the persistence of structural inequality, it is important to keep in mind that changes in school discipline throughout the USA have mirrored broad shifts in how we define and respond to threat and insecurity, generally. These trends have occurred at the same time that we have observed a quadrupling of the US imprisonment rate, for example, without corresponding increases in crime. More importantly, we can think of both trends as part of a widespread shift in how western nations, and especially the USA, have responded to potential and actual crime. In explaining why prison populations have skyrocketed over the past 30 years in the USA and the UK, David Garland (2001) argues that changes in social organization and in widely shared sensibilities (which he calls the culture of control) have shaped crime control arrangements to rely more heavily than before on incarceration. These social shifts are broad and experienced by entire populations of the USA and the UK.

We can also see similarities between the increasing enforcement of school rules and zero-tolerance policing in communities, whereby police crack down on minor offenders who commit 'quality of life crimes' such as public urination or alcohol consumption (Greene, 1999). School discipline resembles this policing approach when schools respond to relatively minor offenses by excluding students from classrooms. For example, Reyes (2006: 35–7) notes that in Texas, the vast majority of students suspended (96%) or expelled (86%) under zero-tolerance laws are punished for a discretionary offense—one for which suspension or expulsion is not required under the policy—rather than for a mandatory offense.

In his recent book, *Governing through crime*, Jonathan Simon (2007) offers a framework for understanding these trends by illustrating how the war against crime has become central to American governance. Simon discusses how policy-makers now use crime discourse as a strategic issue to legitimate interventions and policies related to a wide range of institutions, including housing, public assistance and schools. That is, by drawing citizens' attention to their potential for victimization—either by crime or other social ills—policy makers have mobilized Americans' insecurities and enacted restrictive, fear-based policies that have transformed American governance. Harsh punishments for racial and ethnic minorities, particularly poor African American men, are central to Simon's analysis, since the fear of a black underclass helped to mobilize and legitimate mass incarceration; but he also illustrates that crime control policies have become so pervasive that all Americans now feel their weight. In a chapter devoted entirely to governing through crime in schools, Simon argues that school crime has become the focal point for managing student behaviors, such that social control technologies (police, suspensions, expulsions, surveillance and so on) now compete with pedagogical imperatives in shaping schools' routines and rituals. Moreover, he argues that because of the pervasiveness of governing through crime, these shifts in school social control are occurring in schools across the USA, not only in schools with mostly poor students or students of color. He states: 'the very real violence of a few schools concentrated in zones of hardened poverty and social disadvantage has provided a "truth" of school crime that circulates across whole school systems' (Simon, 2007: 210).

The widespread impact of governing through crime complicates what lessons we should expect contemporary high school students to learn. Although broader trends in punishment have vastly disproportionate effects on different sectors of society (Western, 2006), it is clear that all sectors of society experience the insecurities that correspond with and feed the mission of governing through crime. Furthermore, unlike adults, all children are at a relative power disadvantage within their schools. That is, wealthy, white students with powerful parents still have less immediate power than the adults who make, monitor and enforce the rules of their school; though they have social power, they are still legal minors and thus at the mercy of school employees. With this in mind, it is less clear how school discipline policies are enforced across schools with demographically contrasting student bodies. This puzzle is highlighted by Paul Hirschfield (2008), who considers ways that school discipline varies across school demographics and locations despite increasing punishments and security mechanisms across the USA. He argues that although suburban schools, like urban schools, now rely on security technologies, zero tolerance and police, they do so in different ways:

> criminalization in middle class schools is less intense and more fluid than in the inner city, where proximate or immediate crime threats are overriding concerns. . . . In short, the gated community may be a more apt metaphor to describe the security transformation of affluent schools, while the prison metaphor better suits that of inner-city schools. (Hirschfield, 2008: 84)

Hirschfield's argument is consistent with both cultural reproduction theory and what we know of trends in punishment, generally (see Wacquant, 2001; Western, 2006), though there are few empirical efforts to test these ideas (but see Lyons and Drew, 2006).

Based on numerous prior studies, it is abundantly clear that both racial/ethnic minorities and lower-income youth are more likely than others to be punished *within* schools. Yet for the most part these studies rely on analyses using only individual-level data. As a result, though these within school disparities are clear, we know little about how contemporary school policies are enforced *across* schools, or whether schools with mostly lower-income and/or minority students enforce harsher or a different style of discipline than schools with mostly wealthier, white students. I address this void in the research by considering differences across schools, using empirical data to consider Simon's (2007) argument that schools in all social strata have adopted elements of governing through crime.

Methods

To understand how contemporary discipline practices take shape in schools, I consider ethnographic data collected in four public high schools. The four schools include two in each of two separate states: one Mid-Atlantic state and one Southwestern state. The pair of schools within each state was chosen to provide a demographic contrast, with one school's student body composed of a majority white, middle-class students and the other a majority of non-white, lower-income students. Table 4.6 presents a contrast of key characteristics of each school, as well as each school's pseudonym: Adams High and Clinton High in the Mid-Atlantic state, and Johnson High and Taylor High in the Southwest. Due to variation in residential patterns and school policies (i.e., busing), there is a starker contrast between schools in the Southwestern state than in the Mid-Atlantic one. Nevertheless, each pair offers a comparison between schools with a large proportion of relatively advantaged students (who benefit from dominant social positions along both race and class lines) and a large proportion of relatively disadvantaged students.

Three of the four schools are located in suburban areas. The fourth, Johnson High, is located within a large city, though it is in a region marked more by sprawl than dense population. As a result, the neighborhoods in which all four schools are located share similarities: all four schools are immediately surrounded by single family houses and businesses, with the school occupying an enclosed territory consisting of buildings and athletic fields. The four schools also have a similar number of control-oriented staff members: each has one police officer, two to six security officers or 'interventionists' and one to four administrators handling discipline.

Another important difference among schools that is not represented in Table 4.6 is the architecture of each school. The two schools in each state are very similar to each other in this regard, but with great differences between the two pairs. The Southwestern schools are 'open campus' schools, with large, open layouts consisting of several buildings and courtyards, where students walk between the buildings during class breaks. In contrast, both Mid-Atlantic schools are enclosed buildings, and in both schools students are not allowed outside of these buildings. These architectural differences substantially shape how surveillance is carried out

Table 4.6 Comparison of Sampled Schools (2004–5)

	Southwestern Schools		Mid-Atlantic Schools	
	Johnson High	Taylor High	Adams High	Clinton High
Total students	2227	2739	1506	2067
Student/teacher ratio	16.5	23.1[a]	15.4	18.1
Race/ethnicity (%)				
White	3.5	82.5	36.3	73.5
Hispanic	91.7	11.1	10.9	3.0
Black	3.1	2.3	48.9	20.8
Asian	0.4	2.4	3.7	2.4
American Indian/Alaskan	1.2	1.7	0.2	0.2
Free or reduced lunch eligible (%)	93.8	18.1	41.2	9.1

a. If one calculates the student/teacher ratio using the populations listed on Taylor High's website rather than using the U.S. Department of Education data, the ratio is 18.3, which is consistent with the other three schools.

in the schools; for example, both Mid-Atlantic schools have well-developed surveillance camera systems that monitor their hallways, but neither Southwestern state does, since there is too much outside ground to cover easily with cameras. But the fact that the schools within each state are very similar to one another facilitates comparisons and helps isolate distinctions related to the schools' student bodies.

All data were collected by the author and graduate research assistants. We spent six to 12 months collecting data in each school. During this time, we collected data through both interviews and site observations. A total of 105 semi-structured interviews were conducted across the four sites (at least 26 at each), with each interview taking between 20 minutes and almost two hours; most interviews lasted about 45 minutes. We interviewed a variety of individuals, including school administrators and (non-police) security ($n = 31$), teachers ($n = 16$), police officers ($n = 4$; one in each school), students ($n = 43$) and parents ($n = 11$). School security and administration respondents were selected based on a purposive sample, whereby we interviewed the individuals most involved with discipline; for teachers, students, and parents, we used snowball sampling to collect a sampling frame, and then selectively invited participants so as to maintain a sample that included whites and racial/ethnic minorities as well as males and females. Interviews were digitally recorded and sent to a professional transcriber. The interview guide varied depending on the role of the respondent, though each sought to acquire an understanding of the respondent's views of the school rules and punishments, his/her experiences with school discipline and his/her perceptions of school violence and appropriate responses to it. Researchers began with this guide and probed to explore relevant themes as necessary.

We also logged at least 100 hours of observational time at each school, with visits lasting two to three hours on average. Field notes were written immediately upon leaving each research site, rather than in the field, so as to limit an observation/reaction bias (Bachman and Schutt, 2007). While visiting the schools, researchers would either trail an administrator, police officer or security officer, observe a class or observe common areas in school (e.g., cafeterias, hallways). The principal at each school allowed us full access to the entire campus and to observe any interaction, as long as the participants did not object to our presence, which occurred on only one occasion (when a student's parents met with a principal to discuss the student's removal from school). We noted interactions between adults and students, particularly in response to perceived misbehavior among students. The majority of the interactions we observed were casual conversations in the hallways or classrooms, since this is the most common type of student–staff interaction. We also observed hundreds of meetings between students referred to an administrator (i.e., removed from class and sent 'to the office') and either their dean of discipline, interventionist or assistant principal (whoever handles referrals at each school), as well as arrests on campus and expulsion hearings (though these are far less common).

All data were coded and analyzed in Atlas ti 5.2 to search for patterns and themes that help us understand how school discipline policies take shape across schools. Analyses were guided by three goals: (1) developing a general understanding of common patterns in rule enforcement at each school (i.e., how each school punishes students); (2) carefully considering differences across schools in these patterns; and (3) a grounded theory approach whereby data were coded for any unexpected processes or themes that could further contextualize school discipline.

I focus my analyses here on between-school rather than within-school comparisons for two reasons. One is the difficulty and inappropriateness of making judgments about students. Our ability to judge a student's race/ethnicity or socio-economic status by sight is far from perfect and would be problematic in many cases, yet comparing how different students get treated within a school would require such evaluations (since the school's records are not available when observing students in the hallway). By focusing on between-school comparisons, I can consider how discipline initiatives take shape across student bodies with (relatively) known population characteristics. The other reason is that within school analyses are common in the existing literature, and their conclusions (that poor and minority youth disproportionately receive punishment in school) are very well established, as I discuss above, yet between-school comparisons are relatively unaddressed by the prior research.

Results

As I discuss above, cultural reproduction theory would lead one to predict that school discipline practices reproduce and exacerbate existing social inequalities among students by socializing each group of students into different roles within the social structure: one as the wielders of social power, and the other as a marginalized, hyper-controlled group. I find that this is true, in that there are important differences in the frequency of school punishments and in how school discipline takes shape across schools. However, I also find far more consistency across schools than cultural reproduction theory would lead one to predict. Certain themes found in each of the four schools suggest that students' experiences of a marginalized, hyper-controlled status while in public high schools are widespread.

Distinctions Across Schools

To begin, I focus on the ways in which cultural reproduction theory aptly predicts differences across schools regarding the character and climate of school discipline. I discuss three differences across schools within each state pair: perceptions of threat; the power to appeal punishments; and actual suspension rates.

Perceptions of Treat

In Johnson High, almost all students are Latino/a and come from a very poor neighborhood. Based on interviews and casual conversations with several school staff members, it is clear that their concern about violence centers on gangs, a social problem often associated with Latino/a youth. For example, when asked whether there are certain behaviors that he/she has particularly targeted for enforcement, the principal responded:

> Gang bangers, we went after real hard the first two years because they were running the school, at least they thought they were running the school. They were very active, very violent, very—they would walk around campus in groups and try to intimidate people, and it's like anything [else]: you go after the leaders, you make examples of them, you break them up, and once they don't have that person to lead them, things quieted down.

School staff members here constantly watched for indicators of gang membership such as gang signs, colors and other markers of affiliation. The student dress code that was distributed to students at the beginning of the 2005–6 school year stated that '[Students] shall not wear shirts with numbers 13, 15, 24, 27, 28, 31, 35, 36 (subject to change).' When I asked an administrator about this, he/she said that these numbers are used as gang signs, though the prohibition often changes to keep pace with changing gang signs; I then asked how students know if the rules against certain numbers change, and he/she responded that 'they just know'. The facts that the school is willing to risk appearing arbitrary and inconsistent, and that it prohibits a set of numbers, illustrate the priority of the fear of gangs in governing the school.

In contrast, perceptions of threat in Taylor High, with a majority of middle-class white students, are not centered on any single phenomenon. Instead, staff members discuss the same potential safety threats that administrators and teachers discuss in each school we studied, and presumably in schools across the country: fighting, drugs/alcohol and the potential for a catastrophic 'Columbine-like incident'. These problems are stressed as potential problems of youth and schools in general, and not related to any characteristics of their students.

When considering the two Mid-Atlantic schools, I find similar results—that perceptions of threat differ across the two schools, and in a way that corresponds to racial stereotypes. In Adams High, which has a large proportion of black students, fears of school crime center on a small group of students who are reportedly anti-authority, defiant and generally insubordinate, due to (according to school staff members) a combination of parental neglect, poverty and low school performance. The most common complaint we heard from staff members at this school is that there are several of these problem students, and that they wish these students could be expelled, but that the school cannot get rid of these troublemakers because the school district does not have a sufficient number of alternative placement spots.

These insubordinate students are repeatedly referred to as 'frequent flyers', due to their frequent visits to school disciplinarians. One teacher at this school suggested to me that, since these students have no interest in learning, the school should: 'Round up all the students who are failing, and just sit them in a big room and "make them color Ronald McDonald's nose all day", this would keep them occupied and out of trouble.'

When we observed these youth who are seen as continually insubordinate being punished, they were almost always black students, many of whom lived in poor neighborhoods of the nearby city. The language we repeatedly heard used to describe these students—insubordinate, disrespectful of authority, threatening—closely resembles stereotypes of African Americans as aggressive and disorderly (Ferguson, 2000; see also Quillian, 2006). Moreover, this image of disorder among African American students closely resembles the 1960s segregationists' warnings of disorderly, violent schools if desegregation were to occur.

Of course, these perceptions of danger stem from actual problems the schools face (see Hirschfield, 2008). Though we observed no gang violence at Johnson High, several individuals told us that the surrounding neighborhood does have a gang violence problem, and there are many gang signs and much gang-linked graffiti in it. Additionally, it is common to see students being disruptive and aggressive, either with each other or with teachers, at Adams High. Despite this, the fact that the concerns about violence and disorder in these two schools resemble stereotypes associated with the racial/ethnic groups that compose their student bodies is important, and coincides with prior research that illustrates how social class (Hollingsworth et al., 1984) and race/ethnicity (McCarthy and Hoge, 1987; Ferguson, 2000; Morris, 2005) shape teachers' and administrators' views of disorder within schools. These stereotypes can influence administrators' perceptions of the threat of violence beyond the actual problems they face (see Quillian and Pager, 2001), leading to overly severe punishments to students who display stereotypical behaviors. For example, as the Johnson High School principal's comments about gangs illustrate, students who are believed to be gang-involved are treated more harshly than other students caught doing similar things. These students' punishments are thus influenced by an assumption of gang involvement—an assumption that may be informed by stereotypes and that is extremely difficult to validate.

The Power to Appeal

A second difference across schools that mirrors what one would expect to find is that students in the schools with more middle-class white students have greater power to appeal their punishments. In each of the two mostly middle-class white schools, it is common for teachers, administrators or other school personnel to complain about students and their parents contesting the school's authority to punish. In Taylor High several respondents complained that when students are sent to an administrator for punishment, students often call their parents on the way down to the office, and a parent might appear at the office even before the student arrives to contest any punishment. Here and at Clinton High we often heard complaints about wealthy parents whose children 'could do no wrong' and who blamed the school for their children's misbehaviors.

Most parents of students in the two middle-class schools have more social capital than parents in the lower-income schools. Many of them hold white-collar or managerial jobs and/or are well educated, and we often heard about friendships between parents in these schools and either school administrators or teachers. This social capital empowers both parents and students to challenge the school and equips them with the political savvy of how to do so effectively (Lareau, 2000; Noguera, 2003a). In contrast, when we observed parents interact with school officials or when we heard school officials talk about parents in the two disadvantaged schools, we rarely observed or heard about parents appealing the school's punishments. Parents may either accept the school's authority (Kohn, 1969) or become hostile toward it, but this hostility is usually a general response to perceived unfairness rather than an organized appeal regarding a specific punishment.

The most pronounced effect of this differential opportunity to appeal punishments is the level of care given to following rules and documenting discipline procedures. Rather than students at the more advantaged schools receiving more lenient punishments, teachers and disciplinarians at these schools are more careful to apply the school rules appropriately (i.e., 'by the book') so that they can defend their actions if challenged. For example, at Adams High one of the primary disciplinarians rarely calls the parents of suspended students, despite the fact that this is a requirement of the school, because he claims to be too busy. We never observed violations of punishment procedures like this at either advantaged school. Though students at the advantaged schools likely would have been suspended as well, they (and their parents) might be treated in a way that recognizes their participation in the discipline process rather than as passive subjects of discipline.

Suspension Rates

In Table 4.7, I list the rate of suspensions per 100 students at each of the four schools. There is substantial regional variation in punishment, as the suspension rates are far greater in the Mid-Atlantic state than the Southwestern state. More importantly, though, within each state, the school with more lower-income and minority students has a substantially higher suspension rate. Table 4.7 leaves no doubt that the schools with more disadvantaged youth hand out suspensions far more frequently, which is precisely what one would predict based on cultural reproduction theory.

This result is consistent with results of the prior research on racial disproportionality of school punishment (e.g., Wu et al., 1982; McCarthy and Hoge, 1987; Skiba et al., 2000) as well as on the disproportionate punishment of poor youth (e.g., Hollingsworth et al., 1984), by showing that schools with more lower-class youth and racial/ethnic minority youth use suspension more often than schools with middle-class white students. Yet, as I describe below, a comparison of punishment rates—to

Table 4.7 Suspension Rates in Sampled Schools (2005–6)

State Schools	Suspension Rate per 100 Students
Southwestern state schools	
1. Taylor High	6.1
2. Johnson High	18.9
Mid-Atlantic state schools	
1. Clinton High	17.6
2. Adams High	95.5

NOTE: Suspension rate is calculated as (number of suspensions in the 2005–6 school year/student enrollment) × 100.

which the prior literature has largely been limited—does not tell the entire story, since it fails to capture the way in which similar policies have been adopted across disparate schools, and how these policies influence students' educational experiences and overall socialization.

Similarities Across Schools

Though there certainly are distinctions across schools that correspond to the racial/ethnic and socio-economic statuses of their student bodies, there are also important similarities across schools. That is, my results confirm Simon's (2007) argument by illustrating how the types of policies and practices that were once limited to urban schools (Devine, 1996) or schools serving low-income youth of color (e.g., Ferguson, 2000) are present in all four schools, even though the disciplinary results of these practices are unequally distributed. Additionally, both observations and interviews clearly show that the school discipline policies and practices of all four schools maintain students' powerlessness in the face of the school's authority, and ignore and often exacerbate students' problems. When considering how these policies take shape, it is apparent that school discipline policies at each school reproduce the culture of control.

Similar Policies Across Schools

At the national level, surveillance and policing in schools is pervasive. Though practices such as implementing police and using metal detectors at school entrances might have gained initial popularity only in urban schools (Devine, 1996), similar policies are now used throughout the USA. In fact, it might be the case that wealthier school districts are more likely to implement more costly surveillance tools such as cameras, simply because they are more likely to be able to afford them.

A recent national survey of schools conducted by the National Center for Education Statistics (NCES), a branch of the federal Department of Education, illustrates the pervasiveness of school security policies across social strata. Schools with larger populations of minorities or low-income students (as measured by free/reduced lunch eligibility) are more likely to have metal detectors and to require students to wear ID badges, even if these practices are still not used very frequently (in their peak groups, 11.8 percent of students report schools with ID badge requirements and 11.9 percent report random metal detector scans). Yet schools with few low-income students are somewhat more likely than others to use security cameras, and much more likely to use drug-sniffing dogs. Though, as some prior scholars have argued, surveillance cameras may be used in middle-class schools because they are a fluid technology that expands disciplinary power while promoting self-discipline and protection of students (in contrast to the rigid criminalizing nature of metal detectors—see Hirschfield, 2008), it would be difficult to claim this of random searches using drug-sniffing dogs as well. Despite clear distinctions in how security is practiced across schools, it is not the case that only schools serving low-income or minority youth have imported invasive surveillance and security practices.

The data support the idea that policies and practices meant to police and punish student misbehavior are pervasive, rather than located primarily in schools serving lower-class students or racial/ethnic minorities. Though none of the four schools we studied uses either drug-sniffing dogs or metal detectors, all have full-time SROs on campus and all use some form of a zero-tolerance policy. Each school responds fairly similarly to student misbehavior, in that they are quick to suspend students caught breaking rules. For example, each school within the Mid-Atlantic state publishes a code of conduct that prescribes punishments for a range of infractions, and these stated punishments are relatively similar across the two schools—the distinctions that are evident show harsher punishments at the more advantaged school. Consider a relatively common offense, leaving school without permission: its prescribed punishment (published in the code of conduct) in Clinton High is a detention or suspension for the first offense, and a three to five day suspension for subsequent offenses; in Adams High the code of conduct calls for one to three days of in-school suspension, in sequential order.

One difference that is particularly noticeable is that in one of our four schools, students are routinely arrested if they are involved in a fight—regardless of the severity of the fight or who the instigator was. This policy is based on an explicit agreement between the SRO and the principal, and designed to show students that the school will not tolerate violence. As a result, a student who responds to bullying by striking back, or a student who defends himself/herself is arrested along with the aggressor in the incident. According to administrators and the SRO, this is fair because students have an opportunity to avoid fighting; they can talk to a teacher, administrator or the SRO in advance to alert them of the problem, or they can simply walk away from the incident. Thus, according to this school, even a student who chooses to defend himself/herself physically against an aggressor deserves to be arrested. Based on cultural reproduction theory, one would expect to see a policy like this enforced only in the school with a plurality of racial/ethnic minority students, since they are being socialized to expect a police presence in their lives, harsh punishments for expected or relatively normal behaviors and the likelihood of developing a criminal record. Instead, we found this policy at the more advantaged Clinton High (and observed it being applied to both white and racial/ethnic minority students), illustrating how widespread harsh school discipline is.

Rules Are More Important Than Substantive Problems

Perhaps the most salient and consistent result from my analyses of observations and interviews is how school discipline trumps other issues. The mission of detecting and punishing misbehavior is prioritized over therapeutic, mentoring and even pedagogical goals. As Lyons and Drew (2006) find as well, harsh reactive punishments now take priority over more effective proactive strategies such as counseling or conflict resolution. We observed this in each of the four schools included in our study.

Given this emphasis on school discipline, looking for student misbehavior can take priority over other school functions, such as helping students with their actual problems—including problems which may be prompting their misbehaviors, but that go unaddressed. The following field note illustrates this. In this excerpt, an African American female student, Heather, enters the office of an administrator to ask for a tissue. It is clear that she has been crying, but instead of discussing her problem, the administrator lectures her on the dress code:

> Heather entered Mr. Morris' office and asked if he had a tissue. He said, 'Sure, come on in. Here you are, help yourself' (and held out a box of tissues that was on his desk). Heather took a tissue, said thank you, and turned to walk out. As she did, Mr. Morris said, 'Hold on there, what are you wearing? That shirt is a bit too short.' Heather was wearing a tight shirt that revealed her navel and the small of her back. She pulled it down and said, 'No, it's OK.' She turned to leave again, and when Mr. Morris saw that the back of the shirt was still about three inches over her waist, he said, 'No, it's not. Do you want me to take a picture of it with my camera phone to show you? You can't wear that to school.' Heather mumbled something and slowly turned, again, toward the door. As she did she sniffed, and put the tissue to her eye, as if she had been crying. She left, and Mr. Morris said to me, 'I hate to have to do that, getting on students for how they dress.'

It is important to note that this administrator perceives himself to be a mentor to students, especially the school's African American students, and often encourages students to come talk to him if they are having any problems. Yet when this student approached him, she was reprimanded for how she was dressed. Even when it was obvious that the student had been crying, Mr. Morris did not address the reason why.

This prioritization of rule following over addressing students' underlying problems was also clear in a mediation hearing conducted by two of the school's security guards, each of whom was trained in mediation hearings, and was in response to a minor fight between two students (Jack and Sam, both Latinos) in which nobody was hurt. In this mediation hearing, the reason for the conflict between the two students surfaced after a good deal of dialogue. But rather than teaching strategies for dealing with interpersonal conflict, discussing how each student felt about the incident, or considering behavioral solutions to this and future conflicts, the security guards only discussed the school rules and how one must conform to them (see also Hayward, 2000). This was the only solution or resolution presented—students must follow the rules, or they are wrong. When Jack presented a normative reason for disobeying the instructions of telling an authority when a conflict is brewing, he was told that he had no other option.

It is clear in each school that students' behavioral abnormalities are viewed with an eye toward rule enforcement, not behavioral or emotional counseling. Despite the fact that staff members in each of the four schools told us that students often misbehave due to personal or emotional problems, and most staff members expressed both empathy for students and a desire to help, none of the four schools routinely couples discipline with any counseling or behavioral therapy. We never observed a student referred to a school counselor or psychologist for misbehavior, even when the administrator or other staff member handing out the student's discipline notes to the student that he/she understands the student is experiencing difficulties at home or at school that may be contributing to the problem. Similarly, despite the fact that several teachers we interviewed told us that academic deficits are a common cause of students' classroom misbehavior (they act up to avoid embarrassment at not knowing the course material), the response of many of these teachers to the misbehavior is to remove the student from class. This aggravates the problem, since the punishment is not coupled with any tutoring or other instructional activity—instead the student only falls further behind the class. As evidenced through their words and their deeds, school staff seem to want to help students, but the nearly universal method of helping students we observed at each school is to rely strictly on a rule-orientation rather than responding to students' problems, where advice centers on how to follow rules rather than how to fix underlying problems.

This narrowly focused orientation to problem solving is noticed by students as well as school staff.

The narrow focus on rules and punishments rather than on other issues is clear when students are punished, as well. Rather than treating disciplinary interactions as a teaching opportunity in which students are involved and from which they learn, school staff members tend to treat these interactions as the occasions where punishment is applied without reflection or discussion. Students rarely have a genuine opportunity to discuss their behaviors and present their side to a disagreement, or to have a voice in deciding on their punishment. In fact, we observed several cases in which disciplinarians actually filled out a punishment form—meaning that they had already decided on a punishment—before ever talking to the student involved. This is important because it illustrates the clear lack of a student role in the punishment process, and the lack of any opportunity to present an alternative view of the incident or reasons why it happened. When it leads to suspension such a response is even illegal, given the Supreme Court's decision that schools must hold a hearing to discuss any suspension or expulsion either before or soon after the discipline occurs (*Goss v. Lopez*, 419 US 565, 1975).

In all four schools, punishments often appear to have the goal of asserting the school's authority rather than correcting behavioral problems. For example, one day in Clinton High we observed as John, a white male student, received a suspension for an incident that began when a counselor asked John for his ID badge as she passed John in the hallway. Though the school rules state that all students must have ID badges displayed at all times, we observed this enforced very rarely, and the near universal response is a brief lecture on wearing it next time rather than a detention (the punishment prescribed in the school code of conduct). John did not have his ID, and he gave a false name to the counselor and walked away. According to John (as he explained later), he was only teasing her by giving the false name, and he left her to fetch his ID. The counselor became angry, searched for John, found him and took him to an assistant principal. There he received a three-day suspension (his offense had escalated to insubordination, since he gave false information and avoided the counselor). He became angry, and in response to his raising his voice to an administrator, the punishment was raised to a four-day suspension. John left the office visibly angry, and the SRO stopped him and sat down with him. John complained that the administrator was 'on a power trip' and that it was unfair to be suspended for four days for not having an ID badge, when normally one receives no punishment or a detention at most.

In addition to being unfair, punishments that maintain authority without addressing students' needs or allowing them a voice in the punishment process can have practical consequences. If it teaches students that the school's authority is unfair or unfairly exercised, this can lower students' perceptions of legitimate authority and in turn reduce their willingness to abide by the school rules (see, for example, Gottfredson, 2001; Gottfredson et al., 2005).

Recent evidence also suggests that this brand of reactive punishment is less effective at shaping students' behaviors than proactive positive reinforcement (DeJong, 1999; Mayer, 1999). Moreover, these interactions have an important role in socializing students into their roles in society; the students are taught to be passive recipients of discipline and control. Contrary to what one would expect based on cultural reproduction theory, these lessons are equally likely to occur at each of the four schools we observed.

Discussion

The data thus illustrate how contemporary school discipline and security practices have effects that are more complex than one might assume based on cultural reproduction theory, and that are consistent with Simon's (2007) argument about the ubiquity of governing through crime in schools. Yet there are clear differences between schools that are consistent with cultural reproduction theory as well; most importantly, schools with more lower-income youth and youth of color have substantially higher suspension rates than their more advantaged counterparts. Additionally, the racial/ethnic and social class composition of schools' student bodies can shape perceptions of threat, and distinctions in social capital can influence the discipline process.

When one quantitatively compares the imposition of punishment across or within schools, as the prior research has done, clear distinctions emerge that are consistent with cultural reproduction theory. But when one qualitatively compares how these punishments take shape, the schools seem far more similar than one might expect. Thus the four schools studied here have qualitatively similar discipline policies and approaches but disparate disciplinary results. Each of the schools displays a willingness to intervene punitively by suspending students or referring them to police without inquiring into students' substantive problems, even if suspension rates vary considerably across the schools. By making within-school comparisons that focus almost entirely on what punishments are given and to whom, rather than how they are given out or what policies are in place, the prior research has largely missed this point.

These similarities across schools are even more striking given that the schools are located in very different regions of the USA, situated within disparate political environments. For example, the perceived 'threat' of immigration is politically important in the Southwestern state, but less so in the Mid-Atlantic state. This is important, since 91.7 percent of Johnson High students are Hispanic, and on our first visit to the school the principal volunteered his estimate that about 70 percent of the students there are undocumented immigrants. But despite the unique situation presented by the ethnic composition of this school within the Southwestern political climate, I find that discipline and security at Johnson High follow the same logics and organizing principles as at the other three schools. Additionally, though both are part of the nationwide movement of governing through crime in schools (Simon, 2007), the two states have responded to this movement in somewhat different ways by creating different rules and using different procedures. Despite these variations, I find a strikingly consistent character of school discipline across schools.

Importantly, these results do not suggest that the well-documented class or race divide in school punishment (e.g., Wu et al., 1982) has been leveled. Rather, I argue that one needs to understand class and racial/ethnic inequalities within a contemporary context of school punishment, whereby schools rely on a punitive regime. With harsher punishments in place, students attending schools with mostly lower-income and minority student bodies are more likely to receive them. But also, as a result of these contemporary discipline and security policies, *all* public school students are at a high absolute risk of receiving severe punishment and having their real problems overlooked for the sake of reactive rule enforcement. Thus these data supplement rather than contradict prior research showing that youth of color and lower-income youth face greater risks of being singled out for punishment than white and middle-income youth.

Perhaps the reason for the disjuncture between similar policies and disparate disciplinary results across schools is that more advantaged students are better skilled at navigating disciplinary regimes than less advantaged students. Thus, apparent neutrality of discipline is offset by social skills that correspond to social power and cultural capital. Such an explanation is consistent with the work of Lareau (2002, 2003), who demonstrates how middle-class families engage in 'concerted cultivation', a practice that teaches middle-class children how to force institutions, such as school, to adapt to their preferences. In contrast, working-class and lower-class children are not taught these skills (see also Kohn, 1969). Future research should consider whether disciplinary results vary across schools, despite similar policies, because of the social class-based skills of the students within these schools.

By finding surprising similarities across schools, the data suggest a form of social reproduction in addition to racial/ethnic or class divisions: schools reproduce existing logics of state power by preparing all students to accept and internalize contemporary mechanisms of state control. All students are socialized into the carceral state, in which policy makers govern through crime (Simon, 2007), punishments for perceived wrongdoing are severe and the logics of crime control pervade and are prioritized over other institutional goals, such as behavioral counseling or pedagogy (Lyons and Drew, 2006). This is a disturbing finding, for it suggests that the historically exceptional policies that have spread throughout schools, including SROs and zero-tolerance policies, are or will soon be presumed to be unexceptional among students (Casella, 2001). Future research should consider whether these contemporary policies and practices subsequently shape students' views of governing, of the balance between liberties and security or of crime control.

In addition to being socialized to expect or accept contemporary crime control strategies, it is also the case that harsh school discipline has the potential to diminish youths' educational prospects and/or entangle greater numbers of youth in the criminal justice system. Students who are repeatedly suspended without receiving help for their actual problems are more likely to drop out or fail out of school (Bowditch, 1993; Skiba et al., 2006), which will handicap their future career trajectories. Moreover, the tight coupling between schools and the criminal justice system suggests that more youth will be arrested for behaviors that in years past would have led only to in-school punishments (Wald and Losen, 2003; Rimer, 2004; Reyes, 2006; Hirschfield, 2008). As a result, youth who are arrested for school misbehavior will face greater future difficulties with employment prospects and other life opportunities (e.g., Pager, 2007). It is important for future research to consider the long-term implications of contemporary school discipline for students, and whether the known consequences of school punishment for youth of color (e.g., Bowditch, 1993) apply equally to middle-class white students who now receive a brand of discipline formerly reserved for youth of color and low-income youth.

There are broader potential implications to contemporary school discipline and security as well. Given that a wide array of students is being exposed to the experience of marginalization in the face of governance, it is possible that future civic participation will decline. Our experiences in the schools we studied certainly suggest that students view themselves as powerless to shape the rules they face, and that they respond by either accepting or avoiding authority structures. If this carries over into the realm of civic governance once these students reach the age of majority, it is possible that voting rates will decline from their already low levels.

Increased levels of student misbehavior are another potential consequence of contemporary school discipline and security. Prior research clearly shows relatively low levels of misconduct in schools that establish fair, clear and consistently enforced rules, that provide rewards for rule compliance and punishment for rule infractions and in which caring adults interact regularly with students in ways that teach prosocial norms and expectations (e.g., Bryk and Driscoll, 1988; Mayer and Leone, 1999; Gottfredson, 2001; Arum, 2003; Gottfredson et al., 2005). This research is consistent with procedural justice theory, which predicts that whether an individual complies with laws is largely a result of one's perception that the law is just and is enforced fairly (Tyler, 1990; Tyler and Sunshine, 2003). It seems likely that denying students a voice in discipline will negatively affect their perceptions of procedural justice.

Though these results are important for better understanding how school discipline and security take shape in contemporary schools, it is important to note a few potential limitations. One is generalizability; with only four schools being studied, there is no way to know whether what I describe here is true of other schools across the USA as well. This does seem likely, since the study includes schools in two states that are very distant from one another, yet the processes we observed in each of the four schools are very similar to one another and these schools have adopted strategies and logics that are also being adopted across the country (e.g., SROs, zero-tolerance policies, etc.). But as a qualitative study, the purpose here is to understand how these policies take shape in schools and whether cultural reproduction is valid in this case, not to generalize to schools across the USA. The second limitation is that two important groups are not considered here: private schools and students who have dropped out of school. It seems likely that discipline and security are very different in private schools than in public high schools; it is also possible that the discipline climate in the schools we studied has been changed as a result of the most troubled students leaving school, either by their own volition or by force. A third limitation is that although both race/ethnicity and social class have been shown in prior research to have independent effects on the likelihood of school punishment (see earlier), I am unable to deal with these two statuses separately. Rather, I compare what happens across schools with large numbers of lower-class youth of color and schools with mostly middle-class white youth. As I discuss earlier, making across-school comparisons adds to the literature by contributing a unique and important perspective to the large number of existing studies that make within-school comparisons. Yet this comes with a cost: by relying on qualitative data, in which students' individual socio-economic status is not available through observations, I am unable to determine how social class and race/ethnicity operate in different ways to shape school discipline and security.

References

Apple, Michael (1979) *Ideology and curriculum*. Boston, MA: Routledge & Kegan Paul.

Arum, Richard (2003) *Judging school discipline: The crisis of moral authority*. Cambridge, MA: Harvard University Press.

Bachman, Ronet and Russell K. Schutt (2007) *The practice of research in criminology and criminal justice*, 3rd edn. Los Angeles, CA: Sage.

Bourdieu, Pierre and Jean-Claude Passeron (1990) *Reproduction in education, society and culture*, 2nd edn. Los Angeles, CA: Sage.

Bowditch, Christine (1993) 'Getting rid of troublemakers: High school disciplinary procedures and the production of dropouts', *Social Problems* 40(4): 493–509.

Bowles, Samuel and Herbert Gintis (1976) *Schooling in capitalist America: Educational reform and the contradictions of economic life*. New York: Basic Books.

Bryk, A.S. and M.E. Driscoll (1988) *The school as community: Theoretical foundations, contextual influences, and consequences for students and teachers.* Madison, WI: University of Wisconsin, National Center on Effective Secondary Schools.

Casella, Ronnie (2001) *Being down: Challenging violence in urban schools.* New York: Teachers College Press.

Chamblis, William J. (1973) 'The saints and the roughnecks', *Society* 11(1): 24–31.

Cicourel, Aaron V. and John I. Kitsuse (1963) *The educational decision-makers.* New York: Bobs-Merrill Company.

Cohen, Albert K. (1955) *Delinquent boys: The culture of the gang.* Glencoe, IL: Free Press.

DeJong, William (1999) *Building the peace: The resolving conflict creatively program.* Washington, DC: National Institute of Justice.

Devine, John (1996) *Maximum security: The culture of violence in inner-city schools.* Chicago, IL: University of Chicago Press.

Dinkes, Rachel, Emily Forrest Cataldi, Grace Kena and Katrina Baum (2006) *Indicators of school crime and safety: 2006.* US Departments of Education and Justice. Washington, DC: US Government Printing Office.

Eckert, Penelope (1989) *Jocks and burnouts: Social categories and identity in the high school.* New York: Teachers College Press.

Eitle, Tamela Mcnulty and David James Eitle (2004) 'Inequality, segregation, and the overrepresentation of African Americans in school suspension', *Sociological Perspectives* 47(3): 269–87.

Ferguson, Ann (2000) *Bad boys: Public schools in the making of black masculinity.* Ann Arbor, MI: University of Michigan Press.

Finn, Peter and Jack McDevitt (2000) *National assessment of school resource officer programs final project report.* Washington, CD: National Institute of Justice.

Garland, David (2001) *The culture of control: Crime and social order in contemporary society.* New York: Oxford University Press.

Gee, James P. (1996) *Social linguistics and literacies: Ideology in discourses,* 2nd edn. New York: Taylor & Francis.

Gottfredson, Denise (2001) *Schools and delinquency.* New York: Cambridge University Press.

Gottfredson, Gary D., Denise C. Gottfredson, Allison Ann Payne and Nisha C. Gottfredson (2005) 'School climate predictors of school disorder: Results from a national study of delinquency prevention in schools', *Journal of Research in Crime and Delinquency* 42(4): 412–44.

Greene, Judith A. (1999) 'Zero tolerance: A case study of police policies and practices in New York City', *Crime and Delinquency* 45(2): 171–87.

Hayward, Clarris Rile (2000) *De-facing power.* New York: Cambridge University Press.

Hirschfield, Paul (2008) 'Preparing for prison? The criminalization of school discipline in the USA', *Theoretical Criminology* 12(1): 79–101.

Hollingsworth, Ellen J., Henry S. Lufler, Jr and William H. Clune, III (1984) *School discipline: Order and autonomy.* New York: Praeger.

Illich, Ivan (1971) *De-schooling society.* New York: Harper & Row.

Kohn, Melvin L. (1969) *Class and conformity: A study in values.* Homewood, IL: Dorsey Press.

Lareau, Annete (2000) *Home advantage: Social class and parental interaction in elementary education,* 2nd edn. Lanham, MD: Rowman & Littlefield.

Lareau, Annete (2002) 'Invisible inequality: Social class and childrearing in black families and white families', *American Sociological Review* 67(5): 747–76.

Lareau, Annete (2003) *Unequal childhoods: Class, race, and family life.* Berkeley, CA: University of California Press.

Lyons, William and Julie Drew (2006) *Punishing schools: Fear and citizenship in American public education.* Ann Arbor, MI: University of Michigan Press.

McCarthy, John D. and Dean R. Hoge (1987) 'The social construction of school punishment: Racial disadvantage out of universalistic process', *Social Forces* 65(4): 1101–20.

Mayer, G. Roy (1999) 'Constructive discipline for school personnel', *Education and Treatment of Children* 22(1): 36–54.

Mayer, Matthew J. and Peter E. Leone (1999) 'A structural analysis of school violence and disruption: Implications for creating safer schools', *Education and Treatment of Children* 22(3): 333–56.

Morris, Edward W. (2005) '"Tuck in that shirt!": Race, class, gender and discipline in an urban school', *Sociological Perspectives* 48(1): 25–48.

Morris, Edward W. (2007) '"Ladies" or "loudies"? Perceptions and experiences of black girls in classrooms', *Youth and Society* 38(4): 490–515.

Noguera, Pedro A. (2003a) *City schools and the American dream: Reclaiming the promise of public education.* New York: Teachers College Press.

Noguera, Pedro A. (2003b) 'Schools, prisons and social implications of punishment: Rethinking disciplinary practices', *Theory into Practice* 42(4): 341–50.

Oakes, Jeannie (1985) *Keeping track: How schools structure inequality.* New Haven, CT: Yale University Press.

Pager, Devah (2007) *Marked: Race, crime, and finding work in an era of mass incarceration.* Chicago, IL: University of Chicago Press.

Public Agenda (2004) *Teaching interrupted: Do discipline policies in today's public schools foster the common good?* New York: Public Agenda.

Quillian, Lincoln (2006) 'New approaches to understanding racial prejudice and discrimination', *Annual Review of Sociology* 32: 299–328.

Quillian, Lincoln and Devah Pager (2001) 'Black neighbors, higher crime? The role of racial stereotypes in evaluations of neighborhood crime', *American Journal of Sociology* 107(3): 717–67.

Raffaele Mendez, Linda M. and Howard M. Knoff (2003) 'Who gets suspended and why: A demographic analysis of schools and disciplinary infractions in a large school district', *Education and Treatment of Children* 26(1): 30–51.

Reyes, Augustina H. (2006) *Discipline, achievement, and race: Is zero tolerance the answer?* Lanham, MD: Rowman & Littlefield Education.

Rimer, Sara (2004) 'Unruly students facing arrest, not detention', *New York Times* 4 January: A1.

Rist, Ray C. (1973) *The urban school: A factory for failure.* Cambridge, MA: MIT Press.

Rothstein, Stanley W. (1984) *The power to punish: A social inquiry into coercion and control in urban schools.* New York: University Press of America.

Schiraldi, Vincent and Jason Ziedenberg (2001) *Schools and suspensions: Self-reported crime and the growing use of suspensions.* Washington, DC: Justice Policy Institute.

Schuiteman, John G. (2001) *Second annual evaluation of the DCJS funded school resource officer programs. Report of the Department of Criminal Justice Services, fiscal year 1999–2000.* Richmond, VA: Department of Criminal Justice Services.

Simon, Jonathan (2007) *Governing through crime: How the war on crime transformed American democracy and created a culture of fear.* New York: Oxford University Press.

Skiba, Russell J. (2000) *Zero tolerance, zero evidence: An analysis of school disciplinary practice.* Indiana: Education Policy Center, Research Report #SRS2.

Skiba, Russell J. and Gil G. Noam (eds) (2002) *Zero tolerance: Can suspension and expulsion keep schools safe?* New York: Jossey Bass.

Skiba, Russell J., Robert S. Michael, Abra Carroll Nardo and Reece Peterson (2000) *The color of discipline: Sources of racial and gender disproportionality in school punishment.* Indiana: Education Policy Center, Research Report #SRS1.

Skiba, Russell J., Cecil R. Reynolds, Sandra Graham, Peter Sheras, Jane Close Conoley and Enedina Garcia-Vazquez (2006) *Are zero tolerance policies effective in the schools? An evidentiary review and recommendations* (Report by the American Psychological Association Zero Tolerance Task Force). Washington, DC: American Psychological Association. http://www.apa.org/releases/ZTTF ReportBOD Revisions 5–15.pdf (accessed 24 December 2008).

Tyack, David B. (1974) *The one best system: A history of American urban education.* Cambridge, MA: Harvard University Press.

Tyler, Tom R. (1990) *Why people obey the law.* New Haven, CT: Yale University Press.

Tyler, Tom R. and Jason Sunshine (2003) 'The role of procedural justice for legitimacy in shaping public support for policing', *Law & Society Review* 37(3): 513–48.

Vavrus, Frances and KimMarie Cole (2002) '"I didn't do nothin": The discursive construction of school suspension', *Urban Review* 34(2): 87–111.

Wacquant, Loïc (2001) 'Deadly symbiosis: When ghetto and prison meet and mesh', in D. Garland (ed.) *Mass imprisonment: Social causes and consequences*, pp. 82–120. London: SAGE.

Wald, Johanna and Daniel Losen (2003) *Deconstructing the school-to-prison pipeline: New directions for youth development, number 99.* New York: Jossey-Bass.

Western, Bruce (2006) *Punishment and inequality in America.* New York: Russell Sage Foundation.

Willis, Paul (1977) *Learning to labor: How working class kids get working class jobs.* New York: Columbia University Press.

Wu, Shi-Chang, William Pink, Robert Crain and Oliver Moles (1982) 'Student suspension: A critical reappraisal', *Urban Review* 14(4): 245–303.

DISCUSSION QUESTIONS

1. Describe incidents that occurred during President Clinton's era that led to the creation of School Resource Officers within the public schools. Do you believe that this system is productive?
2. The author speaks of pipelining from school-to-prison. Do you feel that officers within the school system lead to greater imprisonment of those who are subjected to the increased policing within the schools? Explain.
3. Summarize the author's discussion of class and how what is taught in the schools is based on the class system of students. Explain why this is important to understanding policing within schools.

❖

READING

The increase in the number of girls in the juvenile justice system has led to the introduction of gender-specific services and programs. Unlike traditional services and programs, gender-specific approaches address physical and sexual violence, pregnancy and motherhood, family problems, and issues unique to girls. The authors of this article examine how probation officers utilize traditional and **gender-specific programs** and whether or not they are successful with African American girls. The research focuses on placement in either traditional programs or the Reaffirming Young Sisters' Excellence (RYSE) Program in Alameda County, California. RYSE was both a gender- and culture-specific program. The authors conclude that the African American girls in the RYSE program have better success. African American girls had less success with traditional probation services than other races.

The Provision and Completion of Gender-Specific Services for Girls on Probation

Variation by Race and Ethnicity

Angela M. Wolf, Juliette Graziano, and Christopher Hartney

SOURCE: Wolf, A., Graziano, J., & Hartney, C. (2009). The provision and completion of gender-specific services for girls on probation: Variation by race and ethnicity. *Crime & Delinquency*, *55*(2), 294–312.

Introduction

In the past two decades, the number of girls entering the juvenile justice system has risen dramatically at a rate that is much higher than boys (Snyder & Sickmund, 2006). Girls today are more likely to be arrested for more violent crimes, more likely to be detained or committed to residential facilities, and serve more time than girls in years past (Chesney-Lind & Irwin, 2008). This is disproportionately true for girls of color. The over-representation of minority youth has been identified in all stages of the juvenile justice system (Hartney & Silva, 2007), and research has documented variations in the processing, treatment, and needs of system-involved girls of color (Chesney-Lind & Shelden, 2004).

The increasing number of girls in the juvenile justice system is demanding attention from researchers and policy makers in search of explanations for delinquent behavior and effective interventions. To address the unique experiences of girls, practitioners are looking for gender-responsive programming. Within the last decade, guiding principles for gender-specific programming have been developed by Greene, Peters, and colleagues. Although they acknowledge that the specific features of programming will differ due to the goals, size, scope of the programs, and needs of the population, they posit that the common elements of effective gender-specific programming for girls should include organization and management, staffing pattern and training, intake process, education, skills training, promotion of positive development, relationship building, culturally relevant activities, career opportunities, health services, recreational activities, responsive services, mentoring, peer activities, full family involvement, community involvement, specific treatment concerns, reentry into the community, and evaluation (Greene, Peters, & Associates, 1998).

Although the services considered essential for effective girls' programming have been outlined, how well they have been incorporated into gender-responsive interventions remains largely unknown. This is particularly problematic given the dearth of rigorous evaluations of girls' programs. Without examining which services and program elements are beneficial for which groups for girls, our understanding of their effectiveness is severely limited.

Gender-Specific Programming

Influenced by feminist criminologists, gender experts, and juvenile justice leaders, in 1992, the Juvenile Justice and Delinquency Prevention (JJDP) Act was reauthorized (Schaffner, 2006). Central to the JJDP Act was the provision of gender-specific services for the prevention and treatment of juvenile delinquency (JJDP Act, Sec, 223 [8]). In the reauthorization of 2002, providing needed gender-specific services remained a requirement. In response, organizations around the country have been developing girls' programs because gender-responsive interventions may be better positioned than traditional services to address risk factors and meet the treatment needs of delinquent girls.

Gender-responsive programming has been defined as a multidimensional, strengths-based approach based on theoretical perspectives that consider females' pathways into the system and provide interventions that specifically address social, cultural, and psychological factors (Bloom, Owen, & Covington, 2005). Greene et al. (1998) outlined essential services in gender-responsive programs, which address administrative aspects, the provision of needed services, and program evaluation. More specifically, Chesney-Lind (2001) argues that effective programs address physical and sexual violence, the risk of HIV/AIDS, pregnancy and motherhood, substance use, family problems, and stress; include support regarding safe housing, employment training, and unemployment; and develop empowerment and self-efficacy.

This important work led to the proliferation of girls' programs, which have differed substantially in their theoretical orientations, provision of services, and desired outcomes. Interventions have included a variety of services such as girls-only groups, education, life skills sessions, individual and group counseling, parent training, and cultural events. Gender-specific programs have been created as probation and diversion alternatives as well as to address problems such as conduct disorders, gang involvement, sexual risk-taking behavior, or issues related to abuse.

Services for Delinquent Girls

More recent work has examined specific needs of girls. Girls have expressed needs regarding counseling for abuse, sex, sexuality education, and childbirth and parenting classes (Chesney-Lind, Morash, & Stevens, 2008). Holsinger, Belknap, and Sutherland (1999) found that a small percentage of the services that girls stated they needed were actually rendered. For example, 9% of girls actually received services to develop job and career skills, though 70% reported the need. Of the 64% that wanted to learn independent living skills, only 5% received help in this area. Finally, 54% stated they needed family counseling and general health education, though only 14% and 8%, respectively, received these services. In general, traditional programs may not include services and activities that address girls' risk factors and needs. Even programs designed for girls may not be attentive to group differences and the underlying structural issues that place girls at risk of system involvement such as racism and heterosexism.

Although many programs for girls have been created to address delinquency, few have undergone rigorous evaluation to determine their effectiveness. In addition, the specific services and programs have been conceptualized, operationalized, and measured differently because the definition of gender-specific programming was so broad and encompassing. It is crucial for gender-specific programs to be evaluated to ensure that they are effectively meeting girls' needs. Even some feminist researchers have challenged the need for gender-specific programming, arguing that quality evidence-based programs are sufficient and could be equally effective for girls (Kempf-Leonard & Sample, 2000). Empirical reviews of gender-specific interventions that compare traditional and gender-specific services and test for group differences can add important information to this debate.

The Reaffirming Young Sisters' Excellence (RYSE) Program

The RYSE program was designed as an alternative to traditional probation in Alameda County, California. Alameda County had witnessed an increase in the number of girls entering the justice system during the 1980s through the mid-1990s. The goals of the RYSE program were to reduce recidivism rates and increase social, academic, and vocational competencies.

The RYSE program relied on the theoretical assumption that enhancing relationships between each girl and her probation officer and by connecting the girl and the program to the larger community could prevent girls from returning to the justice system. It was theorized that gender-specific interventions administered in a manner that was responsive to individual girl's needs would be more effective than traditional probation in keeping girls out of the system. Therefore, several of the design features and services encouraged and supported relationship building, where probation officers had smaller caseloads (fewer than 25 girls), would be available to the girls via cell phone, and would be located in the girls' home communities. Probation officers would conduct the initial assessments, transport girls to interventions, provide services to family members, and teach or lead some of the interventions.

The RYSE program intended to provide intensive supervision and offer gender- and culturally responsive services in combination with traditional probation services such as required restitution and community service for successful completion. Case plan development and implementation were central to relationship building between each girl and her probation officer. Girls were randomly assigned to the intervention group or the comparison group. RYSE-specific programs were generally divided into two categories: (a) mandatory programs for all girls in the program, and (b) services designed to sanction and/or treat case-specific needs.

The mandatory program interventions aimed to develop life skills in the areas of pregnancy prevention, peer relationships, and teen parenting. The foundation of the RYSE program was the provision of life skills development interventions. Although individual case plans were developed for each girl, participants in the RYSE program began with a rehabilitation strategy that included Sister Friends and Pregnancy Prevention. Girls who were assigned to the Teen Parenting component were not enrolled in the requisite Pregnancy Prevention program. Early on, Sports and Recreation was a mandatory program, but it was later deactivated when staffing changes required it to be so.

Other program services were added as the girls' needs were identified and appropriate community providers were identified and matched with participants. Additional services included anger management, substance use groups, crisis intervention and the provision of funds, family and group counseling, and medical services.

RYSE services were intended to support girls at different developmental stages and from diverse cultural backgrounds and sexual orientations and included activities such as mother-daughter special events and female-focused conferences and workshops. Regarding race, the majority of the girls in the RYSE program were African American; therefore, in an effort to provide culturally congruent services, the intervention team consisted primarily of African Americans, and many of the interventions had an African American focus.

RYSE Evaluation

The National Council on Crime and Delinquency conducted a rigorous program evaluation of the RYSE program (NCCD, 2001). A subsequent examination of the evaluation findings conducted by Le, Arifuku, and Nunez (2003) tested two hypotheses. First, the gender-specific hypothesis argued that girls who received the RYSE intervention would have lower recidivism scores as compared to girls who received traditional probation services. Second, the cultural hypothesis proposed that African American girls who participated in the RYSE intervention would have lower recidivism scores than their Hispanic, Asian, and White counterparts.

The gender-specific hypothesis was not supported as girls who participated in the RYSE intervention did not have lower recidivism scores than the girls in the comparison group. The cultural hypothesis was supported in that African American girls in the RYSE group did significantly better than African American girls in the comparison group.

Findings from the RYSE impact evaluation and analysis that tested gender-specific and cultural hypotheses supported the need to explore racial and ethnic differences in program outcomes. Chesney-Lind et al. (2008, p. 182) note that of the eight contemporary evaluations included in their review of gender-specific programs for girls, only RYSE examined group differences related to program effectiveness. Le et al. (2003) observed that African American girls in RYSE had lower levels of recidivism than African American girls in a comparison group. However, they found no such differences for Hispanic, Asian, and Caucasian participants. Why these outcomes occurred is not explored through the research.

The current article directly addresses this issue. We build on the work of Le et al. (2003) by examining service delivery for girls. Le and her colleagues theorized that the program was more effective for African American girls because some of the RYSE services were developed to be culturally sensitive to African American girls. Contrary to the hypothesis, Le et al. found no overall effect for girls in the RYSE condition but did report that African American girls benefit from their involvement. We used the data available from the evaluation to explore why this might be true.

To explore this issue, in the current article, we focus on how probation officers utilize both traditional and RYSE program services in their interventions with girls. In particular, we examine the number of services that are utilized by probation officers and the percentage of services completed by girls, with special attention given to race/ethnicity.

Method

Hypotheses

The following hypotheses are explored:

> *Hypothesis 1:* There will be no racial/ethnic group difference within the comparison group regarding services assigned, services completed, and the percentage of services completed.

> *Hypothesis 2:* There will be no racial/ethnic group differences within the RYSE group regarding the number of *traditional services* assigned, services completed, and percentage of services completed.

> *Hypothesis 2a:* There will be racial/ethnic group differences within the RYSE group regarding the number of *RYSE interventions* assigned, services completed, and percentage of services completed where African American girls will have higher rates of completion.

> *Hypothesis 3:* There will be no racial/ethnic group differences between the RYSE group and comparison group regarding traditional services assigned, services completed, and the percentage of services completed.

Research Design and Sample

The current article performs secondary data analysis on data collected for the RYSE evaluation. The evaluation of RYSE utilized an experimental design through which girls deposed in the juvenile justice system were randomly assigned into either the intervention group or a comparison group. From the pool of eligible girls, the last digit of each girl's case identification number was used to determine whether she was placed in the experimental or comparison group. The inclusion criteria for RYSE participation included (a) being a female, age 12–17; (b) having no severe emotional problems, as determined by an assessment done by the Youth Guidance Clinic; and (c) having a court date for a pretrial hearing. Each girl's arrest needed to be followed by a charge filed by the District Attorney's office, and a court date must have been set to determine whether or not the girl would be held responsible for the charge (which is equivalent to determining guilt or innocence in adult court).

As in Le et al. (2003), the analyses for the current study consisted of all girls who had complete data for the 12-month follow-up period. However, the current study excluded 17 girls from this original database: 12 girls who were in the program (RYSE or community probation) for less than a month and 5 comparison group girls who had been assigned more than one RYSE-specific service or whose probation officer had RYSE training. The final sample consisted of 333 girls,

249 in the RYSE group and 84 in the comparison group.

Data Sources

Data in this study used the Common Data Elements (CDE). The CDE consists of 118 questions designed by the California Board of Corrections to collect information about Challenge Grant participants and evaluate program effectiveness. The variables include background information and risk factors (demographics, school performance, justice system involvement, and substance use at program entry). Tracking variables were collected for various outcomes for the youth at program exit and at the end of the three follow-up periods. Outcomes include completion of program requirements, completion of conditions of probation, and subsequent delinquent behavior. Finally, the CDE contains information about interventions and referrals regarding the types of services and contacts the client completed during the program intervention period.

Programmatic Elements. There were 60 programmatic elements, requirements, and services (together referred to as "services" in this article) available for assignment to study participants, ranging from restitution and substance abuse treatment to probation officer home visits and one-time community events. Three services-related data points were of particular interest in assessing racial/ethnic differences: (a) number of services assigned, (b) number of services successfully completed, and (c) percentage of assigned services successfully completed.

Number of Services Assigned. The number of services assigned assessed whether there was variation among participants given the opportunity to receive services. It was hypothesized that more services would be assigned to the RYSE group than to the comparison group but that there would be no difference by race/ethnicity in the number of services assigned within each study group.

Number of Services Completed. The number of assigned services successfully completed measure assessed how many services each youth fully received during the study period. This was one of two ways available to assess the "dosage" of services.

Percentage of Services Completed. The percentage of assigned services successfully completed also measured the dosage of services received. This variable was used to assess whether RYSE, with its emphasis on gender and culturally appropriate programming and on probation officers heavily involved in their clients' successful completion of probation, led not only to broader access to services but greater rates of success, as evidenced by service completion. It was hypothesized that RYSE girls would, on average, have higher percentages of completed services than comparison group girls. The argument behind this hypothesis is that girls are more likely to be successful in services that are appropriate to their needs and personalities, including their cultural characteristics. Girls who complete a high percentage of their assigned services are likely to have remained because services were accessible, and their needs were met with appropriate and effective methods.

Type of Services. These three data points were gathered separately for two domains of services: "traditional probation services" and "RYSE services." Traditional probation services are the traditional services associated with community probation and which could be assigned to either comparison or treatment group participants. RYSE services were specifically developed as part of the RYSE program and were available only to RYSE participants.

Results

The 333 girls were aged 11 to 18 years (mean [*M*] = 16.2, standard deviation [*SD*] = 1.36). Just under two thirds of study participants were African American, 15% were Hispanic, 14% were White, and 6% were API (Table 4.8).

Within the comparison group, there were no differences by race/ethnicity for traditional services assigned. There were no significant differences between African Americans and Hispanic or API girls on traditional services completed (see Table 4.9). There was no statistically significant difference between African American and Hispanic girls on completed percentage of traditional services.

Within the RYSE group, there were no differences by race/ethnicity for traditional services assigned. There were no significant differences between African American and Hispanic or African American and API girls on traditional services completed (see Table 4.9).

The ANOVA (race/ethnicity within RYSE group) for percentage of traditional services completed was statistically significant, F (3, 211) = 3.001, $p < .05$. African American girls had a lower percentage of completed traditional services than Whites. African American and Hispanic girls completed approximately the same percentage of traditional services.

- There were no differences by race/ethnicity in the number of RYSE services assigned to girls in the RYSE group.
- There were no differences by race/ethnicity in the number of completed RYSE services by girls in the RYSE group.
- There were no differences by race/ethnicity in the percentage of RYSE services completed by girls in the RYSE group.
- Overall for the RYSE group, a greater number of RYSE services than traditional services were assigned. This was also true for each race/ethnicity.
- Overall for the RYSE group, a greater number of RYSE services than traditional services were successfully completed. This was also true for each race/ethnicity.
- Overall for the RYSE group, there was no statistically significant difference in the completion percentage for traditional services versus RYSE services. By race/ethnicity, statistically significant difference was only found for API girls who completed traditional services at a higher rate than they completed RYSE services (see Table 4.10).

Table 4.8 Racial and Ethnic Count and Percentages by Study Group (N = 333)

		African American	White	Hispanic	API	Total
Treatment (RYSE)	*n*	161	34	38	16	249
	Percentage	65%	14%	15%	6%	100%
Comparison	*n*	52	13	12	7	84
	Percentage	62%	15%	14%	8%	100%

NOTE: API = Asian or Pacific Islander; RYSE = Reaffirming Young Sisters' Excellence.

Table 4.9 Traditional Services Completed by Study Group and Race/Ethnicity

		M	*SD*	*n*
African American	Treatment	2.25	2.04	161
	Comparison	1.06	1.53	52
White	Treatment	3.44	2.35	34
	Comparison	2.69	1.80	13
Hispanic	Treatment	2.18	2.26	38
	Comparison	1.75	2.09	12
API	Treatment	2.56	1.26	16
	Comparison	2.14	1.57	7
Total	Treatment	2.43	2.11	249
	Comparison	1.50	1.75	84

NOTE: API = Asian or Pacific Islander; *M* = mean; *SD* = standard deviation.

Table 4.10 Percentage of Services Completed Within RYSE Group by Race/Ethnicity

	Type of Service	*M*	*SD*	*n*
African American	RYSE	66.03	35.79	138
	Traditional	65.98	38.73	
White	RYSE	76.98	26.97	29
	Traditional	82.33	23.49	
Hispanic	RYSE	57.17	42.68	33
	Traditional	64.75	42.53	
API*	RYSE	66.40	35.54	15
	Traditional	87.78	23.96	
Total	RYSE	66.17	36.03	215
	Traditional	69.52	37.38	

NOTE: API = Asian or Pacific Islander; *M* = mean; RYSE = Reaffirming Young Sisters' Excellence; *SD* = standard deviation.

*$t(14) = -2.62$, $p = .048$.

Discussion

As a gender- and culturally responsive intervention aimed at moving girls out of the juvenile justice system, we would hope and expect that girls involved with RYSE would have less future system involvement, with African American girls having the best outcomes. Le et al. (2003) were only able to support the latter. The current study is an attempt to discuss why.

Well over 100,000 girls are placed on probation every year in the United States, and they are disproportionately girls of color, especially African American. Yet findings here suggest that African American girls are having less success with traditional services than their White and API counterparts. This illustrates the need for continued exploration on how to provide girls of diverse experiences the services they need. In her critique of gender-specific services, Goodkind (2005) argues against the use of an essentialized notion of gender that is inattentive to other identity factors such as race, ethnicity, class, and sexuality. The provision of gender-specific services is at the core of the argument for gender-responsive theory and program development. However, without solid evidence to support their effectiveness, we cannot be sure that we are on the right path toward helping girls reach desired outcomes. The results from this study point to the need to carefully craft, implement, and evaluate gender-responsive intervention.

Outcomes for African American Girls

African American girls were assigned to both traditional and RYSE services equally with other races/ethnicities. This suggests the opportunity for receiving services was equal among study participants—a baseline for moving forward with the other analyses.

African American girls had a lower rate of success in the services to which they were assigned—both RYSE and traditional—compared to other races/ethnicities. This is a disturbing finding and suggests that both traditional probation programming, geared historically toward boys, and new programming, specifically designed to be gender- and culturally sensitive, are not succeeding with African American girls as well as they should. Success or failure in a particular component of probation is a function of a variety of factors, including, of course, characteristics of the girl herself but also including program and service design, service provider training, probation officer characteristics, and other resource issues. It is important to gain a deeper understanding of what barriers may exist for African American girls and whether a lack of accessibility, cultural congruence, or investment was an influential variable.

Assigned at equal rates but succeeding less often than other races/ethnicities, it is not surprising that African American girls successfully completed fewer services than girls of other races. Again, this was true for both traditional and RYSE services. Successfully completing fewer services and other probation services puts African Americans at a disadvantage.

African Americans completed fewer traditional probation services than other racial groups, but African Americans in the RYSE group completed more traditional probation services than African Americans in the comparison group. Despite the disparities in the utilization and success of services for African American girls compared to other races/ethnicities found here, Le et al. (2003) found evidence that African Americans benefited from RYSE.

Traditional Probation Services

Because few gender-responsive programs exist and traditional probation is the standard treatment, it is important to know if there are racial/ethnic differences in the completion of traditional programming. Although African American girls were assigned to traditional probation services similar to other ethnic groups, they did not complete these services at the same level.

Like other races/ethnicities, African American girls in the RYSE group tended to complete traditional services at higher rates than they completed RYSE services. Although there were more RYSE services offered to and completed by RYSE participants than traditional services, girls generally had higher completion rates for traditional services rather than RYSE services, though this was only statistically significant for API girls. This runs counter to the hypothesis that RYSE services would be completed at a higher rate as they would be more individualized and responsive to each girl's needs and experiences. In addition, the girls in the RYSE condition received and completed more RYSE services than they received and completed traditional probation services. So although RYSE girls had traditional probation elements, they also had substantial and successful exposure to RYSE services.

Traditional services may be better suited for some girls and/or some risk factors or treatment issues. Proponents of gender-responsive programming argue that although girls and boys share similar risk factors and treatment needs, there are distinct differences. Traditional services developed primarily for boys may address some of those areas of overlap. Interestingly, despite a wide array of alternative services at their disposal, probation officers in the RYSE condition assigned their girls to the same number of traditional services as probation officers in the comparison group. It is not known whether this speaks to the perceived value of traditional probation services or whether this is a lack of training or buy-in to the alternatives.

Finally, the finding that African Americans in the RYSE program completed more traditional services and had a higher success rate with traditional services than African Americans in the comparison group is somewhat encouraging. In theory, some aspect of the RYSE intervention may have been effective for African American girls in completing traditional services. There also could be an interaction between the girls' experience in the RYSE-specific services and their success in traditional services. In other words, something about RYSE may make it easier for them to succeed in the more traditional aspects of probation. This area is worthy of future investigation.

This area would also need additional analysis to determine the cause. Given that this group had poorer outcomes in the comparison group than Whites and APIs and traditional services are still the norm in probation departments across the United States, exploring in more depth how the intervention supported service completion could provide answers for how better to serve African American girls.

In conclusion, these findings provide preliminary support for the continued analysis of racial and ethnic group differences regarding program outcomes. Conceptually, programs that assume girls are a homogenous group may ignore important differences in race, ethnicity, sexual orientation, and/or class. Because diversity exists within the construct of gender, programs will be limited if they are not attentive to these differences.

Future Directions

Given that the results of the RYSE evaluation are equivocal, combined with the lack of rigorous testing of girls-only interventions reported in the literature, future research regarding which services are most effective in diverting girls from the justice system are direly needed. It is also important to investigate not only which types of services are most effective but to explore how other factors may impact groups differently. In an effort to provide services tailored to meet girls' unique needs, attention should be paid to differences along other axes of identity (Goodkind, 2005). The juvenile justice system has a long history of targeting immigrant girls and girls of color (Chesney-Lind &

Shelden, 2004), so studies should be attentive to their needs and experiences.

References

Bloom, B., Owen, B., & Covington, S. (2005). *Gender-responsive strategies for women offenders: A summary of research, practice, and guiding principles for women offenders.* NIC accession no. 020418. Washington, DC: National Institute of Corrections.

Chesney-Lind, M. (2001). Are girls closing the gender gap in violence? *Criminal Justice Magazine, 16, 1.*

Chesney-Lind, M., & Irwin, K. (2008). *Beyond bad girls: Gender, violence and hype.* New York: Routledge.

Chesney-Lind, M., Morash, M., & Stevens, T. (2008). Girls' troubles, girls' delinquency, and gender responsive programming: A review. *Australian and New Zealand Journal of Criminology, 41,* 162–189.

Chesney-Lind, M., & Shelden, R. G. (2004). *Girls, delinquency, and juvenile justice.* Belmont, CA: West/Wadsworth.

Goodkind, S. (2005). Gender-specific services in the juvenile justice system: A critical examination. *Affilia, 20*(1), 52–70.

Greene, Peters, & Associates. (1998, October). *Guiding principles for promising female programming.* Washington, DC: U.S. Department of Justice, Office of Juvenile Justice and Delinquency Prevention.

Hartney, C., & Silva, F. (2007). *And justice for some: Differential treatment of youth of color in the justice system.* Oakland, CA: National Council on Crime and Delinquency.

Holsinger, K., Belknap, J., & Sutherland, J. L. (1999). *Assessing the gender specific program and service needs for adolescent females in the juvenile justice system.* Columbus, OH: Office of Criminal Justice Studies.

Kempf-Leonard, K., & Sample, L. L. (2000). Disparity based on sex: Is gender-specific treatment warranted? *Justice Quarterly, 17*(1), 89–129.

Le, T., Arifuku, I., & Nunez, M. (2003) Girls and culture in delinquency intervention: A case study of RYSE. *Juvenile and Family Court Journal, 54,* 25–34.

National Council on Crime and Delinquency. (2001, December). *Evaluation of the RYSE Program: Alameda County Probation Department.* Oakland, CA: National Council on Crime and Delinquency. Available at http://www.nccd-crc.org/nccd/pubs/2001dec_ryse_ report.pdf.

Schaffner, L. (2006). *Girls in trouble with the law.* New Brunswick, NJ: Rutgers University Press.

Snyder, H. N., & Sickmund, M. (2006). *Juvenile offenders and victims: 2006 national report.* Washington, DC: U.S. Department of Justice, Office of Justice Programs, Office of Juvenile Justice and Delinquency Prevention.

DISCUSSION QUESTIONS

1. The Office of Juvenile Justice and Delinquency Prevention (OJJDP) believed that there is a need for gender/race specific programs. Explain why you agree or disagree with their perspective.
2. What makes delinquent females different from their delinquent male counterparts?
3. Explain why there is a need for different types of programs for the female juvenile offender.
4. What factors contribute to African American females being the majority within the female juvenile justice system?

Policing

SECTION HIGHLIGHTS

- Overview of Policing in America
- History of Policing
- Race and Policing
- Contemporary Issues in Race and Policing
- Racial Profiling
- Summary
- Edited Readings

The police are the primary agents of social control responsible for order maintenance, law enforcement, and crime prevention. Race and policing has received much more attention in the past two decades as a result of the Rodney King incident, the OJ Simpson Trial, the Jena 6, the arrest of Blacks in Tulia, Texas and elsewhere on fabricated drug charges, unwarranted **racial profiling** during traffic stops, the use of **Tasers**, and recent tactics to control illegal immigration. Police agencies employ many more minorities (and women) today than in eras past, and considerable progress has been made by African Americans and other minorities in police leadership, especially in urban areas. Their advancement is often overshadowed by the unequal treatment minorities continue to receive from some police and the hostility that still exists between the two groups in many jurisdictions.

In this section, we provide a brief overview of policing in America, the major **components of the policing industry**, and information about recent employment patterns. The history of policing and of race and policing are included to contextualize problems in **police–community relations** that still exist today. The section concludes with a discussion of two contemporary race and policing issues: public opinion and citizen satisfaction with police and racial profiling.

Overview of Policing in America

Police are the most visible symbol of governmental authority in our country. In some communities and commercial settings they are seen on a daily basis, in others they are only seen when called upon, usually after a crime has occurred. The components of the policing industry include federal, local, and state agencies; Native American (tribal) police agencies; special police agencies with limited jurisdiction (e.g., transit police and school districts); and private police. Police agencies vary in size, and most are bureaucratic and quasi-military in structure. The roles and functions of police agencies are specified in federal and state statutes and local ordinances. The traditional roles of police (maintaining order, law enforcement, and crime prevention and control) in local agencies (police and sheriff departments) have remained the same over time. Sworn personnel in sheriffs' departments have court-related duties as well as traditional policing roles. Federal and state police have more investigative functions than local police agencies. Discretion (decisional latitude) is inherent in police work, and officers are authorized to use force in the performance of their duties. The police work closely with other local, state, and federal police agencies to address specific problems, including gangs, homeland security, immigration issues, narcotics law enforcement, and terrorism.

According to the most recent statistics available from the Bureau of Justice Statistics, in 2004 there were 17,876 state and local law enforcement agencies in the United States. In 2008, sworn officers accounted for 69.2% of all law enforcement personnel (FBI, 2009). Most sworn police are employed in local police departments, even though many of these agencies employed fewer than 10 full-time officers, some had only 5 officers, and 12% of these agencies had only 1 full-time officer or only part time officers (Reaves, 2007). Throughout American history, efforts to make policing a more diverse profession were often met with resistance by police officers and the citizenry. Legislation and court challenges led to changes in police hiring practices and growth in the representation of minorities in law enforcement during the latter part of the 20th century. Despite considerable progress, minorities are still underrepresented in law enforcement.

The most recent (2004) census of state and local agencies did not report the race and gender of sworn police. In 2000, in large cities, minority representation in police departments was 38.1%—20.1% Black and 14.1% Hispanic (Reaves & Hickman, 2002). Minority officers outnumbered White officers in some agencies, although the ratio of minority police officers to minority group members in large cities was .63, .74 for Blacks, .56 for Latinos, and .37 for other minorities (Reaves & Hickman, 2002). This means that there were 63 minority officers for every 100 minority citizens, 74 Black officers for every 100 citizens, and so on. Minority representation in smaller police departments as well as in state and federal agencies was still relatively low. Minorities comprised 22.7% of local sworn police officers and 17.1% of sworn officers in sheriffs' departments (Hickman & Reaves, 2003; Reaves & Hickman, 2003). Relying on percentages has a tendency to mask the actual representation of minorities in policing. For example, in 2000, 22.7% of the 440,000 sworn officers in local police agencies equated to about 101,000 officers, and 17.1% of police in sheriffs' agencies represented only about 30,000 sworn officers (nationwide).

At the federal level, passage of the Homeland Security Act in 2002 created the **Department of Homeland Security** (DHS) in order to provide a more integrated approach to security in the United States. The legislation transferred either all or part of 22 federal agencies to the DHS, making it the largest employer of federal law enforcement officers, and created the Transportation Security Agency (Reaves & Bauer, 2003). The 2004 Census of Federal Law Enforcement Officers identified 105,000 full-time personnel authorized to arrest and carry firearms. Most federal officers are White males, and about one third are members of a racial or ethnic minority group (Reaves, 2006). In agencies with more than 500 employees—the U.S. Customs and Border Protection (CBP) employs the most (28,200) federal officers with arrest and firearm authority—46.8% are minorities, and 36.9% are Hispanic or Latino. Other federal agencies had much lower minority representation, including the Federal Bureau of Investigation (17.2%), Drug Enforcement Administration (19.4%), and Bureau of Alcohol, Tobacco, Firearms and Explosives (19.9%) (see Table 5.1) (Reaves, 2006).

Table 5.1 Gender and Race or Ethnicity of Federal Officers With Arrest and Firearm Authority, Agencies Employing 500 or More Full-Time Officers, September 2004

		Percent of Full-Time Federal Officers With Arrest and Firearm Authority						
			Racial/Ethnic Minority					
Agency	Number of Officers	Female	Total Minority	American Indian	Black or African American	Asian or Pacific Islander	Hispanic or Latino, Any Race	Other Race
U.S. Customs and Border Protection	28,200	15.3%	46.8%	0.6%	5.0%	4.2%	36.9%	0.0%
Federal Bureau of Prisons	15,361	13.3	39.7	1.3	24.2	1.5	12.7	0.0
Federal Bureau of Investigation	12,414	18.5	17.2	0.4	5.8	3.6	7.4	0.0
U.S. Immigration and Customs Enforcement	10,691	13.7	33.9	0.6	8.6	2.7	22.0	0.0
U.S. Secret Service	4,780	10.5	19.6	0.6	11.2	2.6	5.2	0.0
Drug Enforcement Administration	4,500	8.9	19.4	0.4	7.6	2.5	8.9	0.0
Administrative Office of the U.S. Courts	4,166	44.2	32.2	0.5	15.3	1.6	14.1	0.6
U.S. Marshals Service	3,233	10.2	20.0	0.7	7.3	2.3	9.6	0.1
U.S. Postal Inspection Service	2,999	19.6	36.4	0.5	21.6	4.7	9.6	0.0

(Continued)

Table 5.1 (Continued)

Agency	Number of Officers	Percent of Full-Time Federal Officers With Arrest and Firearm Authority: Female	Racial/Ethnic Minority: Total Minority	American Indian	Black or African American	Asian or Pacific Islander	Hispanic or Latino, Any Race	Other Race
Internal Revenue Service, Criminal Investigation	2,791	30.0	24.0	0.8	10.2	4.5	8.1	0.4
Veterans Health Administration	2,474	6.9	40.1	0.9	26.8	2.5	10.0	0.0
Bureau of Alcohol, Tobacco, Firearms & Explosives	2,398	13.3	19.9	1.1	9.3	2.1	7.5	0.0
National Park Service–Ranger Division	1,547	18.2	10.3	2.1	2.5	2.4	3.0	0.3
U.S. Capitol Police	1,535	18.8	34.7	0.3	28.9	1.2	4.2	0.0
Bureau of Diplomatic Security, Diplomatic Security Service	825	11.8	20.0	0.7	9.7	3.4	5.5	0.7
U.S. Fish and Wildlife Service	713	8.7	13.6	3.5	1.7	1.4	7.0	0.0
National Park Service–U.S. Park Police	612	11.4	18.8	0.0	10.9	2.8	5.1	0.0
USDA Forest Service	604	17.5	17.4	6.5	3.3	1.3	6.3	0.0

History of Policing

The history of policing from the colonial period to the present varies from time to time and place to place. Most of the available early historical information focuses on the northeast region of the country. During the colonial era, there were no formal police departments in the original colonies. Like their British counterparts, the colonists initially made policing the responsibility of every citizen and later utilized sheriffs, constables, and watches (Uchida, 1997). In some northern cities like Boston (MA) and New Amsterdam (NY), night watches were established, whereas in the South, **slave patrols** were more common. Over time, social disorder and crime increased so much, especially in northern cities, that the early forms of policing proved ineffective and were gradually replaced with more formal police agencies patterned after the British model (Fogelson, 1977; Lane, 1967; Monkkonen, 1981; Richardson, 1970). Unlike the British police, American police agencies were decentralized, locally controlled, and influenced by politics.

According to Emsley (1983), "The history of American police during the nineteenth century is the history of separate forces in separate cities" (p. 101). For example, **White immigrants** dominated police forces in some northern cities, and slave patrollers in the South were usually poorer Whites. The first African American police were "free men of color" who served in police organizations in New Orleans, Louisiana, between 1805 and 1830. For the most part, they were responsible for slaves (Dulaney, 1996). D. Johnson (1981) mentioned that social tensions among immigrants, Blacks, and native Whites often resulted in conflicts and crime. Examples of these conflicts include verbal and physical abuse of abolitionists, race riots, labor strikes, and draft riots (Barlow & Barlow, 2000). Outside the urban areas, especially on the frontier, policing was mostly accomplished by vigilantes.

Although paid police forces that emerged in the 1800s were viewed as better than the night-and-day watches of the colonial era, social disorder and crime continued to be challenges. As a result, private police agencies, such as the Pinkerton Agency, began to appear. Early police agencies were plagued by political control and corruption that led to two major reform efforts in the late 1800s and early 1900s. Many of the reforms that began in the early 20th century, including changes in personnel, policy, and training, did not occur until much later in the century. Poor police-community relations, which were a problem both before and after World War II, were not adequately addressed until the 1960s. It was at that time that civil unrest led to close scrutiny of police. Several U.S. Supreme Court decisions, including *Mapp v. Ohio* (1961), *Escobedo v. Illinois* (1964), and *Miranda v. Arizona* (1966), attempted to balance police power and citizens' due process guarantees. The first major crime related legislation, the Omnibus Crime and Control and Safe Streets Act of 1968 created the Law Enforcement Assistance Administration to improve and strengthen law enforcement. Between 1970 and the present, policing has changed dramatically due to even more legislation and court decisions, technological developments, the research revolution, and, most recently, the threat of terrorism after September 11, 2001.

Before what some describe as the Homeland Security era in policing, community-oriented policing (COP) was believed to be an alternative to traditional policing models that often excluded the citizenry and distanced the police from those they served. COP is a proactive approach that strives to bring police and citizens closer together in their efforts to reduce crime and disorder and solve related problems. COP was attractive to many progressive police administrators because it could be tailored to fit the needs of a particular neighborhood or jurisdiction. Other administrators and police officers resisted COP because it required a completely different police role; crime control was replaced with addressing not only crime, but also problems of disorder. COP received a major boost when the Crime Control Act of 1994 made federal funds available for hiring COP officers. At the time, although many agencies had adopted COP programs, most others were not convinced of its utility.

During the past decade, research on COP addressing numerous topics and varying methodologies, including descriptive studies of implementation, organizational issues, evaluative studies, and analyses of citizen and officer perceptions of COP, informs us about its progress and obstacles. Most COP programs have a problem-solving component that originated in problem-oriented policing (POP). Today, many police agencies have aspects of the COP philosophy, including in their mission statements whether or not they still are engaged in COP at the same level as they were before September 11, 2011. Proponents of COP thought cooperation between minority communities and the police would improve. More research is needed to determine whether or not and to what extent this has occurred.

Race and Policing

> The fact that the legal order not only countenanced but sustained slavery, segregation, and discrimination for most of our nation's history—and the fact that the police were bound to uphold that order—set a pattern for police behavior and attitudes toward minority communities that has persisted until the present day. The existence of this pattern . . . meant that, while important changes were occurring in policing during our Nation's history, members of minority groups benefited less than others from these changes. (Williams & Murphy, 1990, p. 2)

As the quote indicates, it is impossible to separate the history of policing minority groups from the general history of the experiences of minorities in the United States, which were presented in Section 1. Historical information about policing for Native Americans, African Americans, Asians, and Latinos is presented next.

Native Americans

While federally recognized tribes have sovereignty and the right to administer justice within their jurisdiction, the reduction of their land ownership to reservations took hundreds of years. Since the colonial era, Native Americans have been controlled by numerous treaties, federal laws, and judicial decisions that minimized their legitimacy and political autonomy. The U.S. Indian Police were established in 1878 by congress for tribes and reservations that continued to exist. By 1881 there were 40 agencies, 162 officers, and 653 privates (Tyler, 1973). During the 1880s, the West was becoming rapidly developed and settled by Whites, which precipitated the demand for the acquisition of more Indian land and resources. According to Tyler (1973), there were chiefs of Indian police on the reservations who often mediated between White man's law and Indian custom. At the same time, the decimation of tribal leadership often resulted in the breakdown of social control.

The FBI's first major homicide investigation involved Native Americans. During the 1800s, oil was discovered on the land of the Osage Indian tribe of Oklahoma. By the early 1900s, the tribe was extremely wealthy considering that "in 1923 alone, the Osage Tribe received $27 million. In two decades, the Osage would receive more money from oil than all the old west gold rushes combined had yielded" (Hogan, 1998, p. 28). Eventually, this made them the target of elaborate schemes to defraud them of their wealth. After asking for assistance from the government, during the 1920s, the FBI infiltrated the tribe and uncovered a major scheme that involved intermarriage and murder. In the end, the FBI solved the case but had local officials make the arrests "since Special

Agents of the FBI did not have the power of arrest (or the authority to carry firearms) at the time" (Hogan, 1998, p.194).

On August 15, 1953, **Public Law 280** transferred federal responsibility for criminal and civil jurisdiction, including law enforcement duties, to six states (Alaska, California, Minnesota, Nebraska, Oregon, and Wisconsin) and made it optional for several other states to assert jurisdiction (Luna-Firebaugh, 2003; Tyler, 1973). Although P.L. 280 did not terminate tribal jurisdiction, it was the belief that states and sheriffs were now responsible for law enforcement. When it was widely recognized that states were not providing adequate policing services, some tribal governments sought to reestablish and strengthen tribal police services. In 1974, almost a century after the federal government first established police in Indian country, police protection on reservations was described as follows:

> On reservations where state laws apply, police activities are administered in the same manner as elsewhere. On reservations where State laws do not apply, tribal laws or Department of the Interior regulations are administered by personnel employed by the Bureau of Indian Affairs, or by personnel employed by the tribe, or by a combination of both. (Bureau of Indian Affairs, 1974, p. 27)

In the 1990s, more than 56 million acres of land were owned and policed by tribal nations in the United States. "Indian country" includes reservations in 34 states, most of which are located west of the Mississippi River (Wakeling et al., 2001). Tribal police have responsibility for large land areas and often share criminal jurisdiction with federal and state agencies, "depending upon the particular offense, the offender, the victim and the offense location" (M. Hickman, 2003, p. 4).

According to the *Census of State and Local Law Enforcement Agencies, 2004*, there were 154 tribal police agencies with 2,490 sworn personnel (Reaves, 2007). The typical department on a reservation is small, and therefore police protection is considerably lower than in other urban and rural agencies. The workload of officers in Indian police departments has increased as a result of several factors, including more reliance on the police (instead of traditional methods) and more crime and emergencies (Wakeling et al., 2001). Today, there are several administrative arrangements for policing Native Americans that include cross-deputization agreements with other law enforcement agencies.

African Americans

African Americans have posed a unique problem for America since their arrival as slaves in the 16th century. By the early 18th century, most of the early colonies regulated the movement and activities of free and enslaved Negroes by enacting special codes to totally control them. During the antebellum period, slaves were unprotected from crimes including murder, rape, and assault by slave owners (Kennedy, 1997). Slave patrols carried out numerous duties, including checking passes of slaves leaving plantations, routinely searching slave quarters for stolen property, and administering whippings (Websdale, 2001). Slave revolts were of increasing concern and, along with slavery, mandated a brutal policing mechanism to both protect Whites and dehumanize Blacks (Jones, 1977).

During the 1800s, in the North and South, both before and after emancipation, free Blacks were treated like slaves. Kennedy (1997) described the unwillingness of Southern

Whites to recognize Blacks' rights to protection and the failure of local authorities to restrain or punish violence against them. During the late 19th and early 20th century, Blacks continued to lack legal protection from lynching and race riots.

In 1938, Gunnar Myrdal undertook a comprehensive study of the Negro in the United States. His findings were reported in *An American Dilemma*, where he stated the following:

> The average Southern policeman is a promoted poor White with a legal sanction to use a weapon. His social heritage has taught him to despise the Negroes, and he has had little education which could have changed him. . . . The result is that probably no group of Whites in America have a lower opinion of the Negro people and are more fixed in their views than Southern policemen. (Myrdal, 1944, pp. 540–541)

Blacks entered law enforcement during the Reconstruction, although early gains were erased in the 1890s (Dulaney, 1996). There were approximately 50 Negro policemen in 1940, and by the 1970s, the integration of more police departments began to occur.

Asian Americans

As discussed in Section I, many Chinese immigrated to the United States as laborers. The fact that many Chinese immigrants were illegal did not seem to matter as much as their opium smoking and **opium dens**. Opium smoking was common among Chinese immigrants and was confined to them between 1850 and 1870. Soon after, opium and opium dens gained popularity with the underworld of gamblers, prostitutes, and other criminals (Courtwright, 2001). Many believe that opium dens were targeted by the police and other governmental officials over concerns that Whites were mixing with Chinese, viewed by some as "polluting" (Institute of Texan Cultures, 1998). In the 1870s and 1880s, federal, municipal, and state governments passed laws that penalized opium smoking. By 1909, federal legislation banned the importation of opium for smoking by stipulating that it could be imported only for medicinal purposes.

During most of the 20th century, Asian Americans were more likely to remain in cultural enclaves and less likely to be involved in crime in their communities. Thus, although Asian gangs are still involved in drug distribution (e.g., heroin, ice), prostitution, and other illegal activities, they remain insulated from police attention due, at least in part, to their cultural values, ethnic isolation, and language barriers. More recent Southeast Asian immigrants and some second-generation immigrants target other Asian immigrants, Asian Americans, and businesses (Know Gangs, n.d.) and are more likely to come to the attention of police today.

Latinos

Research on the experiences of Mexican Americans in the Southwest and in Los Angeles, California is more readily available than studies of the historical experiences with the police of other Latino groups such as Puerto Ricans, Dominicans, Colombians, and others. Trujillo (1974/1995) described how American capitalists who colonized the Southwest during the 1850s and 1860s created a cheap labor force and perpetrated an atmosphere of violence against Chicano immigrants. He maintained that repression of Chicanos by the police, military, and vigilantes led to the formation of protective guerilla units and bandits that are misrepresented in American history. Brutality against Mexican Americans included lynchings and murders. The number of brutal incidents in California and Texas prompted the Mexican ambassador to formally protest the mistreatment of Mexicans in 1912 (Kanellos, 1977). According to Chabrán and Chabrán (1996), Latino migrant workers in the Southwest received the harshest treatment. Because many of them were illegal immigrants, they were not as protected by the American legal system.

In the 1931 Wickersham Commission Report on Crime and the Foreign Born, three chapters specifically address the Mexican American immigrant (National Commission on Law Observance and Enforcement, 1931). By the 1940s, police–Chicano relations in Los Angeles, where many Mexican Americans resided, had deteriorated to what Escobar (1999) described as extreme hostility and suspicion toward each other, culminating in the **Zoot Suit Riots** (or sailor riots) in June, 1943. During the latter part of the 20th century, Latinos, like African Americans, continued to have strained relations with the police. The problems of illegal immigration, human smuggling, and drug smuggling, especially in the Southwest region of the country, have increased the amount of contact between Latinos and state, local, and federal police agencies.

White Immigrants

The police experiences of White immigrants were drastically different from those of Native Americans, African Americans, Asian Americans, and Latinos. First, it was easier for foreign-born Whites to gradually blend into American society. Second, many White immigrants were able to secure jobs as police officers. Third, White immigrants often were assisted by the police in their transition to life in a new country. As early as the 1850s, the Boston police provided firewood and other necessities to Irish immigrants. Decades later, one function of the Boston police department was to distribute free soup in station houses, especially during the winter (Lane, 1967). Police also assisted parents looking for lost children (Monkkonen, 1981) and accommodated overnight lodgers (Lane, 1967; Monkkonen, 1981). By the late 1800s, immigration was seen by Progressive Era reformers as a threat to democracy, social order, and American identity (Graham, 2004). Poverty, illiteracy, unemployment, and underemployment in the ethnic ghettos meant that various types of criminal enterprises, including gambling, prostitution, and theft, and criminals, such as con men, were common (Fogelson, 1977).

In the early 20th century, policing of White immigrants depended on whether the police were controlled by political machines friendly to either immigrants or Progressive Era reformers seeking to restrict the immorality of immigrants (Brown & Warner, 1992). Later in the 20th century, serial killers, including Theodore Bundy, David Berkowitz, and John Wayne Gacy; White supremacists Randy Weaver and the Ruby Ridge incident; and domestic terrorists Timothy McVeigh and Terry Nichols, who bombed the Alfred P. Murrah Federal Building in Oklahoma City, were key factors in the development of criminal profiles and revisions to training and policy, especially at the federal level. As noted in Section I, over time, White ethnics assimilate into the general population. Whether or not they are new or recent immigrants and how they are treated by the police is not as controversial as police-minority relationships.

Today, the face of immigration has changed dramatically. Twenty-two percent of **nonresident immigrants** (foreign nationals who are legally admitted into the United States for specific, temporary purposes and whose classes of admission are associated with long stays) are from India, 8% are from Canada, 8% are from South Korea, and 17% are from Europe (Baker, 2008). Even though we don't know the number of illegal immigrants, they too come from many countries around the world, and some blend into society easier than others. Those that don't are more likely to be subjected to surveillance and monitoring techniques quite different from earlier time periods. Concerns about illegal immigrants and their supposed involvement in crime are not much different from those of the 19th and 20th centuries. Contemporary issues in race and policing are presented in the next section.

Contemporary Issues in Race and Policing

Traditional policing and **community policing** strategies both require good police–community relations in order for police to perform their duties. This is especially true in minority communities and neighborhoods where criminality and victimizations are serious threats to safety, order, and stability. Before citizens willingly cooperate with police, they need to feel respected and safe when interacting with them. There are many critical race and policing issues today, including police use of deadly force, police brutality, the use of Tasers, police corruption, **driving while Black/Brown**, selective enforcement, and **police accountability**, that impact support for police. Here we focus on two contemporary issues in race and policing: public opinion and citizen satisfaction with police and racial profiling.

Research and data on public opinion and citizen satisfaction with police include a range of topics, such as confidence in the police, determinants of attitudes toward police, police encounters, racial bias, racial profiling, and police reform (Brunson, 2007; McCluskey, McCluskey, & Enriquez, 2008; Reisig & Parks, 2002; Skogan, 2005; Tuch & Weitzer, 1997; Weitzer & Tuch, 2004, 2006). Today, many cities use surveys to gauge both citizens' satisfaction and expectations, as do some police departments. Reisig and Parks (2002) identified two important factors related to satisfaction with the police: perceptions about quality of life issues (such as disorder and safety) and how police behave when they interact with residents. More recently, Skogan (2005) found that citizen satisfaction with the police in Chicago was impacted by their treatment during a police encounter. Politeness, fairness, attentiveness, and respect were important. Weitzer and Tuch (2006) found that several factors influenced perceptions about racially biased policing, including personal experience, vicarious experience, mass media reporting, and neighborhood conditions. Citizen distrust of the police among African Americans is a consistent finding in the research literature.

The ***Sourcebook of Criminal Justice Statistics*** (Maguire & Pastore, 2003, 2007) provides information on public attitudes toward several police topics, including confidence in the police, racial profiling, police brutality, police performance and fairness, honesty, and ethics. The majority of Americans have confidence in the police. In 2003, while 65% of Whites had a great deal of confidence in the police, only 43% of non-Whites did (Maguire & Pastore, 2003). In 2007, 90% of Whites, 75% non-Whites, and 65% of Blacks reported confidence in the police (i.e., a great deal or some) (Maguire & Pastore, 2007). In 2009, 88% of all respondents had a great deal or some confidence in the police. Table 5.2 presents

Table 5.2 Reported Confidence in the Police

By demographic characteristics, United States, 2009

Question: "I am going to read you a list of institutions in American society. Please tell me how much confidence you, yourself, have in each one—a great deal, quite a lot, some, or very little: the police?"

	Great Deal/Quite a Lot	Some	Very Little	None[a]
National	59%	29%	10%	1%
Sex				
Male	59	30	9	1
Female	59	28	10	1
Race				
White	63	30	6	1
Nonwhite	51	27	20	3
Black	38	31	27	4
Age				
18 to 29 years	50	32	18	1
30 to 49 years	60	27	10	2
50 to 64 years	63	29	7	1
50 years and older	64	28	6	1
65 years and older	65	27	6	(b)
Education				
College post graduate	66	29	5	(b)
College graduate	69	23	7	2
Some college	57	30	10	2
High school graduate or less	55	30	13	1
Income				
$75,000 and over	70	27	3	(b)
$50,000 to $74,999	65	30	4	2
$30,000 to $49,999	52	33	14	1
$20,000 to $29,999	52	31	10	4
Under $20,000	50	25	23	1
Region				
East	60	31	9	1
Midwest	62	30	5	3
South	60	27	12	(b)
West	58	28	12	2

(Continued)

Table 5.2 (Continued)

	Great Deal/Quite a Lot	Some	Very Little	None[a]
Politics				
Republican	71	26	2	0
Democrat	53	30	14	1
Independent	56	30	11	2
Ideology				
Conservative	66	25	7	1
Moderate	61	29	8	1
Liberal	49	38	12	1

NOTE: Sample sizes vary from year to year; the data for 2009 are based on telephone interviews with a randomly selected national sample of 1,011 adults, 18 years of age and older, conducted June 14–17, 2009. The "don't know/refused" category has been omitted; therefore percents may not sum to 100.
a. Response volunteered.
b. Less than 0.5%.

the 2009 responses to the question about confidence in the police. The differences by race were similar to previous years: 93% of Whites, 78% of non-Whites, and only 69% of Blacks had a great deal or some confidence in the police (Maguire, 2010).

The policy implications of citizen distrust and lack of confidence in the police include (1) a reluctance to assist the police and (2) an overall lack of faith in the criminal justice system (Brunson, 2007). Both are problematic for the police and minorities. To overcome this, police agencies will need to identify new strategies that are race neutral (Weitzer, 2000). The Consortium for Police Leadership in Equity (2011) works with participating police departments to address equity issues. One of their foci is racial profiling, which is discussed in the next section.

Racial Profiling

There are several definitions of racial profiling. Russell-Brown (2004) defined racial profiling as "any action that results in the heightened racial scrutiny of minorities—justified or not" (Russell-Brown, 2004, pp. 98–99). In recent years, profiling has become a subspecialty within policing and has produced countless articles and books on the topic (for a summary of the extant literature, see Withrow, 2006). Profiling research includes racial profiling during traffic stops, **consumer racial profiling** in retail settings (Gabbidon, 2003; Gabbidon, Craig, Okafo, Marzette, & Peterson, 2008; Gabbidon & Higgins, 2007; Higgins & Gabbidon, 2009), and profiling of passengers at airports. Public opinion polls about racial profiling indicate that most Americans believe it exists (Barlow & Barlow, 2002; McMahon, Garner, Davis, & Kraus, 2002). Racial profiling has a deleterious impact on cooperation between police and minorities. It undermines law enforcement, is ineffective as a strategy to control drugs, and undermines national unity (Amnesty International, 2010).

During the 1990s, driving while Black/Brown (DWB) was the most visible form of racial profiling (Russell, 2002). Profiling on the highways and in the streets is dangerous because it is based on beliefs about those who might commit crimes (predictive), rather than those who have committed them (descriptive), and is less formal (based on empirical support) and more informal (based on personal experiences) (Harris, 2002). In 1996, in their controversial *Whren v. United States* decision, the U.S. Supreme Court exacerbated the DWB problem by granting police officers the power to stop persons suspected of drug crimes under the pretext of probable cause for a traffic violation. For many observers, *Whren* ignored the importance of an officer's racial prejudices and opened the door to racial profiling during traffic stops (Russell, 2002). Since *Whren*, the Supreme Court has granted police even greater powers over drivers and passengers (American Civil Liberties Union, 1999).

Numerous studies provide overwhelming support for the overrepresentation of Blacks and Latinos in traffic stops (see for example, Becker, 2004; Higgins, Vito, & Walsh, 2008; Russell-Brown, 2004). The Racial Profiling Data Collection Resource Center (RPDCRC) at Northeastern University provides a state-by-state list of jurisdictions collecting racial profiling data. At the federal level, the Bureau of Justice Statistics collected data on police-citizen contacts in 2005 in a supplement to the NCVS that included 63,943 respondents ages 16 or older (Durose, Smith, & Langan, 2007). An estimated 19% of U.S. citizens (over age 16) had face-to-face contact with a police officer in 2005. About 41% of all contacts were for traffic stops, and most drivers were stopped for speeding. Of those stopped, Black drivers were more likely to be arrested, and Hispanics were more likely to receive a ticket. The rate of drivers stopped was similar for Whites, Blacks, and Hispanics in 2002 and 2005, although minorities were more likely to be searched by police (Durose, Smith, & Langan, 2007). One issue that is absent from the racial profiling research is whether traffic stops are used as a pretext for curtailing illegal immigration.

Consumer racial profiling is less visible and has not received as much attention in the research literature as profiling during traffic stops. This is due, at least in part, to the fact that retailers have their own security guards and are not subjected to as much scrutiny as public police. Data on consumer racial profiling is not readily available and might only surface during litigation. In the 2004 Gallup poll, 45% of Whites, 65% of Blacks, and 56% of Hispanics believed that racial profiling was widespread in retail settings, and fewer minorities felt that it was justified. Twenty five percent of Whites, 19% of Blacks, and 38% of Hispanics felt it was justified (Pastore & Maguire, 2010). Two studies using self-reporting methods found that Blacks are much more likely than Whites to experience consumer racial profiling (Gabbidon et al., 2008; Gabbidon & Higgins, 2007; Higgins & Gabbidon, 2009).

Racial and ethnic **profiling at airports** has received little attention in the scholarly research (Gabbidon, Penn, Jordan, Higgins, 2009). In 2004, fewer Americans (45%) felt that racial profiling was justified at airports than in 2010. In the latest poll, 70% of Americans favored profiling airline passengers to prevent terrorism (Maguire, 2010).

DNA profiling (formerly DNA fingerprinting) is an investigative tool in law enforcement used both nationally and internationally. State and federal DNA databanks collect and store DNA from arrestees and convicted felons. According to the ACLU (2007), "This trend not only represents a grave threat to privacy and the 4th Amendment, but it also turns the legal notion that a person is 'innocent until proven guilty' on its head" (ACLU, 2007). INTERPOL is fostering an international partnership and cooperation amongst its members on the use of DNA profile comparison (Interpol, 2010). DNA profiling will require monitoring in order to determine whether or not it has a negative impact on minorities and people of color.

Police accountability strategies provide opportunities to improve public opinion of and citizen satisfaction with the police and to reduce the occurrence of racial and ethnic profiling. External strategies such as lawsuits and oversight by the federal government are helpful, but accountability (and change) must come from inside police departments as well. Video cameras in police vehicles are a useful accountability tool that discourages abuses of power. Monitoring of citizens complaints with early warning systems ensures accountability as well. Police administrators that have made progress in strengthening public support of the police can serve as models for departments in locales that haven't made enough progress.

Summary

- The policing industry is comprised of federal, state, local, tribal, private, and special police agencies.
- Most sworn officers are employed in large local police departments.
- Most sworn officers at the federal, state, and local levels are White males. Minorities comprised 22.7% of local sworn police and 17.1% of sworn officers in sheriff's departments in 2002.
- Police misconduct and attitudes toward members of minority communities have existed since the colonial era.
- Public confidence in the police varies by racial groups, with Whites having more confidence than Blacks and other minorities.
- Several factors influence perceptions about racially biased policing, including personal encounters, vicarious experience, mass media reporting, and neighborhood conditions.
- Consumer racial profiling, profiling at airports, and DNA profiling are of concern for racial and ethnic minorities.
- Police accountability strategies can improve public opinion of and citizen satisfaction with the police and reduce profiling incidents.

KEY TERMS

community policing

components of the policing industry

consumer racial profiling

Department of Homeland Security

DNA profiling

driving while Black/Brown

nonresident immigrants

opium dens

police accountability

police-community relations

profiling at airports

Public Law 280

racial profiling

slave patrols

Sourcebook of Criminal Justice Statistics

Tasers

White immigrants

Zoot Suit Riots

DISCUSSION QUESTIONS

1. Why is race and policing an important issue in the study of race and crime?
2. Do you think public confidence in the police will improve in minority communities during the next decade? Explain your answer.
3. Should police agencies conduct citizen satisfaction surveys on a regular basis?
4. In what circumstances, if any, do you believe racial profiling is justified?
5. Is community policing an effective approach for improving the relationship between the police and the citizenry they serve?

WEB RESOURCES

The Center for Institutional and Social Change: http://changecenter.org/

Northeastern University: http://www.northeastern.edu/research/centers_institutes/crime/

Amnesty International USA: http://www.amnestyusa.org

READING

Tasers are conductive energy devices (CEDs) that were thought to be a nonlethal alternative for police officers in dangerous encounters. They have received considerable attention in the news during the past several years, primarily as a result of the injuries and deaths that have resulted from their use. Race has always been an issue in the police use of force because minorities are disproportionally victims of police brutality and use of deadly force. In this article, Gau, Mosher, and Pratt examine race and police use of Tasers using data from a state patrol agency. The authors found that resistance was the strongest predictor of Taser use, that officers' race was a significant predictor of Taser use, and that Hispanic suspects were more likely than Blacks, Whites, and others to be tased. The authors present possible explanations for the more frequent use of Tasers on Hispanics and suggest future directions for policy and research.

An Inquiry Into the Impact of Suspect Race on Police Use of Tasers

Jacinta M. Gau, Clayton Mosher, and Travis C. Pratt

Introduction

Police use of force captures the interest of scholars and the public alike. The legal authority to inflict verbal or physical violence on citizens is a pivotal characteristic of the institution of policing; it is, as the now-classic argument goes, the defining characteristic of police that sets them apart from private citizens and from other agents of the state (Bittner, 1970; Klockars, 1985). Scholars have devoted considerable attention to both deadly (e.g., Sparger & Giacopassi, 1992) and less-than-lethal police force (e.g., Klinger, 1995), yet they have been slow to take on one of the issues that is currently at the forefront of police use of force: Tasers. The carrying and use of Tasers and other conductive energy devices (CEDs) have proliferated over the past few decades, and CEDs are now commonplace in many police departments and have been incorporated into existing use-of-force policies (White & Ready, 2007).

There is simultaneously both a plethora and a paucity of research on CEDs. On the plethora side are the numerous medical studies and descriptive reports that have been released concerning the prevalence of officers' use of CEDs and the potential dangers these devices pose to suspects' health and lives. On the paucity side are scholarly research articles that embed CEDs within current theoretical and empirical knowledge about police use of force. The existing academic literature is largely descriptive in nature and includes topics such

Source: Gau, M. J., Mosher, C., & Pratt, T. C. (2010). An inquiry into the impact of suspect race on police use of Tasers. *Police Quarterly, 13*(1), 27–48.

Authors' note: The data used in this study were gathered under the National Highway Traffic Safety Administration Grant-Funded Study on Racial Profiling Phenomena (OGRD 107828).

as how the rise of CEDs has affected officer and suspect injury rates (e.g., Smith, Kaminski, Rojek, Alpert, & Mathis, 2007), the physiological effects these electromuscular devices have on suspects (see Downs, 2007; Vilke & Chan, 2007, for reviews), and the possible implications of CEDs for police officers' civil liability (Smith, Petrocelli, & Scheer, 2007). These studies have contributed much to the understanding of CEDs, but work remains to be done.

What is missing from the literature are analyses that go beyond simple descriptions to instead probe for patterns and apply theory and prior research to add depth to the study of electromuscular technologies' use in the field. As the scholarly literature advances, both academics' and practitioners' understanding of the social and political implications of CEDs will be enhanced. One of the most pressing inquiries in this respect is whether the prevalence of CED usage is spread equally across all races or whether it is concentrated among persons of particular racial groups. This question is important for understanding police behavior and use of force and for informing the literature on police-minority relations.

The development of policing in the United States has been heavily influenced by the historical tensions between police and minorities (Williams & Murphy, 1990). Minorities face disproportionately high odds of being the subjects of pedestrian and vehicle stops (Fagan & Davies, 2000; Meehan & Ponder, 2002), and many Black citizens express resentment at what they perceive to be unwarranted police scrutiny (Weitzer, 1999, 2000; see also Gau & Brunson, in press). People who feel they were subjected to particular treatment on the basis of their race can be left feeling victimized (Weitzer & Tuch, 2005a). Resentment spurred by negative police encounters is, moreover, not limited to the individual who feels personally affronted by unfair treatment—that person may share his or her experiences with friends and family, which leads to vicarious victimization among those who were not personally involved but who feel the emotional effects of the negative experience (Brunson, 2007; Rosenbaum et al., 2005). With regard to Tasers specifically, media publicity surrounding Taser-related incidents (Ready, White, & Fisher, 2008) could spark animosity or distrust among other members of the public whose opinions about police may be shaped or altered by these reports (see Weitzer, 2002), thereby dramatically widening the scope of vicarious victimization.

The academic research on race and policing has been hampered by the traditional practice of focusing on the differences either between Whites and Blacks or between Whites and so-called non-Whites, a catchall category that lumps Blacks, Latinos, and persons of other races into a single group (see, e.g., Alpert, Dunham, & MacDonald, 2004; see also Mastrofski et al., 2002). Much literature has examined contacts, including but not limited to contacts involving physical force, between police and African Americans, but there is as yet relatively little information about police-Latino encounters (Weitzer & Tuch, 2005b). The studies that have deliberately gone beyond the traditional Black-White differences to include Latinos (Cheurprakobkit, 2000; Rosenbaum et al., 2005; Skogan, 2005) have concentrated on racial variation in citizens' satisfaction with police and their perceptions of the quality of the treatment they receive from officers—they have not addressed use of force.

The present study offers two primary contributions to the literature. First, it analyzes police use of Tasers, which is a topic that has yet to be fully elucidated in academic literature. Second, it broadens the Taser inquiry to examine potential differences between Black, White, and Hispanic suspects. The present study employs use-of-force data from a state patrol agency in a Pacific Northwest state to examine whether and to what extent there appear to be racial disparities in Taser use. The results have implications for police policy and for future research.

Police Use of Force

Police use of force encompasses an array of behaviors ranging from simple verbal commands to the actual taking of a suspect's life. The precise rate of the use of verbal and/or physical force is unknown and difficult to estimate (Garner, Maxwell, & Heraux, 2002), due in no small part to a lack of data-collection efforts among police departments (Alpert & MacDonald, 2001; Alpert & Smith, 1994), the rather unscientific nature of most of the efforts that have been undertaken (Alpert & Smith, 2000), or problems involving researchers' measurement of police behavior (Mastrofski & Parks, 1990). What is clear is that relatively few police-citizen encounters result in the use of force and an even smaller portion result in the use of physical—as opposed to verbal—force (Klinger, 1995), though the precise rate of use of force does vary depending on how force is measured (see Garner et al., 2002; see also Hoffman & Hickey, 2005). A multitude of police-citizen interactions take place every day, however, so even a low rate can translate into a substantial absolute number. The study of police use of deadly force has a lengthy history in academia (Fyfe, 1981; Garner et al., 2002; Klinger, 1995, 2001; Langworthy, 1986; MacDonald, Kaminski, Alpert, & Tannenbaum, 2001; Meyer, 1980; Reiss, 1980; Robin, 1963; Smith, 2004; Sparger & Giacopassi, 1992), and less-than-lethal force has also taken its place in academic and policy studies. Examinations of less-than-lethal physical force, which surfaces more frequently in the day-to-day interactions between police and citizens, are more informative from a practical standpoint (Garner et al., 2002).

A fair amount of attention has been devoted to identifying the particular characteristics of suspects, officers, and situations that make the occurrence of force more or less likely. One of the most obvious suspect characteristics that may influence use of force is race. Theories such as Black's (1976) proposition regarding social asymmetry between officers and suspects would offer reason to predict that non-White suspects will receive harsher treatment by police due to the former's lower social status. In empirical studies, however, suspect race has actually born an inconsistent relationship with the likelihood of police use of force. Some studies do suggest that police are more likely to apply force against non-White suspects as compared to Whites (Alpert et al., 2004; Sparger & Giacopassi, 1992), whereas others have reported no such effect (McCluskey, Terrill, & Paoline, 2005) or even the opposite result (Ho, 1993; see Garner et al., 2002, for a review of mixed findings). Still others indicate that race effects are confounded with neighborhood context. High crime rates and area levels of concentrated disadvantage can impact officers' decision making and can help determine what actions they take, under what circumstances they take those actions, and how serious their response to a given incident will be (Kane, 2002; Klinger, 1997; Smith, 1986; Terrill & Reisig, 2003). The issue of suspect race and police use of force, then, is still cloudy and merits continued attention.

CEDs and Use of Force

Police agencies are under social and legal pressures to enforce the law effectively but without inflicting undue violence. The prevalence of CEDs today is emblematic of the growing demand over the past few decades for police to reduce reliance on lethal and otherwise severe weapons (see Vilke & Chan, 2007). In the 1960s, heavy-handed crowd-control techniques earned the police condemnation from the public and sparked the search for effective but less dangerous weapons (Johnston, 1981; White & Ready, 2007, in press). The need for less-than-lethal substitutes for deadly force was codified into law in 1985, when the fatal shooting of an unarmed juvenile fleeing a burglary scene prompted the U.S. Supreme Court to interpret the Fourth Amendment as permitting deadly force only against suspects who pose clear and immediate public safety threats (*Tennessee v. Garner*, 1985). Four years after the *Garner* decision, the court added more detail to the law surrounding the Fourth Amendment's restrictions on all forms of force—deadly and otherwise—and held that any amount of force that surpasses what is necessary to subdue a combative suspect is by definition 'excessive' and a violation of the Fourth Amendment's reasonableness requirement (*Graham v. Connor*, 1989). The definition of 'reasonable' and 'unreasonable' force has been the subject of much debate (Alpert & Smith, 1994), and methods for guiding and assessing the proportionality between the intensity of suspect resistance and officers' responding force—such as use-of-force continua—have been produced to help clarify this ambiguity (Terrill, Alpert, Dunham, & Smith, 2003).

Many less-than-lethal alternatives have sprung up over the past few decades in response to social, political, and legal pressures to balance effectiveness and evenhandedness. They ranged from weapons still common today (e.g., chemical sprays) to some odd creations such as the super banana peel, a slippery goo police smeared on sidewalks to make rioters fall down (unfortunately, it also made police fall down; this idea was abandoned quickly), to large nets that were thrown over suspects to ensnare and immobilize them (Johnston, 1981). CEDs—including but not limited to Tasers—appeared on the market in the 1970s (Government Accountability Office [GAO], 2005). Early reports claimed that CEDs were highly effective, posed minimal risk to suspects beyond the pain caused by the device itself, and minimized officer injuries by making physical combat with suspects unnecessary (Meyer, 1992). Electromuscular devices also sidestep the dangers of impact munitions weapons (such as rubber bullets and bean-bag rounds) that although generally not dangerous to those on the receiving end, have been linked to some serious injuries and deaths (Klinger, 2007). Nearly half of the law enforcement agencies in the United States now issue CEDs to some or all of their officers, and there have been more than 70,000 estimated deployments of these devices (GAO, 2005).

Human rights groups have not been as enthusiastic about CEDs as law enforcement agencies have been. The intense pain caused by these instruments, combined with reports of possible CED-related deaths among suspects with physical or mental vulnerabilities, have led Amnesty International to twice plead for a moratorium on CED use (Amnesty International, 2006). The International Association of Chiefs of Police (IACP) has also noted the potential risks and liabilities associated with CEDs and has admonished police departments to develop guidelines to regulate their use (IACP, 1999; see also the Commission for Public Complaints Against the Royal Canadian Mounted Police, 2008; Welch, 2008). There is marked variation in the location of CEDs on police agencies' use-of-force continua (Adams & Jennison, 2007), though available evidence suggests that the device is often placed toward the lower end (Amnesty International, 2006; see also GAO, 2005).

Current Focus: Race and Tasers

Racial stereotypes can play a prominent role, as Blacks and Hispanics (particularly young males belonging to these groups) are, all else being equal, considered more dangerous than their White counterparts (Steffensmeier, Ulmer, & Kramer, 1998). Police officers who encounter a suspect on the street generally possess precious little knowledge about that person (Piliavin & Briar, 1969) and they must make consequential decisions—including decisions regarding the use of force (Hontz, 1999)—quickly and on the basis of this sparse information. Symbolic cues such as the neighborhood in which the encounter takes place (Brunson, 2007; Gau & Brunson, in press; Jones-Brown, 2007) and the personal characteristics of the suspect (Piliavin & Briar, 1969; Skolnick, 1966) act as heuristic cues to help officers form snap judgments about the nature of and appropriate response to suspects' actions. Racial minorities have been paired with crime for so long that the assumption of criminality may be entirely unconscious (Harris, 2007; Jones-Brown, 2007). Race also functions as a proxy for social and economic status (Bonilla-Silva, 1996), so although officers on-scene may not have information concerning a suspect's status, they may infer it from his or her race (see Piliavin & Briar, 1969). Race and socioeconomic status factor into a general social standing consideration, wherein police are more likely to use force against those persons they perceive as relatively powerless (Black, 1976; see also Kane, 2002; Skolnick, 1966; Terrill & Reisig, 2003). The present study, therefore, focused on the potential relationship between suspect race and police officers' use of Tasers. The research question under examination was as follows: Are police more likely to use Tasers against Black and/or Hispanic suspects than against White suspects?

The research question was addressed in two different ways using two separate but similar models. First, a model was constructed with a dependent variable measuring whether officers used Tasers at all or whether they opted for some other type of force. This model assessed whether racial differences emerged in the use of Tasers. In the second model, the sample was restricted to the first use of force and excluded any subsequent attempts. This model measured the use of Tasers as a first resort in that they were the first weapon employed to subdue the suspect. To the extent that racial biases and stereotypes lurk subconsciously and manifest as automatic responses that people may not even recognize as being discriminatory (see Harris, 2007; Jones-Brown, 2007), a race effect in the second model could be interpreted as evidence of biases at work.

Method

Data

The two hypotheses described above were tested with use-of-force data gathered from a state patrol agency in a single state between the years 2005 and 2007. Troopers who were involved in any use-of-force incident were required to document the event in a case file. Relevant data were then culled from these records and recorded electronically. The result was a data set containing 1,209 uses of force. Toward the end of the data-collection period, one of the researchers on the project drew a random sample of the original case files to cross-check the accuracy of the data set; the records matched and the accuracy was thus confirmed. It is worth emphasizing that these data include use-of-force incidents only; it is not a data set of all trooper-suspect encounters, and it is not, therefore, necessarily representative of more routine incidents that do not involve force. In all the incidents included in the present analysis, something happened during the encounter that prompted the officer to use force against the suspect. The question is not whether there was force but, rather, what type of force was used.

Using state patrol data departs from the custom among prior use-of-force studies of employing data from municipal and county agencies (e.g., Alpert et al., 2004; Alpert, Kenney, & Dunham, 1997; Alpert & MacDonald, 2001; Klinger, 1995; Terrill & Reisig, 2003). The form and function of state patrol agencies differs in many respects from those of municipal or county agencies; however, descriptive statistics from the present data showed that the Taser was the weapon of first choice in 19.2% of force-involved encounters and that it was used at some point in time (either immediately or after unsuccessful application of a different method) in 48.8% of encounters for which data were available. There was, then, sufficient prevalence of Taser use among state patrol troopers to permit a meaningful analysis. To the extent that state patrol agencies differ from municipal agencies, the results of the present study should be interpreted accordingly and generalized with caution.

State patrol data have the advantage of helping to avoid context effects that can confound race-force analyses. As noted above, the location of a police-suspect encounter and the characteristics of the neighborhood or community wherein an encounter transpires can impact the way that an officer and a suspect approach one another and the ultimate outcome of the incident (Klinger, 1997; Terrill & Reisig, 2003; see also Kane, 2002). State patrol agencies, in contrast to municipal police, do not patrol specific neighborhoods. This reduces the threat that differential exposure could bias the results. Stops, moreover, take place on highways rather than in suspects' neighborhoods of residence, which minimizes the possibility of officers utilizing contextual cues and enhances the probability that the outcome of a trooper–suspect encounter is truly the product of the interaction between those two people and not an artifact of the social or structural environment.

Table 5.3 contains the study agency's force continuum, which ranks the different types of force from the least to the most severe. Officers are required by federal and state law, as well as agency regulation, to use only as much force as is necessary to take control of the situation and subdue the suspect.

As Table 5.3 shows, this agency places the Taser just below the middle of its continuum, indicating that the Taser is not treated lightly, but neither is it considered a particularly severe form of force. Suspects would need to show a moderate, though not too serious, amount of resistive or combative behavior in order for officers to justify a Taser response. This use-of-force continuum is not necessarily representative of that used in other police organizations, but it is included here to give context to the study of troopers' use of force in this agency. Based on reports of other police departments (Amnesty International, 2006; GAO, 2005), it is likely that the present agency's classification of the Taser is not atypical.

Dependent Variables

As described above, two models were estimated that differed from one another only in the dependent variable used in each analysis. The first dependent variable was Taser use on any force application and was a dichotomous measure indicating whether an officer responded to a suspect's resistive behaviors by using a Taser

Table 5.3 State Patrol Agency's Use-of-Force Continuum

Force Level	Force Description
1	Physical takedowns, leg sweeps, or any technique that forcibly requires the subject to end up on the ground from means other than his/her own
2	Use of maximum restraints
3	Use of OC-10
4	Use of the Taser
5	Striking with hand/fist or foot
6	Any use of an impact tool, whether designed for that function or not
7	Neck restraint hold
8	Any action that results in a complaint of injury and/or any form of visible injury to a suspect
9	Use of the Pursuit Immobilization Technique at 40 miles per hour or higher
10	Use of a vehicle in an act of intentional intervention
11	Use of any firearm (including accidental discharge), except as outlined in the Animal Destruction policy

(coded as 1) or by using some other type of force, such as chemical spray or a physical takedown (coded as 0) during any force application. The second dependent variable was Taser use on the first force application (1 = *Taser on first*; 0 = *some other type on first*) and measured officers' propensity to reach for the Taser as a weapon of first resort when encountering a difficult suspect. The dichotomous nature of the dependent variables' coding scheme allowed for an estimation of the likelihood of a suspect being tased relative to the likelihood of that suspect having a different type of weapon/tactic used against him or her. Binary logistic regression was employed for both models.

Independent Variables

The same set of independent variables was used in both models. Suspect race was the primary predictor. Race was coded as a series of dummy variables indicating whether a suspect was White, Hispanic, Black, or Other (e.g., Asian, American Indian), with Whites left out as the reference category. This allowed for the generation of odds ratios and the computation of probabilities to assess whether minority suspects were more likely than White suspects to have Tasers used against them.

Situational controls were also included. The first control was suspect resistance type and was coded as dummy variables indicating whether resistance was active, assaultive, or other noncompliant, with passive resistance left out as the reference category. Officers were permitted to place suspects into multiple resistance categories, so for the analyses, the most serious category was selected and the suspect placed in that classification (e.g., a suspect who displayed passive resistance that escalated into active resistance would be considered an active resistor to avoid double-counting that person). Suspect resistance or combativeness is an obvious factor in the use of force by police (Bazley, Lersch, & Mieczkowski, 2007; Klinger, 2001). Police are empowered and required to use physical force when necessary (Bittner, 1970; see also Klockars, 1985), yet they are bound by *Garner*, *Connor*, and various departmental policies to use only that force that is commensurate with the level of resistance displayed by a suspect. Minorities tend to express more negative attitudes about police (Rosenbaum et al., 2005), which could lead to racially-systematic differences in suspect resistance. Controlling for resistance type was therefore necessary to guard against spuriousness in any race–Taser relationship that surfaced in the analyses.

Other situational controls included whether the incident was a traffic stop (1 = *traffic stop*; 0 = *other encounter*), whether it was light outside (1 = *light*; 0 = *dark*) during the encounter, and a continuous scale measuring the ratio of officer-to-suspect height and weight. We controlled for the encounter type because prior researchers have argued that there are qualitative differences between traffic stops and other types of encounters. The action taken to address this is sometimes to exclude traffic stops altogether (e.g., Klinger, 1994), but we find the systematic exclusion of a given type of encounter problematic both conceptually (differences should be explored, not ignored) and statistically (more than 40% of encounters involving Taser use and more than 60% of all force-involved encounters originated as traffic stops). Controlling for encounter type served as an acknowledgement that traffic stops present unique circumstances and dilemmas to officers. The light variable measured whether officers had the benefit of daylight to assist them or whether they were operating with limited visibility. The height and weight ratio scale accounted for any potential propensity for officers who are at a physical disadvantage to suspects to resort to Tasers faster than officers who may be able to subdue suspects without using weapons. Officers' age (years), sex (1 = *female*; 0 = *male*), and race (1 = *White*; 0 = *non-White*) were also entered into the model. Officers' years of service was substituted for age in both models and was nonsignificant; therefore, only age was included in the models so as to avoid collinearity. Suspect controls were age (years) and sex (1 = *female*; 0 = *male*).

Results

Table 5.4 contains the characteristics of officers, suspects, and situations in the entire sample of use-of-force incidents and in the subsample of uses of force that involved Tasers. Officers and suspects in the whole sample had a similar mean age of mid-30s. Most officers (96%) were men, as were most suspects (80.34%).

Only 10.2% of the officers were non-White, whereas approximately 11% of suspects were Hispanic and just under 10% were Black. Nearly two thirds of the encounters were traffic stops. Active resistance was the most common type of misbehavior displayed by suspects (47.02%), trailed by just over one quarter of suspects who displayed assaultive behavior and

Table 5.4 Descriptive Statistics for the Entire Sample (N = 1,209) and Subsample Taser on Any Force Application (n = 596)

	Whole Sample		Taser Subsample	
	M (SD)	Valid Percent	*M (SD)*	Valid Percent
Officers				
Age	34.52 (6.35)		34.19 (6.36)	
Female		4.00		5.03
White		89.80		89.43
Suspects				
Age	33.79 (11.66)		33.95 (11.89)	
Female		19.66		14.86
White		71.90		72.32
Hispanic		11.36		11.74
Black		9.34		8.89
Other		7.41		7.05
Situational				
Traffic stop		61.69		66.61
Passive resistance		11.23		13.26
Active resistance		47.02		50.36
Assaultive behavior		27.58		28.52
Other noncompliant		14.17		7.89
Taser use on any application		48.75		—
Taser use on first application		19.15		—
Light outside		37.00		36.00
Height/weight ratio scale	2.22 (0.53)		2.21 (0.60)	

approximately 11% who resisted passively. Tasers were used in nearly half (48.75%) of all use-of-force incidents and were the first-used type of force in 19.15%. The mean of the height and weight ratio summed scale was 2.22, indicating that on average officers and suspects were of similar physical stature (a 1 on each of the height and weight ratios meant that there was no difference between officer and suspect height or weight).

Prior to the logistic regression analyses, the independent and dependent variables were entered into ordinary least squares regression models to obtain collinearity diagnostics. All variance inflation factors (VIFs) were below 2.5, indicating the absence of harmful collinearity. The tolerances were high, but the condition indices both slightly exceeded 20. The variables that appeared potentially problematic were the resistance-type measures (active, assaultive, and other). These variables had low VIFs but their tolerances were borderline (.419, .441, and .667, respectively). To ensure that collinearity did not present a threat to the analyses, both of the models presented below were rerun using a dichotomous measure of resistance (1 = *passive resistance*; 0 = *any other type of resistance*). This reduced all VIFs, tolerances, and condition indices to acceptable limits. The logistic regression model results did not change when this binary variable was substituted for the ordinal resistance measure, so the original variables were retained.

The results of the logistic regression models predicting Taser use on any force application are shown in Table 5.5. As can be seen, resistance was the strongest predictor of Taser use. Active and assaultive resistance had large effects on the likelihood of Taser use ($\exp(b) =$ 0.335 and 0.315, respectively), indicating that suspects who actively resisted or who attempted to assault police officers were less likely than passive resistors to be tased. The most probable explanation for this is that officers used more serious forms of force against combative individuals, as these suspects may have presented an immediate threat to officers' safety or even their lives (the assaultive group contained suspects who wielded a knife or gun). It is also possible, though not directly observable in the present data set, that some troopers used the Taser against passive resistors preemptively; that is, they may have tried to defuse the situation before passive resistance escalated into physical combativeness. The fact that passive resistors were the most likely group to be tased, though, presents a question of the propriety of current Taser practices that is worthy of further examination in future research.

Officer race was a significant predictor of Taser use, with White officers being less likely to employ the Taser relative to officers of other races ($\exp(b) = 0.567$). Female suspects were less likely ($\exp(b) = 0.525$), than male suspects to be tased at any point during the encounter. Suspect race was not significant in this model, indicating no racial disparities in the likelihood that Tasers would be used at any point during a use-of-force encounter. Examination of the classification tables with and without suspect race included in the model showed that the full model correctly classified 62.5% of cases, and the model with race omitted yielded 62.8% correct classification. This confirmed that suspect race was not an important predictor of Taser use on any application of force.

Table 5.6 contains the results for the model restricted to the first force encounter. This second model was similar to the first in that active resistance ($\exp(b) = 0.360$), and assaultive behavior ($\exp(b) = 0.169$), were the strongest predictors of Taser use, and suspects who displayed one of these types of resistance were less likely than passive resistors to be tased. White officers were, again, significantly less likely to use Tasers relative to other forms of force ($\exp(b) = 0.411$). Traffic stops were also somewhat less likely than other types of encounters to result in the use of the Taser as the first type of force ($\exp(b) = 0.634$). The most striking result from this model was the large effect for Hispanics: Hispanic suspects faced twice the

Table 5.5 Logistic Regression Results for Taser Use on Any Application of Force

	Taser Use on Any Force Application		
	b	*SE*	Exp(*b*)
Officer age	0.000	.014	1.000
Officer female	0.592	.405	1.808
Officer White	−0.567**	.280	0.567
Suspect age	−0.005	.007	0.995
Suspect female	−0.644***	.239	0.525
Suspect Hispanic	0.197	.273	1.218
Suspect Black	0.416	.305	1.516
Suspect other	0.091	.364	1.095
Traffic stop	−0.181	.183	0.834
Active resistance	−1.093****	.277	0.335
Assaultive behavior	−1.154****	.298	0.315
Other noncompliant	−1.108***	.398	0.330
Light outside	0.020	.186	1.020
Height/weight ratio scale	−0.086	.176	0.918
Constant	1.618**	.680	5.044

NOTE: $n = 596$. Nagelkerke $R^2 = .094$.
*$p < .10$. **$p < .05$. ***$p < .01$. ****$p < .001$.

odds that Whites faced (exp(b) = 2.236) of having the first force attempt be a Taser.

Resistance level was controlled for, meaning that the effect for Hispanic race/ethnicity was not an artifact of differential resistance. Black suspects (exp(b) = 0.364), and those belonging to other races (exp(b) = 0.238), were significantly less likely than Whites to be tased on the first force application, which was unexpected given the increase in odds for Hispanics. The statistical significance of these two findings was marginal, though ($p < .10$), so they should be interpreted with caution.

The predicted probabilities of Taser use on the first application of force were .170 for Whites, .314 for Hispanics, .077 for Blacks, and .066 for the other category. The differences in Whites' and Hispanics' respective probabilities lends support to the conclusion that there were meaningful differences between these two groups and that, even controlling for relevant factors like resistance, Hispanics were more likely than Whites, Blacks, or other races to be tased. Classification results showed that 84.2% of cases were predicted correctly. The percentage dropped to 82.9 when suspect race was omitted from the model. This shows that suspect race, although statistically significant, was a modest predictor of Taser use on the first application. This is likely due to the fact that only Hispanics emerged as significantly different from Whites—no other suspect racial classification achieved statistical significance at $p < .05$. Officers' use of force was likely driven primarily by suspects' behavior rather than by their personal characteristics, though Hispanic ethnicity did increase the chances of Taser use. Racial disparities, then, were apparent

Table 5.6 Logistic Regression Results for Taser Use on First Application of Force

	Taser Use on First Force Application		
	b	*SE*	Exp(*b*)
Officer age	−0.004	.019	0.996
Officer female	−0.115	.540	0.891
Officer White	−0.889***	.332	0.411
Suspect age	0.003	.010	1.003
Suspect female	−0.576	.352	0.562
Suspect Hispanic	0.805**	.314	2.236
Suspect Black	−1.010*	.551	0.364
Suspect Other	−1.437*	.756	0.238
Traffic stop	−0.455*	.239	0.634
Active resistance	−1.021***	.300	0.360
Assaultive behavior	−1.780****	.380	0.169
Other noncompliant	−0.383	.440	0.682
Light outside	−0.050	.246	0.951
Height/weight ratio scale	0.059	.207	1.060
Constant	0.574	.875	1.776

NOTE: $n = 594$. Nagelkerke $R^2 = .153$.
$^{*}p < .10$. $^{**}p < .05$. $^{***}p < .01$. $^{****}p < .001$.

but temperate. This conclusion is elaborated on in the following section.

Discussion

This study's purpose was to add to academic knowledge concerning police officers' use of Tasers and to spur a dialogue regarding the possibility of racial disparities. Two logistic regression analyses were run. The first determined that there was not a statistically significant relationship between a suspect's race and the likelihood that an officer tased the suspect at some point during the use-of-force encounter. The second model tested the effect of suspect race on the likelihood that the Taser would be an officer's first tool of choice when dealing with a difficult suspect. The results of this model suggested that although suspect resistance type was the largest predictor of Taser use, there were racial differences as well; in particular, Hispanic/Latino suspects were twice as likely as White suspects to be tased. This finding has implications for research and policy.

First, it must be emphasized that race—no less than any other suspect, officer, or situational characteristic—does not exist in a vacuum. Officer and citizen characteristics and each actor's behavior toward the other influence the outcome of an incident (McCluskey, Mastrofski, & Parks, 1999); however, every officer-suspect encounter is embedded in a sociostructural context that has very real potential to alter that outcome (Alpert & MacDonald,

2001; Bonilla-Silva, 1996; Jacobs & Britt, 1979; Jacobs & O'Brien, 1998; Kane, 2002; Kania & Mackey, 1977; Klinger, 1997; MacDonald et al., 2001; Meehan & Ponder, 2002; Terrill & Reisig, 2003; see also Sampson & Bartusch, 1998). Officers may bring racial stereotypes and preconceived notions to bear in a confrontation with a suspect (Harris, 2007; Jones-Brown, 2007; Skolnick, 1966), and suspects may do likewise with regard to stereotypes and assumptions about police (see Cheurprakobkit, 2000; Mastrofski et al., 2002; Sampson & Bartusch, 1998; Weitzer & Tuch, 2002).

In this mix of factors, however, suspect race is an important consideration. Prior research provides testament to the historical importance of race in officer-suspect encounters (Meyer, 1980; Robin, 1963; Skogan, 2005; Sparger & Giacopassi, 1992; see also Williams & Murphy, 1990), even apart from ecological factors (MacDonald et al., 2007). As Tasers and other CEDs proliferate, therefore, suspect race serves as a viable avenue for pursuit of a deeper understanding of these implements' use. Findings from the present study confirmed that suspect race was, indeed, a factor influencing the likelihood that officers in this agency would use Tasers rather than other types of force. The fact that the race effect surfaced only in the model predicting Taser use on the first force application—but not in that predicting Taser use at any point during the encounter—seems to point in one of two directions. The first possibility is that there was something qualitatively different in the interactions police in this agency had with Hispanic suspects. The models presented here controlled for resistance type, and a supplementary multinomial logistic regression model predicting resistance type (not shown; available on request) confirmed that suspect race was not related to resistance type; that is, there was no systematic tendency for Hispanic suspects to engage in any particular type of resistance. No data were available to test for cultural or language barriers that may have frustrated officer-suspect communication or for the potential that Hispanics approached officers with a more hostile demeanor that, although not captured in officers' official recording of resistance type, may have caused troopers to interpret Hispanics' behavior as more dangerous than that of White suspects.

The possible existence of hidden systematic differences between Hispanic suspects and suspects of other races was explored using a series of bivariate analyses. The results of these tests suggested no marked differences between Hispanics and others in terms of officers' demographic characteristics, suspect sex, or situational factors. The only potentially influential difference between the groups was in age: Hispanic suspects were significantly younger (M = 28.69) than White suspects (M = 34.89; F = 9.423, $p < .001$). Younger suspects may be more impulsive or aggressive during police encounters, and prior research has shown that age and race interact (Steffensmeier et al., 1998). To ensure that age differences did not confound the race effect, the sample was split into four age groups based on the distribution of the age variable (minimum = 15; maximum = 82; M = 33.79): 15–24, 25–34, 35–44, and 45 and older. The Taser on first application model was run individually for each of the four age groups, and predicted probabilities for Whites and Hispanics were obtained. The pattern of results across the age groups mirrored that for the entire sample, suggesting that Hispanics' younger mean age was not the driving force behind this group's disproportionately high likelihood of being tased. All of the supplementary analyses, then, indicated that suspect race was not confounded with any other predictor in this study.

The potential for there to be racial differences in officers' interpretations of suspects' behavior segues into the second possibility, which is that officers' differential interpretation of Hispanics' and Whites' behaviors was racially based rather than premised on actual variations in behavior. Stereotypes can lead criminal justice actors of all sorts to interpret the behavior of racial minorities as being more dangerous than identical behavior engaged in by Whites (see, e.g., Jones-Brown, 2007; see also the extensive body of literature concerning race and sentencing). The pattern of results found here—that Hispanics suffered no greater likelihood of Taser use in the any-application model but twice the odds of Whites in the first-application model—is consistent with stereotype-driven behavior. The unconscious, automatic nature of bias (Skolnick, 1966) is perhaps most apparent in split-second decisions, as opposed to perceptions that form and decisions that are made more gradually and with the benefit of time. To that end, it could be that race does not affect officers' decision making when they respond to suspect resistance by graduating progressively up the force continuum but that it does leak into decisions that are made rapidly on the basis of limited information. This proposed explanation for the present results is, of course, tentative and not directly falsifiable or confirmable here. We urge researchers to continue this line of investigation and put the current findings to the test using data from other police agencies.

The results of this study have policy implications. The first and most important is that police officers in the agency studied here did seem to use suspect behavior, as opposed to race, as the primary determinate of their use of Tasers. This is, of course, appropriate. The question of where Tasers should be placed on use-of-force continua or what standards of training and supervision should be in place to govern Taser use (Adams & Jennison, 2007) is a legitimate debate but is beyond the scope of this article. Without speaking to that controversy, we can offer the preliminary conclusion that Taser use in this particular agency did not appear overtly problematic within current bounds of acceptable Taser deployment.

The second policy implication turns on the apparent discrepancies in Taser use on the first application. The race effect was small but extant, with Hispanic suspects being twice as likely as Whites to be tased when the Taser was the force type of first resort. This finding warrants further investigation both by academic researchers and by police departments seeking to root out discriminatory practices. The enhanced use of Tasers against Hispanic suspects can be interpreted as akin to racial profiling in the sense that it involves disparate treatment of suspects on the basis of race, and to that extent, it raises the same questions concerning the accuracy of officers' judgments about the dangerousness of individual suspects (Harris, 2002) and the damage that can be done to police-citizen relationships on a grand scale (Spitzer, 1999; Stoutland, 2001; see also Alpert, Dunham, & Smith, 2007). An officer-citizen encounter is rarely an isolated event, particularly if it yields a negative outcome for the citizen: That person will tell friends and family, who may themselves experience vicarious feelings of victimization (Brunson, 2007; Rosenbaum et al., 2005). It is of paramount importance, then, for officers to be mindful when they encounter an individual citizen that their actions in this single, seemingly-isolated instance have the potential to resonate throughout the community.

A third policy implication from this study mirrors some prior calls for further research into the circumstances under which Taser use is (in)appropriate. Supplementary frequency analyses on the data used here showed that 25.6% of suspects who resisted passively were tased on the first application of force. The fact that a full fourth of passive resistors' efforts were met with the Taser raises the concern that police are substituting this weapon for verbal de-escalation and other skilled ways of calming suspects down without hurting them. This is a possibility worthy of examination so that any trend that may be developing can be squelched immediately.

More research on Tasers' effects and patterns of use is warranted to fully understand this device and its use. Research should determine whether the findings in the present study generalize to other areas of the country with a variety of racial compositions. Studies should include all types of police organizations, including city, county, and state agencies.

The finding here that Black and Hispanic suspects differed notably in their odds of being tased also underscores the need for researchers to stop analyzing simple White/non-White differences in tests designed to identify possible racial disparities in police behavior. A growing stock of evidence (Cheurprakobkit, 2000; Meyer, 1980; Rosenbaum et al., 2005; Skogan, 2005; Weitzer & Tuch, 2005b), to which the present study adds, suggests that there are very real differences between Blacks and Hispanics (and probably between other races, too) in perceptions of police and in the behavior manifested by officers during encounters. Patterns in Taser use might also change over time, which raises the need for trend monitoring. CEDs are relatively novel and officers' employment of them could shift longitudinally. The more academics and practitioners learn about Taser and other CED use, the better equipped they will be to ensure that utilization is appropriate and that the Taser is an advance in, rather than a setback to, the professionalism and effectiveness of the police.

References

Adams, K., & Jennison, V. (2007). What we do not know about police use of Tasers. *Policing: An International Journal of Police Strategies and Management, 30,* 447–465.

Alpert, G. P., Dunham, R. G., & MacDonald, J. M. (2004). Interactive police–citizen encounters that result in force. *Police Quarterly, 7,* 475–488.

Alpert, G. P., Dunham, R. G., & Smith, M. R. (2007). Investigating racial profiling by the Miami–Dade Police Department: A multimethod approach. *Criminology & Public Policy, 6,* 25–56.

Alpert, G. P., Kenney, D. J., & Dunham, R. (1997). Police pursuits and the use of force: Recognizing and managing "the pucker factor"—A research note. *Justice Quarterly, 14,* 371–385.

Alpert, G. P., & MacDonald, J. M. (2001). Police use of force: An analysis of organizational characteristics. *Justice Quarterly, 18,* 393–409.

Alpert, G. P., & Smith, M. R. (2000). Police use-of-force data: Where we are and where we should be going. *Police Quarterly, 2,* 57–78.

Alpert, G. P., & Smith, W. C. (1994). How reasonable is the reasonable man? Police and excessive force. *Journal of Criminal Law & Criminology, 85,* 481–501.

Amnesty International. (2006). *Continuing concerns about Taser use* (Publication No. AMR 51/030/2006). Available at http://www.amnesty.org/en/library/asset/AMR51/151/2007/en/dom-AMR511512007en.pdf

Bazley, T. D., Lersch, K. M., & Mieczkowski, T. (2007). Officer force versus suspect resistance: A gendered analysis of patrol officers in an urban police department. *Journal of Criminal Justice, 35,* 183–192.

Bittner, E. (1970). *The functions of the police in modern society.* Cambridge, MA: Oelgeschlager, Gunn & Hain.

Black, D. (1976). *The behavior of law.* New York: Academic Press.

Bonilla-Silva, E. (1996). Rethinking racism: Toward a structural interpretation. *American Sociological Review, 62,* 465–480.

Brunson, R. K. (2007). "Police don't like Black people": African American young men's accumulated police experiences. *Criminology & Public Policy, 6,* 71–102.

Cheurprakobkit, S. (2000). Police–citizen contact and police performance: Attitudinal differences between Hispanics and non-Hispanics. *Journal of Criminal Justice, 28,* 325–336.

Commission for Public Complaints Against the Royal Canadian Mounted Police. (2008). Retrieved December 1, 2009, from http://www3.thestar.com/static/PDF/080618_CPC_RCMP_Report.pdf

Downs, R. L. (2007). Less lethal weapons: A technologist's perspective. *Policing: An International Journal of Police Strategies and Management, 30,* 358–384.

Fagan, J., & Davies, G. (2000). Street cops and broken windows: Terry, race, and disorder in New York City. *Fordham Urban Law Journal, 28,* 457–504.

Fyfe, J. J. (1981). Observations on police deadly force. *Crime & Delinquency, 27,* 376–389.

Garner, J. H., Maxwell, C. D., & Heraux, C. G. (2002). Characteristics associated with the prevalence and severity of force used by the police. *Justice Quarterly, 19,* 705–746.

Gau, J. M., & Brunson, R. K. (in press). Procedural justice and order maintenance policing: A study of inner-city young men's perceptions of police legitimacy. *Justice Quarterly.*

Government Accountability Office. (2005). *Use of Tasers by select law enforcement agencies* (Publication No.

GAO-05-464). Retrieved December 1, 2009, from http://www.gao.gov/new.items/d05464.pdf

Graham v. Connor, 490 U.S. 386 (1989).

Harris, D. A. (2002). *Profiles in injustice.* New York: New Press.

Harris, D. A. (2007). The importance of research on race and policing: Making race salient to individuals and institutions within criminal justice. *Criminology & Public Policy, 6,* 5–24.

Ho, T. (1993). Individual and situational determinants of the use of deadly force: A simulation. *American Journal of Criminal Justice, 18,* 41–60.

Hoffman, P. B., & Hickey, E. R. (2005). Use of force by female police officers. *Journal of Criminal Justice, 33,* 145–151.

Hontz, T. A. (1999). Justifying the deadly force response. *Police Quarterly, 2,* 462–476.

International Association of Chiefs of Police. (1999). *Electro-muscular disruption technology: A nine-step strategy for effective deployment.* Available at http://www.theiacp.org/research/CuttingEdge/EMDT9Steps.pdf

Jacobs, D., & Britt, D. (1979). Inequality and police use of deadly force: An empirical assessment of a conflict hypothesis. *Social Problems, 26,* 403–412.

Jacobs, D., & O'Brien, R. M. (1998). The determinants of deadly force: A structural analysis of police violence. *American Journal of Sociology, 103,* 837–862.

Johnston, D. (1981). Stop! Or I'll throw my net at you. *Police Magazine, 4*(2), 23–28.

Jones-Brown, D. (2007). Forever the symbolic assailant: The more things change, the more they remain the same. *Criminology & Public Policy, 6,* 103–122.

Kane, R. J. (2002). The social ecology of police misconduct. *Criminology, 40,* 867–896.

Kania, R. R. E., & Mackey, W. C. (1977). Police violence as a function of community characteristics. *Criminology, 15,* 27–48.

Klinger, D. A. (1994). Demeanor or crime? Why "hostile" citizens are more likely to be arrested. *Criminology, 32,* 475–493.

Klinger, D. A. (1995). The micro-structure of nontlethal force: Baseline data from an observational study. *Criminal Justice Review, 20,* 169–186.

Klinger, D. A. (1997). Negotiating order in patrol work: An ecological theory of police response to deviance. *Criminology, 35,* 277–306.

Klinger, D. A. (2001). Suicidal intent in victim-precipitated homicide: Insights from the study of "suicide-by-cop." *Homicide Studies, 5,* 206–226.

Klinger, D. A. (2007). Impact munitions: A discussion of key information. *Policing: An International Journal of Police Strategies and Management, 31,* 385–397.

Klockars, C. B. (1985). *The idea of police.* Beverly Hills, CA: SAGE.

Langworthy, R. H. (1986). Police shootings and criminal homicide: The temporal relationship. *Journal of Quantitative Criminology, 2,* 377–388.

MacDonald, J. M., Kaminski, R. J., Alpert, G. P., & Tannenbaum, A. N. (2001). The temporal relationship between police killings of civilians and criminal homicide: A refined version of the danger-perception theory. *Crime & Delinquency, 47,* 155–172.

MacDonald, J. M., Stokes, R. J., Ridgeway, G., & Riley, K. J. (2007). Race, neighbourhood context and perception of injustice by the police in Cincinnati. *Urban Studies, 44,* 2567–2585.

Mastrofski, S., & Parks, R. B. (1990). Improving observational studies of police. *Criminology, 28,* 475–496.

Mastrofski, S. D., Reisig, M. D., & McCluskey, J. D. (2002). Police disrespect toward the public: An encounter-based analysis. *Criminology, 40,* 519–551.

McCluskey, J. D., Mastrofski, S. D., & Parks, R. B. (1999). To acquiesce or rebel: Predicting citizen compliance with police requests. *Police Quarterly, 2,* 389–416.

McCluskey, J. D., Terrill, W., & Paoline, E. A. (2005). Peer group aggressiveness and the use of coercion in police-suspect encounters. *Police Practice and Research, 6,* 19–37.

Meehan, A. J., & Ponder, M. C. (2002). Race and place: The ecology of racial profiling African American motorists. *Justice Quarterly, 19,* 399–430.

Meyer, G. (1992). Nonlethal weapons: Where do they fit? Part II. *Journal of California Law Enforcement, 26*(2), 53–58.

Meyer, M. W. (1980). Policing shootings at minorities: The case of Los Angeles. *Annals of the American Academy of Political and Social Science, 452,* 98–110.

Piliavin, I., & Briar, S. (1969). Police encounters with juveniles. In D. R. Cressey & D. A. Ward (Eds.), *Delinquency, crime, and social processes* (pp. 154–165). New York: Harper & Row.

Ready, J., White, M. D., & Fisher, C. (2008). Shock value: A comparative analysis of news reports and official police records on TASER deployments. *Policing: An International Journal of Police Strategies and Management, 31,* 148–170.

Reiss, A. J., Jr. (1980). Controlling police use of deadly force. *Annals of the American Academy of Political and Social Science, 452,* 122–134.

Robin, G. D. (1963). Justifiable homicide by police officers. *Journal of Criminal Law, Criminology, and Police Science, 54,* 225–231.

Rosenbaum, D. P., Schuck, A. M., Costello, S. K., Hawkins, D. F., & Ring, M. K. (2005). Attitudes toward the police: The effects of direct and vicarious experience. *Police Quarterly, 8,* 343–365.

Sampson, R. J., & Bartusch, D. J. (1998). Legal cynicism and (subcultural?) tolerance of deviance: The neighborhood context of racial differences. *Law & Society Review, 32,* 777–804.

Skogan, W. G. (2005). Citizen satisfaction with police encounters. *Police Quarterly, 8,* 298–321.

Skolnick, J. (1966). *Justice without trial.* New York: Wiley.

Smith, B. W. (2004). Structural and organizational predictors of homicide by police. *Policing: An International Journal of Police Strategies and Management, 27,* 539–557.

Smith, D. A. (1986). The neighborhood context of police behavior. In A. J. Reiss, Jr. & M. Tonry (Eds.), *Communities and crime* (pp. 313–341). Chicago: University of Chicago Press.

Smith, M. R., Kaminski, R. J., Rojek, J., Alpert, G. P., & Mathis, J. (2007). The impact of conducted energy devices and other types of force and resistance on officer and suspect injuries. *Policing: An International Journal of Police Strategies and Management, 30,* 423–446.

Smith, M. R., Petrocelli, M., & Scheer, C. (2007). Excessive force, civil liability, and the Taser in the nation's courts. *Policing: An International Journal of Police Strategies and Management, 30,* 398–422.

Sparger, J. R., & Giacopassi, D. J. (1992). Memphis revisited: A reexamination of police shootings after the *Garner* decision. *Justice Quarterly, 9,* 211–225.

Steffensmeier, D., Ulmer, J., & Kramer, J. (1998). The interaction of race, gender, and age in criminal sanctioning: The punishment cost of being young, Black, and male. *Criminology, 36,* 763–797.

Stoutland, S. (2001). The multiple dimensions of trust in resident/police relations in Boston. *Journal of Research in Crime and Delinquency, 38,* 226–256.

Tennessee v. Garner, 471 U.S., 1 (1985).

Terrill, W., Alpert, G. P., Dunham, R. G., & Smith, M. R. (2003). A management tool for evaluating police use of force: An application of the force factor. *Police Quarterly, 6,* 150–171.

Terrill, W., & Reisig, M. D. (2003). Neighborhood context and police use of force. *Journal of Research in Crime and Delinquency, 40,* 291–321.

Vilke, G. M., & Chan, T. C. (2007). Less lethal technology: Medical issues. *Policing: An International Journal of Police Strategies and Management, 30,* 341–357.

Weitzer, R. (1999). Citizens' perceptions of police misconduct: Race and neighborhood context. *Justice Quarterly, 16,* 819–846.

Weitzer, R. (2000). Racialized policing: Residents' perceptions in three neighborhoods. *Law & Society Review, 34,* 129–155.

Weitzer, R. (2002). Incidents of police misconduct and public opinion. *Journal of Criminal Justice, 30,* 397–408.

Weitzer, R., & Tuch, S. A. (2002). Perceptions of racial profiling: Race, class, and personal experience. *Criminology, 40,* 435–456.

Weitzer, R., & Tuch, S. A. (2005a). Determinants of public satisfaction with the police. *Police Quarterly, 8,* 279–297.

Weitzer, R., & Tuch, S. A. (2005b). Racially biased policing: Determinants of citizen perceptions. *Social Forces, 83,* 1009–1030.

Welch, D. (2008). *Police slammed over Taser plan.* Available from http://www.smh.com.au

White, M. D., & Ready, J. (2007). The Taser as a less lethal force alternative: Findings on use and effectiveness in a large metropolitan police agency. *Police Quarterly, 10,* 170–191.

Williams, H., & Murphy, P. V. (1990). The evolving strategy of police: A minority view. In J. K. Stewart & M. H. Moore (Eds.), *Perspectives on policing* (Vol. 13, pp. 27–50). Washington, DC: National Institute of Justice.

DISCUSSION QUESTIONS

1. What are the advantages and disadvantages of police use of Tasers?
2. Why is police use of Tasers an important issue in the study of race and policing?
3. Summarize the major findings and limitations of the study.

READING

The authors of this article provide an overview of Elijah Anderson's "code of the street" to help understand why some individuals resort to violence and victimization to settle disputes. Stewart, Schreck, and Brunson point to structural neglect and inequality in some inner-city areas as factors that contribute to the failure of civic institutions and neighborhood social networks. Residents in these areas believe that legal systems, including the police, have failed them. As a result, they resort to an informal system governing the use of violence. The street code requires that residents are tough and often display a violent demeanor to gain and keep respect. Those that lack respect are the most likely to be victimized. The authors present some recommendations to reduce reliance on the street code and improve the legitimacy of the police and other legal institutions. Repressive police tactics and poor police–community relations can be addressed by working with residents and community institutions such as churches and schools.

Lessons of the Street Code

Policy Implications for Reducing Violent Victimization Among Disadvantaged Citizens

Eric A. Stewart, Christopher J. Schreck, and Rod K. Brunson

More than a decade ago, Gottfredson and Hirschi (1995) characterized crime control policy as being unguided by theory. Rather, they asserted that the philosophy that lay behind favored policies reflected the parochial aims of "administrative criminology," where the solutions to crime resided within the criminal justice system. Should the crime problem be perceived by anyone as too high, the policy maker's invariable solution is to demand more resources for law enforcement (including additional personnel, firepower, and hi-tech gadgetry), fewer restrictions on troublesome civil liberties so the authorities can "do their jobs," and a toughening of criminal sanctions. Unfortunately, as violent crime begins to move upward after years of decline, there is no evidence that officials have learned anything new. We are already beginning to hear more demands for tax monies to support the usual crime control policies that claim to protect society from criminal elements (Rosenfeld, 2007; Tonry, 2007).

The response of administrative criminology toward stricter enforcement, reflecting as it does the interests of political leaders and practitioners, nevertheless proves problematic for some segments of society (Rose & Clear, 1998). The consequences of these initiatives are indeed often dire, particularly in the most disadvantaged stretches of American inner cities where violence is endemic (Wilson, 1987) and African Americans are disproportionately exposed to violence as offenders and victims in socially

Source: Stewart, E. A., Schreck, C. J., & Brunson, R. K. (2008). Lessons of the street code: Policy implications for reducing violent victimization among disadvantaged citizens. *Journal of Contemporary Criminal Justice, 24*, 137–147.

isolated and disadvantaged neighborhoods (Bureau of Justice Statistics, 2003; Hawkins, Laub, Lauritsen, & Cothern, 2000; Lauritsen, 2003; Moore & Tonry, 1998; Reiss & Roth, 1993). Consequently, a significant portion of the U.S. prison population consists of African American males from the inner city (Pettit & Western, 2004). Concern about the high rates of violence and incarceration among African Americans has made identification of contributing factors a research priority (Anderson, 1999; Reiss & Roth, 1993).

In the current article, we focus on a crime control perspective that is shaped by theory and research on violence in disadvantaged areas and that provides us with ideas for curbing violence. Furthermore, we examine the context of areas where few economic an[illegible] social opportunities for advancement exis[illegible] particular, we look at the persistent di[illegible]antage, racial segregation, and structur[illegible]equality that African Americans i[illegible]ese areas endure, which leads to what [illegible]ah Anderson (1999) calls the "code of th[illegible]reet." We believe that policy makers who are serious about reducing violence in the inner city must consider how neighborhood structural problems fuel violence. In the sections that follow, we discuss the meaning of the code of the street, and how police practices facilitate the development of the street code, and how police-citizen interactions can improve order in areas where the street code is solidly entrenched as a way of reducing violence.

The Special Problem of the Code of the Street

Subculture-of-violence theories are not new in the fields of criminology and sociology (Cohen, 1955; Curtis, 1975; Magura, 1975; Miller, 1958; Wolfgang & Ferracuti, 1967). In fact, such theories have been extensively studied by scores of researchers (Agnew, 1994; Austin, 1980; Ball-Rokeach, 1973; Bernard, 1990; Cao, Adams, & Jensen, 1997; Erlanger, 1974; Felson, Liska, South, & McNulty, 1994; Heimer, 1997; Luckenbill & Doyle, 1989; Markowitz & Felson, 1998; Sampson & Bartusch, 1998). Among this grouping is Elijah Anderson (1999), who provides the most detailed accounting of the complexities that underlie the code of the street for many African Americans. In Anderson's book *Code of the Street*, he presents a co[illegible]ex illustration of the interplay in which s[illegible]ural inequalities give rise to cultural a[illegible]ations. His basic argument is that partic[illegible]areas of one's life are governed by sets of[illegible]ns and expectations that are often not i[illegible]e with the legal system. This does not m[illegible]that people mindlessly act out in a viol[illegible]anner simply because local norms f[illegible]violence. Rather, the conditions on the [illegible]reet might force residents into a position where they have to choose between violence and suffering repeated victimization. In the view of residents from disadvantaged areas, the legal system, which had a monopoly on legitimate violence, has effectively failed, and it behooves residents to maintain order as best they can—by unilaterally assuming control of violence.

Anderson further explains that at the heart of the code of the street is "a desperate search for respect" (p. 9). Residents of disadvantaged, racially, and socially isolated neighborhoods do not trust the police to provide security; they feel the need to resort to a kind of "people's law" based on "street justice" (p. 10). The code of the street is thus in large measure an adaptation to "a lost sense of security of the local inner-city neighborhood and, by extension, a profound lack of faith in the police and judicial system" (p. 323). In these disadvantaged neighborhoods, residents must cultivate and maintain respect or they become vulnerable to victimization, especially physical attack. Accordingly, people develop a heightened sensitivity to signs of disrespect and feel compelled to display a predisposition to violence. The code of the street thus increases the likelihood that violence will become commonplace in social interactions.

How does a community get to the point where violence is the most viable option for self-preservation? The simple answer is continual structural neglect and inequality of an area and its residents. According to Anderson (1999), the code of the street emerges in predominantly African American inner-city areas where high rates of poverty, joblessness, violence, racial discrimination, alienation, mistrust of police, and hopelessness are characteristic (Bruce, Roscigno, & McCall, 1998; Miller, 1958; Sampson & Wilson, 1995; Wilkinson, 2003; Wilson, 1987). In addition, within these areas, civic institutions have either failed or are ineffective such that they have lost legitimacy in the eyes of residents. For example, the police are the most visible social institution in distressed communities. However, it does not follow that the police contribute meaningfully—at least in a benign sense—to order within the neighborhood. Their purpose is primarily repressive, their responses are ineffectual and arbitrary, and residents are mistrustful (Jacobs & Wright, 2006). Moreover, in areas where there is confidence in institutions, disputes are nonviolently resolved. There are courts available, or neighbors can settle their differences informally (Ellickson, 1991). But within the primarily minority inner city, these institutions and alternatives have catastrophically failed or are grossly unrealistic given the circumstances. Disadvantaged citizens tend to have less access to the court system (e.g., Black, 1976). Informal peaceful means of control fail as well, given the isolated and weakened nature of neighborhood social networks in socially disorganized areas (Sampson, Raudenbush, & Earls, 1997). Lacking any legitimate means of recourse, residents have few means short of violence with which to compel order. Anderson and others have noted that violence characterizes disadvantaged neighborhoods (e.g., Sampson & Lauritsen, 1994); and violence is thought to be one of the most important resources for gaining status, respect, and street credibility among those who subscribe to the street culture (Wilkinson, 2003).

What, then, is the code of the street? According to Anderson (1999), the code of the street is an informal system governing the use of violence, especially among young African American males. The code of the street emphasizes that one must maintain the respect of others through a violent and tough identity, and a willingness to exact retribution in the event of disrespect, or else risk being "rolled on" or physically assaulted (p. 73). As Anderson notes, "An important part of the code is not to allow others to chump you, to let them know that you are 'about serious business' and not to be trifled with" (p. 130). Implicit in Anderson's work is the notion that responsibility for order and safety has essentially devolved on the individual. Excessive and violent retribution is the consequence of victimization or disrespect. Safety comes from having a "reputation" for using violence. The toughness and aggressiveness, as prescribed by the street culture, should communicate to others that one is dangerous and best left alone. In addition, displaying a violent demeanor not only commands respect but also serves to discourage others from "testing" or "challenging" those exhibiting the street code style. Anderson points out that "for those who are invested in the code, the clear object of their demeanor is to discourage strangers from even thinking about testing their manhood" (p. 92). And if the street code demeanor is properly displayed, it should "check others who would violate one's person, and it also helps build a reputation that works to prevent future challenges" (p. 92). Thus, on the street, the message must be that you are not a pushover and there are penalties for disrespect (p. 130). According to Anderson, the desire to protect oneself from victimization is one of the primary reasons for the emergence of the street code, which leads to "rough justice" in the streets if one is disrespected or experiences a perceived injustice (Baron, Kennedy, & Forde, 2001).

Alternatively, by not responding to victimization, a person becomes a "chump." Chumps also try to rely on "legitimate" authorities to solve their problems. They are frequently objects of contempt, ridicule, and victimization. According to Anderson's (1999) description, on the streets an individual who is seen as a chump or not streetwise "gets little or no respect, and those who resemble him are the ones who most often get picked on, tried or tested, and become victims of robbery and gratuitous violence" (p. 131). One earns respect by personally paying back others. Interestingly, such views have been recorded regarding medieval times as well, when governing institutions were primitive and ineffective.

Accordingly, adoption of street code behavior inherently leads to some form of violence or victimization. Baron et al. (2001) found that street culture behaviors (e.g., toughness, aggression, and retribution) were negatively related to victimization. The authors speculated that adherence to the street code may serve a protective function against victimization. In another study, Jacobs (2004) interviewed 33 street offenders who followed the street code. He found that these hard-core individuals used retaliation or the threat of retaliation to reduce their risk of victimization and to earn, maintain, or enhance respect. As such, those individuals following the street code must be ready to use violence for protection and let others on the street know that there are consequences for transgressions (Tedeschi & Felson, 1994). To let transgressions go unchallenged, even small ones, demonstrates that one is soft and weak; therefore, all transgression must be avenged (Anderson, 1999; Courtwright, 1996; Horowitz, 1983; Jacobs, 2004; Rich & Grey, 2005). Similarly, Kubrin and Weitzer (2003) studied homicide victimization in disadvantaged St. Louis neighborhoods and observed that a disproportionate number of homicides were retaliatory, based in part on street code values. Furthermore, they found that disputes and disrespect had to be settled violently as a way to achieve status and protect against future transgressions because individuals involved in the homicides deemed local law enforcement as unresponsive.

Although the results of the above studies are consistent with Anderson's arguments, we found contradictory evidence of the street code or victimization link. In 2006, Stewart, Schreck, and Simons examined whether the norms of the street code subculture protected individuals from violent victimization. A primary interest of this study was determining if those who followed the street code were indeed safer from being targeted for victimization. The results showed that following the street code worsened victimization risk even after controlling for actual offending behavior and risky settings (e.g., neighborhood danger and deviant peers). This study, along with the aforementioned research, highlights the notion that street code norms are related to violence, either through victimization or perpetration of violence (also see Brunson & Stewart, 2006; Lauritsen, Sampson, & Laub, 1991).

The Street Code and Victimization Prevention Policy

An understanding of the street code offers valuable lessons for the prevention of victimization. In the following paragraphs, we highlight some of the areas where this understanding could inform victimization prevention policy, such as improving police–citizen interactions and providing meaningful and effective opportunities for residents in a dispute to peacefully settle their differences.

The problem of the street code is that individuals feel obliged to take violence into their own hands to resolve grievances, rather than rely on formal or informal peaceful means of dispute resolution. The origin of the problem, according to theory and research, is not so much the individual's preference but rather the context (Anderson, 1999; Kane, 2005; Reisig & Parks, 2000; Sampson & Bartusch, 1998; Walker, Spohn, & DeLone, 2000; Weitzer, 1999). The specific structural conditions in neighborhoods, and the presence of local institutions lacking effectiveness and legitimacy, foster the street code. Individuals, whether through their own choice or the policy makers' design, might choose on their own to settle disputes peacefully, but the external reality of the neighborhood will frequently punish such decisions. Peaceful dispute resolution and trust in the authorities—at least as a matter of individual choice—is not often seen as realistic given the circumstances. To expect otherwise would be effectively to demand that residents act against what they see as their own interests. The implication, then, is that the conditions making the street code the only feasible source of order must change.

The entrenched structural problems described earlier create the natural conditions that allow the street code to flourish. Thus, the only permanent solution is to create environments where peaceful dispute resolution might occur. Or put another way, government must invest in the revitalization of the infrastructure and institutions within the disorganized neighborhood, politically empower its residents, and alleviate poverty. Less intensive (and perhaps more realistic) alternatives, which we will focus on here, might prove successful as well; however, one must be mindful that these expedients represent fundamentally artificial conditions for the peaceful resolution of conflicts that—should a city withdraw support—would not be self-perpetuating. When these conditions are removed and institutions begin to fail, the behavior of residents would naturally revert to the default rules of conduct appropriate to the external situation: the street code.

With this caveat in mind, one approach for mitigating the street code and reducing victimization is to promote the broad legitimacy of legal institutions. Because many residents of structurally disadvantaged communities feel estranged from formal institutions, they may lack much social and/or political capital to engage law enforcement to address various problems within their neighborhood. In addition, residents often complain of dissatisfaction with the police, inadequate police protection, and police abuse, with the consequence being strained relationships between residents and legal authorities (Anderson, 1999; Klinger, 1997; Smith, 1986; Walker et al., 2000). Repressive law enforcement tactics reinforce the street code and further destroy the legitimacy of legal authorities. If the public perceives that procedural injustice is widespread, they are less likely to view the law and agents of the criminal justice system as fair and moral (Tyler, 2006).

To combat skepticism about the police, and build trust, it is necessary to improve police–citizen interactions and form *meaningful* partnerships between citizens and the police. Although there have been mixed results as to whether community policing is effective at improving police–citizen relations (Piquero, Greene, Fyfe, Kane, & Collins, 2000; Reisig & Parks, 2004; Skogan & Frydl, 2007), there is still some possible benefit for community policing to improve these strained relationships depending on how it is implemented (Stoutland, 2001). The goal of community policing initiatives vary, and include reducing crime or fear of crime, enforcing the laws fairly and competently, and providing courteous, responsive service to citizens (Stoutland, 2001). Police departments, and the larger criminal justice system, should work with community residents, churches, and schools to improve relationships with citizens in a neighborhood. Reisig and Parks (2004, p. 163) argue that community policing methods should incorporate mechanisms that allow for citizen input on police actions in their neighborhood, thereby possibly improving strained police–citizen relations. When residents are part of the community policing process, they may have the opportunity to have their own and their group's concerns addressed by law enforcement officials. Weitzer and Tuch (2004) note that "While most blacks and Hispanics desire more law enforcement and crime control, they are simultaneously interested in ensuring that police minimize abuses . . . of minority citizens, who are disproportionately the recipients of mistreatment" (p. 321). Furthermore, improving police-citizen relationships could improve trust and legitimacy among residents. Researchers have observed that when citizens believe they have been treated fairly and with respect, they tend to grant more legitimacy to the police and are more likely to comply with the police (Mastrofski, Snipes, & Supina, 1996; Tyler, 2006; Tyler & Wakslak, 2004). We believe that strengthening police and community relationships in disadvantaged areas where the street code is most pronounced might reduce an individual's risk of violence as either an offender or a victim.

The recent trend in the criminal justice system toward mediation techniques, as with restorative justice, might yield greater legitimacy for the peaceful resolution of disputes (for more, see Dignan, 2005). A major goal of restorative justice is to conciliate victims and offenders, and the process is highly informal compared to that of a criminal court. There are no attorneys, and neither are the police involved. During the mediation process, both the victims and the offenders work together to reach a compromise that both can live with. Research indicates that participants in such programs, when they are implemented properly, tend to be more satisfied (e.g., Sullivan & Tifft, 2001; Viano, 1990). If these programs promote higher levels of understanding between residents at the community level, then the street code should become less necessary for order maintenance.

We have focused on improving police-citizen interactions and providing peaceful dispute resolution options to reduce violence and mediate the effects of the street culture. However, we would be remiss if we overlooked the harsh structural pressures of joblessness, poverty, segregation, and racial prejudice that many African American families face in disadvantaged neighborhoods (Sampson & Wilson, 1995; Wilson, 1987, 1996). Although we did not focus on this issue, we believe that it is imperative that structural pressures have to be addressed in disadvantaged African American neighborhoods to see long-term and sustained reductions in violence. For example, implementation of policies aimed at increasing employment opportunities and promoting harmony among neighborhood residents will serve to build community and possibly neighborhood social connections (Sampson, 1988).

References

Agnew, R. S. (1994). The techniques of neutralization and violence. *Criminology, 32,* 555–580.

Anderson, E. (1999). *Code of the street: Decency, violence, and the moral life of the inner city.* New York: Norton.

Austin, R. L. (1980). Adolescent subcultures of violence. *Sociological Quarterly, 21,* 545–561.

Ball-Rokeach, S. J. (1973). Values and violence: A test of the subculture of violence thesis. *American Sociological Review, 38,* 736–749.

Baron, S. W., Kennedy, L. W., & Forde, D. R. (2001). Male street youths' conflict: The role of background, subcultural, and situational factors. *Justice Quarterly, 18,* 759–789.

Bernard, T. J. (1990). Angry aggression among the truly disadvantaged. *Criminology, 28,* 73–96.

Black, D. (1976). *The behavior of law.* New York: Academic Press.

Bruce, M. A., Roscigno, V. J., & McCall, P. (1998). Structure, context, and agency in the reproduction of Black-on-Black violence. *Theoretical Criminology, 2,* 29–55.

Brunson, R. K., & Stewart, E. A. (2006). Young African American women, the street code, and violence: An exploratory analysis. *Journal of Crime and Justice, 29,* 1–19.

Bureau of Justice Statistics. (2003). *Criminal victimization in the United States: 2001 statistical tables.* Washington, DC: Author.

Cao, L., Adams, A., & Jensen, V. J. (1997). A test of the Black subculture of violence thesis: A research note. *Criminology, 35,* 367–379.

Cohen, A. K. (1955). *Delinquent boys: The culture of the gang.* Glencoe, IL: Free Press.

Courtwright, D. T. (1996). *Violent land: Single men and social disorder from the frontier to the inner city.* Cambridge, MA: Harvard University Press.

Curtis, L. A. (1975). *Violence, race, and culture.* Lexington, MA: D. C. Heath.

Dignan, J. (2005). *Understanding victims and restorative justice*. Berkshire, UK: Open University Press.

Ellickson, R. C. (1991). *Order without law: How neighbors settle disputes*. Cambridge, MA: Harvard University Press.

Erlanger, H. S. (1974). The empirical status of the subculture of violence thesis. *Social Problems, 22*, 280–291.

Felson, R. B., Liska, A. E., South, S. J., & McNulty, T. J. (1994). The subculture of violence and delinquency: Individual vs. school context effects. *Social Forces, 73*, 155–174.

Gottfredson, M. R., & Hirschi, T. (1995). National crime control policy. *Society, 32*, 30–36.

Hawkins, D. F., Laub, J. H., Lauritsen, J. L., & Cothern, L. (2000). *Race, ethnicity, and serious and violent juvenile offending. Juvenile justice bulletin*. Washington, DC: U.S. Department of Justice, Office of Juvenile Justice and Delinquency Prevention.

Heimer, K. (1997). Socioeconomic status, subcultural definitions, and violent delinquency. *Social Forces, 75*, 799–833.

Horowitz, R. (1983). *Honor and the American dream: Culture and identity in a Chicano community*. New Brunswick, NJ: Rutgers University Press.

Jacobs, B. (2004). A typology of street criminal retaliation. *Journal of Research in Crime and Delinquency, 41*, 295–323.

Jacobs, B. A., & Wright, R. (2006). *Street justice: Retaliation in the criminal underworld*. New York: Cambridge University Press.

Kane, R. J. (2005). Compromised police legitimacy as a predictor of violent crime in structurally disadvantaged communities. *Criminology, 43*, 469–498.

Klinger, D. A. (1997). Negotiating order in patrol work: An ecological theory of police response to deviance. *Criminology, 35*, 277–306.

Kubrin, C. E., & Weitzer, R. (2003). Retaliatory homicide: Concentrated disadvantage and neighborhood culture. *Social Problems, 50*, 157–180.

Lauritsen, J. L. (2003). *Juvenile victims of violence: Individual, family, and community factors. Juvenile justice bulletin*. Washington, DC: U.S. Department of Justice, Office of Juvenile Justice and Delinquency Prevention.

Lauritsen, J. L., Sampson, R. J., & Laub, J. H. (1991). The link between offending and victimization among adolescents. *Criminology, 29*, 265–291.

Luckenbill, D. F., & Doyle, D. P. (1989). Structural position and violence: Developing a cultural explanation. *Criminology, 27*, 801–818.

Magura, S. (1975). Is there a subculture of violence? *American Sociological Review, 40*, 831–835.

Markowitz, F. E., & Felson, R. B. (1998). Social-demographic attitudes and violence. *Criminology, 36*, 117–138.

Mastrofski, S. D., Snipes, J. B., & Supina, A. E. (1996). Compliance on demand: The public's response to specific police requests. *Journal of Research in Crime and Delinquency, 33*, 269–305.

Miller, W. B. (1958). Lower class culture as a generating milieu of gang delinquency. *Journal of Social Issues, 14*, 5–19.

Moore, M. H., & Tonry, M. (1998). Youth violence in America. In M. Tonry & M. H. Moore (Eds.), *Crime and justice: A review of research* (pp. 1–29). Chicago: University of Chicago Press.

Pettit, B., & Western, B. (2004). Mass imprisonment and the life course: Race and class inequality in U.S. incarceration. *American Sociological Review, 69*, 151–169.

Piquero, A., Greene, J., Fyfe, J., Kane, R., & Collins, P. (2000). Implementing community policing in public housing developments in Philadelphia: Some early results. In G. Alpert & A. Piquero (Eds.), *Community policing: Contemporary readings* (2nd ed., pp. 95–122). Prospect Heights, IL: Waveland.

Reisig, M. D., & Parks, R. B. (2000). Experience, quality of life, and neighborhood context: A hierarchical analysis of satisfaction with police. *Justice Quarterly, 17*, 607–630.

Reisig, M. D., & Parks, R. B. (2004). Can community policing help the truly disadvantaged? *Crime & Delinquency, 50*, 139–167.

Reiss, A. J., & Roth, J. A. (1993). *Understanding and preventing violence*. Washington, DC: National Academy Press.

Rich, J. A., & Grey, C. M. (2005). Pathways to recurrent trauma among young Black men: Traumatic stress, substance use, and the code of the street. *American Journal of Public Health, 95*, 816–824.

Rose, D. R., & Clear, T. R. (1998). Incarceration, social capital, and crime: Implications for social disorganization theory. *Criminology, 36*, 441–480.

Rosenfeld, R. (2007). Transfer the uniform crime reporting program from the FBI to the Bureau of Justice Statistics. *Criminology and Public Policy, 6*, 825–834.

Sampson, R. J. (1988). Local friendship ties and community attachment in mass society: A multi-level systemic model. *American Sociological Review, 53*, 766–779.

Sampson, R. J., & Bartusch, D. J. (1998). Legal cynicism and (subcultural?) tolerance of deviance: The neighborhood context of racial differences. *Law and Society Review, 32*, 777–804.

Sampson, R. J., & Lauritsen, J. L. (1994). Violent victimization and offending: Individual-, situational-, and community-level risk factors. In A. J. Reiss & J. A. Roth (Eds.), *Understanding and preventing violence: Social influences on violence* (pp. 1–114). Washington, DC: National Academy Press.

Sampson, R. J., Raudenbush, S. W., & Earls, F. (1997). Neighborhoods and violent crime: A multilevel study of collective efficacy. *Science, 277*, 918–924.

Sampson, R. J., & Wilson, W. (1995). Toward a theory of race, crime, and urban inequality. In J. Hagan & R. D. Peterson (Eds.), *Crime and inequality* (pp. 37–56). Stanford, CA: Stanford University Press.

Skogan, W., & Frydl, K. (Eds.). (2007). *Fairness and effectiveness in policing: The evidence.* Washington, DC: National Academies Press.

Smith, D. A. (1986). The neighborhood context of police behavior. In A. Reiss & M. Tonry (Eds.), *Communities and crime* (pp. 313–341). Chicago: University of Chicago Press.

Stewart, E. A., Schreck, C., & Simons, R. (2006). "I ain't gonna let no one disrespect me": Does the code of the street reduce or increase violent victimization among African American adolescents? *Journal of Research in Crime and Delinquency, 43*, 427–458.

Stoutland, S. E. (2001). The multiple dimensions of trust in residents/police relations in Boston. *Journal of Research in Crime and Delinquency, 38*, 226–256.

Sullivan, D., & Tifft, L. (2001). *Restorative justice: Healing the foundations of everyday lives.* Monsey, NY: Willow Tree.

Tedeschi, J., & Felson, R. B. (1994). *Violence, aggression, and coercive action.* Washington, DC: American Psychological Association Books.

Tonry, M. (2007, November). *Presidential address: Why are human rights ideas absent from American punishment policies?* Presented at the annual meeting of the American Society of Criminology, Atlanta, GA.

Tyler, T. R. (2006). *Why people obey the law.* Princeton, NJ: Princeton University Press.

Tyler, T. R., & Wakslak, C. J. (2004). Profiling and police legitimacy: Procedural justice, attributions of motive, and acceptance of police authority. *Criminology, 42*, 253–281.

Viano, E. (1990). The recognition and implementation of victims' rights in the United States: Developments and achievements. In E. Viano (Ed.), *The victimology handbook: Research findings, treatment, and public policy* (pp. 319–336). New York: Garland.

Walker, S., Spohn, C., & DeLone, M. (2000). *The color of justice: Race, ethnicity, and crime in America* (2nd ed.). Belmont, CA: Wadsworth.

Weitzer, R. (1999). Citizen's perceptions of police misconduct: Race and neighborhood context. *Justice Quarterly, 16*, 819–846.

Weitzer, R., & Tuch, S. A. (2004). Race and perceptions of police misconduct. *Social Problems, 51*, 305–325.

Wilkinson, D. L. (2003). *Guns, violence, and identity among African American and Latino youth.* New York: LFB.

Wilson, W. J. (1987). *The truly disadvantaged: The inner city, the underclass, and public policy.* Chicago: University of Chicago Press.

Wilson, W. J. (1996). *When work disappears: The world of the new urban poor.* New York: Random House.

Wolfgang, M. E., & Ferracuti, F. (1967). *The subculture of violence: Towards an integrated theory of criminology.* London: Tavistock.

DISCUSSION QUESTIONS

1. After reading the previous information, how would you describe "street codes," and do you feel that this is true within impoverished communities?
2. Do you agree with Anderson when he suggests that street codes are effective within communities where minorities reside?
3. What policies can be adapted to prevent street codes within these communities?

READING

Negative perceptions about law enforcement contribute to ongoing tension between police and African Americans. Taylor, Holleran, and Topalli undertook this study to determine whether or not police clearance of criminal cases can explain African Americans' attitudes toward the police. They review research on both over-enforcement and under-enforcement actions by the police. The National Incident Based Reporting System (NIBRS) 2002 data is used to examine whether or not race impacts police clearance rates. If the under-enforcement perspective is correct, crimes involving minority victims might not be cleared as often as when victims are White. The authors examined characteristics of 50,000 incidents involving a single-offender and a single victim for murders, aggravated assaults, rapes, and robberies reported to NIBRS by participating police agencies. They found that victims' race had a modest affect on police clearance in the cross-tabulations, but little affect in the regression analyses. The article concludes with a discussion of the implications of their findings for the police and criminal justice.

Racial Bias in Case Processing

Does Victim Race Affect Police Clearance of Violent Crime Incidents?

Terrance J. Taylor, David Holleran, and Volkan Topalli

Introduction

Tyler (2004, 2006) provides a framework illustrating the importance of "legitimacy" of the law and its enforcement agents as a key part of a functional, free, fair society. Specifically, Tyler argues that societies rely on citizens' self-regulation to effectively accept and comply with social control efforts. When legitimacy is diminished, tensions between citizens and social control actors are heightened, compliance and cooperation decreases, and the social order is compromised. Recent studies on this topic have illustrated the decreased legitimacy of the police and resultant consequences among many African American citizens (Baumer, 2002; Brunson, 2007; Brunson & Miller, 2006; Carr, Napolitano, & Keating, 2007; Rosenbaum, Schuck, Costello, Hawkins, & Ring, 2005; Sunshine & Tyler, 2003; Tyler & Huo, 2002).

While tensions between police and African Americans are well documented, it is unclear whether this is primarily due to a function of a tenuous history, current discriminatory practices, or a combination of the two. Additionally, questions remain as to whether over-enforcement of the law against African American offenders, under-enforcement of crimes with African American victims, or a combination of the two accounts for racial differences in attitudes toward the criminal justice system. For example, the use of police to subjugate African Americans and maintain social policies such as slavery and segregation has been well documented (Bass,

Source: Taylor, T. J., Holleran, D., & Topalli, V. (2009). Race bias in case processing: Does victim race affect police clearance of violent crime incidents? *Justice Quarterly, 26*(3), 562–591.

2001a, 2001b; Johnson, 2003; Websdale, 2001). This historical context, coupled with perceptions that police engaged in discrimination against racial/ethnic minorities (particularly in terms of over-enforcing crimes involving African American offenders), produced a deepening and longstanding sense of antipathy between law enforcement and many African American residents. Indeed, some scholars suggest that the 1960s incidents of civil unrest may be attributed to police repressive actions in an already volatile context of minority discontent (Johnson, 2003; Perez, Berg, & Myers, 2003). Additionally, extensive media coverage of these incidents brought widespread attention to police-community tensions. These factors illustrate the importance of over-enforcement in police-community relations.

Conversely, Hawkins (1987) and Kennedy (1997) have argued that under-enforcement of the law is a more serious problem because it allows criminogenic forces to fester (see Tonry, 1995). While it remains unclear whether over- or under-enforcement of the law is more problematic, the view that police treat crimes involving minorities differently may have contributed to findings of African Americans' reduced levels of trust, perceived legitimacy, and support of police relative to their white peers (see Brown & Benedict, 2002; Decker, 1981; Tuch & Weitzer, 1997; for reviews, see also Frank, Brandl, Cullen, & Stichman, 1996). For example, African Americans are more likely than white citizens to view criminal justice interventions as unfair regardless of outcome (Engel, 2005), and these attitudinal differences may further strain the relationships between African Americans and the criminal justice system as a whole (Albrecht & Green, 1977; Tyler & Huo, 2002).

While numerous studies have examined the role of victim race in criminal justice case processing, these inquiries have generally been conducted on the later stages of the system (such as prosecutorial decisions about whether to file charges and sentencing). The relationship between the race of the victim in a crime and police clearance of criminal cases, however, has received less scholarly attention. Additionally, extant research on the topic is limited by a number of conceptual and methodological issues including a failure to fully explore the role of race in case clearance. Specifically, studies have typically focused on a single offense and have failed to examine the interaction between victim and offender race.

The current study seeks to expand the research that has examined the effect of race on criminal justice processing and African Americans' perceptions of the legitimacy of the police. Using data from the 2002 National Incident-Based Reporting System (NIBRS) (U.S. Department of Justice, 2004a), we examine the role of victim race on the likelihood that police will clear violent crimes (i.e., homicide, forcible rape, robbery, and aggravated assault). Using Tyler's framework, our research builds upon findings from previous studies of other system stages (i.e., filing of charges, trial and bail decisions, verdicts, and sentencing outcomes) to explore the possibility that effects of victim race on police case clearance may be conditioned by other factors (particularly offender race). We conclude with discussions of ways in which history and current practices shape perceptions of fairness and legitimacy among African Americans specifically and society generally.

Theoretical Framework and Prior Literature

African Americans generally have been found to have less favorable attitudes toward the police than whites (see Brown & Benedict, 2002; Decker, 1981; Tuch & Weitzer, 1997; for reviews, see also Frank et al., 1996). One potential issue that arises from this consistent finding involves the legitimacy of police as agents of social control in the eyes of African Americans. According to Tyler (2004, 2006), the law and its enforcement agents must be viewed as legitimate in order to maintain social order. Perceptions of legitimacy are established through individual experiences with the criminal justice system, as well as "vicarious" experiences, whereby other individuals' experiences are transmitted between citizens through communication about those events. Experiences perceived as procedurally fair and satisfactory in outcome tend to increase perceptions of legitimacy.

Law-abiding behavior is primarily based on individual self-regulation, as "police must be able to rely upon widespread, voluntary law-abiding behavior to allow them to concentrate their resources on those people and situations in which compliance is difficult to maintain" (Tyler, 2004, p. 85). Police are also reliant upon citizen cooperation in a number of ways, such as reporting crimes, assisting in investigations, and complying with police directives. As the legally sanctioned agents of enforcing the laws and often the "first responders" to crimes, police are also the most visible agents of the criminal justice system. Thus, when the legitimacy of the police is diminished, social control is compromised, potentially disrupting the larger social order. This may take a variety of forms, including engaging in less law-abiding behavior generally, failing to report crimes when they occur, reduced satisfaction in encounters, failing to cooperate in criminal investigations, and failing to comply with police directives.

Recent research suggests that police have "lost legitimacy" among many African Americans. As Bass (2001a, 2001b) has highlighted, the police have historically been responsible for enforcing laws intended to maintain racially and spatially based formal and informal social order, which has created an experience unique to African Americans. Police over-enforcement of the law is a partial explanation of the loss of legitimacy among many African Americans.

Hawkins (1987) and Kennedy (1997) have suggested that under-enforcement of the law is more common and problematic, consistent with Tonry's (1995) proposition that the American criminal justice system operates under a model of "malign neglect" when applied to racial and ethnic minorities. Klinger (1997) has suggested that police often adjust the rigor of their enforcement of criminal laws in communities or neighborhoods based upon their view of the "normality" of deviance in those areas. Those with higher levels of deviance—often disproportionately inhabited by minority residents—receive less stringent enforcement because crime is viewed as "normal" in these areas. If true, this orientation supports the possibility that police and other criminal justice actors may under-enforce the law in crimes involving minority victims as evidenced through delays in response to calls for service, lax enforcement and investigation of criminal offenses in communities inhabited primarily by racial/ethnic minorities (and thus typically involving minority victims), and more lenient treatment of cases involving minority victims.

This paradox (i.e., the perception that both over-enforcement and under-enforcement processes are at work) is highlighted by Brunson's (2007) study of young males residing in St. Louis. The young men interviewed expressed frustration with what they viewed as both overly aggressive (e.g., stops, searches, use of violence) and lax (e.g., slow response times, prioritization of calls for service, and a general sentiment that police were incapable of effective crime solving and prevention) police practices. Equally important in Brunson's work, young black men were found to develop their perceptions both through direct encounters with police as well as through "vicarious experiences" relayed by friends and family members. Similarly, Rosenbaum et al.'s (2005) examination of Chicago residents found that negative vicarious (as opposed to direct) experiences were particularly important for African Americans (relative to other racial/ethnic groups). While African Americans have also been found to have less tolerance for deviance in their communities relative to whites (Sampson & Bartusch, 1998), it appears that a potential loss of police legitimacy may be leading to situations where African American citizens are reluctant to report crimes (Baumer, 2002; Carr et al., 2007). But do the perceptions of differential treatment of criminal cases represent current police practices?

Victim Race and Police Clearance

There has been a resurgence in studies examining factors affecting police clearance of criminal cases, thus providing an additional foundation for the current study. According to the FBI (U.S. Department of Justice, 2004b; see also U.S. Department of Justice, 2000), cases are considered "cleared" either through the arrest of a subject or through "exceptional" means (i.e., a suspect is identified and evidence is gathered to support an arrest, but factors beyond the control of police prohibit arrest). The under-enforcement perspective would suggest that crimes involving minority victims may be considered "lower profile" and result in less police time, energy, and resources allocated to clear these cases (Corsianos, 2003). Consequently, such cases would be less likely to be cleared than cases involving white victims. Whether such differences in case clearances exist remains to be seen, but it is clear that African Americans view under-enforcement of the law in African American communities (and thus with predominantly African American victims) as a continuing problem (Brunson, 2007).

Prior studies provide insight into the extent to which victim characteristics affect police case clearance. For example, findings by Smith and colleagues (Smith, 1987; Smith & Visher, 1981; Smith, Visher, & Davidson, 1984) have found that African American victims were denied the same degree of protection of the law offered to white victims (Smith et al., 1984) and that victim characteristics were more important than offender characteristics in police handling of violent criminal encounters (Smith, 1987). The effects of victim race, however, were found to be less salient than factors such as seriousness of the offense, presence of evidence, use of weapons, preference of the victim, and relational distance between victims and offenders (Black, 1971; Smith, 1987; Smith & Visher, 1981; Smith et al., 1984).

With the exception of homicide research (discussed below), our search for more recent studies using NIBRS data turned up only two results remotely addressing this issue. Stolzenberg, D'Alessio, and Eitle (2004) used 2000 NIBRS data to examine macro-level processes associated with the "racial threat hypothesis" to determine whether police would make an arrest in violent crime cases in 182 cities. Their results were not supportive of the racial threat hypothesis, and their primary focus was on the probability of arrest involving cases involving African American offenders; the findings related to victim race, however, were particularly relevant to the current study. Specifically, crimes involving white victims and African American offenders were most likely to result in an arrest in segregated cities. Expanding on this study, Eitle, Stolzenberg, and D'Alessio (2005) used 2000 data from NIBRS, Law Enforcement Management and Administrative Statistics (LEMAS), and U.S. Census to examine how police organizational characteristics affected police clearance of assault cases. Of particular relevance for the current study, the likelihood of arrest for simple and aggravated assaults was higher for white offenders than African American offenders, and police organizational characteristics moderated the relationship between offender race and probability of arrest for simple assaults but not aggravated assaults.

While highly prevalent, recent studies focusing on factors affecting police clearance of homicide cases have provided little support for the under-enforcement of crimes involving minority victims. They have generally found that the race of the victim has no statistically significant effect on police clearance of homicide cases (Litwin, 2003; Marche, 1994; Puckett & Lundman, 2003; Roberts, 2007) or that cases involving African American victims are slightly more likely to be cleared than cases involving white victims (Regoeczi, Kennedy, & Silverman, 2000) once other factors are controlled. While homicides occurring in predominantly minority neighborhoods are less likely to be cleared than homicides committed in predominantly white neighborhoods, this does not appear to be the result of differential police treatment attributable to victim race (Puckett & Lundman, 2003). Rather, racial differences in case clearance has typically been explained by racial differences in factors such as witness cooperation (Litwin, 2003; Puckett & Lundman, 2003), the relationship between the victim and offender (Regoeczi et al., 2000), and/or circumstances surrounding the incident, including the type of weapon used (Puckett & Lundman, 2003), or contemporaneous crimes associated with the homicide (Puckett & Lundman, 2003; Regoeczi et al., 2000). A number of other factors have been found to affect police clearance of homicide cases including victim age (Puckett & Lundman, 2003; Regoeczi et al., 2000) and sex (Regoeczi et al., 2000), presence of evidence (Litwin, 2003; Regoeczi et al., 2000), detective caseload (Marche, 1994; Puckett & Lundman, 2003), and police organizational culture (Litwin, 2003).

Limitations of Prior Research on Police Clearance

The recent research on factors affecting police clearance of criminal cases is limited in a number of ways. Prior studies have generally focused exclusively on homicide (Litwin, 2003; Marche, 1994; Puckett & Lundman, 2003; Regoeczi et al., 2000; Roberts, 2007; see also Eitle et al., 2005; Stolzenberg et al., 2004). The factors affecting homicide case clearance, however, may be different than for other crimes. Homicide cases are typically considered "high profile" crimes (Puckett & Lundman, 2003), which have been found to result in greater time, energy, and resources devoted to solving the case (Corsianos, 2003). Prior research also has found that extralegal variables are more highly correlated with police case clearance in less serious incidents and those less visible to the public (Engel, Sobol, & Worden, 2000); extralegal factors are less likely to correlate with higher profile cases involving more serious and/or visible crimes. Thus, the discrepancy in case clearance between minority victims and non-minority victims may be smaller in homicide cases, compared with less serious (but more common) offenses. Additionally, homicide cases are typically handled by investigators who are evaluated solely on their ability to solve these crimes (adding incentive to clear as many homicide cases as possible), while case clearance is one of many factors used to evaluate patrol officers, who are often involved in clearing other types of crime (Puckett & Lundman, 2003).

Perhaps most importantly, studies have failed to fully explore the possibility that the effect of victim race may interact with offender race to affect police clearance of violent crimes. This is somewhat surprising given important differences found at other stages of the criminal justice system as a result of the interaction between victim and offender race. LaFree (1980), for example, found that racial composition of the case participants had no effect on the likelihood of arrest, prosecution, trial, or verdict. The victim/offender race combination, however, influenced the sentence imposed, with African American offenders convicted of victimizing whites receiving the harshest sentences and African American offenders convicted of victimizing African American victims receiving the most lenient sentences (see also Baldus, Woodworth, & Pulaski, 1990; Bowers & Pierce, 1980; Gross & Mauro, 1984; Kingsnorth, Lopez, Wentworth, & Cummings, 1998; Paternoster, 1984; Sorensen & Wallace, 1999; Spohn, 1994; Spohn & Spears, 1996; Walsh, 1987; Wolfgang & Riedel, 1973). Thus, prior research has illustrated the importance of the "victim-offender dyad" in examinations of criminal justice case processing.

The current study extends research examining police clearance of criminal cases as one potential explanation of African Americans' less favorable attitudes toward the police. Our primary question of interest is: Does the race of the victim in a criminal case affect the likelihood that it will be cleared by police? Our inquiry improves on prior research in three ways. First, our research question and findings are couched within the larger context of African Americans' experiences with and attitudes toward the police. Secondly, we examine four types of crime, varying in severity. Finally, we draw from research focused on other stages of the criminal justice system to more specifically examine the interaction between offender and victim race, thereby providing a more nuanced examination of the role of victim race on police case clearance.

Methodology

Data Source

Data used in the current study were collected from law enforcement agencies as part of the 2002 National Incident-Based Reporting System (NIBRS), which is publicly available at the National Archive of Criminal Justice Data (U.S. Department of Justice, 2004a). The NIBRS program was conceptualized in 1984 to meet the needs of local law enforcement agencies, with incident-level data being collected by the end of the 1980s on 22 Group A offenses (encompassing 46 specific crimes) and 11 Group B offenses (U.S. Department of Justice, 2004b). The NIBRS data are unique because they contain information about offenders, victims, situational characteristics involved in the incident, and police arrest/clearance status. As of 2002, the NIBRS data collected information from law enforcement agencies in 23 states. While the NIBRS data are not a nationally-representative sample of law enforcement agencies or criminal incidents and do not capture crimes that fail to come to the attention of law enforcement agencies (Maxfield, 1999), they are one of the few multi-jurisdictional data sources available allowing for a rigorous, quantitative assessment of the role that incident-level characteristics play in the clearance of crime by police.

Data File Structure

As publicly released, the NIBRS data are divided into 13 separate data segments. We recreated a full rectangular data structure following instructions provided by the codebook (U.S. Department of Justice, 2004a, p. 12) provided with the archived data and the procedures outlined by Akiyama and Nolan (1999). After the full NIBRS file was reconstructed, a smaller "working file" including only incidents involving single victims and single offenders in communities with more than 100,000 residents was created for analyses. This analysis file included a total of 49,639 observations spanning 39 individual agencies.

Variable Description

The dependent variable in this study is *police case clearance* (1 = case cleared; 0 = case not cleared). *Victim race* was restricted to two categories (1 = African American; 0 = white). The same restriction and coding scheme were used for *offender* race. Racial characteristics were examined independently and in combination (i.e., African American victim/African American offender, white victim/white offender, African American victim/white offender, white victim/African American offender). We also focused on four *offense types:* murder, aggravated assault, rape, and robbery. A number of additional variables identified as correlating with other decision points in the criminal justice system were also examined. *Victim age* and *offender age* are included as controls. The *victim-offender relationship* is represented across three categories: stranger, acquaintance, and unknown. *Type of injury* is organized into three categories: no injury, minor injury, and major injuries. *Type of weapon* used in the incident includes no weapon, personal weapon, gun, knife, or other weapon. *Regional variations* are examined by grouping agencies into one of four regions within the USA: West (i.e., Colorado, Idaho, and Utah), Northeast (i.e., Connecticut and Massachusetts), Midwest (i.e., Iowa, Kansas, Michigan, and Ohio), and South (i.e., South Carolina, Tennessee, Texas, and Virginia).

Unit of Analysis and Sample Description

The unit of analysis in the current study is the criminal case (i.e., incident). As presented in Table 5.7, these included 508 murders (1% of sample), 26,615 aggravated assaults (53.6%), 3,835 rapes (7.7%), and 18,681 robberies (37.6%). Forty-eight percent of the incidents involved African American victims and 57% involved male victims. Sixty-seven percent involved an African American offender and 85% involved a male offender. Forty-eight percent involved someone known to the victim, and approximately 31% involved strangers; the victim-offender relationship was unknown in approximately 21% of the incidents. Weapons were present in approximately 95% of all incidents, with guns being the most common (32%), followed by personal weapons (29%), and knives (16%). Slightly less than one half (46.5%) of all incidents resulted in some sort of injury to the victim, with minor injuries more common than serious injuries. Overall, approximately 66% of these incidents occurred in the South, and approximately 29% of all offenses in the analysis sample were cleared.

Table 5.7 Sample Characteristics

	Total	Murder	Aggravated Assault	Rape	Robbery
White victim	25,795	167	12,726	2297	10,605
%	52.0	32.9	47.8	59.9	56.8
African American victim	23,844	341	13,889	1,538	8,076
%	48.0	67.1	52.2	40.1	43.2
Male victim	28,378	392	15,568	31	12,387
%	57.2	77.3	58.5	0.8	66.4
Female victim	21,234	115	11,034	3,804	6,281
%	42.8	77.3	41.5	99.2	33.6
Victim age (mn)	31.22	30.97	30.27	22.18	34.44
White offender	16,376	132	10,892	1,695	3,657
%	33.0	26.0	40.9	44.2	19.6
African American offender	33,263	376	15,723	2,140	15,024
%	67.0	74.0	59.1	55.8	80.4
Male offender	42,243	457	20,318	3,812	17,656
%	85.1	90	76.3	99.4	94.5
Female offender	7,396	51	6,297	23	1,025
%	14.9	10	23.7	0.6	5.5

	Total	Murder	Aggravated Assault	Rape	Robbery
Offender age (mn)	27.81	28.95	29.20	28.07	25.44
Acquaintance	23,823	243	18,261	2,590	3,089
%	48.5	47.8	69.0	67.6	16.6
Stranger	15,150	65	4,390	684	5,552
%	30.9	12.8	16.6	17.8	29.8
Unknown relationship	10,123	200	3,812	559	10,011
%	20.6	39.4	14.4	14.6	53.7
No injury	26,149	—	10,834	2,637	12,676
%	53.5	—	41.0	68.8	70.0
Minor injury	14,372	—	8,771	905	4,694
%	29.4	—	33.2	23.6	25.2
Severe injury	8,399	—	6,815	290	1,279
%	17.2	—	25.8	7.6	6.9
No weapon	2,450	0	427	589	1,404
%	5.2	0.0	1.8	16.4	7.9
Personal weapon	13,346	56	4,691	2,615	5,984
%	28.9	12.0	19.3	72.8	33.5
Gun	14,579	329	6,031	129	8,090
%	31.6	70.8	24.9	3.6	45.3
Knife	7,560	59	6,013	133	1,355
%	16.4	12.7	24.8	3.7	7.6
Other weapon	8,253	21	7,087	125	1,020
%	17.9	4.5	29.2	3.5	5.7
South	32,263	363	17,457	2,056	12,787
%	65.5	71.5	65.6	53.6	68.4
West	4,643	37	2,571	695	1,340
%	9.4	7.3	9.7	18.1	7.2
Midwest	9,120	91	4,187	948	3,894
%	18.4	17.9	15.7	24.7	20.8
Northeast	3,213	17	2,400	136	660
%	6.5	3.3	90.	3.5	3.5
Cleared	14,334	369	10,116	705	3,144
%	28.9	72.6	38.0	18.4	16.8
N	49,639	508	26,615	3,835	18.681

Differences between offense types on the key variables are readily apparent. Clearance rates varied from a high of 72.6% of murder incidents to a low of 16.8% of rape incidents. The characteristics associated with different offense types can also clearly be seen. Offense types differed in terms of the race, sex, and age of offenders and victims. Additionally, situational characteristics such as the victim-offender relationship, presence and type of weapons used, and severity of injury also varied by offense type. Finally, regional differences also exist, with an overwhelming majority of incidents occurring in the South. Thus, it is important to examine offenses separately in addition to an overall examination of crime incidents.

Results

Table 5.8 presents the results of cross-tabulations of police clearance by victim race and offense type. The strength of the relationship between police case clearance and victim race for all offenses and individually, as determined by the value of Cramer's V, is weak. For all offense types combined, the differences observed in police case clearance across white victims (29.5%) and African American victims (28.1%) is less than 2%. The smallest percentage difference, not surprisingly, exists for the offense of murder; police case clearance is nearly uniform for white victims and African American victims, while the clearance of rape and robbery differ by a maximum of 2%. The relationship between clearance and victim race for aggravated assault cases, however, indicates nearly a 6% advantage of police clearance for white victims over African American victims.

To examine whether victim race and offender race interact in police case clearance, cross-tabulations for police clearance by victim race and offender race for all offenses combined and individually are also explored. For all offenses and for each individual offense other than aggravated assault, cases involving an African American offender and a white victim have the lowest police case clearance. Conversely, for all offenses and for aggravated assault, robbery, and murder, cases involving a white offender and a white victim have the highest police case clearance. These analyses illustrate larger percentage differences across the groups than when examining victim race without controlling for offender race. For example, overall incidents involving white offenders and white victims were 16% more likely to be cleared than offenses involving African American offenders and white victims. For each separate offense type, however, the differences across groups were less pronounced (7.8% for aggravated assault, 6.1% for rape, 9.9% for robbery, and 9.2% for murder).

Table 5.9 features binary logistic regression estimates for police clearance for the offenses of aggravated assault, rape, and robbery in the aggregate. The dependent variable is a dichotomous variable indicating whether a case is cleared (no/yes). Victim race, particularly as it is related to offender race, is the variable in which we are most interested. Three columns of data are presented in the regression tables: the nonstandardized logistic regression coefficient, the odds ratio, and the difference in predicted probability.

The regression estimates indicate that, with the exception of victim's age, victim characteristics exert a minimal influence on the probability of police clearance. The differences in predicted probabilities in police clearance between victims within the 25th and 75th percentiles are quite small. Modest effects are observed for offender characteristics. Interestingly, incidents involving African American offenders are nearly 4% less likely than incidents involving white offenders to be cleared, and incidents involving male offenders are nearly 5% less likely than incidents involving female offenders to be cleared. Incidents among acquaintances are slightly more than 6% more likely than incidents involving strangers to be cleared. We also included the type of weapon used in the incident as a control

Table 5.8 Cross Tabulation of Police Case Clearance by Victim Race and Offense Type

	All Offenses			Aggravated Assault			Rape			Robbery			Murder		
	Not Cleared	Cleared	Total	Not Cleared	Cleared	Total	Not Cleared	Cleared	Total	Not Cleared	Cleared	Total	Not Cleared	Cleared	Total
African American victim	17,093	6,669	23,762	4,850	4,850	13,826	1,232	304	1,536	6,792	1,268	8,060	93	247	340
%	71.9	28.1	100	35.1	35.1	100	80.2	19.8	100	84.3	15.7	100	27.4	72.7	100
White victim	18,104	7,563	25,667	5,179	5,179	12,624	1,897	400	2,297	8,716	1,863	10,579	46	121	167
%	70.5	29.5	100	41.0	41.0	100	82.6	17.4	100	82.4	17.6	100	27.5	72.5	100
Pearson chi-square		11,796		99,115	99,115			3,470			11,548			.002	
Cramer's V		0.015		0.061	0.061			–0.030			0.025			0.002	

Table 5.9 Binary Logistic Regression Estimates of Police Clearance for All Offenses (n = 44,711)

	b	e^b	Prob. Diff.
African American victim (reference = white victim)	–0.003	0.997	–0.06
African American offender (reference = white offender)	–0.198	0.821	–3.82
Male victim (reference = female victim)	–0.009	0.991	–0.16
Male offender (reference = female offender)	–0.233	0.792	–4.62
Victim age	–0.005	0.995	–1.79
Offender age	0.028	1.028	7.51
Acquaintance (reference = stranger)	0.327	1.387	6.33
Unknown relationship	–0.160	0.852	–2.73
No injury (reference = major injury)	–0.161	0.851	–3.11
Minor injury	–0.065	0.937	–1.28
Guns (reference = no weapons)	–0.450	0.637	–8.65
Knives	0.004	1.004	0.09
Personal weapons	–0.157	0.855	–3.22
Other weapons	–0.336	0.714	–6.64
Rape (reference = aggravated assault)	–1.009	0.365	–17.28
Robbery	–0.580	0.560	–11.11
West (reference = South)	0.417	1.518	8.24
Midwest	0.164	1.179	3.06
Northeast	0.950	2.585	20.66
Intercept	–0.855		

NOTE: The difference in predicted probabilities (Prob. Diff.) for offender age and victim age represent the difference between the predicted probabilities at the 25th and 75th percentiles. The differences in predicted probabilities for all design variables have been computed with the predicted probability for the reference category as the baseline.

variable. Those involving guns are nearly 9% less likely than incidents involving no weapon to result in clearance.

The most noticeable effects involve type of offense and region. Aggravated assault incidents are a little more than 17% more likely than rape cases to be cleared and a little more than 11% more likely than robbery incidents to be cleared. The clearance in aggravated assault is likely explained by the fact that more than 76% of aggravated assaults involved acquaintances. Region produced the largest effects in the regression equation. Agencies located in the southern USA are least likely to clear incidents. The largest difference is observed between the Northeastern and Southern regions. Agencies in the northeastern USA are more than 20% more likely than those in the South to clear incidents.

Table 5.10 illustrates the effect of the victim/offender race dyad on police clearance rates for all offenses combined.[1] These results again show small effects of victim characteristics on police

[1]The offense of murder was again excluded on the basis of insufficient data representation and variability.

Table 5.10 Binary Logistic Regression Estimates of Police Clearance for All Offenses Disaggregated by Victim and Offender Race ($n = 44{,}711$)

	b	e^b	Prob. Diff.
White offender/African American victim (reference = African American victim/African American offender)	0.165	1.179	3.2
African American offender/white victim	−0.005	0.995	−0.1
White offender/white victim	0.201	1.223	3.9
Male victim (reference = female victim)	−0.008	0.992	−0.1
Male offender (reference = female offender)	−0.233	0.792	−4.6
Victim age	−0.005	0.995	−1.8
Offender age	0.028	1.028	−7.5
Acquaintance (reference = stranger)	0.325	1.384	6.3
Unknown relationship	−0.161	0.851	−2.7
No injury (reference = major injury)	−0.161	0.851	−3.1
Minor injury	−0.065	0.937	−4.0
Guns (reference = no weapons)	−0.451	0.637	−4.4
Knives	0.005	1.005	4.3
Personal weapons	−0.157	0.855	−1.0
Other weapons	−0.336	0.715	−2.4
Rape (reference = aggravated assault)	−1.009	0.365	−7.9
Robbery	−0.580	0.560	−3.2
West (reference = South)	0.417	1.518	8.2
Midwest	0.165	1.179	3.0
Northeast	0.951	2.587	20.7
Intercept	−0.855		

NOTE: The difference in predicted probabilities (Prob. Diff.) for offender age and victim age represents the difference between the predicted probabilities at the 25th and 75th percentiles. The differences in predicated probabilities for all design variables have been computed with the predicted probability for the reference category as the baseline.

case clearance. Compared with violent crime incidents involving African American victims and African American offenders, cases involving white victims and white offenders were approximately 4% more likely to be cleared. Offender characteristics were also weakly associated with case clearance, with cases involving male offenders and older offenders less likely to be cleared. Region again showed the strongest relation to police case clearance, with incidents in the Northeast and West more than 20% and 8% more likely to be cleared than incidents in the South, respectively.

The relationships between offense characteristics on police clearance were slightly reduced when victim and offender race were considered in combination. Rapes and robberies were approximately 8% and 3% less likely to be cleared than aggravated assaults. Additionally, incidents involving no injuries (relative to incidents not involving weapons) were slightly less likely to be cleared. Finally, cases involving acquaintances were approximately 6% more likely to be cleared than cases involving strangers.[2]

Given that victim race had a modest effect on police clearance in the cross-tabulation tables, it is not surprising that it exerts little influence [on] police clearance in the regression models. Other noteworthy findings, however, emerge from these estimates. Offender race exhibits modest effects for aggravated assault and robbery incidents, with aggravated assaults involving African American offenders approximately 3% less likely to be cleared than those involving white offenders, and rapes involving African American offenders approximately 5% less likely to be cleared than those involving white offenders. Rape incidents involving younger victims are more likely to be cleared than incidents involving older victims. Not surprisingly, incidents involving an acquaintance are more likely than those involving strangers to result in a clearance for all three crimes. A completed act of rape is nearly 10% more likely to be cleared than an attempted rape. Again, region exhibits the largest effects, with incidents in the Northeastern USA approximately 20% more likely to be cleared than incidents in the South. The difference between the Midwestern and Southern regions in rape clearance, however, is negligible.

Discussion

Police-community relations have received substantial attention in academic circles, as well as the popular press. As visible maintainers of the social order, police must be viewed as "legitimate" within the eyes of the citizens in order to gain cooperation and compliance. This is best accomplished through a process of individual self-regulation, where cooperation with the law and its agents of enforcement is based upon feelings of responsibility and obligation.

While citizens generally have been found to hold positive attitudes toward the police, African American citizens' perceptions have consistently been found to be less favorable than those of whites (see Brown & Benedict, 2002; Decker, 1981; Tuch & Weitzer, 1997; for reviews), potentially fostering distrust in the criminal justice system more generally (Albrecht & Green, 1977; Tyler & Huo, 2002).

For urban African Americans, the perceived legitimacy of the police has been found to be particularly strained (Brunson, 2007; Tyler & Huo, 2002), possibly resulting in behavioral changes such as reductions in reporting crimes or calling for service (Baumer, 2002; Carr et al., 2007).

The current study examined the influence of victim race on the likelihood that police would clear cases involving incidents of serious violent crime as one potential explanation of African Americans' relatively less favorable perceptions of police. Using data from the 2002 NIBRS, we analyzed approximately 50,000 single-offender, single-victim incidents involving four types of serious crime, varying in severity—murder/non-negligent manslaughter, aggravated assault, robbery, and rape—in the largest cities participating in the NIBRS program. While differences in the likelihood that police would clear crimes were apparent across offense type, results of our analyses suggest that victim race had a minimal relationship with the likelihood that serious violent criminal cases are cleared by police, relative to other factors. Incidents involving African American offenders were slightly less likely to be cleared than incidents involving white offenders overall, and for aggravated assault and robbery (but not rape). When results were disaggregated by victim and offender race, cases involving African American offenders and white victims were the *least* likely to be cleared,

[2]Cases where the victim-offender relationship was unknown were approximately 3% less likely to be cleared than cases involving strangers.

and cases involving white victims and white offenders were the *most* likely to be cleared.

Our bivariate estimates show that cases involving African American victims were 1.4% less likely than whites to be cleared for all offenses, 5.9% for aggravated assault, and 2.4% for rape; these differences were enhanced when the race of both the victim and offender were considered in combination. Multivariate results show that cases involving African American victims were approximately 0.6% less likely to be cleared than cases involving white victims for all crimes combined, 0.35% for robberies, and 1.5% for aggravated assault.

We note that the *pure number* of cases where victim race, particularly in combination with offender race, may be obscured through an emphasis on percentage differences. Additionally, it is important to note that each of these cases affect not only the individuals directly involved, but also their family members, friends, employers, neighbors, and others close to them. Put simply, our results suggest that racial disparities in police clearance of violent criminal cases remain troublesome.

Given recent findings that African Americans are particularly apt to develop their attitudes toward police specifically and the criminal justice system generally through both direct and vicarious experiences (Brunson, 2007; Rosenbaum et al., 2005), it is essential for criminal justice agents and agencies to recognize and address real and/or perceived disparities in case processing. Even modest disparities in actual case processing have the potential of a greater reduction in the perceived legitimacy of authorities, particularly among African Americans, as assessments of government institutions are likely to change over time through an incremental, additive learning process where actual and vicarious experiences with the criminal justice system drive changes in attitudes (Tyler, Casper, & Fisher, 1989). An absence of procedural fairness (in direct experiences) and/or a presence of continuous and widespread negative information regarding treatment of minorities by the police (through awareness of historical racism and accumulated vicarious experiences with incidents of racism) has the potential of reducing perceptions of legitimacy even more. These processes make the police function more difficult, but also potentially contribute to decay in urban African American communities where criminogenic forces may fester without interference of formal social control (Hawkins, 1987; Kennedy, 1997; Tonry, 1995).

In order for true change to occur, sweeping changes may be required. The vestiges of historical inequality must continue to be recognized and addressed. A movement away from segregated housing projects to scattered site housing and a thorough restructuring of the system of funding municipal agencies and public schools, coupled with a renewed emphasis on integration, is advised (Massey & Denton, 1993). Focusing on enhancing informal social bonds, communication, and control (Sampson, Raudenbush, & Earls, 1997) in integrated neighborhoods is crucial. Broader policies—drug treatment instead of incarceration, enhancing community capacities and economic development, job training, and programs encouraging healthy living and development—are also mechanisms of forwarding social justice ends (Bass, 2001a, p. 172) and potentially enhancing legitimacy. To wit, Frank et al.'s (1996) study of Detroit residents found that African Americans perceptions of the police were actually *more* favorable than those of whites, a situation they attributed to the representation of African Americans in visible governmental positions in the city.

Having said this, our results suggest that the relationship between victim race (alone, or in combination with offender race) has a less salient effect on police clearance of violent criminal incidents than a number of other factors. The type of offense was important, as rape and robbery incidents were less likely to be cleared than aggravated assault incidents. Situational characteristics such as the relationship between the victim and offender, presence and type of weapon used, and presence and severity of injury resulting from the incident were also salient. Finally, clearance rates varied substantially by region of the country.[3] We hope that future research continues to examine these important factors.

Limitations and Future Directions

A number of limitations of the current study are apparent. First, while the NIBRS data provide the richest source of information on criminal incidents, the scope of the program is not representative of all law enforcement agencies. One glaring issue is the lack of coverage of large cities. Larger cities are more likely to be racially diverse, while the predominance of smaller jurisdictions participating in the NIBRS program includes a disproportionate amount of racial homogeneity. Additionally, while providing a rich source for incident-level data, there are key factors that are not included. Specifically, the lack of solid measures of evidence related to the criminal incidents poses problems for examinations of police clearance. Finally, as with all law-enforcement based data, these data are limited to criminal incidents that come to the attention of authorities, which may or may not be representative of all criminal incidents that occur.

A separate limitation that must be considered is the exclusive focus on the four serious offenses in the current study. When examining law enforcement data, it is generally agreed that the most serious offenses provide the most valid data (O'Brien, 1985). The most serious offenses, however, are often the ones allowing officers (and other criminal justice practitioners) the least latitude in how cases are handled and adjudicated. In this sense, it is perhaps not surprising that victim race was found to exert little influence on police clearance of these types of offenses. Policing research has consistently demonstrated that factors such as seriousness of the offense, presence of evidence, presence of weapons, and relational distance are typically the most important determinants of whether an arrest occurs (see, for example, Black, 1971; Smith, 1987; Smith & Visher, 1981; Smith et al., 1984). Our findings are generally consistent with those of extant research on the topic. This convergence in findings is important, as much of the prior research on policing has focused on large, urban areas.

Despite these limitations, we feel that our study presents an important contribution to understanding racial differences in criminal justice processing and citizens' perceptions of the police. While our findings suggest relatively small effects of victim race on police case clearance, these differences were enhanced when the victim-offender race dyad was examined. Additionally, while racial differences were virtually non-existent in homicide case clearance, they were more apparent in less serious felonies. We hope that future research continues this line of inquiry, as well.

Conclusions

Examining racial/ethnic issues related to policing must be continued. Given the importance of both direct and vicarious encounters with police in shaping attitudes, particularly among African Americans (Brunson, 2007; Rosenbaum et al., 2005), small differences in case processing may take on a much larger role in shaping perceptions of legitimacy of the criminal justice system. It may take innovative strategies, such as partnerships between police and other

---

[3]As raised by an anonymous reviewer, the differences in clearance across offense types and jurisdictions may be due to differences in police expertise and/or resources. We agree that this is a plausible explanation worthy of additional study. Since the purpose of the current study is primarily descriptive in its examination of the effect of victim race on police clearance as a potential explanation of African Americans' relatively unfavorable view of the police, we do not specifically focus on reasons for regional variations or some of the other control variables. We hope that future research tackles this and other related topics.

community stakeholders (e.g., residents, churches, schools) to improve police-community relations in minority neighborhoods (Bass, 2001a; Stewart, 2007).

We remain cognizant that other studies, such as those of Stolzenberg et al. (2004), illustrate that aggregate patterns such as those examined herein may mask effects at other levels, such as the neighborhood or individual. There is, after all, reason to expect that police practices vary by neighborhood (Klinger, 1997). We hope that future researchers continue to examine issues related to race, ethnicity, and policing, particularly through the use of different methodologies and in varying social contexts, as evidence of racial disparities is often difficult to detect and interpret (Bass, 2001a; Weitzer, 1996; Zatz, 1987, 2000). Such approaches are unquestionably fruitful in determining variations in communities and police agencies and practices. We also hope, however, that this is not done to the exclusion of "big picture" studies, which provide an important context of their own.

References

Akiyama, Y., & Nolan, J. (1999). Methods for understanding and analyzing NIBRS data. *Journal of Quantitative Criminology, 15,* 225–238.

Albrecht, S. L., & Green, M. (1977). Attitudes toward the police and the larger attitude complex: Implications for police-community relationships. *Criminology, 15,* 67–86.

Baldus, D., Woodworth, G., & Pulaski Jr., C. A. (1990). *Equal justice and the death penalty: A legal and empirical analysis,* Boston, MA: Northeastern University Press.

Bass, S. (2001a). Policing space, policing race: Social control imperatives and police discretionary decisions. *Social Justice, 28,* 156–176.

Bass, S. (2001b). Out of place: Petit apartheid and the police. In D. Milovanovic & K. K. Russell (Eds.), *Petit apartheid in the U.S. criminal justice system* (pp. 43–54). Durham, NC: Carolina Academic Press.

Baumer, E. (2002). Neighborhood disadvantage and police notification by victims of violence. *Criminology, 40,* 579–616.

Black, D. J. (1971). The social organization of arrest. *Stanford Law Review, 23,* 1087–1111.

Bowers, W., & Pierce, G. (1980). Arbitrariness and discrimination under post-Furman capital statutes. *Crime & Delinquency, 26,* 563–635.

Brown, B., & Benedict, W. R. (2002). Perceptions of the police: Past findings, methodological issues, conceptual issues and policy implications. *Policing: An International Journal of Police Strategies & Management, 25,* 543–580.

Brunson, R. K. (2007). "Police don't like Black people:" African American young men's accumulated police experiences. *Criminology & Public Policy, 6,* 71–102.

Brunson, R. K., & Miller, J. (2006). Young Black men and urban policing in the United States. *British Journal of Criminology, 46,* 613–640.

Carr, P. J., Napolitano, L., & Keating, J. (2007). We never call the police and here is why: A qualitative examination of legal cynicism in three Philadelphia neighborhoods. *Criminology, 45,* 445–480.

Corsianos, M. (2003). Discretion in detectives' decision making and "high profile" cases. *Police Practice & Research, 4,* 301–314.

Decker, S. H. (1981). Citizen attitudes toward the police: A review of past findings and suggestions for future policy. *Journal of Police Science and Administration, 9,* 81–87.

Eitle, D., Stolzenberg, L., & D'Alessio, S. (2005). Police organizational factors, the racial composition of the police, and the probability of arrest. *Justice Quarterly, 22,* 30–57.

Engel, R. S. (2005). Citizens' perceptions of distributive and procedural injustice during traffic stops with police. *Journal of Research in Crime & Delinquency, 42,* 445–481.

Engel, R. S., Sobol, J. J., & Worden, R. E. (2000). Further exploration of the demeanor hypothesis: The interaction effects of suspect's characteristics and demeanor on police behavior. *Justice Quarterly, 17,* 235–258.

Frank, J., Brandl, S., Cullen, F., & Stichman, A. (1996). Reassessing the impact of race on citizens' attitudes toward police: A research note. *Justice Quarterly, 13,* 321–334.

Gross, S., & Mauro, R. (1984). Patterns of death: An analysis of racial disparities in capital sentencing and homicide victimization. *Stanford Law Review, 37,* 27–153.

Hawkins, D. (1987). Beyond anomalies: Rethinking the conflict perspective on race and criminal punishment. *Social Forces, 65,* 719–745.

Johnson, M. S. (2003). *Street justice: A history of police violence in New York City.* Boston, MA: Roscoe Press.

Kennedy, R. (1997). *Race, crime, and the law.* New York: Pantheon Books.

Kingsnorth, R., Lopez, J., Wentworth, J., & Cummings, D. (1998). Adult sexual assault: The role of racial/ethnic composition in prosecution and sentencing. *Journal of Criminal Justice, 26,* 359–372.

Klinger, D. A. (1997). Negotiating order in patrol work: An ecological theory of police response to deviance. *Criminology, 35,* 277–306.

LaFree, G. (1980). The effect of sexual stratification by race on official reactions to rape. *American Sociological Review, 5,* 842–854.

Litwin, K. J. (2003). A multilevel multivariate analysis of factors affecting homicide clearances. *Journal of Research in Crime & Delinquency, 41,* 327–351.

Marche, G. E. (1994). The production of homicide solutions: An empirical analysis. *American Journal of Economics and Sociology, 53,* 385–401.

Massey, D. S., & Denton, N. A. (1993). *American apartheid: Segregation and the making of the underclass.* Cambridge, MA: Harvard University Press.

Maxfield, M. G. (1999). The National Incident-Based Reporting System: Research and policy implications. *Journal of Quantitative Criminology, 15,* 119–149.

O'Brien, R. M. (1985). *Crime and victimization data.* Beverly Hills, CA: Sage Publications.

Paternoster, R. (1984). Prosecutorial discretion in requesting the death penalty: A case of victim-based racial discrimination. *Law & Society Review, 18,* 437–478.

Perez, A. D., Berg, K. L., & Myers, D. J. (2003). Police and riots, 1967–1969. *Journal of African American Studies, 34,* 153–182.

Puckett, J. L., & Lundman, R. J. (2003). Factors affecting homicide clearances: Multivariate analysis of a more complete conceptual framework. *Journal of Research in Crime & Delinquency, 40,* 171–193.

Regoeczi, W. C., Kennedy, L. W., & Silverman, R. A. (2000). Uncleared homicides: A Canada/United States comparison. *Homicide Studies, 4,* 135–161.

Roberts, A. (2007). Predictors of homicide clearance by arrest: An event history analysis of NIBRS incidents. *Homicide Studies, 11,* 82–93.

Rosenbaum, D. P., Schuck, A. M., Costello, S. K., Hawkins, D. F., & Ring, M. K. (2005). Attitudes toward the police: The effects of direct and vicarious experiences. *Police Quarterly, 8,* 343–365.

Sampson, R. J., & Bartusch, D. J. (1998). Legal Cynicism and (subcultural?) tolerance of deviance: The neighborhood context of racial differences. *Law & Society Review, 32,* 777–804.

Sampson, R. J., Raudenbush, S. W., & Earls, F. (1997). Neighborhoods and violent crime: A multilevel study of collective efficacy. *Science, 15,* 918–924.

Smith, D. A. (1987). Police response to interpersonal violence: Defining the parameters of legal control. *Social Forces, 65,* 767–782.

Smith, D. A., & Visher, C. A. (1981). Street-level justice: Situational determinants of police arrest decisions. *Social Problems, 29,* 167–177.

Smith, D. A., Visher, C. A., & Davidson, L. A. (1984). Equity and discretionary justice: The influence of race on police arrest decisions. *Journal of Criminal Law and Criminology, 75,* 234–249.

Sorensen, J., & Wallace, D. H. (1999). Prosecutorial discretion in seeking death: An analysis of racial disparity in the pre-trial stages of case processing in a midwestern county. *Justice Quarterly, 16,* 559–578.

Spohn, C. (1994). Crime and the social control of African Americans: Offender/victim race and the sentencing of violent offenders. In G. S. Bridges & M. A. Myers (Eds.), *Inequality, crime and social control* (pp. 249–268). Boulder, CO: Westview.

Spohn, C., & Spears, J. W. (1996). The effect of offender and victim characteristics on sexual assault case processing decisions. *Justice Quarterly, 13,* 649–679.

Stewart, E. A. (2007). Either they don't know or they don't care: Black males and negative police experiences. *Criminology & Public Policy, 6,* 123–130.

Stolzenberg, L., D'Alessio, S. J., & Eitle, D. (2004). A multilevel test of racial threat theory. *Criminology, 42,* 673–698.

Sunshine, J., & Tyler, T. R. (2003). The role of procedural justice and legitimacy in shaping public support for policing. *Law & Society Review, 37,* 513–548.

Tonry, M. (1995). *Malign neglect: Race, crime, and punishment in America.* New York: Oxford University Press.

Tuch, S. A., & Weitzer, R. (1997). Trends: Racial differences in attitudes toward the police. *Public Opinion Quarterly, 61,* 642–663.

Tyler, T. R. (2004). Enhancing police legitimacy. *Annals of the American Academy of Political and Social Science, 593,* 84–99.

Tyler, T. R. (2006). *Why people obey the law.* New Haven, CT: Yale University Press.

Tyler, T. R., Casper, J. D., & Fisher, B. (1989). Maintaining allegiance toward political authorities: The role of prior attitudes and the use of fair procedures. *American Journal of Political Science, 33,* 629–652.

Tyler, T. R., & Huo, Y. J. (2002). *Trust in the law: Encouraging public cooperation with the police and courts.* New York: Russell Sage Foundation.

U.S. Department of Justice. (2000). *National Incident-Based Reporting System Volume I: Data collection guidelines.* Washington, DC: U.S. Department of Justice, Federal Bureau of Investigation.

U.S. Department of Justice. (2004a). *National Incident-Based Reporting System, 2002* (Computer file, compiled by the U.S. Department of Justice, Federal Bureau of Investigation, edited by ICPSR). Ann Arbor, MI: Inter-university Consortium for Political and Social Research (producer and distributor).

U.S. Department of Justice. (2004b). *Uniform crime reporting handbook.* Washington, DC: U.S. Department of Justice, Federal Bureau of Investigation.

Walsh, A. (1987). The sexual stratification hypothesis and sexual assault in light of the changing conception of race. *Criminology, 25,* 152–173.

Websdale, N. (2001). *Policing the poor: From slave plantation to public housing.* Boston, MA: Northeastern University Press.

Weitzer, R. (1996). Racial discrimination in the criminal justice system: Findings and problems in the literature. *Journal of Criminal Justice, 24,* 309–322.

Wolfgang, M., & Riedel, M. (1973). Race, judicial discretion, and the death penalty. *Annals, 407,* 119–133.

Zatz, M. S. (1987). The changing forms of racial/ethnic biases in sentencing. *Journal of Research in Crime* & Delinquency, *24,* 69–92.

Zatz, M. S. (2000). The convergence of race, ethnicity, gender, and class on court decisionmaking: Looking toward the 21st century. In J. Horney (Ed.), *Policies, processes, and decisions of the criminal justice system: Vol. 3. Criminal Justice 2000* (pp. 503–552). Washington, DC: U.S. Department of Justice, Office of Justice Programs.

DISCUSSION QUESTIONS

1. Describe the information collected in the National Incident Based Reporting System and the limitations of the data.
2. What factors were found to influence police clearance of violent criminal incidents?
3. Do you think that the race of the victim and offender are important to understanding either violent crime clearance or attitudes toward the police?

Courts and Sentencing

SECTION HIGHLIGHTS

- Overview of American Courts and Sentencing
- Contemporary Issues in Race and the Courts
- Contemporary Issues in Race and Sentencing
- Summary
- Edited Readings

The American courts are one of the key components of the criminal justice system. They are the places in which justice is believed to be carried out. That is, courts are the place where citizens believe that injustices will be remedied—if injustices were committed at earlier stages of the criminal justice process. They are also where victims perceive that justice occurs on their behalf. The competing interests of defendants and victims make the courts a place where there are intense debates about the merits of cases and whether someone is innocent or guilty. While American courts are glamorized on television with compelling trials and charismatic attorneys and judges, the reality is that most courts are really in the negotiation business, with more than 95% of all cases resolved through the **plea bargaining** process. Thus, this is the stage where defense attorneys fight for their clients and prosecutors attempt to secure justice on behalf of the victims.

Nationally, the courts represent an entity in which billions of dollars are spent each year. Moreover, according to the Bureau of Justice Statistics, in 2006, more than 1.1 million adults were convicted of felonies in state-level courts (Rosenmerkel, Durose, & Farole, 2009). Of these felony convictions, 38% were of Blacks (Rosenmerkel et al., 2009).

Considering the significance of courts and sentencing in the race and crime discourse, this section examines the ways in which race and ethnicity matter during the court process and the sentencing phase.

Overview of American Courts and Sentencing

Like so many other facets of American life, the American court system owes much to the English justice system (Chapin, 1983). In general, as American society gained its independence, the courts became more complex with the development of the federal court system and the Supreme Court (Shelden, 2001). Today, because of these early changes, the U.S. court system is referred to as a ***dual court system***. There are both state and federal courts, each with trial courts at the lowest level and appellate courts at the top of the hierarchy. The federal court system starts with U.S. magistrate courts, "who hear minor offenses and conduct preliminary hearings" (Shelden & Brown, 2003, p. 196). U.S. district courts are trial courts that hear both civil and criminal cases. Positioned above the U.S. district courts are the U.S. courts of appeals, which are the final step before reaching the Supreme Court. The Supreme Court represents the highest court in the land and has the final say on matters that make it to that level (see Photo 6.1). The American court system (at both the state and federal level) involves several actors and processes. Subsequently, over time, some of these actors and processes have come under scrutiny for a variety of reasons, including race- and class-related concerns (Reiman, 2007). The court is generally comprised of three main figures: the judge, the prosecutor, and the defense attorney. Although the system is theoretically based on the ancient system of "trial by combat," in practice, it has been suggested that these main figures are part of the "courtroom work group" who actually work together to resolve matters brought before the court (Neubauer, 2002).

▲ **Photo 6.1** Supreme Court 2009

There are several processes involved when one is navigating through the court system. First there is a pretrial process, where the decision is made on whether to move forward with a particular case. If the case is moved forward, the question of pretrial detention and **bail** is decided next. Other processes in the court system include the preliminary hearing, grand jury proceedings, and the arraignment, where a defendant first enters his or her plea. Although plea bargaining determines the outcome in most of the cases, if the case happens to go to trial, there are other processes that move the case along. Once the decision to go to trial is made, unless the case is going to be decided solely by a judge (referred to as a *bench trial*), the next process is jury selection. Following the completion of jury selection, the trial begins. If the defendant is found guilty, the sentencing phase follows.

Sentencing is the stage of the criminal justice process where, following conviction, a defendant is given a sanction for committing his or her offense. Sanctions that are regularly used because they are not in violation of the Eighth Amendment's cruel and unusual punishment clause include fines (which cannot be excessive); being placed on probation, given an intermediate sanction (something in between probation and incarceration), and/or incarceration; and the death penalty. Many of the contemporary issues pertaining to race, the courts, and sentencing are related to whether there is race or gender discrimination in the various court processes (Free, 2002a, 2002b; Walker, Spohn, & DeLone, 2007).

Contemporary Issues in Race and Courts

Bail and the Pretrial Process

Although bail is not guaranteed by the Constitution, the Eighth Amendment does state that when given, it should not be excessive. Since the creation of this amendment, various types of **pretrial release** options have been used. During the early 1950s and 1960s, the Vera Institute of New York conducted studies on bail practices in Philadelphia and New York City. This early research found that those defendants who received bail were more likely to be acquitted than those defendants who could not afford bail (Anderson & Newman, 1998). In the 1960s, the Vera Institute created the Manhattan Bail Project, which was meant to see whether those released on their own recognizance (ROR) absconded any more often than those released on monetary bail. The project convincingly showed that "the rate of return for ROR releases was consistently equal to or better than the rate for those on monetary bail" (Anderson & Newman, 1998, p. 215). Mann (1993) noted that many of the defendants in the pioneering Manhattan Bail Project were minorities, the majority of whom did return for trial. Even with these findings, during the Reagan presidency, the Bail Reform Act of 1984 provided judges with more discretion as to who could be given pretrial release. In general, judges can hold defendants in jail if they consider them either a risk for flight or a danger to the community (Robinson, 2002). Because of risk concerns, the courts consider a variety of factors when making the decision as to whether to grant pretrial release on bail. In fact, some states, such as New York, have bail statutes that, when deciding whether to grant bail, require judges to consider risk factors such as the nature of the offense, prior record, previous record in appearing when required in court, employment status, community ties, and the weight of the evidence against a defendant (Inciardi, 1999).

There are generally three broad categories of pretrial release: nonfinancial release, financial release, and emergency release (Reaves & Perez, 1994). Nonfinancial release is when someone is released without having to provide any monetary collateral. This typically comes in the form of ROR or citation releases, which are typically administered by law enforcement. Other such releases include a conditional release that involves having to either contact or report to an official to ensure compliance with the conditions of release (e.g., drug treatment). Under this type of release, a third party can also be entrusted to ensure the defendants return (Anderson & Newman, 1998). According to Reaves and Perez (1994), "about 2 in 5 defendants released before case dispositions received that release through financial terms involving a surety, full cash, deposit, or property bond. Deposit, full cash, and property bonds are posted directly with the court, while surety bonds involve the services of a bail bond company" (p. 3). The final release is referred to as an *emergency release,* and it occurs when, due to jail crowding, the defendant is given pretrial release under generally nonstringent release conditions.

Race and Pretrial Release

Analyzing pretrial release data on 28,000 felony defendants from 75 of the largest American counties, Reaves and Perez (1994) provided one of the few examinations of race and the pretrial process. A review of the racial characteristics of the various types of releases showed that Blacks, Whites, and Hispanics appeared to have access to financial, nonfinancial, and emergency releases. Undoubtedly, some of these figures were tied to the nature of the offenses committed by each defendant. Though dated, Reaves and Perez's national data still provides some useful information on the race of those who failed to appear and those who were rearrested.

Data on felony defendants who failed to appear, by race, showed that 72% of Blacks, 81% of Whites, 86% of Others, and 70% of Hispanics made all court appearances. Of those who failed to appear, 19% of Blacks, 13% of Whites, 9% of Others, and 17% of Hispanic defendants eventually returned to court. Only 8% of Blacks, 6% of Whites, and 5% of Other persons remained fugitives. In the case of Hispanics, 13% remained fugitives (Reaves & Perez, 1994).

Of those who were released prior to trial on any type of release, 85% of Blacks, 91% of Whites, 94% of Others, and 84% of Hispanics were not rearrested (Reaves & Perez, 1994). Hispanics (12%) and Blacks (11%) were rearrested for felonies more often than Whites (7%) and Others (6%). A similar pattern emerged when the authors reviewed the racial characteristics of defendants who were charged with some sort of misconduct (e.g., new charge, failure to appear, technical violation) when they were on pretrial release: Hispanics (38%) and Blacks (35%) had the highest rates, with Whites (25%) and Others (19%) having lower rates.

Although nearly 95% of criminal defendants are charged in state courts (Wolf Harlow, 2000), the remaining 5%—or 57,000 other defendants—are charged with a federal offense (Scalia, 1999). Federal officials also adhere to the Bail Reform Act of 1984 to decide who will receive pretrial release and under what circumstances. In general, persons who had committed violent offenses, had a history of pretrial misconduct, or had no ties with the community were more likely to be detained prior to trial (Scalia, 1999).

More than one third (34%) of federal defendants were ordered detained prior to trial. Hispanic defendants were detained at the highest rate (46.7%), with Blacks (35.9%), Others (32.8%), and Whites (19.3%) following behind (Scalia, 1999). According to Scalia (1999), the high rate of detention for Hispanics was because they were identified as noncitizens, which contributed in part to them not being able to show established community ties in America. In addition, they were often charged with the more severe drug-trafficking offenses (Scalia, 1999). Like Hispanics, Blacks were also charged with the more serious drug-trafficking offenses. They also had more serious criminal histories, with 75% of them having been arrested on a prior occasion (as opposed to 61% of Whites and 57% of Hispanics). Moreover, "38.9% of Black defendants had been arrested at least five times compared to 23.1% of Hispanics, 24% of Whites, and 15% of other non-White defendants" (Scalia, 1999, p. 10). Nearly half (46%) of the Black defendants had been previously convicted of a felony, with half of them convicted of a violent felony and another 33% convicted of a drug offense. Given these figures, scholars have sought to determine whether discrimination (race or gender) plays any role in the bail and pretrial process.

Free (2002a) conducted a comprehensive review of studies related to race and pretrial release and found that most studies did find that race and gender were significant factors in the decision to grant pretrial release. Demuth and Steffensmeier (2004) examined 75 of the most populous counties in the United States (from 1990 to 1996) and found that, "in general, female defendants receive more favorable decisions and outcomes than males across all racial-ethnic groups" (p. 234). In addition, the research found that Hispanic and African American males were less likely than White males to be granted pretrial release. Overall, however, Hispanics received the least favorable pretrial decisions. This finding has also been confirmed by additional research (Schlesinger, 2005; Turner & Johnson, 2005).

Legal Counsel

As a result of the blatant racism found in the notorious Scottsboro case, since 1932, the U.S. Supreme Court has mandated that indigent defendants in capital cases have the right to adequate counsel (see *Powell v. Alabama*, 1932). Four decades later, in *Gideon v. Wainwright* (1963), the Court ruled that all felony defendants have a right to counsel, a ruling that was expanded in 1972 when the Court mandated that counsel be provided for defendants in misdemeanor cases where there was the possibility of incarceration (see *Argersinger v. Hamlin*, 1972). To meet these Supreme Court mandates, states created several legal defense systems. Many states have adopted a **public defender system** where, as with a district attorney, the local or state government hires a full-time attorney to provide legal counsel for indigent defendants. In other cases, defendants are assigned counsel from a list of private attorneys who are selected on a case-by-case basis by a judge. Another option is the use of contract attorneys. These people are also private attorneys who are contracted to provide legal representation to an indigent defendant (DeFrances & Litras, 2000).

Defense Counsel

In 2005, the federal government has conducted studies to determine the state of counsel in criminal cases (DeFrances, 2001; DeFrances & Litras, 2000; Wolf Harlow, 2000). Recent figures show that there are nearly 1,000 public defender offices handling nearly 6 million cases (Farole & Langton, 2009). Most observers of indigent defense wonder whether there are different outcomes depending on whether you are represented by public or private counsel. Looking at the outcomes of cases at both the state and federal levels, Wolf Harlow (2000) found that conviction rates were the same and that most defendants were convicted with either type of attorney. One difference noted in his study was that at both court levels, those represented by public defense were more likely to be incarcerated. At the federal court level, the difference was 11% (88% public vs. 77% private). On the state level, however, the differences were more dramatic: "In large State courts 71% with public counsel and 54% with private attorneys were sentenced to incarceration" (Wolf Harlow, 2000, p. 1). It is also interesting to note that more than 90% of federal defendants were found guilty irrespective of type of counsel (Wolf Harlow, 2000). A recent study on legal counsel in federal cases found that public defenders outperformed (lower conviction rates and sentence lengths) private attorneys who were retained on an hourly basis (Iyengar, 2007). Turning to the representation of those who were incarcerated, minorities used public defense systems more than Whites (Wolf Harlow, 2000). Approximately 75% of Black and Hispanic state inmates and 69% of Whites had public defenders or assigned counsel (Wolf Harlow, 2000). In the case of federal inmates, 65% of Black inmates had public defenders, and Hispanics and Whites used public defense at a similar level (56% vs. 57%).

Using a statewide study from Pennsylvania as an example, we examine how the public defense system is working in the sixth most populous state. In Pennsylvania, 80% of all criminal defendants rely on public defense (Pennsylvania Supreme Court, 2003). The study found a system filled with public defenders that fit the stereotype of overburdened and underpaid. In most instances, there were few resources to carry out independent investigations of the facts of cases or to hire crucial expert witnesses. Such findings suggest that, in Pennsylvania, defendants who are poor and people of color are being represented by inadequate counsel. Given these facts, it is no wonder that plea bargaining pervades court systems across the country.

Plea Bargaining

Before actually proceeding to the trial phase, in any given year, an estimated 96% of convictions are reconciled through a guilty plea in the plea-bargaining process (Reaves, 2001). Early in American history, however, plea bargaining was frowned on by justice system officials and, as a result, comprised a small percentage of how cases were resolved. Only since the 20th century have courts accepted it as an important part of the criminal justice process (Shelden & Brown, 2003). Predictably, a process involving no real oversight and such broad discretion has come under scrutiny because of concerns related to race and class. The intersection of race and class is well articulated by M. Robinson (2002), who wrote, "Plea bargaining results in a bias against poor clients, who are typically minorities, as well as the uneducated, who may not even know what is being done to them in the criminal justice process" (p. 247).

An example of how racial bias can influence the plea-bargaining process can be seen by one of the few comprehensive studies on the topic. In 1991, the *San Jose Mercury News* conducted an analysis of California criminal cases. Using a computer analysis of nearly 700,000 criminal cases from 1981 to 1990, the study found the following:

> At virtually every stage of pretrial plea bargaining Whites were more successful than minorities. All else being equal, Whites did better than African Americans and Hispanics at getting charges dropped, getting cases dismissed, avoiding harsher punishment, avoiding extra charges, and having their records wiped clean. (Donzinger, 1996, p. 112)

In addition, the study found that, although one third of Whites who started out with felony charges had their charges reduced to misdemeanors, African Americans and Hispanics received this benefit only 25% of the time (Donzinger, 1996). Seeking to explain some of these results, one California judge stated that there was no conspiracy among judges to produce such outcomes. A public defender explained the disparities this way:

> If a White person can put together a halfway plausible excuse, people will bend over backward to accommodate that person. It's a feeling, "You've got a nice person screwing up," as opposed to the feeling that "this minority person is on track and eventually they're going to end up in state prison." It's an unfortunate racial stereotype that pervades the system. It's an unconscious thing. (Donzinger, 1996, p. 113)

One can only imagine the compounded impact of such attitudes if they are pervasive nationwide. In the rare event that a case is not resolved during the plea-bargaining process, the next stage of the process requires the preparation for a jury trial. Jury selection begins this phase of the process.

Jury Selection

Once it is decided that a case is going to trial, the case is decided by either a jury or a judge in a bench trial (where a judge is responsible for the determination of guilt or innocence). In the event of a jury trial, the jury selection process begins with a *venire*, or the selection of a jury pool. This provides the court with a list of persons from which to select the final jury members. The Constitution requires that citizens are entitled to a jury of their peers. Those in the legal profession generally agree that this should translate into juries being representative of the communities in which the defendant resides. In the jury selection process, however, race and gender concerns have continued to pervade the process. Although times have changed, in some jurisdictions, when minorities are underrepresented on juries in their communities, questions have been raised. But in other instances, the courts have refused to intervene.

In some states, it has been found that there are key barriers that restrict minorities and women from serving on juries. For example, in Pennsylvania, minorities received fewer summonses for jury duty and had transportation issues, child-care issues, and employer issues (Pennsylvania Supreme Court, 2003).

Turning to the underrepresentation of women on juries, research in Pennsylvania revealed some of the interconnections between race and gender. Women were generally the ones responsible for child care; therefore, they were often unable to serve on juries. Women often had difficulty reaching the courthouse, a concern shared by non-White men. In certain situations, women, like men, were also unable to serve on juries due to economic hardships. A final gender-related concern was "[the finding of] evidence that the interpersonal dynamics within the jury room can operate to the detriment of female jurors" (Pennsylvania Supreme Court, 2003, p. 106). More specifically, "women in Pennsylvania were less likely than men to be chosen as presiding jurors" (Pennsylvania Supreme Court, 2003, p. 106).

The opportunity for race and gender bias does not end once the jury pool is formed. There have been concerns with the subsequent ***voir dire*** process, where jurors are screened for their fitness to serve on a particular case.

Voir Dire

Considering the difficulty in locating non-White jurors, it would seem that once the final juror selection process began, non-White jurors would not be the targets for removal. To the surprise of some, this is not the case. Both the defense and prosecution often use their **peremptory challenges** to remove jurors based, in large part, on their race. In general, peremptory challenges can be used to remove jurors without cause. This was challenged in the 1965 case of *Swain v. Alabama.* In the case, Robert Swain, a Black teenager, was accused and convicted of raping a White teenager (Cole, 1999). During the case, the prosecution "struck all six prospective Black jurors," and after investigation, it was revealed "that no Black had ever served on a trial jury in Talladega County, Alabama," (Cole, 1999, p. 119) despite the fact that Blacks made up 25% of the county population. Based on this information, the conviction was challenged, and the Supreme Court decided to hear the case. However, the Supreme Court found no problem with striking the prospective Black jurors, indicating among other things that, "in the quest for an impartial and qualified jury, Negro and White, Protestants and Catholic, are alike subject to being challenged without cause" (cited in Cole, 1999, p. 119). But according to the 1986 Supreme Court decision in ***Batson v. Kentucky***, race or gender must not be the deciding factor. It is notable that, six years later, in *Hernandez v. New York* (1991), the Supreme Court ruled as follows:

> A criminal defendant's Fourteenth Amendment rights to equal protection were not violated when a prosecutor exercised a peremptory challenge excluding potential Latino/a jurors who understood Spanish on the basis that they might not accept the court interpreter's version as the final arbiter in the case. The defendant had argued that the elimination of potential Latino/a jurors violated his right to a trial by his peers in violation of his constitutional rights. (Cited in Morin, 2005, p. 78)

In the eyes of the Supreme Court, the prosecutor's reason for the removal of Latino/a jurors was "race neutral" (Morin, 2005, p. 78). Prior to the *Batson* (1986) decision, studies of jurisdictions in Texas and Georgia found that peremptory challenges were used to strike 90% of Black jurors (Cole, 1999). In fact, in large cities such as Philadelphia, district attorneys were given clear instructions to strike non-White jurors. A now infamous training tape by one Philadelphia assistant district attorney made this declaration:

> Young Black women are very bad. There's an antagonism. I guess maybe they're downtrodden in two respects. They are women and they're Black . . . so they somehow want to take it out on somebody, and you don't want it to be you. (Cole, 1999, p. 118)

Scholars have also noted that, in certain instances, defense attorneys follow similar practices (Cole, 1999).

Since the *Batson* (1986) decision, prosecutors have turned to deception to strike non-White jurors. According to Cole (1999), prosecutors are masking their race-based actions by using neutral explanations to remove jurors:

> Courts have accepted explanations that the juror was too old, too young, was employed as a teacher or unemployed, or practiced a certain religion. They have accepted unverifiable explanations based on demeanor: the juror did not make eye contact or made too much eye contact, appeared inattentive or headstrong, nervous or too casual, grimaced or smiled. And they have accepted explanations that might often be correlated to race: the juror lacked education, was single or poor, lived or worked in the same neighborhood as the defendant or a witness, or had previously been involved with the criminal justice system. (pp. 120–121)

Gabbidon, Kowal, Jordan, Roberts, and Vincenzi (2008) confirmed these findings after reviewing 5 years worth of litigation in which plaintiffs sued because they felt alleged race-neutral peremptory challenges were race-based. Based on an analysis of 283 cases from the U.S. Court of Appeals, the researchers found that Blacks were the ones most likely to be removed from juries. As for the explanations used to justify their removal, some included questionable body language, questionable mannerisms, medical issues, child-care issues, limited life experiences, and unemployment. The courts accepted these explanations, considering that 79% of the appellants lost their cases (Gabbidon et al., 2008). For those who actually won their appeal, there was an extremely high burden of proof. Central to winning was being able to show some inconsistency on the part of the attorney who made the removals. For example, Gabbidon et al. found that in one instance, the prosecutor struck a juror "because he was concerned that she did not seem to understand or respond appropriately to certain dire questions" (p. 64). But after further review, "the courts ruled against the prosecutor because they found that the prosecutor declined to strike White jurors whose answers were far more inappropriate or unresponsive" (p. 64).

Jury Nullification

Given the numerous measures being taken in some jurisdictions to diversify jury pools, one would think that keeping non-Whites on the jury would be a high priority. On the contrary, as discussed in the previous section on peremptory challenges, prosecutors and defense attorneys alike often eliminate jurors based on race if they believe it will help them secure a victory. The underlying premise behind such thinking is surely a lack of trust, particularly of non-White jurors. Why else would someone not want non-Whites on juries? The concern relates to the practice of **jury nullification.** According to Walker et al. (2007), the following is true:

> Jury nullification . . . occurs when a juror believes that the evidence presented at trial establishes the defendant's guilt, but nonetheless votes to acquit. The juror's decision may be motivated either by a belief that the law under which the defendant is being prosecuted is unfair or by an application of the law to a particular defendant. (p. 223)

There has been debate and concern about jury nullification (Butler, 1995). Krauss and Schulman (1997) see the general concern of Black juror nullification as being based on anecdotal evidence. In their analysis, the discussion comes down to the following equation: "Black defendant + Black jurors + non-conviction = miscarriage of justice"

(Krauss & Schulman, 1997, p. 2). In their view, those who believe in this equation ignore the fact that, in some of these cases, "Black jurors are being condemned for doing exactly what jurors are supposed to do: demanding that the prosecution prove its case beyond a reasonable doubt" (Krauss & Schulman, 1997, p. 2). Furthermore, they view the continuing outrage over jury nullification as a response to an article published in the *Wall Street Journal* shortly after the conclusion of the O. J. Simpson trial in 1995. The article provided figures showing that nationwide there was an overall acquittal rate of 17%, whereas in jurisdictions such as the Bronx, New York, and Washington, D.C., the acquittal rates were 47.6% and 28.7%, respectively. The authors countered these figures, showing that the acquittal rate nationally was closer to 28% (Krauss & Schulman, 1997). Subsequently, contrary to the notion of jury nullification, the authors noted that the Bronx rate was likely a result of "(1) jurors doing their jobs well, [and] (2) prosecutors who are not doing their jobs well" (Krauss & Schulman, 1997, p. 3). Krauss and Schulman (1997) also noted that there is the belief that only White jurors can be color-blind. They responded that it is impossible to have a color-blind jury because race is the first thing that people see in others. Another important point discussed by the authors relates to police testimony. Although in many instances the testimony of police officers is believed without challenge, the authors pointed out that, because of their historically negative experiences with police officers, persons of color give equal weight to police testimony and that of other witnesses even when they differ (Krauss & Schulman, 1997).

Contemporary Issues in Race and Sentencing

The sentencing phase has considerable potential for discrimination and errors. It is important to consider, however, that, like the laws that set the criminal justice process in motion, state and federal legislatures are primarily responsible for determining the appropriate sentence for each offense. Although the legislature has a significant role to play in the creation of sentences, in many instances, judges also have considerable discretion in the sentencing process. Therefore, a variety of legislative enactments (e.g., sentencing guidelines) have been created to "equalize" or reduce the disparities in the sentencing process, yet judicial discretion remains a place where sentences can be influenced appreciably. Because of this, over the years, the actions of the judiciary have been scrutinized more closely by citizens and social scientists alike.

In 2006, more than 1.1 million adults were convicted of a felony in state courts; 69% of them were sentenced to either jail (28%) or prison (41%), with the remainder being sentenced to nonincarceration (Rosenmerkel et al., 2009; see Table 6.1). In 2006, the average felony sentence was 38 months. For those who committed murder and nonnegligent manslaughter, the average was 20 years. In general, most persons who committed homicide received a sentence of incarceration, with only 4% not receiving a sentence involving confinement. In line with the arrest statistics, most persons convicted for felony offenses were Whites; however, Blacks were overrepresented in nearly every category (see Table 6.2). In 2006, for example, Blacks, who made up approximately 13% of the population, represented 38% of those persons convicted of a felony and 39% of convicted violent felons (Rosenmerkel et al., 2009). Other races (American Indians, Alaska Natives, Asian and Pacific Islanders) represented 2% of all felony convictions and

3% of convictions for violent crime (Rosenmerkel et al., 2009). Given the large numbers of Blacks convicted of felony offenses, the next question is whether they are convicted and sentenced fairly. Since the 1990s, there has been an explosion of literature investigating this question (Chircos & Crawford, 1995; Crow & Johnson, 2008; Mitchell, 2005; Pratt, 1998; Spohn, 2000; Zatz, 1987). Much of this literature examined **sentencing disparities** during the height of the **"War on Drugs"** in the 1980s.

Table 6.1 Types of Felony Sentences Imposed in State Courts, by Offense, 2006

		Percent of Felons Sentenced to –					
		Incarceration			Nonincarceration		
Most Serious Conviction Offense	Total	Total	Prison	Jail	Total	Probation	Other
All offenses	100%	69	41	28	31	27	4
Violent offenses	100%	77	54	23	23	20	3
Murder/nonnegligent manslaughter	100%	95	93	2	5	3	2
Sexual assault	100%	81	64	18	19	16	3
Rape	100%	86	72	15	14	10	4
Other sexual assault[a]	100%	77	58	20	23	20	2
Robbery	100%	85	71	14	15	13	2
Aggravated assault	100%	72	43	30	28	25	3
Other violent[b]	100%	70	39	30	30	26	4
Property offenses	100%	67	38	29	33	29	4
Burglary	100%	73	49	24	27	24	3
Larceny	100%	69	34	34	31	28	3
Motor vehicle theft	100%	83	42	41	17	15	2
Fraud/forgery[c]	100%	59	32	27	41	35	6
Drug offenses	100%	65	38	28	35	30	4
Possession	100%	63	33	31	37	33	4
Trafficking	100%	67	41	26	33	29	4
Weapon offenses	100%	73	45	28	27	25	2
Other specified offenses[d]	100%	70	36	34	30	27	3

NOTE: For persons receiving a combination of sentences, the sentence designation came from the most severe penalty imposed, with prison being the most severe, followed by jail, probation, and then other sentences, such as a fine, community service, or house arrest. Prison includes death sentences. In this table, *probation* is defined as straight probation. Columns may not sum to total shown because of rounding. Data on sentence type were reported for 98% of the estimated total of 1,132,290 convicted felons. Percentages are based on reported data.

a. Includes such offenses as statutory rape and incest with a minor.

b. Includes such offenses as negligent manslaughter and kidnapping.

c. Includes embezzlement.

d. Comprises nonviolent offenses such as vandalism and receiving stolen property.

Table 6.2 Gender and Race of Persons Convicted of Felonies in State Courts, by Offense, 2006

		Percent of Convicted Felons				
		Gender		Race		
Most Serious Conviction Offense	Total	Male	Female	White	Black	Other[a]
All offenses	100%	83	17	60	38	2
Violent offenses	100%	89	11	58	39	3
Murder/nonnegligent manslaughter	100%	90	10	46	51	3
Sexual assault	100%	97	3	74	24	2
Rape	100%	96	4	70	28	2
Other sexual assault[b]	100%	97	3	77	21	2
Robbery	100%	91	9	42	57	1
Aggravated assault	100%	86	14	59	39	3
Other violent[c]	100%	88	12	69	28	3
Property offenses	100%	75	25	65	33	2
Burglary	100%	90	10	66	32	2
Larceny	100%	75	25	64	34	2
Motor vehicle theft	100%	86	14	70	26	5
Fraud/forgery[d]	100%	59	41	66	32	2
Drug offenses	100%	82	18	55	44	1
Possession	100%	80	20	62	36	2
Trafficking	100%	83	17	50	49	1
Weapon offenses	100%	95	5	43	55	2
Other specified offenses[e]	100%	87	13	67	30	3

NOTE: Data on gender were reported for 86% of convicted felons and data on race for 74%. Columns may not sum to total shown because of rounding. Racial categories include persons of Latino or Hispanic origin.

a. Includes American Indians, Alaska Natives, Asians, Native Hawaiians, and other Pacific Islanders.

b. Includes offenses such as statutory rape and incest with a minor.

c. Includes offenses such as negligent manslaughter and kidnapping.

d. Includes embezzlement.

e. Comprises nonviolent offenses such as vandalism and receiving stolen property.

Sentencing Disparities and the "War on Drugs"

The War on Drugs that began to take shape in the 1980s rang in a new era of punitive sanctions. Unfortunately, as has been noted by several researchers, minorities have been impacted most by the war (Donzinger, 1996; Miller, 1996; Tonry, 1995). On the federal level alone, Tonry (1995) noted that, in 1980, drug offenders represented 22% of the admissions to institutions, but by 1989, this had risen to 39%, and by 1990, this had risen to 42%. Strikingly, by 1992, 58% of federal inmates were drug offenders (Tonry, 1995). At the state level, Shelden and Brown (2003) noted that, "between 1980 and 1992, sentences on drug charges increased by more than 1,000%" (p. 252). They continued by noting that when taking race into consideration, "The number of African Americans sentenced to prison on drug charges increased by over 90%, almost three times greater than White offenders" (p. 252). Shelden and Brown also pointed to figures that show that, during the 10-year period of 1985 to 1995, "the number of African American inmates sentenced for drug offenses increased by 700%" (p. 252).

During this same period (1985–1995), crack cocaine became a significant concern for the government, which led to the formulation of differential mandatory minimum penalties. For example, someone with 500 grams of powder cocaine would receive a mandatory minimum sentence of 5 years, whereas someone with 5 grams of crack cocaine would receive the same 5-year mandatory minimum penalty. For those caught with 50 grams of crack cocaine, the mandatory minimum penalty was 10 years, whereas those caught with 5,000 grams of powder cocaine also received a 10-year mandatory minimum sentence. Unfortunately, although minorities are overrepresented in the use of crack cocaine, the majority of those who use crack cocaine are White—yet most of those serving time under these federal policies are African Americans and Hispanics (Russell-Brown, 2004).

Tracing the origin of this much maligned 100-to-1 crack cocaine-to-powder cocaine sentencing differential, Russell-Brown (2009) suggested that the sudden death of University of Maryland basketball star Len Bias contributed to this "moral panic," or unsupported fear about crack cocaine (Brownstein, 1996; Jenkins, 1994). Because Bias' death was linked to crack cocaine, a cheaper form of cocaine, initially, many public officials felt that this was a sign that crack would devastate the Black community.

According to Kennedy (1997), during the ensuing legislative debates, Black legislators such as Charles Rangel and Major Owens argued vociferously for their legislative colleagues to move quickly in drafting legislation to head off a potential epidemic in the African American community. Although Kennedy (1997) noted that the legislators didn't call for the differential penalties that ensued, "eleven of the twenty-one Blacks who were then members of the House of Representatives voted in favor of the law which created the 100–1 crack-powder differential" (p. 370).

Many observers agree the early efforts to stave off an impending epidemic were noble, but others, however, argue that, because of these actions, an "incarceration epidemic" ensued (Mauer, 1999; Radosh, 2008; Tonry, 1995). Moreover, once it became clear that the sentencing differential was leading to massive incarceration disparities, in 1995 and 1997, the government had two opportunities to rectify the situation. But according to Russell (1998), Congress overwhelmingly voted against taking such action, although it was recommended by the **U.S. Sentencing Commission.** To the surprise of many in the African American community, President Clinton did not follow the recommendations of the Commission. In response to this inaction, prisoners at several federal correctional facilities rioted (Russell, 1998). Congress returned to the matter in 2002, when the Senate held hearings on the federal cocaine policy (see U.S. Senate, 2002). In preparation for this congressional hearing, in 2002, the U.S. Sentencing Commission produced the report, *Cocaine and Federal Sentencing Policy.*

The Commission based its report on empirical analyses on federal cocaine offenders sentenced in 1995 and 2000, a survey of state cocaine sentencing policies, public opinion, and public hearings. From these sources, the Commission reported the following four major findings: (1) current penalties exaggerate the relative harmfulness of crack cocaine, (2) current penalties sweep too broadly and apply most often to lower-level offenders, (3) current quantity-based penalties overstate the seriousness of most crack cocaine offenses and fail to provide adequate proportionality, and (4) current penalties' severity impact mostly minorities (U.S. Sentencing Commission, 2002).

With the first finding, the Commission recognized that the form of cocaine is irrelevant; both crack and powder cocaine produce "the same physiological and psychotropic effects" (U.S. Sentencing Commission, 2002, p. v). In addition, speaking to the short-lived, unsuccessful, and, some believe, racism-based attempt of some states (e.g., South Carolina and Kentucky) to prosecute mothers (who happened to be overwhelmingly Black) who used drugs during pregnancy (Kennedy, 1997; Russell-Brown, 2004), the Commission noted that "the negative effects of prenatal crack cocaine exposure are identical to the negative effects of prenatal powder cocaine exposure and are significantly less severe than previously believed" (U.S. Sentencing Commission, 2002, pp. v–vi). Equally important, the Commission added that "the negative effects from prenatal cocaine exposure are similar to those associated with prenatal tobacco exposure and less severe than the negative effects of prenatal alcohol exposure" (U.S. Sentencing Commission, 2002, p. vi).

Under the second finding, the Commission noted that more than a quarter of the federal crack cocaine offenses involved small quantities (less than 25 grams). In contrast, "Only 2.7% of federal powder cocaine offenses involved less than 25 grams of the drug, perhaps because the statutory minimum penalties would not apply to such a small quantity of powder cocaine" (U.S. Sentencing Commission, 2002, p. vi). If what the Commission surmised is true, then those dealing in powder cocaine actually have the law on their side. To further illustrate the nature of the sentencing disparity in practice, the commission provided the following figures:

> Defendants convicted of trafficking less than 25 grams of powder cocaine received an average sentence of 13.6 months, just over one year. In contrast, defendants convicted of trafficking an equivalent amount of crack received an average sentence of 64.8 months, over five years. (U.S. Sentencing Commission, 2002, p. vi)

The third finding by the Commission argued that the crack cocaine–violence link was unsupported by the empirical evidence. As they reported, "In 2000 . . . three-quarters of federal crack cocaine offenders had no personal weapon involvement, and only 2.3% discharged a weapon" (U.S. Sentencing Commission, 2002, p. vii). In the Commission's view, the penalty was inflexible and did not acknowledge that, although some crack cocaine offenders do engage in violence, the majority do not (U.S. Sentencing Commission, 2002). The final finding discussed by the Commission was that minorities were hit hardest by the current cocaine penalties. They noted that, in 2000, 85% of those impacted by the crack cocaine penalties were Black, whereas only 31% of those affected by the powder cocaine laws were Black (U.S. Sentencing Commission, 2002).

Taking their findings into consideration, the Commission provided three recommendations. First, they recommended "increas[ing] the five-year mandatory minimum threshold quantity for crack cocaine offenses to at least 25 grams and the ten-year threshold quantity to at least 250 grams (and repeal[ing] the mandatory minimum for simple possession of crack cocaine)" (U.S. Sentencing Commission, 2002, p. viii). Second, rather than having a blanket mandatory minimum sentence, they recommended providing sentencing enhancements based on the nature of the offense. Such enhancements would take into consideration whether a weapon was used, bodily injury occurred, the person was a repeat offender, and so on. Finally, the Commission recommended maintaining the current powder cocaine thresholds, but also incorporating the said sentencing enhancements (U.S. Sentencing Commission, 2002).

Five years later, the U.S. Sentencing Commission (2007) returned to the topic with another report, *Cocaine and Federal Sentencing Policy.* The Commission returned to similar themes from the 2002 report, noting the continuing "universal criticism from representatives of the Judiciary, criminal justice practitioners, academics, and community interest groups" (U.S. Sentencing Commission, 2007, p. 2). In addition, the report noted that the major conclusions from the 2002 report remained valid.

During 2007, however, the Commission had the benefit of two Supreme Court cases that provided additional impetus to change the disparity: *Blakely v. Washington* (2004) and *United States v. Booker* (2005), both of which involved issues related to sentencing. In the *Blakely* case, the Court ruled that judges could not enhance penalties based on facts outside of those noted by the jury and the offender. In doing so, they violated one's Sixth Amendment rights to a jury trial. In the *Booker* case, the Court affirmed this decision. Thus, when mandatory sentences are in place and they go against a jury's findings, the judge can view such mandatory penalties as only advisory. Thus, the draconian mandatory crack cocaine sentences could be seen as advisory, and with these decisions, judicial discretion was permissible. In December 2007, the Supreme Court ruled in the case of *Kimbrough v. United States* that mandatory crack penalties were advisory in nature and judges could take into account the crack and powder cocaine disparities when sentencing. Given these significant decisions and the long-standing efforts of numerous entities, the Commission's recommended changes were partially adopted and made "sentences for crack offenses between two and five times longer than sentences for equal amounts of powder" (*Kimbrough v. United States*). The changes in the federal guidelines were made retroactive and took effect in early 2008. In August 2010, President Obama signed the Fair Sentencing Act that reduced the crack-cocaine powder-cocaine penalty to 18:1, as opposed to the 100:1 (crack to powder penalty) (Sentencing Project, 2010).

Throughout the last 30 years, some citizens (particularly racial and ethnic minorities) have questioned the neutrality of judges when racial disparities were revealed. Consequently, a consistent theme in policy considerations related to the judiciary is that if there were more minority judges, the courts would be run more equitably.

Minority Judges

More than 150 years ago, Robert Morris became the first African American to be appointed as a judge (Washington, 1994). Less than 20 years later, during the Reconstruction period, another milestone was reached when Jonathan Jasper Wright was elected to the Supreme Court of South Carolina in 1872 (Washington, 1994). Since these early breakthroughs, few minorities have served as judges. Although this could be a product of the fact that in

2002 Blacks and Hispanics combined represented less than 8% of American lawyers (up from 3% in 1983), proactive measures have resulted in some increases in minority judicial appointments (U.S. Bureau of the Census, 2003).

Looking at judicial appointments to the U.S. district courts over the last 40 years, one does notice a considerable improvement in diversity, but only during the tenure of two presidents (Carter and Clinton) were there substantial gains. During the Carter era, nearly 14% of the appointments were African American and nearly 7% were Hispanic (Pastore & Maguire, 2007). During this span, significant gains were also made for women. In the Johnson era, only 1.6% of the appointees were women, while during the presidency of George W. Bush, 20% of the appointments were women. During the period selected, President George W. Bush also had the highest average rating for his appointees; nearly 70% of them were rated by the American Bar Association to be exceptionally qualified or well qualified. This figure was followed by the Clinton presidency at 59% (Pastore & Maguire, 2007). It is also notable that during Bush's presidency the percentage of Latino appointees to the U.S. district courts was higher than at any other point in history.

Turning to judicial appointments for the U.S. Court of Appeals, the Clinton presidency stands out (1993–2000). During his presidency, nearly 33% of his appointments were female, and nearly 25% were racial minorities (13.1% Black, 11.5% Hispanic) (Pastore & Maguire, 2007). Contrary to some concerns about minority judicial appointments, nearly 79% of Clinton's judicial appointments were rated as either exceptionally well qualified or well qualified by the American Bar Association, a figure that surpassed the appointment records of all other presidents over the last 40 years.

Two things stand out from these data. First, Asian Americans and Native Americans are minimally represented in the appointment figures. The absence of qualified Native American judges could be a product of many of them serving in such positions on reservations. In the case of Asian Americans, although their population figures are low, by now there are surely an ample number of potential nominees. Nevertheless, for minorities who have made it to the judiciary, are there differences between their decisions and those of White judges? We explore this question next.

Most people are familiar with the instant classic *Black Robes, White Justice* by New York State Judge Bruce Wright (1987). Judge Wright's poignant criticism of the justice system served as a much-needed case study of how, in his experience, race operated within the courts. Since the publication of his work, several observers have investigated the impact of minority judges, such as Wright, to see whether they are bringing balance to the bench. In essence, because many minority judges have experienced racism along the way, some observers believe they will be more sensitive to the plight of minorities who come before them. Other observers believe that because of the nature of the judicial role, minority or female judges are more apt to conform to the norm so they can fit in (Spohn, 2002).

Reviewing the literature on the subject, Spohn (2002) noted that there were few differences between the sentences dispensed by Black, Hispanic, and White justices. In fact, in some instances, both Black and White judges sentenced Black defendants more harshly than White offenders. Spohn posited that minority judges could be more sensitive to the justice given to Black *victims,* as opposed to being sensitive to the plight of Black offenders. In addition, "the fact that Black judges might see themselves as potential victims of

Black-on-Black crime, could help explain the harsher sentences imposed on Black offenders by Black judges" (Spohn, 2002, p. 110). Yet others contend that at times Black judges hand down longer sentences because they work in high-crime areas (Adkins, 2002). Worse yet, minority judges might buy into the idea that minorities are more dangerous than Whites. One thing is clear from Spohn's review: The current body of macro-level studies does not provide definitive answers to this question.

Could it be that we expect too much from minority judges? In line with this question, the late Judge A. Leon Higginbotham noted, "No Black judge should work solely on racial matters. I think that would be a profoundly inappropriate abstention, and I would further argue that there is no special role that a Black jurist should play" (cited in Washington, 1994, p. 4). Reviewing the decision of Supreme Court Justice Clarence Thomas in the case of *Hudson v. McMillian* (1992), where a Black prisoner was assaulted by two prison guards while he was shackled at the hands and feet, Higginbotham added the following:

> A Black judge, like all judges, has to decide matters on the basis of the record. But you would hope that a Black judge could never be as blind to the consequences of sanctioning violence and racism against Blacks by state officials as Clarence Thomas was in the *Hudson* case. (Cited in Washington, 1994, p. 5)

Thus, barring exceptional cases, according to one of the leading African American jurists of the 20th century, we should not expect anything different from minority judges; irrespective of race, the facts should dictate case outcomes. The larger issue likely relates to opportunity. How a minority or female judge rules is, in some ways, beside the point. The more central issue is that qualified minority and female attorneys should be afforded equal opportunities to serve in these important roles. Although it could be that in modern times race discrimination continues to be a factor in not appointing more minority attorneys, such a trend could also be tied to politics. That is, which political party is in office might be an equally strong explanation as to why some minorities are selected for the judiciary while others are not.

Summary

- Race, ethnicity, class, and gender have played a role in the American courts since colonial times.
- Public defense systems are grossly underfunded and are often the only choice for racial and ethnic minorities.
- Racial bias in the courts is more subtle today with the use of peremptory challenges to remove Black and Hispanic jurors. These race-based challenges are often used by defense attorneys and prosecutors.
- The War on Drugs has led to sentencing practices that resulted in Blacks and Hispanics being overrepresented in the prison system.
- The appointment of Black and Hispanic judges has been viewed as a way to minimize sentencing disparities. The research on the impact of a diversified judiciary has been mixed.

KEY TERMS

bail

Batson v. Kentucky

dual court system

jury nullification

peremptory challenges

plea bargaining

pretrial release

public defender system

sentencing disparities

U.S. Sentencing Commission

voir dire

War on Drugs

DISCUSSION QUESTIONS

1. Do you believe jury nullification is a viable way to fight injustices in the criminal justice system? Why or why not?
2. Should peremptory challenges be eliminated from the juror selection process?
3. How did the War on Drugs exacerbate racial disparities in the justice system?
4. Do you believe more racial and ethnic minorities in the judiciary will result in more fairness in justice system outcomes?
5. Do you believe the crack-cocaine powder-cocaine laws will ever be equivalent? Why or why not?

WEB RESOURCES

The Sentencing Project: http://www.sentencingproject.org/template/index.cfm

U.S. Courts:
www.uscourts.gov/FederalCourts/UnderstandingtheFederalCourts/CourtofAppeals.aspx

READING

This article examines the controversial use of peremptory challenges. Used to exclude jurors who lawyers feel cannot be impartial, peremptory challenges provide wide discretion for both the defense and prosecution; unfortunately, the use of race and other characteristics (e.g., ethnicity, gender) that the Supreme Court has said cannot be used to strike jurors remains a concern. Even though empirical research has shown that race is being used to remove jurors when lawyers are confronted with a *Batson* challenge or an allegation that race was the reason for removal, attorneys are presenting race-neutral explanations for the removal. This article uses an experiment including undergraduates, college students, law students, and attorneys to determine whether race is considered when presented with a scenario calling for the removal of a juror. The study found that race was considered in the removal of jurors, with Blacks being removed more frequently than Whites. The results also found that the participants used race-neutral explanations as to why they removed the Black juror.

Race-Based Judgments, Race-Neutral Justifications

Experimental Examination of Peremptory Use and the Batson *Challenge Procedure*

Samuel R. Sommers and Michael I. Norton

> This case illustrates, once again, the difficulties confronting defense counsel and prosecutors, Massachusetts trial judges and appellate courts . . . despite vigilant efforts to eliminate race-based and other impermissible peremptory challenges, it is all too often impossible to establish whether a peremptory challenge has been exercised for an improper reason.
>
> Chief Justice Margaret Marshall, Massachusetts Supreme Judicial Court (*Commonwealth v. Maldonado,* 2003)

In selecting a jury, attorneys have two means at their disposal for removing members of the venire. First, they may issue a *challenge for cause,* an attempt to convince the judge that a prospective juror cannot be impartial. The second option is to use one of a limited number of *peremptory challenges,* which allow for exclusion of individuals without explanation or evidence of potential bias. Peremptory use in the United States was, in effect, unrestricted for two centuries before the Supreme Court ruled in 1986 that prospective jurors could not be challenged solely on the basis of membership in a "cognizable racial group"

SOURCE: Sommers, S. R., & Norton, M. I. (2007). Race-based judgments, race-neutral justifications: Experimental examination of peremptory use and the Batson Challenge Procedure. *Law and Human Behavior, 31*(3), 261–273.

(Batson v. Kentucky).[1] Subsequent rulings have extended *Batson* to apply to cases when the defendant and prospective juror are not of the same race *(Powers v. Ohio*, 1991) and to peremptories based on gender (*J. E. B. v. Alabama*, 1994).

The Court's willingness to break with precedent and change the very nature of the peremptory challenge is consistent with the conclusions that removal of venire members based on race violates a defendant's equal protection rights as well as the rights of the prospective jurors themselves. Such concerns are bolstered by evidence demonstrating the effects of racial composition on jury performance. Several archival analyses of real cases, mock juror experiments, and meta-analyses converge on the conclusion that jury racial composition—and, thus, the use of race-based peremptories—has the potential to affect decision-making processes and outcomes (e.g., Baldus, Woodworth, Zuckerman, Weiner, & Broffitt, 2001; Bowers, Steiner, & Sandys, 2001; Mitchell, Haw, Pfeifer, & Meissner, 2005; Sommers, 2006; Sommers & Ellsworth, 2003; Sweeney & Haney, 1992). In sum, both Constitutional and performance considerations suggest that *Batson* marked a significant step forward in the effort to curtail racial bias in the jury system.

Unfortunately, as illustrated by the excerpt with which we opened, it is less evident that the implementation of *Batson* has met its lofty objectives (Kovera, Dickinson, & Cutler, 2002). As we mark the 20th anniversary of the decision, many critical assumptions and questions regarding race and peremptory use have yet to be resolved. Intuition and theory suggest that race likely has an observable, pervasive influence on jury selection judgments, but such a causal relationship has not been confirmed through experimentation. Furthermore, though anecdotal and correlational evidence suggests that requiring attorneys to justify suspicious peremptory use—as is the practice post-*Batson*—fails to provide judges with information useful for identifying the influence of race, experimental manipulation remains essential for determining whether the race-neutrality typically conveyed in these justification indicates true colorblindness or rather the masking of bias. The present research provides such an experimental assessment of the influence of race on peremptory judgments and justifications.

Batson Challenges

As *Batson* placed the first practically meaningful restrictions on peremptory use, its enforcement necessitated a new two-step procedure. Specifically, when a defense attorney believes that her counterpart has based a peremptory challenge on race, she may now initiate a *Batson* challenge by establishing a prima facie case of racial discrimination.[2] If the trial judge is satisfied by these arguments, the burden shifts to the prosecution to articulate a race-neutral justification. It is ultimately left to the judge to determine whether the defense has proven its assertion that the prospective juror was excused because of race.

Thus, the *Batson* challenge procedure is based on two assumptions regarding race and

[1]The Court considered the issue of race and peremptory challenges 20 years earlier in *Swain v. Alabama* (1965). In denying Swain's appeal of his conviction and death sentence by an all-White jury, the Court agreed that systematic and intentional effort to exclude members of a racial group from jury service across several trials was not permissible, but ruled that such purposeful discrimination was not proven in Swain's case. Though this ruling outlined circumstances under which race-based peremptories would be unconstitutional, the decision had little practical effect as it set the bar for proving discrimination unattainably high.

[2]Though *Batson* applies to peremptories used by the prosecution in a criminal trial, subsequent rulings extended the prohibition to defense attorneys *(Powers v. Ohio*, 1991) and civil trials *(Edmonson v. Leesville Concrete Co.*, 1991). Nonetheless, the vast majority of *Batson* challenges are still levied against prosecutors in criminal trials (Melilli, 1996). As such, this investigation focuses on this most common form of *Batson* challenge.

jury selection judgments: (1) under some circumstances, a prospective juror's race influences attorneys' peremptory use, and (2) racial bias during jury selection can be reduced by requiring attorneys to justify suspicious peremptories. The first proposition, though unexamined by experimental design, is rather uncontroversial. It is well-established that the process of jury selection is often guided by attorneys' intuitions and stereotypes (Broderick, 1992; Kovera et al., 2002), and even the dissenting opinion in *Batson* conceded that at least in some instances, race likely affects peremptory use. Consistent with these conclusions, studies that have analyzed jury selection in actual criminal trials indicate that prosecutors are more likely than defense attorneys to exclude Black venire members, while the opposite is true for White venire members (Baldus et al., 2001; MeGonigle, Becka, LaFleur, & Wyatt, 2005; Rose, 1999; Turner, Lovell, Young, & Denny, 1986).

No published experiments have examined the second assumption above, that questioning attorneys is likely to elicit clear evidence of the influence of race, thereby facilitating the effort to curtail racial bias. Such a proposition would be supported either by evidence that attorneys readily admit to the influence of race, or that judges are able to distinguish genuinely race-neutral justifications from ostensibly neutral justifications that belie the influence of race. A review of the psychological literature on social judgment suggests that neither tendency is likely. Many researchers have demonstrated that people can offer compelling explanations for their behavior even when unaware of the factors—such as race—that are actually influential (e.g., Nisbett & Wilson, 1977; Norton, Vandello, & Darley, 2004; Shafir, Simonson, & Tversky, 1993). But even if attorneys consciously and strategically consider race during jury selection, they would be unlikely to admit it. Such an admission would have immediate consequences, as it would comprise a *Batson* violation. More generally, psychologists have noted that behavior is often influenced by the desire to appear nonprejudiced and to avoid the social sanctions that can follow from the appearance of racial bias (e.g., Gaertner & Dovidio, 1986; Norton, Sommers, Apfelbaum, Pura, & Ariely, in press; Plant & Devine, 1998; Sommers & Norton, 2006).

Analysis of actual *voir dire* proceedings supports the conclusions that attorneys are unlikely to cite race as influential and judges are unlikely to deem challenges to be in violation of *Batson*. Melilli (1996) examined every published decision of federal and state courts for the first 7 years after *Batson*, identifying 2,994 *Batson* challenges. In only 533 (17.8%) of these instances was the attorney unable to persuade the judge that the peremptory challenge in question was race-neutral, and in only 55 instances (1.8% of the sample) did the attorney admit that race influenced peremptory use (see also McGonigle et al., 2005; Raphael & Ungvarsky, 1993). Indeed, even before *Batson*, very few attorneys cited race in explaining their jury selection judgments. Diamond, Ellis, and Schmidt (1997) reported on a pre-*Batson* sample of 102 peremptory challenges in the U.S. District Court for the Northern District of Illinois (see also Diamond & Zeisel, 1974). Even absent explicit prohibitions against considering race, on only 8 occasions (7.8%) did attorneys cite a race-related reason for issuing a peremptory when interviewed by the researchers.[3]

One explanation for these findings is that race did not affect the challenges. However, this conclusion would be inconsistent with theoretical predictions and archival evidence regarding the influence of race on jury selection

[3]An even more direct test of the effects of *Batson* would examine the racial composition of juries before and after the decision, but as Diamond et al. (1997) observe, such an investigation has not been published. In a related analysis, Baldus et al. (2001) examined peremptory use in Philadelphia and found no reliable difference in the number of Black venire members challenged in the years preceding and following *Batson*.

judgments. As one—albeit egregious—example, consider that at the time of the Supreme Court's ruling in *Swain v. Alabama* (1965), no Black "within the memory of persons [then] living [had] ever served on any petit jury in any civil or criminal case tried in Talladega County, Alabama" (pp. 231–232). Moreover, such a conclusion that race is not influential would also stand in stark contrast to anecdotal evidence, such as prosecutorial jury selection manuals and training videos that emphasize the importance of considering race during *voir dire* (see Baldus et al., 2001; *Miller-El v. Dretke*, 2005). It would seem likely that race did bias many peremptories examined in the studies reviewed above, but attorney self-reports did not provide judges with sufficient evidence to find a *Batson* violation. To test these competing possibilities, the two assumptions underlying *Batson* must be considered simultaneously and experimentally. That is, a true assessment of the influence of race on jury selection must assess both the extent to which race affects peremptory use, as well as the usefulness of self-report for discerning this influence.

The Present Research

Psychological theory not only suggests that decision-makers infrequently admit to the influence of social category information such as race, but also demonstrates the ease with which ostensibly neutral explanations can be recruited to justify these judgments. For example, Norton et al. (2004) presented participants with a job hiring task that required choosing between male and female candidates for a stereotypically male job. In one condition the male had less work experience but more education than the female; in the other the male had more experience but less education. The majority of participants "hired" the male applicant regardless of qualifications, yet very few cited gender as influential. Instead, when the male was better educated, they listed education as the primary basis for their decision; when he had more experience, they used experience to justify their choice. Norton and colleagues interpret these findings as resulting from casuistry, the tendency to engage in specious reasoning to justify questionable behavior.

In combination with the broader psychological literature on social judgment, these findings suggest that reliance on judicial assessment of attorney self-reports is problematic on several counts. For one, self-report measures rarely capture the true influence of variables such as race. Furthermore, social judgments of the type made during jury selection are based on criteria so ambiguous and subjective that it is easy to generate race-neutral justifications in most cases (Norton, Sommers, Vandello, & Darley, 2006), a conclusion consistent with archival analyses of peremptory use (McGonigle et al., 2005; Melilli, 1996; Raphael & Ungvarsky, 1993). The present research examines these issues experimentally by exploring casuistry in the context of peremptory challenge judgments. Specifically, we address three questions: (1) To what extent does race affect jury selection judgments? (2) How accurately and completely do self-report measures capture this influence? (3) If decision-makers fail to report the influence of race on jury selection judgments, how do they justify their decisions?[4]

We used one experimental procedure and three participant populations. College students, advanced law students, and practicing

[4]We do not examine the other key empirical question surrounding race and jury selection, namely judges' accuracy in identifying *Batson* violations. Clearly, such a study would be of great interest, but it requires access to a specialized sample outside the scope of the present investigation. Because archival analyses indicate that only a small percentage of peremptories are ultimately rejected by judges, we focused instead on explaining why it is so difficult for judges to conclude that a challenge was based on race by identifying the psychological tendencies underlying peremptory use and justification.

attorneys were presented with information about a trial with a Black defendant, shown profiles of two prospective jurors, and asked to play the role of a prosecutor with one peremptory remaining. Our manipulation involved race: one prospective juror was identified as White and the other as Black, but this racial group membership varied across condition. In other words, for half of the participants, the first prospective juror was White and the second Black; for the other half, the first prospective juror was Black and the second White. Prospective jurors' background and *voir dire* responses remained identical across conditions. Of course, in actual jury selection, attorneys evaluate more than two members of the venire and their peremptory use is not limited to one either/or decision. The advantage of the present experimental design is the simplicity that enables conclusions regarding the extent to which race—and race alone—affects judgments. The aggregate data obtained allow for identification of systematic bias and comparison of the actual influence of race with self-reports of its influence. However, the important issue of generalizability to real trials is considered in more detail in the Discussion.

Experiment

Method

Trial Scenario

We created a summary of a robbery and aggravated assault trial in which the defendant allegedly beat a male homeowner with a blunt object after being confronted in the midst of a burglary. Because the victim could not identify his attacker, the prosecution's case relied on DNA, hair, and footprint analysis.

Pretesting

Forty-six college students were presented with the trial scenario and descriptions of seven prospective jurors. For each prospective juror, participants were asked to respond to the following statement on a scale of 1 *(strongly disagree)* to 9 *(strongly agree)*: "As a prosecutor, I would not want this individual on the jury." Each juror description included one characteristic that could be unattractive to a prosecutor. For example, one prospective juror reported that he believed O.J. Simpson was framed by police. The race of the defendant and jurors was not specified. Pretesting identified two prospective juror profiles that were rated as relatively comparable in terms of unattractiveness to a prosecutor: a journalist who wrote about police misconduct ($M = 7.85$) and an executive skeptical of statistics and forensic analysis ($M = 7.28$). We chose these two profiles for use in the experiment.

Prospective Juror Profiles

We expanded the pre-testing information for these two profiles, adding details regarding marital status, age, jury experience, educational background, and career history. In the final prospective juror profiles, Juror #1 was a 43-year-old married male with no previous jury experience. He was a journalist who, several years earlier, had written articles about police misconduct. Juror #2 was a 40-year-old divorced male who had served on two previous juries. He was an advertising executive with little scientific background who stated during *voir dire* that he was skeptical of statistics because they are easily manipulated. Both prospective jurors were described as having responded to *voir dire* questioning with clear statements that their personal experiences and beliefs would not prevent them from being impartial in the case.

Participants

College students. We first recruited a convenience sample of 90 undergraduates. The issues raised by the use of college participants in investigations of legal decision making have been detailed by numerous researchers (see Bornstein, 1999; MacCoun, 1989; Sommers & Ellsworth, 2001). In the domain of jury selection, however, research suggests that college students, law students, and even experienced trial attorneys demonstrate similar judgment styles and strategies in evaluating prospective jurors (Olczak, Kaplan, & Penrod, 1991). Of the 90 students who participated in partial completion of a course requirement, 63 (70%) were female; 65 (72%) identified themselves as White, 17 (19%) as Asian, 3 (3%) as Black, 1 (1%) as Latino, and 4 (4%) used other racial identifiers.[5]

Law students. We recruited a sample of 81 second- and third-year students at a Top-10 law school.[6] These students participated as part of a class exercise. Of the 81, 36 (45%) were female; 65 (80%) identified as White, 3 (4%) as Asian, 3 (4%) as Black, 2 (3%) as Latino, and 7 (9%) used other racial identifiers. Participant age ranged from 23–35 with an average of 26 years.

Attorneys. We recruited 28 practicing attorneys with jury trial experience (M = 3.1 jury trials; range = 1–15). Attorneys were recruited through personal contact and participated on a voluntary basis. Of the 28, 13 (46%) were female; 22 (79%) identified as White, 3 (11%) as Asian, 2 (7%) used other racial identifiers, and 1 did not identify race. Participant age ranged from 26–63 with an average of 38 years.

Procedure

Participants were given a questionnaire with instructions to assume the role of a prosecuting attorney. They were then presented with the trial scenario described above, along with a photo of the defendant, a 24-year-old Black male (the race of the victim remained unspecified). College participants were provided

Table 6.3 Peremptory Challenge Use by Prospective Juror Race Across Three Participant Samples

	Juror #1		Juror #2	
	When Black(%)	When White(%)	When Black(%)	When White(%)
College students (n = 90)	80	59	41	20
Law students (n = 81)	73	51	49	27
Attorneys (n = 28)	79	43	57	21

NOTE: Values represent the percentage of participants who chose to excuse the prospective juror. One prospective juror was always depicted as Black and the other as White, thus the first and last columns present the two prospective jurors presented to participants in one experimental condition (and sum to 100%), and the second and third column represent the two prospective jurors presented to participants in the other condition.

[5]As our focus is not limited to the judgments of individuals of a particular race, results are based on data from all participants. Across the three samples, analyses indicated no significant between-race differences in responses.

[6]Per 2006 ratings from *U.S. News and World Report*, available at http://www.usnews.com/usnews/edu/grad/rankings/law/brief/lawrank_brief.php.

with background information about the jury selection process, information that was not given to the two legal samples. They were told that as a prosecutor they would be able to eliminate a certain number of prospective jurors "because (a) you don't think they would be able to be fair jurors or (b) you do not think they would be sympathetic to your case." Instructions for the law students and attorneys simply stated, "As a prosecutor, you will be able to eliminate a certain number of individuals using peremptory challenges."

The second page of the questionnaire included the two prospective juror profiles, each with a photograph. In one condition Juror #1 was depicted as Black and Juror #2 as White. In the other condition, information about Jurors #1 and #2 remained the same, but #1 was depicted as White and #2 as Black. The third page informed participants that they had one challenge remaining and required them to identify which prospective juror they would excuse. An open-ended question then instructed them to explain to the trial judge why they challenged the individual they did. Finally, for college participants only, we were able to assess direct perceptions of the two prospective jurors by obtaining a rating of how likely it would have been for each individual to vote guilty after the trial, on a scale of 1 *(very unlikely)* to 7 *(very likely)*.

Discussion

Across three samples, this investigation provides clear empirical evidence that a prospective juror's race can influence peremptory challenge use and that self-report justifications are unlikely to be useful for identifying this influence—findings that are strikingly similar in direction as well as magnitude to the conclusions of archival analyses of real peremptory use (e.g., Baldus et al., 2001; McGonigle et al., 2005). College students, law students, and attorneys playing the role of a prosecutor trying a case with a Black defendant were more likely to challenge a prospective juror when he was Black as opposed to White; mediational analyses using college participants indicated that beliefs about the prospective jurors' predispositions towards the case drove this effect. When justifying these judgments, participants rarely cited race as influential, focusing instead on the race-neutral characteristics associated with the Black prospective juror. That is, when Juror #l was Black, participants tended to justify their judgments by citing his familiarity with police misconduct as their reason for excluding him. When Juror #2 was Black, on the other hand, participants reported his skepticism about statistics to be more important than the police misconduct issue. These data serve as important experimental validation of the correlational and anecdotal conclusions of previous researchers regarding race and jury selection processes.

The practical implications of these findings are clear: even when attorneys consider race during jury selection, there is little reason to believe that judicial questioning will produce information useful for identifying this bias. Because judgments such as those made during jury selection are based on multiple, subjective criteria, myriad justifications are typically available (Norton et al., 2006). In fact, recent Supreme Court decisions have held that a peremptory justification need not be plausible nor even relevant to the case in question for it to comply with *Batson,* as long as it is literally race-neutral (Page, 2005). Justifications for peremptories therefore leave judges with little basis for rejecting them, as demonstrated by archival analyses (Melilli, 1996; Raphael & Ungvarsky, 1993). Even in extreme instances of bias—such as the exclusion of every Black member of the venire—the present findings imply that it would be relatively easy to generate multiple, race-neutral justifications. We observed bias against Black venire members only when examining decisions made by several participants; indeed, for any given participant, we are unable to determine whether the peremptory was influenced by race or whether the justification provided was valid. Only in the aggregate does evidence of racial bias emerge, and in the real world, such data are often unavailable.

One of the few instances when it seems possible for biased peremptory use to be identified is when an attorney challenges a Black member of the venire on the basis of characteristics also possessed by an empaneled White juror (Melilli, 1996; Raphael & Ungvarsky, 1993). Such occurrences provide the judge with aggregate data across juror race—the same type of data examined in the current investigation. But even when such comparisons are available, the determination of racial bias remains no easy task. Consider, for example, the *Maldonado* (2003) case from our opening quotation. When the district attorney was questioned about using peremptories for the only two African Americans in the venire, she explained that she challenged one individual because he was 55 years old and childless. The judge pressed further, reminding her that Whites without children were not similarly challenged. But even when confronted with this argument, the attorney responded as follows: "It's just a feeling. That's why I used my peremptory. I mean it's not because of his color. It's certainly not that" (Burge, 2003).

Another example is provided by the recent Supreme Court decision in *Miller-El* v. *Dretke* (2005), which includes close analysis of the questioning of Billy Jean Fields, a Black member of the venire challenged by the prosecution. During *voir dire,* Fields professed support for the death penalty and stated that its administration is consistent with God's will. In justifying the challenge of Fields, the prosecutor cited concern about his religious and death penalty beliefs, even though Fields seemed to be a stronger proponent of capital punishment than many of the empaneled Whites. Whereas the Court majority cited this example as evidence that the peremptory was based on race, the dissenting opinion suggested that the challenge was more ambiguous. Quoting different excerpts from the same *voir dire,* the dissenting Justices concluded that Fields was, in many respects, unattractive to the prosecution. Furthermore, they argued that other race-neutral factors, including the order in which prospective jurors were questioned, provide legitimate justification for the challenge. These contradictory opinions based on the same *voir dire* provide further support for our conclusion that the subjectivity underlying peremptory challenges renders it extremely difficult for judges to reach conclusive determinations of racial bias.

Once again, though, our findings are consistent with those of more generalizable correlational studies. Moreover, as our discussion of *Maldonado* (2003) and *Miller-El* (2005) demonstrates, an increased number of prospective jurors and juror characteristics in a case do not necessarily make it easier to detect racial bias. We might also suggest, albeit speculatively, that the pressure to deny or disguise the influence of race on jury selection judgments would be far greater during actual interrogation from a trial judge than it was in the present paradigm, indicating that our findings may underestimate the effects of race (and the difficulty inherent in identifying these effects) in real *voir dire* settings.

Future Questions

The present studies also raise interesting questions for future consideration. We focused this investigation on prosecutorial peremptory use since the vast majority of *Batson* challenges continue to be levied against prosecutors who exclude Black prospective jurors (Melilli, 1996). Nonetheless, it would be useful to determine whether similar processes are exhibited by a prosecutor trying a case with a White defendant, or by defense attorneys (see Baldus el al., 2001 for archival analysis of these variables). Such investigations would generalize the present conclusions, and could also confirm that the present data do not simply reflect a general belief that Black jurors are always inferior jurors.

Conclusion

Intuition, anecdote, and psychological theory suggest that race affects jury selection judgments, though identifying this influence is difficult. The present investigation tests these assumptions empirically, providing the first experimental evidence of a causal relationship between race, peremptory challenge use, and peremptory justification. This research also sheds light on the potential psychological processes through which race exerts its influence. Specifically, the present data suggest that decision makers are remarkably facile at recruiting race-neutral characteristics to justify jury selection judgments, and this tendency poses a threat to current restrictions on peremptory use. Finally, it is worth emphasizing that our findings do not identify limitations specific only to the *Batson* challenge procedure, but rather suggest more generally that the very idea of using self-report measures to assess and curtail the influence of race on legal judgment is untenable.

References

Baldus, D. C., Woodworth, G. G., Zuckerman, D., Weiner. N. A., & Broffit, B. (2001). The use of peremptory challenges in capital murder trials: A legal and empirical analysis. *University of Pennsylvania Journal of Constitutional Law, 3,* 3–169.

Batson v. Kentucky (1986). 476 U.S. 79.

Bornstein, B. H. (1999). The ecological validity of jury simulations: Is the jury still out? *Law and Human Behavior, 23,* 75–91.

Bowers, W. J., Steiner, B. D., & Sandys, M. (2001). Death sentencing in Black and White: An empirical analysis of jurors' race and jury racial composition. *University of Pennsylvania Journal of Constitutional Law, 3,* 171–275.

Broderick, R. J. (1992). Why the peremptory challenge should be abolished. *Temple Law Review, 65,* 369–423.

Burge, K. (May 24, 2003). SJC urges limits on juror rejections, *Boston Globe,* p. Al.

Commonwealth v. Maldonado (2003). No. SJC-08878 (Mass. SJC May 23).

Diamond, S. S., Ellis, L., & Schmidt, E. (1997). Realistic responses to the limitations of *Batson v. Kentucky. Cornell Journal of Law and Public Policy, 7,* 77–95.

Diamond, S. S., & Zeisel, H. (1974). A courtroom experiment on juror selection and decision-making. *Personality and Social Psychology Bulletin, 1,* 276–277.

Edmonson v. Leesville Concrete Co. (1991). 500 U.S. 614.

Gaertner, S. L., & Dovidio, J. F. (1986). The aversive form of racism. In J. Dovidio & S. Gaertner (Eds.), *Prejudice, discrimination, and racism* (pp. 61–89). Orlando, EL: Academic Press.

J. E. B. v. Alabama (1994). 511 U.S, 127.

Kovera, M. B., Dickinson, J. J., & Cutler, B. L. (2002). *Voir dire* and jury selection. In A. M. Goldstein (Ed.), *Comprehensive handbook of psychology, Volume II: Forensic psychology* (pp. 161–175). New York: John Wiley and Sons.

MacCoun, R. J. (1989). Experimental research on jury decision-making. *Science, 244,* 1046–1050.

McGonigle, S., Becka, H., LaFleur, R., & Wyatt, T. (2005). Striking differences. *Dallas Morning News.* Retrieved March 15, 2006 from http://www.dallasnews.com/s/dws/spe/2005/jury/index-jury.html

Melilli, K. J. (1996). *Batson* in practice: What we have learned about *Batson* and peremptory challenges. *Notre Dame Law Review, 71,* 447–503.

Miller-El v. Dretke (2005). 545 U.S.

Mitchell, T. L., Haw, R. M., Pfeifer, J. E., & Meissner, C. A. (2005). Racial bias in mock juror decision-making: A meta-analytic review of defendant treatment. *Law and Human Behavior, 29,* 621–637.

Nisbett, R. E., & Wilson, T. D. (1977). Telling more than we can know. *Psychological Review, 84,* 231–259.

Norton, M. I., Sommers. S. R., Apfelbaum, E. P., Pura, N., & Ariely, D. (in press). Colorblindness and interracial interaction: Playing the "political correctness game." *Psychological Science.*

Norton, M. I., Sommers, S. R., Vandello, J. A., & Darley, J. M. (2006). Mixed motives and racial bias: The impact of legitimate and illegitimate criteria on decision-making. *Psychology, Public Policy, and Law, 12,* 36–55.

Norton, M. I., Vandello, J. A., & Darley, J. M. (2004). Casuistry and social category bias. *Journal of Personality and Social Psychology, 87,* 817–831.

Olczak, P. V., Kaplan, M. F., & Penrod, S. (1991). Attorneys' lay psychology and its effectiveness in selecting jurors: Three empirical studies. *Journal of Social Behavior and Personality, 6,* 431–452.

Page, A. (2005). Bauson's blind-spot: Unconscious stereotyping and the peremptory challenge. *Boston University Law Review, 85,* 155–262.

Plant, E. A., & Devine, P. G. (1998). Internal and external motivation to respond without prejudice. *Journal of Personality and Social Psychology, 69,* 811–832.

Powers v. *Ohio* (1991). 499 U.S. 400.

Raphael, M. J., & Ungvarsky, E. J. (1993). Excuses, excuses: Neutral explanations under *Batson v. Kentucky. University of Michigan Journal of Law Reform, 27,* 229–275.

Rose, M. R. (1999). The peremptory challenge accused of race or gender discrimination? Some data from one county. *Law and Human Behavior, 23,* 695–702.

Shafir, E., Simonson, I., & Tversky, A. (1993). Reason-based choice. *Cognition, 49,* 11–36.

Sommers, S. R. (2006). On racial diversity and group decision-making: Identifying multiple effects of racial composition on jury deliberations. *Journal of Personality and Social Psychology, 90,* 597–612.

Sommers, S. R., & Ellsworth, P. C. (2001). White juror bias: An investigation of racial prejudice against Black defendants in the American courtroom. *Psychology, Public Polity, and Law, 7,* 201–229.

Sommers, S. R., & Ellsworth, P. C. (2003). How much do we really know about race and juries? A review of social science theory and research. *Chicago-Kent Law Review, 78,* 997–1031.

Sommers, S. R., & Norton, M. I. (2006). Lay theories about White racists: What constitutes racism (and what doesn't). *Group Processes and Intergroup Relations, 9,* 117–138.

Swain v. Alabama (1965). 380 U.S, 202.

Sweeney, L. T., & Haney, C. (1992). The influence of race on sentencing: A meta-analytic review of experimental studies. *Behavioral Sciences and the Law, 10,* 179–195.

Turner, B. M., Lovell, R. D., Young, J. D., & Denny, W. P. (1986). Race and peremptory challenges during *voir dire*: Do prosecution and defense agree? *Journal of Criminal Justice, 14,* 61–69.

DISCUSSION QUESTIONS

1. Do you think that the *Batson* decision effectively addressed the issue of racial bias during the *voir dire* process? Why or why not?

2. Why do the authors decided to use an experimental procedure in order to study the effect of race when deciding whether to use peremptory challenges? Would you have studied this phenomenon differently? Explain.

3. Did the authors find that race was a factor used when deciding whether to use a preemptory challenge? Do you believe that the way the study was conducted could have influenced the findings? Why or why not?

READING

For decades, scholars and activists have argued that the key to solving some of the racial disparities in the criminal justice system rests on diversifying the workers in the system. In policing, this created a big push to hire a more diverse police force and to also promote qualified Blacks within police organizations. In the courts, there has been a sizeable body of literature that examines the impact of the diversification of the judiciary; however, there has been less of an emphasis on the diversification of all levels of workers in the courts. The authors examine whether the presence of Black workers in the federal district court system reduces sentencing disparities. They also examine the influence of the diversification of probation officers and whether this also impacts racial disparities in sentencing. While the results suggest that Black defendants do positively benefits from a diversified federal court workforce, there were some less promising results as they pertain to the increased presence of Black probation officers.

Race Effects of Representation Among Federal Court Workers

Does Black Workforce Representation Reduce Sentencing Disparities?

Amy Farrell, Geoff Ward, and Danielle Rousseau

The significance of racial and ethnic diversity among court workers has escaped close attention in sentencing research considering assumptions about its symbolic and substantive significance to court decision making. Studies tend to be limited to examining racial and ethnic characteristics of individual decision makers and sole categories of workers (especially judges), without considering broader workforce and racial and ethnic group relations of which these are a part. These oversights may limit understanding of diversity in the justice workforce, including the race effect of court workforce representation on sentencing and other outcomes.

This article employs data on the district-level racial diversity of federal courts to consider whether more equitable black representation among decision makers increases racial parity in the sentencing of black and white defendants. Our model is distinguished from prior research in two ways. First, we consider how racial group representation among several categories of federal court workers—judges, prosecutors, defenders, and probation officers—relates to sentencing. Second, we conceptualize

Source: Farrell, A., Ward, G., and Rousseau, D. (2009). Race effects of representation among federal court workers: Does black workforce representation reduce sentencing disparities? *Annals of the American Academy of Political and Social Science, 623*, 121–133.

representation as a contextual characteristic of courts. Whereas prior research has focused on diversity—proportions of blacks and other minorities among decision makers—our model asks whether racially equitable statistical representation among court workers relates to racially equitable court outcomes.

Prior research on racial and ethnic group diversity in justice administration mainly focuses on whether race differentiates attitudes and behaviors of individual actors, such as prison workers, police, and judges (for a review, see Ward 2006). Results of these studies are mixed and inconclusive. Status characteristics of workers, including race, hold limited significance in comparison to occupational roles, political ideology, and professional goals (Raganella and White 2004), but minorities do bring distinct perspectives to bear on the idea and practice of justice (Bennett and Johnson 2000). Research is similarly inconclusive regarding consequences of decision maker diversity on justice processes and outcomes. Several studies find no substantial race of decision maker effect on outcomes (Mastrofski, Reisig, and McCluskey 2002; Spohn 1990a, 1990b), while others report significant but marginal effects (Holmes et al, 1993; Johnson 2006; Schanzenbach 2005; Scherer 2004; Steffensmeier and Britt 2001). This inconsistency may reflect limits in the conceptualization and measurement of decision maker diversity and its relation to justice processes and outcomes (Ifill 2000; Scherer 2004). In this article, we aim to advance research on the significance of diversity in justice-related occupations by considering race effects of racial group representation among several categories of federal court workers on federal criminal sentencing severity and disparity.

Race, Representation, and Sentencing in Federal Courts

Sentencing research has established that social organizational factors influence decision making in courts (Ulmer 1997; Ulmer and Johnson 2004; Ulmer and Kramer 1996). The "court community" concept has been used to describe how court organizations vary according to contextual characteristics internal and external to courts. These characteristics form the basis of "subcultures of justice" that may develop among court workgroups and court organizations overall. These can, in turn, affect court processing and outcomes (Dixon 1995; Nardulli, Eisenstein, and Flemming 1988). While many factors have been associated with court organization, research has yet to adequately consider the contextual significance of workforce racial and ethnic diversity to court subcultures and case outcomes. Design limitations of existing decision-maker diversity research contribute to this gap in the understanding of court communities.

Existing research on diversity in courts and other contexts of justice administration generally lacks social contextualization, limiting its conceptualization and measurement of racial and ethnic group representation in decision making. Research on decision-maker diversity and court outcomes has neglected to consider racial group representation among multiple categories of workers involved in shaping outcomes. While court studies have typically focused on the diversity of the judiciary (Scherer 2004; Spohn 1990a, 1990b; Steffensmeier and Britt 2001), sentence outcomes may be significantly influenced by the attitudes and decisions of several other court actors. This is especially likely in courts where structured decision making has limited and displaced the discretion of judges. Research demonstrates that structured sentencing systems, such as federal sentencing guidelines, do not eliminate discretion, but shift authority from judges to nonjudicial actors, particularly prosecutors, whose decisions about the severity and number of charges have the most direct effect on sentencing (e.g., Engen and Steen 2000; Steffensmeier and Demuth 2000). Following adjudication, federal prosecutors and defenders can influence sentencing, by advocating directly with the judge to increase or reduce sentences within the guideline range, arguing for or against departures from the guidelines to reduce sentence outcomes, and controlling the evidence introduced throughout the sentencing process. Like attorneys, federal probation officers also serve important yet often overlooked roles in federal courts, with implications for sentencing. These include providing presentencing investigation reports that judges consult in sentencing decisions and making decisions about probation violations (Bridges and Steen 1998; Kingsnorth et al, 1998).

Despite the importance of these and other court actors, decision-maker diversity research generally ignores the role of nonjudicial actors in sentencing. In the federal contexts, some research examines prosecutorial discretion generally (Miller and Eisenstein 2005; Misner 1996) as well as the impact of guideline sentencing on defense counsel (Hall 1999) and probation officer activity (D'Anca 2001). Yet no study that we have found considers racial group representation among these workers and its potential relation to race-related court outcomes.

The challenge is not merely to assess individual-level differences among nonjudicial actors but to incorporate multiple categories of workers in measures of workforce diversity (Ward 2006). Given the established importance of "workgroups" to decision making in courts, decision-making *groups* seem to be the appropriate contextual unit for assessing the race effect of representation in sentencing (Nardulli, Eisenstein, and Flemming 1988). Our analysis considers racial diversity within multiple categories of court workers—judges, prosecutors, defense attorneys, and probation officers—as a means of assessing the influence of racial group *workforce representation.* Because we lack data on the specific workers who form decision-making groups in specific cases, we conceptualize workgroups as occupationally defined collectives and use the term *workforce*, rather than *workgroup*, to emphasize this focus.

We also contextualize our analysis of court workforce racial diversity by considering racial demographics of the population served by the court. Rather than measuring diversity as a basic proportional characteristic of courts, our model considers whether racially *representative* courts yield more racially equitable case outcomes. To do so, we ground our measures of diversity among court workers by comparing them to diversity in the population, resulting in a basic measure of statistical representation. Calls for increasing diversity among criminal justice decision makers often suggest that doing so will symbolically and substantively enhance the quality and legitimacy of justice administration, in part by infusing the interests, sensibilities, and skill sets of a more representative cross-section of society (Pope and Lovell 2000; U.S. Department of Justice 2003). However, there has been little effort to determine what constitutes a "representative" court workforce, or what forms or degrees of workforce diversity yield specific symbolic or substantive outcomes. We theorize that variable levels of racial and ethnic group representation within and across categories of workers may meaningfully differentiate court organizations, with implications for sentencing outcomes.

More equitable racial and ethnic group representation among decision makers is typically expected to benefit minority groups. Such group representation in criminal justice decision making, for example, is advocated as a means to advance symbolic and substantive interests of underrepresented groups, including equitable court outcomes (Kerner Commission 1968; U.S. Department of Justice 2003). While research evidence is limited and mixed, some of it indicates that racially representative courts may mitigate inequality in the administration of justice (Bridges and Steen 1998; Holmes et al, 1993; Scherer 2004). Scholarship focused on other public and private sectors also suggests that active representation in decision making yields more substantively fair and symbolically legitimate processes (Krislov 1974; Thomas and Ely 2001). As black Americans have historically been subject to unwarranted disparity in sentencing severity, we consider whether greater black representation among various federal court decision makers corresponds with less disparity between the sentences of white and black defendants. We test the following general hypothesis:

> Disparities between black and white defendants in the likelihood of being sentenced to prison are reduced in districts with greater black representation among judges, prosecutors, defenders, and probation officers.

Research Design and Methods

The current research uses a series of multilevel models to consider how individual defendant characteristics; the social context of the court; and levels of racial group representation among judges, prosecutors, defenders, and probation officers relate to district-level differences in sentencing. Individual defendant case decisions were obtained through the Monitoring Federal Criminal Sentencing (MFCS) data acquired from the United States Sentencing Commission, which include information on all federal cases sentenced between October 1, 2000, and September 30, 2002. The MFCS data contain information on case-level factors such as offender characteristics, offense severity, criminal history background, other relevant guidelines, court processing information, and the sentence imposed. Because we are interested in examining the effect of black courtroom representation on the sentencing of black defendants, we include only cases with non-Hispanic black or white defendants ($N = 51{,}782$). This final sample also excludes cases that have missing data for any variable in the analyses (8.5 percent of all cases).

Discussion and Conclusion

This study advances our understanding of the contextual determinants of sentencing by considering race effects of federal court workforce representation on federal criminal sentencing severity and disparity. We find that variation in racial group representation in court organizations is moderately related to the likelihood of imprisonment and racial disparities in this likelihood. Black defendants are more likely to be sentenced to prison than their white counterparts, even after controlling for legally relevant variables, but when black defendants are sentenced in districts with increased representation of black prosecutors, they have a decreased likelihood of being imprisoned, which results in more racially equitable sentences. We find the opposite effect of black representation among probation officers. For judges and defense attorneys, racial representation has no impact on disparities in being sentenced to prison. These analyses do not explain why variation in racial representation among decision-making groups differentially affects sentence outcomes. This question awaits further research. Nonetheless, our findings illustrate (1) the need to conceptualize workforce diversity as a complex group dynamic and (2) the value of considering an array of decision-making groups who weigh in on sentencing outcomes.

Black defendants are more likely to be sentenced to prison than their white counterparts, even after controlling for legally relevant variables, but when black defendants are sentenced in districts with increased representation of black prosecutors, they have a decreased likelihood of being imprisoned, resulting in more racially equitable sentences.

Our conclusions are also tempered by research limitations. This is a study of workforce representation and sentencing comparing only blacks and whites in the federal court context within a particular period. Our models also consider sentencing decisions under strict federal guidelines. Different dynamics likely exist in other court contexts, such as juvenile or state courts, or in different time periods. For example, we do not know how these relationships are unfolding now that guidelines have become advisory. Furthermore, one needs to go beyond a focus on sentencing to understand disparities in justice processing. Police and other criminal justice officials with varying levels of racial representation make decisions at earlier stages that impact selection into prosecution and sentencing. Finally, our models only identify relationships between court workforce representation, sentence severity, and racial parity in sentence outcomes, controlling for certain case and context characteristics; they do not *explain* how the orientations and behaviors of courtroom workgroups are related to race and specific case outcomes. More in-depth qualitative and quantitative research is needed to understand how racial and ethnic diversity in courtroom workgroups relates to the "social world of sentencing" (Ulmer 1997).

Despite limitations, this study offers a wide-angle view of federal court workforce representation in the United States and its relation to criminal sentencing outcomes. Our modeling of workforce representation across multiple categories of court workers in relation to population advances sociological understanding on the substantive significance of decision-maker racial diversity. At the same time, the study has policy relevance. It suggests that greater representation of workers of color in the justice system can contribute to more equitable treatment of racial groups. Specifically, equity would be improved with greater representation of blacks among prosecutors. Yet tradeoffs are possible given the countervailing, albeit smaller, effect of racial representation among probation officers in increasing black–white disparities in imprisonment. Future theoretical and empirical research on multiple justice-related occupation and decision points will help to advance understanding of the influence of the racial and ethnic composition of the justice workforce on the administration of equal justice.

References

Bennett, Katherine, and Wesley Johnson, 2000. African American wardens: Managerial perspectives and attitudes. *Corrections Management Quarterly* 4:52–63.

Bridges, George S., and Sara Steen, 1998. Racial disparities in official assessments of juvenile offenders: Attributional stereotypes as mediating mechanisms. *American Sociological Review* 63:554–70.

D'Anca, Alfred, 2001. The role of the federal probation officer in the guidelines sentencing system. *Federal Probation* 65:65–67.

Dixon, Jo, 1995. The organizational context of criminal sentencing. *American Journal of Sociology* 100: 1157–98.

Engen, Rodney, and Sarah Steen, 2000. The power to punish: Discretion and sentencing reform in the war on drugs. *American Journal of Sociology* 105:1357–95.

Hall, Joseph, 1999. Guided to injustice? The effect of the sentencing guidelines on indigent defendants and public defense. *American Criminal Law Review* 36:1331–70.

Holmes, Malcolm, Harmon M. Hosch, Howard C. Daudistel, Dolores A. Perez, and Joseph B. Graves, 1993. Judges' ethnicity and minority sentencing: Evidence concerning Hispanics. *Social Science Quarterly* 74:496–506.

Ifill, Sherrilyn, 2000. Racial diversity on the bench: Beyond role models and public confidence. *Washington and Lee Law Review* 57:405–95.

Johnson, Brian, 2006. The multilevel context of criminal sentencing: Integrating judge and county-level influences. *Criminology* 44:259–98.

Kerner Commission, 1968. *Report of the National Advisory Commission on Civil Disorders*. Washington, DC: Government Printing Office.

Kingsnorth, Rodney, Debra Cummings, John Lopez, and Jennifer Wentworth, 1998. Criminal sentencing and court probation officers: The myth of individualized justice revisited. *Justice System Journal* 20:255–73.

Krislov, Samuel, 1974. *Representative bureaucracy*. Englewood Cliffs, NJ: Prentice Hall.

Mastrofski, Stephan, Michael Reisig, and John McCluskey, 2002. Police disrespect toward the public: An encounter-based analysis. *Criminology* 40:519–52.

Miller, Lisa, and James Eisenstein, 2005. The federal/state criminal prosecution nexus: A case study in cooperation and discretion. *Law and Social Inquiry* 30:239–68.

Misner, Robert, 1996. Recasting prosecutorial discretion. *Journal of Criminal Law and Criminology* 86:717–77.

Nardulli, Peter, James Eisenstein, and Roy Flemming, 1988. *The tenor of justice: Criminal courts and the guilty plea process.* Urbana: University of Illinois Press.

Pope, Carl, and Rick Lovell, 2000. *Synthesis of disproportionate minority confinement (DMC) literature.* Washington, DC: U.S. Department of Justice.

Raganella, Anthony, and Michael White, 2004. Race, gender, and motivation for becoming a police officer: Implications for building a representative police department. *Journal of Criminal Justice* 32:501–13.

Schanzenbach, Max, 2005. Racial and sex disparities in prison sentences: The effect of district-level judicial demographics. *Journal of Legal Studies* 34:57–88.

Scherer, Nancy, 2004. Blacks on the bench. *Political Science Quarterly* 119:655–74.

Spohn, Cassia, 1990a. Decision making in sexual assault cases: Do black and female judges make a difference? *Women and Criminal Justice* 2:83–105.

———, 1990b. The sentencing decisions of black and white judges expected and unexpected similarities. *Law and Society Review* 24:1197–1216.

Steffensmeier, Darrell, and Chester Britt, 2001. Judge's race and judicial decision making: Do black judges sentence differently? *Social Science Quarterly* 82:749–64.

Steffensmeier, Darrell, and Stephen Demuth, 2000. Ethnicity and sentencing outcomes in the U.S. federal courts: Who is punished more harshly? *American Sociological Review* 65:705–29.

Thomas, David, and Robin Ely, 2001. Cultural diversity at work: The effects of diversity perspectives on work group processes and outcomes. *Administrative Science Quarterly* 46:229–66.

Ulmer, Jeffery T, 1997. *Social worlds of sentencing: Court communities under sentencing guidelines.* Albany: State University of New York Press.

Ulmer, Jeffery T., and Brian Johnson, 2004. Sentencing in context: A multilevel analysis. *Criminology* 42:137–77.

Ulmer, Jeffery T., and John H. Kramer, 1996. Court communities under sentencing guidelines: Dilemmas of formal rationality and sentencing disparity. *Criminology* 34:383–407.

U.S. Department of Justice, 2003. Justice department initiates new diversity program. Press release 03-070, February 5. Washington, DC: U.S. Department of Justice.

Ward, Geoff, 2006. Race and the justice workforce: A system perspective. In *The many colors of crime: Inequalities of race, ethnicity, and crime in America,* ed. R. Peterson, L. Krivo, and J. Hagan, 67–87. New York: New York University Press.

DISCUSSION QUESTIONS

1. Which factors do you believe could help explain the authors' findings that there were less racial disparities in sentencing in districts with higher numbers of Black prosecutors?
2. What type of policy changes should be advocated for based on the findings of this study? Explain.
3. Does the authors' decision to examine the representation of just Blacks and Whites in the federal court system limit the findings of this study? Why or why not?

READING

Asian Americans have largely been left out of the race and crime discussion. This is likely because they tend to be underrepresented in official measures of crime and victimization. Thus, even as it relates to criminal justice, they are considered the "model minority." This article explores the sentencing of Asian Americans in federal district courts. The researchers found that the sentencing patterns of Asian Americans mirrored those of Whites as opposed to the patterns of Hispanics and Blacks. In short, the authors found that the model minority label was a positive attribute in federal district courts and resulted in leniency toward Asian American defendants—particularly those born in the United States.

Punishing the "Model Minority"

Asian-American Criminal Sentencing Outcomes in Federal District Courts

Brian D. Johnson and Sara Betsinger

Social discourse on race relations in the legal system represents a major undertaking of contemporary scholarship in criminology and law. Historically, its purview has been restricted to the dichotomy between black and white. This limited approach is manifest in classic sociological and criminological treatments of racial inequality and discrimination in the justice system (e.g., Blumstein, 1982; Hacker, 1995; Hagan and Albonetti, 1982; Kerner Commission, 1968; Piliavin and Briar, 1964; Sellin, 1935). Although more contemporary work argues persuasively for expanding the racial ken to include Hispanic ethnicity (e.g., Albonetti, 1997; Martinez, 2002; Steffensmeier and Demuth, 2000; Zatz, 1984), conspicuously little attention is devoted to Asian-American offenders—discrimination and inequality among Asian Americans in the justice system remain virtually uninvestigated. Although shifting population demographics clearly highlight the need for broader approaches to racial dynamics in society, the traditional focus on blacks and Hispanics remains the dominant research paradigm. This persists despite widespread acknowledgment of "the need to develop better information concerning the punishment of racial and ethnic minorities other than those that are most sizable" (Ruth and Reitz, 2003: 32). The current study argues for the theoretical and empirical importance of examining criminal punishments for Asian-American offenders, and it offers the first systematic investigation of racial disparities in sentencing for this often overlooked minority group within the federal justice system.

The lack of attention paid to the treatment of Asian-American groups in the criminal justice system is noteworthy given their increasing prominence. According to recent U.S. Census figures, the population of Asian Americans has increased steadily during the past several decades, approximately doubling between 1980 and 1990 (from 3.7 to 7.3 million) and expanding to 11.9 million by 2000 (Barnes and Bennett, 2002). In fact, the percent increase in population size for Asian Americans in the past two decades has been greater than for any other racial or ethnic group. Not only has the Asian-American population been growing rapidly, but also the population of Asian Americans in federal and state prisons has increased appreciably in recent years. Recent estimates suggest that nearly 10,000 Asian-American offenders are in prison (Stephan and Karberg, 2003). As the fastest growing minority group in the United States, now constituting a sizeable incarcerated population, research on the criminal processing of Asian offenders is timely and needed.

The absence of scholarship on Asian offenders is unfortunate given their unique niche in contemporary race relations in American society. Whereas blacks and Hispanics occupy socially disadvantaged socioeconomic positions (McKinnon and Bennett, 2005; Ramirez, 2004), the relative standing of Asian Americans tends to be much closer to the white majority. Relative to other minority groups, Asian Americans have a higher mean level of education, they have lower rates of poverty and unemployment, and they are underrepresented in official crime statistics (Reeves and Bennett, 2004; Sampson and Lauritsen, 1997). Unlike other minority groups who have been demonstrated to have negative stereotypes associated with them in the criminal justice system (Bridges and Steen, 1998), Asian Americans have, at least in recent years, been favorably perceived in popular discourse. As one prominent scholar has noted, "The academic achievement of [Asian] American children has gained public attention, resulting in a positive stereotype as a model minority" (Zhou, 2000: 331). This epithet carries with it different connotations from those of other racial and ethnic groups, which suggests that the treatment of Asian offenders in the justice system may differ in important ways from other minority groups. Given their unique status, an examination of the criminal processing of this understudied racial group offers an important opportunity to expand current research and theorizing on racial and ethnic disparities in criminal punishment.

Using sentencing data from the United States Sentencing Commission (USSC), the current study examines the treatment of Asian-American offenders in the federal justice system. In doing so, it contributes to the extensive literature on the sociology of punishment by broadening current discourse and conceptualizations of racial and ethnic disparities, by examining criminal sentences for a variety of offense types in U.S. federal district courts, and by clarifying the theoretical linkages among conflict, consensus, and organizational perspectives on criminal court decision making. It begins with a review of extant literature on racial and ethnic effects in sentencing, followed by a theoretical depiction of the Asian-American "model minority" stereotype. It then develops competing theoretical hypotheses about the treatment of Asian-American offenders and proceeds to test them by examining key decision-making outcomes in federal district courts.

Race/Ethnicity and Criminal Sentencing Outcomes

Few topics have received as much attention from criminal justice researchers as the presence of racial and ethnic disparities in criminal sentencing. A vast and growing literature focuses on the extent to which white offenders receive beneficial treatment at sentencing (e.g., Albonetti, 1997; Bridges and Crutchfield, 1988; Bridges and Steen, 1998; Bushway and Piehl, 2001; Hagan, 1974; Johnson, 2006; Mitchell, 2005; Peterson and Hagan, 1984; Steffensmeier, Ulmer, and Kramer, 1998; Thomson and Zingraff, 1981; Ulmer, 1997). Despite considerable theoretical and empirical advances (Zatz, 1987), extant research remains focused on black/white comparisons (e.g., Crawford, Chiricos, and Kleck, 1998; Kautt and Spohn, 2002; Kramer and Steffensmeier, 1993; Spohn, Gruhl, and Welch, 1981–1982; Steffensmeier, Ulmer, and Kramer, 1998; Unnever, Frazier, and Henretta, 1980) and, to a lesser extent, black/white/Hispanic comparisons (e.g., Albonetti, 1997, 2002; Demuth, 2003; Johnson, 2003; Spohn and Holleran, 2000; Steffensmeier and Demuth, 2000, 2001). Overviews of racial and ethnic effects in punishment exist elsewhere (e.g., Hagan and Bumiller, 1983; Kleck, 1981; Klepper, Nagin, and Tierney, 1983; Mitchell, 2005; Sampson and Lauritsen, 1997; Spohn, 2000; Zatz, 2000) and suggest that despite some inconsistencies, the weight of the evidence indicates minority groups are often disadvantaged at sentencing. Importantly, however, the effects of race and ethnicity are often subtle, indirect, and typically small relative to legal considerations like seriousness of the present offense. However, as Sampson and Lauritsen (1997: 364) opined, "we know very little about criminal justice processing other than for blacks and whites. Quite simply, there is little empirical basis from which to draw firm conclusions for Hispanic, Asian, and Native Americans."

Recent research has answered the call for additional investigations incorporating Hispanic offenders. Findings from this work highlight important differences in court processing and criminal sanctioning by offender ethnicity (Albonetti, 1997, 2002; Johnson, 2003; LaFree, 1985; Steffensmeier and Demuth, 2000, 2001; Welch, Spohn, and Gruhl, 1985; Zatz, 1984). Recent studies of Hispanic offenders in federal district courts, for instance, concur that they are not only punished more severely than both their white and black counterparts, but also they are less likely to receive sentencing discounts such as favorable departures from the federal sentencing guidelines (Albonetti, 1997; Johnson, Ulmer, and Kramer, 2008; Mustard, 2001; Steffensmeier and Demuth, 2000). Evidence suggests that Hispanic offenders are punished at least as severely as black offenders. The limited work on Native American offenders reaches a similar conclusion (e.g., Alvarez and Bachman, 1996; Bynum, 1981; Bynum and Paternoster, 1984; Hagan, 1975, 1977). According to Spohn (2000: 428), these findings "suggest that race and ethnicity do play an important role in contemporary sentencing decisions," such that "the 'discrimination thesis' cannot be laid to rest."

What is conspicuously absent from modern discourse on racial and ethnic disparities in criminal punishment, however, is consideration of the way Asian Americans are processed through the justice system. Our review of contemporary research on race and sentencing revealed only one study that incorporated Asian-American offenders in any capacity. Everett and Wojtkiewicz (2002) analyzed the relative placement of racial groups within four different strata of federal sentencing guideline recommendations. Their results suggested that, within conforming guidelines ranges, Asian offenders were punished similarly to white offenders for all offenses except immigration, where they received slightly more severe punishments. Although this study represents an important contribution, it does not focus on punishments for Asian Americans, it provides little theoretical discussion of its findings, and it is limited to sentences that conform to guideline recommendations. Because the federal sentencing guidelines comprise narrow, restrictive sentencing ranges, meaningful differences among racial and ethnic groups are likely to remain uncaptured (Mustard, 2001). Overall, little remains known about the subtleties and complexities of criminal punishments for Asian-American offenders.

The lack of scholarly attention to Asian offenders is partly a consequence of common data limitations, including insufficient numbers or a lack of detail on Asian Americans. However, data limitations alone cannot account for the dearth of research. The growing interest in the treatment of other ethnic groups has not spread to Asian Americans in part because of the perception that Asian Americans are not a disadvantaged racial group in society. Whereas other minority groups are equated with the socially disadvantaged, Asian Americans have been labeled an American success story. Given their underrepresentation in official crime statistics (Sampson and Lauritsen, 1997), the relative recentness of appropriate data, and the general success image associated with the "model minority" stereotype, it is not surprising that few empirical studies have focused on Asian offenders—in many ways, they represent a unique racial group. Yet it is exactly this uniqueness that establishes the need for empirical research. Because Asian Americans occupy a singular niche in American race relations, an examination of their punishment outcomes provides a useful opportunity to expand current theoretical conceptions of the courtroom decision-making process. Some brief historical background on the model minority stereotype is provided before elaborating its theoretical importance in more detail.

From Yellow Peril to Model Minority

For most of American history, Asian Americans have endured similar racial subordinations as blacks and other minority groups, serving as targets of racial violence, segregation, and discrimination in housing, employment, education, and the justice system. Their early subjugation was tied to multiple factors, including nativistic anti-immigrant sentiments, language and cultural barriers, perceptions of racial and economic threat, and international relations, including U.S. military involvements in Asian countries (Ancheta, 2006). Early U.S. Supreme Court decisions ruled that Asian Americans should be legally classified as blacks. Yet Asians exhibit their own unique cultural legacy of contentious race relations in America. Beginning in the mid-nineteenth century with the California gold rush and the building of the transcontinental railroad, the dramatic influx of Chinese laborers into the United States fueled widespread anti-Asian prejudice in America (Fredrickson, 2003). A unique specter of racial threat, one tied to both racism and nativism, culminated in several infamous government interventions. The Chinese Exclusion Act of 1882 summarily prohibited all immigration from China. The legacy of that legislation was not fully redressed until the Immigration Act of 1965 removed national origin immigration quotas. Similar experiences characterized other Asian ethnic groups. During World War II, more than 100,000 Japanese were forcibly detained in military-style internment camps after the bombing of Pearl Harbor (Daniels, 1993). This was emblematic of a profound sense of anti-Asian fear and prejudice that pervaded America in the early twentieth century. Much of the early anti-Asian sentiment was tied to economic threat perpetuated by early labor movements that feared the influx of a foreign labor group, as well as racial threat fueled by widespread American fears associated with the rubric "yellow peril," which according to Miller (1969: 201), conjured stereotypical images of "deceit, cunning, idolatry, despotism, xenophobia, cruelty, infanticide, and intellectual and sexual perversity."

Despite continuing prejudices and subjugations, the post-war popular image of Asian Americans in society has been dramatically overhauled. In just a few decades, "the past negative image of the Asian population in the United States has been transformed into a positive one" (Hurh and Kim, 1989: 516). This transformation has been variously attributed to the professional employment status and upward social mobility of early Asian immigrant groups (Lyman, 1974: 119), the recent influx of more college-educated Asian groups (Hurh and Kim, 1989), and the political utility of an exemplar racial minority group during periods of racial tension (Chun, 1980). Whatever the reasons for the historic transformation, by the mid-1960s, the popular press had begun to highlight the success stories of Asian Americans, identifying them as the "model minority"—a stereotype that "represents a number of positive qualities supposedly unique to Asian Americans, such as a superior work ethic, high levels of educational achievement, and a highly refined business and economic sensibility" (Paek and Shah, 2003: 226).

Today, stereotypical attributions linking Asian Americans to social and economic success in this country are firmly entrenched in popular discourse. As Ancheta (2006: 6) argues, "contemporary race relation controversies appear to have elevated Asian Americans to the status of honorary whites." Asian Americans as a group therefore hold a unique place in American racial relations. Although the model minority appellation has been widely criticized for being overly simplistic (Wong, 1994), at least some objective evidence supports its thesis—as a group, Asian Americans outperform other minority groups across a variety of social welfare indices (Cheng, 1997). They earn higher median salaries, are more likely to earn their Bachelor's degree, and are more likely to be employed in management, professional and related occupations compared with the general population (Reeves and Bennett, 2004).

Criminological research substantiates these claims even more. Using data from the National Longitudinal Study of Adolescent Behavior (Add Health), McNulty and Bellair (2003) reported that Asian youth are significantly less likely to be involved in serious acts of violence, live in less structurally disadvantaged and more stable communities, and have parents with significantly more education and higher average incomes. Asian adolescents also report substantially higher levels of school attachment and higher average grades, relative to both other minority groups and the white majority (see also Jang, 2002). Official crime statistics also indicate that Asian offenders are underrepresented in virtually all offense categories (Sampson and Lauritsen, 1997; Uniform Crime Reports, 2005). Whereas other racial and ethnic minority groups tend to be over-represented in felony crime statistics, Asian Americans "account for 1.0 percent of all arrests, yet make up 2.9 percent of the population" (Sampson and Lauritsen, 1997: 325). Some scholars have therefore concluded, "in comparison to African Americans and even Mexican-Americans, Asian-Americans appear to be on their way to being assimilated by the European-American majority" (Fredrickson, 2003: 10).

The unique niche occupied by Asian Americans in the racial stratification system of the United States has important theoretical implications for understanding punishment in society. Racially, Asians remain a subordinate status group, but socially and economically, they have been labeled a success story. Their unique status as a racial minority group with positive stereotypes therefore provides a rare opportunity to test competing theoretical propositions on the role of race and ethnicity in the punishment process.

Data and Methods

Data for this study come from the USSC for FY1997-FY2000. These data collate information from presentence reports, court orders, and reports on sentencing hearings and are particularly apt to the present purposes because they contain information on a relatively large number of Asian American offenders. The data were limited to the 88 federal districts that had sentenced Asian offenders (excluding foreign territories and the District of Columbia), resulting in a total sample size of 188,937 federal offenders. Consistent with prior research (e.g., Johnson, 2005), analyses of guidelines departures are limited to cases that are eligible for these discounts, resulting in a reduced sample size of 165,632 cases (cases in Zone A of the guidelines cannot receive downward departures). For analyses of sentence length, we examine only the 157,276 cases that received incarceration.

Discussion

For nearly a century, social researchers have studied racial disparities and racial discrimination in the criminal justice system; yet this voluminous scholarship has paid virtually no attention to the growing population of Asian offenders, despite their unique position in the racial strata of society. Drawing from multiple theoretical frameworks, the current work offers an investigation of Asian sentencing in the federal justice system. According to traditional conflict perspectives, racial minority groups occupy a subordinate position in America's system of social stratification—one that should translate into harsher punishment in the justice system. Traditional consensus theories, however, argue that racial status has minimal impact on punishment decisions. Rather, consensual values of fairness and equality translate into similar punishments among groups. More contemporary perspectives collectively argue for a more nuanced and situational interpretation of race and ethnicity in the justice system. Racial attributions are expected to influence court actor perceptions of dangerousness and culpability in ways that vary across racial groups and decision-making contexts. The relatively positive stereotypes of Asians as a minority group should result in less punitive outcomes than for other racial and ethnic minority groups in society.

Table 6.4 summarizes support for our specific predictions, which is varied and often dependent on the outcome of interest. Taken as a whole, these findings suggest that membership in a racial minority group exerts neither uniformly detrimental nor null effects on punishment outcomes. Instead, punishments seem to be race graded; that is, black and Hispanic offenders typically receive more severe outcomes than their similarly situated white counterparts, whereas Asian offenders do not. Although Asians are somewhat less likely to receive downward departures from federal judges, they are substantially more likely to receive substantial assistance motions from U.S. attorneys. This is consequential because 5K1.1 departures exert strong effects on incarceration and sentence lengths, and they even allow judges to "demandatorize" federal sentences (Kramer and Ulmer, 2002). Taken together, our findings are largely consistent with the interpretation that positive stereotypes associated with the model minority image translate into more favorable outcomes for Asian offenders in the federal justice system relative to other racial minority groups like blacks and Hispanics.

Moreover, in line with theoretical predictions, young males tend to receive the harshest punishments among Asian offenders, but young Asian males are not punished as severely as young male black or Hispanics offenders, particularly in the case of federal incarceration decisions. Somewhat surprisingly, citizenship status also exerted more deleterious effects on blacks and Hispanics compared with Asian offenders. The influence of racial status across offense types was varied and complex. Few significant differences emerged for violent crimes, and racial differences in immigration were constrained to offsetting effects for downward and substantial assistance departures. For drug crimes, however, blacks and Hispanics clearly fared worse, whereas Asians fared best for fraud crimes.

This pattern of results suggests that racial identity is an important conditioner of punishments across crime type, but the pattern is not simply one of greater punishments for less typical crimes, as suggested by Hawkins (1987). It may be that heterogeneous categories such as fraud or violent crime are simply too broad to capture meaningful differences among offenses, or it may be that the specific meaning and interpretation of racial identities varies in more complex ways with additional factors such as situational and organizational contexts (Steen, Engen, and Gainey, 2005). Future research is clearly needed to disentangle interrelationships among race, ethnicity, and offense types in the federal justice system.

Still, the current results indicate that federal punishments are race graded in important ways. Although this observation gives pause for concern, it also may provide reason for optimism. Even though important variation exists among Asian subgroups, and prejudice, racism, and racial violence remain prevalent today,[7] as an aggregate group, Asian Americans can in many ways be viewed as a socioeconomic and educational success story in the United States (Reeves and Bennett, 2004). It may be, then, that economic equality is a precursor to social

[7]Between 1995 and 2002, there were more than 3,500 racially motivated incidents of violence against Asian Americans in the United States (Ancheta 2006: 7). Moreover, several highly publicized incidents of anti-Asian violence have occurred, such as in 1982, when two disgruntled automobile workers mistakenly identified Vincent Chen as Japanese and beat him to death in response to the perceived loss of jobs in the automobile industry.

Table 6.4 Summary of Support for Hypotheses of Asian Offenders in Federal Sentencing

		Outcome			
Hypothesis	Prediction	Substantial Assistance Departure	Downward Departure	Incarceration	Ln Sentence Length
1	Asian offenders will be sentenced more severely than white offenders.	–	+	–	+
2	Asian offenders will be sentenced no differently than white offenders.	–	–	–	–
3	Asian offenders will be sentenced less severely than other minority groups.	+	+/–	+	ns
4	Young, male, Asians will be sentenced more severely than other young, male, minorities.	+/–	+/–	+	+/–
5	Young, male, Asians will be sentenced more severely than other Asian offenders.	ns	+/–	+/–	+/–
6	Asian noncitizens will be sentenced more severely than Asian citizens.	ns	ns	+	+
7	Asian-American punishments will vary across offense types.	+/–	+	+	+/–

Abbreviations: Ln = natural logarithm; ns = no significant effects.

Key: + = hypothesis supported; – = hypothesis not supported; +/– = hypothesis partially supported.

justice—that is, striving to improve the relative socioeconomic standing of other racial and ethnic minority groups may have important ripple effects that translate into more favorable societal stereotypes and greater equality of punishment within the American justice system itself (cf. Wilson, 1980).

Conclusion

Given the prodigious scholarly attention devoted to the importance of racial stratification in the justice system, it is unfortunate that so little work examines ethnic minority groups other than blacks and Hispanics. Asians represent the fastest growing minority group in America, and they now constitute a sizeable number of federal inmates. Moreover, their unusual position in the racial hierarchy of society provides a unique opportunity to assess competing theoretical perspectives vis-à-vis the intersection of race and punishment in society. The current research, therefore, broadens contemporary debates on racial disparity by systematically examining sentencing decisions for Asian offenders in U.S. federal courts.

Our findings lend credence to contemporary theoretical perspectives that emphasize the situational meaning of race and ethnicity in the justice system, but they also provide overarching evidence that broad patterns of racialized justice continue to characterize contemporary punishment decisions. In the aggregate, Asian offenders often, although not always, are treated similarly to or even more leniently than their white counterparts, and they are often sentenced to less severe punishments than black and Hispanic offenders. Although these race effects are typically small in comparison with the cumulative effects of legal case characteristics, they are sizeable enough to be substantively important. Whereas this offers evidence of differential punishment, it is important to note it does not necessarily equate with discrimination on the part of federal justice personnel. Federal judges and U.S. attorneys may well have valid reasons for giving individual punishments that appear as a disparity in aggregate statistical analyses. Future work incorporating qualitative methods represents an important next step in understanding the role of model minority stereotypes in federal punishment decisions.

Although the current study provides an important foundation for future research on understudied racial and ethnic groups, it also raises several additional research questions. Paramount among them is the role that social context plays in conditioning individual race disparities. Future research is needed that delves into this issue more acutely. Like other minority groups, Asian offenders tend to be spatially grouped, with high concentrations in a limited number of federal districts. If the meaning of racial identity is locally varying, then punishment outcomes are also likely to demonstrate geographic variation. We capture district-level differences using fixed effects that control for, but preclude examination of, inter-district variation in sentencing. Future work examining differences in the treatment of Asian and other offenders across federal districts therefore provides an important opportunity to expand our understanding of racial variations in punishment.

Another productive avenue for future work is the examination of within-group differences in punishment. As with Hispanic offenders, Asian Americans vary widely in their national origins and immigration experiences. Some groups have arrived recently, whereas others have long-standing histories in the United States. Broad variation also characterizes the socioeconomic, social, and political backgrounds of different Asian-American groups. Far East Asians like Chinese and Japanese may receive different punishments from more socioeconomically disadvantaged Southeast Asians groups. Although the current work includes proxies for socioeconomic status (SES), such as educational attainment, it does not have direct measures of SES. This is an important limitation that characterizes most research on criminal sentencing (Zatz, 2000), and it should clearly be a priority of future research to develop more refined measures of SES along with finer racial and ethnic distinctions.

Finally, future research is needed that examines the extent to which relative leniency for Asian minorities is maintained across additional decision-making outcomes. Both offender and court actor decisions that predate sentencing outcomes are of cardinal significance, stretching back all the way to the causes of crime (Bushway and Piehl, 2007). With few exceptions (e.g., Jang, 2002; McNulty and Bellair, 2003), studies of racial differences in offending suffer from the same myopic focus on two or three racial groups, and we are aware of no studies that include Asian Americans in analyses of arrests or prosecutorial charging practices. Because sentencing decisions are intricately tied to earlier decision-making stages, the ultimate goal should be to track the treatment of Asian offenders and other racial/ethnic groups across decision-making phases of punishment. Only by accurately accounting for cumulative racial group differences in case processing can we begin to identify the collective influence of racial identity and societal stereotypes in the punishment process of American courtrooms.

References

Albonetti, Celesta A., 1997. Sentencing under the federal sentencing guidelines: Effects of defendant characteristics, guilty pleas, and departures on sentence outcomes for drug offenses, 1991–1992. *Law & Society Review* 31:789–322.

Albonetti, Celesta A., 2002. The joint conditioning effect of defendant's gender and ethnicity on length of imprisonment under the federal sentencing guidelines for drug trafficking-manufacturing offenders. *Journal of Gender, Race, and Justice* 6:39–60.

Alvarez, Alexander, and Ronet Bachman, 1996. American Indians and sentencing disparity: An Arizona test. *Journal or Criminal Justice* 24:549–61.

Ancheta, Angelo, 2006. *Race, Rights and the Asian American Experience,* 2nd ed. Newark, NJ: Rutgers University Press.

Barnes, Jessica, and Claudette Bennett, 2002. *The Asian Population: 2000 Census Brief.* Washington, DC: U.S. Census Bureau.

Blumstein, Alfred, 1982. On the racial disproportionality of United States' prison populations. *The Journal of Criminal Law and Criminology* 73:1259–81.

Bridges, George S., and Robert D. Crutchfield, 1988. Law, social standing, and racial disparities in imprisonment. *Social Forces* 66:699–724.

Bridges, George S., and Sara Steen, 1998. Racial disparities in official assessments of juvenile offenders: Attributional stereotypes as mediating mechanisms. *American Sociological Review* 63:554–70.

Brown, Imogen, and Roy Hullin, 1992. A study of sentencing in the Leeds magistrates' courts: The treatment of ethnic minority and white offenders. *British Journal of Criminology* 32:41–53.

Bushway, Shawn D., and Anne M. Pichl, 2001. Judging judicial discretion: Legal factors and racial discrimination in sentencing. *Law & Society Review* 35:733–764.

Bushway, Shawn D., and Anne M. Piehl, 2007. Social science research and the legal threat to presumptive sentencing guidelines. *Criminology & Public Policy* 6:461–82.

Bynum, Tim, 1981. Parole decision making and Native Americans. In *Race, Crime, and Criminal Justice,* eds. R. L. McNeely and Carl Pope. Thousand Oaks, CA: Sage.

Bynum, Tim, and Raymond Paternoster, 1984. Discrimination revisited: An exploration of frontstage and backstage criminal justice decision making. *Sociology and Social Research* 69:90–108.

Cheng, Cliff, 1997. Are Asian American employees a model minority or just a minority? *The Journal of Applied Behavioral Science* 33:277–90.

Chun, Ki-Taek, 1980. The myth of Asian American success and its educational ramifications. In *The Asian American Cultural Experience,* eds. Don Nakanishi and Tina Nishida. New York: Routledge.

Crawford, Charles, Ted Chiricos, and Gary Kleck, 1998. Race, racial threat, and sentencing of habitual offenders. *Criminology* 36:481–512.

Daniels, Roger, 1993. *Prisoners without Trial: Japanese Americans in World War II.* New York: Hill & Wang.

Demuth, Stephen, 2003. Racial and ethnic differences in pretrial release decisions and outcomes: A comparison of Hispanic, black, and white felony arrestees. *Criminology* 41:873–908.

Everett, Ronald S., and Roger A. Wojtkiewicz, 2002. Difference, disparity, and race/ethnic bias in federal sentencing. *Journal of Quantitative Criminology* 18:189–211.

Fredrickson, George, 2003. The historical construction of race and citizenship in the United States. Paper presented to UNRISD, pp. 465–80. www.unrisd.org.

Hacker, Andrew, 1995. *Two Nations: Black and White, Separate, Hostile, Unequal.* New York: Macmillan.

Hagan, John, 1974. Parameters of criminal prosecution: An application of path analysis to a problem of criminal justice. *Journal of Criminal Law & Criminology* 65:536–44.

Hagan, John, 1975. The social and legal construction of criminal justice: A study of the pre-sentencing process. *Social Problems* 22:620–37.

Hagan, John, 1977. Criminal justice in rural and urban communities: A study of the bureaucratization of justice. *Social Forces* 55:597–612.

Hagan, John, and Celesta A. Albonetti, 1982. Race, class, and the perception of criminal injustice in America. *American Journal of Sociology* 88:329.

Hagan, John, and Kristin Bumiller, 1983. Making sense of sentencing: A review and critique of sentencing research. In *Research on Sentencing: The Search for Reform, Vol. II,* eds. Alfred Blumstein, Jacqueline

Cohen, Susan E. Martin, and Michael H. Tonry. Washington, DC: National Academy Press.

Hawkins, Darnell F., 1987. Beyond anomalies: Rethinking the conflict perspective on race and criminal punishment. *Social Forces* 65:719–45.

Hurh, Won Moo, and Kwang Chung Kim, 1989. The "success" image of Asian Americans: Its validity, and its practical and theoretical implications. *Ethnic and Racial Studies* 12:512–37.

Jang, Sung Joon, 2002. The effects of family, school, peers, and attitudes on adolescents' drug use: Do they vary with age? *Justice Quarterly* 19:97–126.

Johnson, Brian D., 2003. Racial and ethnic disparities in sentencing departures across modes of conviction. *Criminology* 41:449–90.

Johnson, Brian D., 2006. The multilevel context of criminal sentencing: Integrating judge- and county-level influences. *Criminology* 44:259–98.

Johnson, Brian D., Jeffery Ulmer, and John Kramer, 2008. The social context of guidelines circumvention: The case of U.S. district courts. *Criminology* 46: 737–783.

Kautt, Paula, and Cassia Spohn, 2002. Cracking down on black drug offenders? Testing for interactions among offenders' race, drug type, and sentencing strategy in federal drug sentences. *Justice Quarterly* 19:1–35.

Kerner Commission, 1968. *Report of the National Advisory Commission on Civil Disorders.* Washington, DC: U.S. Government Printing Office.

Kleck, Gary, 1981. Racial discrimination in criminal sentencing: A critical evaluation of the evidence with additional evidence on the death penalty. *American Sociological Review* 46:783–805.

Klepper, Steven, Daniel S. Nagin, and Luke-Jon Tierney, 1983. Discrimination in the criminal justice system: A critical appraisal of the literature. In *Research on Sentencing: The Search for Reform, Vol. 2,* eds. Alfred Blumstein, Jacqueline Cohen, Susan E. Martin, and Michael H. Tonry. Washington, DC: National Academy Press.

Kramer, John, and Darrell Steffensmeier, 1993. Race and imprisonment decisions. *Sociological Quarterly* 34:357–76.

Kramer, John, and Jeffery Ulmer, 2002. Downward departures for serious violent offenders: Local court "corrections" to Pennsylvania's sentencing guidelines. *Criminology* 40:897–932.

LaFree, Gary, 1985. Official reactions to Hispanic defendants in the Southwest. *Journal of Research in Crime and Delinquency* 22:213–37.

Lyman, Stanford, 1974. *Chinese Americans.* New York: Random House.

Martinez, Ramiro, Jr., 2002. *Latino Homicide: Immigration, Violence and Community.* New York: Routledge.

McKinnon, Jesse, and Claudette Bennett, 2005. *We the People: Blacks in the United States, Census 2000 Special Report.* CENSR-25. Washington, DC: Bureau of the Census.

McNulty, Thomas L., and Paul E. Bellair, 2003. Explaining racial and ethnic differences in serious adolescent violent behavior. *Criminology* 41:709–48.

Miller, Stuart C, 1969. *The Unwelcome Immigrant: The American Image of the Chinese, 1785–1882.* Berkeley: University of California Press.

Mitchell, Ojmarrh, 2005. A meta-analysis of race and sentencing research: Explaining the inconsistencies. *Journal of Quantitative Criminology* 21:439–66.

Mustard, David B, 2001. Racial, ethnic, and gender disparities in sentencing: Evidence from the U.S. federal courts. *Journal of Law and Economics* 44:285–314.

Paek, Hye Jin, and Hemant Shah, 2003. Racial ideology, model minorities, and the "not-so-silent partner:" stereotyping of Asian Americans in U.S. magazine advertising. *Howard Journal of Communication* 14:225–43.

Peterson, Ruth D., and John Hagan, 1984. Changing conceptions of race: Towards an account of anomalous findings of sentencing research. *American Sociological Review* 49:56–70.

Piliavin, Ivan, and Scott Briar, 1964. Police encounters with juveniles. *American Journal of Sociology* 70:206–14.

Ramirez, Roberto, 2004. *We the People: Hispanics in the United States, Census 2000 Special Report.* CENSR-18. Washington, DC: Bureau of the Census.

Reeves, Terrence J., and Claudette E. Bennett, 2004. *We the People: Asians in the United States, Census 2000 Special Report.* CENSR-17. Washington, DC: Bureau of the Census.

Ruth, Henry, and Kevin R. Reitz, 2003. *The Challenge of Crime: Rethinking our Response.* Cambridge, MA: Harvard University Press.

Sampson, Robert J., and Janet L. Lauritsen, 1997. Racial and ethnic disparities in crime and criminal justice in the United States. *Crime and Justice* 21:311–74.

Sellin, Thorsten, 1935. Race prejudice in the administration of justice. *American Journal of Sociology* 41:212–7.

Spohn, Cassia, 2000. *Thirty years of Sentencing Reform: The Quest for a Racially Neutral Sentencing Process.* Washington, DC: National Institute of Justice.

Spohn, Cassia, John Gruhl, and Susan Welch, 1981–1982. The effect of race on sentencing: A re-examination of an unsettled question. *Law & Society Review* 16:71–88.

Spohn, Cassia, and David Holleran, 2000. The imprisonment penalty paid by young, unemployed black and Hispanic male offenders. *Criminology* 38:281–306.

Steen, Sara, Rodney L. Engen, and Randy R. Gainey, 2005. Images of danger and culpability: Racial stereotyping, case processing, and criminal sentencing. *Criminology* 43:435–68.

Steffensmeier, Darrell, and Stephen Demuth, 2000. Ethnicity and sentencing outcomes in U.S. federal courts: Who is punished more harshly? *American Sociological Review* 65:705–29.

Steffensmeier, Darrell, and Stephen Demuth, 2001. Ethnicity and judges' sentencing decisions: Hispanic-black-white comparisons. *Criminology* 39:145–78.

Steffensmeier, Darrell, Jeffery Ulmer, and John Kramer, 1998. The interaction of race, gender, and age in criminal sentencing: The punishment cost of being young, black, and male. *Criminology* 36:763–98.

Stephan, James J., and Jennifer C. Karberg, 2003. *Census of State and Federal Correctional Facilities, 2000.* Report NCJ-198272. Washington, DC: Bureau of Justice Statistics.

Thomson, Randall J., and Matthew T. Zingraff, 1981. Detecting sentencing disparity: Some problems and evidence. *American Journal of Sociology* 86:869–80.

Ulmer, Jeffery, 1997. *Social Worlds of Sentencing: Court Communities under Sentencing Guidelines.* Albany: State University of New York Press.

Uniform Crime Reports, 2005. *Crime in the United States 2005.* Uniform Crime Reports. Washington, DC: U.S. Department of Justice, Federal Bureau of Investigation, www.fbi.gov/ucr/ucr.htm

Unnever, James D., Charles E. Frazier, and John C. Henretta, 1980. Race differences in criminal sentencing. *Sociological Quarterly* 21:197–205.

Welch, Susan, Cassia Spohn, and John Gruhl, 1985. Convicting and sentencing differences among black, Hispanic, and white males in six localities. *Justice Quarterly* 2:67–80.

Wilson, William J, 1980. *The Declining Significance of Race: Blacks and Changing American Institutions.* Chicago, IL: University of Chicago Press.

Wong, William, 1994. Covering the invisible "model minority." *Media Studies Journal* 8:49–60.

Zatz, Marjorie, 1984. Race, ethnicity, and determinate sentencing: A new dimension to an old controversy. *Criminology* 22:147–71.

Zatz, Marjorie, 1987. The changing forms of racial/ethnic biases in sentencing. *Journal of Research in Crime and Delinquency* 24:69–92.

Zatz, Marjorie, 2000. *The Convergence of Race, Ethnicity, Gender and Class on Court Decision Making: Looking Toward the 21st Century.* Washington, DC: National Institute of Justice.

Zhou, Min, 2000. Social capital in Chinatown: The role of community-based organizations and families in the adaptation of the younger generation. In *Contemporary Asian America: A Multidisciplinary Reader,* eds. Min Zhou and James Gatewood. New York: NYU Press.

DISCUSSION QUESTIONS

1. Why have criminal justice scholars largely overlooked the study of Asian Americans in the criminal justice system?
2. Which of the three theories discussed—conflict, consensus, and organizational theory—best explain the influence of race in the criminal justice system?
3. What do the authors mean when they state that Asian Americans hold an unusual position in the racial hierarchy? How does this unusual position affect their representation in the criminal justice system?

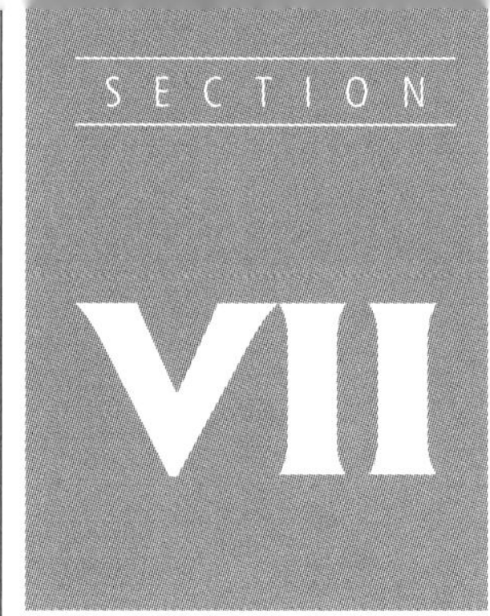

The Death Penalty

SECTION HIGHLIGHTS

- Overview of Race and the Death Penalty
- Significant Death Penalty Cases
- Current Statistics on the Death Penalty
- Public Opinion on the Death Penalty
- Wrongful Convictions
- Summary
- Edited Readings

The **death penalty** has been part of the American punishment process from the early 1600s. Colonists were not satisfied with simply brutally maiming offenders who violated colonial laws—they decided that certain offenses warranted the ultimate punishment: execution. The first person to receive a death sentence was Captain George Kendall, who was executed in 1608 for spying (Death Penalty Information Center, 2010). This first execution set the stage for the continued use of the death penalty. Since Kendall's execution, thousands of Americans have been executed for crimes ranging from stealing grapes to premeditated homicide.

Today, because of several landmark Supreme Court decisions, the death penalty is reserved for those who commit homicide. Yet there remains a sizeable segment of the American population that opposes the death penalty. The passions on both sides of the debate make the death penalty one of the most highly charged criminal justice practices. The passions intensify when the role of race becomes intertwined with debates about the death penalty. This section examines various aspects of the race and death penalty debate. The section begins with an historical overview of the death penalty and is followed by a discussion of several significant death penalty cases. The section also includes current death penalty statistics and a review of public opinion on the death penalty. Though **wrongful convictions** occur for all offenses, the wave of death penalty cases that have involved wrongful convictions has brought increased attention to the issue. This section includes a discussion of the nuances of wrongful convictions.

Overview of Race and the Death Penalty

The death penalty in America followed colonists from their homeland, where English law provided for so many offenses resulting in death that it was referred to as the ***bloody code.*** In a pioneering article on the death penalty as it relates to Native Americans, Baker (2007) noted that in addition to the well-known early genocidal actions of Europeans, since their arrivals, there have been at least 450 formal executions of Native Americans. He pointed to the 1639 execution of Nepauduck as the first execution of a Native American. According to Baker, during the 16th century there were 157 executions of Native Americans.

Besides the execution of Native Americans, Banner (2002) noted that the colonies had numerous death penalty **statutes** that were solely applied to Blacks. There were a variety of such statutes, beginning in New York in 1712. However, it was in the South where many of these statutes prevailed. Because of the greater number of slaves in the South, there was considerable concern that they might rebel; therefore, as a means of deterrence, there were wide-ranging capital statutes. For example, "In 1740 South Carolina imposed the death penalty on slaves and free Blacks for burning or destroying any grain, commodities, or manufactured goods; on slaves for enticing other slaves to run away; and on slaves maiming or bruising Whites" (Banner, 2002, pp. 8–9). Other statutes made it punishable by death for slaves to administer medicine (to guard against poisoning), "strike Whites twice, or once if a bruise resulted," or burn a house (Banner, 2002, p. 9). It is noteworthy that Black female slaves were not spared the death penalty. Thus, unlike White women who rarely received the death penalty, states did not hesitate to execute Black women. Baker (2008) noted that the first recorded execution of a Black woman was in 1681, when Maria, a slave, was executed for arson and murder. After this initial execution, 58 more slave women were executed before 1790, with another 126 executed prior to the Civil War (Baker, 2008).

The obvious undercurrent with early death penalty statutes was that landowners were intent on controlling the slave population by fear and state-sanctioned brutality. As Banner (2002) noted, colonial officials "streamlined" the process by cutting out juries and using local justices of the peace to ensure that "justice" was rapid. It is likely that although a host of capital offenses also applied to Whites, the processes that prevailed in the slave era resulted in disparities. Looking at one state, North Carolina, the record shows that "at least one hundred slaves were executed in the quarter-century between 1748 and 1772, well more than the number of Whites executed during the colony's entire history, spanning a century" (Banner, 2002, p. 9). These early disparities have persisted into the 21st century.

Over the last 40 years, there has been considerable debate about the merits of the death penalty as a form of punishment. These debates have led to challenges to the constitutionality of the death penalty. The following section reviews some significant death penalty cases.

Significant Death Penalty Cases

The continued use of the death penalty in America can be credited to the strong historical and continuing public sentiment in favor of its use and a series of Supreme Court cases, which, over the last three decades, have reaffirmed its constitutionality. The first of these was the 1972 decision in ***Furman v. Georgia.*** The case centered on a 25-year-old Black man (William Henry Furman) with an IQ of 65 who was charged with killing a 30-year-old White man (Bohm, 2007). Because of the lack of instructions given to jury members about deciding which cases warrant the death penalty and which ones do not, Furman's lawyers argued that the way the death penalty was being administered was in violation of his Fourteenth Amendment right to due process and was also a violation of the **Eighth Amendment**, which protects citizens from cruel and unusual punishment. In a decision where the nine justices each wrote a separate opinion, the majority agreed that the death penalty was being administered in an arbitrary and capricious manner. That is, there was little uniformity across states as to who should receive the death penalty and under what circumstances. Those in the majority also pointed out that the death penalty had been applied in a discriminatory manner. Concurring with the majority decision, Justice Douglas, for example, wrote the following:

> It is cruel and unusual punishment to apply the death penalty selectively to minorities whose numbers are few, who are outcasts of society, and who are unpopular, but whom society is willing to see suffer though it would not countenance general application of the same penalty across the boards. (*Furman v. Georgia*, 1972, p. 247)

Given some of these considerations, Furman's sentence was eventually commuted to life in prison. (He was paroled in 1985.) Baker (2003) noted the following:

> The aftermath of *Furman* saw the Court vacate 120 cases immediately before it and some 645 other cases involving death row inmates. The decision rendered defective the death penalty statutes of thirty-nine states, the District of Columbia, and the federal government. (p. 180)

The *Furman* decision, however, stood for only 4 years. In the 1976 case of ***Gregg v. Georgia***, the Court indicated that states that used **guided discretion** statutes removed concerns regarding previous procedures that were considered to be arbitrary and capricious. According to Bohm (1999), such statutes

> set standards for juries and judges when deciding whether to impose the death penalty. The guided discretion statutes struck a reasonable balance between giving the jury some discretion and allowing it to consider the defendant's background and character and circumstances of the crime. (p. 25)

The year following the *Gregg* decision, the Court provided states with further guidance on the application of the death penalty. Specifically, in ***Coker v. Georgia*** (1977), the Court ruled that sentencing rapists to death was cruel and unusual punishment. Considering that between 1930 and the 1970s, 405 Black men were executed in the South for the crime of rape, whereas only 48 Whites were executed for the same offense during this period (Holden-Smith, 1996), it is perplexing that the Court skirted the racial dynamics of the historical use of executions for rapists. With about 90% of such death sentences being given to Blacks, it appears that this punishment was historically reserved for Blacks.

In June of the same year as the *Coker* decision, the court also ruled in *Eberheart v. Georgia* (1977) that kidnappings not resulting in death could not be punished with the death penalty. A decade later, the 1987 decision in ***McCleskey v. Kemp*** represented another important Supreme Court case, which challenged the constitutionality of the death penalty based on race discrimination in its application.

Warren McCleskey, a Black man, was convicted of the 1978 shooting of a White police officer during an armed robbery. Once caught, tried, and convicted following Georgia's death penalty statute, the jury found beyond a reasonable doubt that the murder had occurred with one of their statutorily defined aggravating circumstances. In this case, however, there were two aggravating circumstances. First, McCleskey had committed the murder during an armed robbery; and second, the victim was a police officer. In the course of his appeals, McCleskey claimed that Georgia's death penalty process was being administered in a racially discriminatory manner, which violated his Eighth and Fourteenth Amendment rights. As evidence of this discrimination, McCleskey's defense showed what follows:

> Even after taking account of 39 non racial variables, defendants charged with killing Whites were 4.3 times more likely to receive a death sentence in Georgia as defendants charged with killing Blacks, and that Black defendants were 1.1 times as likely to receive a death sentence as other defendants. (*McCleskey v. Kemp*, 1987, p. 287)

After working its way through the courts, the case finally made its way to the Supreme Court in 1986. In an opinion written by Justice Powell and joined by four other justices (Rehnquist, White, O'Connor, and Scalia), here is what the majority held:

> The statistical evidence was insufficient to support an inference that any of the decision makers in the accused's case acted with discriminatory purpose in violation of the equal protection clause of the Fourteenth Amendment, since (a) the accused offered no evidence of racial bias specific to his own case, and (b) the statistical evidence alone was not clear enough to prove discrimination in any one case; (2) the study was insufficient to prove that the state violated the equal protection clause by adopting the capital punishment statute and allowing it to remain in force despite its allegedly discriminatory application; and (3) the study was insufficient to prove that the state's capital punishment system was arbitrary and capricious in application and that therefore the accused's death sentence was excessive in violation of the Eighth Amendment. (*McCleskey v. Kemp,* 1987, pp. 279–281)

Conversely, the dissenting justices in the case (Brennan, Marshall, Stevens, and Blackmun) provided a host of contrasting points. First, as noted in previous cases, justices Brennan and Marshall reiterated that the death penalty was cruel and unusual and therefore violated the Eighth and the Fourteenth Amendments. Furthermore, in their eyes, the statistical evidence was valid and showed that racial prejudice likely influenced his sentence (*McCleskey v. Kemp*, 1987). In his dissenting opinion, Justice Blackmun, who was joined by justices Marshall and Stevens, suggested that the statistical data showed the following:

> (1) The accused was a member of a group that was singled out for different treatment, (2) the difference in treatment was substantial in degree, and (3) Georgia's process for seeking the death penalty was susceptible to abuse in the form of racial discrimination. (*McCleskey v. Kemp*, 1987, pp. 245–365)

The study that was debated by the majority has come to be known as the "Baldus study" (see Baldus, Woodworth, & Pulaski, 1990). Leading up to the *McCleskey* case, Baldus, Woodworth, and Pulaski (1990) had conducted two important death penalty studies: the procedural reform study and the charging and sentencing study. The first study was designed to

> compare how Georgia sentenced defendants convicted of murder at trial, before and after the statutory reforms prompted by *Furman v. Georgia*, and to assess the extent to which those reforms affected the levels of arbitrariness and discrimination observed in its sentencing decisions. (p. 42)

For the second study, Baldus and his colleagues (1990) were hired by the NAACP Legal Defense Fund to conduct the study "with the expectation that the results might be used to challenge the constitutionality of Georgia's death sentencing system as it has been applied since *Gregg v. Georgia* (1976)" (p. 44). The second study was the one considered and rejected in the McCleskey decision. Using a sophisticated methodological design, which controlled for hundreds of variables, the Baldus study remains the standard when examining race and the death penalty. Probably the most discussed and important finding from the study was the strong race-of-the-victim effect, which showed that Black offenders in Georgia who victimized Whites were considerably more likely to receive death sentences than White persons who victimized Blacks. In fact, looking at this dynamic nationally over a 370-year period (1608–1978), only 30 Whites in the United States have been executed for killing African Americans (Radelet, 1989).

It has been suggested that had the Supreme Court ruled in McCleskey's favor, it would have opened "a Pandora's box of litigation" (Kennedy, 1997, p. 333). In short, ruling in McCleskey's favor would have, as Justice Powell stated, "throw[n] into serious question the principles that underlie our entire criminal justice system" (cited in Kennedy, 1997, p. 333). Moreover, he noted that such a decision would have produced similar claims "from other members of other groups alleging bias" (Kennedy, 1997, p. 333). The fact remains that the supporters of the death penalty outnumber those who oppose it.

Current Statistics on the Death Penalty

Using the year following the *Gregg* decision as a reference point, from 1977 to 2008, there were 1,136 inmates executed (Snell, 2009). Since 1977, of those persons receiving the death penalty, 34% have been Black. At the end of 2008, there were 3,207 persons under a death sentence at the federal and state levels (see Table 7.1). When reviewing data on the elapsed time from sentence to execution, for those on death row in December 2008, Hispanics averaged 131 months, Blacks averaged 149 months, and Whites averaged 150 months. Strikingly, the following five states accounted for nearly two thirds of the executions since 1977: Texas (423), Virginia (102), Oklahoma (88), Missouri (66), and Florida (66) (Snell, 2009). In addition, 98% of these persons were male, with more than 90% of them having a high school diploma/GED or less. More than half of them had never been married (54.7%). Of those under sentence of death, 41.7% were Blacks and 56.1% were Whites. Hispanics accounted for 13.2% of those prisoners under death sentence, whereas all other races accounted for 2.2%. In 2008, 37 persons were executed. Of these, 20 were White (Hispanics were included under this classification) and 17 were Black. On average, these persons had been serving a death sentence for approximately 12 years.

Table 7.1 Demographic Characteristics of Prisoners Under Sentence of Death, 2008

	Prisoners Under Sentence of Death, 2008		
Characteristic	**Year End**	**Admissions**	**Removals**
Total inmates	3,207	111	119
Gender			
Male	98.2%	97.3%	99.2%
Female	1.8	2.7	0.8
Race[a]			
White	56.1%	58.6%	61.3%
Black	41.7	39.6	37.0
All other races[b]	2.2	1.8	1.7
Hispanic origin			
Hispanic	13.2%	19.8%	8.1%
Non-Hispanic	86.8	80.2	91.9
Number unknown	384	5	8
Education			
8th grade or less	13.5%	17.1%	19.2%
9th-11th grade	36.5	31.7	36.4
High school graduate/GED	40.8	41.5	35.4
Any college	9.2	9.8	9.1

Characteristic	Prisoners Under Sentence of Death, 2008 Year End	Admissions	Removals
Median	12th	12th	11th
Number unknown	528	29	20
Marital status			
Married	22.2%	18.3%	20.2%
Divorced/separated	20.1	19.5	27.9
Widowed	2.9	4.9	1.9
Never married	54.7	57.3	50.0
Number unknown	371	29	15

NOTE: Calculations are based on those cases for which data were reported. Columns may not sum to total shown due to rounding.

a. Includes persons of Hispanic/Latino origin.

b. At year end 2008, inmates in the "all other races" category consisted of 27 American Indians, 35 Asians, and 9 self-identified Hispanics. During 2008, 1 American Indian and 1 Asian were admitted, and 1 Asian and 1 self-identified Hispanic were removed.

Public Opinion and the Death Penalty

According to Bohm (2007), public opinion on the death penalty is important for the following five reasons. First, strong public support for the death penalty is the likely reason that it is still used as a punishment in the United States. Consequently, politicians will continue to support the death penalty as long as support from the public remains high. Second, because the public wants the death penalty, Bohm believes that prosecutors are willing to appease them by seeking the death penalty in cases where other penalties might be more suitable. Third, feeling the pressure from public sentiment, judges, like prosecutors, might feel undue pressure to impose death sentences. Fourth, governors are also swayed by public opinion in their decisions to commute sentences. If public support for the death penalty is strong, few governors are willing to risk political favor to go against such sentiment. Finally, because state supreme courts and the U.S. Supreme Court consider public sentiment in their decisions regarding whether the death penalty is cruel and unusual punishment, the results of public opinion polls take on an added measure of significance.

Recent polls continue to indicate strong support for the death penalty, with overall support at 69% (Gallup Organization, 2007). In some instances, even when given the option of choosing between the death sentence and life in prison without the possibility of parole, the majority of Americans (53%) remain supportive of the death penalty (Jones, 2003). The differences in levels of support for the death penalty have been attributed to a variety of characteristics, including race, political party affiliation, region, education level, occupations, religion, and gender (Longmire, 1996). Such differences have remained constant over time.

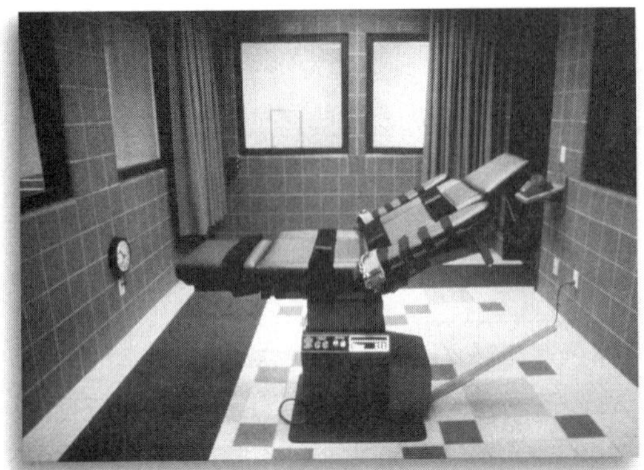

▲ **Photo 7.1** Terre Haute, Indiana: Death Chamber

Racial differences in support for the death penalty have also been consistent. Characteristics such as age, income, education, marital status, and political affiliation all have an impact on which Blacks supported the death penalty. Blacks in the middle and upper classes are more supportive of the death penalty (Arthur, 1998). In addition, Blacks who are married and conservative support the death penalty. Although as a whole more educated Blacks support the death penalty (high school diploma and above), out of this educated group, those with only high school diplomas report the strongest support for the death penalty (Arthur, 1998). As for regional considerations, "Blacks who live in large metropolitan districts and suburbs are more likely than those who live in 'other urban' and rural places to favor the death penalty for murder" (Arthur, 1998, p. 165). Research on the geographic variation in attitudes about capital punishment has also noted the significance of political affiliation, percentage of Blacks in the population, and areas with higher levels of homicides in predicting higher levels of support for the death penalty (Baumer, Messner, & Rosenfeld, 2003).

Barkan and Cohn (1994) explored the notion that racial prejudice plays a role in racial differences in support for the death penalty. Using 1990 General Social Survey (GSS) data, they examined questions that are related to prejudice, such as whether Whites strongly favored or strongly opposed "living in a neighborhood where half your neighbors were Black" and "having a close relative or family member marry a Black person" (Barkan & Cohn, 1994, p. 203). Based on questions on the survey, they constructed a racial stereotyping scale out of questions that were meant to measure "the degree to which they thought Blacks were lazy, unintelligent, desirous of living off welfare, unpatriotic, violent, and poor" (p. 203). Barkan and Cohn's results showed that "many White people are both prejudiced against Blacks and are more likely to support the death penalty" (p. 206).

Bobo and Johnson's (2004) research on attitudes toward the death penalty found that more than 80% of Whites and slightly more than 50% of Black respondents favored the death penalty. Such support was not mediated when the researchers introduced respondents to concerns regarding bias in the administration of criminal justice. There was, however, an effect when respondents were told that when someone murdered a White person they were more likely to receive the death penalty than when they murdered a Black person. This caveat significantly reduced Black support for the death penalty, whereas White support was not significantly affected. When Bobo and Johnson posed a hypothetical question involving executing innocent people on death row, there were only slight changes in the views of Whites and Blacks toward support for the death penalty.

Analyzing 14 years of GSS data, spanning from the 1970s to 2002, related to attitudes toward the death penalty, Unnever and Cullen (2007) also reported that African Americans were significantly more likely than Whites to oppose the death penalty. In general, this study, like other recent ones, found considerable support for the "racial divide" in public opinion on the death penalty (see also Cochran & Chamlin, 2006). Another consideration related to the death penalty public opinion research includes the so-called **Marshall hypotheses.**

The Marshall Hypotheses

Drawing on the statements of the late Supreme Court Justice Thurgood Marshall (see Photo 7.2) in *Furman v. Georgia*, researchers have presented hypotheses derived from his suggestions that (a) "American citizens know almost nothing about capital punishment," and (b) "[people] fully informed as to the purposes of the penalty and its liabilities, would find the penalty shocking, unjust, and unacceptable" (p. 363). Marshall qualified his second supposition by noting that this would not be the case if someone adhered to the retributive sentencing philosophy.

▲ **Photo 7.2** Supreme Court Justice Thurgood Marshall

On the whole, scholars have found support for Marshall's first hypothesis—that the public is uninformed about the death penalty (Bohm, Clark, & Aveni, 1991; Lambert & Clarke, 2001). However, very few studies have been conducted to examine Marshall's second hypothesis. Cochran and Chamlin (2005) used a pretest-posttest design to determine whether students' views on the death penalty would be influenced by exposure to materials presented in a course on the death penalty. The authors found mixed support for the supposition that "death penalty attitudes and beliefs were inversely associated with student's level of knowledge" (Cochran & Chamlin, 2005, p. 582). The researchers also found that knowledge about the death penalty decreased the level of support for capital punishment and increased students' support for life without parole as an alternative to capital punishment (see also Cochran, Sanders, & Chamlin, 2006).

Mitchell (2006) also examined whether Marshall's suppositions could be supported using a pretest-posttest approach with a seminar course as the experimental stimulus. An interesting finding from his research was that White and Hispanic views were minimally impacted by taking the seminar. On this result, he wrote "Only black respondents showed a significant change in the level of support for the death penalty. After undergoing the seminar, blacks increased their opposition toward the death penalty" (Mitchell, 2006, p. 9). Mitchell attributed this finding to the legacy of Blacks being disproportionately sentenced to the death penalty. When comparing the experimental group to a control group that did not take the seminar, the study did find that the seminar increased the participants' knowledge of the death penalty.

Wrongful Convictions

Concerns regarding innocent people being convicted are not new. Early on, both American (Borchard, 1932) and British (Brandon & Davies, 1973) scholars investigated this issue. In general, most Americans understand that, given the nature of our justice system, at times the guilty will go free and at times innocent people will be sent to jail or prison. This was confirmed by a 2003 Gallup Poll in which 74% of Americans supported the death penalty, although 73% responded yes when asked the following question:

> How often do you think that a person has been executed under the death penalty who was, in fact, innocent of the crime he or she was charged with—do you think this has happened in the past five years, or not? (Jones, 2003)

Therefore, when it comes to criminal justice, we generally adhere to a utilitarian philosophy. That is, because the system works for most citizens, Americans are willing to tolerate the risk that a small number of citizens are wrongfully convicted. Essentially, this is the price we are willing to pay to maintain our adversarial "trial by combat" justice system. Although such a philosophy might be acceptable if the stakes were low, that is not the case with the American justice system. Considering that the United States still maintains the death penalty, adhering to such a system leaves us open to executing innocent people. In fact, pioneering research in this area suggests that the United States has already executed hundreds of innocent people (Radelet, Bedau, & Putnam, 1992).

In the last decade, numerous authors have elucidated the major contributors to wrongful convictions (Castelle & Loftus, 2002; Christianson, 2004; S. Cohen, 2003; Harmon, 2001, 2004; Huff, 2004; Huff, Rattner, & Sagarin, 1996; Leo, 2002; Martin, 2002; Zimmerman, 2002). Of these, the most consistent contributors include (a) eyewitness error, (b) police misconduct, (c) prosecutorial misconduct, (d) plea bargaining, (e) community pressure for conviction, (f) inadequacy of counsel, (g) false confessions, (h) mistaken identity, (i) fabrication of evidence, (j) having a criminal record, (k) misinformation from criminal informants, and (l) race.

Bedau and Radelet (1987) were among the first to discuss race as a factor in wrongful conviction cases: Of the 350 capital cases they reviewed, 40% involved instances in which Blacks were wrongly accused. Huff et al. (1996) also noted that historically there have been disproportionate numbers of Blacks and Hispanics among those wrongly convicted. He and his coauthors alluded to the fact that many of the early instances of wrongful convictions involving minorities were likely a result of being tried by racist prosecutors, who also had all-White, prejudiced juries on their sides.

According to Parker, Dewees, and Radelet (2002), the 40% figure generally holds true across studies. One exception to this is the research done by Barry Scheck and Peter Neufeld, in which their **Innocence Project** (housed at Cardozo Law School at Yeshiva University in New York) found that, of those exonerated by the use of DNA, 57% were Black (Parker et al., 2002). Parker et al. also surmised that, based on past criminal justice practices, "Among those wrongly convicted of felonies, Black defendants are significantly less likely than White defendants to be vindicated" (p. 118).

Although there are numerous case studies that highlight the racial tenor of wrongful conviction cases, one of the most notable is the *Central Park Jogger* case. Although not a capital case, it represents an example in which many of the contributors to wrongful convictions, especially race, played roles in the unfortunate outcome. In the case, in April 1989, a White, 28-year-old investment banker was seriously injured when, according to the original reports, she was allegedly brutally attacked and raped by several Harlem teenagers. That night, 40 teenagers from Harlem were alleged to have engaged in "randomly molesting, robbing, and assaulting strangers who were jogging or bicycling through the Upper East Side of the park" (Cohen, 2003, p. 255). Following the incident, as Cohen (2003) noted, "The term '*wilding*' [was] introduced to the vernacular of oppression" (p. 255; italics original). Eventually, five Black youths between the ages of 15 and 17 were charged with the offense. Reviewing the facts of the case, Cohen (2003) wrote this statement:

> The only physical evidence the police had were hairs on the clothing of one of the boys that were said to be consistent with the hair of the jogger. But all five youths would soon be offering detectives what passed for confessions of guilt. The videotaped statements were the backbone of the prosecutor's case. (p. 256)

All of the youth were eventually convicted of all or some of the charges. A year later (in 1990), however, it was found that "semen found in the victim did not come from any of the five youths convicted of the crime" (Cohen, 2003, p. 257). Strikingly, not until 2002, when a convicted rapist admitted to a New York correctional officer that he had committed the offense, did anyone pay any additional attention to the fate of the youths. Although the youths were eventually released and partially exonerated (some officials continued to insist some of the youths participated in the crime), the racial element of the case cannot be overstated. One of the most disturbing elements of this case was that, although officials centered on the five innocent youths and looked past the obvious inconsistencies in their confessions and the overall weak evidence, the real rapist, Matias Reyes, went on "raping, assaulting, and tormenting" women (Cohen, 2003, p. 259). In fact, in the weeks following the arrest of the five youths, he also murdered a pregnant woman (Cohen, 2003). In the end, had the racial elements of the case not fanned the fears of Whites, it is likely that the evidence in the case would have led them to conduct a more thorough investigation, which would have surely exonerated the youths shortly after their arrest.

In recent years, more high-profile cases have occurred, such as the 2006 Duke University case in which lacrosse players were arrested on charges of raping a Black stripper. The stripper provided sordid details of the incident, which was later proved to be a hoax. Not long after the Duke case, the Jena 6 case reached the national spotlight. In the small town of Jena, Louisiana, a Black youth asked one of his high school teachers for permission to sit under a tree that was believed to be reserved for White youths. He received permission to sit under the tree and did so; the following day, there were three nooses hanging from the tree. The details of what happened after this remain murky. It has been suggested that six Black youths (Robert Bailey, Carwin Jones, Bryant Purvis, Theodore Shaw, Jesse Beard, and Mychal Bell [the Jena 6]) got into an altercation with two White youths who were believed to have placed the nooses on the tree. During the altercation, one of the White youth, Justin Barker, was injured; as a result, the Black youths were charged with attempted second-degree murder and conspiracy (Sims, 2009). As one of the Black youth, Mychal Bell, moved through the justice system, there was increasing outrage concerning the case. Observers wondered why such serious charges were being levied against the Black youth while nothing had happened to the White youths. This disparity in treatment led to nationwide protests, as well as a significant protest march in Jena that was attended by tens of thousands of protesters, including national civil rights leaders. In the wake of these protests, the District Attorney, Reed Walters, reduced the charges of the youths. In addition, it was later ruled that some of the youths should have been tried as juveniles; thus, their cases were moved to the juvenile court. It is likely that without national attention the Black youths would have been the victims of a rogue district attorney who overcharged the Black youths while neglecting to file any charges against the White youths. Again, such a case had the potential to lead to youths being wrongly prosecuted.

All three cases highlighted here illustrate the problems related to the rush to judgment that often takes place when high-profile cases involving race occur. However, this approach often leads to both mistakes and unethical cover-ups that can often lead to misguided prosecutions or, in the worst-case scenarios, wrongful convictions. Because of the high-profile nature of wrongful conviction cases in which persons on death row have been exonerated, scholars have continued to call for an increased emphasis on wrongful convictions in the discipline (Leo, 2005), as well as continuing to investigate the nature and scope of wrongful convictions (see Denov & Campbell, 2005; Ramsey & Frank, 2007; Zalman, 2006).

Summary

- The heavy reliance on the death penalty in colonial times can be traced to the *bloody code*, or the extensive use of the death penalty as a punishment in England.
- Research shows that the death penalty has been applied in a discriminatory fashion since colonial times.
- The Supreme Court has decided several cases related to the death penalty and the use of executions. In *McCleskey v. Kemp* the Court ruled that statistical evidence alone is not enough to prove that racial discrimination was involved in the decision to administer the death penalty.
- Public opinion has consistently shown that Whites are more likely to support the death penalty than Blacks. Researchers believe that this finding is likely the result of the longstanding racial disparities in the administration of the death penalty.
- The Marshall hypotheses are based on two suppositions articulated by Thurgood Marshall in *Furman v. Georgia* (1972). The first was that Americans know very little about the death penalty. The second was that, if Americans were fully informed about the death penalty, they would find it shocking, unjust, and unacceptable. Scholars have found some support for both of Marshall's suppositions.
- Racial and ethnic minorities are overrepresented among those who have been wrongfully convicted. In recent years, Innocence Projects across the country have been used to exonerate offenders of all races and ethnicities.

KEY TERMS

bloody code
Coker v. Georgia
death penalty
Eighth Amendment
Furman v. Georgia
Gregg v. Georgia
guided discretion
Innocence Project
Marshall hypotheses
McCleskey v. Kemp
statutes
wrongful convictions

DISCUSSION QUESTIONS

1. Do you think the bloody code, or executing offenders for more offenses than homicide, would be an effective deterrent in modern day America?
2. Explain why public opinion on the death penalty is so critical.
3. Explain why *Coker v. Georgia* was significant for African Americans.
4. Explain the significance of the Baldus study.
5. Discuss some of the strategies that can be used to prevent wrongful convictions.

WEB RESOURCES

Capital Jury Project: http://www.albany.edu/scj/CJPhome.htm

Death Penalty Information Center: http://www.deathpenaltyinfo.org

Center on Wrongful Convictions: http://www.law.northwestern.edu/wrongfulconvictions/

The Justice Project: http://www.thejusticeproject.org/national/ipa/

READING

Although much of the existing research on the administration of the death penalty has focused on African Americans, there has been an emerging interest in whether Hispanics are also at a disadvantage in death penalty cases. In previous research on African Americans there has consistently been a race-of-the-victim effect. That is, when African Americans kill Whites the likelihood of them receiving the death penalty is enhanced. This article examines research on the death penalty conducted in San Joaquin, California, where, using a decade worth of death penalty data, the authors examined how the death penalty was applied to Hispanics. The research uncovered a race-of-the-victim effect, with Hispanic defendants who killed Whites and Asians being more likely to receive a death sentence. Cases in which women were the victim also increased the defendants' likelihood of receiving a death sentence.

Hispanics and the Death Penalty

Discriminatory Charging Practices in San Joaquin County, California

Catherine Lee

Introduction

Debates over fairness and constitutionality of the death penalty recently reentered the political and media limelight. Governor George Ryan of Illinois, for example, generated a political firestorm when he commuted the death sentences of all of the state's death row inmates before leaving office in January 2003, citing concerns over error in determining guilt and sentencing in death penalty cases. Stories about innocence and claims of wrongful convictions may grab the headlines, yet what social scientists have carefully and quietly documented over the last three decades was evidence of racial and gender bias against defendants and victims at all stages of the death penalty system, from charging to conviction and sentencing. Despite these consistent findings, questions remained. One crucial unknown was whether or not racial bias uncovered in investigations of African Americans and Whites also negatively impacted members of other minority groups, in particular the largest minority group in the U.S.—Hispanics. Are Hispanics, as both victims and defendants, treated more like non-Hispanic Whites or African Americans? This study was the first to answer this question.

How Hispanics fare in the criminal justice system with respect to the death penalty may have broad implications for understanding race and ethnicity in the United States. The death penalty system's treatment of Hispanics may indicate how the color line in the U.S. is being drawn as their numbers rise. Historians of race and ethnicity showed that throughout the

Source: Lee, C. (2007). Hispanics and the death penalty: Discriminatory charging practices in San Joaquin County, California. *Journal of Criminal Justice, 35,* 17–27.

nineteenth and first half of the twentieth centuries, the color line in the U.S. was drawn between White/non-White (Jacobson, 1998; Roediger, 1991). What mattered and was privileged was whiteness. Following the rise of post-1965 immigration from Asia and Latin America, some immigration scholars suggested that the color line is now between Black/non-Black (Foner, 2005; Lee, Bean, & Stevens, 2003). Lee et al. (2003) found that Hispanics and Asian Americans were more likely than African Americans to marry Whites. Their children were also discovered to identify more often as "multicultural," while children of Black/White unions were more likely to identify as Black or African American. Foner (2005) and Lee et al. (2003) argued that what mattered now was the distinction between Black and non-Black. An understanding of how Hispanic victims and defendants were treated by the criminal justice system will not provide a definitive explanation of the process of racialization nor how racialized groups interact. An empirical investigation, nevertheless, of how Hispanics fared in the criminal justice system may help social scientists to consider potentially broader changes taking afoot with respect to race and ethnicity in the United States.

Finally, as patterns of prosecutorial or jury discretion have led to capricious outcomes, legal scholars and social scientists must question whether the comparative-proportionality review process, instituted by states that sought to address concerns raised in the Supreme Court's overturning of existing death penalty statutes in *Furman v. Georgia* (1972), were adequately resolved by the Court's decision in *Gregg v. Georgia* (1976).

This article considers these questions by examining death-eligible cases that arose in the period immediately following the reinstatement of the death penalty in California. Specifically, the study investigated homicide cases from August 1977 through 1986 in San Joaquin County, California. An exploration of this place and time are interesting for two important reasons. The study enabled an examination of the death penalty system in the post-*Gregg* era. This research also demonstrated the role of race and ethnicity in death penalty cases, involving Hispanics and not just Black and White defendants and victims. This permitted an analysis of whether or not discriminatory practices that affected African American victims and defendants, which had been documented by prior research, similarly impacted other minority groups. In previous death penalty studies, researchers mainly made Black/White racial comparisons since many of the studies were conducted for litigation in which the defendants were African American and/or there were insufficient numbers of other minorities in the data utilized. A large Hispanic population in San Joaquin County provided the opportunity to focus on Hispanics.

Data and Methods

Data on death-eligible homicide cases from San Joaquin County from August 1977, when California's current death penalty statute became effective, through 1986 were gathered. There were 250 non-vehicular homicides between August 1977 and 1986. Of these 250 cases, seventy case reports could not be examined further. Reports for these seventy cases were missing key pages, in poor condition, or simply lost. There did not appear to be a pattern, however, to the seventy cases. They were not all cases, for example, from one time period or one city in the county. Of the 180 homicides, 128 cases were serious enough to warrant the *possibility* of a special circumstance attachment to the murder charge, which would have made it death-eligible. This means that a special circumstance such as multiple victims, killing of a police officer, or commission of a contemporaneous felony like kidnapping or robbery could have been added to the murder charge.

Analysis and Discussion

Sample characteristics are presented in Table 7.2. Most victims in San Joaquin County were White. Forty-five percent of the victims were White. Hispanics constituted the second largest group of victims with 28 percent of all cases. African American victims made up 23 percent of the total. The smallest group was Asian, accounting for just 6 percent of the sample. Victims were more likely to have been male in the study. Seventy-three percent of victims were men, whereas 27 percent were women.

Two-thirds of all defendants were White or Hispanic. Thirty-four percent of defendants were White, and 33 percent were Hispanic. Twenty-five percent of defendants were African American, while just 7 percent were Asian American. These defendants were accused of committing a contemporaneous felony in 26 percent of the cases.

Table 7.3 shows that twenty percent of all cases resulted in a death-eligible charge. It was expected that murders committed during the commission of a contemporaneous felony such as burglary or robbery led to a death-eligible charge since this is one of the aggravating factors that warrant a death-eligible charge. In cases where there was a contemporaneous felony committed, defendants in 59 percent of the cases received a death-eligible charge. In 94 percent of the cases in which there were no additional felonies committed, no death-eligible charges were filed.

Table 7.2 Sample Characteristics ($N = 122$)

Victim's race	
White	45% (54)
Hispanic	28% (34)
African American	23% (27)
Asian American	6% (7)
Victim's sex	
Female	27% (33)
Male	73% (89)
Defendant's race	
White	34% (42)
Hispanic	33% (41)
African American	25% (31)
Asian American	7% (8)
Contemporaneous felony	
Yes	26% (32)
No	74% (90)

Table 7.3 Death-Eligible Charges Made by Case Characteristics (N = 122)

	Death-Eligible Charge Made	Death-Eligible Charge Not Made
All cases	20% (24)	80% (98)
Contemporaneous felony		
Involved	59% (19)	41% (13)
Not involved	6% (5)	94% (85)
Victim's race		
White	30% (16)	70% (38)
Hispanic	6% (2)	94% (32)
African American	9% (5)	81% (22)
Asian American	17% (1)	83% (6)
Victim's sex		
Female	48% (16)	52% (17)
Male	9% (8)	91% (81)
Defendant's race		
White	26% (11)	74% (31)
Hispanic	10% (4)	90% (37)
African American	29% (9)	71% (22)
Asian American	0% (0)	100% (8)

Table 7.3 also shows that White victim cases netted the most death-eligible charges. While 30 percent of White victim cases yielded a death-eligible charge, only 6 percent of Hispanic victim cases and 9 percent of African American victim cases led to a death-eligible charge. Defendants in 17 percent of Asian American victim cases faced a death-eligible charge; however, this was just a single murder case. Defendants were also more likely to face a death-eligible charge if the victim was female. In 48 percent of such cases, defendants were held to answer to a death-eligible charge, while defendants in just 9 percent of male-victim cases did.

Previous research suggested that the race of the defendant sometimes played a role in the charging outcome. A death-eligible charge was never levied against Asian American defendants. Death-eligible charges were brought up against 10 percent of Hispanic defendants. Black defendant cases had the highest rate of death-eligible charges with 29 percent, while White defendant cases had the second highest rate with 26 percent.

Conclusion

The findings from this study showed that a pattern of racial and gender discrimination existed in death-eligible charging practices in San Joaquin County, California from 1977 through 1986, immediately following reforms instituted by the state. The results replicated previous findings, discovering that defendants in White victim cases (and perhaps to some extent Asian American victim cases) faced much greater odds of being charged with a death-eligible offense than did defendants in Black victim cases. This investigation also permitted Hispanic/White comparisons. Defendants in White victim cases faced greater odds of being charged with capital homicide than defendants in Hispanic victim cases.

Aside from these race-of-victim effects, this research also found that killing a woman versus a man increased a defendant's odds of facing a capital homicide charge. Every attempt was made to find any plausible legal explanation that could "explain away" these racial and gender results. The commission of a contemporaneous felony, having planned the murder, or having left fingerprint(s) on the murder weapon raised a defendant's chances of facing a death-eligible charge. These and additional variables such as the relationship between the defendant and victim, weapon(s) used, and whether the defendant had a prior serious record, however, could not eliminate the racial and gender outcomes.

References

Foner, N. (2005). *In a new land: A comparative view of immigration.* New York: New York University Press.

Jacobson, M. (1998). *Whiteness of a different color: European immigrants and the alchemy of race.* Cambridge, MA: Harvard University.

Lee, J., Bean, F., & Stevens, G. (2003). Immigration and race-ethnicity in the United States. In F. Bean & G. Stevens (Eds.), *America's newcomers and the dynamics of diversity* (pp. 11-42). New York: Russell Sage Foundation.

Roediger, D. (1991). *The wages of whiteness: Race and the making of the American working class.* London: Verso.

Cases Cited

Furman v. Georgia, 408 U.S. 238 (1972).

Gregg v. Georgia, 428 U.S. 153 (1976).

DISCUSSION QUESTIONS

1. What factors could help explain the finding that Hispanics had the least number of death-eligible charges brought against them? Explain.
2. After reading this article, has your opinion of the death penalty changed? Why or why not?
3. Several studies, including this one, highlight how race is a significant factor in death penalty cases. Are there any changes that could be made to the criminal justice system to eliminate the role of race?

READING

Using the case study approach, the authors examine how a high-profile killing in Delaware led to changes in the application of the death penalty in the state. The authors examined both the role of the media and the legislature in shaping the death penalty debate around the location of where crimes were emanating from (Philadelphia) and the people who were causing the problems (non-White invaders from Philadelphia). The authors provide a nuanced discussion of how the debate actually produced a more punitive approach to the death penalty and resulted in Delaware prosecutors more easily securing death sentences.

Governing Through Crime as Commonsense Racism

Race, Space, and Death Penalty "Reform" in Delaware

Benjamin D. Fleury-Steiner, Kerry Dunn, and Ruth Fleury-Steiner

> Whatever else they do, laws define categories of subjects to which consequences, negative and positive, attach.
>
> Jonathan Simon, *Governing Through Crime*

The enactment, enforcement, and toughening of criminal laws is a dynamic process that takes place in highly contingent fields of social, political, and economic conditions. A question that is central for exploring Simon's (2007) theory of governing through crime is then: How are these conditions tied to current understandings of *place* and *identity?* Such a question must be investigated with attention to the particular circumstances of the site under inquiry. For example, *how* politicians govern through crime in a non-death penalty state such as Vermont will obviously differ from how they do so in the USA's premier killing state, Texas. Specifically, we explore governing through crime in the context of one specific instance: Delaware's 1991 reform of its death penalty statute. Local media reports and legislative debate illuminate how constructions of particular places and persons appropriated by lawmakers enabled them to push through a far more punitive capital statute in little more than forty-eight hours after a high profile, racially charged case ended in four life sentences.

Source: Fleury-Steiner, B. D., Dunn, K., & Fleury-Steiner, R. (2009). Governing through crime as commonsense racism: Race, space, and death penalty "reform" in Delaware. *Punishment & Society, 11*, 5–24.

In Part I, we review empirical and theoretical literature on the racialization of popular and official conceptions of crime and criminals and the attendant consequences on legal action and lawmaking. We argue that integrating Haney-Lopez's conception of commonsense racism with Simon's governing through crime allows us to contribute a more nuanced conception of how crime, space, and race are pervasively tied to lawmaking practices. Part II investigates the events that led to sweeping reforms of Delaware's death penalty laws. We highlight the pervasive use of spatial narratives in the Delaware media and in a special legislative session that led to a radical revamping of the state's death penalty law. In this way, we shed light on how commonsensical narratives of 'good' or 'decent' persons and places were presented and subsequently influenced one 'just' action on behalf of the Delaware General Assembly. In Part III, we reflect on the Delaware case in the context of broader systems of social inequality and democratic decision making. In the concluding section, we reflect on death penalty reform in Delaware as it speaks to lawmaking practices as governing through crime.

Governing Through Crime as Commonsense Racism

In *Governing Through Crime* (2007), Simon provides several examples of how government actors value some spaces over others and create idealized and demonized legal subjects. Since the enforcement of laws against 'highway bandits' of the 1930s, the defense of mythical, 'good' places and persons has played an important role in the enactment of various tough on crime policies. For example, the passage of anti-car-jacking laws is a relatively new criminal sanction that is obviously imbued with dominant conceptions of locale and identity. Thus, an important contribution of Simon's work is that it forces us not only to view how state power is extended through tough sanctions, but how the rhetoric that accompanies implementation creates new forms of knowledge of space, self, and the other. We argue that an overarching racialized narrative of 'dangerous outsiders' from Philadelphia made dramatic reform of Delaware's death penalty law the 'commonsense' and 'morally just' thing to do.

More broadly, we argue that racialized representations of person and place are a catalyst for the mobilization of new, tougher criminal laws. We make this case through the exploration of one high profile crime and the subsequent radical reforming of Delaware's death penalty law. In the wake of the killing of two white armored car drivers by four black men from Philadelphia and the subsequent failure of the prosecution to secure a death sentence for the killers, the Delaware state legislature made a radical amendment to its death penalty statute. Following the enactment of the new death penalty law, death sentences in Delaware increased dramatically and the state now has, per capita, one of the highest execution rates in the country. Moreover, recent research on death sentencing outcomes in Delaware finds that cases involving black defendants and white victims are significantly more likely to result in a death sentence (e.g., Blume et al., 2008).

In *Racism on Trial*, Ian Haney-Lopez (2003) presents an important framework for understanding the pervasive ways race is routinized in public knowledge of crime and the enforcement of criminal law practices. Focusing on the infamous 'East LA Thirteen' and 'Biltmore Six' trials, Haney-Lopez's study demonstrates how disproportionate under representation of Latinos from grand juries was the result of the racial commonsense of judges. Racial commonsense, according to Haney-Lopez (2003: 123), is a widely shared, taken-for-granted set of ideas within a culture'. As a result of racial common-sense, legal and governmental actors do *not* have to act intentionally for racism to occur. Racism occurs any time one acts according to taken-for-granted scripts of racialized persons, places, and channels that enforce racial hierarchy (i.e., actions that hurt minorities and favor whites).

Haney-Lopez's theory of commonsense racism is critical for understanding how contemporary policy makers govern through crime; taken-for-granted beliefs in a 'black crime problem' pervade state-level criminal lawmaking and enforcement practices. Indeed, as Haney-Lopez (2003: 250) concludes 'We are still, and long will be, living in the distant past . . . in which race powerfully defines social and material relations in the United States.' Thus in an overwhelming drive to appear 'tough on crime' policy makers define the problem in terms of 'thugs', 'super predators', 'gangsters', and other racialized code words for the inhabitants of 'criminal spaces'. That is to say, according to this logic, the 'war' must be aggressively waged against the threatening outsiders (poor, non-whites) and their disorderly territories (ghettos, barrios, etc.).

What is important in these studies is the demonstration of how commonsense understandings of racialized spaces and identities infect the discretion of legal officials and laypersons acting on behalf of the state. However, lawmaking provides a different context for studying commonsense racism. As we will discuss in subsequent sections, lawmakers are given incredible power to actually *change* or *create* laws based on their own taken-for-granted understandings of 'threatening outsiders'. In this way, our contribution to the literature on death penalty lawmaking is to call attention to the power of legislators to literally construct or, in this instance, reconstruct laws based on symbolic maps they enact that re-draw stark lines between racialized insiders and outsiders.

'Invaders' From Philadelphia: The Brooks Armored Car Case

Capital punishment in the USA has suffered a number of important setbacks in recent years, including complete abolition in New Jersey in 2007 (e.g., Peters, 2007). However, we are not convinced that other states will uniformly follow New Jersey's lead. In fact, if the constellation of events that occurred in Delaware is at all indicative further expansion and entrenchment of capital punishment may occur in other US states. Calling attention to the subtle ways commonsense racism of space and person infuses lawmaking we believe sheds important light on the perpetuation of the USA's ongoing crime war or what Simon (2002) aptly calls the 'severity revolution' in American criminal justice practices of the last several decades. Moreover, we believe that calling attention to the awesome power of lawmakers in such instances as not simply examples of being tough on crime but illustrative of the subtle ways commonsense racism of person and space enables state elites to narrow debate and block dissent.

The Case

On 12 December 1990 four African American men from Philadelphia, Kenneth Rodgers, Christopher Long, James Llewellyn, and Paul 'Scotty' Robertson, traveled across state lines in a rental van to commit a planned robbery of a Brooks armored car as it delivered $613,600 to a Delaware Trust bank. At least two of the men wore bullet proof vests and were heavily armed. It is nearly indisputable that their intent was to execute the two bank truck guards and take as much of the money as possible. Their plan seemed, at least at first, to have worked exactly according to plan. The Brooks Car arrived and two men in bullet proof vests quickly emerged from a van gunning down both guards at point blank range. Michael Salvatore was shot four times and died instantly at the scene of the crime. The second guard, Vincent Monterosso, was shot five times, but did not die until 12 January 1991, less than 13 hours after the birth of his third son.

Rodgers, Long, Llewellyn, and Robertson immediately fled the scene. But police response was rapid; officers tracked down the rental van on a New Jersey highway in the vicinity of the

Commodore Barry Bridge. A gun fight ensued, but all four men were eventually apprehended and charged with two counts of capital murder by Delaware prosecutors.

In the first month after the crime and arrests of Rodgers, Long, Llewellyn, and Robertson, the case received prominent news coverage in Delaware's most widely read newspaper the *News Journal*. In the first two days after the arrests, perhaps not surprisingly given the drama of the crime and the televised coverage of the subsequent police chase across state lines, there was near saturation coverage in the local media. On 13 December 1991, five separate front page stories of the case appeared, including the most prominent, 'Guard dies in armored car heist'. Subsequent media coverage of the trial of the defendants who had come to be widely known as the 'Philadelphia Four' portrayed them as dangerous, immoral outsiders who *must* receive the death sentence in order to send a message to surrounding states that such conduct will not be tolerated in Delaware (Caddell, 1991b: A1). This coverage focused heavily on the detailed backgrounds of the two guards as 'fathers', 'husbands', 'upstanding citizen' (Gutierrez-Mier and Amster, 1990: A1; Stewart, 1990: A1; Gutierrez-Mier, 1991: A1) and little on the particular identities of the four Philadelphia men beyond their offensive behavior during the trial and brief coverage of their family's pleas for mercy (Caddell, 1991a: A3). Such coverage had the effect of creating a stark dichotomy between 'good' and 'bad' people. Descriptions of the bank as a 'vulnerable institution' and the surrounding area as 'upstanding community' all served to heighten the stakes of the trial.

Sentencing of the 'Philadelphia Four'

On 23 October 1991, approximately 10 months after the incident, the trial of the 'Philadelphia Four' began. All four defendants were convicted of capital murder and now faced death or life without possibility of parole (LWOP). But the ultimate sentence for the Philadelphia 'outlaws' was not to be. In little more than two and a half hours, the New Castle County jury returned with LWOP sentencing verdicts for all four men.

The next day the *News Journal* ran a cover spread of the Brooks case sentencing verdict with large photographs of all four men in shackles—clearly connoting a highly racialized, menacing 'Willie Horton' like presence—the images took up approximately one-fourth of the paper's front cover. Letters to *News Journal* editors in the days just after the sentencing verdict also conveyed a similar outrage toward the verdict, and underscored the belief in the death penalty's deterrent effect and the need for Delaware to defend itself from predatory outsiders: *The Philadelphia Four came to our state for one reason—to commit a crime. . . . The state had better start using the death penalty or more hideous crimes are going to occur here.*

Death Penalty 'Reform' in Delaware

Only two days had passed since the Brooks verdict, but on 24 October 1991 an unscheduled debate over Delaware's death penalty was thrust before the General Assembly. Attorney General Ross captured the tenor of the debate that would follow:

> The Brooks case was a freak situation because the General Assembly probably wouldn't have passed it if they had just waited six months. When it came to the regular session they might have sent it to a committee, they might have studied it a bit more. But the special session was organized to accomplish the law-change in one day, and it was only put on the agenda for that one day.

Time or lack thereof is an essential factor for understanding a pervasive subtext to death penalty law reform in Delaware. But as the analysis that follows reveals, urgency was just one aspect of how rapid reform would take place. Beyond the knee-jerk hysteria of right and wrong, there was a far more commonsensical story of particular persons and spaces that enabled lawmakers to defend the 'freak situation' of momentous law change as the only way to protect the 'fragile' and 'vulnerable' state.

Legislative Debate, 24 October 1991

By debate standards this one was remarkably short. The legislative transcript contains approximately 25 pages of actual dialogue—that is, only a few legislators and witnesses spoke very much. On the one hand, this relative *lack* of discourse may be a product of the unannounced session and legislators being caught by surprise. Other possible reasons for voting may also have resulted from deals legislators made with the bill's sponsors and or the intense political pressure they felt to demonstrate they were 'tough on crime'. On the other hand, when members of the Delaware General Assembly did speak several interesting themes emerge.

Legislators draw heavily on the very recent local media bonanza of the last 48 hours for source material. Indeed, they often echo the 'criminalized' space and person themes captured in the local media. But the debate also brings to light a broader commonsense that is revealing in its pervasive representations of 'us and them' and a conception of 'post-Brooks' Delaware.

Although discussion of the particularities of the law reform does feature prominently in the debate, the squabbles over technicalities are far overshadowed by a deeper subtext. At the heart of the debate is a test of legislators' commitment to protecting Delaware's law abiding citizens. Indeed, the potential consequences of passing the new law received comparatively little attention among legislators. The overriding tenor of the debate is thus one of a 'duty to act' in the face of impending emergency. At the same time, not a single legislator presented reflections on the serious risk of racial bias in the application of a far more aggressive death sentencing law in the state, a concern now confirmed by a recent empirical study documenting significant racial biases in Delaware's death penalty (e.g., Blume et al., 2008).

Legislators as Moral Cartographers

From a strict geographic orthodoxy, cartographers construct maps of particular places that emphasize spatial representations of an environment or location at a specific time in history. For example, one of the resources cartographers rely on for creating maps is information on the landscape such as population density. However, social geographers have long demonstrated that cartography is also an inextricably *political* activity in which places deemed to be on the margins of society become increasingly difficult to find or, importantly for our purposes, are altogether left out. As Dennis Wood (1992: 43) writing in *The power of maps*, a trenchant analysis of the politics of mapmaking throughout time, argues, cartography itself can be seen as 'a form of political discourse concerned with the acquisition and maintenance of power' especially *state power.*

Lawmakers as moral cartographers classify populations, impute boundaries, and emphasize difference. Delaware legislators literally re-construct a map of the state's moral order that leaves out any minority voices and serves as a template for justifying the passage of new and tougher laws—laws that ironically will have the greatest impact on poor, racial minorities. Legislators defend a particularistic map of a world that excludes representation of the racially aggrieved, poor communities from which the 'Philadelphia Four' come from and are also present especially in the poorest sections of Wilmington, Delaware. But the state's own racially marginalized communities and the protracted history of injustices perpetrated against such places (i.e., redlining) and persons (i.e., racial profiling) are left out of state elites' mapping. There is simply no room for such complexities in a context dominated by static dichotomies between 'good' and 'evil'. Indeed, the criminal law is an ideal place to do this because it is set up to individualize, to determine individual blame—even mitigation does not allow for structural arguments. In this way, adapting a law to exterminate more outsiders represents a powerful tightening of such boundaries; a *territorializing* that has no sympathy for anything perceived as threatening the normative order. As Steve Herbert (1996: 568) cogently articulates in his analysis of police territoriality:

> An understanding of police territoriality is enhanced by deployment of the concept of 'normative order,' understood here as a set of rules and practices structured around a central value. The concept thus ties together the rules that structure social action and the values that provide meaning to the action.

In the context of death penalty lawmaking in Delaware, the central value is to enable the state to use lethal force more aggressively against those racialized outsiders that are represented as threatening to the 'decent' (i.e., white, middle class) insiders. The next section turns to the particular spatial practices Delaware lawmakers employed in their reaffirmation of the moral boundaries that were threatened by the Brooks case and all it had come to represent.

'Plotting and Murdering'

One of the prevailing themes in Delaware legislators' discourse is of an urgent assault on decent communities. By emphasizing dwindling time and ever present danger, legislators defended moral boundaries in the absence of any meaningful discussion about real places and persons *most directly impacted* by legislator's actions. The Brooks case is never analyzed by legislators in terms of what it may reveal about racial segregation, social isolation, or other toxic racial inequalities that are important for situating the crime in the context of a more accurate account of space and person. Instead, Delaware legislators focused on a generalized threat as a sweeping defense against archetypal, immoral outsiders. As Representative Merrill stated during the hearing:

> We're talking about a form of organized crime that plots and schemes and *comes into this state* and commits brutal acts, fully aware of what they're doing. And if one examines the laws in the contiguous states relative to capital punishment or how that is imposed, then the citizens of Delaware are very vulnerable to this sort of activity in the future. (Legislative debate before the Delaware House of Representatives, 24 October 1991, emphasis added)

Representative Merrill's reference to Delaware's 'vulnerability' in relation to 'contiguous states' reveals a clear example of lawmaking as moral cartography: the assessment is one of comparing the extant geography in terms of another state's death penalty laws as they pertain to four poor, black men from that state. Pennsylvania—the state most mentioned in local news coverage as having a tough death penalty law that Delaware should adopt—has a higher violent crime rate than Delaware. But the actual utility of the death penalty for addressing crime as a complex social problem not easily separated from prevailing structural inequalities is rendered irrelevant.

Risk is assessed purely in moral terms—by enabling the state to sentence outsiders to death more easily 'we' are upholding the prevailing order. There is no assessment in terms of how hastening death sentences may lead to a heightened risk of condemning the innocent. Likewise the debate never involves ensuring greater due process protections for the accused. The focus on death as a barometer for ensuring safety relative to other states is thus not one of genuine concerns about fairness, but a punitive dogma of 'protecting our surroundings' and the need to reaffirm the prevailing order by increasing the possibility of a death sentence alone.

'One Juror Acting Arbitrarily'

The post-Brooks world of capital punishment in Delaware redefines 'arbitrary' as 'not imposing death'. Despite having absolutely no knowledge as to why one juror may oppose the death sentence in a given case—indeed, recent research on jury discretion in death cases strongly suggests that life holdouts may in fact be both reasonable in their decision to oppose the death sentence and serve to educate their fellow jurors about the complexity of a defendants invariably horrible childhood (e.g., Bowers et al., 2001; Fleury-Steiner, 2004)—in Delaware all death holdouts are 'less intelligent' than judges and thus prone to arbitrary, irrational behavior in the jury room.

Conclusion

What has been the impact of the law change in Delaware since 1991? On the one hand it is easy to be skeptical of its influence, especially when considering that for 46 years not a *single* execution occurred in the state. And from 1976–91, only *seven* individuals were on Delaware's death row. Could a law change in Delaware really achieve the overriding goals of more death sentences and executions in a historically weak killing state?

The answer has overwhelmingly been *yes.* On average about *four times* as many people were sentenced to death since the 1991 law change than were sentenced before the law change. Interestingly, official statistics also reveal that no other state has experienced such dramatic changes after 1991, with some states' death sentencing rates showing a slight decrease. Bureau of Justice Statistics (BJS) data on state death sentences from 1976 to 2004 show on average that about four times as many people were sentenced to death each year after the 1991 law change than were sentenced before the law change. In terms of other states' averages over these periods, only Louisiana showed a substantial change since 1992 (two times as many death sentences).

Remarkably, Delaware prosecutors secured death sentences in less than 1 in 10 capital cases before 1991, but since the law change they did so in nearly *50 percent* of all capital cases. Indeed, a recent analysis of BJS data conducted by the Death Penalty Information Center (DPIC) on state executions since 1976 shows that Delaware ranks number 13 out of the 29 states that have had conducted executions. However, when the numbers are considered per capita, as of 2000, Delaware shoots up to *number one* with 1.66 executions per 100,000 residents beating number two, Oklahoma, with 1.45, and number three, Texas, with 1.25 (Death Penalty Information Center, 2000).

In terms of the racial effects of death penalty 'reform' in Delaware, recent research by Blume et al. (2008) is very instructive. Death sentences in the state are imposed in black defendant and white victim cases *twice* as often than in any other capital case. Comparing these findings in Delaware to research they have conducted in Georgia, Indiana, Maryland, Nevada, Pennsylvania, and South Carolina, Blume et al. (2008) observe: 'The highest death sentencing rate in black-defendant white victim cases previously observed was 10.1%. Delaware death sentencing rate is almost twice as high.'

Death penalty 'reform' in Delaware cannot be seen solely in terms of formal legality but driven by a deeper ideology 'that constitutes the social order not just by overt or purposeful activity' (Frohmann, 1997: 553). Even though the Brooks case involved black outsiders who murdered white bank truck drivers, it was not the racial composition of the crime *alone* that drove the punitive backlash in the state. Instead, it was the *re*-creation of a particular political geography of capital punishment in which marginalized voices are silenced and jurors' voices are muted. Indeed, the representation of New Castle County jurors as *incapable* of confronting this fundamental breech in the states moral order catalyzed legislators to dramatically curtail the role of jurors in capital cases.

The grief and outrage over the Brooks case is not easily separated from perceptions of a state long plagued by race and class inequalities. The 'invaders' are constituted by a local knowledge of the 'violent' and 'volatile' urban metropolis of Philadelphia. Why such folk knowledge is readily accepted in Delaware, the state's own tumultuous racial history is also instructive. Indeed, the General Assembly's decision to rush through a far more punitive death penalty law must be viewed against a longstanding backdrop of persistent racial segregation and racial conflict in Delaware.

References

Blume, John, Theodore Eisenberg, Sheri Johnson and Valerie Hans (2008) *The death penalty in Delaware: An empirical study.* Cornell Law School Legal Research Paper No. 08–025. http://papers.ssrn.com/sol3/papers.cfm?abstract_id=1207882

Bowers, William J., Benjamin D. Steiner and Marla Sandys (2001) 'Death sentencing in black and white: An empirical analysis of juror race and racial composition', *University of Pennsylvania Journal of Constitutional Law* 3(1): 171–274.

Caddell, Ted (1991a) 'Moms convicted killers seek mercy from jury', *News Journal,* 19 October.

Caddell, Ted (1991b) 'Death penalty study omits too-forgiving Delaware', *News Journal,* 10 November.

Death Penalty Information Center (2000) *Executions as of April 2000.* Texans for Public Justice. www.tpj.org/docs/2000/09/reports/sos/chapter5.pdf

Fleury-Steiner, Benjamin and Victor Argothy (2004) 'Lethal borders: Elucidating jurors' racialized discipline to punish in Latino defendant death cases', *Punishment & Society* 6(1): 67–84.

Frohmann, Lisa (1997) 'Convictability and discordant locales: Reproducing race, class, and gender ideologies in prosecutorial decision making', *Law & Society Review* 31: 531–56.

Gutierrez-Mier, John (1991) 'Hours after son's birth, armored car guard dies of wounds', *News Journal,* 13 January.

Gutierrez-Mier, John and Sarah-Ellen Amster (1990) 'Slain guard had almost stayed home', *News Journal,* 13 October.

Haney-Lopez, Ian (2003) *Racism on trial: The Chicano fight for justice.* Cambridge, MA: Belknap Press of Harvard University Press.

Herbert, Steve (1996) 'The normative ordering of police territoriality: Making and marking space with the Los Angeles Police Department', *Annals of the Association of American Geographers* 86(3) 567–82.

Simon, Jonathan (2002) 'Sanctioning government: Explaining America's severity revolution', *Miami Law Review* 56: 217–53.

Simon, Jonathan (2007) *Governing through crime: How the war on crime transformed democracy and created a culture of fear.* New York: Oxford University Press.

Stewart, Ann (1990) 'Guard dies in armored car heist', *News Journal,* 13 October.

Wood, Dennis (1992) *The power of maps.* New York: Guilford Press.

DISCUSSION QUESTIONS

1. What do the authors mean when they state that government entities do not have to act intentionally in order for racism to occur? Does this statement make you reconsider your views on what is or is not racism?

2. According to the reading, what role does race play in perpetuating the cycle of commonsense racism? Explain.

3. It is suggested that state legislators in Delaware used scare tactics, stating that "dangerous outsiders" were taking over the state, in order to push their death penalty reform. How does race fit into this argument?

READING

This article examines public opinion of race and the death penalty. Attempting to determine whether public opinion on the death penalty is malleable, the authors conducted an experiment using a nationwide sample. Specifically, the research investigated whether Blacks or Whites are willing to change their views based on a series of argument frames. The researchers find that Blacks, in general, are more likely to change their views when presented with frames related to the unfairness of the death penalty and innocence concerns. The authors conducted supplementary analyses that help better explain the racial differences in the willingness to change one's views.

Persuasion and Resistance

Race and the Death Penalty in America

Mark Peffley and Jon Hurwitz

The conventional wisdom on public opinion toward the death penalty in the United States, as summarized nicely by Ellsworth and Gross, is that people "feel strongly about the death penalty, know little about it, and feel no need to know more" (1994,19). As a consequence of these feelings, the authors argue, attitudes tend to be relatively crystallized and, therefore, unresponsive to question phrasing or arguments that are contrary to an individual's belief.

We must wonder, then, why views of the death penalty vary so dramatically over time and across contexts. Gallup surveys document a sharp increase in support for capital punishment between 1966 and 1994, clearly in response to rising violent crime rates during this period (e.g., Page and Shapiro 1992). However, with the dramatic surge in arguments questioning the fairness of the sentence (due, in part, to DNA exonerations of death row inmates) in the national media in the late 1990s (Baumgartner, De Boef, and Boydstun 2004), support then began to wane, falling from 80% in 1994 to 66% in 2000. Moreover, approval varies substantially depending on the characteristics of the target and the alternatives posed, with much lower support for putting juveniles and the mentally ill to death (26% and 19%, respectively, in 2002) and for the alternative of life imprisonment without the possibility of parole (52%; Bohm 2003; Gallup 2005). Given the fact that attitudes toward this policy are often responsive to events, to characteristics of the target, and to alternatives, the conventional wisdom—that death penalty attitudes are impervious to change—is surely overstated. Accordingly, any analysis of death penalty attitudes must account for the responsiveness of such attitudes, as well as their reputed *resistance* to change.

Authors' Note: This project was funded by National Science Foundation Grant #9906346.

Such an analysis is essential because attitudes toward the death penalty are consequential in ways that most other public attitudes are not. According to McGarrell and Sandys (1996), the U.S. Supreme Court has used public support for the policy as its barometer of "evolving standards of decency," a criterion the Court in turn uses to settle the "cruel and unusual" question (Soss, Langbein, and Metelko 2003, 398). The decisions of state jurists, as well, have been found to be influenced by public opinion on this issue. For example, Brace and Hall (1997) determined that, in states with citizens supportive of capital punishment, supreme court justices are significantly more likely to uphold the death sentence (or less likely to dissent from a prodeath majority) when they face "competitive electoral conditions" (e.g., they are close to the end of a judicial term or they won by narrow margins).

Legislatures are also influenced by the public. Congress (and President Clinton), for example, mandated the death penalty for certain federal crimes as a part of the Violent Crime Control and Law Enforcement Act of 1994, largely in response to growing public concerns with escalating crime rates. There are also numerous studies finding an impact of public opinion on state death penalty statutes (e.g., Mooney and Lee 2000) and state implementation rates (e.g., Norrander 2000). And capital punishment offers a form of direct democracy that is found in no other area of public policy. Citizen jurists often make the decision to take or spare the life of a convict in capital cases, thereby *directly* translating their beliefs into public policy.

Because such attitudes are both responsive and so extraordinarily important, we need to know a great deal more about what, exactly, shapes them. We need to understand the conditions under which these attitudes change, the types of arguments that are most persuasive, and the types of individuals who are most susceptible. But most importantly, we need to understand the differential responses of whites and African Americans to these arguments. As we will argue, the death penalty has become an extremely racialized policy in the United States, necessitating an analysis that is both inter- and intraracial. And as we will show, not only do whites and African Americans hold quite different beliefs about the death penalty, but they also respond quite differently to arguments against it.

Survey Experiment and Hypothesis

In the aggregate, consistent with numerous studies (e.g., Bobo and Johnson 2004; Bohm 2003), we expect whites to support the death penalty more than do African Americans (H_1). We also expect the framing of the antideath penalty arguments to vary inter racially. Given the heightened skepticism of many blacks toward the policy and toward the fairness of the criminal justice system in general, we anticipate that anticapital punishment arguments—of either variety—emphasizing a lack of fairness should be more persuasive with blacks than with whites (H_{2a}) because, relative to whites, African Americans are attitudinally predisposed to accept such arguments, which are more consistent with their prior predispositions that both the death penalty and the justice system are unfair. Whites, for whom antideath penalty attitudes are more inconsistent, should be less persuaded.

While we expect African Americans to be persuaded by both (i.e., discrimination and innocent) arguments, we hypothesize (H_{2b}) that many whites should be particularly unimpressed with the racial argument. While they may, in other words, be *somewhat* persuaded by the argument that innocent individuals are being executed, there is ample research (e.g., Hurwitz and Peffley 2005) documenting a naive faith among whites that the criminal justice system is racially fair. There is also, as we will document, ample evidence that most whites believe African Americans to be disproportionately inclined to criminal behavior (rather than being victims of discrimination) and, consequently, that they deserve to be treated more punitively. The racial fairness argument, consequently, is anathema to many whites and may therefore be wholly rejected, perhaps even to the degree that it produces a reactance or boomerang effect.

How exactly should attributional beliefs (regarding the causes of crime) affect support for the death penalty? Disregarding the race of the respondent and the experimental manipulation, we expect to find that respondents who believe that individuals engage in crime for dispositional (i.e., internal) reasons should be more supportive of the death penalty than those who attribute crime to structural (i.e., external) reasons (H_3). But how, if at all, does the relationship between attributional beliefs and capital punishment attitudes differ across experimental treatments? And do attributional beliefs play the same role for both whites and blacks?

In order to examine the racial elements of death penalty attitudes (and their responsiveness to argument), it is necessary to put both the argument itself and the criminal in a racial context. As noted, one of our two antideath penalty arguments is inherently racialized inasmuch as it suggests that the policy is biased against African Americans. Additionally, in asking about the causes of criminal behavior, we ask specifically about the perceived causes of *black* criminal behavior—whether African Americans get into trouble due to some internal failing or, instead, to the biases of the justice system. Specifically, respondents hear the following: "Statistics show that African Americans are more often arrested and sent to prison than are whites. The people we talk to have different ideas about why this occurs. I'm going to read you several reasons, two at a time, and ask you to choose which is the *more important* reason why, in your view, blacks are more often arrested and sent to prison than whites.

- First, the police and justice system are biased against blacks, OR blacks are just more likely to commit more crimes?
- Next, the police and justice system are biased against blacks, OR many younger blacks don't respect authority?"

For each comparison, therefore, respondents are instructed to choose between a dispositional ("just more likely to commit more crimes" and "don't respect authority") and a structural ("the police and justice system are biased against blacks") explanation of black crime.[1] The resulting additive index, Causes of Black Crime, ranges from 0 to 4, with higher values indicating more dispositional attributions of the causes of black crime. Whites are far more likely than African Americans to attribute the greater arrest rate of blacks to the failings of blacks who run afoul of the law than to the biases of the criminal justice system, and these sharp interracial differences are revealed in both the average (mean = 2.5 for whites vs. 1.5 for blacks; sd = 1.4 for both races) and the modal response of the scale (4 for whites, 0 for blacks).[2]

---

[1]For each question, choosing a structural cause was coded as 0, a dispositional cause as 2, and volunteering that both causes are equally important was coded as 1.

[2]These interracial differences are not surprising and are reminiscent of whites' failure to recognize discrimination in the economic realm (e.g., Sigelman and Welch 1991), where such beliefs have been viewed as a more subtle form of prejudice (e.g., Bobo, Kluegel, and Smith l997),an argument on which we elaborate in the conclusions.

More importantly, we also expect interracial differences in the degree to which explanations of black crime influence capital punishment beliefs across the three experimental groups. Framing research demonstrates how different messages can affect what prior beliefs (in this case, attributional beliefs) are used to evaluate the messages. Given the conflation of race and crime in the minds of many whites, the racial argument against capital punishment should activate beliefs about the origins of black crime. In the baseline and innocent conditions, however, beliefs about the causes of black crime are much less germane. We do not expect, consequently, causal beliefs about black crime to strongly predict attitudes toward capital punishment in these two treatments. In the race condition, however, such causal beliefs are, doubtless, activated by the question itself and should, therefore, become strong determinants of whites' attitudes toward the death penalty (H_{4a}).

Analysis

Data

The data for the analysis are from the National Race and Crime Survey (NRCS), a nationwide random-digit telephone survey administered by the Survey Research Center (SRC) at the University of Pittsburgh. Between October 19, 2000, and March 1, 2001, the SRC completed half-hour interviews with 603 (non-Hispanic) whites and 579 African Americans, for an overall response rate (RR3) of 48.64% (www.aapor.org). White respondents were selected with a variant of random-digit dialing, and an over-sample of black respondents was randomly selected using stratified sampling techniques. Details on the sample are available from the authors on request.

Support for the Death Penalty Across Race and Experimental Conditions

How does support for the death penalty vary across the races and the experimental conditions? Table 7.4 shows the percentage of whites (top portion of the table) and blacks (bottom portion) who favor and oppose the death penalty in the baseline (no argument), racial, and innocent treatment conditions. Focusing first on levels of support in the baseline condition, our study confirms our first hypothesis (H_1): there is a substantial race gap in support for the death penalty, with 65% of whites supporting the policy, compared to only 50% among African Americans (significant at $p < .01$). Of greater interest is how support changes across the baseline (no argument) and the two (argument) conditions for blacks and whites. Consistent with our second hypothesis, we find that blacks are significantly more receptive to both arguments against the death penalty than are whites. In response to the argument that "the death penalty is unfair because too many innocent people are being executed," support for the policy drops by 16% among blacks; support drops by 12% when blacks are exposed to the argument that "the death penalty is unfair because most of the people who are executed are African Americans."

As a whole, however, whites are not receptive to either argument. Not only do they appear resistant to persuasion when presented with an argument against the death penalty, but *support for the death penalty actually increases in the racial argument condition.* Statistically speaking, the trivial decrease (.68%) from the baseline to the innocent condition is not significant. But the more substantial 12% *increase* in response to the racial argument is significant at the .01 level. To repeat, whites overall not only reject the racial argument against the death penalty, but some move strongly in the direction *opposite* to the

Table 7.4 Percentage Support for the Death Penalty Across Race and Experimental Conditions

	Baseline Condition (No Argument)	Racial Argument	Innocent Argument
	Do you favor or oppose the death penalty for persons convicted of murder?	Some people say* that the death penalty is unfair because most of the people who are executed are African Americans. Do you favor or oppose the death penalty for persons convicted of murder?	Some people say* that the death penalty is unfair because too many innocent people are being executed. Do you favor or oppose the death penalty for persons convicted of murder?
Whites			
Strongly oppose	17.95%	11.38%	20.09%
Somewhat oppose	17.09	11.79	15.63
Somewhat favor	29.06	25.20	29.46
Strongly favor	35.90	51.63	34.82
% favor	64.96%[b]	76.83%[b]	64.28%[b]
% favor vs. baseline		+12% favor[ab]	–.68% favor[b]
N	117	246	224
Blacks			
Strongly oppose	34.17%	43.60%	45.98%
Somewhat oppose	15.83	18.48	20.09
Somewhat favor	22.50	17.54	18.75
Strongly favor	27.50	20.38	15.18
% favor	50%	37.92%	33.93%
% favor vs. baseline		–12% favor[a]	–16% favor[a]
N	120	211	224

NOTE: Statistical significance was computed by estimating an ordered probit equation for the pooled data that regressed support for the death penalty on two dummies for argument condition (baseline versus innocent argument, baseline versus racial argument), a dummy for race of respondent, and two race × argument condition interactions.

* The experiment also randomly manipulated the source of the argument as either "some people" or "FBI statistics show that," which had no discernible influence on support for the death penalty.

a. Difference across baseline and argument condition is statistically significant (< .05).

b. Difference across race of respondent is statistically significant (< .05).

argument. For example, whereas 36% of whites strongly favor the death penalty in the baseline condition, 52% strongly favor it when presented with the argument that the policy is racially unfair.

Summary and Conclusions

While there have been numerous studies of death penalty attitudes, few have examined the resistance of these attitudes to arguments against capital punishment among both whites and blacks, two groups central to any debate on the issue. Our survey experiment examines the power of two arguments against capital punishment—one racial, one not—to reshape support for the policy. We find that such frames may result in either persuasion or resistance, depending on the characteristics of the message and of the recipient.

The dominant theme of the empirical story is that whites and blacks diverge substantially in their support for the death penalty *and* their receptivity to arguments against it. We find, quite clearly, that African Americans are much more responsive to persuasive appeals that are both racial and nonracial (i.e., innocence) in nature, likely because such arguments are consistent with their existing predispositions. Given their belief that the criminal justice system is racially unfair, blacks appear receptive to any argument against the death penalty that frames the issue in terms of fairness. Whites, in contrast, seem immune to persuasion and, in the case of the racial argument, exhibit a response in the direction opposite of the message. Indeed, our most startling finding is that many whites actually become more supportive of the death penalty upon learning that it discriminates against blacks.

On this count, we believe that the conventional wisdom, which holds that death penalty attitudes are virtually immune to the types of pressures that give most political attitudes their lability (Ellsworth and Gross 1994), is a far more accurate characterization of whites than of blacks. While we would never label the opinions of African Americans as flimsy or random, we do believe that many blacks are willing to reconsider their support for punitive crime policies when presented an argument that is consistent with their belief that the criminal justice system is racially, and generally, unfair. Although the laboratory studies reviewed by Ellsworth and Gross benefit from high levels of internal validity, it is safe to say that they did not examine the effectiveness of arguments against the death penalty among a large number of minority participants, thereby exaggerating the perseverance of attitudes toward the policy.

The interracial differences in the nature and role of naive beliefs about the causes of black crime are no less intriguing. In the first place, as noted, African Americans are substantially more likely to attribute the disproportionate black crime rate to external (i.e., a discriminatory justice system) rather than internal causes, a belief that is consistent with the large body of scholarly evidence documenting substantial de facto procedural discrimination in our legal system (e.g., Lauritsen and Sampson 1998). It is also wholly consistent with the personal experiences of many blacks who are subjected to unfair treatment by police and the courts. Whites, on the other hand, are much more likely to view black criminality as being dispositionally caused, believing the reason blacks are more likely to be arrested and imprisoned than whites is that blacks commit more crimes (and thus deserve the punishment), not because the criminal justice system is biased against them.

Not only do blacks and whites hold different causal beliefs regarding black crime, but they also employ them in quite different ways when responding to questions about the death penalty. Blacks who believe that African American criminality is due more to biases in the justice system are less supportive of the death penalty, regardless of how the argument is framed. Even when race is not explicitly mentioned (as in the baseline and innocent conditions), these respondents are influenced by their causal beliefs, presumably because capital punishment is an inherently racialized issue for many in the African American community. Whites, by contrast, employ such causal beliefs more selectively. When confronted with the argument that the death penalty is racially unfair, whites who believe that black crime is due more to blacks' dispositions than to a biased justice system end up rejecting the racial argument with such force that they become even more supportive of the death penalty.

The different reactions of blacks and whites are consistent with studies in persuasion finding that, for important issues like the death penalty, one's prior beliefs affect whether one resists or responds to a message. Blacks overall are more responsive to arguments against the death penalty because they are more consistent with their beliefs about the lack of fairness of the CJS. Many whites, on the other hand, come to the table with a very different set of beliefs that prompt them to react to these same arguments with intense skepticism. Their response to the racial argument, in particular, is consistent with studies in persuasion that find when people are presented with arguments that run counter to their convictions, they are often rejected so strongly that attitude change runs in the direction opposite to the argument.

Our findings also help to extend recent studies documenting the limits of issue frames as tools of persuasion (e.g., Druckman 2001). In theory, issue frames work by altering the importance individuals attach to certain beliefs used to evaluate the message (Nelson and Oxley 1999). In reality, framing the argument against the death penalty in terms of racial discrimination does not appear to have worked as intended for either blacks or whites. Among blacks, the importance of their causal beliefs for shaping support for the death penalty was not altered by the arguments but remained constant across all three argument conditions, presumably because when blacks are asked about capital punishment such beliefs are chronically salient regardless of how the issue is framed. And among whites, although the racial argument successfully activated their beliefs about the causes of black crime, their prior beliefs prompted them to strongly *reject* the racial argument.[3] The lesson for elites who use frames as persuasive tools is that frames can have a variety of unintended consequences and can be less efficacious than is often suggested.

A similar lesson is gained from Chong and Druckman's recent study of competing frames, where the authors find evidence for what they term a "contrast effect," when a weak frame backfires when "matched against a strong frame by causing individuals to move *away* from the position advocated by the weak frame" (2006, 20; emphasis in original). If whites in our study viewed the racial discrimination argument as weak compared to the proposition of using the death penalty to punish murderers (an implicit "strong" frame), the backlash effect we find could be interpreted as being consistent with such a contrast effect. The difference is that in the Chong and Druckman study, people rejected the weak frame, whereas in our study, whites did not reject the racial *frame*, which served to activate their naive causal beliefs. Rather, their more salient causal beliefs prompted them to reject the racial *argument*.

Still other interpretations of the "backlash" effect among whites are possible. It has been suggested, for example, that instead of rejecting the racial argument, whites may be ignoring the first part of the manipulation arguing against the death penalty, focusing instead on the death penalty as a punishment for *black* convicted murderers. In other words, the manipulation may have framed the death penalty as a punishment for black offenders and because many whites view black criminals as particularly violent or beyond redemption, they are more supportive of the punishment. While plausible, we

[3]We note that rejecting the argument is fundamentally different from rejecting the frame.

see two problems with this interpretation. First, it assumes that whites ignore the main thrust of the introduction of the racial argument ("some people think the death penalty is unfair") that contains a very powerful stimulus—"unfair," a word that should not be ignored given its prominence in the justice system. Second, if whites are reacting to their images of black offenders, as suggested by this alternative explanation, surely antiblack stereotypes should play a more direct role in shaping whites' responses to the racial argument than we found to be the case. Clearly, the microtheoretical mechanisms underlying such backlash effects deserve more attention in future research.

A wholly different interpretation of the backlash effect is that it is a "principled" reaction to the racial argument driven by the conservative beliefs held by many whites about the causes of black crime (e.g., Feldman and Huddy 2005; Sniderman and Carmines 1997). A closer look at our instrumentation and findings suggests otherwise, however. As noted, whites' views about the causes of black crime are not independent of their antiblack stereotypes ($r = .23$). Thus, racial prejudice contributes indirectly to whites' reactions to the racial argument. In addition, the popular belief among whites that black crime is attributable to the failings of blacks, with no real weight given to biases in the criminal justice system, can be interpreted as constituting a more subtle form of prejudice. In the economic sphere, for example, whites' denial of racial discrimination has been termed "laissez-faire racism" (Bobo, Kluegel, and Smith 1997) because, it is argued, the maintenance of racial hierarchies no longer requires widespread endorsement of the idea that blacks are genetically inferior. Rather, it presumes that all major obstacles facing blacks as a group have been removed, making government-sponsored efforts to reduce racial inequality unnecessary.

By the same token, by denying the discrimination that blacks face in the justice system, whites are free to "blame the victim" or turn a blind eye to the many injustices that blacks suffer at the hands of the police and the courts. Thus, whites' resistance to racial arguments against the death penalty is likely motivated, at least in part, by racial animus, or at the very least, a mixture of racial insensitivity and ignorance about the reality of discrimination in the justice system.

Put differently, we do not take exception to the findings generated by Bobo and Johnson (2004), or Soss, Langbein, and Metelko (2003), who find racial prejudice to be linked to prodeath penalty attitudes. In one way or another, racism (even if defined as a denial of the de facto discrimination that is rampant in the justice system) surely affects many whites' beliefs regarding this policy. But whatever the precise explanation for our finding, the results are clear—i.e., a majority of whites supports capital punishment, a majority of whites believes that high levels of black criminality can be attributable mainly to dispositional characteristics, and a majority of whites refuses to abandon support for the death penalty despite evidence that the policy is highly flawed.

We must, as always, accept these results alongside the usual caveats, the most important in our case being the fact that we only provided respondents with antideath penalty arguments. It is always possible that arguments supportive of the policy would catalyze a fundamentally different dynamic, both intra- and interracially. It is possible, for example, that African Americans would have demonstrated greater resistance if they had been "pressured" with procapital punishment messages.

Nonetheless, our results are strongly suggestive that future research should further explore the tendency of blacks and whites to respond to the death penalty in quite different ways. To date, we know comparatively little about blacks' views on the issue—an unfortunate deficiency because of the unique role that they have played in the criminal justice system, generally, and the administration of the death penalty, specifically. As such, they provide an important contrast group that enables us to understand better the views not just of African Americans but of whites, as well.

One important practical implication of our findings is that groups (or politicians) who attempt to mobilize opposition to the death penalty face an acute political dilemma. While such groups clearly need the support of blacks, who are likely to comprise an important part of any antideath penalty coalition, direct appeals based on the claim that the policy discriminates against African Americans are likely to create a backlash among whites who see no real discrimination in the criminal justice system. Once a racial argument against the death penalty has been introduced, even a majority (62%) of whites at the extreme liberal (i.e., structural) end of the causes of black crime scale supports capital punishment. Because most whites do not see widespread racial discrimination in the criminal justice system (or any other domain, see Sigelman and Welch 1991), direct appeals based on claims of discrimination are unlikely to win their support.

Our results suggest that a more effective argument for encouraging opposition to the death penalty is one that frames the unfairness of the policy more generally, without focusing on race, thereby avoiding whites' resistance to more direct racial appeals. The argument that many innocent people are being executed may not move whites in great numbers toward opposition, but neither does it precipitate a white backlash. In addition, as we have seen, such nonracial arguments against the death penalty can and do elicit blacks' opposition to the policy because many blacks already have a deep suspicion about the fairness of the legal system. Thus, making more general arguments against the lack of fairness of the death penalty without making a direct reference to race may constitute a successful "stealth" strategy that appeals to blacks but does not produce countermobilization among whites.

In many respects, whites' responses in our study provide a more general rationale for focusing more on resistance in studies of political persuasion. Not only did many whites appear immune to persuasive appeals, but they also exhibited the type of "bolstering" (or boomerang) effect noted in the literature (Johnson and Eagly 1989). We know, if only experientially, that instances of resistance are commonplace—witness the large numbers of supporters of George W. Bush who continued to believe in the existence of weapons of mass destruction in Iraq despite months of media coverage to the contrary. But nonfindings seldom receive placement in journals, and students of opinion and persuasion are typically more interested in agents that are persuasive than in those that are not.

Appendix Table Predicting Support for the Death Penalty, Pooled Across Condition

	Whites	Blacks
Predictors		
Black crime attrib.	.01 (.08)	.15* (.08)
General crime attrib.	.14* (.08)	.08 (.09)
Antiblack ster.	.02 (.02)	−.02 (.02)
Fear of crime	−.15 (.13)	.08 (.11)

(Continued)

Appendix Table (Continued)

	Whites	Blacks
Punitiveness	−.24*** (.09)	.01 (.07)
Party ID	−.07 (.06)	.10 (.07)
Ideology	.06 (.08)	.03 (.05)
Education	−.08 (.08)	−.02 (.09)
Female	−.56** (.24)	−.47** (.22)
Income	.15** (.08)	−.00 (.08)
Age	−.01 (.01)	−.01 (.01)
Conditions and interactions		
Racial argument (1 = Condit.)	−1.02 (1.12)	.15 (1.01)
Innocent argument (1 = Condit.)	−.61 (1.15)	−.61 (1.00)
Racial * Black crime attrib.	.21** (.10)	.01 (.11)
Racial * Gen. crime attrib.	.03 (.10)	−.10 (.11)
Racial * Antiblack ster.	−.00 (.03)	−.01 (.02)
Racial * Fear of crime	.24 (.16)	−.11 (.14)
Racial * Punitiveness	.05 (.10)	−.18** (.09)
Racial * Party ID	.14* (.08)	−.02 (.09)
Racial * Ideology	−.11 (.09)	−.05 (.07)
Racial * Education	−.07 (.10)	−.02 (.12)
Racial * Female	.04 (.29)	.89*** (.29)
Racial * Income	−.01 (.10)	.05 (.10)
Racial * Age	.00 (.01)	.01 (.01)
Innocent * Black crime attrib.	.09 (.10)	.02 (.11)
Innocent * Gen. crime attrib.	−.10 (.10)	.02 (.10)
Innocent * Antiblack ster.	.04 (.03)	−.01 (.02)
Innocent * Fear of crime	.21 (.16)	−.14 (.14)
Innocent * Punitiveness	.06 (.11)	−.12 (.09)
Innocent * Party ID	−.01 (.08)	−.07 (.09)

	Whites	Blacks
Innocent * Ideology	.06 (.09)	.00 (.07)
Innocent * Education	–.00 (.10)	.22* (.11)
Innocent * Female	.24 (.29)	.58** (.29)
Innocent * Income	–.16* (.09)	–.08 (.10)
Innocent * Age	.00 (.01)	.01 (.01)
Cutpoint1	2.42 (.97)	–.08 (.82)
Cutpoint2	1.85 (.97)	.44 (.82)
Cutpoint	–.98 (.96)	1.08 (.82)
N	584	546

NOTE: Entries are ordered probit regression coefficients with standard errors in parentheses. Variable coding is in the test. The omitted condition is the baseline condition.

*$p < .10$; **$p < .05$; ***$p < .01$.

References

Baumgartner, Frank R., Suzanna De Boef, and Amber E. Boydstun, 2004. "An Evolutionary Factor Analysis Approach to the Study of Issue-Definition." Paper prepared for presentation at the annual meeting of the Midwest Political Science Association.

Bobo, Lawrence D., and Devon Johnson, 2004. "A Taste for Punishment: Black and White Americans' Views on the Death Penalty and the War on Drugs." *Du Bois Review* 1(1): 151–80.

Bobo, Lawrence D., James R. Kluegel, and R. A. Smith, 1997. "Laissez Faire Racism: The Crystallization of a 'Kinder, Gentler' Antiblack Ideology." In *Racial Attitudes in the 1990s: Continuity and Change,* ed. Steven A. Tuch and Jack K. Martin. Greenwood, CT: Praeger, pp. 93–120.

Bohm, Robert M. 2003. "American Death Penalty Opinion: Past, Present and Future." In *America's Experiment with Capital Punishment,* 2nd ed., ed. James Acker, Robert Bohm, and Charles Lanier. Durham, NC: Carolina Academic Press.

Brace, Paul R., and Melinda Gann Hall, 1997. "The Interplay of Preferences, Case Facts, Context, and Rules in the Politics of Judicial Choice." *Journal of Politics* 59(November); 1206–31.

Chong, Dennis, and James N. Druckman, 2006. "Democratic Competition and Public Opinion." Paper presented at the annual meeting of the American Political Science Association, Philadelphia.

Druckman, James N, 2001. "The Implications of Framing Effects for Citizen Competence." *Political Behavior* 23(3): 225-56.

Ellsworth, Phoebe C., and Samuel R. Gross, 1994. "Hardening of the Attitudes: Americans' Views on the Death Penalty." Journal of Social Issues 50(1): 19–52.

Feldman, Stanley, and Leonie Huddy, 2005. "Racial Resentment and White Opposition to Race-Conscious Programs: Principles or Prejudice?" *American Journal of Political Science 49*(1): 168–83.

Gallup Poll, 2005. "Death Penalty." Princeton, NJ: The Gallup Organization. http://poll.gallup.com/

Hurwitz, Jon, and Mark Peffley, 2005. "Explaining the Great Racial Divide: Perceptions of Fairness in the U.S. Criminal Justice System." *Journal of Politics* 67(3): 762–83.

Johnson, Blair, and Alice Eagly, 1989. "Effects of Involvement on Persuasion: A Meta-Analysis." *Psychological Bulletin* 106(2): 290–314.

Lauritsen, Janet L., and Robert J. Sampson, 1998. "Minorities, Crime, and Criminal Justice" In *The Handbook of Crime and Punishment,* ed. Michael

H. Tonry. New York: Oxford University Press, pp. 30–56.

McGarrell, Edmund F., and Marla Sandys, 1996. "The Misperception of Public Opinion toward Capital Punishment." *American Behavioral Scientist* 39(4): 500–513.

Mooney, Christopher Z., and Mei-Hsien Lee, 2000. "The Influence of Values on Consensus and Contentious Morality Policy: US. Death Penalty Reform. 1956–82." *Journal of Politics* 62(1): 223–39.

Nelson, Thomas E., and Zoe M. Oxley, 1999. "Issue Framing Effects and Belief Importance and Opinion." *Journal of Politics* 61(4): 1040–67.

Norrander, Barbara, 2000. "The Multi-Layered Impact of Public Opinion on Capital Punishment Implementation in the American States." *Political Research Quarterly* 53: 771–93.

Page, Benjamin, and Robert Shapiro, 1992. *The Rational Public.* Chicago: University of Chicago Press.

Sigelman, Lee, and Susan Welch, 1991. *Black Americans' Views of Racial Inequality: The Dream Deferred.* Cambridge: Cambridge University Press.

Sniderman, P. M., and E. G. Carmines, 1997. *Reaching Beyond Race.* Cambridge, MA: Harvard University Press.

Soss, Joe, Laura Langbein, and Alan R. Metelko, 2003. "Why Do White Americans Support the Death Penalty?" *Journal of Politics* 65(2): 397–421.

DISCUSSION QUESTIONS

1. Why is it important to study the difference in beliefs between White and Black citizens regarding the death penalty?
2. What factors do you think could help explain the difference in effect persuasion had on both Blacks and Whites? Explain.
3. Do you believe that factors other than race play a part in the disproportionate representation of Blacks on death row? Explain.

Corrections

SECTION HIGHLIGHTS

- Overview of Corrections
- Race and Corrections in Historical Context
- Contemporary Issues in Race and Corrections
- Summary
- Edited Readings

Overview of Corrections

Corrections refer to federal, state, and local agencies that are responsible for persons found guilty in a court of law. State and federal prisons and local jails held over 2,297,400 inmates under their authority in midyear 2009 (West, 2010). The terms *corrections* and *incarceration* are often used interchangeably, even though most persons under correctional supervision are on **probation**. In 2008, of the 5,095,200 offenders under community supervision, 4,270,917 (84%) were probationers and 828,169 (16%) were parolees (Glaze & Bonczar, 2009). Sometimes referred to as ***community corrections***, probation and **parole** require that the person either serve their sentence (probation) or the remainder of their sentence (parole) under supervision in the community. The disproportionate number of minorities under correctional supervision is an important issue in the study of race and crime. Table 8.1 presents the estimated number of inmates who were held in custody between 2000 and 2009. During the 10-year period, minority males outnumbered Whites in custody every year, and Black males outnumbered White and Hispanic males behind bars. When Black and Hispanic females are combined, minority females outnumber White females in custody as well.

Table 8.1 Estimated Number of Inmates Held in Custody in State or Federal Prison, or in Local Jails, by Sex, Race, and Hispanic Origin, June 30, 2000–2009

	Males				Females			
Year	Total[a]	White[b]	Black[b]	Hispanic	Total[a]	White[b]	Black[b]	Hispanic
2000	1,775,700	663,700	791,600	290,900	156,200	63,700	69,500	19,500
2001	1,800,300	684,800	803,400	283,000	161,200	67,700	69,500	19,900
2002	1,848,700	630,700	818,900	342,500	165,800	68,800	65,600	25,400
2003	1,902,300	665,100	832,400	363,900	176,300	76,100	66,800	28,300
2004	1,947,800	695,800	842,500	366,800	183,400	81,700	67,700	28,600
2005	1,992,600	688,700	806,200	403,500	193,600	88,600	65,700	29,300
2006	2,042,100	718,100	836,800	426,900	203,100	95,300	68,800	32,400
2007	2,090,800	755,500	814,700	410,900	208,300	96,600	67,600	32,100
2008	2,103,500	712,500	846,000	427,000	207,700	94,500	67,800	33,400
2009	2,096,300	693,800	841,000	442,000	201,200	92,100	64,800	32,300

NOTE: Detailed categories exclude persons who reported two or more races. All totals include persons under age 18.

a. Includes American Indians, Alaska Natives, Asians, Native Hawaiians, and other Pacific Islanders, and persons identifying two or more races.

b. Excludes persons of Hispanic or Latino origin.

This section provides information about the purpose of corrections, its history in America, components of the corrections industry, employment trends, types of facilities, and recent trends in the number of prisoners, jail inmates, and persons on probation and parole. It provides a brief historical overview of race and corrections in American history since the colonial era. The section concludes with a discussion of two contemporary issues in the study of race and crime: racial disparities in corrections and **prisoner reentry**. The original purpose of corrections and prisons in America was to provide an alternative to the barbaric forms of punishment that existed during the colonial era and in the 1800s. Other purposes of corrections and punishment more generally are deterrence, incapacitation, and retribution. Reforming individuals through **rehabilitation** was an important goal of imprisonment and corrections that emerged in the late 19th century and lasted well into the 20th century. Today, the major purpose of punishment—especially in regard to those behind bars—is justice or *just deserts*, a term used to convey that offenders should be held accountable for their criminal behavior and that punishment is deserved (Schmalleger, 2006). The **justice model** and "get tough laws" legislated in the 1980s and 1990s created mandatory sentences and abolished parole in many jurisdictions. As a result, overcrowding in prisons and, more recently, in jails became dramatic. This overcrowding coincided with the decline in support for rehabilitation. During the early 1970s, a large majority (76%) of Americans supported rehabilitation (Flanagan, 1996). By 1980, only a little more than 50% of the public supported such an approach. Summarizing the public opinion literature from 1968 to 1982, Flanagan (1996) wrote, "The proportion of Americans selecting rehabilitation as the main emphasis of prisons declined 40%; the proportion selecting punishment rose 171%, and the proportion of protection of society rose 166%" (p. 79).

The early prisons that emerged during colonial times in America were similar to correctional facilities in England and Europe at that time. Like today, jails and prisons were expensive to build and maintain (Chapin, 1983). Most offenders were rarely sentenced to prison, with fines, corporal punishments (e.g., whippings), and banishment serving as the most common punishments (Chapin, 1983; Shelden, 2001). In addition, early colonists who fled from England seeking religious freedom, like the Quakers, were critical of harsh corporal punishments and sought reforms. In 1790, the **Walnut Street Jail** became America's first correctional facility. Chapin (1983) noted that "jails were used most commonly to hold persons accused of serious crimes before trial and to detain convicted persons until they could pay fines or make restitution" (p. 52). The Quakers believed that solitary confinement at all times was required for prisoners in the Walnut Street Jail. This served as a model for another early prison: the Newgate Prison that opened in New York in 1797. The Auburn Prison (NY, 1819) became a popular model as well due to its use of congregate labor that was profitable (Manatu-Rupert, 2002). When the Walnut Street facility became overcrowded, the Pennsylvania legislature approved the construction of two prisons: Western Penitentiary (1826) and Eastern Penitentiary (1829). Prisoner Number 1, who arrived at the Eastern Penitentiary (near Philadelphia) on October 25, 1829, was "Charles Williams, an 18-year-old African American from Delaware County, Pennsylvania . . . serving a two-year sentence for larceny" (Clear & Cole, 2000, p. 35). Another early corrections facility was the Elmira Reformatory that opened in 1876. Designed for younger offenders, it emphasized rehabilitation (Reid, 2008).

In 1930, the Federal **Bureau of Prisons** (BOP) was established to provide for federal inmates in the 11 federal prisons that existed at that time (U.S. Federal Bureau of Prisons [BOP], 2010). Throughout the 20th century and into the 21st, the federal government and most states continued to build prisons. In 1993, there were 74 new prison projects planned (Camp & Camp, 1993). According to the *Census of State and Federal Correctional Facilities, 2000*, there were 84 federal facilities, 1,023 state, 101 private confinement facilities, and 460 community-based facilities; 297 were state-run and 163 were private facilities (Stephan & Karberg, 2003). In 2006, there were approximately 1,325 state prisons (Smallager, 2006), 115 federal institutions, and 28 federal community corrections offices (BOP, 2010). Spending on corrections has increased to more than $50 billion in the past two decades (Pew Center on the States, 2010a).

Federal and state prisons include three types of facilities: minimum-, medium-, and maximum-security prisons. **Risk assessment** is used for inmate classification and placement (Latessa & Lovins, 2010). Types of confinement facilities include reception and diagnostic centers, boot camps, substance abuse treatment programs, those for youthful offenders, work release/prerelease, and others (BJS, 2004). Nationwide, there are also approximately 57 "supermax" prisons in 40 states (Mears & Watson, 2006). According to Clear and Cole (2003), "These institutions are designed to hold the most disruptive, violent, and incorrigible prisoners" (p. 252). These units and facilities are more expensive than other prisons because of their construction requirements, sophisticated security systems, and requisite electronic systems (Riveland, 1999).

Persons who are awaiting trial and are unable to secure bail, and those who are sentenced to a year or less, are held in local jails. Some states contract with jails to house prisoners because of overcrowding (Allen, Simonsen, & Latessa, 2004). Non-incarcerative options for offenders placed in the community (usually on probation) include fines, community service, drug and alcohol treatment, home confinement, and **intensive probation** supervision. These options are less expensive than placement in confinement.

The growth in the corrections industry has resulted in employment opportunities in many locales. For example, in 1983, there were 146,000 correctional officers (U.S. Bureau of the Census, 2003); however, just over two decades later, in 2006, there were 451,000 correctional officers. Blacks (24.2%) and Hispanics (7.4%) were beneficiaries of this growth (U.S. Bureau of the Census, 2008).

Imprisonment trends have earned the United States a reputation as the world's incarceration leader. In midyear 2009, there were 1,617,478 prisoners being held in state and federal prisons. The number of offenders overshadows two important facts: (1) This was an increase of only .5% compared to 2008, and (2) most prison growth occurred at the federal level (West, 2010). *Prison Count 2010* reports that as of January, 2010, there were 1,404,053 persons under the jurisdiction of state prison authorities—4,777 fewer than in December, 2008. According to the report, the following is true:

> This marks the first year-to-year drop in the nation's state prison population since 1972. . . . The prison population declined in 26 states, while increasing in 24 states and in the federal system. (Pew Center on the States, 2010b)

Table 8.2 presents the age, race, and gender of inmates held in federal and state prisons and jails at midyear 2009. Most of the persons in custody were between the ages of 25 and 29 (360,800), 30 and 34 (326,400), and 20 and 24 (318,800). Most Black and Hispanic males were between the ages of 25 and 29, while most white males were between 40 and 44 years of age. The majority of females, as well as of Black and White females in custody, were between the ages of 35 and 39. Most of the Hispanic females in custody were between the ages of 25 and 29 (West, 2010).

State and federal prisoners held in private facilities (126,248) increased by 6.8% in midyear 2008. Most inmates were either in the federal system (32,712), Texas (19,851) or Florida (9,026) (DOJ, 2009). At midyear 2009, there were 127,688 inmates, most of them in the same three systems. Most prisoners (58,102) were in private facilities located in the South (West, 2010).

Unlike prisons, jails are local facilities that confine persons for several reasons, including those (1) awaiting completion of their trial, conviction, and sentencing; (2) transferring to other facilities; (3) serving as witnesses in court; and (4) on probation, parole, and bail-bond violators (BJS, 2010). Like in prisons, incarceration in jails continued to increase between 2000 and 2008, from 621,149 in 2000 to 785,556 in 2008 (Glaze & Bonczar, 2009). At midyear 2009, there were 767,620 inmates being held in jails. For the first time, jail occupancy dropped to 90% of capacity in 2009, compared to 92% in 2000 and 95% in 2008 (BJS, 2010).

Every year, BJS conducts the annual Survey of Jails in Indian Country (SJIC), which surveys facilities that are operated by tribal authorities or the Bureau of Indian Affairs.

Table 8.2 Estimated Number of Inmates Held in Custody in State or Federal Prisons or in Local Jails, by Sex, Race, Hispanic Origin, and Age, June 30, 2009

	Males				Females			
Year	Total[a]	White[b]	Black[b]	Hispanic	Total[a]	White[b]	Black[b]	Hispanic
Total[c]	2,096,300	693,800	841,000	442,000	201,200	92,100	64,800	32,300
18-19	68,200	21,100	29,400	14,300	4,200	1,800	1,400	1,000
20-24	318,800	92,300	135,000	76,600	26,700	12,200	8,800	5,600
25-29	360,800	101,100	149,700	90,800	30,400	14,000	10,700	5,800
30-34	326,400	96,500	130,400	80,900	33,600	14,800	11,600	5,500
35-39	308,100	103,500	123,800	61,700	37,700	17,000	12,300	5,200
40-44	278,600	103,900	108,000	47,400	32,400	15,000	10,300	3,800
45-49	203,900	77,200	80,600	33,500	19,700	9,200	5,900	2,600
50-54	111,800	43,900	43,600	17,400	8,900	5,000	2,000	1,400
55-59	58,000	26,200	19,500	9,400	3,900	1,800	600	700
60-64	25,200	12,900	7,000	4,300	1,600	500	400	200
65 or older	21,000	11,500	5,600	2,800	1,100	500	100	100

NOTE: Detailed categories exclude persons who reported two or more races.

a. Includes American Indians, Alaska Natives, Asians, Native Hawaiians, other Pacific Islanders, and persons identifying two or more races.

b. Excludes persons of Hispanic or Latino origin.

c. Includes persons under age 18.

These facilities include jails, detention centers (youth), and confinement and other types of correctional facilities. In 2008, the 82 facilities included in the survey reported 2,135 inmates. Unlike other correctional facilities, these jails saw a decline in the inmate population (–1.3%) (Minton, 2009). It is important to note, however, that Native Americans are also held in other correctional facilities.

As previously stated, most of the persons under correctional supervision are placed in the community. In 2000, there were 4,550,000 persons in the community. In 2008, there were 5,095,200 offenders under community supervision. The majority—4,270,917—were on probation, including 1,528,485 Whites, 786,499 Blacks, and 371,015 Hispanics. The growth in the probation population has slowed since 2003, and the parole population slowed in 2008. In spite of this, the number of persons on both probation and parole has steadily increased between 2000 and 2008 (Glaze & Bonczar, 2009). The next section provides a temporal perspective on race and corrections.

Race and Corrections in Historical Context

During the antebellum period (prior to the Civil War), economic considerations meant that it was rare to find slaves, Native Americans, or indentured servants incarcerated. On this subject, Collins (1997) wrote the following:

> Jailing of slaves was not profitable for the slave owners, so very few slaves were ever incarcerated for an extended period of time. Instead, prior to the Civil War, Black slaves would be imprisoned in plantation built jails and punished for crimes committed (for example, running away, stealing, assaulting an overseer, or disobeying an order) by the slave master who had unlimited power, including deadly force. (p. 6)

To legitimize their actions, slave masters created "Negro courts," which meted out punishments (Sellin, 1976).

In a review of early prison records from the North (1795–1826), McIntyre (1992) noted that the free African American population in Philadelphia ranged from 4.6% in 1790 to 9.4% in 1810. When she looked at prisoner statistics from the Walnut Street Jail, McIntyre (1992) found the following:

> Throughout the period from 1795 to 1826 in Philadelphia City and County, Blacks comprised 35% with "Mulattoes" equaling an additional 9%. This 44% reflected an inmate population for African Americans more than 13 times greater than the state's and nearly 5 times greater than the city's total African American population. (pp. 170–171)

Inmate records from 1829 to 1841 at the Eastern Penitentiary show that that there were 1,353 prisoners from 1829 to 1841, "with a breakdown of 846 White inmates (823 males and 23 females) and 508 Black inmates (456 males and 52 females). The Black men represented 37.5% of all males, and the Black women equaled 66% of the females" (McIntyre, 1992, p. 171).

Other states had similar trends in relation to the racial composition of early correctional facilities. For example, from 1812 to 1832, the Maryland state prison in Baltimore "held 45% African American males and 68% African American females for a 51% overall Black inmate population" (McIntyre, 1992, p. 172). Over a 10-month period, from 1832 to 1833, records show that in Richmond, Virginia, African American men represented 22% of male inmates; African American women represented 100% of the female inmates (McIntyre, 1992). As noted in Section I, after emancipation in 1863 and the passage of the Thirteenth Amendment in 1865, southern landowners were devastated. Sellin (1976) noted that, following the passage of the Thirteenth Amendment, the following was true:

> The penal laws of the southern states became applicable to all offenders regardless of race. This was a distressing prospect for states which had created industrial penitentiaries for offenders from the master class and now faced the rapidly growing criminality of poor, unskilled, bewildered ex-slaves cast into a freedom for which few of them were prepared. (p. 145)

Sellin (1976) added that, although Blacks were legally free, southern landowners "did not change their opinions on the status of Blacks in a society dominated by Whites" (p. 145). Because of Whites' "reluctance to labor," they created a system to maintain an able-bodied labor force (Sellin, 1976).

Taking advantage of the language in the Thirteenth Amendment, which allowed for slavery and involuntary servitude, southern landowners created the **convict-lease system**, whose sole aim was financial profit to the states. Over time, the racial composition of prison populations (especially in the South) changed dramatically (Oshinsky, 1996). By 1880, the convict populations were overwhelmingly Black. For example, records from Georgia prisons in the late 1800s showed that Blacks were serving sentences twice as long as Whites, with 50% of the inmates serving sentences of more than 10 years (Oshinsky, 1996).

In the decades between the Reconstruction period and 1960, although much changed in terms of overall advancements for racial minorities, there wasn't much change in mass incarceration. Blacks continued to be overrepresented in state and federal correctional institutions.

Prior to the 1960s, Black inmates essentially accepted their status without any resistance (Reasons, Conley, & Debro, 2002). Reasons, Conley, and Debro (2002) noted that, although Blacks were exposed to inhumane conditions, they did not protest because "(1) the courts had a hands-off policy with respect to penal conditions and issues, and (2) the institutions were located primarily in rural areas and thus functioned in relative isolation, and the guards were all White" (p. 271). Discussing the importance of the mass migration from the South to northern and western states among African Americans, Reasons et al. wrote, "This demographic shift made racial segregation more difficult and expensive to maintain in all institutions, including penal institutions" (p. 271). Another contributor to change was the fact that leaders from the civil rights movement (e.g., Martin Luther King, Jr., Ralph Abernathy, and Medgar Evers), Black Panther movement (e.g., Stokely Carmichael, H. Rap Brown, Huey Newton, and Angela Davis), and Black Muslim movement (most notably, Malcolm X) were all incarcerated at some point and spoke out about their experiences (Reasons et al., 2002). It was, however, the Black Muslim and Black Panther movements that had the greatest influence on correctional systems in their quest for religious freedom and other privileges now referred to as *prisoners' rights.*

Since the 1960s, several contemporary issues have emerged in the study of race and corrections, including prison riots and disturbances, prison gangs, segregation in prison, the use of chain gangs, and felon disenfranchisement. In the next section, we discuss two other issues: ongoing racial disparities in corrections and prisoner reentry after incarceration.

Racial Disparities in Corrections

The historical account of race and corrections provides an important temporal context for understanding racial disparities in corrections today. Without question, racial minorities are disproportionately affected by what some have called America's "imprisonment binge" (Austin & Irwin, 2001). Consider the following:

- More than three quarters of a million Black men are behind bars (Brewer & Heitzeg, 2008, p. 628).
- Black men are eight times more likely to be incarcerated than whites (Western & Wildman, 2009, p. 228).
- For Black male dropouts born since the mid-1960s, 60% to 70% go to prison (Western & Wildman, 2009, p. 231).
- More than college graduation or military service, incarceration has come to typify the biographies of African American men born since the late 1960s (Western & Wildman, 2009, p. 233).
- Black (non-Hispanic) males were incarcerated at a rate more than 6 times higher than White (non-Hispanic) males and 2.6 times higher than Hispanic males (West, 2010, p. 2).
- African American women are 3 times more likely than Latinas and 6 times more likely than White women to be in prison (Brewer & Heitzeg, 2008, p. 628).
- One in every 300 Black females was incarcerated, compared to about 1 in every 1,099 White females and 1 in every 704 Hispanic females (West, 2010, p. 2).
- The incarceration rate for American Indians was 921 per 100,000, about 21% higher than the overall national incarceration rate of 759 per 100,000 persons (Minton, 2009, p. 2).

Explaining why these facts exist is problematic. Are minorities more criminal? Are they more likely to commit serious crimes? Does discrimination play a role in the disparity dilemma? The arrest data presented in Section II indicated that Blacks are more likely to be arrested for two violent personal crimes—homicide and robbery—and that they are disproportionately arrested for other serious crimes as well. Another issues presented in Section II was that, in 2008, the majority of persons were arrested for drug abuse offenses. Some of the contemporary disparities in corrections are related to sentences for drug crimes, discussed in Section VI. Historically, discrimination manifested itself in social control, including incarceration—especially after emancipation. Several scholars (Alexander, 2010; Glasser, 2006; Scotti & Kronenberg, 2001) have referred to drug laws and mass incarceration as a new form of Jim Crow. Alexander (2010) used the term ***New Jim Crow*** to refer to similarities between current and past racialized systems of social control and made the following statement:

> What is painfully obvious when one steps back from individual cases and specific policies is that the system of mass incarceration operates with stunning efficiency to sweep people of color off the streets, lock them in cages, and then release them into an inferior second-class status. Nowhere is this more true than in the War on Drugs. (p. 100)

In the early 1980s, scholars began to examine racial disparities in corrections (see, e.g., Christianson, 1981; Petersilia, 1983). Blumstein (1982) investigated the role of discrimination in Black overrepresentation in prisons. Taking into account arrest patterns of Blacks and Whites, Blumstein found that "80% of the actual racial disproportionality in incarceration rates is accounted for by differential involvement in arrest" (pp. 1267–1268).

Blumstein noted that while this explained the majority of the racial differences in incarceration, if the 20% that was unexplained (which at the time translated into 10,500 prisoners) "were attributable to discrimination, that would be a distressing level of discrimination" (p. 1268). Even he acknowledged that several factors, including racial discrimination, could not be ruled out. It is important to note that Blumstein's analysis was based on arrest statistics, which, as noted in Section II, have serious limitations.

Hawkins (1986) found that from 1978 to 1979 in North Carolina, 30% of the prison disproportionality was explained by arrest patterns. For the subsequent 2 years, Hawkins (1986) noted that the figures increased to 40% and 42%. In line with Blumstein's (1982) earlier supposition for certain crimes, Hawkins's research showed that "fewer Blacks than White assault offenders received prison sentences. Fewer Blacks than Whites also received prison terms for larceny and armed robbery" (p. 260). These findings were in line with Hawkins's (1983) earlier work, which noted that, in certain contexts, Black life was devalued, which resulted in justice officials minimizing Black-on-Black offenses and assigning less serious punishments for such offenses. In another study, Hawkins and Hardy (1989) used state-level arrest and prison data for 39 states (with a 1% or greater Black population), found some variation across states, and concluded that Blumstein's figure of 80% did not seem to be a good approximation for all states (p. 79). In another study, Blumstein (1993) found 24% of the disproportionality of Blacks in prison was not explained by offending patterns. Blumstein (1993) surmised that, because of the increased level of discretion in less serious offenses (i.e., drug offenses), factors such as discrimination could be contributing to the disparity.

In the 1990s, two nonprofit organizations, the Sentencing Project and the National Center on Institutions and Alternatives (NCIA), published reports that highlighted the control rates for African Americans. Russell-Brown (2004) noted that such rates "refer to the percentage of a population that is under the jurisdiction of the criminal justice system—on probation, parole, in jail, or in prison. It provides a snapshot of a group's overall involvement in the justice system" (pp. 123–124). One report showed that "almost one in four African American males in the age group of 20–29 was under some form of criminal justice supervision" (Mauer, 1990). Two years later, J. G. Miller (1992) of the NCIA reported the following:

> On an average day in 1991, 21,800 (42%) of Washington, D.C.'s 53,375 African American males ages 18 through 35 were either in jail or prison, on probation or parole, out on bond awaiting disposition of criminal charges or being sought on an arrest warrant. (p. 1)

It was during the 1990s that concerns about the increasing expenditures on prisons and the decreasing spending on education were raised (Chambliss, 1991). Sometime during the decade, prisons became hot commodities that were desirable for their economic impact (Lotke, 1996).

Huling (2002) noted that, prior to 1990, 36% of prisons were built in nonmetropolitan areas. According to her figures, "Between 1990 and 1999, 245 prisons were built in rural and small town communities—with a prison opening somewhere in rural America every fifteen days" (p. 198). Noting that the economic impact is often overstated, she pointed to the "hidden" costs, such as increasing costs for local court and police services, the negative impact on investments by other industries, and the prevalence of racism in many rural communities.

Some researchers (Dyer, 2000; Parenti, 1999) have argued that government and citizens were profiting from the mass incarceration of principally African Americans and Hispanics. Private prison companies such as Corrections Corporation of America, which constitutes the sixth largest prison system in the nation, were in some cases found unknowingly in the retirement portfolios of many Americans (Dyer, 2000). As such, society was investing in prisons, which obviously relied on an ample supply of prisoners to keep the prison boom going (Dyer, 2000; Hallett, 2006; Price, 2006). Other writers of the period stressed the rebirth of the convict-lease system in the form of the modern-day use of cheap prison labor by private companies partnering with state corrections departments (Davis, 1997, 2000, 2003). Overall, scholars of this genre believed that because of the continuing need for bodies to keep the prison-industrial complex going, disparities in corrections will likely persist.

In the 2000s, scholars have continued to examine disparities (Crutchfield, 2004; Fernandez & Bowman, 2004; Mauer, 2004, 2006; Sorenson, Hope, & Stemen, 2003; Western, 2006). Today, information on disparities is more readily available. For example, the Sentencing Project provides a useful tool on its website to examine data for the states that includes current information on their corrections population, racial and ethnic disparity in incarceration, juveniles in custody, corrections expenditures, and felony disenfranchisement, as well as other information. Another development during this decade has been an emphasis on the consequences of mass incarceration on communities in general and minority communities in particular (see Clear, 2007; Western & Wildeman, 2009). Alexander (2010) described how the system of mass incarceration concludes with a period of *invisible punishment* (a term coined by Jeremy Travis) once the offender is released. Exoffenders, families, and communities continue to suffer.

The American Bar Association (ABA) adopted criminal justice standards on collateral sanctions for convicted persons in 2003 to address the prohibitions and disqualifications convicted persons face upon release, including "access to government benefits and housing benefits; restrictions on employment; voting and other forms of participation in civic life; and issues affecting family life" (The Reentry of Exoffenders Clinic, 2007, p. 6). Prisoner reentry garnered a great deal of attention during the 2000s. In the next section we examine some of these recent developments, including strategies for addressing **collateral consequences**.

Prisoner Reentry

The mass incarceration that took place in the 1980s and 1990s resulted in thousands of offenders being released back into society (Petersilia, 2003; Travis, 2005). As stated previously, there were more than 828,169 persons on parole at midyear 2008 (Glaze & Bonczar, 2009). In addition to those on parole, thousands of persons "max out," or complete their entire sentences and leave prison without any supervision, as do millions released from jails. Since minorities represent a large portion of those in jails and prisons, it is only logical that they represent the majority. Petersilia (2003) defined *prisoner reentry* as "all activities and programming conducted to prepare ex-convicts to return safely to the community and to live as law-abiding citizens" (p. 3). The major goals of reentry strategies are (1) to promote public safety by reducing **recidivism** and

(2) to reintegrate inmates by promoting positive interactions upon their release (Travis, Crayton, & Mukamal, 2009).

In the preface to his book titled *But They All Come Back*, Jeremy Travis (2005) tells the story about a question Attorney General Janet Reno asked following a meeting in spring 1999: "What are we doing about all the people coming out of prison?" Travis, at the time the director of the National Institute of Justice, and Laurie Robinson, at that time the assistant attorney general for justice programs, didn't know the answer (Travis, 2005, p. xi). Shortly thereafter, Travis became a leading advocate for prisoner reentry research, courts, and other initiatives before leaving NIJ and later at the Urban Institute. Travis (2005) identified several reentry policy challenges, including public safety, public health, families and children, employment, and civic identity.

Perhaps the most challenging aspect of reentry is recidivism. *Recidivism* refers to committing crimes after one's release. Persons placed in the community on probation recidivate, as do parolees and those released from prisons and jails without supervision. According to Petersilia (2002), some of the key factors that contribute to failure on both probation and parole (which has been eliminated at the federal level and in some states) include the following:

> Conviction crime (property offenders have higher rates), prior criminal record (the more convictions the higher the recidivism), employment (unemployment is associated with higher recidivism), age (younger offenders have higher rates), family composition (persons living with spouse or children have lower rates) and drug use (heroin addicts have the highest recidivism rates). (p. 491)

Because minorities are more likely to fit some of these characteristics, they are at even higher risk for reentry problems (Pager, 2007a, 2007b). And recidivism in many minority communities is high as well. In a 1994 study it was estimated that two thirds of inmates followed for 3 years in 15 states were rearrested, and 52% were reconvicted (Langan & Levin, 1994). Visher, Yahner, and La Vigne (2010) followed 652 men (76% African American, 8% Latino) before and after release in Chicago, Illinois, Cleveland, Ohio, and Houston, Texas. They found that one in five (22%) reoffended and that 70% of reoffenders had technical violations. Two of the biggest challenges to recidivism and reentry are prior convictions and drug dependency. Travis, Crayton, and Mukamal (2009) identified several guidelines for reducing recidivism, including targeting high-risk offenders, using risk assessment instruments, beginning treatment in prison, and continuing intensive interventions in the community for 6 months, the period of time in which re-arrests are most likely to occur.

The federal government has funded several reentry initiatives during the 2000s, including the U.S. Department of Labor's Ready4Work program, the BOP's Transition From Prison to Community Initiative, and the National Institute of Justice's Prisoner Reentry Initiative. In 2000, the Office of Justice Programs (OJP) launched a Reentry Court Initiative (RCI) in nine states (California, Colorado, Delaware, Florida, Iowa, Kentucky, Ohio, New York, and West Virginia). Initially proposed by Travis (2005), reentry courts were designed to improved offender accountability and to provide support services during the reentry process (Delaware Judicial Information Center, 2009). The Second Chance Act, signed into law in April, 2008, authorized federal grants to government agencies and nonprofit organizations to provide assistance to exoffenders to improve outcomes and reduce recidivism (National Reentry Resource Center, 2010). In 2009, more than $28 million dollars was awarded to fund adult and juvenile mentoring programs, adult and juvenile demonstration programs, and the National Reentry Resource Center.

More than a decade after then Attorney General Janet Reno wanted to know what the federal government was doing about exoffenders, many continue to wonder what difference research and programs are making. Recidivism data would help to determine progress that has been made. Exoffenders are still unable to successfully transition back home. The so-called invisible punishment is actually in plain view as the revolving door of corrections continues. A major part of the challenge of successful reentry is that there simply aren't enough resources to effectively meet the needs of exoffenders. Structural barriers will require more legislative changes and advocates for change. As in the past, exoffenders themselves and faith-based organizations are at the forefront of community efforts to help prisoners transitioning back home before and after their release. Coalitions with other interest groups will be necessary. The impact on minorities of disparities in corrections will require different strategies as well. The collateral consequences of incarceration should be better understood and integrated into crime prevention efforts, especially in communities where crime is accepted as normal. Knowing the challenges one faces upon the completion a criminal sanction might prevent and deter crime.

Summary

- Corrections includes federal, state, and local confinement facilities, as well as community corrections.
- Most persons under correctional supervision are on probation under supervision in the community.
- Racial disparities in corrections began centuries ago.
- Imprisonment rates have increased dramatically since the 1980s, following the introduction of mandatory sentences and other "get tough" policies.
- Today, minorities outnumber Whites in confinement; explaining why continues to be debatable.
- In 2010, the number of persons in confinement decreased for the first time in 38 years.
- Reentry programs attempt to address the collateral consequences of imprisonment.

KEY TERMS

Bureau of Prisons	intensive probation	probation
collateral consequences	justice model	recidivism
community corrections	New Jim Crow	rehabilitation
convict-lease system	parole	risk assessment
Corrections	prisoner reentry	Walnut Street jail

DISCUSSION QUESTIONS

1. Do you think the number of minorities in secure confinement and community corrections will decrease during the next decade?
2. What is the best explanation for racial disparities in corrections?
3. Do you agree with Alexander that mass incarceration is a newer form of the Jim Crow that existed in the late 1800s?
4. Will prisoner reentry courts prove helpful in reducing recidivism?
5. Do you thing that at-risk youth and young adults should be informed of the collateral consequences of involvement in crime before they get into trouble?

WEB RESOURCES

National Reentry Resource Center: http://www.nationalreentryresourcecenter.org/

The Sentencing Project: http://www.sentencingproject.org/template/index.cfm

Pew Center on the States: http://www.pewcenteronthestates.org/

READING

In this article, Brewer and Heitzeg posit that the escalation in criminalization and incarceration in the United Stated can be traced to the war on drugs and to mandatory sentencing. They argue that criminal justice and the prison industrial complex have racist and classist roots that must be made transparent. They use critical race theory to help the reader understand how legal constructions of race created economic, social, and political disadvantages in our society. The authors believe that social justice requires coalitions between academicians and grassroots organizations who must work together to address the dilemmas of crime and punishment.

The Racialization of Crime and Punishment

Criminal Justice, Color-Blind Racism, and the Political Economy of the Prison Industrial Complex

Rose M. Brewer and Nancy A. Heitzeg

The post–civil rights era explosion in criminalization and incarceration is fundamentally a project in racialization and macro injustice. It is, too, a project deeply connected to political economic changes in advanced capitalism. Multinational globalization in search of cheaper and cheaper labor and profit maximization is part and parcel of the growth of the prison industrial complex. The ideological underpinnings of racialization and the political economy of inequality are at the core of this discussion. It is the latest in a historically uninterrupted series of legal and political machinations designed to enforce White supremacy with its economic and social benefits both in and with the law; "all domination is, in the last instance, maintained through social control strategies" (Bonilla-Silva, 2001, p. 103). As movements for abolition and civil rights end the institutions of slavery, lynching, and legalized segregation, new and more indirect mechanisms for perpetuating systemic racism and its economic underpinnings have emerged. In this era of color-blind racism, there has been a corresponding shift from de jure racism codified explicitly into the law and legal systems to a de facto racism where people of color, especially African Americans, are subject to unequal protection of the laws, excessive surveillance, extreme segregation, and neo–slave labor via incarceration, all in the name of crime control. It is the current manifestation of the legal legacy of the racialized transformations of plantations into prisons, of Slave Codes into Black Codes, of lynching into state-sponsored executions. The "imputation of crime to color" (Douglass, cited in Foner, 1955, p. 379) continues to the present as racial profiling and culminates ultimately in the new plantation—in the prison industrial complex.

SOURCE: Brewer, R. M., & Heitzeg, N. A. (2008). The racialization of crime and punishment: Criminal justice, color-blind racism, and the political economy of the prison industrial complex. *American Behavioral Scientist, 51*, 625–644.

Social justice requires that the role of civil justice in racialization be made transparent. This requires social justice projects that emanate from the micro level, from stories and struggle. Using the theory and methods of Critical Race Theory (CRT), this article will attempt to begin this work. CRT proceeds from the premise that racial privilege and related oppression are deeply rooted in both our history and our law, thus making racism a "normal and ingrained feature of our landscape" (Delgado & Stefancic, 2000, p. xvii). CRT acknowledges the myriad ways in which the legal constructions of race have produced and reproduced systemic economic, political, and social advantages for Whites. Challenges to racism require micro-level efforts to expose the deep structures of racism first made possible by the legal benefits of what Harris (1993) called "whiteness as property." "Whiteness" produced both tangible and intangible value to those who possessed it:

> The concept of whiteness was premised on white supremacy rather than mere difference. "White" was defined and constructed in ways that increased its value by reinforcing its exclusivity. Indeed, just as whiteness as property embraced the right to exclude, whiteness as a theoretical construct evolved for the very purpose of racial exclusion. Thus, the concept of whiteness is built on both exclusion and racial subjugation. This fact was particularly evident during the period of the most rigid racial exclusion, as whiteness signified racial privilege and took the form of status property. (Harris, 1993, p. 116)

Removing White supremacy from the law did not, of course, erase its property benefits, nor did a shift to color-blindness in the law eradicate racism. CRT offers a critique of civil rights legal reforms by noting that they failed to fundamentally challenge racial inequality. As Bell (2000) noted, "the subordination of blacks seems to reassure whites of an unspoken, but no less certain, property right in their whiteness" (p. 7). In the post–civil rights era, this subordination continues via color-blind legal mechanisms, particularly criminal justice.

(It should be noted that whereas all communities of color suffer from racism in general and its manifestation in criminal justice in particular, "Black" has been the literal and figurative counterpart of "White." For this reason, in combination with the excessive overrepresentation of African Americans in the criminal justice system and the prison industrial complex, our analysis will largely focus on the ways in which the law has been a tool for the oppression of African Americans.)

CRT also offers the use of narratives and context to surface these deep structures. We adopt these methods here, relying on the narratives and counternarratives of both judicial opinions and political prisoners/prisoners of conscience, referred to by James (2003) as "imprisoned intellectuals." The dominant story and the dissent reveal the deep roots of current practices and the extent to which methods of legally enforcing White supremacy merely shift and change shape over time. These competing narratives provide a micro-level foundation for exposing and challenging the systemic injustice that has persisted over centuries. The words of those empowered to interpret the racial meanings of the Constitution and the words of those oppressed by these very same decisions will illuminate the law and its application as a consistent, albeit subtly changing, project in racialization.

Current Situation of Criminal Injustice

There is no dispute as to the extent of the dramatic escalation in criminalization and incarceration in the United States that has occurred during the past 35 years. Much of this increase can be traced to the war on drugs and the rise of mandatory minimum sentences for drug crimes and some other felonies.

There is also no dispute that the poor and people of color, particularly African Americans, are dramatically overrepresented in these statistics at every phase of the criminal justice system.

And there is no dispute as to the devastating impact of these policies and practices on communities of color. The current expansion of criminalization and mass incarceration is accompanied by legislation that further limits the political and economic opportunities of convicted felons and former inmates. Felony disenfranchisement is permanent in 14 states. Forty-eight states do not permit prison inmates to vote, 32 states disenfranchise felons on parole, and 28 states prohibit probationers from voting. Nationally, 40 million felons are disenfranchised; 2% of the nation on average cannot vote as a result of a felony conviction. Of African American males, 13% are disenfranchised; in 7 states, 1 in 4 are permanently barred from voting. Twenty-five states bar felons from ever holding public office, 33 states place a lifetime ban on gun ownership for convicted felons, and all states require driver's license suspension for convicted drug felons. States have also increased the occupational bans for convicted felons, prohibiting them from teaching, child care work, related work with children, or law enforcement. This is accompanied by eased access to criminal records, an increase in all employers' checking criminal backgrounds, and new technology, which facilitates quick checks. Drug felons are permanently barred from receiving public assistance such as Temporary Assistance for Needy Families, Medicaid, food stamps, or Supplemental Security Income. Drug use, possession, or sales are the only offenses other than welfare fraud that result in a ban on federal assistance. The welfare fraud ban is limited to 10 years. Probation or parole violations also result in the temporary suspension of federal assistance. Drug felons are also permanently prohibited from receiving federal financial aid for education. Those convicted of drug felonies "or violent criminal activity or other criminal activity which would adversely affect the health, safety, or right to peaceful enjoyment of the premises by others" (Rubenstein & Mukamal, 2002) are permanently barred from public housing or Section 8. A growing number of private rental properties also screen for convicted felons. A felony conviction by anyone in the household is grounds for eviction from public housing. Recent legislation also creates barriers for families and has particularly devastating consequences for women. Certain convicted felons are prevented from being approved as adoptive or foster parents. Congress has accelerated the termination of parental rights for children who have been in foster care for 15 of the most recent 22 months. Nineteen states regard felony conviction as grounds for parental termination; 29 states identify felony conviction as grounds for divorce (Chesney-Lind, 2002; Ritchie, 2002). And finally, the conditions of incarceration contribute to physical illnesses (e.g., Hepatitis B and C, HIV/AIDS, tuberculosis, general lack of adequate medical care), injuries (e.g., physical and sexual assaults from correctional officers and other inmates), and mental disorders that continue to plague former inmates, families, and their communities on release (Fellner, 2004).

The reasons for this unprecedented explosion in criminalization and incarceration, however, are in dispute. The rhetoric of color-blind racism would have us believe that this situation is the unfortunate result of disproportionate Black and Latino participation in crime. These so-called "racial realists" (Brown et al., 2005) argue that racism is over, successfully eradicated by civil rights legislation, and that if racial inequality persists, it is "the problem of the people who fail to take responsibility for their own lives" (Brown et al., 2005, p. vii). This adherence to the ideology of color-blindness (a co-optation and subversion of the dream of Dr. King) pervades conservative political and intellectual discourse, the corporate media, and the minds of the public. Racism is widely held to be an individual problem, rather than structural and systemic, an integral feature of what Bonilla-Silva (2001) referred to as "racialized social systems" (p. 57). From this vantage point, the issue then is crime, not race, and certainly not racism.

The scale, scope, and extremes of negative consequences—both direct and collateral—for communities of color are new, especially for women, but the role of criminal justice in policing, prosecuting, imprisoning, and executing people of color has deep historical roots. What is not new is the racist and classist economic and political agenda that is foundational. The paradigms shift from essentialist to color-blind and the practices of oppression are refined and renamed, but the resulting inequality remains much the same. The law and its attendant machinery were, and still are, enforcers of both White supremacy and capitalist interests.

The Past Is the Present

It is well established that our Constitution was written with a narrowly construed view of citizenship that at the time included only White, property-holding men. This property included both wives and children, but the most lucrative property of all—indeed that property that made any economic survival, let alone prosperity, possible—was slaves. By the time of the Constitutional Convention of 1787, the racial lines defining slave and free had already been rigidly drawn—White was free, and Black was slave. The Three Fifths Clause, the restriction on future bans of the slave trade, and limits on the possibility of emancipation through escape were all clear indications of the significance of slavery to the founders. Any doubt as to the centrality of White supremacy was erased a few decades later in the case of *Scott v. Sandford* (1857), where a majority of the Supreme Court denied the citizenship claims of Dred Scott and went further to declare that the Missouri Compromise requirement of balance between free and slave states in the expanding United States was a violation of the due process rights of slaveholders. Referring to the legal status of African Americans, Justice Taney's opinion for the majority makes it painfully clear:

> They are not included, and were not intended to be included, under the word "citizens" in the Constitution, and can therefore claim none of the rights and privileges which that instrument provides for and secures to citizens of the United States. On the contrary, they were at that time considered as a subordinate and inferior class of beings, who had been subjugated by the dominant race, and, whether emancipated or not, yet remained subject to their authority, and had no rights or privileges but such as those who held the power and the Government might choose to grant them.

The growing abolition movement could not overcome this legal bar with debates, written appeals, or legislative action. The economic and political interests of the slave states were too dependent on the rising trade in slaves and cotton.

The abolition of slavery did not result in the abolition of essentialist racism in the law; it merely called for new methods of legally upholding the property interests of Whiteness. In the presence of now freed Black labor, the vote was now offered to unpropertied White men and, as Du Bois and others have argued, Whiteness played a central role in the reduction of class tensions.

Postslavery, White supremacy in the law was accomplished by the introduction of a series of segregationist Jim Crow laws, a new model for an essentialist racial paradigm that was now legitimated by so-called biology; the laws did not mandate that Blacks be accorded equality under the law because nature—not man, not power, not violence—has determined their degraded status (Harris, 1993, p. 118). The courts were complicit and explicit in their support for the purity and attendant property rights of Whiteness. This is made most dramatically clear in *Plessy v. Ferguson* (1896). In a challenge to the legalized segregation of public transportation in the state of Louisiana, Plessy argued that these laws denied him equality before the law. The majority disagreed and set forth the principle of separate but equal.

After decades of resistance via legal challenges, grassroots organizing, boycotts, *Letters from the Birmingham Jail,* sit-ins, jail-ins, marches, and mass protest, legalized segregation began to come undone. Indeed, part of its undoing was the role that activists played in exposing the official and extralegal violence that had previously been cloaked in the legitimacy of the law. Emitt Till, Birmingham, Bloody Sunday, and more bared the lie. In the historic 1954 *Brown v. Board of Education* decision, *Plessy* was overturned; the essentialist racist paradigm was no longer codified in law. This was complete with the passage of the Civil Rights Act of 1964, the Voting Rights Act of 1965, and the passage of the 24th Amendment to the Constitution. Whereas there was once hope that the law itself could be pressed into the service of racial equality, those victories now seem bittersweet. Legally supported essentialist racism was about to be replaced with a more insidious counterpart—the paradigm of color-blindness.

Following the end of legalized racial discrimination, there was an especially concerted effort to escalate the control of African Americans via the criminal justice system. The criminal justice system provides a convenient vehicle for physically maintaining the old legally enforced color lines as African Americans are disproportionately policed, prosecuted, convicted, disenfranchised, and imprisoned. The criminal justice system and its culmination in the prison industrial complex also continues to guarantee the perpetual profits from the forced labor of inmates, now justifying their slavery as punishment for crime. Finally, the reliance on the criminal system provides the color-blind racist regime the perfect set of codes to describe racialized patterns of alleged crime and actual punishment without ever referring to race.

There were early warnings about the potentially devastating interconnections between race, crime, and the law in the era of late capitalism. The mid-20th-century criticism of the criminal justice system as foundationally racist initially emanated from the Black Power Movement's critique of institutionalized racism and police brutality in communities of color. The writings of political prisoners (e.g., Angela Davis, Huey P. Newton, Assata Shakur) and prisoners of conscience (e.g., Malcolm X and George Jackson) brought racism and its intimate connection with the penitentiary to light. The 10 Point Program of the Black Panther Party began to make the connections between capitalist exploitation of the Black community and the criminal justice system. Their demands provided the foundations for the contemporary critiques of the role of criminal justice in upholding both capitalism and White supremacy.

Perhaps the most significant barrier to the pursuit of equality before the law comes in the case of *McCleskey v. Kemp* (1987). After a series of death penalty cases wherein the court decried racial discrimination in the application of the criminal laws' ultimate penalty, it is here that the Supreme Court, in a 5 to 4 decision, clearly defined discrimination as individual, not institutionalized. Citing statistical evidence from the now famous Baldus study, McCleskey argued that the application of the death penalty in Georgia was fraught with racism. Defendants charged with killing White victims were more likely to receive the death penalty, and in fact, cases involving Black defendants and White victims were more likely to result in a sentence of death than cases involving any other racial combination. The majority did not dispute the statistical evidence but feared the consequences. If the court were to accept McCleskey's claim, then the Equal Protection Clause of the 14th Amendment would apply to patterns of discrimination, to institutionalized racism and sexism, and to questions of structured inequality.

Color-blind racism, with its call to ignore race and its treatment of any residual racism as individual and intentional, was now ensconced. Equal protection of the law was for individuals, not oppressed groups, and discrimination must be intentional and similarly individual. *McCleskey* closed off the last avenue for remedying structural inequality with the law and left us imprisoned by the past, imprisoned with the present.

Intersections: Criminal Injustice, Race, and Political Economy

The legal entrenchment of color-blind racism allowed White supremacist political and economic advantage to be pursued—unchecked by either law or public discourse—under the guise of criminal justice.

As before, this newest political and legal construction of White supremacy is intimately interconnected with capitalist economic interests. The extreme racialization of criminal justice and the rise of the prison industrial complex are directly tied to the expansion of global economy, the decline of the industry and rise of the minimum wage service sector in the United States, and the growth of privatization of public services. The internationalization of the labor force and the turn to robotics, computers, and hi-tech are having a profound impact on labor in the United States and globally. The prison industrial complex is an expression and rearticulation of the political economy of late capitalism. The intense concentration and privatization of wealth in a few hands continues unchecked in this country. Indeed, the unparalleled growth of corporate power is at the heart of the economic inequality African Americans and all working people are confronting.

This quest for dispensable labor increasingly includes women of color who, in light of globalization, deindustrialization, and the dismantling of social services, are propelled by state economic interests into the slave labor markets of the prison industrial complex.

> The prison industrial complex is not a conspiracy, but a confluence of special interests that include politicians who exploit crime to win votes, private companies that make millions by running or supplying prisons and small town officials who have turned to prisons as a method of economic development. (Silverstein, 1997)

This complex now includes more than 3,300 jails, more than 1,500 state prisons, and 100 federal prisons in the United States. Nearly 300 of these are private prisons. More than 30 of these institutions are super-maximum facilities, not including the super-maximum units located in most other prisons. The prison industrial complex consumes vast amounts of tax dollars at the expense of education and other social programs. Each year, the United States spends more than $146 billion dollars on the criminal justice system, including police, the judiciary and court systems, and corrections. More than $50 billion of this is spent directly on corrections, with the majority of those expenditures going toward incarceration and executions—the two most expensive sentencing options (Bureau of Justice Statistics, 2004). The quest for profit has led to international U.S. expansion of the prison industrial complex in the United States. Both private companies and the U.S. military industrial complex rely on the global proliferation of both U.S. prisons and their internal practices at Basra, Abu Ghraib, Guantanamo Bay, and untold other locations.

In essence, the prison industrial complex is a self-perpetuating machine where the vast profits (e.g., cheap labor, private and public supply and construction contracts, job creation, continued media profits from exaggerated crime reporting, and crime/punishment as entertainment) and perceived political benefits (e.g., reduced unemployment rates, "get tough on crime" and public safety rhetoric, funding increases for police, and criminal justice system agencies and professionals) lead to policies that are additionally designed to ensure an endless supply of "clients" for the criminal justice system (e.g., enhanced police presence in poor neighborhoods and communities of color; racial profiling; decreased funding for public education combined with zero-tolerance policies and increased rates of expulsion for students of color; increased rates of adult certification for juvenile offenders; mandatory minimum and three-strikes sentencing; draconian conditions of incarceration and a reduction of prison services that contribute to the likelihood of recidivism; collateral consequences—such as felony disenfranchisement, prohibitions on welfare receipt, public housing, gun ownership, voting and political participation, and employment—that nearly guarantee continued participation in crime and return to the prison industrial complex following initial release).

In sum, Black workers, men and women, are at the center of this prison industrial process. They are used again as exploited labor and as consumers—of products produced by prison labor. African Americans and other working people are less needed in the free labor market under current conditions of globalization. Highly exploited global workers match cheap prison labor. So the processes of deindustrialization and economic restructuring contribute to the process of accumulation for capital and the increasing immiseration of the Black poor, and this is true because many of the decisions are explicitly racial in form. Corporate actors choose to move out of Black communities on racial grounds (Brewer, 1983). Thus, private prisons play a key role in the political economy of transnational capital. But so do public prisons.

This exploitation of Black labor continues, made permissible, indeed possible, with the law. Although the names and legal legitimations have changed, there is little to distinguish the plantation from the penitentiary. Nevertheless, in the United States, Blacks have been a central political force in checking unabashed profit realization. Historically, this occurs through political struggle. We contend that it is only through organized political struggle and radical pedagogies for change that the current situation will be transformed for social justice.

Transparency, Political Struggle, and Radical Pedagogies for Social Justice

As we have seen, the call for social justice cannot rely on civil justice or macro-level remedies alone; law has been the handmaiden of what hooks (1992) has termed "the white supremacist capitalist patriarchy" in the ever-evolving political and economic exploitation of persons of color. To paraphrase Bell (1992), the 14th Amendment cannot save us. The call for social justice requires more.

As the latest project in racialization, criminal justice and the prison industrial complex have fundamentally racist and classist roots that must be exposed and abolished. The work of justice must begin at the micro level; it must emerge from the grass roots. Drawing links between the movements to abolish slavery and segregation, Davis (2003) asked us to imagine the abolition of prisons and the creation of alternatives to mass incarceration with all its racist and classist corollaries. Davis (1998) identified three key dimensions of this work—public policy, community organizing, and academic research:

> In order to be successful, this project must build bridges between academic work, legislative and other policy interventions, and grassroots campaigns calling, for example, for the decriminalization of drugs and prostitution, and

> for the reversal of the present proliferation of prisons and jails. (pp. 71–72)

Much of this work is in progress. Organizations such as The Sentencing Project (http://www.sentencingproject.org/), the Prison Moratorium Project (http://www.nomoreprisons.org), Critical Resistance (http://www.criticalresistance.org), Families Against Mandatory Minimum Sentencing, Amnesty International, Human Rights Watch, and the Prison Activist Resource Center (http://www.prisonactivist.org) have successfully linked a large and growing body of research with a critique of current practices and a call for legislative and policy change.

The true underpinnings of criminal justice and the prison industrial complex must become transparent. They must be surfaced by micro-level social justice projects. They must be surfaced via radical and relentless pedagogies of resistance; they must be surfaced in the stories, the narratives, of political prisoners and prisoners of conscience; they must be surfaced through the research, writing, and teaching of those whom Mumia Abu-Jamal (2005) called "radical intellectuals" and ultimately through the coalitions between the two that bridge the lines of difference between freedom and incarceration, as well as those of race, class, and gender.

As noted earlier, the writings of political prisoners and prisoners of conscience sounded the early warning about the role of the police, the courts, and prisons in economic and political repression of people of color. These works publicly clarified the extent to which there were political prisoners in the United States and served to raise the consciousness of what, in 1970, were the 200,000 mostly Black and Brown inmates in prisons and jails. Just as the writings of George Jackson, Assata Shakur, Huey P. Newton, and the early Angela Davis inspired an earlier generation of activists, so too do new voices rise in dissent from our prisons and jails. Leonard Peltier, Sanykia Shakur, Paul Wright's *Prison Legal News* (http://www.prisonlegalnews.org), Marilyn Buck, and the prolific Mumia Abu-Jamal have given voice to the more than 2 million who are now incarcerated in increasingly harsh and isolated conditions. They have made the invisible horrors of the prison industrial complex visible and again sparked the call for resistance. They offer both an insider's view and a deep critique of the law.

The call to social justice, especially when addressing complex and cloaked systems of racialization, requires critical and systematic documentation, the surfacing of deep political and economic structures, and bold confrontation. It requires the analytical tools and methods of multiple disciplines, as we have attempted to offer here. The dismantling of the White supremacist and capitalist machinery of criminal justice requires coalitions between intellectuals of all sorts.

Ultimately, the realization of social justice will require still broader coalitions. Criminal justice and the prison industrial complex represent particular manifestations of the entanglements of racialization, the law, and the global economy in late capitalism. Truly challenging this project in racialization calls for coalitions with those who are addressing different aspects of these foundation dilemmas. Audre Lorde (1984) reminded us that much of Western European history conditions us to see human differences in simplistic opposition to each other: dominant/subordinate, good/bad, up/down, superior/inferior. In a society where the good is defined in terms of profit rather than in terms of human need, there must always be some group of people who, through systematized oppression, can be made to feel surplus, to occupy the place of the dehumanized inferior. Within this society, that group is made up of Black and Third World people, working-class people, older people, women, gays/lesbians, and physically different and physically challenged people.

Most important, we must organize, continuing the legacy of struggle. We must come together across boundaries of national identity, gender, race, class, and ethnicity. We must work in alliance to realize the vision that another world is possible.

References

Abu-Jamal, M. (2005). Intellectuals and the gallows. In J. James (Ed.), *Imprisoned intellectuals: America's political prisoners write on life, liberation and rebellion* (p. 179). New York: Rowman and Littlefield.

Bell, D. (1992). *Faces at the bottom of the well: The permanence of racism.* New York: Basic Books.

Bell, D. (2000). After we're gone: Prudent speculations on America in a post-racial epoch. In R. Delgado & J. Stefancic (Eds.), *Critical race theory: The cutting edge* (2nd ed., pp. 2–8). Philadelphia: Temple University Press.

Bonilla-Silva, E. (2001). *White supremacy and racism in the post-civil rights era.* Boulder, CO: Lynne Rienner.

Brewer, R. (1983). Black workers and corporate flight. *Third World Socialists, 1,* 9–13.

Brown v. Board of Educ., 347 U.S. 483 (1954).

Brown, M. K., Carnoy, M., Currie, E., Duster, T., Oppenheimer, D. B., Schultz, M. K., et al. (2005). *Whitewashing race: The myth of a color-blind society.* Berkeley: University of California Press.

Bureau of Justice Statistics. (2004). *Sourcebook of criminal justice statistics.* Washington, DC: Government Printing Office.

Chesney-Lind, M. (2002). Imprisoning women: The unintended victims of mass incarceration. In M. Mauer & M. Chesney-Lind (Eds.), *Invisible punishment: The collateral consequences of mass imprisonment* (pp. 79–94). New York: New Press.

Davis, A. (1998). Race and criminalization: Black Americans and the punishment industry. In J. James (Ed.), *The Angela Y. Davis reader* (pp. 61–73). New York: Blackwell.

Davis, A. (2003). *Are prisons obsolete?* New York: Seven Stories Press.

Delgado, R., & Stefancic, J. (Eds.). (2000). *Critical race theory: The cutting edge* (2nd ed.). Philadelphia: Temple University Press.

Foner, P. S. (Ed.). (1955). *The life and writings of Frederick Douglass: Vol. 4. Reconstruction and after.* New York: International.

Harris, C. (1993). Whiteness as property. In D. R. Roediger (Ed.), *Black on White* (pp. 103–118). New York: Schocken.

hooks, b. (1992). *Black looks.* Boston: South End.

James, J. (Ed.). (2003). *Imprisoned intellectuals: America's political prisoners write on life, liberation and rebellion.* New York: Rowman and Littlefield.

Lorde, A. (1984). *Sister outsider: Essays and speeches.* Freedom, CA: Crossing Press.

McCleskey v. Kemp, 482 U.S, 279 (1987).

Plessy v. Ferguson, 163 U.S. 537 (1896).

Ritchie, B. (2002). The social impact of the mass incarceration of women. In M. Mauer & M. Chesney-Lind (Eds.), *Invisible punishment: The collateral consequences of mass imprisonment* (pp. 136–149). New York: New Press.

Rubenstein, G., & Mukamal, D. (2002). Welfare and housing—Denial of benefits to drug offenders. In M. Mauer & M. Chesney-Lind (Eds.), *Invisible punishment: The collateral consequences of mass imprisonment* (pp. 37–50). New York: New Press.

Scott v. Sandford, 60 U.S. 393 (1857).

Silverstein, K. (1997, June). America's private gulag. *Prison Legal News.*

DISCUSSION QUESTIONS

1. According to critical race theory, what factors would likely lead to a minority person becoming incarcerated? Do you think there are other factors that lead to a minority person becoming incarcerated?

2. Over the past decade, African Americans have accounted for the highest percentage of incarcerated persons in prison, especially women. Why? What factors associated with racism or crime would account for this increase?

3. Do you agree or disagree with the notion that racism within the criminal justice system is an individual problem?

READING

The authors of this article argue that risk assessment is widely used in many correctional settings and is critical to reducing reoffending. They identify eight major risk factors and emphasize that high risk offenders have multiple risk factors. As a result, high risk offenders require more intensive treatment in order to reduce recidivism. Even though intensive treatment is used for low risk offenders, it may actually increase their recidivism. The authors believe distinguishing high risk from low risk offenders is critical to reducing reoffending. Several obstacles to good risk assessment are presented by the authors, as well as some costs associated with using an assessment tool. The authors believe identifying and reducing the number of high risk offenders is an important aspect of protecting the public that should not be overlooked.

The Role of Offender Risk Assessment

A Policy Maker Guide

Edward J. Latessa and Brian Lovins

Introduction

One of the foundations of developing effective correctional practices and programs is the need to conduct risk assessment. According to national and international professional correctional organizations (National Institute of Corrections, American Probation and Parole Association, International Community Corrections Association, American Correctional Association, and the American Association of Community Justice Professionals), offender risk assessment is a component of best practices. The concept of risk assessment is really quite simple and can be understood through one basic question—"What is the probability that this person will reoffend?" Being able to classify offenders into risk levels (e.g., low, moderate, high, very high) has come a long way over the years, and has evolved from using "gut feelings" and intuition to working with instruments that focused primarily on past behavior (static indicators)—to what are now called fourth generation instruments that include changeable or dynamic indicators as well as an integrated case plan system (Bonta & Wormith, 2008). We will discuss this progression of risk assessment in much greater detail later, but for now it is important to review why assessment is so critical to the correctional enterprise.

Why Is Offender Assessment Important?

The importance of using validated and objective offender assessment tools cannot be overstated. Assessment is the engine that drives effective

Source: Latessa, E. J., & Lovins, B. (2010). The role of offender risk assessment: A policy maker guide. *Victims and Offenders*, 5(3) 203–219.

intervention with offenders and is important for a number of reasons (Latessa, 2004).

Offender assessment

- helps identify the offenders most at risk for recidivating,
- identifies who needs the most intervention (or none at all),
- identifies crime producing needs that should be targeted for change,
- helps guide decision making by providing more information in a systematic manner,
- helps reduce bias by following objective criteria rather than personal intuition and judgment,
- improves the placement of offenders,
- improves the utilization of resources, and
- enhances public safety.

What Is the National Picture?

Risk assessment is used at some level in all states, and across a wide range of correctional settings—including pretrial, probation, parole, community corrections, and prisons. Risk assessment is used by courts to help make bond and pretrial decisions, to arrive at sentencing decisions, and during revocation hearings. Probation and parole agencies use risk assessment to decide levels of supervision (i.e., intensive, regular, or even nonreporting) and placement in programs (e.g., substance abuse, day reporting centers, halfway houses). Parole boards often use risk assessment to help make release decisions, and prison and jail systems use it to help develop inmate classification systems and to decide which offenders should receive programs or be granted early release (Holsinger, Lurigio, & Latessa, 2001).

A national survey of probation and parole agencies concerning the use and practices surrounding offender assessment (Jones, Johnson, Latessa, & Travis, 1999) found that the vast majority of community correctional agencies reported using some actuarial instrument to assess and classify offenders, among a number of other findings.

- Almost 75% of probation and parole agencies and about 56% of community corrections service providers reported that they assess offender risk using standardized and objective instruments.
- Large agencies were more likely to assess offenders than small agencies.
- More that 83% of the respondents reported that it was "absolutely" or "very necessary" to classify on risk, and 66% reported it was necessary to classify on needs.
- Nearly all respondents agreed that offender assessment made their jobs easier, benefits the offender, creates a more professional environment, helped staff make better decisions, increased the effectiveness of service delivery, and enhanced fairness in decision making.
- Use of these tools addressed officer workload (75%), staff deployment (54%), development of specialized caseloads (47%), and helped with sentencing decisions (20%).

While there is a good deal of evidence that risk assessment is widely used and valued in corrections, there is a great deal of variation in its application and implementation. For example, some states have adopted and implemented standardized assessment tools that are used throughout the state and across a wide range of settings, while others have taken a less systematic approach. Examples of states that have developed or adopted risk assessment at a major level of the correctional system include Arizona, Pennsylvania, Maryland, Washington, Idaho, Colorado, North Dakota, Nebraska, Oklahoma, Iowa, Georgia, New Jersey, Illinois, and Indiana. Noteworthy is Ohio, which has recently funded a project to develop a statewide risk assessment process that includes all levels of the correctional system (from pretrial to parole) and will include a Web-based application that will allow correctional staff across the state to assess offenders using the same tools.

What Is Risk Assessment?

It is important that we define the concept of "risk" as it pertains to offender recidivism. For some, "risk" is a concept associated with the seriousness of the crime—for example, in the sense that a felon is higher risk than a misdemeanant. In actuality, however, though a felon has been convicted of a more serious offense than a misdemeanant, their relative risk of reoffending may have nothing to do with the seriousness of the crime.

For our purposes, "risk" refers to the probability of reoffending. A low risk offender is one with a relatively low probability of committing a new offense (i.e., relatively prosocial people with few risk factors), while a high risk offender has a much greater probability (i.e., more antisocial with many risk factors). The application of the concept in corrections is similar to that in most actuarial sciences. For example, life insurance is cheaper for a nonsmoker in his 40s than a smoker of the same age. The reason insurance costs more for the smoker is that smokers have a risk factor that is significantly correlated with health problems. Similarly, an offender who uses drugs and is unemployed has a higher chance of reoffending than someone who does not use drugs and has steady employment. Figure 8.1 shows how a distribution of offenders might be classified according to risk. Note that the probability of someone in the low risk category reoffending is 10%, for moderate risk it is 30%, while for high risk it is 50%.

Figure 8.1 Example of Distribution of Risk Scores and Recidivism

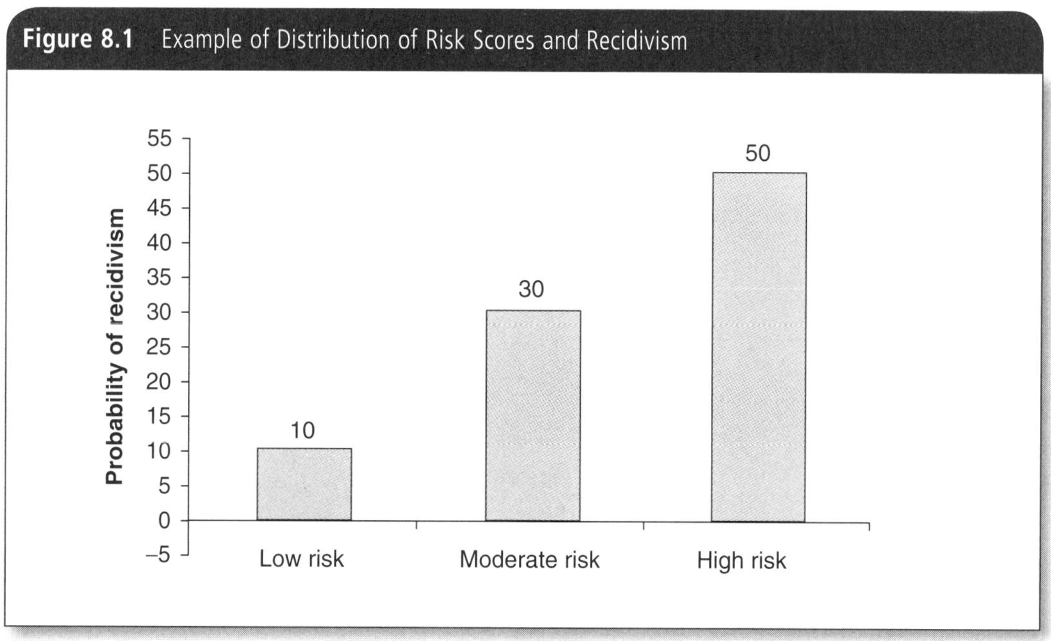

Risk, Needs, and Responsivity

Three important principles in the assessment process are risk, needs, and responsivity. Below we will briefly examine each principle.

Risk Principle

In 1990, Andrews, Bonta, and Hoge discussed the importance of the risk principle as it relates to the assessment of offenders. There are three important elements to the principle.

- Target those offenders with a higher probability of recidivism.
- Provide the most intensive treatment to higher risk offenders.
- Intensive treatment for lower risk offenders can increase recidivism.

Since 1990, considerable research has investigated how adhering to the risk principle can impact a correctional program's effectiveness. Here is one way to think of the risk principle—suppose that half of the offenders that are released from prison never return. Which half are we worried about? The obvious answer is the half that will return to prison, and this is the group to whom we want to provide the most intensive programs and services (since they pose the greatest risk to reoffend). The more troubling aspect of the risk principle is the fact that providing intensive interventions for low risk offenders can actually increase failure rates (Lowenkamp & Latessa, 2004). Figure 8.2 shows effects on recidivism rates when we target high risk and low risk offenders.

The question that arises is why a correctional intervention or program can produce a reduction in recidivism for higher risk offenders,

Figure 8.2 The Risk Principle and Correctional Intervention Results From Meta-Analysis

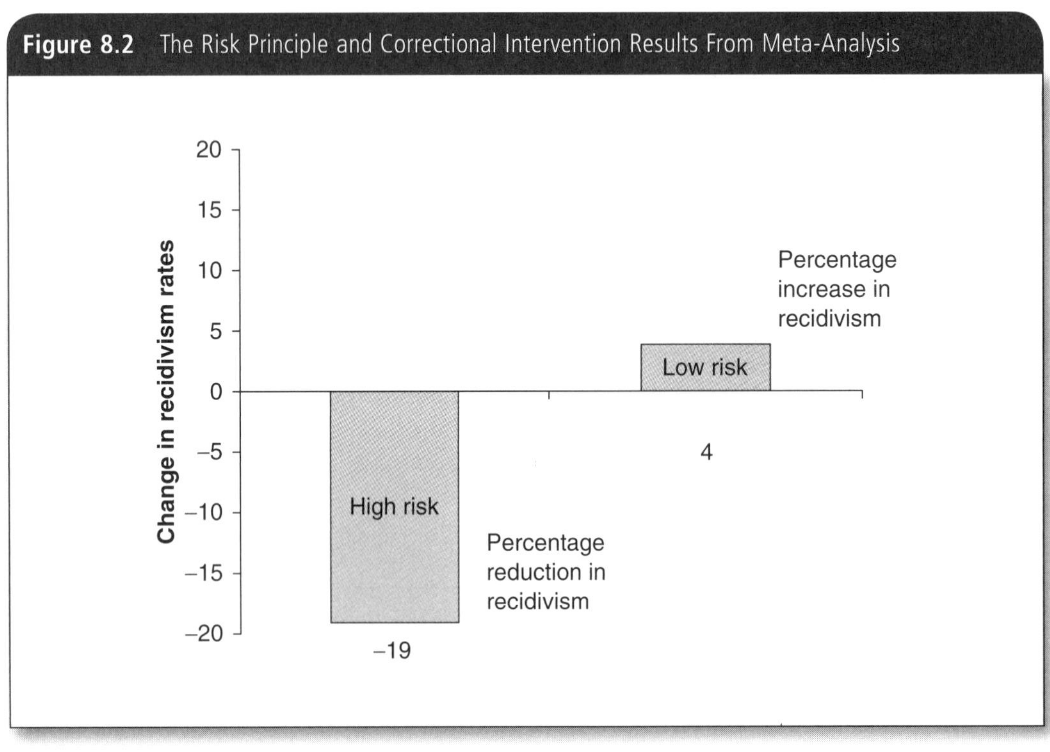

but have undesired and unintended consequences for lower risk offenders? The increased failure rates of low risk offenders can largely be understood when considering the following three explanations. First, when we place low risk offenders in the more intense correctional interventions we are likely exposing them to higher risk offenders—and the learning that is transmitted is often antisocial. Practically speaking, placing high risk and low risk offenders together is never a good strategy. If you had a son or daughter that got into some trouble would you want them placed in a group with high risk offenders? Second, when we take lower risk offenders—who by definition are fairly prosocial (if not they would not be considered low risk)—and place them in a highly structured, restrictive program, we actually disrupt the factors that make them low risk. For example, if most prosocial people were placed in a correctional treatment program for six months they would lose their job, experience family disruption, and their prosocial attitudes and contacts would be cut off and replaced with antisocial thoughts and peers—their neighbors would probably not have a "Welcome Home from the Correctional Program" party when they got out. In other words, risk would be increased due to the disruption of prosocial networks. Third, other factors such as IQ, intellectual functioning, and maturity might be at work. It could be the case that there are some low functioning, low risk offenders that are manipulated by more sophisticated, higher risk, predatory offenders (Lowenkamp, Latessa, & Holsinger, 2006).

What all this means for corrections is that low risk offenders should be identified and excluded, as a general rule, from intensive correctional programs. The first step in meeting the risk principle is the identification of appropriate targets (higher risk offenders). To achieve this goal, agencies must assess offenders with standardized and objective risk assessment instruments. To be clear, this is not to imply that low risk offenders should not be held accountable for their actions—they did break the law. However, less intense, less intrusive interventions would be recommended since they are less costly and potentially less harmful.

Need Principle

Research by Andrews and Bonta (1998) and Gendreau, Little, and Goggin (1996) have identified eight major risk factors associated with criminal conduct.

1. Antisocial/procriminal attitudes, values, and beliefs
2. Procriminal associates and isolation from prosocial people
3. Temperament and personality factors such being impulsive, adventurous, and pleasure seeking
4. History of antisocial behavior
5. Family factors such as family criminality or lack of caring and cohesiveness
6. Low levels of educational, vocational, or financial achievement
7. Lack of prosocial leisure activities
8. Abuse of drugs and alcohol

While these are all considered major, it is important to note that the first four are referred to as the "Big Four" and are considered the strongest risk factors among the set.

If we look carefully at these areas we can see that some can be influenced or changed while others cannot. Those that cannot be changed are called "static." Examples include prior record or family criminality. For instance, early onset of criminal behavior is a very good predictor of future behavior, but it is a risk factor that cannot be changed—if you were first arrested at age ten you will always have been first arrested at age ten. Similarly, if your father was in prison it may help explain why you are in trouble (i.e., social learning), but the fact that your father was in prison cannot be changed.

Those factors that can be changed are called "dynamic." They include factors like who an offender associates with, attitudes and values, a lack of problem solving skills, substance use, and employment status. All these are correlated with recidivism, and all can be targeted for change. These dynamic factors are also called *criminogenic needs:* crime producing factors that are strongly correlated with risk. Combining static and dynamic factors together gives us the best picture of the overall risk of recidivism (Latessa & Lowenkamp, 2005b), We can illustrate this by showing the risk factors associated with having a heart attack—age (over 50), sex (male), family history of heart problems, high blood pressure, being overweight, lack of exercise, stress, smoking, and high cholesterol. Some of these factors are static and others are dynamic. To *understand* your risk you would factor in all of them; to *affect*—and lower—your risk, you would focus on the dynamic ones.

Applying the same logic to effective correctional intervention, researchers have come up with the need principle as a way to choose the "what" to target for change in an offender—namely, dynamic factors or criminogenic needs that are highly correlated with criminal conduct. Programs should assess and target crime producing needs, such as antisocial attitudes, antisocial peer associations, substance abuse, lack of empathy, lack of problem solving and self-control skills, and other factors that are highly correlated with criminal conduct (Dowden & Andrews, 1999).

It is important to note that most offenders are not at high risk for recidivism because they have one risk or need factor, but rather are high risk because they have multiple factors. As a result, programs that target only one may not produce the desired effects (Lowenkamp, Latessa, & Holsinger, 2006). For example, while unemployment is correlated with criminal conduct for many probationers and parolees, by itself it is not that strong of a risk factor. After all, if most of us lost our job we would not start selling drugs or robbing people; we would simply start looking for another job. But if you think a job is for someone else, if you have no problem letting someone else support you, or if you think you can make more in a day illegitimately than someone can make in a month legitimately, then being unemployed does add considerably to your risk of offending. Identifying criminogenic needs is an important part of offender risk assessment—it tells us what to focus on to reduce risk.

Responsivity Principle

In addition to risk factors, there are often personal characteristics of an individual that should be assessed, since these factors can affect their engagement in treatment. These would include areas like mental and emotional problems, cognitive functioning, and level of motivation and readiness to change. For example, an offender might be moderate risk to offend, but due to a low level of cognitive functioning they would not be successful in a program that required normal functioning. Assessment of these areas can often improve the placement of offenders and the effectiveness of correctional treatment.

Actuarial Versus Clinical Assessment

The two basic ways to assess offenders are through actuarial (also called statistical) and clinical assessment. Actuarial risk assessment is similar to what insurance companies use to calculate rates. Actuarial instruments are based on statistical analysis of records and other information, resulting in the development of probability tables: if you score X, you have an X chance of reoffending. On the other hand, clinical assessment usually involves gathering information about the offender and then using experience, skills, and judgment to form a conclusion about the likelihood of success or failure. Studies dating back over 50 years have consistently demonstrated that actuarial prediction is more accurate than clinical prediction (Meehl, 1954).

Types of Assessment Tools

Assessment tools in corrections can be grouped into three basic categories: screening instruments, comprehensive risk/need assessments, and specialized tools.

Screening instruments are usually quick to complete and easy to use. They consist primarily of static items (e.g., prior arrests) and can be useful for in-or-out decisions (detain, release on recognizance, etc.). Static instruments can also be useful to sort offenders into risk categories (i.e., low, moderate, or high) but beyond that they have limited utility, since they do little to identify criminogenic factors.

Comprehensive risk/need assessment tools cover all major risk and need factors. They take longer to administer (and thus cost more), require more extensive training, and produce levels of risk/need that are correlated with outcome measures like recidivism. These instruments are also more dynamic and can be useful in reassessment (to determine if risk has changed after some intervention or program). The advantage of these types of tools is that they facilitate the development of case and treatment plans since they take into account the full range of factors associated with risk (Latessa & Lowenkamp, 2005a).

Specialized tools are usually used to assess specific domains (like substance abuse) or special populations (i.e., sex offenders, mentally ill offenders, psychopaths, etc.). These instruments may require special training to administer and should be used in conjunction with more comprehensive risk/need assessments. For example, if your risk/need assessment indicates that substance abuse is a contributing factor to an offender's behavior, then a more detailed assessment of this area using an instrument specifically designed for the purpose may be in order.

In many instances jurisdictions develop an assessment process that involves all three types. For example, a screening instrument might be used at pretrial, or to screen out low risk offenders from further assessment. For those offenders who continue to move through the system and are higher risk, a more comprehensive assessment tool should be used. Specialized assessment will also be used on an "as needed" basis. Following this approach can increase efficiency, since not all offenders will be thoroughly assessed, but those offenders who appear to pose the greatest risk to reoffend will be examined much more closely (Flores, Russell, Latessa, & Travis, 2005).

Methods of Assessment

There are several different approaches that are used for the assessment process, depending on the instrument selected. Some instruments, like screening tools, are based primarily on file or record information—although the person being assessed may be asked some questions as well. The assessor examines the file or record, checks the appropriate indicators, and then adds up the score and determines the appropriate risk category. More comprehensive assessment tools may require both file and record information and a structured interview with the offender or a questionnaire to be completed. Most assessment tools involve the gathering of information about the offender (through file review, interviews, questionnaires, third party information, etc.). In addition to questions about the nature of the assessment tool itself, there are a number of practical issues to consider.

- What will the tool be used for?
- How long does it take to complete the tool?
- How much training is involved?
- What is the cost?
- How complex is the tool to use and understand?
- When will it be done?
- Where will it be done?
- Who will do it?
- What is the level of staff commitment to using the instrument?
- Is the assessment tool reliable (do we get consistent results)?
- Is the assessment valid (does it measure what we want it to measure)?

The last two questions highlight important considerations regarding the use of assessment tools—reliability and validity.

Reliability

One of the considerations involved in the administration of a risk assessment tool is reliability, or the consistency of the assessment tool. A reliable tool results in the same decisions being made about the same kind of offenders irrespective of who is using the tool. This means that if different people assess the same offender they should come to similar conclusions about the risk of reoffending. This is usually easier to achieve with static instruments since they often depend on file or historical information. Reliability is more of an issue with instruments that include dynamic factors (such as gauging the attitudes or values of the offender), which is why training is so important when using these types of tools. An instrument that is not reliable cannot be valid, but an instrument can be reliable but not valid—we can all come to the same conclusion but all be wrong. When this occurs the instrument is not considered valid (Lowenkamp, Holsinger, & Latessa, 2004).

Validity

While there are different forms of validity, the one we are most concerned about with risk assessment tools is predictive validity—the ability of the instrument to predict what we think it is predicting. Predictive validity is usually measured as the correlation between the score on the tool and its correlation with some outcome measure, such as a new conviction; the stronger the correlation the more valid the tool. Of course, no instrument is 100% accurate—however strong a case can be made for actuarial risk assessment, it is not a perfect science. Although statistical risk assessment reduces uncertainty about an offender's probable future conduct, it is subject to errors and should be regarded as advisory rather than peremptory (Clear, 1985). Even with large data sets and advanced analytical techniques, the best models are usually able to predict recidivism with about 70% accuracy (Petersilia & Turner, 1987)—provided it is completed by trained staff. Assessment results are invariably susceptible to two types of classification errors: false positives and false negatives. False positives occur when offenders who are predicted to fail actually succeed, whereas false negatives occur when predicted successes actually fail. False negatives are more visible and damaging because they can actually involve new offenses that cause harm to victims and jeopardize public safety. False negatives are potentially very costly; hence most assessment strategies err on the conservative side. Controlling false positives and false negatives is important in order to maximize the utility of assessment practices (Farrington, 1987).

The Recent Progression of Risk Assessment

Although the criminal justice field has moved past "gut feelings" as its primary form of assessment, there still remains significant variation in the implementation of risk assessment. In Ohio, for example, the Ohio Department of Youth Services conducted a survey of the 88 counties and found that there were 77 different risk assessments used to assess youth's risk to reoffend. Assessments ranged from homegrown, unstructured assessments to the Youthful Level of Service/Case Management Inventory (Modry & Gies, 2005). Even among academics there is strong discourse between two specific camps.[1]

The first camp, lead primarily by Christopher Baird, argues that the current fourth generation risk assessment is problematic and that criminogenic needs should not be included in the measurement of risk. Instead he argues that risk should be measured by historical variables (or static factors) and that needs should be separated and assessed using need-specific assessments (Baird, 2009). The second camp, lead by Don Andrews and his colleagues, posits that fourth generation tools are not only practical but are just as predictive as "risk only" measures (Bonta & Wormith, 2008). Depending on in which camp one resides, there are either very few advancements (Baird camp) or significant advancements (Andrews) in assessing risk over the past ten years. For this reason, the following section will briefly discuss the advancement of risk assessment from second and third generation tools to fourth generation risk/needs assessments.[2]

For the past 20 years, corrections have focused primarily on the implementation of second and third generation risk assessment instruments. Though these instruments have demonstrated over time they are valid measures of recidivism, they have not been successfully integrated into practice. Lowenkamp, Latessa, and Holsinger (2006) suggest that until a risk assessment translates academic-based endeavors into practical measures of risk, the system will not fully adopt risk/need assessments.

Bonta and Wormith (2008) argue a similar point, suggesting that the utility of risk assessment is directly correlated to the eagerness of officers to adopt it. This is where the fourth generation tools provide a significant step forward compared to second and third generation tools. Fourth generation tools are designed to integrate the results of the risk/need assessment directly into the case plan process to ensure that agents of change target those criminogenic needs that are tied specifically to reoffending. Examples of fourth generation tools are the Youthful Level of Service/Case Management Inventory (YLS/CMD), the Ohio Youth Assessment System (OYAS), the Level of Service/Case Management Inventory (LS/CMI), and the Ohio Risk Assessment System (ORAS).

These instruments use dynamic risk factors to measure initial risk and then reassess on these items to determine if the offender has made any significant changes in the risk they pose to society. In addition to targets of change, the fourth generation tools allow for departments to focus their resources on those domains (broad areas of need) that are moderate to high risk. Ultimately, if the criminal justice system can significantly reduce the recidivism rates for offenders, this will result in increased public safety. The fourth generation tools provide agents of change with a specific "road map" to address the needs of the offenders, manage limited resources, and protect public safety.

Obstacles to Good Practice

Here are some of the more common obstacles that exist with regard to offender assessment.

1. Offenders are assessed, but the process ignores important factors. Sometimes this is because the tool selected is comprised mainly of static predictors, or the assessment process focuses on one or two domains (like substance abuse) to the exclusion of other important risk factors.
2. Offenders are assessed, but the process does not distinguish quantifiably determined levels (i.e., high, moderate, low). This is common with narrative assessments, and the result is often that the summaries all read the same—e.g., "offender is a risk to reoffend unless they get substance abuse treatment." This type of information tells us little about the actual risk of reoffending or the level of need in specific areas. This is common with clinical assessment processes.
3. Even when offenders are comprehensively assessed, the results are not used—everyone gets the same treatment. As we will discuss below, adopting a risk assessment tool is only one step in the process. If the information is not going to be used, then why assess?
4. Staff members often are not adequately trained in use of the instruments, or they are only trained when the new instrument is selected. When a decision to use a new instrument is made everyone is trained, but as time goes on and new employees are hired little refresher training may be done—new staff simply learn how to use the tools by watching the older staff. The result is that reliability and validity suffer, and stakeholders lose confidence in the results of the assessment.
5. Staff resistance is one of the most persistent obstacles to overcome. Some of the common refrains include "I just need to talk to them for five minutes to determine their level of risk," "we don't have time to conduct an assessment" "they are all high risk," and "they all get the same treatment anyway so why assess them?" While staff resistance can be a challenge, it is not insurmountable; as the Jones survey found, most community correctional agencies understand the importance and value of using a valid and reliable risk assessment tool.

Some Points to Consider

To avoid these and other mistakes and to derive the full value from assessments, there are some points to consider.

- There is no "one size fits all" assessment tool. Some domains or types of offenders will require specialized assessments, such as sex offenders or mentally disturbed individuals. In addition the use or purpose will vary. For example, the assessment tool for making a decision about whether to grant pretrial release may be different from one for making a decision about whether to grant probation.
- Actuarial assessment is more accurate than clinical assessment, but no process is perfect and there will always be false positives and false negatives; sometimes low risk offenders reoffend, and sometimes high risk offenders are successful.
- Assessment is usually not a "one-time" event, especially if the offender is under

some form of community control. Offender risk and need factors change, so it is important to consider assessment as an ongoing process.

- Assessments help guide decisions, but they do not make them—professional discretion is part of good assessment-aided decision making.
- While the new dynamic assessment tools can produce more useful information, they require more effort to ensure reliability—they require staff training and continual monitoring of the assessment process. Like just about everything we do, fidelity and quality assurance make a difference.
- Remember, good risk assessment serves a number of functions and helps guide decisions by providing reliable information in a systematic and objective manner. It can be the cornerstone of a more effective, efficient, and just system.
- Develop a flexible process that expands as needed—higher risk offenders need more assessment.
- Standardize the process and instruments so that everyone is speaking the same language with regard to risk assessment.
- Regardless of the assessment tool used, staff should be thoroughly trained on the rationale and use of a risk assessment tool. Proper training will ensure that the staff understands the advantages of risk assessment and that they use the tool in an appropriate and consistent manner. The level and amount of staff "buy in" can drastically affect the level of success in implementing a risk assessment process or tool (Lowenkamp, Holsinger, & Latessa, 2004).
- Following training, agency administrators should establish quality assurance processes such as periodic audits of assessments, refresher training, or even certification of assessors.
- Use the assessment results to develop case supervision and treatment plans and to assign offenders to programs.
- Share information with service providers so that they understand the risk of the offender they are involved with as well as the criminogenic factors that need to be targeted.
- An assessment tool should be validated on the population for which it is being used. There are several widely used actuarial instruments that have been validated in numerous settings and across several subgroups (i.e., males, females, different racial and ethnic groups). Nonetheless, agencies should still analyze assessment results based on the population for which the tool is being used.

What Is the Impact of Offender Assessment?

Numerous studies have demonstrated the importance of risk assessment in developing effective correctional programming, but what is not known is how much is saved through the use of assessment tools. Undoubtedly there is a cost savings when we are able to divert low risk offenders from intensive and costly correctional programs. There is also the matter of improving public protection by identifying those offenders who pose the greatest risk of continuing their criminal behavior. When we are able to identify the higher risk offender, providing an appropriate correctional response that can reduce that risk, we have achieved a level of public protection through risk reduction. One of the major benefits of offender assessment and classification is that it allows agencies to allocate resources and staff more optimally and effectively (Lowenkamp & Latessa, 2005).

What Is the Cost of an Assessment Tool?

There are a number of costs to consider when implementing a risk assessment tool. These include cost of the instruments, costs of training, staff time to administer the tool, possible automation, and validation studies. As for the cost of the tool itself, it depends on whether an agency chooses a proprietary instrument or a nonproprietary (public domain) instrument. While the former incur a per unit or license cost to use, they have several advantages—including regular upgrades of the instrument, automated versions of the tools, and technical assistance from the vendor. The exact cost usually depends on the volume used and can range between one and a couple of dollars per assessment. Some agencies have elected to develop their own instruments, usually through contracting with a consultant, in which case they "own" the tool and can use it without charge. For large agencies this may be a viable option; however, development and validation can take several years to complete. Whether a public domain or proprietary tool is used, training cost, time required for administration, and automation costs all need to be considered.

The implementation of an actuarial risk assessment tool is a daunting task, particularly in a large jurisdiction or organization, and the decision of what instrument to use can be perplexing enough without the focus on issues of consistency, reliability, validity, training, and quality assurance. Most experts, however, believe that the potential benefits of using a risk assessment instrument far outweigh the costs, particularly over a long period of time.

Notes

1. Although it could be argued that there is a third camp led by Barbara Bloom (2000) and Meda Chesney-Lind (2000) regarding the appropriateness of actuarial risk assessments for females, the purpose of this paper is to not debate the appropriateness of risk assessment, but instead to provide a review of the advancements in assessing risk over the past ten years.

2. This chapter's focus is to outline the use of risk assessment, the conditions in which risk assessment is appropriate, and the advancements of risk assessment over the past ten years. For this reason, we will not be comparing and contrasting second generation tools with third and fourth generation tools. For further critiques of these tools see Baird (2009).

References

Andrews, D. A., & Bonta, J. (1998). *The psychology of criminal conduct.* Cincinnati, OH: Anderson Publishing.

Andrews, D. A., Bonta, J., & Hoge, R. (1990). Classification for effective rehabilitation: Rediscovering psychology. *Criminal Justice and Behavior, 17,* 19–52.

Baird, C. (2009). *A question of evidence: A critique of risk assessment models used in the justice system.* Madison, WI: National Council on Crime and Delinquency.

Bloom, B. (2000). Beyond recidivism: Perspectives on evaluation of programs for female offenders in community corrections. In M. McMahon (Ed.), *Assessment to assistance: Programs for women in community corrections* (pp. 107–138). Lanham, MD: American Correctional Association.

Bonta, J., & Wormith, S. J. (2008). Risk and need assessment. In G. Mclvor & P. Raynor (Eds.), *Developments in social work with offenders* (pp. 131–152). London: Jessica Kingsley Publishers.

Chesney-Lind, M. (2000). What to do about girls? Thinking about programs for young women. In M. McMahon (Ed.). *Assessment to assistance: Programs for women in community corrections* (pp. 139–170). Lanham, MD: American Correctional Association.

Clear, T. R. (1985). Managerial issues in community corrections. In L. F. Travis (Ed.), *Probation, parole, and community corrections* (pp. 33–46). Prospect Heights, IL: Waveland Press.

Dowden, C., & Andrews, D. A. (1999). What works in young offender treatment: A meta-analysis. *Forum on Corrections Research, 11,* 21–24.

Farrington, D. P. (1987). Predicting individual crime rates. In D. M. Gottfredson & M. Tonry (Eds.), *Prediction and classification: Criminal justice decision making* (pp. 151–181). Chicago: University of Chicago Press.

Flores, A. W., Russell, A. J., Latessa, E. J., & Travis, L. F. (2005). Evidence of professionalism or quackery: Measuring practitioner awareness of risk/need, factors and effective treatment strategies. *Federal Probation, 69*(2), 9–14.

Gendreau, P., Little, T., & Goggin, C. (1996). A meta-analysis of the predictors of adult offender recidivism: What works! *Criminology, 34,* 575–607.

Holsinger, A. M., Lurigio, A. J., & Latessa, E. J. (2001). Practitioners' guide to understanding the basis of assessing offender risk. *Federal Probation, 65*(1), 46–50.

Jones, D. A., Johnson, S., Latessa, E. J., & Travis, L. F. (1999). Case classification in community corrections: Preliminary findings from a national survey. In *Topics in community corrections* (pp. 4–10). Washington, DC: Department of Justice.

Latessa, E. J. (2004). Best practices of classification and assessment. *Journal of Community Corrections, 12(2),* 4–6, 27–30.

Latessa, E. J., & Lowenkamp, C. T. (2005a). The role of offender risk assessment tools and how to select them. *For the Record, 4th Quarter,* 18–20.

Latessa, E. J., & Lowenkamp, C. T. (2005b). What are criminogenic needs and why are they important? *For the Record, 4th Quarter,* 15–16.

Lowenkamp, C. T., Holsinger, A., & Latessa, E. J. (2004). Assessing the inter-rater agreement of the Level of Service Inventory Revised. *Federal Probation, 65*(3), 34–38.

Lowenkamp, C. T., & Latessa, E. J. (2004). Understanding the risk principle: How and why correctional interventions can harm low-risk offenders. In *Topics in community corrections* (pp. 3–8). Washington, DC: Department of Justice.

Lowenkamp, C. T., & Latessa, E. J. (2005). Increasing the effectiveness of correctional programming through the risk principle: Identifying offenders for residential placement. *Criminology and Public Policy, 2*(4), 15–24.

Lowenkamp, C. T., Latessa, E. J., & Holsinger, A. (2006). The risk principle in action: What we have learned from 13,676 offenders and 97 correctional programs. *Crime and Delinquency, 62*(1), 1–17.

Meehl, P. E. (1954). *Clinical versus statistical prediction.* Minneapolis: University of Minnesota Press.

Modry, L., & Gies, R. (2005). *The state of risk assessment in Ohio.* Unpublished report.

Petersilia, J., & Turner, S. (1987). Guideline-based justice: Prediction and racial minorities. In D. M. Gottfredson & M Tonry (Eds.), *Prediction and classification: Criminal justice decision making* (pp. 151–181). Chicago: University of Chicago Press.

DISCUSSION QUESTIONS

1. Explain why offender risk assessment is important.
2. According to the authors, what are the three principles of risk assessment?
3. Do you think improvements in risk assessment will reduce racial disparities that exist in corrections?
4. Do you believe that assessing both risk and need of high risk offenders will reduce recidivism?

READING

Western and Wildeman argue that mass incarceration is concentrated among disadvantaged minority men and women. Unlike traditional life course researchers, they argue that the life course for these individuals is more negatively impacted after incarceration because their changes of employment and marriage are less likely. They point out that the Black family suffers in many ways. Black male prisoners are viewed as less desirable as mates, their children grow up without fathers in the home, and separation strains family and other relationships as well. Though they are fewer in number, incarcerated Black females face similar challenges. The authors conclude that the inequalities of mass incarceration could persist beyond the lifetime of an offender and impact their families and communities for generations to come.

The Black Family and Mass Incarceration

Bruce Western and Christopher Wildeman

Today, we read Daniel Patrick Moynihan's 1965 report, *The Negro Family: The Case For National Action*, with a sense of lost opportunity. The report drew attention to the problems of chronic idleness, addiction, and serious violence in minority urban neighborhoods of concentrated poverty. Moynihan traced these problems to the breakdown of the African American family. High nonmartial birth rates, divorce and separation, and single-parenthood, in Moynihan's analysis, all contributed to ghetto poverty, crime, and other dislocations. Although Moynihan did not offer a detailed policy solution, he understood that the social problems of the urban poor stood in the way of the historic promise of full African American citizenship demanded by the civil rights movements.

Sounding the alarm over ghetto poverty in 1965, Moynihan named a social problem and suggested a direction for its solution. Viewed in hindsight, the report marked a fork in the road. Many of the social problems Moynihan identified have subsequently worsened. Joblessness among young, black, noncollege men climbed through the 1960s and 1970s. Crime rates and rates of single-parenthood also escalated. While Moynihan called for increased social investment to avert the problems of crime and poverty, public policy turned instead in a punitive direction, massively expanding the role of the criminal justice system. By the early 2000s, more than a third of young black noncollege men were incarcerated. Among black men younger than forty, there were nearly twice as many prison records as bachelor's degrees. The spectacular growth of the American penal system has transformed the institutional context of urban poverty in a way that was wholly unexpected by Moynihan or other students of social policy of his time.

Source: Western, B., & Wildeman, C. (2009). The black family and mass incarceration. *The Annals of the American Academy of Political and Social Science, 621*, 221–242.

In this article, we describe the main contours of the American prison boom and its effect on the lives and structure of poor African American families. We argue that in the wake of the Moynihan Report, economic conditions among the ghetto poor continued to deteriorate. Instead of a movement for social investment in the urban poor that Moynihan supported, politics turned to the right. Political currents flowed to law and order and away from rehabilitative criminal justice policy. Retribution and incapacitation were embraced as the main objectives of criminal punishment. As a result, the prison population ballooned through the 1980s and 1990s, producing astonishing incarceration rates among young African American men. Although family breakdown was not the immediate cause of the American prison boom, mass incarceration has had potentially profound effects on the family life of those caught in the web of the criminal justice system. Research is still in its infancy, but we conclude by describing what we see as the most important questions linking mass incarceration to the family life of America's urban poor.

Political and Economic Roots of the Prison Boom

Mass imprisonment of the late 1990s can be traced to two basic shifts in politics and economics. The growth of harsh sentencing policies and a punitive approach to drug control began with a rightward shift in American politics, first visible at the national level in the mid-1960s. The Republican campaign of 1964 linked the problem of street crime to civil rights protest and the growing unease among whites about racial violence.

Historically, responsibilities for crime control were divided mostly between state and local agencies. The Republicans had placed the issue of crime squarely on the national agenda. What is more, by treating civil rights protest as a strain of social disorder, veiled connections were drawn between the crime problem, on one hand, and black social protest, on the other.

The social problem of crime became a reality as rates of murder and other violent crimes escalated in the decade following the 1964 election. Throughout the 1960s, urban riots in Los Angeles, New York, Newark, Detroit, and dozens of other cities provided a socially ambiguous mixture of disorder and politics. Despite Goldwater's defeat, support grew for the new law and order message, particularly among southern whites and northern working-class voters of Irish, Italian, and German descent who turned away from the Democratic Party in the 1970s (Edsall and Edsall 1991).

Elevated crime rates and the realigned race relations of the post–civil rights period provided a receptive context for the law and order themes of the Republican Party. In state politics, Republican governors and legislators increased their representation through the South and West and placed themselves in the vanguard of the movements for mandatory minimum sentences, sentence enhancements for repeat offenders, and expanded prison capacity (Western 2006; Davey 1998; Jacobs and Carmichael 2001). Quantitative analyses show that incarceration rates grew fastest under Republican governors and state legislators (Western 2006, chap. 3).

Although Republicans were quick to promote prison expansion and tough new criminal sentences, Democrats also came to support punitive criminal justice policy. Perhaps the clearest signal that Democrats too were tough on crime was sent by President Clinton's Violent Crime Control and Law Enforcement Act (1994). The Clinton crime bill earmarked $9.9 billion for prison construction and added life terms for third-time federal felons (Windelsham 1998, 104–7). By the 1990s, Democrats and Republicans had come to support the sentencing policies and capital construction campaigns that grew the penal population.

Shifts in politics and policy, however, are only half the story. The newly punitive system of criminal sentencing would have had largely symbolic significance but for the ready supply of chronically idle young men that came to swell the nation's prisons and jails. Urban deindustrialization eroded the labor market for unskilled young men while punitive politics gained momentum in the 1970s and 1980s.

From 1969 to 1979, central cities recorded enormous declines in manufacturing and blue collar employment. New York, for example, lost 170,000 blue-collar jobs through the 1970s, another 120,000 jobs were shed in Chicago, and blue-collar employment in Detroit fell by 90,000 jobs (Kasarda 1989, 29). For young black men in metropolitan areas, employment rates fell by 30 percent among high school dropouts and nearly 20 percent among high school graduates. Job loss was only a third as large among young noncollege whites (Bound and Holzer 1993, 390).

Variation in imprisonment is closely linked to variation in wages and employment. Weekly earnings for young low-education men declined through the 1980s and 1990s while imprisonment rates were rising. Among black men, unemployment increased steeply with declining education. One study estimates that if wages and employment had not declined among low-education men since the early 1980s, growth in prison admission rates would have been reduced by as much as 25 percent by 2001 (Western, Kleykamp, and Rosenfeld 2004).

Idle young men in poor minority neighborhoods supplied a large share of the inmates that drove the prison boom. The path from concentrated economic disadvantage to mass imprisonment runs partly through the mechanism of crime, but policy also played a vital role. At any given point in time, crime among young disadvantaged men is higher than in the rest of the population. For example, the murder rates—victimization and offending—are about twenty-five times higher for black men aged eighteen to twenty-four than for white men aged twenty-five and older (Pastore and Maguire 2006). Violent crime is also a more serious problem in poor communities than affluent ones (e.g., Sampson 1987; see also the review of Braithwaite 1979). The criminal involvement of young, economically disadvantaged men makes them more likely at a given point in time to go to prison than others who are less involved in crime.

Crime cannot explain, however, why disadvantaged young men were so much more likely to go to prison by the end of the 1990s than two decades earlier. Indeed, survey data show that poor male youth were much less involved in crime at the height of the prison boom, in 2000, than at its inception, in 1980. To explain the growing risk of imprisonment over time, the role of policy is decisive. Because the system of criminal sentencing had come to rely so heavily on incarceration, an arrest in the late 1990s was far more likely to lead to prison time than at the beginning of the prison boom in 1980 (Blumstein and Beck 1999).

The drug trade itself became a source of economic opportunity in the jobless ghetto. High rates of joblessness and crime, and a flourishing street trade in illegal drugs, combined with harsher criminal penalties and intensified urban policing to produce high incarceration rates among young unskilled men in inner cities. In the twenty-five years from 1980, the incarceration rate tripled among white men in their twenties, but fewer than 2 percent were behind bars by 2004. Imprisonment rates for young black men increased less quickly, but one in seven were in custody by 2004. Incarceration rates are much higher among male high school dropouts in their twenties. Threefold growth in the imprisonment of young white male dropouts left 7 percent in prison or jail by 2004. The incarceration rate for young low-education black men rose by 22 points in the two decades after 1980. Incredibly, 34 percent of all young black male high school dropouts were in prison or jail on an average day in 2004, an incarceration rate forty times higher than the national average (Western 2006, chap. 1).

Tough sentences for drug and repeat offenders, strict policing and prosecution of drug traffic and public order offending, and unforgiving parole supervision broadened the use of imprisonment from its traditional focus on serious crime. Certainly sentences increased for serious crime, and this contributed to incarceration rates too. For example, time served for murderers increased from five to eleven years, from 1980 to 1996 (Blumstein and Beck 1999, 36). But growth in the share of less serious offenders in state prison increased much more rapidly (Blumstein and Beck 1999, 24, 37). Growth in the numbers of drug offenders, parole violators, and public order offenders reflects the use of penal policy as a surrogate social policy, in which a troublesome and unruly population is increasingly managed with incarceration.

Mass Incarceration

The scale of the penal system is usually measured by an incarceration rate. The incarceration rate records the number of people in prison or jail on a given day per 100,000 of the population. Figure 8.3 compares the United States' incarceration rate in 2004 to the incarceration rates of the long-standing democracies of Western Europe. The penal systems of Western Europe locked up, on average, about 100 per 100,000. The United States by contrast incarcerated more than seven times the European

Figure 8.3 Incarceration Rates per One Hundred Thousand Residents, United States and Western Europe, 2004

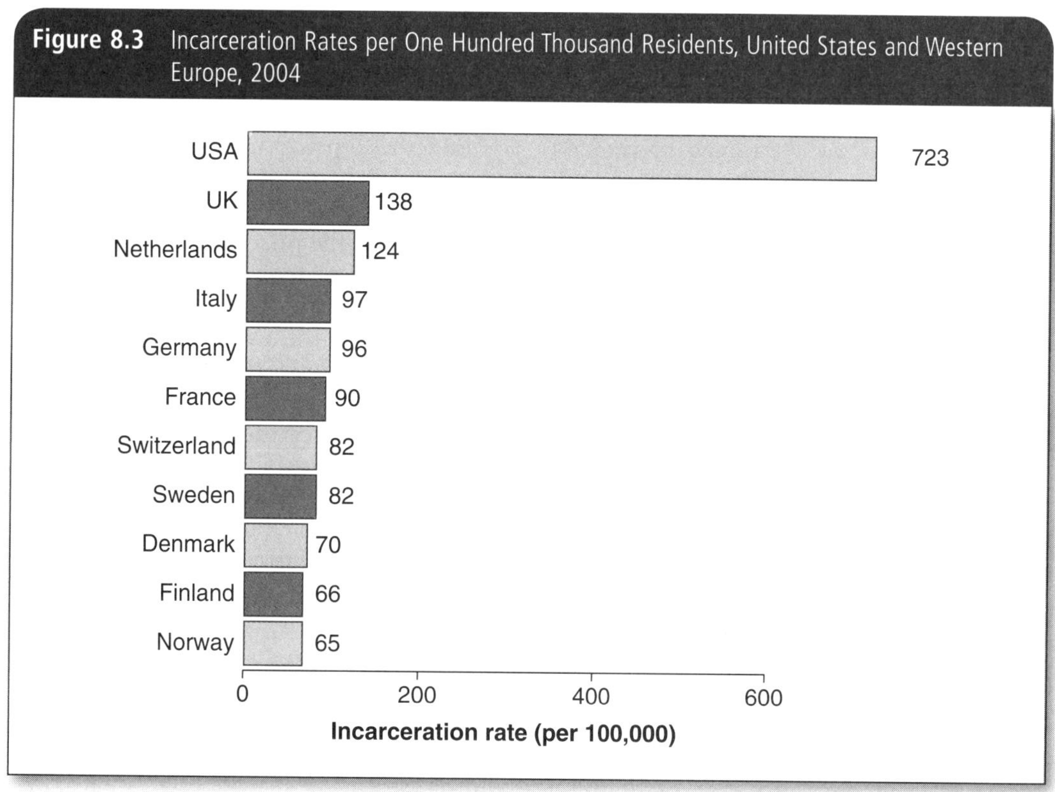

Source: Aebi (2005), Harrison and Beck (2006).

average, with an incarceration rate of more than 700 per 100,000.

Beginning in 1974, the prison population began to grow, and the incarceration rate increased continuously for the next three decades. By 2005, nearly 2.2 million people were in custody, either in prison for felony convictions or in local jails awaiting trial or serving short sentences. These figures do not fully reflect the contemporary correctional population. In 2005, another 784,000 men and women were under community supervision on parole, while 4.1 million people were on probation. The total population under correctional supervision thus includes more than 7 million people, or about 3.1 percent of all U.S. adults (Glaze and Bonczar 2006).

The broad significance of the penal system for American social inequality results from extreme social and economic disparities in incarceration. More than 90 percent of all prison and jail inmates are men. Women's incarceration rates have increased more quickly than men's since 1980, but much higher rates persist for men, leaving women to contend with raising children while their partners cycle in and out of jail. These men are young, of working age, many with small children. About two-thirds of state prisoners are over eighteen years old but under age thirty-five. With this age pattern, only a small number of people are incarcerated at any point in time, but many more pass through the penal system at some point in their lives.

Incarceration is also concentrated among the disadvantaged. High incarceration rates among low-status and minority men are unmistakable. The 1997 survey of state and federal prisoners shows that state inmates average less than eleven years of schooling. A third were not working at the time of their incarceration, and the average wage of the remainder is much lower than that of other men with the same level of education. African Americans and Hispanics also have higher incarceration rates than whites, and together the two groups account for about two-thirds of the state prison population.

The black-white difference in incarceration rates is especially striking. Black men are eight times more likely to be incarcerated than whites, and large racial disparities can be seen for all age groups and at different levels of education. The large black-white disparity in incarceration is unmatched by most other social indicators. Racial disparities in unemployment (two to one), nonmarital childbearing (three to one), infant mortality (two to one), and wealth (one to five) are all significantly lower than the eight to one black-white ratio in incarceration rates (see Western 2006). If white men were incarcerated at the same rate as blacks, there would be more than 6 million people in prison and jail, and more than 5 percent of the male working-age population would be incarcerated.

Age, race, and educational disparities concentrate imprisonment among the disadvantaged. From 1980 to 2004, the percentage of young white men in prison or jail increased from 0.6 to 1.9 percent. Among young white men with only a high school education, incarceration rates were about twice as high. At the dawn of the prison boom, in 1980, the incarceration rate for young black men, 5.7 percent, was more than twice as high as that for low-education whites. By 2004, 13.5 percent of black men in their twenties were in prison or jail. Incarceration rates were higher in the lower half of the education distribution. More than one in five young noncollege black men were behind bars on a typical day in 2004.

Incarceration rates offer a snapshot of the extent of penal confinement. Time series of incarceration rates tell us how the extent of penal confinement has shifted historically. We can also study, not the level of incarceration at a point in time, but how the risk of incarceration accumulates over an individual's life. This kind of life course analysis asks, What is the likelihood an individual will go to prison by age twenty-five, thirty, or thirty-five. Instead of providing a snapshot of the risk of incarceration, this analysis describes a typical biography.

The life course perspective provides a compelling account of social integration. In this account, the passage to adulthood is a sequence of well-ordered stages that affect life trajectories long after the early transitions are completed. In modern times, arriving at adult status involves moving from school to work, then to marriage, to establishing a home and becoming a parent. Completing this sequence without delay promotes stable employment, marriage, and other positive life outcomes. The process of becoming an adult thus influences success in fulfilling adult roles and responsibilities.

As an account of social integration, life course analysis has attracted the interest of students of crime and deviance. Criminologists point to the normalizing effects of life course transitions. Steady jobs and good marriages build social bonds that keep would-be offenders in a daily routine. They enmesh men who are tempted by crime in a web of supportive social relationships. Strong family bonds and steady work restrict men's opportunities for antisocial behavior and offer them a stake in normal life. For persistent lawbreakers, the adult roles of spouse and worker offer a pathway out of crime (Sampson and Laub 1993; Warr 1998; Hagan 1993). Those who fail to secure the markers of adulthood are more likely to persist in criminal behavior. This idea of a normalizing, integrative life path offers a powerful alternative to claims that criminality is a stable trait possessed by some but absent in others. Above all else, the life course account of crime is dynamic, describing how people change as their social context evolves with age.

Imprisonment significantly alters the life course. Working life is disrupted as workers with prison records try to find jobs from employers who are deeply suspicious of applicants with criminal records. Ex-prisoners are also less likely to get married or cohabit with the mothers of their children (Lopoo and Western 2005). By eroding opportunities for employment and marriage, incarceration may also lead ex-inmates back to a life of crime. In short, imprisonment is a turning point in which young crime-involved men acquire a new status involving diminished life chances.

To place the risks of imprisonment in the context of the life course, we report new estimates of the cumulative risks of imprisonment by age thirty to thirty-four, for five-year birth cohorts born through the postwar period (see Table 8.3). Because most inmates enter prison for the first time before age thirty-five, these cumulative risks of imprisonment roughly describe lifetime risks of imprisonment. We emphasize that these lifetime risks of incarceration are for imprisonment, as opposed to jail incarceration. Imprisonment here describes a sentence of twelve months or longer for a felony conviction, now about twenty-eight months of time served, at the median.

The oldest cohort was born just after World War II, and its members reached their mid-thirties in 1979, just at the takeoff of the prison boom. In this group, just over 1 percent of whites and 9 percent of blacks would go to prison. As incarceration rates climbed through the 1980s, lifetime imprisonment risks also increased. The big jump in imprisonment separates men born in the 1950s and earlier from those born in the 1960s and later. The pervasive presence of the criminal justice system in the lives of African American men only emerges among those born since the mid-1960s who were reaching their midthirties from the end of the 1990s. Like the long time series of incarceration rates, these figures on postwar birth cohorts underscore the historic novelty of mass incarceration. Only through the 1990s did the penal system figure prominently in the lives of young black men.

Like incarceration rates, lifetime risks of imprisonment are also steeply stratified by education. We report cumulative risks of imprisonment for men who have had at least some college education and for all those with just a

Table 8.3 Cumulative Risk of Imprisonment by Age Thirty to Thirty-Four by Race and Education for Men Born 1945 Through 1949 to 1975 Through 1979 (in Percentages)

	1945–1949	1950–1954	1955–1959	1960–1964	1965–1969	1970–1974	1975–1979
White men							
High school dropouts	4.2	7.2	8.0	8.0	10.5	14.8	15.3
High school only	0.7	2.0	2.1	2.5	4.0	3.8	4.1
All noncollege	1.8	2.9	3.2	3.7	5.1	5.1	6.3
Some college	0.7	0.7	0.6	0.8	0.7	0.9	1.2
All men	1.2	1.9	2.0	2.2	2.8	2.8	3.3
Black men							
High school dropouts	14.7	19.6	27.6	41.6	57.0	62.5	69.0
High school only	10.2	11.3	9.4	12.4	16.8	20.3	18.0
All noncollege	12.1	14.1	14.7	19.9	26.7	30.9	35.7
Some college	4.9	3.5	4.3	5.5	6.8	8.5	7.6
All men	9.0	10.6	11.5	15.2	20.3	22.8	20.7

SOURCE: Data sources and methods are described in Pettit and Western (2004).
NOTE: Estimates for the cohorts born after 1969 are based on data from the 2004 Survey on Inmates of States and Federal Correctional Facilities.

high school education. Among those with just a high school education, we separate high school dropouts and high school graduates. We report figures for all noncollege men because—particularly for African Americans—those without college education have remained an approximately constant proportion of the population. Educational attainment has increased across birth cohorts chiefly because the proportion of high school dropouts has declined.

At the very bottom of the education distribution, among high school dropouts, prison time has become extraordinarily prevalent. For black male dropouts born since the mid-1960s, 60 to 70 percent go to prison. For this very poorly schooled segment of the population, serving time in prison has become a routine life event on the pathway through adulthood. Indeed, we need only go back several decades to find a time when incarceration was not pervasive in the lives of young black men with little schooling.

From a life course perspective, we can compare imprisonment to other significant life events that are commonly thought to mark the path through young adulthood. Life course researchers have previously studied college graduation, military service, and marriage as key milestones that move young men forward in life to establishing a household and a steady job. Comparing imprisonment to these life events suggests how the pathway through adulthood has been changed by the prison boom.

The risks of each life event are different for blacks and whites, but racial differences in imprisonment greatly overshadow any other inequality. By their early thirties, whites are more than twice as likely to hold a bachelor's degree compared with blacks, whereas blacks are about 50 percent more likely to have served in the military. However, black men in their early thirties are about seven times more likely than whites to have a prison record. Indeed, recent birth cohorts of black men are more likely to have prison records (22.4 percent) than military records (17.4 percent) or bachelor's degrees (12.5 percent). The share of the population with prison records is particularly striking among noncollege men. Whereas few noncollege white men have prison records, nearly a third of black men with less than a college education have been to prison. Noncollege black men in their early thirties in 1999 were more than twice as likely to be ex-felons as veterans (see Table 8.4).

By 1999, imprisonment had become a common life event for black men that sharply distinguished their pathway through adulthood from that of white men.

The empirical markers of mass imprisonment are more slippery in this case. When will the incarceration rate be high enough to imprison, not the individual, but the group? The picture painted by the statistics in this article helps us answer this question. Not only did incarceration become common among young black men at the end of the 1990s, but its prevalence also exceeded that of other life events that we usually associate with passage through the life course. More than college graduation or military service, incarceration has come to typify the biographies of African American men born since the late 1960s.

Table 8.4 Percentage of Non-Hispanic Black and White Men, Born 1965 to 1969, Experiencing Life Events by 1999

Life Event	Whites	Blacks
All men		
Prison incarceration	3.2	22.4
Bachelor's degree	31.6	12.5
Military service	14.0	17.4
Marriage	72.5	59.3
Noncollege men		
Prison incarceration	6.0	31.9
High school diploma/GED	73.5	64.4
Military service	13.0	13.7
Marriage	72.8	55.9

Source: Pettit and Western (2004).
Note: The incidence of all live events except prison incarceration were calculated from the 2000 Census. To make the incarceration risks comparable to census statistics, the estimates are adjusted to describe the percentage of men, born 1965 to 1969, who have ever been imprisoned and survived to 1999.

Mass Incarceration and Family Life

As imprisonment became common for low-education black men by the end of the 1990s, the penal system also became familiar to poor minority families. By 1999, 30 percent of non-college black men in their midthirties had been to prison, and through incarceration, many were separated from their wives, girlfriends, and children. Women and children in low-income urban communities now routinely cope with absent husbands and fathers lost to incarceration and adjust to their return after release. Poor single men detached from family life are also affected, bearing the stigma of a prison record in the marriage markets of disadvantaged urban neighborhoods.

Discussions of the family life of criminal offenders typically focus on the crime-suppressing effects of marriage, not the effects of incarceration on family life. Researchers find that marriage offers a pathway out of crime for men with histories of delinquency. Not a wedding itself, but marriage in the context of a warm, stable, and constructive relationship, offers the antidote to crime (Sampson and Laub 1993; Laub, Nagin, and Sampson 1998). Wives and family members in such relationships provide the web of obligations and responsibilities that restrains young men and reduces their contact with the male friends whose recreations veer into antisocial behavior (Warr 1998).

The prison boom places the link between crime and marriage in a new light. If a good marriage is important for criminal desistance, what is the effect of incarceration on marriage?

Poverty researchers closely followed the changing shape of American families. Growing numbers of female-headed families increased the risks of enduring poverty for women and children. Growing up poor also raised a child's risk of school failure, poor health, and delinquency. The combination of high incarceration rates with a large proportion of fathers among inmates means many children now have incarcerated fathers. Data from surveys of prison and jail inmates can be used to calculate the numbers of children with fathers in prison or jail. A time series for 1980 to 2000 shows that the total number of children with incarcerated fathers increased sixfold from about 350,000 to 2.1 million, nearly 3 percent of all children nationwide in 2000. Among whites, the fraction of children with a father in prison or jail is relatively small—about 1.2 percent in 2000. The figure is about three times higher (3.5 percent) for Hispanics. Among African Americans, more than a million, or one in eleven, black children had a father in prison or jail in 2000. The numbers are higher for younger children: by 2000, 10.4 percent of black children under age ten had a father in prison or jail. Just as incarceration has become a normal life event for disadvantaged young black men, parental incarceration has become commonplace for their children.

Table 8.5 reports the risks of parental imprisonment by age fourteen for children born in 1978 and 1990 (see Wildeman forthcoming). Among white children born in 1978 who reached their teenage years in the early 1990s, around 2 percent experienced a parent being sent to prison. Among African American children born in the same year, around 14 percent had a parent sent to prison by age fifteen. Twelve years later, among children born in 1990, about a quarter of all black children had a parent sent to prison. Indeed, the proportion of black children who had a mother sent to prison (a relatively rare event) nearly equaled the proportion of white children who had a father sent to prison.

The children of low-education parents were far more exposed to the criminal justice system than the population in general. These estimates indicate that among children born in the late 1970s to noncollege African American parents, about one in seven had a parent sent to prison by the time they reached their teenage years. Just over a decade later, more than a quarter of the children of noncollege black parents experienced parental imprisonment. For

Table 8.5 Cumulative Risks of Paternal and Maternal Imprisonment for Children Born in 1978 and 1990, by Parents' Race and Education (in Percentages)

	Whites		Blacks	
	Maternal	**Paternal**	**Maternal**	**Paternal**
Born 1978				
All	0.2	2.1	1.4	13.4
High school dropout	0.2	4.0	1.9	21.4
High school graduate	0.2	2.0	0.9	9.9
All noncollege	0.2	2.8	1.5	15.1
Some college	0.2	1.4	1.2	7.1
Born 1990				
All	0.6	3.6	3.2	24.5
High school dropout	1.0	7.1	5.0	49.4
High school graduate	0.7	4.7	2.6	20.0
All noncollege	0.8	5.5	3.6	24.5
Some college	0.3	1.7	2.6	13.2

SOURCE: Sources, methods, and figures are reported in Wildeman (forthcoming).

black children whose parents dropped out of high school, around half had a parent sent to prison by the early 2000s. Just as imprisonment had become a normal life event for young black male dropouts, so had parental imprisonment become normal for their children.

The incapacitation effect captures only part of the impact of the prison boom on marriage. Incarceration reduces men's wages, slows the rate of wage growth, increases unemployment, and shortens job tenure. If a poor employment record damages the marriage prospects of single men and contributes to the risk of divorce among those who are married, the economic effects of incarceration will decrease the likelihood of marriage among men who have been to prison and jail.

While poor women care about men's economic status, they also worry about men's honesty and respectability. Just as the stigma of incarceration confers disadvantage in the labor market, it also undermines a man's prospects in the marriage market. Men in trouble with the authorities cannot offer the respectability that many poor women seek from their partners. A prison record—the official stamp of criminality—can convey trouble to mothers looking for a stable home.

Quantitative analysis of survey data is generally consistent with the field research. Black single men are especially likely to remain unmarried if they have prison records. The gap in marriage rates between black noninmates and ex-inmates is estimated to be anywhere from 20 to 200 percent. Survey data point more strongly to the destabilizing effects of incarceration on couples. Consider an analysis of the Fragile Families Survey of Child Wellbeing—a survey of poor urban couples with infant children. The survey shows that men who are living with the mothers of their newborn children are three times more likely to separate within the year if they have a history of incarceration (Western 2006, chap. 7).

Unanswered Questions

Moynihan traced the dilapidated state of the black family of the early 1960s to the burdens of slavery and a history of discrimination. In the early 2000s, however, the family life of poor African Americans in urban neighborhoods of concentrated poverty is also strained by mass incarceration. Emerging only in the closing years of the 1990s, mass incarceration has routinely drawn young noncollege black men and their families into the orbit of the penal system.

While a handful of ethnographic studies are beginning to shed light on the effects of incarceration on the family life of the urban poor, and several quantitative studies have examined the effects of incarceration on marriage and divorce, research is still in its infancy. We close our discussion by describing what we see as the central research questions and offering some hypotheses for understanding the family life of the urban poor in the era of mass incarceration.

What are the financial consequences of incarceration for poor families? The costs of visiting far-flung facilities, accepting collect calls, and retaining legal representation all add to the financial strains of poor families. The extent of these costs is largely unknown. The economic effect of mass incarceration on families is thus fundamentally an empirical question. Research on the pay and employment of ex-prisoners suggests that the economic effects of mass incarceration on families may be large, but this hinges on the strength of the connection between crime-involved men and their families before and after incarceration.

What are the effects of incarceration on the supervision and socialization of children? We have seen that rates of maternal incarceration are much lower, but incarcerated mothers are more likely to be living with their children at the time of imprisonment. Again, the effects of imprisonment depend on the quality of the relationship between parent and child, and here relatively little is known. While the loss of a parent to the criminal justice system likely affects the socialization of children, children's aspirations and sense of self-worth are likely to be affected by the stigma of imprisonment.

We have argued here that the emergence of mass imprisonment has transformed the institutional context of America's urban poor. In this sense, this new era of mass incarceration adds another chapter to Moynihan's original analysis of urban poverty and its social correlates. The data suggest that the prison boom has been massively corrosive for family structure and family life, but much work remains to be done. In the background of this research agenda is the key question of the durability of urban poverty in the era of mass incarceration. If pervasive imprisonment undermines family life and disrupts the developmental path of children into young adulthood, the inequalities produced by mass incarceration may be exceptionally enduring. If the children of the prison boom are at greater risk of poverty and violence and are more involved in crime themselves, they too will risk following their parents into prison. Under these circumstances, the inequalities of mass incarceration will be sustained not just over a lifetime, but from one generation to the next.

References

Aebi, Marcel, 2005. *Council of Europe annual penal statistics.* Strasbourg, France: Council of Europe.

Blumstein, Alfred, and Allen J. Beck, 1999. Population growth in U.S. prisons, 1980–1996. In *Crime and justice: Prisons*, Vol. 26, ed. Michael Tonry and Joan

Petersilia, 17–62. Chicago: University of Chicago Press.

Bound, John, and Harry Holzer, 1993. Industrial shifts, skill levels, and the labor market for white and black men. *Review of Economics and Statistics* 75: 387–96.

Braithwaite, John, 1979. *Inequality, crime and public policy*. London: Routledge.

Davey, Joseph D, 1998. *The politics of prison expansion: Winning elections by waging war on crime*. Westport, CT: Praeger.

Edsall, Thomas B., and Mary D. Edsall, 1991. *Chain reaction: The impact of race, rights, and taxes on American politics*. New York: Norton.

Glaze, Lauren E., and Thomas P. Bonczar, 2006. *Probation and parole in the United States, 2005*. Washington, DC: U.S. Department of Justice.

Hagan, John, 1993. The social embeddedness of crime and unemployment. *Criminology* 31: 465–91.

Harrison, Paige M., and Allen J. Beck, 2006. Prison and jail inmates at midyear 2005. *Bureau of Justice Statistics Bulletin*. NCJ 208801. Washington, DC: U.S. Department of Justice.

Jacobs, David, and Jason T. Carmichael, 2001. The politics of punishment across time and space: A pooled time-series analysis of imprisonment rates. *Social Forces* 80: 61–91.

Kasarda, Jack, 1989. Urban industrial transition and the underclass. *The Annals of the American Academy of Political and Social Sciences* 501: 26–47.

Laub, John H., Daniel S. Nagin, and Robert J. Sampson, 1998. Trajectories of change in criminal offending: Good marriages and desistance processes. *American Sociological Review* 63: 225–38.

Lopoo, Leonard M., and Bruce Western, 2005. Incarceration and the formation and stability of marital unions. *Journal of Marriage and the Family* 65: 721–34.

Pastore, Ann L., and Kathleen Maguire, eds, 2006. *Sourcebook of criminal justice statistics*. http://www.albany.edu/sourcebook/(accessed December 2007).

Pettit, Becky, and Bruce Western, 2004. Mass imprisonment and the life course: Race and class inequality in U.S. incarceration. *American Sociological Review* 69: 151–69.

Sampson, Robert, 1987. Urban black violence: The effect of male joblessness and family disruption. *American Journal of Sociology* 93: 348–82.

Sampson, Robert J., and John H. Laub, 1993. *Crime in the making: Pathways and turning points through life*. Cambridge, MA: Harvard University Press.

Warr, Mark, 1998. Life-course transitions and desistance from crime. *Criminology* 36: 183–216.

Western, Bruce, 2006. *Punishment and inequality in America*. New York: Russell Sage Foundation.

Western, Bruce, Meredith Kleykamp, and Jake Rosenfeld, 2004. Crime, punishment, and American inequality. In *Social inequality*, ed. Katherine Neckerman, 771–96. New York: Russell Sage Foundation.

Wildeman, Christopher. Forthcoming. Parental imprisonment, the prison boom, and the concentration of childhood disadvantage. *Demography*.

Windelsham, Lord, 1998. *Politics, punishment and populism*. New York: Oxford University Press.

DISCUSSION QUESTIONS

1. Why would policy makers choose to deal with the problems facing African Americans by incarcerating them at higher rates?
2. What are some solutions to solving the problem of increasing crime rates without disproportionately affecting minorities?
3. According to the authors, 34% of young Black male high school dropouts were in prison or jail on an average day in 2004. Why is it that more punitive treatment of less serious crimes has not led to fewer crimes committed by minorities?

Glossary

Adjudication: The process of disposing of (or settling) a juvenile or criminal matter.

Arrest rates: Refers to the number of arrests per 100,000 persons for all persons 18 years or older. These arrest rates are reported by police agencies to the FBI and are reported annually in the *Uniform Crime Report.*

Assimilation: The merging of cultural traits from previously distinct cultural groups.

Bail: Money, property, or other security offered in exchange for the release from custody of an arrested person and to guarantee the person's appearance at trial. Bail is forfeited if the accused does not appear in court.

Batson v. Kentucky: Batson, a Black man in Kentucky, was convicted by an all-White jury of second-degree burglary. The prosecutor used all of his peremptory challenges to exclude the few prospective Black jurors from the jury pool. In the 1986 landmark case, the U.S. Supreme Court decided that peremptory challenges could not be used for a racially discriminatory purpose. Thus, creating an all-White jury by deliberately eliminating all prospective Black candidates was discriminatory. The Supreme Court ruled in favor of Batson.

Best practices: A best practice is a technique, method, or process that is believed to be most effective at delivering a particular outcome given the same conditions or circumstances.

Black child savers: The child savers were civic actors who led social movements during the 19th and 20th century to establish and develop the juvenile justice system and other child welfare reform in the United States and elsewhere. The Black child savers were those Black civic actors who were effective in reconfiguring prevailing color lines of juvenile social control, not by making race insignificant, but by pushing Black youth and community stakeholders into child welfare networks of juvenile social control—uplifting the deliberative radical democracy of American juvenile justice.

Black codes: Laws which were enacted shortly after the Civil War in the ex-confederate states to restrict the liberties of the newly freed slaves to ensure an ample supply of cheap agricultural labor and to maintain White economic prosperity in the South.

Bloody code: The name given to the English legal system from the late 17th century to the early 19th century. It was known as the *bloody code* because of the huge numbers of crimes for which the death penalty could be imposed. At that time, the attitudes of the wealthy men who made the law were unsympathetic. They felt that people who committed crimes were sinful, lazy, or greedy and deserved little mercy. Since the rich made the laws, they made laws that protected their interests. Any act that threatened their wealth, property, or sense of law and order was criminalized and made punishable by death.

Bracero Program: Created in 1942 by an executive order, it allowed Mexican nationals to take temporary agricultural work in the United States. Lasting for more than 22 years, more than 4.5 million Mexican nationals were legally contracted for work in the United States. Mexican peasants, desperate for cash work, were willing to take jobs at wages scorned by most Americans. The Braceros' presence had a significant effect on the business of farming and the culture of the United States.

Bureau of Justice Statistics (BJS): The branch of the Office of Justice Programs (OJP) within the U.S. Department of Justice that promotes the collection and analysis of crime data in the states and territories.

Bureau of Prisons: Established in 1930, the Bureau consists of 115 institutions, 6 regional offices, a Central Office (headquarters), 2 staff training centers, and 28 community corrections offices. The Bureau protects public safety by ensuring that Federal offenders serve their sentences of imprisonment in facilities that are safe, humane, cost-efficient, and appropriately secure. The Bureau helps reduce the potential for future criminal activity by encouraging inmates to participate in a range of programs that have been proven to reduce recidivism.

Centers for Disease Control and Prevention (CDC): A research and funding arm of the Public Health Service, U.S. Department of Health and Human Services. The CDC, as it is known, oversees an ambitious research agenda on myriad health problems, including homicide, suicide, and intentional injuries. It is also the sponsor of the periodic *Youth Risk Behavior Survey*, a survey of U.S. high school students about their recent experiences with sexual activity and high-risk behaviors.

Cesare Lombroso: An Italian doctor, often referred to as the "father of criminology," who took a scientific approach to studying crime during the end of the 19th century. His influence spread not only throughout Europe, but to the United States and other countries as well. His theory was based on the idea of atavism, in which he deemed that criminals were an evolutionary throwback to an earlier stage in human evolution. His theory led to his classification of criminals in categories such as born criminals, criminaloids, and insane criminals, as well as to research on female offenders.

Child savers: Civic actors during the 19th and 20th centuries who led to the establishment and development of autonomous juvenile justice systems and other welfare reforms in the United States and elsewhere.

Chinese Exclusion Act (1882): The first major and the only federal legislation that banned immigrants explicitly based on a specific nationality. The Act excluded Chinese laborers and those employed in mining from entering the country for 10 years under penalty of imprisonment and deportation.

Code of the street: A theory developed by Yale professor Elijah Anderson that presents an explanation for high rates of violence among African American adolescents. Anderson contends that economic disadvantage, separation from mainstream society, and racial discrimination encountered by some African American adolescents may lead to antisocial attitudes and to violent behavior.

Coker v. Georgia: Coker was convicted of raping a woman and was sentenced to death. In this 1977 landmark case, the United States Supreme Court overturned his death sentence, saying that death sentences are inappropriate punishments for rapes in which the life of the rape victim is not taken as well.

Collateral consequences: Unintended or unknown consequences certain offenders face for committing a crime, in addition to the penalties included in the criminal sentence. An example is the loss of voting rights for a convicted felon.

Collective efficacy: The tendency of members of a neighborhood or community to look out for one another's interests, including serving as surrogate parents.

Colonial model: A theory used to explain racial disparities in arrests and imprisonment. It builds upon the early writings of Frantz Fanon, who examined the relations between majority and minority groups in colonial settings. In an effort to explain high rates of crime and violence among Blacks, some criminologists have used the colonial model to analyze the psychological impact on those living in a society where the colonizer (often Whites) creates a race- and caste-based society based on racism. The colonial system, which devalues and discredits the culture and traditions of the colonized, leaves the colonized in a psychological state that results in self-hate and destructive behaviors such as crime (mostly intraracial).

Colonization: Occurs when one group forcibly takes over the country of another group. During this process, those who are colonized are then forced to adhere to the norms of the colonizer.

Community corrections: The spectrum of sentencing alternatives that permit the convicted offender to remain in the community as opposed to serving time in a remote correctional facility. Community corrections include, but are not limited to, community-based correctional facilities, halfway houses, day reporting centers, probation, and parole.

Community policing: A philosophy of policing that emphasizes identifying and solving a wide range of community problems that are thought to lead to crime and social disorder. In community-oriented policing, often simply termed community policing, the beat officer and community residents form a bond that permits the regular exchange of information to promote safety and improve the overall quality of life in the neighborhood.

Components of the policing industry: Refers to local police, state police, federal police, special jurisdiction police, and tribal police agencies that have law enforcement functions.

Conflict theory: A theoretical perspective in criminology that holds that opposing political, social, or other forces in society are responsible for a variety of social ills, including crime and delinquency.

Consumer racial profiling (CRP): Profiling of consumers that occurs in racial settings and other locations. This type of profiling is discriminatory when consumers are suspected of criminal activity because of their race/ethnicity.

Convict-lease system: After the Civil War, southern states leased prison inmates to private companies that used them as forced laborers. This system of enforced labor ran from 1865 to 1920.

Corrections: The component of the criminal justice system concerned with the imprisonment, control, and rehabilitation of convicted offenders. Corrections include the administration and study of prisons, community-based sanctions, parole, probation, and less intrusive alternatives.

Crime rates: The number of crimes per unit of population, most often 100,000. The crime rate per 100,000 is calculated by dividing the actual population of the jurisdiction in question by 100,000. That quotient is then divided into the number of actual crimes. See *Uniform Crime Reports.*

Crime statistics: Statistical data compiled by the police and the courts and routinely published by governments as indices of the extent of crime.

Death penalty: Punishment for a crime that results in the execution of the defendant.

Department of Homeland Security: Created in 2002 to prevent terrorist attacks within the United States, to reduce vulnerability to terrorism, and to minimize the impact from and assist in the recovery from terrorist attacks. (Note: Taken from http://www.dhs.gov/xabout/laws/law_regulation_rule_0011.shtm)

Disposition: The conclusion of juvenile or criminal court proceedings, often with an *adjudication* in a juvenile case or the *imposition* of a sentence in a criminal case.

Disproportionate minority confinement and contact: The confinement in detention, jail, prison, or other facilities of minorities, particularly juveniles, in percentages out of proportion to their representation in the general population.

DNA profiling: The use of deoxyribonucleic acid (DNA) evidence to exacerbate existing racial bias in the American criminal justice system and to subject ethnic minorities to disproportionate surveillance by law enforcement agencies.

Driving while Black/Brown: Coined in the 1990s, this is an expression used to describe the practice by law enforcement officers of targeting Black and other minority motorists for traffic stops when there is no violation of the law.

Dual court system: Refers to the judicial branch of American government consisting of both state and federal courts.

Eighth Amendment: The Amendment to the United States Constitution, also a part of the Bill of Rights, which prohibits the federal government from imposing excessive bail, excessive fines, or cruel and unusual punishments.

Ethnicity: Refers to a group of people who identify with each other through a common heritage, consisting of a common language, a common culture (often including a shared religion), and a tradition of common ancestry.

Furman v. Georgia: In this landmark case, Furman, a Black man, was accused of murder. Despite evidence at his trial that he was mentally deficient, he was convicted of murder and sentenced to death. He appealed his sentence on the grounds that his Fourteenth Amendment rights were violated. At the time of this case, disproportionately more Black murderers were being given the death sentence than White murderers. In 1972, the United States Supreme Court set aside Furman's death penalty saying that the death penalty was administered in a racially discriminatory way in Georgia. In addition, the Court stated this constituted cruel and unusual punishment. The case led to a moratorium on capital punishment in the United States until 1976.

Gender-specific programs: Programs for at-risk and delinquent girls that meet needs given their age and development. Gender-specific programs address such issues as teenage pregnancy, eating disorders, body self-image, and sexually transmitted diseases.

General strain theory: Robert Agnew's revision of the strain theory extended Robert Merton's anomie theory that was based on the general idea that economic strains are the primary contributor to crime. Agnew's theory also refers to the strains caused by the removal of positive stimuli (e.g., loss of a spouse, girlfriend/boyfriend, etc.) or the introduction of noxious stimuli (e.g., child abuse, criminal victimization, etc.), which can also contribute to criminal behavior.

Gregg v. Georgia: Gregg was convicted of robberies and murders in Atlanta. Georgia. This landmark case put an end to the moratorium set in *Furman v. Georgia* in 1972. The Supreme Court decision in *Gregg* rejected the legal argument that capital punishment in and of itself constituted "cruel and unusual punishment" and thus violated the Eighth Amendment of the U.S. Constitution. *Gregg* led to new death penalty statutes. Some state legislatures reformed their death penalty statutes to deal with the problem of undue jury discretion identified in *Furman* by mandating capital punishment for all persons convicted of first degree murder. In addition, the newly accepted provisions required two-stage trials in all death penalty cases, in which guilt or innocence would be determined in the first stage and the penalty would be assessed in the second stage.

Guided discretion: A term adopted from the landmark U.S. Supreme Court case *Gregg v. Georgia* that refers to the two stage death penalty trial process. Under this approach, if a defendant was convicted of first degree murder or another death-eligible offense, the prosecutor could ask the court to conduct a second "penalty stage" of the trial. After this second proceeding, the jury could impose the death sentence only if it found that the prosecution had proven a statutorily specified "aggravating circumstance," such as that the murder was committed for financial gain.

Hate crime: A criminal offense motivated by hatred of a specific race, ethnicity, religion, or sexual orientation. The Federal Bureau of Investigation only recently began systematically collecting data on hate crimes. In many states, hate crimes are codified as offenses distinguished from the core offenses, such as assault, vandalism, and intimidation. In addition, hate crimes newly qualify for enhanced sentencing.

Healthy People 2020: Healthy People provides science-based, 10-year national objectives for promoting health and preventing disease. Every 10 years, the U.S. Department of Health and Human Services (HHS) leverages scientific insights and lessons learned from the past decade, along with new knowledge of current data, trends, and innovations. Healthy People 2020 assesses major risks to health and wellness, changing public health priorities, and emerging issues related to our nation's health preparedness and prevention.

Houses of refuge: Facilities for juveniles opened in the 1800s as the result of increased juvenile presence on the streets after an influx of immigrant families entering the United States in the late 1700s and early 1800s.Although houses of refuge existed presumably to protect potentially criminal youth from being easily influenced by the negative aspects of society, some critics argue that the use of houses of refuge was discriminatory, affecting only poor White immigrants while excluding Blacks.

Innocence Project: The Innocence Project uses DNA testing to establish the innocence of wrongfully convicted offenders. It was founded by civil rights attorneys Peter J. Neufeld and Barry C. Scheck in 1992 at Benjamin N. Cardoza School of Law, located at Yeshiva University in New York City.

Intake: The point at which a youth formally becomes involved in the juvenile justice process.

Intensive probation: A form of probation that involves an extra measure of supervision and control by the probation officer. ISP is often used for chronic and other high-risk offenders who pose a great probability of reoffending.

Intimate partner violence: Physical or sexual violence between those living together or romantically involved, most often a spouse or significant other.

IQ: An intelligence quotient (IQ) is a purported measure of an individual's general intellectual ability. Over the past century, there have been repeated attempts to link low intelligence with propensity to commit criminal acts and frequent claims that some supposed racial groups have lower intelligence than others. Critics have rejected such claims as racist pseudoscience.

Jury nullification: The disregard by a jury of the evidence presented and the rendering of its verdict based on other criteria

Justice model: A philosophy and its associated policies that emerged in the wake of the 1970s *nothing works* movement. The justice model emphasizes predictability of legal consequences for offenders.

Juvenile court: A court of law, sometimes a subdivision of a common pleas court or domestic relations court, that has jurisdiction over matters pertaining to the delinquency and unruliness of persons who have not yet attained adulthood.

Juvenile justice system: Refers to the agencies and processes designed to meet the needs of delinquent and dependent youth.

Lynching: The practice of illegally taking the life of another by hanging, generally accomplished by a mob and often motivated by racial or ethnic hatred. Now infrequent, lynching in the United States is associated with White supremacists and their targeting of Blacks.

Marshall hypotheses: A series of conjectures by Supreme Court Justice Thurgood Marshall in *Furman v. Georgia* regarding the value of opinion poll data on public sentiments about capital punishment. Because the results of such polls can be of great importance to the U.S. Supreme Court's assessment of the constitutionality of various statutes and policies and practices, the validity of these data is especially important. The Marshall hypotheses are as follows: (1) Americans know almost nothing about the death penalty, and (2) those citizens who were fully informed about the purposes of the penalty and its liabilities would find the penalty shocking, unjust, and unacceptable.

McCleskey v. Kemp: McCleskey, a Black man, was convicted and sentenced to death for murdering a police officer during a grocery store robbery in 1978. Introducing into evidence that statistically more Black criminals receive the death penalty than White criminals and claiming that such disproportion is unconstitutional, McCleskey appealed. In 1987, the United States Supreme Court rejected the appeal, claiming Georgia's death penalty was not arbitrary and capricious, nor was it being applied in a discriminatory manner, regardless of the statistical evidence to the contrary.

Minority: The term *minority* typically refers to a socially subordinate ethnic group (understood in terms of language, nationality, religion, and/or culture). Other minority groups include people with disabilities, "economic minorities" (working poor or unemployed), "age minorities" (who are younger or older than a typical working age), and sexual minorities. Members of minority groups are prone to differential treatment in the communities in which they live. This discrimination may be directly based on an individual's perceived membership in a minority group, without consideration of that individual's personal achievement. It may also occur indirectly, due to social structures that are not equally accessible to all.

Model minority: Used in social sciences to describe a racial minority group that has excelled in the United States despite prejudice and discrimination. This stereotype has become synonymous with the Asian American population

National Crime Victimization Survey (NCVS): A survey of citizens 12 years of age and older conducted by the U.S. Bureau of the Census for the Bureau of Justice Statistics. The NCVS measures the respondents' experiences as victims of rape, robbery, assault, burglary, larceny, and motor vehicle theft.

National Incident-Based Reporting System (NIBRS): The crime reporting system designed to replace the *Uniform Crime Report.* NIBRS collects detailed data on the offender, time, place, and other aspects of the incident for each criminal offense reported by police agencies in participating agencies.

National Youth Risk Behavior Survey (NYRBS): A biannual survey of high school youth about their dietary habits, substance abuse, fighting, and other behaviors that pose a risk to health. The NYRBS is sponsored by the Centers for Disease Control and Prevention (CDC).

New Jim Crow: A term used to refer to the idea that mass incarceration as a system of social control has replaced the historical Jim Crow and legal racial segregation.

Nonresident immigrant: Someone who has relocated from another country, applied for citizenship, but is not yet a resident of the country.

Office of Juvenile Justice and Delinquency Prevention (OJJDP): A branch of the U.S. Department of Justice's Office of Justice Programs. OJJDP is charged with promoting a variety of programs to reduce juvenile delinquency and to improve the administration of juvenile justice. Authorized by the Juvenile Justice and Delinquency Prevention Act of 1974, the OJJDP administers discretionary and formula grant programs and provides technical assistance to state and local governments.

OJJDP Statistical Briefing Book (SBB): An online tool that enables users to access information via OJJDP's website to learn more about juvenile crime and victimization and about youth involved in the juvenile justice system. Developed for OJJDP by the National Center for Juvenile Justice, SBB provides timely and reliable statistical answers to the most frequently asked questions from policy makers, the media, and the general public. In addition, the data analysis and dissemination tools available through the SBB give users quick and easy access to detailed statistics on a variety of juvenile justice topics.

Opium dens: Establishments where opium was sold and smoked, prevalent in many parts of the world in the 19th century, most notably China, Southeast Asia, North America, and France. Opium smoking began in North America with the first migration of the Chinese laborers who were addicted from the British expansionist policy of trade in opium. The first opium dens in the United States were located in the Chinese community.

Parole: The conditional release under supervision of a convict prior to the expiration of the sentence. Parole is generally granted by a parole board. Upon release on parole, the offender reports to a parole officer, who ensures compliance with specified conditions.

People of color: A term primarily used in the United States to refer to non-Whites. The term has been used to replace the term *minority.*

Peremptory challenges: The right during voir dire to challenge the seating of jurors without citing a specific cause.

Plea bargaining: The process and result of an agreement between a prosecuting attorney and defense counsel to reduce the seriousness or number of charges in a criminal case in return for a guilty plea.

Police accountability: The premise that police officers should be held responsible for their actions and treat members of the community in a respectful and lawful manner—without regard to race or ethnicity. Particularly, sworn officers will not abuse their power and use more force than necessary, nor will they exhibit bias against any group of persons.

Police-community relations: Efforts to create a positive relationship between police and citizens. An earlier initiative that relates to community policing, a philosophy of policing that emphasizes identifying and solving a wide range of community problems that are thought to lead to crime and social disorder. In community policing, the beat officer and community residents form a bond that permits the regular exchange of information to promote safety and improve the overall quality of life in the neighborhood.

Prejudice: When someone fosters a negative attitude toward a particular racial/ethnic group. This is usually in the form of acerbic stereotypes that often result in people making unfavorable generalizations about an entire group.

Pretrial release: The practice of conditionally releasing criminal defendants prior to trial without formal posting of bail. Those who participate in pretrial release generally must have stable residence and employment as well as other ties to the community that suggest they are likely to appear for trial.

Prisoner reentry: The return of offenders, probationers, parolees, and those released from jails to their community. Prisoner reentry involves the use of programs targeted at promoting the effective reintegration of offenders back to communities upon release from prison and jail. These programs are intended to assist offenders in acquiring the life skills needed to succeed in the community and become law-abiding citizens. These programs include prerelease programs, drug rehabilitation and vocational training, and work programs.

Probation: The suspension of a sentence of a convicted offender and granting of freedom for a period of time under specified conditions. Probation is generally granted in lieu of confinement.

Profiling at airports: A term that became popular after the events of September 11, 2001. It refers to the targeting for a more intrusive inspection by airport security officials of Arabs, people of Middle Eastern descent, or those who appear to be Muslim. This practice has also been referred to as *flying while Arab.*

Public defender systems: A federal, state, or local criminal justice agency that provides legal counsel for criminal defendants who have been accused or convicted of a crime or crimes and are too poor to hire a private attorney. Public defenders are attorneys paid as salaried government employees. The public defender system began in Los Angeles County in 1914 and has since become the most typical method of representing indigent defendants in court.

Public Law 280: A federal statute enacted by Congress in 1953 that enabled states to assume criminal, as well as civil, jurisdiction in matters involving American Indians as litigants on reservation land.

Race: Refers to the classification of humans into populations or groups based on various factors such as culture, language, social practice, or heritable characteristics.

Racial discrimination: The act of preventing someone from receiving or withholding social benefits, facilities, services, opportunities, and so on, on the basis of race, color, or national origin.

Racial profiling: Any police-initiated action that relies on the race, ethnicity, or national origin of an individual rather than the behavior of an individual or information that leads the police to a particular individual who has been identified as being, or having been engaged in, criminal activity (as quoted in Gabbidon & Greene, 2009, p. 120).

Recidivism: Reoffending after an offender has been released from probation or corrections. The term includes re-arrest during terms of probation and arrest for technical violations/conditions of supervision.

Reformatories: State correctional facilities intended to rehabilitate youthful or otherwise non-serious offenders. Reformatories were first used in the 1800s. Reformatories were originally intended to reform and educate young offenders rather than punish them.

Rehabilitation: A rationale for punishment that emphasizes correcting offender behavior through treatment. The goal of rehabilitation is to change behavior. Punishments that are in accordance with this theory are community service, probation orders, and any form of punishment that entails any form of guidance and aftercare toward the offender.

Relocation centers: In U.S. history, a camp in which Japanese and Japanese Americans were interned during World War II. The U.S. internment camps were overcrowded and provided poor living conditions.

Risk assessment: The systematic process of determining the potential and likelihood of reoffending.

Self-report studies: Studies in which survey respondents or interviewees are asked to reveal the nature and extent to which they have engaged in crime or delinquency. Self-report surveys, which can employ surveys or interviews, gained increasing popularity with the acknowledgement that traditional crime statistics such as the *Uniform Crime Reports* had severe limitations in their ability to accurately measure crime.

Sentencing disparities: Differences in sentences that include cases with similarly situated offenders. Sentencing disparities can be the result of legislative differences between jurisdictions or judicial or prosecutorial discretion.

Slave patrols: Organized groups that regularly patrolled both rural and urban areas of the Southern United States to enforce restrictions that White colonists placed upon enslaved African Americans during the 18th and 19th centuries. Slave patrols were responsible for apprehending runaways, breaking up unsanctioned gatherings and celebrations of enslaved people as well as other functions.

Social buffers: A term used to refer to working class and middle class role models in areas where there are significant concentrations of poverty. These individuals provide examples of success and serve as social buffers until they abandon these communities. Without these social buffers, residents of these communities become socially isolated and lack exposure to mainstream individuals (Gabbidon & Green, 2009).

Social disorganization: Social disorganization theory argues that crime and delinquency rates are a direct result of heterogeneous, transitional, and poverty-stricken neighborhoods. Neighborhoods characterized by social disorganization also include some of the following factors: large numbers of families on welfare, large numbers of condemned buildings, large numbers of renters, and high truancy rates.

Statutes: A law formulated by a legislative body that governs a particular jurisdiction and is aimed at requiring or prohibiting something.

Strain theory: A theoretical perspective in criminology that is often tied to Robert Merton. The theory proposes that in every society there are culturally prescribed goals (e.g., American Dream) and institutionally accepted means (e.g., education, work, etc.) to achieve them. When citizens aspire to the societal goal but are unable to achieve them through institutionally approved means, a strain occurs that can lead them to commit crime and to engage in other illicit and harmful behaviors (e.g., drug abuse, alcoholism, etc.).

Supplemental Homicide Reports (SHRs): An addition on criminal homicide reported routinely by local law enforcement agencies as part of their participation in the *Uniform Crime Reports* program. Data collected through SHRs include the offender's age, gender, and race; the victim's age, gender, and race; the circumstances of the offense; the offender–victim relationship; and the type of weapon. SHR's have largely been replaced by the *National Incident Based Reporting System (NIBRS).*

Tasers: Electronic weapons that work by discharging high-voltage electrodes attached to long wires that, when they penetrate human flesh, render the individual temporarily immobile. Originally designed for self-protection by law enforcement, security, and other well-meaning, innocent persons, they have been used by criminals for committing assault.

Theory: A set of statements or principles devised to explain a group of facts or phenomena. A theory is one that generally has been repeatedly tested or is widely accepted and can be used to make predictions about natural phenomena.

Truly disadvantaged: Refers to a segment of the American population often referred to as the *underclass* or the *ghetto underclass*, predominately Black, who often live in inner cities and urban areas stricken with poverty, family instability, unemployment, a poor educational system, and crime.

Uniform Crime Report (UCR): A crime statistics program of the Federal Bureau of Investigation (FBI). The UCR has been the national reporting system since the 1930s. UCR collects summary-based information from law enforcement agencies on offenses reported and arrests made as well as more detailed data on homicides.

United States Sentencing Commission: An independent agency of the judicial branch of the federal government. It has the following three purposes: (1) to establish policy, procedure, and sentencing practices related to the punishment of federal crimes; (2) to advise Congress regarding the creation of crime policies; and (3) to research, analyze, and distribute information on federal crimes and sentencing issues.

Victimization data: Information received from the National Crime Victimization Survey (NCVS). The data include type of crime; month, time, and location of the crime; relationship between victim and offender; characteristics of the offender; self-protective actions taken by the victim during the incident and the results of those actions; consequences of the victimization; type of property lost; whether the crime was reported to the police and reasons for reporting or not reporting; and offender use of weapons, drugs, and alcohol. Basic demographic information, such as age, race, gender, and income, is also collected to enable analysis of crime by various subpopulations.

Victimization rates: A calculated percentage using victimization data to measure the existence of actual rather than reported crimes obtained from the victims themselves. This information is obtained from the National Crime Victimization Survey (NCVS).

Voir dire: The process of selecting jurors prior to the commencement of a criminal trial. During the voir dire, prospective jurors are questioned by both the prosecutor and the defense attorney to learn about their backgrounds and possible biases.

Walnut Street Jail: A prison in Philadelphia in which prisoners spent their time alone in their cells.

War on Drugs: Term used to describe the attempt by the federal and state authorities to control the supply and distribution of illegal drugs. The war on drugs has drawn criticism for its emphasis on supply reduction, likened by many to Prohibition, which failed in its efforts to stem the flow of alcohol.

W.E.B. Du Bois: Considered by some to be one of the first major sociological criminologists. William Edward Burghardt Du Bois was also an American civil rights activist, leader, Pan-Africanist, sociologist, educator, historian, writer, editor, poet, and scholar. Du Bois's life and work were an inseparable mixture of scholarship, protest activity, and polemics. All of his efforts were geared toward gaining equal treatment for Black people and toward marshaling and presenting evidence to refute the myths of racial inferiority. Du Bois was among the founders of the National Association for the Advancement of Colored People (NAACP) in 1910 and was founder and editor of the NAACP's journal *The Crisis*.

White ethnic: A term used in the United States to refer to Whites who are not of Northeastern European background. The term *White ethnic* almost always carried the connotation of being blue-collar and referred to White immigrants and their descendants from southern and eastern Europe. In the early 20th century, many White ethnics claimed to have been placed in a low socioeconomic level due to discrimination and ethnic stereotypes by the White Anglo-Saxon Protestants, commonly referred to as WASP, elite.

White immigrants: Refers to British, German, Italian, Irish, French, Spanish, and other White ethnic groups that came to the United States as early as the 1500s. Most early White immigrants, including Jewish immigrants, came from European countries.

Wrongful convictions: A conviction in court of an accused person who, in fact, did not commit the alleged offense.

Zoot Suit Riots: A term used to describe a series of conflicts that occurred in Los Angeles, California in the summer of 1943 between servicemen and Mexican American youths. Zoot suits were outfits popular among Mexican American youth at the time of the riots.

Appendix

Race and Crime Timeline

1500s–1700s

1565 First permanent European settlement in the United States at St. Augustine, Florida by the Spanish[1]

1598 Spanish immigrants settle in what is now Texas and New Mexico[1]

1619 First Africans arrive in Virginia[1]

1622 Jamestown Massacre

1639 First execution of a Native American (Nepauduck)

1680 First major slave codes enacted

1681 Execution of Maria, a slave

1793 Fugitive Slave Act

1800s

1800–1820 First great wave of immigration to the United States (British, Irish, German)[1]

1824 Bureau of Indian Affairs created

1831 Nat Turner Slave Revolt

1848 Mexican-American War ends with the signing of the Treaty of Guadalupe-Hidalgo[1]

1849 Significant Chinese migration to the United States begins[1]

1851 Irish migration to the United States increases[1]

1857 *Dred Scott v. Sandford*

1863 New York City Draft Riots

1864 Fort Pillow Massacre[4]

1865 Thirteenth Amendment formerly abolishes slavery except for punishment for a crime

1866 New Orleans Riot

Memphis Riot

Ku Klux Klan founded

1869 Fourteenth Amendment guarantees due process and equal protection under the law

1871 Anti-Chinese Riot, Los Angeles

Ku Klux Klan Act made it a federal offense to deny individuals their civil rights

1876 Battle of Little Bighorn

1882 Immigration Act (Chinese Exclusion Act)

1885–1886 Anti-Chinese Riots in Seattle, Washington[1]

1886–1887 German-American anarchists incite the Haymarket riot and kill police officers[1]

1890 Wounded Knee Massacre (South Dakota)

1891 New Orleans Anti-Italian Riot

Omaha Race Riot

1894 Buffalo, New York Riot (Irish and Italian Americans)

1892 Federal immigration reception center opens on Ellis Island[1]

First department of sociology opens at the University of Chicago

1896 *Plessy v. Ferguson*

1899 *The Philadelphia Negro: A Social Study 1899* by W.E.B. Du Bois

1900s

1901–1910 Largest number of immigrants arrives in the United States[1]

1906 Pure Food and Drug Act

1909 Opium Exclusion Act prohibits the importation of opium from the Philippines

1910 Mann Act

National Association for the Advancement of Colored People founded

1913 Anti-Defamation League is established in New York

1914 Harrison Narcotics Tax Act

1915 The controversial film *Birth of a Nation* premieres

1917 Immigration Act banned and criminalized immigrants who were illiterate

1919 Red Summer: Race riots in Chicago, Illinois; Washington, DC; Charleston, South Carolina; Omaha, Nebraska; Knoxville, Tennessee; and Elaine, Arkansas

Volstead Act

1921 Tulsa (Oklahoma) Race Riot

1923 *Moore v. Dempsey*

Rosewood, Florida massacre

1924 Indian Citizenship Act

1925 Marcus Garvey imprisoned in the federal penitentiary in Atlanta[2]

1929 League of United Latin American Citizens formed

1931 Scottsboro Boys arrested in Alabama

1932 *Powell v. Alabama*

1935 Harlem Race Riot

Norris v. Alabama

1936 *Brown v. Mississippi*

1937 Marijuana Tax Act

1940 NAACP Legal Defense Fund founded

1942 Executive Order 9066 authorized the removal of Japanese Americans from the West Coast

Bracero Program

1943 Detroit Race Riot

Zoot Suit Riots, Los Angeles, California

Harlem Race Riot

1953 Public Law 280 enacted

1954 *Brown v. Board of Education*

Operation Wetback

1955 Emmett Till murdered

1956 FBI Counterintelligence Programs (COINTELPRO) begin

1961 *Mapp v. Ohio*

1963 16th Street Baptist Church bombing

1964–1968 Civil disturbances and riots

1964 Civil Rights Act

Escobedo v. Illinois

1965 Voting Rights Act

Swain v. Alabama

Los Angeles Race Riot

1966 *Mapp v. Arizona*[5]

Black Panther Party founded by Huey P. Newton and Bobby Seal in Oakland, California

1967 Thurgood Marshall appointed to the US Supreme Court

Detroit Riot

1968 American Indian Movement began

Indian Civil Rights Act

Omnibus Crime Control and Safe Streets Act

Terry v. Ohio

1969 National American Indian Court Judges Association founded

1971 George Jackson shot at San Quentin Prison

New York State Prison at Attica Riot[2]

National Criminal Justice Association founded

Wilmington 10 arrests

1972 *Furman v. Georgia*

National Council of La Raza founded

1973 Wounded Knee II

1974 National Association of Blacks in Criminal Justice founded

1975 Indian Self-Determination Act

1976 *Gregg v. Georgia*

Castaneda v. Partida

National Organization of Black Law Enforcement Executives founded

1977 *Coker v. Georgia*

1978 New York Juvenile Offender Act (Willie Bosket Law)

Oliphant v. Suquamish Indian Tribe

1979 Atlanta Child Murders begin

Alliance for Justice founded

1980 Miami Riot following Mariel

Cuban Migrants arrive in the United States[5]

1984 Crime Control Act

Bernard Goetz shoots four African American males on the 2 train in New York City

1985 *Tennessee v. Garner*

1986 Anti-Drug Abuse Act

Batson v. Kentucky

1987 *McCleskey v. Kemp*[5]

1988 Juvenile Justice and Delinquency Prevention Act amended to address Disproportionate Minority Confinement

Anti-Drug Abuse Act

Skinhead murder of Ethiopian immigrant Mulugeta Seraw in Portland, Oregon

1989 Central Park Jogger Attack

Graham v. Connor

1990 Hate Crime Statistics Act

1991 Crown Heights Riots following the killing of 7-year-old Gavin Cato

Clarence Thomas appointed to the U.S. Supreme Court

Rodney King police brutality incident (March 3)

Los Angeles Christopher Commission examines use of excessive force

1992 Acquittal of officers in the Rodney King beatings sparks the Los Angeles Riot Innocence Project established by Peter J. Neufeld and Barry C. Scheck

1993 National Native American Law Enforcement Association founded

Colin Ferguson opens fire on a Long Island Railroad train resulting in 6 deaths and numerous persons injured

1994 Hate Crime Sentencing Enhancement Act

Violent Crime Control and Law Enforcement Act

1995 Bombing of the Murrah Federal Building in Oklahoma City by Timothy McVeigh[5]

First O. J. Simpson trial ends in acquittal

1996 Illegal Immigration Reform and Immigrant Responsibility Act

State v. Soto

U.S. v. Armstrong

Whren v. U.S.

1997 *Maryland v. Wilson*[5]

1998 Matthew Sheppard murder[3]

James Byrd, Jr. murder

1999 Columbine, Colorado high school shootings

Tulia Texas Drug Sting

2000s

2000 *Illinois v. Wardlow*

2001 September 11th attacks

Cincinnati Riots following the killing of Timothy Thomas, an unarmed Black teenager, by a White police officer

2002 DC Sniper shooting and killing spree begins on October 2nd

Homeland Security Act

2005 *U.S. v. Booker*

2006 Duke lacrosse incident

2007 *Kimbrough v. United States*

Jena 6 arrested after an incident at Jena High School (Louisiana)

2008 *Kennedy v. Louisiana*

O. J. Simpson convicted of robbery

2009 Sonia Sotomayor appointed to the U.S. Supreme Court

Matthew Shepard and James Byrd, Jr. Hate Crimes Prevention Act

2010 Fair Sentencing Act

Notes

1. Immigration Timeline, www.unc.edu/~perreira/198timeline.html
2. www.blackpast.org
3. http://social.jrank.org/pages/1361/Legal-System-Hate-Crime-Overview.html
4. *Encyclopedia Britannica's Guide to Black History* http://www.britannica.com/blackhistory
5. *Encyclopedia of Race and Crime.*

Credits and Sources

Section I: Overview of Race, Ethnicity, and Crime

Photo 1.1: Wikimedia, http://upload.wikimedia.org/wikipedia/commons/thumb/9/93/Johann_Friedrich_Blumenbach.jpg/445px-Johann_Friedrich_Blumenbach.jpg

Table 1.1: http://quickfacts.census.gov/qfd/states/00000.html

Photo 1.2: United States Department of the Interior, http://en.wikipedia.org/wiki/File:Posted_Japanese_American_Exclusion_Order.jpg

Section II: Extent of Crime and Victimization

Figure 2.1: U.S. Department of Justice, http://bjs.ojp.usdoj.gov/content/homicide/intimates.cfm

Table 2.2: Federal Bureau of Investigation, http://www2.fbi.gov/ucr/hc2008/data/table_01.html

Section III: Theoretical Perspectives on Race and Crime

Photo 3.1: Library of Congress, http://en.wikipedia.org/wiki/File:WEB_DuBois_1918.jpg

Figure 3.1: Shaw, C., & McKay, H. (1972). *Juvenile delinquency in urban areas* (p. 69). Chicago: University of Chicago Press. Copyright © by the University of Chicago Press. All rights reserved.

Photo 3.2: Robert K. Merton courtesy of the Columbia University Archives.

Section IV: Juvenile Justice

Table 4.1: Derived from State DMC compliance plans submitted in fiscal year 2008, http://www.ncjrs.gov/pdffiles1/ojjdp/228306.pdf

Table 4.2: Federal Bureau of Investigation, 2009, *Crime in the United States, 2008.* Table 43. Washington, DC: Author.

Table 4.6: Institute of Education Statistics, U.S. Department of Education.

Section V: Policing

Table 5.1: Bureau of Justice Statistics, http://bjs.ojp.usdoj.gov/content/pub/pdf/fleo04.pdf

Table 5.2: Bureau of Justice Statistics, http://www.albany.edu/sourcebook/tost_2.html#2_aw. Table constructed by SOURCEBOOK staff from data provided by The Gallup Organization Inc.

Section VI: Courts and Sentencing

Photo 6.1: Collection of the Supreme Court of the United States, photographer Steve Petteway. Available from http://commons.wikimedia.org/wiki/File:Supreme_Court_US_2009.jpg

Table 6.1: Rosenmerkel et al., Felony Sentences in State Courts 2006-Statistical. Tables, Bureau of Justice Statistics

Table 6.2: Rosenmerkel et al., Felony Sentences in State Courts 2006—Statistical Tables, Bureau of Justice Statistics

Section VII: The Death Penalty

Table 7.1: Snell, T. L. (2009). *Capital punishment, 2008—Statistical tables.* Washington, DC: Bureau of Justice Statistics.

Photo 7.1: © Scott Olson/Getty

Photo 7.2: Federal Government

Section VIII: Corrections

Table 8.1: U.S. Department of Justice, http://bjs.ojp.usdoj.gov/content/pub/pdf/pim09st.pdf

Table 8.2: U.S. Department of Justice, http://bjs.ojp.usdoj.gov/content/pub/pdf/pim09st.pdf

References

Abril, J. C. (2007). Perceptions of crime seriousness, cultural values, and collective efficacy among Native American Indians and non-Indians within the same reservation community. *Applied Psychology in Criminal Justice, 3,* 172–196.

Adkins, S. (2002, December 27). Judges' characteristics are a factor. *York Daily Record.* Retrieved on July 29, 2003, from http://ydr.com/story/justice/4962/printer/

Agnew, R. (1992). Foundation for a general strain theory of crime and delinquency. *Criminology, 30,* 47–87.

Agozino, B. (2003). *Counter-colonial criminology: A critique of imperialist reason.* London: Pluto Press.

Akers, R. L. (2000). *Criminological theories: Introduction, evaluation, and application.* Los Angeles: Roxbury.

Alexander, M. (2010). *The new Jim Crow.* New York: The New Press.

Allen, H. E., Simonsen, C. E., & Latessa, E. J. (2004). *Corrections in America: An introduction.* Upper Saddle River, NJ: Prentice Hall.

Allen, T. W. (1994). *The invention of the White race: Vol. 1. Racial oppression and social control.* New York: Verso.

American Civil Liberties Union. (1999). *Driving while Black: Racial profiling on our nation's highways.* New York: Author.

American Civil Liberties Union. (2007). *Forensic DNA databanks.* Retrieved on July 17, 2010, from http://www.aclu.org/technology-and-liberty/forensic-dna-databanks

Amnesty International. (2010). *The truth about racial profiling: Five Facts.* Retrieved on July 27, 2010, from http://www.amnestyusa.org/us-human-rights/other/rp-five-facts-about-racial-profiling/page.do?id=1106649

Anderson, C. (1994). *Black labor, White wealth.* Edgewood, MD: Duncan & Duncan.

Anderson, E. A. (1994, May). The code of the streets. *Atlantic Monthly,* pp. 81–94.

Anderson, E. A. (1999). *The code of the streets: Decency, violence, and the moral life of the inner city.* New York: Norton.

Anderson, P. R., & Newman, D. J. (1998). *Introduction to criminal justice* (6th ed.). New York: McGraw-Hill.

Argersinger v. Hamlin, 407 U.S, 25 (1972).

Arthur, J. A. (1998). Proximate correlates of Blacks support for capital punishment. *Journal of Crime and Justice, 21,* 159–172.

Austin, J., & Irwin, J. (2001). *It's about time: America's imprisonment binge* (3rd ed.). Belmont, CA: Wadsworth.

Austin, R. (1983). The colonial model, subcultural theory, and intragroup violence. *Journal of Criminal Justice, 11,* 93–104.

Bachman, R. (1991). An analysis of American Indian homicide: A test of social disorganization and economic deprivation at the reservation county level. *Journal of Research in Crime and Delinquency, 28,* 456–471.

Baker, B. C. (2008). *Estimates of the resident nonimmigrant population in the United States: 2008.* Retrieved on July 26, 2010, from http://www.dhs.gov/xlibrary/assets/statistics/publications/ois_ni_pe_2008

Baker, D. V. (2003). The racist application of capital punishment to African Americans. In M. Free (Ed.), *Racial issues in criminal justice: The case of African Americans* (pp. 177–201). Westport, CT: Greenwood.

Baker, D. V. (2007). American Indian executions in historical context. *Criminal Justice Studies, 20,* 315–373.

Baker, D. V. (2008). Black female executions in historical context. *Criminal Justice Review, 33,* 64–88.

Baldus, D. C., Woodworth, G., & Pulaski, C. A. (1990). *Equal justice and the death penalty: A legal and empirical analysis.* Boston: Northeastern University Press.

Banner, S. (2002). *The death penalty: An American history.* Cambridge, MA: Harvard University Press.

Barak, G., Flavin, J., & Leighton, P. (2010). *Class, race, gender, and crime* (3rd ed.). New York: Rowman & Littlefield.

Barkan, S. F., & Cohn, S. F. (1994). Racial prejudice and support for the death penalty by Whites. *Journal of Research in Crime and Delinquency, 31,* 202–209.

Barlow, D. E., & Barlow, M. H. (2000). *Police in a multicultural society.* Prospect Heights, IL: Waveland.

Barlow, D. E., & Barlow, M. H. (2002). Racial profiling: A survey of African American police officers. *Police Quarterly, 5,* 334–358.

Batson v. Kentucky, 476 U.S. 79, 108 (1986).

Baumer, E., Horney, J., Felson, R., & Lauritsen, J. (2003). Neighborhood disadvantage and the nature of violence. *Criminology, 41,* 39–71.

Baumer, E., Messner, S., & Rosenfeld, R. (2003). Explaining spatial variation in support for capital punishment: A multilevel analysis. *American Journal of Sociology, 108,* 844–875.

Becker, S. (2004). Assessing the use of profiling in searches by law enforcement personnel. *Journal of Criminal Justice, 32,* 183–193.

Bedau, H. A., & Radelet, M. L. (1987). Miscarriage of justice in potentially capital cases. *Stanford Law Review, 40,* 21–179.

Bell, J. (2010). *Disproportionate minority confinement/contact.* Webinar. Retrieved July 8, 2010, from http://burns.live2.radicaldesigns.org/article.php?id=220

Blakely v. Washington, 542 US 296 (2004).

Blalock, H. M. (1967). *Toward a theory of minority group relations.* New York: Wiley.

Blauner, R. (1969). Internal colonialism and ghetto revolt. *Social Problems, 16,* 393–408.

Blauner, R. (1972). *Racial oppression in America.* New York: Harper & Row.

Blumer, M. (1984). *The Chicago school of sociology: Institutionalization, diversity, and the rise of sociological research.* Chicago: University of Chicago Press.

Blumstein, A. (1982). On the racial disproportionality of the United States' prison populations. *Journal of Criminal Law & Criminology, 73,* 1259–1281.

Blumstein, A. (1993). Racial disproportionality of U.S. prison populations revisited. *University of Colorado Law Review, 63.* Retrieved from Lexis-Nexis database on August 25, 2002.

Bobo, L. D., & Johnson, D. (2004). A taste for punishment: Black and White Americans' views on the death penalty and the war on drugs. *Du Bois Review, 1,* 151–180.

Bohm, R. M. (1999). *Deathquest: An introduction to the theory and practice of capital punishment.* Cincinnati, OH: Anderson.

Bohm, R. M. (2001). *A primer on crime and delinquency theory* (2nd ed.). Belmont, CA: Wadsworth/Thomson Learning.

Bohm, R. M. (2007). *Deathquest: An introduction to the theory and practice of capital punishment* (3rd ed.). Cincinnati, OH: Anderson.

Bohm, R. M., Clark, L., & Aveni, A. (1991). Knowledge and death penalty opinion: A test of the Marshall hypotheses. *Journal of Research in Crime and Delinquency, 28,* 360–387.

Borchard, E. M. (1932). *Convicting the innocent: Sixty-five actual errors of criminal justice.* Garden City, NY: Doubleday.

Bosworth, M., & Flavin, L. (Eds.). (2007). *Race, gender, & punishment: From colonialism to the war on terror.* New Brunswick, NJ: Rutgers University Press.

Brandon, R., & Davies, C. (1973). *Wrongful imprisonment: Mistaken convictions and their consequences.* London: Archon Books.

Brewer, R. M., & Heitzeg, N. A. (2008). The racialization of crime and punishment: Criminal justice, color-blind racism, and the political economy of the prison industrial complex. *American Behavioral Scientist, 51,* 625–644.

Brezina, T., Agnew, R., Cullen, F. T., & Wright, J. P. (2004). The code of the street: A quantitative assessment of Elijah Anderson's subculture of violence thesis and its contribution to youth violence research. *Youth Violence and Juvenile Justice, 2,* 303–328.

Brown, M. C., & Warner, B. D. (1992). Immigrants, urban politics and policing in 1900. *American Sociological Review, 57,* 293–305.

Brown v. Board of Education of Topeka et al., 347 US 483 (1954).

Brownstein, H. H. (1996). *The rise and fall of a violent crime wave: Crack cocaine and the social construction of a crime problem.* Guilderland, NY: Harrow & Heston.

Brunson, R. K. (2007). "Police don't like Black people": African American young men's accumulated police experiences. *Criminology & Public Policy, 6*(1), 71–102.

Brunson, R. K., & Stewart, E. A. (2006). Young African American women, the street code, and violence: An exploratory analysis. *Journal of Crime and Justice, 29,* 1–19.

Bureau of Indian Affairs. (1974). *The American Indians: Answers to 101 questions.* Washington, DC: U.S. Department of the Interior.

Bureau of Justice Statistics. (2005). *Criminal victimization in the United States, 2004.* Washington, DC: U.S. Department of Justice.

Bureau of Justice Statistics. (2009). *Criminal victimization in the United States, 2008.* Washington, DC: U.S. Department of Justice. Retrieved July 8, 2010, from http://bjs.ojp.usdoj.gov/content/pub/pdf/cv08.pdf

Bureau of Justice Statistics. (2010). *Victims.* Retrieved on July 1, 2010, from http://bjs.ojp.usdoj.gov/index.cfm?ty=tp&tid=9

Burgess, E. W. (1925). The growth of the city: An introduction to a research project. In R. Park, E. W. Burgess, & R. D. McKenzie (Eds.), *The city* (pp. 47–62). Chicago: University of Chicago Press.

Bushway, S., Stoll, M., & Weiman, D. F. (Eds.). (2007). *Barriers to reentry? The labor market for released prisoners in post-industrial America.* New York: Russell Sage.

Butler, P. (1995). Racially based jury nullification: Black power in the criminal justice system. *The Yale Law Journal, 105,* 677–725.

Camp, G. M., & Camp, C. G. (1993). *The corrections yearbook 1993.* Middleton, CT: Criminal Justice Institute.

Carlson, D. K. (2004). *Racial profiling seen as pervasive, unjust.* Retrieved on January 17, 2010, from http://www.gallup.com/poll/12406/racial-profiling-seen-pervasive-unjust.aspx

Castelle, G., & Loftus, E. F. (2002). Misinformation and wrongful convictions. In S. Westervelt & J. A. Humphrey (Eds.), *Wrongly convicted: Perspectives on failed justice* (pp. 17–35). New Brunswick, NJ: Rutgers University Press.

Catalano, S. M. (2006). *Criminal victimization, 2005.* Washington, DC: U.S. Department of Justice, Office of Justice Programs, Bureau of Justice Statistics.

Centers for Disease Control and Prevention. (2010). *Healthy people 2020.* Retrieved on July 1, 2010, from http://www.healthypeople.gov/

Center for the Study and Prevention of Violence. (2008). *Center for the study and prevention of violence.* Retrieved on July 1, 2010, from http://www.colorado.edu/cspv/infohouse/publications.html

Cernkovich, S. A., Giordano, P. C., & Rudolph, J. L. (2000). Race, crime, and the American dream. *Journal of Research in Crime and Delinquency, 37,* 131–170.

Chabrán, R., & Chabrán, R. (1996). *The Latino encyclopedia.* Tarrytown, NY: Marshall Cavendish Corporation.

Chambliss, W. J. (1991). *Trading textbooks for prison cells.* Baltimore: National Center for Institutions and Alternatives.

Chapin, B. (1983). *Criminal justice in colonial America, 1606–1660.* Athens: University of Georgia Press.

Chilton, B. (2004). Regional variations in lethal and nonlethal assaults. *Homicide Studies, 8,* 40–56.

Chircos, T. G., & Crawford, C. (1995). Race and imprisonment: A contextual assessment of the evidence. In D. Hawkins (Ed.), *Ethnicity, race, and crime* (pp. 281–309). Albany: State University of New York Press.

Christianson, S. (1981). Our Black prisons. *Crime and Delinquency, 27,* 364–375.

Christianson, S. (2004). *Innocent: Inside wrongful conviction cases.* New York: New York University Press.

Clarke, H. J. (1992). *Christopher Columbus and the Afrikan holocaust.* Brooklyn, NY: A & B.

Clear, T. R. (2007). *Imprisoning communities: How mass incarceration makes disadvantaged neighborhoods worse.* New York: Oxford University Press.

Clear, T. R., & Cole, G. F. (2000). *American corrections* (5th ed.). Belmont, CA: Wadsworth.

Clear, T. R., & Cole, G. F. (2003). *American corrections* (6th ed.). Belmont, CA: Wadsworth.

Clear, T. R., Rose, D. R., & Ryder, J. A. (2001). Incarceration and the community: The problem of removing and returning offenders. *Crime & Delinquency, 47,* 335–351.

Clear, T. R., Rose, D. R., Waring, E., & Scully, K. (2003). Coercive mobility and crime: A preliminary examination of concentrated incarceration and social disorganization. *Justice Quarterly, 20,* 33–64.

Cochran, J. K., & Chamlin, M. B. (2005). Can information change public opinion? Another test of the Marshall hypotheses. *Journal of Criminal Justice, 33,* 573–584.

Cochran, J. K., & Chamlin, M. B. (2006). The enduring racial divide in death penalty support. *Journal of Criminal Justice, 34,* 84–99.

Cochran, J. K., Sanders, B., & Chamlin, M. B. (2006). Profiles in change: An alternative look at the Marshall hypotheses. *Journal of Criminal Justice Education, 17,* 205–226.

Cohen, S. (2003). *The wrong man: America's epidemic of wrongful death row convictions.* New York: Carroll & Graf.

Coker v. Georgia, 429 U.S. 815 (1977).

Cole, D. (1999). *No equal justice.* New York: New Press.

Collins, C. F. (1997). *The imprisonment of African American women.* Jefferson, NC: McFarland.

Consortium for Police Leadership in Equity. (2011). *Areas of emphasis.* Retrieved on January 28, 2011, from http://cple.psych.ucla.edu/areas-of-emphasis/

Courtwright, D. T. (2001). *Dark paradise.* Cambridge, MA: Harvard University Press.

Covington, J. (1995). Racial classification in criminology: The reproduction of racialized crime. *Sociological Forum, 10,* 547–568.

Crow, M. C., & Johnson, K. A. (2008). Race, ethnicity, and habitual-offender sentencing: A multilevel analysis of individual and contextual threat. *Criminal Justice Policy Review, 19,* 63–83.

Crutchfield, R. D. (2004). Warranted disparity? Questioning the justification of racial disparity in criminal justice processing. *Columbia Human Rights Law Review, 36,* 15–40.

Curran, D. J., & Renzetti, C. M. (2001). *Theories of crime.* Boston: Allyn & Bacon.

D'Alessio, S. J., Eitle, D., & Stolzenberg, L. (2005). The impact of serious crime, racial threat, and economic inequality on private police size. *Social Science Research, 34,* 267–282.

Daniels, R. (1988). *Asian America: Chinese and Japanese in the United States since 1850.* Seattle: University of Washington Press.

Davis, A. Y. (1981). *Women, race & class.* New York: Random House.

Davis, A. Y. (1997). Race and criminalization: Black Americans and the punishment industry. In W. Lubiano (Ed.), *The house that race built: Black Americans, U.S. terrain* (pp. 264–279). New York: Pantheon.

Davis, A. Y. (2000). From the convict lease system to the super-max prison. In J. James (Ed.), *States of confinement: Policing, detention, and prisons* (pp. 60–74). New York: St. Martin's Press.

Davis, A. Y. (2003). *Are prisons obsolete?* New York: Seven Stories Press.

Davis, K., & Sorensen, J. R. (2010, March 4). Disproportionate minority confinement of juveniles: A national examination of Black-White disparity in placements, 1997–2006. *Crime & Delinquency* (DOI:10.1177/0011128709359653).

Death Penalty Information Center. (2010). *Introduction to the death penalty.* Washington, DC: Author. Retrieved on July 31, 2010, from http://www.deathpenaltyinfo.org/part-i-history-death-penalty#intro

DeFrances, C. J. (2001). *State-funded indigent defense services, 1999.* Washington, DC: U. S. Bureau of Justice Statistics.

DeFrances, C. J., & Litras, M. F. X. (2000). *Indigent defense services in large counties, 1999.* Washington, DC: Bureau of Justice Statistics.

De Las Casas, B. (1993). *The devastation of the Indies: A brief account.* Baltimore: John Hopkins University Press. (Original work published 1552).

Delaware Judicial Information Center. (2009). *Reentry court.* Retrieved August 4, 2010, from http://courts.delaware.gov/

Demuth, S., & Steffensmeier, D. (2004). The impact of gender and race-ethnicity in the pretrial release process. *Social Problems, 51,* 222–242.

Denov, M. S., & Campbell, K. M. (2005). Criminal injustice: Understanding the causes, effects, and responses to wrongful convictions in Canada. *Journal of Contemporary Criminal Justice, 21,* 224–249.

DiLulio, J. (1996). My Black crime problem, and ours. *City Journal, 6,* 14–28.

Dinnerstein, L., & Reimers, D. M. (1982). *Ethnic Americans* (2nd ed.). New York: Harper & Row.

Donzinger, S. R. (Ed.). (1996). *The real war on crime.* New York: Harper Perennial.

Du Bois, W.E.B. (1899/1996). *The Philadelphia Negro: A social study.* Philadelphia: The University of Pennsylvania Press. (Original work published 1899)

Du Bois, W.E.B. (1901). The spawn of slavery: The convict lease system in the south. *Missionary Review of the World, 14,* 737–745. (Reprinted in *African American classics in criminology and criminal justice,* pp. 83–88, by S. L. Gabbidon, H. Taylor Greene, & V. Young, 2002. Thousand Oaks, CA: Sage.)

Dulaney, W. M. (1996). *Black police in America.* Bloomington: Indiana University Press.

Durose, M. R., Smith, E. L., & Langan, P. A. (2007). *Contacts between police and the public, 2005.* Washington, DC: U.S. Department of Justice.

Dyer, J. (2000). *The perpetual prisoner machine: How America profits from crime.* Boulder, CO: Westview Press.

Eberheart v. Georgia, 433 U.S. 917 (1977).

Eitle, D., & Turner, R. J. (2003). Stress exposure, race, and young male adult crime. *Sociological Quarterly, 44,* 243–269.

Ellis, L., & Walsh, A. (2000). *Criminology: A global perspective.* Needham Heights, MA: Allyn & Bacon.

Empey, L. T., Stafford, M. C., Hay, C. H. (1999). *American delinquency: Its meaning and construction* (4th ed.). Belmont, CA: Wadsworth.

Emsley, C. (1983). *Policing and its context, 1750–1870.* New York: Schocken Books.

Escobar, E. J. (1999). *Race, police, and the making of a political identity: Mexican Americans and the Los Angeles Police Department, 1900–1945.* Berkeley: University of California Press.

Escobedo v. Illinois, 378 U.S. 478, 84 S. Ct, 1758 (1964).

Farole, D. J., & Langton, L. (2009). *Public defender offices, 2007 statistical tables.* Washington, DC: Bureau of Justice Statistics.

Feagin, R. F., & Feagin, C. (2008). *Racial and ethnic relations* (8th ed.). Upper Saddle River, NJ: Prentice Hall.

Federal Bureau of Investigation. (1995). *Section I, Summary of the uniform crime reporting program.* Retrieved on June 12, 2010, from http://www.fbi.gov/ucr/Cius_97/95CRIME/95crime1.pdf

Federal Bureau of Investigation. (2001). *Crime in the United States, 2000.* Washington, DC: Author. Retrieved July 1, 2010, from http://www.fbi.gov/about-us/cjis/ucr

Federal Bureau of Investigation. (2002). *Crime in the United States, 2001.* Washington, DC: Author. Retrieved July 1, 2010, from http://www.fbi.gov/about-us/cjis/ucr

Federal Bureau of Investigation. (2003). *Crime in the United States, 2002 Section IV arrests.* Retrieved June 12, 2010, from http://www.fbi.gov/ucr/cius_03/pdf/03sec4.pdf

Federal Bureau of Investigation. (2004). *Crime in the United States, 2003.* Washington, DC: Government Printing Office. Retrieved June 12, 2010, from http://www.fbi.gov/ucr/cius_02/pdf/4section four.pdf

Federal Bureau of Investigation. (2005a). *Crime in the United States, 2004 Section IV arrests.* Retrieved June 12, 2010, from http://www.fbi.gov/ucr/05cius/arrests/index.html

Federal Bureau of Investigation. (2005b). *Hate crime statistics, 2004.* Retrieved June 12, 2010 from http://www.fbi.gov/stats-services/publications

Federal Bureau of Investigation. (2006). *Crime in the United States, 2005.* Washington, DC: Author. Retrieved July 1, 2010, from http://www.fbi.gov/about-us/cjis/ucr

Federal Bureau of Investigation. (2009a). *Crime in the United States, 2008. Section IV Arrests.* Retrieved July 1, 2010, from http://www.2.fbi.gov/ucr/cius2008/data/table_43.html

Federal Bureau of Investigation. (2009b). *Full-time law enforcement employees by population group percent male and female, 2008*. Table 74. Retrieved on July 17, 2010, from http://www2.fbi.gov/ucr/cius2008/data/table_74.html

Feld, B. (1999). *Bad kids: Race and the transformation of the juvenile court*. New York: Oxford University Press.

Fernandez, K. E., & Bowman, T. (2004). Race, political institutions, and criminal justice: An examination of the sentencing of Latino offenders. *Columbia Human Rights Law Review, 36*, 41–70.

Flanagan, T. J. (1996). Reform or punish: Americans' views of the correctional system. In T. J. Flanagan & D. R. Longmire (Eds.), *Americans view crime and justice: A national public opinion survey* (pp. 75–92). Thousand Oaks, CA: Sage.

Fogelson, R. (1977). *Big-city police*. Cambridge, MA: Harvard University Press.

Fox, J. A., & Swatt, M. L. (2008). *The recent surge in homicides involving young Black males and guns: Time to reinvest in prevention and crime control*. Boston: Northeastern University.

Fox, J. A., & Zawitz, M. W. (2003). *Homicide trends in the United States: 2000 update* (NCJ 197471). Washington, DC: Department of Justice.

Fox, J. A., & Zawitz, M. W. (2007). *Homicide trends in the United States*. Washington, DC: U.S. Department of Justice, Office of Justice Programs, Bureau of Justice Statistics.

Free, M. D. (2002a). Race and presentencing decisions in the United States: A summary and critique of the research. *Criminal Justice Review, 27*, 203–232.

Free, M. D. (2002b). Racial bias and the American criminal justice system: Race and presentencing revisited. *Critical Criminology, 10*, 195–223.

Frey, C. P. (1981). The house of refuge for colored children. *Journal of Negro History, 66*, 10–25.

Furman v. Georgia, 408 U.S, 238 (1972).

Gabbidon, S. L. (1999). W. E. B. Du Bois on crime: American conflict theorist. *The Criminologist, 24*, 1, 3, 20.

Gabbidon, S. L. (2003). Racial profiling by store clerks and security personnel in retail establishments: An exploration of "shopping while Black." *Journal of Contemporary Criminal Justice*, 19, 345–364.

Gabbidon, S. L. (2007). *W. E. B. Du Bois on crime and justice: Laying the foundations of sociological criminology*. Aldershot, UK: Ashgate Publications.

Gabbidon, S. L. (2010). *Race, ethnicity, crime, and justice: An international dilemma*. Thousand Oaks, CA: Sage.

Gabbidon, S. L., Craig, R., Okafo, N., Marzette, L. N., & Peterson, S. A. (2008). The consumer racial profiling experiences of Black students at historically Black colleges and universities: An exploratory study. *Journal of Criminal Justice, 36*, 354–361.

Gabbidon, S. L., & Greene, H. T. (2009). *Race and crime* (2nd ed.). Thousand Oaks, CA: Sage.

Gabbidon, S. L., & Higgins, G. E. (2007). Consumer racial profiling and perceived victimization: A phone survey of Philadelphia residents. *American Journal of Criminal Justice, 32*(1–2), 1–11.

Gabbidon, S. L., Kowal, L., Jordan, K. L., Roberts, J. L., & Vincenzi, N. (2008). Race-based peremptory challenges: An empirical analysis of litigation from the U.S. Court of Appeals, 2002–2006. *American Journal of Criminal Justice, 33*, 59–68.

Gabbidon, S. L., Penn, E. B., Jordan, K. L., Higgins, G. E. (2009). The influence of race/ethnicity on the perceived prevalence and support for racial profiling at airports. *Criminal Justice Policy Review, 20*, 344–358.

Gallup Organization. (2007). *Sixty-nine percent of Americans support Death Penalty: Majority say death penalty is applied fairly*. Retrieved February 14, 2008, from http://www.gallup.com/poll/101863/sixtynine-percent-americans-support-death-penalty.aspx

Georges-Abeyie, D. (1989). Race, ethnicity, and the spatial dynamic. *Social Justice, 16*, 35–54.

Gideon v. Wainwright, 372 U.S. 335 (1963).

Glasser, I. (2006, July 10). Drug busts = Jim Crow. *The Nation*.

Glaze, L. E., & Bonczar, T. P. (2009). *Probation and parole in the United States, 2008*. Washington, DC: Bureau of Justice Statistics. Retrieved July 31, 2010, from http://bjs.ojp.usdoj.gov/content/pub/pdf/ppus08.pdf

Gordon, M. (1964). *Assimilation in American life: The role of race, religion, and national origins*. New York: Oxford University Press.

Gossett, T. (1963). *Race: The history of an idea in America.* Dallas, TX: Southern Methodist University Press.

Gould, L. A. (2000). White male privilege and the construction of crime. In The Criminal Justice Collective of Northern Arizona University (Eds.), *Investigating difference: Human and cultural relations in criminal justice* (pp. 27–43). Boston: Allyn & Bacon.

Gould, S. J. (1996). *The mismeasure of man.* New York: Norton.

Graham, O. L., Jr. (2004). *Unguarded gates: A history of America's immigration crisis.* Lanham, MD: Rowman & Littlefield.

Green, H. T., & Gabbidon, S. L. (2009). *Encyclopedia of race and crime.* Thousand Oaks, CA: Sage.

Gregg v. Georgia, 428 U.S, 153 (1976).

Hagan, F. E. (2002). *Introduction to criminology: Theories, methods, and criminal behavior.* Belmont, CA: Wadsworth.

Hallett, M. A. (2006). *Private prisons in America: A critical race perspective.* Urbana: University of Illinois Press.

Harmon, T. R. (2001). Guilty until proven innocent: An analysis of post-*Furman* capital errors. *Criminal Justice Policy Review, 12,* 113–139.

Harmon, T. R. (2004). Race for your life: An analysis of the role of race in erroneous capital convictions. *Criminal Justice Review, 29,* 76–96.

Harrell, E. (2007). *Black victims of violent crime.* Washington, DC: U.S Department of Justice, Office of Justice Programs, Bureau of Statistics.

Harrell, E. (2009, March). *Asian, Native Hawaiian, and Pacific Island victims of crime, 2009* (NCJ 225037). Washington, DC: U.S. Department of Justice, Office of Justice Programs, Bureau of Statistics.

Harris, D. A. (2002). *Profiles in injustice.* New York: New Press.

Hawkins, D. F. (1986). Race, crime type, and imprisonment. *Justice Quarterly, 3,* 251–269.

Hawkins, D. F. (1987). Beyond anomalies: Rethinking the conflict perspective on race and capital punishment. *Social Forces, 65,* 719–745.

Hawkins, D. F., & Hardy, K. A. (1989). Black-White imprisonment rates: A state-by-state analysis. *Social Justice, 16,* 75–94.

Healey, J. F. (2003). *Race, ethnicity, gender, and class: The sociology of group conflict and change* (3rd ed.). Thousand Oaks, CA: Pine Forge Press.

Healey, J. F. (2004). *Diversity and society: Race, ethnicity, and gender.* Thousand Oaks, CA: Pine Forge Press.

Healey, J. F. (2006). *Race, ethnicity, gender, and class: The sociology of group conflict and change* (4th ed.). Thousand Oaks, CA: Pine Forge Press.

Healey, J. F. (2007). *Diversity and society: Race, ethnicity, and gender* (2nd ed.). Thousand Oaks, CA: Pine Forge Press.

Hernandez v. New York, U.S. 352 (1991).

Herrnstein, R. J., & Murray, C. (1994). *The bell curve: Intelligence and class structure in American life.* New York: Free Press.

Hickman, L. J., & Suttorp, M. J. (2008). Are deportable aliens a unique threat to public safety? Comparing the recidivism of deportable and nondeportable aliens. *Criminology & Public Policy, 7,* 59–82.

Hickman, M. J. (2003). *Tribal law enforcement, 2000.* Washington, DC: U.S. Department of Justice.

Hickman, M. J., & Reaves, B. A. (2003). *Sheriffs' offices 2000.* Washington, DC: U.S. Department of Justice.

Higgins, G. E., & Gabbidon, S. L. (2009). Perceptions of consumer racial profiling and negative emotions: An exploratory study. *Criminal Justice & Behavior, 36,* 77–88.

Higgins, G. E., Gabbidon, S. L., & Martin, F. (2010). The influence of race/ethnicity and race relations on public opinion related to the immigration and crime link. *Journal of Criminal Justice, 38,* 51–56.

Higgins, G. E., Vito, G. F., & Walsh, W. F. (2008). Searches: An understudied area of racial profiling. *Journal of Ethnicity in Criminal Justice, 6,* 23–40.

Hirschi, T., & Hindelang, M. (1977). Intelligence and delinquency: A revisionist review. *American Sociological Review, 42,* 571–587.

Hogan, L. J. (1998). *The Osage Indian murders.* Frederick, MD: Amlex.

Holden-Smith, B. (1996). Inherently unequal justice: Interracial rape and the death penalty. *Journal of Criminal Law & Criminology, 86,* 1571–1583.

Hooton, E. A. (1939). *Crime and the man.* Cambridge, MA: Harvard University Press.

Howell, J. C. (2003). *Preventing and reducing juvenile delinquency: A comprehensive framework.* Thousand Oaks, CA: Sage.

Hudson v. McMillian, 503 U.S, 1 (1992).

Huff, C. R. (2004). Wrongful convictions: The American experience. *Canadian Journal of Criminology and Criminal Justice, 46,* 107–120.

Huff, C. R., Rattner, A., & Sagarin, E. (1996). *Convicted but innocent: Wrongful conviction and public policy.* Thousand Oaks, CA: Sage.

Huling, T. (2002). Building a prison economy in rural America. In M. Mauer & M. Chesney-Lind (Eds.), *Invisible punishment: The collateral consequences of mass imprisonment* (pp. 197–213). New York: New Press.

Ignatiev, N. (1996). *How the Irish became White.* New York: Routledge.

Inciardi, J. A. (1999). *Criminal justice* (6th ed.). New York: Harcourt Brace.

Institute of Texan Cultures. (1998). *The El Paso Chinese colony.* Retrieved December 16, 2004, from http://www.texancultures.utsa.edu/txtext/chinese/chineseelpaso.htm

Interpol. (2010). *DNA profiling.* Retrieved on July 27, 2010, from http://www.interpol.int/public/forensic/dna/default.asp

Iyengar, R. (2007). *An analysis of the performance of federal indigent defense counsel.* Cambridge, MA: National Bureau of Economic Research.

Jackson, P. I. (1989). *Minority group threat, crime, and policing.* New York: Praeger.

Jang, S. J., & Johnson, B. R. (2003). Strain, negative emotions, and deviant coping among African Americans: A test of general strain theory. *Journal of Quantitative Criminology, 19,* 79–105.

Jang, S. J., & Johnson, B. R. (2005). Gender, religiosity, and reactions to strain among African Americans. *The Sociological Quarterly, 46,* 323–357.

Jang, S. J., & Lyons, J. A. (2006). Strain, social support, and retreatism among African Americans. *Journal of Black Studies, 37,* 251–274.

Jenkins, P. (1994). The ice age: The social construction of a drug panic. *Justice Quarterly, 11,* 7–31.

Johnson, D. R. (1981). *American law enforcement: A history.* St. Louis, MO: Forum Press.

Jones, J. (2003). *Support for the death penalty remains high at 74%: Slight majority prefers death penalty to life imprisonment as punishment for murder.* Retrieved on March 2, 2003, from www.gallup.com/content/print.asp

Jones, N. (2010). *Between good and ghetto.* New Brunswick, NJ: Rutgers University Press.

Jones, T. (1977). The police in America: A Black viewpoint. *The Black Scholar, 9*(2), 22–39.

Kanellos, N. (1977). *The Hispanic-American almanac.* Detroit, MI: Gale Research.

Kennedy, R. (1997). *Race, crime, and the law.* New York: Pantheon Books.

Kim, H. C. (1999). *Koreans in the hood: Conflict with African Americans.* Baltimore, MD: Johns Hopkins University Press.

Kim, H. C. (2001). The Filipino Americans. *Journal of American Ethnic History,* 20, 135–137.

Kimbrough v. US, 128 S. Ct. 558 (2007).

King, R. D. (2007). The context of minority group threat: Race, institutions, and complying with hate crime law. *Law & Society Review, 41,* 189–224.

Know Gangs. (n.d.). *Southeast Asian gangs.* Retrieved on July 1, 2010, from www.knowgangs.com/gang_resources/sea/southeast_asian_gangs_001.htm

Krauss, E., & Schulman, M. (1997). The myth of Black jury nullification: Racism dressed up in jurisprudential clothing. *Cornell Journal of Law and Public Policy, 7,* 57–76.

Krivo, L. J., & Peterson, R. D. (1996). Extremely disadvantaged neighborhoods and urban crime. *Social Forces, 75,* 619–650.

Krivo, L. J., & Peterson, R. D. (2000). The structural context of homicide: Accounting for racial differences in process. *American Sociological Review, 65,* 547–559.

Kubrin, C. E. (2005). Gangstas, thugs, and hustlas: Identity and the code of the streets in rap music. *Social Problems, 52,* 360–378.

Kupchik, A. (2009). Things are tough all over: Race, ethnicity, class and school discipline. *Punishment & Society, 11,* 291–317.

Lambert, E., & Clarke, A. (2001). The impact of information on an individual's support of the death penalty: A partial test of the Marshall hypothesis among college students. *Criminal Justice Policy Review, 12,* 215–234.

Lane, R. (1967). *Policing the city: Boston, 1822–1885.* Cambridge, MA: Harvard University Press.

Lanier, C., & Huff-Corzine, L. (2006). American Indian homicide: A county level analysis utilizing social disorganization theory. *Homicide Studies, 10*, 181–194.

Lanier, M. M., & Henry, S. (1998). *Essential criminology.* Boulder, CO: Westview.

Latessa, E. J., & Lovins, B. (2010). The role of offender risk assessment: A policy maker guide. *Victims and Offenders 5*(3), 203–219.

Lee, M. T., & Martinez, R. (2002). Social disorganization revisited: Mapping the recent immigration and Black homicide relationship in northern Miami. *Sociological Focus, 35*, 363–380.

Leiber, M. J. (2002). Disproportionate minority confinement (DMC) of youth: An analysis of state and federal efforts to address the issue. *Crime & Delinquency, 48*, 3–45.

Leo, R. A. (2002). False confessions: Causes, consequences, and solutions. In S. Westervelt & J. A. Humphrey (Eds.), *Wrongly convicted: Perspectives on failed justice* (pp. 36–54). New Brunswick, NJ: Rutgers University Press.

Leo, R. A. (2005). Rethinking the study of miscarriages of justice: Developing a criminology of wrongful conviction. *Journal of Contemporary Criminal Justice, 21*, 201–223.

Lilly, R. J., Cullen, F. T., & Ball, R. A. (2001). *Criminological theory: Context and consequences.* Thousand Oaks, CA: Sage.

Lombroso, C. (1911). *Criminal man.* New York: Putnam. (Original work published 1876)

Longmire, D. R. (1996). Americans' attitudes about the ultimate weapon: Capital punishment. In T. J. Flanagan & D. R. Longmire (Eds.), *Americans view crime and justice: A national public opinion survey* (pp. 93–108). Thousand Oaks, CA: Sage.

Lopez, R., Roosa, M. W., Tein, J. T., & Dinh, K. T. (2004). Accounting for Anglo-Hispanic differences in school misbehavior. *Journal of Ethnicity in Criminal Justice, 2*, 27–46.

Lotke, E. (1996). *The prison-industrial complex.* Baltimore: National Center on Institutions and Alternatives.

Luna-Firebaugh, E. M. (2003, July 28–30). *Tribal law enforcement in P.L. 280 states.* Paper presented at the annual conference on Criminal Justice Research and Evaluation, Washington, DC.

Maguire, K. (2010). Reported confidence in police, 2009, Table 2.12. In *Sourcebook of criminal justice statistics.* Retrieved on July 17, 2010, from http://www.albany.edu/sourcebook/pdf/t2122009.pdf

Maguire, K., & Pastore, A. L. (Eds.). (2003). *Sourcebook of criminal justice statistics.* Retrieved on July 17, 2010, from http://www.albany.edu/sourcebook/pdf/t213.pdf

Maguire, K., & Pastore, A. L. (Eds.). (2004). Reported confidence in the police: Table 2.13. In *Sourcebook of criminal justice statistics.* Retrieved on July 17, 2010, from www.albany.edu/sourcebook/

Maguire, K., & Pastore, A. L. (Eds.). (2007). *Sourcebook of criminal justice statistics* [Online]. Washington, DC: U. S. Department of Justice, Bureau of Justice Statistics.

Maltz, M. (1977). Crime statistics: A historical perspective. *Crime & Delinquency, 23*, 32–40.

Manatu-Rupert, N. (2002). Prison reform. In D. Levinson (Ed), *Encyclopedia of crime and punishment* (pp. 1225–1231). Thousand Oaks, CA: Sage.

Mann, C. R. (1993). *Unequal justice: A question of color.* Bloomington: Indiana University Press.

Mapp v. Ohio, 367 U.S, 1081, 81 S.CT (1961).

Marger, M. (Ed.). (1997). *Race and ethnic relations: American and global perspectives* (4th ed.). Belmont, CA: Wadsworth.

Martin, D. L. (2002). The police role in wrongful convictions: An international comparative study. In S. Westervelt & J. A. Humphrey (Eds.), *Wrongly convicted: Perspectives on failed justice* (pp. 77–95). New Brunswick, NJ: Rutgers University Press.

Martinez, R. (2002). *Latino homicide.* New York: Routledge.

Martinez, R. (2003). Moving beyond Black and White violence: African American, Haitian, and Latino homicides in Miami. In D. F. Hawkins (Ed.), *Violent crime: Assessing race and ethnic differences* (pp. 22–43). New York: Cambridge University Press.

Martinez, R. (2006). Coming to America: The impact of the new immigration on crime. In R. Martinez & A. Valenzuela (Eds.), *Immigration and crime: Race, ethnicity, and violence* (pp. 1–19). New York: New York University Press.

Martinez, R., Lee, M. T., & Nielsen, A. L. (2001). Revisiting the Scarface legacy: The victim/offender relationship and Mariel homicides in

Miami. *Hispanic Journal of Behavioral Sciences, 23,* 37–56.

Martinez, R., & Valenzuela, A. (Eds.). (2006). *Immigration and crime: Race, ethnicity, and violence.* New York: New York University Press.

Massey, D. S., & Denton, N. A. (1993). *American apartheid.* Cambridge, MA: Harvard University Press.

Mauer, M. (1990). *Young African American men and the criminal justice system: A growing national problem.* Washington, DC: The Sentencing Project.

Mauer, M. (1999). *Race to incarcerate.* New York: New Press.

Mauer, M. (2004). Extended view: Racial disparity and the criminal justice system: An assessment of causes and responses. *SAGE Race Relations Abstracts, 29,* 34–56.

Mauer, M. (2006). *Race to incarcerate* (Rev. ed.). New York: New Press.

McCleskey v. Kemp, 481 U.S, 279 (1987).

McCluskey, C. P. (2002). *Understanding Latino delinquency: The applicability of strain theory by ethnicity.* New York: LFB Scholarly Publishing.

McCluskey, J. B., McCluskey, C. P., & Enriquez, R. (2008). Comparison of Latino and White citizen satisfaction with police. *Journal of Criminal Justice, 36*(6), 471–477.

McGee, Z. T. (1999). Patterns of violent behavior and victimization among African American youth. *Journal of Offender Rehabilitation, 30,* 47–64.

McGee, Z. T. (2003). Community violence and adolescent development: An examination of risk and protective factors among African American youth. *Journal of Contemporary Criminal Justice, 19,* 293–314.

McGee, Z. T., & Baker, S. R. (2002). Impact of violence on problem behavior among adolescents. *Journal of Contemporary Criminal Justice, 18,* 293–314.

McGee, Z. T., Barber, A., Joseph, E., Dudley, J., & Howell, R. (2005). Delinquent behavior, violent victimization, and coping strategies among Latino adolescents. *Journal of Offender Rehabilitation, 42,* 41–56.

McIntyre, C. C. L. (1992). *Criminalizing a race: Free Blacks during slavery.* New York: Kayode.

McMahon, J., Garner, J., Davis, R., & Krause, A. (2002). *How to correctly collect and analyze racial profiling data: Your reputation depends on it.* Washington, DC: US Department of Justice, Office of Community Oriented Policing Services.

Mears, D. P., & Watson, J. (2006). Towards a fair and balanced assessment of supermax prisons. *Justice Quarterly, 23,* 232–270.

Meier, A., & Rudwick, E. (1970). *From plantation to ghetto* (Rev. ed.). New York: Hill & Wang.

Mennel, R. M. (1973). *Thorns and thistles.* Hanover: University of New Hampshire Press.

Merton, R. K. (1938). Social structure and anomie. *American Sociological Review, 3,* 672–682.

Miller, J. (1992). *Hobbling a generation: Young African American males in Washington, DC's, criminal justice system.* Baltimore: National Center for Institutions and Alternatives.

Miller, J. (1996). *Search and destroy: African American males in the criminal justice system.* New York: Cambridge University Press.

Miller, J. (2001). Breaking the individual back in: A commentary on Wacquant and Anderson. *Punishment & Society, 3,* 153–160.

Minton, T. D. (2009). *Jails in Indian country* (NCJ 22871). Washington, DC: Department of Justice, Office of Justice Programs, Bureau of Justice Statistics.

Miranda v. Arizona, 384 U.S. 436,86 S. Ct, 1602 (1966).

Mirande, A. (1987). *Gringo justice.* Notre Dame, IN: Notre Dame University Press.

Mitchell, A.D. (2006). The effect of the Marshall hypothesis on attitudes towards the death penalty. *Race, Gender & Class, 13,* 221–239.

Mitchell, O. (2005). A meta-analysis of race and sentencing research: Examining the inconsistencies. *Journal of Quantitative Criminology, 21,* 439–466.

Monkkonen, E. H. (1981). *Police in urban America, 1860–1920.* Cambridge, NY: Cambridge University Press.

Morin, J. L. (2005). *Latino/a rights and justice in the United States: Perspectives and approaches.* Durham, NC: Carolina Academic Press.

Myers, M. A. (1998). *Race, labor, & punishment in the new south.* Columbus: Ohio State University Press.

Myrdal, G. (1944). *An American dilemma: The Negro problem and modern democracy.* New York: Harper & Brothers.

National Commission on Law Observance and Enforcement. (1931). *Crime and the foreign born* (Report No. 10). Washington, DC: Government Printing Office.

National Reentry Resource Center. (2010). *Reentry courts: An emerging trend.* Retrieved August 4, 2010, from http://www.nationalreentryresourcecenter.org

Neubauer, D. (2002). *America's courts and the criminal justice system* (7th ed.). Belmont, CA: Wadsworth.

Neverdon-Morton, C. (1989). *Afro-American women of the south and the advancement of the race, 1895–1925.* Knoxville: University of Tennessee Press.

Office of Juvenile Justice and Delinquency Prevention. (2009). *Disproportionate minority contact.* Washington, DC: OJJDP in Focus. Retrieved July 8, 2010, from http://ojjdp.ncjrs.gov/dmc/about.html

Onwudiwe, I. D., & Lynch, M. J. (2000). Reopening the debate: A reexamination of the need for a Black criminology. *Social Pathology: A Journal of Reviews, 6,* 182–198.

Oshinsky, D. M. (1996). *"Worse than slavery": Parchman farm and the ordeal of Jim Crow justice.* New York: Free Press.

Pager, D. I. (2007a). *Marked: Race, crime, and finding work in an era of mass incarceration.* Chicago: University of Chicago Press.

Pager, D. I. (2007b). Two strikes and you're out: The intensification of racial and criminal stigma. In D. Weiman, S. Bushway, & M. Stoll (Eds.), *Barriers to reentry? The labor market for released prisoners in post-industrial America* (pp. 151–173). New York: Russell Sage.

Parenti, C. (1999). *Lockdown America: Police and prisons in the age of crisis.* New York: Verso.

Parker, K. F., Dewees, M. A., & Radelet, M. L. (2002). Racial bias and the conviction of the innocent. In S. Westervelt & J. A. Humphrey (Eds.), *Wrongly convicted: Perspectives on failed justice* (pp. 114–131). New Brunswick, NJ: Rutgers University Press.

Pastore, A. L., & Maguire, K. (Eds.). (2007). *Sourcebook of criminal justice statistics* [Online]. Retrieved on July 17, 2010, from http://www.albany.edu/sourcebook

Pastore, A. L., & Maguire, K. (Eds.). (2010). *Sourcebook of criminal justice statistics* [Online]. Table 2.12. Retrieved on July 17, 2010, from http://www.albany.edu/sourcebook/pdf/t2122009.pdf

Pennsylvania Supreme Court. (2003). *Pennsylvania Supreme Court committee on racial and gender bias in the justice system* (Final report). Retrieved on February 2, 2011, from http://www.friendsfw.org/PA_Courts/Race_Gender_Committee.pdf

Perry, B. (2000). Perpetual outsiders: Criminal justice and the Asian American experience. In The Criminal Justice Collective of Northern Arizona University (Eds.), *Investigating difference: Human and cultural relations in criminal justice* (pp. 99–110). Boston: Allyn & Bacon.

Perry, B. (2002). Defending the color line: Racially and ethnically motivated hate crime. *American Behavioral Scientist, 46,* 72–92.

Perry, S. W. (2004). *American Indians and crime: A BJS statistical profile, 1992–2002.* Washington, DC: U.S. Department of Justice, Bureau of Justice Statistics. Retrieved on July 3, 2010, from http://bjs.ojp.usdoj.gov

Petersilia, J. (1983). *Racial disparities in the criminal justice system.* Santa Monica, CA: RAND.

Petersilia, J. (2002). Community corrections. In J. Q. Wilson & J. Petersilia (Eds.), *Crime: Public policies for crime control* (pp. 483–508). Oakland, CA: Institute for Contemporary Studies.

Petersilia, J. (2003). *When prisoners come home: Parole and prisoner reentry.* New York: Oxford University Press.

Peterson, R. D., & Krivo, L. J. (1993). Racial segregation and Black urban homicide. *Social Forces, 71,* 1001–1026.

Peterson, R. D., & Krivo, L. J. (2005). Macrostructural analyses of race, ethnicity, and violent crime: Recent lessons and new directions for research. *Annual Review of Sociology, 31,* 331–356.

Pew Center on the States. (2010a). *Corrections and public safety.* Retrieved August 8, 2010, from http://www.pewcenteronthestates.org

Pew Center on the States. (2010b). *Prison count 2010: State population declines for the first time in 38 years.* Retrieved July 31, 2010, from http://www.pewcenteronthestates.org

Platt, A. (1969). *The child savers: The invention of delinquency.* Chicago: University of Chicago Press.

Plessy v. Ferguson, 163 U.S. 537 (1896).

Polk, W. R. (2006). *The birth of America: From Columbus to the revolution.* New York: HarperCollins.

Powell v. Alabama, 287 U.S. 45 (1932).

Pratt, T. C. (1998). Race and sentencing: A meta-analysis of conflicting empirical research results. *Journal of Criminal Justice, 26,* 513–523.

Price, B. E. (2006). *Merchandizing prisoners: Who really pays for prison privatization?* Westport, CT: Praeger.

Quetelet, A. Q. (1984). *Research on the propensity for crime at different ages.* Cincinnati, OH: Anderson. (Original work published 1833)

Radelet, M. L. (1989). Executions of Whites for crimes against Blacks: Exceptions to the rule? *The Sociological Quarterly, 30,* 529–544.

Radelet, M. L., Bedau, H. A., & Putnam, C. E. (1992). *In spite of innocence: The ordeal of 400 Americans wrongly convicted of crimes punishable by death.* Boston: Northeastern University Press.

Radosh, P. F. (2008). War on drugs: Gender and race inequities in crime control strategies. *Criminal Justice Studies, 21,* 167–178.

Ramsey, R. J., & Frank, J. (2007). Wrongful convictions: Perceptions of criminal justice professionals regarding the frequency of wrongful convictions and system errors. *Crime & Delinquency, 53,* 436–470.

Rand, M. R. (2009). *Criminal victimization, 2008.* Washington, DC: U.S. Department of Justice. Retrieved on July 3, 2010, from http://bjs.ojp.usdoj.gov/content/pub/pdf/cv08.pdf

Reasons, C. E., Conley, D. C., & Debro, J. (Eds.). (2002). *Race, class, gender, and justice in the United States.* Boston: Allyn & Bacon.

Reaves, B. A. (2001). *Felony defendants in large urban counties, 1998.* Washington, DC: Bureau of Justice Statistics.

Reaves, B. (2006). *Federal law enforcement officers, 2004.* Washington, DC: U.S. Department of Justice. Retrieved February 16, 2008, from http://bjs.ojp.usdoj.gov/content/pub/pdf/fleo04.pdf

Reaves, B. (2007). *Census of state and local law enforcement agencies, 2004.* Washington, DC: U.S. Department of Justice.

Reaves, B., & Bauer, L. (2003). *Federal law enforcement officers, 2002.* Washington, DC: U.S. Department of Justice.

Reaves, B., & Hickman, M. (2002). *Census of state and local law enforcement agencies, 2000.* Washington, DC: U.S. Department of Justice.

Reaves, B., & Hickman, M. (2003). *Local police departments, 2000.* Washington, DC: U.S. Department of Justice.

Reaves, B., & Perez, J. (1994). *Pretrial release of felony defendants, 1992.* Washington, DC: Bureau of Justice Statistics.

Reentry of Exoffenders Clinic. (2007). *A report on the collateral consequences of criminal convictions in Maryland.* Baltimore, MD: University of Maryland School of Law. Retrieved on February 2, 2011 from http://www.courts.state.tx.us/pdf/MDCollateralConsequencesReport12007.pdf

Reid, I. De A. (1957). Race and crime. *Friends Journal, 3,* 772–774.

Reid, S. T. (2008). *Criminal Justice* (8th ed.). Mason, OH: Thomson Custom Solutions.

Reiman, J. (2007). *The rich get richer and the poor get prison: Ideology, class, and criminal justice* (8th ed.). Boston: Allyn & Bacon.

Reisig, M. D., & Parks, R. B. (2002). *Satisfaction with police: What matters?* Washington, DC: National Institute of Justice.

Richardson, J. F. (1970). *The New York police.* New York: Oxford University Press.

Riveland, C. (1999). *Supermax prisons: Overview and general considerations.* Washington, DC: National Institution of Corrections.

Robinson, M. B. (2002). *Justice blind? Ideals and realities of American criminal justice.* Upper Saddle River, NJ: Prentice Hall.

Rocque, M. (2008). Strain, coping mechanisms, and slavery: A general strain theory application. *Crime, Law, and Social Change, 49,* 245–269.

Rose, D. R., & Clear, T. R. (1998). Incarceration, social capital, and crime: Implications for social disorganization theory. *Criminology, 36,* 441–479.

Rosenmerkel, S., Durose, M., & Farole, D. (2009). *Felony sentences in state courts, 2006–statistical tables.* Washington, DC: Bureau of Justice Statistics.

Russell, K. K. (1998). *The color of crime.* New York: New York University Press.

Russell, K. K. (2002). "Driving while Black": Corollary phenomena and collateral consequences. In C. E. Reasons, D. J. Conley, & J. Debro (Eds.), *Race, class, gender, and justice in the United States* (pp. 191–200). Boston: Allyn & Bacon.

Russell-Brown, K. K. (2004). *Underground codes: Race, crime, and related fires.* New York: New York University Press.

Russell-Brown, K. K. (2009). *The color of crime: Racial hoaxes, White fear, Black protectionism, police harassment, and other macroaggressions* (2nd ed.). New York: New York University Press.

Sale, K. (1990). *The conquest of paradise: Christopher Columbus and the Columbian legacy.* New York: Knopf.

Saleh-Hanna, V. (Ed.). (2008). *Colonial systems of control: Criminal justice in Nigeria.* Ottawa, Ontario, Canada: University of Ottawa Press.

Sampson, R. J. (1987). Urban Black violence: The effects of male joblessness and family disruption. *American Journal of Sociology, 93,* 348–382.

Sampson, R. J., & Bean, L. (2006). Cultural mechanisms and killing fields: A revised theory of community-level racial inequality. In J. Hagan, R. Peterson, & L. Krivo (Eds.), *The many colors of crime: Inequalities of race, ethnicity, and crime in America* (pp. 8–36). New York: New York University Press.

Sampson, R. J., & Groves, W. B. (1989). Community structure and crime: Testing social-disorganization theory. *American Journal of Sociology, 94,* 774–802.

Sampson, R. J., Raudenbush, S. W., & Earls, F. (1997). Neighborhoods and violent crime: A multilevel study of collective efficacy. *Science, 277,* 918–924.

Sampson, R. J., & Wilson, W. J. (1995). Toward a theory of race, crime, and urban inequality. In J. Hagan & R. D. Peterson (Eds.), *Crime and inequality* (pp. 37–54). Stanford, CA: Stanford University Press.

Scalia, J. (1999). *Federal pretrial release and detention, 1996.* Washington, DC: Bureau of Justice Statistics.

Schlesinger, T. (2005). Racial and ethnic disparity in pretrial case processing. *Justice Quarterly,* 22, 170–192.

Schmalleger, F. (2006). *Criminal justice: A brief introduction.* Upper Saddle River, NJ: Pearson Prentice Hall.

Scotti, R., & Kronenberg, S. (2001, Spring). U.S. drug laws: The new Jim Crow? *Temple Political and Civil Rights Law Review 2000 Symposium,* 303–310.

Sellin, T. (1928). The Negro criminal: A statistical note. *The American Academy of Political and Social Sciences, 130,* 52–64.

Sellin, T. (1935). Race prejudice in the administration of justice. *The American Journal of Sociology, 41,* 212–217.

Sellin, T. (1976). *Slavery and the penal system.* New York: Elsevier.

Sentencing Project. (2010). *Fair sentencing act signed by President Obama.* Retrieved on February 2, 2011, from http://www.sentencingproject.org/detail/news.cfm?news_id=984&id=164

Sesardic, N. (2010). Race: A social destruction of a biological concept. *Biological Philosophy, 25,* 143–162.

Sharp, E. B. (2006). Policing urban America: A new look at the politics of agency size. *Social Science Quarterly, 87,* 291–307.

Shaw, C., & McKay, H. D. (1969). *Juvenile delinquency in urban areas.* Chicago: University of Chicago Press. (Original work published 1942)

Shelden, R. G. (2001). *Controlling the dangerous classes.* Needham Heights, MA: Allyn & Bacon.

Shelden, R. G., & Brown, W. (2003). *Criminal justice in America: A critical view.* Needham Heights, MA: Allyn & Bacon.

Sherman, L. W. (1997). Communities and crime prevention. In L. W. Sherman, D. C. Gottfredson, D. L. MacKenzie, J. E. Eck, P. Reuter, & S. D. Bushway (Eds.), *Preventing crime: What works, what doesn't, and what's promising.* Washington, DC: National Institute of Justice.

Sickmund, M. (2009). *Delinquency cases in juvenile court, 2005* (OJJDP Fact Sheet NCJ 224538). Washington, DC: Office of Juvenile Justice and Delinquency Prevention.

Siegel, L. J. (2002). *Juvenile delinquency: The core.* Belmont, CA: Wadsworth/Thomson Learning.

Simons, R. L., Chen, Y. F., Stewart, E. A., & Brody, G. H. (2003). Incidents of discrimination and risk for delinquency: A longitudinal test of strain theory with an African American sample. *Justice Quarterly, 20*(4), 827–854.

Simons, R. L., Gordon Simons, L., Burt, C. H., Brody, G. H., & Cutrona, C. (2005). Collective efficacy, authoritative parenting and delinquency: A longitudinal test of a model integrating community- and family-level processes. *Criminology, 43,* 989–1029.

Sims, Y. (2009). Jena 6. In H. T. Greene & S. L. Gabbidon (Eds.), *Encyclopedia of race and crime* (pp. 409–411). Thousand Oaks, CA: Sage.

Skogan, W. G. (2005). Citizen satisfaction with police encounters. *Police Quarterly, 8*(3), 298–321.

Snell, T. L. (2009). *Capital punishment, 2008—statistical tables.* Washington, DC: Bureau of Justice Statistics.

Snyder, H. N. (1997). *Juvenile arrests 1995.* Washington, DC: Office of Juvenile Justice and Delinquency Prevention.

Snyder, M., & Sickmund, M. (2008). *Juvenile offenders and victims: 2006 national report.* Washington, DC: Office of Juvenile Justice and Delinquency Prevention.

Sorenson, J., Hope, R., & Stemen, D. (2003). Racial disproportionality in state prison admissions: Can regional variation be explained by differential arrest rates? *Journal of Criminal Justice, 31,* 73–84.

Sowell, T. (1981). *Ethnic America: A history.* New York: Basic Books.

Spilde, K. (2001). *The economic development journey of Indian Nations.* Retrieved on August 6, 2004, from http://www.indiangaming.org/library/articles/the-economic-development-journey.shtml

Spohn, C. S. (2000). Thirty years of sentencing reform: The quest for a racially neutral sentencing process. In Julie Horney (Ed.), *Policies, processes and decisions of the criminal justice system* (pp. 427–501). Washington, DC: National Institute of Justice.

Spohn, C. S. (2002). *How do judges decide? The search for fairness and justice in punishment.* Thousand Oaks, CA: Sage.

Staples, R. (1975). White racism, Black crime, and American justice: An application of the colonial model to explain crime and race. *Phylon, 36,* 14–22.

Stephan, J. J., & Karberg, J. C. (2003). *Census of state and federal correctional facilities, 2000.* Washington, DC: US Dept of Justice, Bureau of Justice Statistics.

Stewart, E. A., Schreck, C. J., & Brunson, R. K. (2008). Lessons of the street code: Policy implications for reducing violent victimization among disadvantaged citizens. *Journal of Contemporary Criminal Justice, 24,* 137–147.

Stewart, E. A., Schreck, C. J., & Simons, R. L. (2006). I ain't gonna let no one disrespect me: Does the code of the street reduce or increase violent victimization among African American adolescents? *The Journal of Research in Crime and Delinquency, 43,* 427–457.

Stewart, E. A., & Simons, R. L. (2006). Structure and culture in African Americans adolescent violence: A partial test of the "code of the street" thesis. *Justice Quarterly, 23,* 1–33.

Stewart, E. A., & Simons, R. L. (2010). Race, code of the street, and violent delinquency: A multilevel investigation of neighborhood street culture and individual norms of violence. *Criminology, 48,* 569–606.

Stewart, E. A., Simons, R. L., & Conger, R. D. (2002). Assessing neighborhood and social psychological influences on childhood violence in an African American sample. *Criminology, 40,* 801–829.

Stowell, J.I. (2007). *Immigration and crime: Considering the direct and indirect effects of immigration on violent criminal behavior.* New York: LFB Scholarly Press.

Sutherland, E. H. (1931). Mental deficiency and crime. In K. Young (Ed.), *Social attitudes* (pp. 357–375). New York: Henry Holt and Company.

Swain v. Alabama, 380 U.S, 202 (1965).

Takaki, R. (1989). *Strangers from a different shore: A history of Asian Americans.* Boston: Little & Brown.

Tarver, M., Walker, S., & Wallace, H. (2002). *Multicultural issues in the criminal justice system.* Boston: Allyn & Bacon.

Tatum, B. L. (1994). The colonial model as a theoretical explanation of crime and delinquency. In A. T. Sulton (Ed.), *African American perspectives on crime causation, criminal justice administration, and prevention* (pp. 33–52). Engelwood, CO: Sulton Books.

Tatum, B. L. (2000). *Crime, violence and minority youths.* Aldershot, UK: Ashgate.

Taylor Greene, H., & Gabbidon, S. L. (2000). *African American criminological thought.* Albany: State University of New York Press.

Taylor Greene, H., & Penn, E. (2005). Reducing juvenile delinquency: Lessons learned. In E. Penn,

H. Taylor Greene, & S. L. Gabbidon (Eds.), *Race and juvenile justice* (pp. 223–241). Durham, NC: Carolina Academic Press.

Texeira, E. (2005, August, 28). Should the term "minority" be dropped? Word confuses, insults people some critics say. *Patriot-News*, A15.

Tonry, M. (1995). *Malign neglect.* Oxford, UK: Oxford University Press.

Travis, J. (2005). *But they all come back: Facing the challenges of prisoner reentry.* Washington, DC: Urban Institute Press.

Travis, J., Crayton, A., & Mukamal, D. (2009, December). A new era in inmate reentry. *Corrections Today, 71*(6), 38–41.

Trujillo, L. (1995). La evolucion del "bandido" al "pachuco": A critical examination and evaluation of criminological literature on Chicanos. In A. S. Lopes (Ed.), *Criminal justice and Latino communities* (pp. 21–45). New York: Garland. (Reprinted from *Issues in Criminology, 74*(9), 44–67, 1974.)

Tuch, S. A., & Weitzer, R. (1997). The poll trends, racial differences in attitudes toward the police. *Public Opinion Quarterly, 61*(4), 642–663.

Tulchin, S. H. (1939). *Intelligence and crime.* Chicago: University of Chicago Press.

Turner, K. B., & Johnson, J. B. (2005). A comparison of bail amounts for Hispanics, Whites, and African Americans: A single county analysis. *American Journal of Criminal Justice, 30*, 35–53.

Tyler, S. L. (1973). *A history of Indian policy.* Washington, DC: U.S. Department of Interior.

Uchida, C. (1997). The development of American police. In R. G. Dunham & G. P. Alpert (Eds.), *Critical issues in policing* (pp. 18–35). Prospect Heights, IL: Waveland Press.

Ulmer, J. T., & Johnson, B. (2004). Sentencing in context: A multilevel analysis. *Criminology, 42*, 137–177.

United States v. Booker, 543 U.S. 220 (2005).

Unnever, J. D., & Cullen, F.T. (2007). Reassessing the racial divide in support for capital punishment: The continuing significance of race. *Journal of Research in Crime and Delinquency, 44*, 124–158.

U.S. Bureau of the Census. (2003). *Statistical abstract of the United States.* Washington, DC: Author.

U.S. Bureau of the Census. (2008). *Statistical abstract of the U.S.* Retrieved from www.census.gov/compendia/statab/

U.S. Census Bureau. (2000). Retrieved on April 15, 2003, from http://www.census.gov/main/www/cen2000.html

U.S. Census Bureau. (2004). U.S. interim projections by age, race, and Hispanic origin. Retrieved on January 18, 2008, from www.census.gov

U.S. Department of Justice. (2009, March 31). *Growth in prisons and jail populations slowing: 16 states report declines in the number of prisoners.* Retrieved August 4, 2010, from http://www.ojp.usdoj.gov/newsroom/pressreleases/2009/BJS090331.htm

U.S. Federal Bureau of Prisons. (2010). *About the Bureau of Prisons.* Retrieved July 31, 2010, from http://www.bop.gov/about/index.jsp

U.S. Senate. (2002). *Senate hearing before the Subcommittee on Crime and Drugs of the Committee on the Judiciary, United States* (107–911). Washington, DC: U.S. Government Printing Office.

U.S. Sentencing Commission. (2002). *Cocaine and federal sentencing policy.* Retrieved March 19, 2008, from http://www.ussc.gov/Legislative_and_Public_Affairs/Congressional_Testimony_and_Reports/Drug_Topics/200205_RtC_Cocaine_Sentencing_Policy/20020

U.S. Sentencing Commission. (2007). *Cocaine and federal sentencing policy.* Retrieved March 19, 2008, from http://www.ussc.gov/r_congress/cocaine2007.pdf

Velez, M. B. (2006). Toward an understanding of the lower rates of homicide in Latino versus Black neighborhoods: A look at Chicago. In J. Hagan, R. Peterson, & L. Krivo (Eds.), *The many colors of crime: Inequalities of race, ethnicity, and crime in America* (pp. 91–107). New York: New York University Press.

Venkatesh, S. A. (2006). *Off the books: The underground economy of the urban poor.* Cambridge, MA: Harvard University Press.

Visher, C., Yahner, J., & La Vigne, N. (2010). *Life after prison: Tracking the experiences of male prisoners returning to Chicago, Cleveland, and Houston.* Washington, DC: The Urban Institute. Retrieved August 9, 2010, from http://www.urban.org

Vold, G. B., Bernard, T. J., & Snipes, J. B. (1998). *Theoretical criminology* (4th ed.). Oxford, UK: Oxford University Press.

Wacquant, L. (2002). Scrutinizing the street: Poverty, morality, and the pitfalls of urban ethnography. *American Journal of Sociology, 107,* 1468–1532.

Wakeling, S., Jorgensen, M., Michaelson, S., Begay, M., Hartmann, F., & Wiener, M. (2001). *Policing on Indian reservations.* Washington, DC: U.S. Department of Justice.

Walker, S., Spohn, C., & DeLone, M. (2007). *The color of justice* (4th ed.). Belmont, CA: Thomson Learning.

Ward, G. (2001). *Color lines of social control: Juvenile justice administration in a racialized social system, 1825–2000.* Unpublished doctoral dissertation, University of Michigan, Ann Arbor.

Washington, L. (1994). *Black judges on justice: Perspectives from the bench.* New York: New Press.

Websdale, N. (2001). *Policing the poor: From slave plantation to public housing.* Boston: Northeastern University Press.

Weitzer, R. (2000). Racialized policing: Residents' perceptions in three neighborhoods. *Law & Society Review, 34,* 129–156.

Weitzer, R., & Tuch, S. A. (2004). Reforming the police: Racial differences in public support for change. *Criminology, 42,* 391–416.

Weitzer, R., & Tuch, S. A. (2006). *Race and policing in America: Conflict and reform.* Cambridge, NY: Cambridge University Press.

West, H. C. (2010). *Prison inmate at midyear 2009–Statistical tables* (NCJ 230113). Washington, DC: Bureau of Justice Statistics. Retrieved July 30, 2010, from http://bjs.ojp.usdoj.gov/index.cfm?ty=pbdetail&iid=2200

Western, B. (2006). *Punishment and inequality in America.* New York: Russell Sage Foundation.

Western, B., & Wildeman, C. (2009). The Black family and mass incarceration. *The Annals of the American Academy of Political and Social Science, 621,* 221–242.

Williams, H., & Murphy, P. (1990). *The evolving strategy of police: A minority view.* Washington, DC: National Institute of Justice.

Wilson, W. J. (1987). *The truly disadvantaged.* Chicago: University of Chicago Press.

Withrow, B. L. (2006). *Racial profiling: From rhetoric to reason.* Upper Saddle River, NJ: Prentice Hall.

Wolf, A., Graziano, J., & Hartney, C. (2009). The provision and completion of gender-specific services for girls on probation: Variation by race and ethnicity. *Crime & Delinquency, 55,* 294–312.

Wolf Harlow, C. (2000). *Defense counsel in criminal cases.* Washington, DC: Bureau of Justice Statistics.

Work, M. (1900). Crime among the Negroes of Chicago. *American Journal of Sociology, 6,* 204–223.

Work, M. (1913). Negro criminality in the South. *Annals of the American Academy of Political and Social Sciences, 49,* 74–80.

Wright, B. (1987). *Black robes, White justice.* New York: Carol Publishing.

Wright, J. P. (2009). Inconvenient truths: Science, race, and crime. In A. Walsh & K. M. Beaver (Eds.), *Biosocial criminology: New directions in theory and research* (pp. 137–153). New York: Routledge.

Wu, F. H. (2002). *Yellow: Race in America beyond Black and White.* New York: Basic Books.

Xu, Y., Fiedler, M. L., Flaming, K. H. (2005). Discovering the impact of community policing: The broken windows thesis, collective efficacy, and citizens' judgment. *Journal of Research in Crime and Delinquency, 42,* 147–186.

Young, V. (1993). Punishment and social conditions: The control of Black juveniles in the 1800s in Maryland. In A. G. Hess & P. F. Clement (Eds.), *History of juvenile delinquency: A collection of essays on crime committed by young offenders, in history and in selected countries* (pp. 557–575). Aalen, Germany: Scientia Verlag.

Zalman, M. (2006). Criminal justice system reform and wrongful convictions: A research agenda. *Criminal Justice Policy Review, 17,* 468–492.

Zangrando, R. L. (1980). *The NAACP crusade against lynching, 1900–1950.* Philadelphia: Temple University Press.

Zatz, M. S. (1987). The changing form of racial/ethnic biases in sentencing. *Journal of Research in Crime and Delinquency, 24,* 69–92.

Zimmerman, C. S. (2002). From the jailhouse to the courthouse: The role of informants in wrongful convictions. In S. Westervelt & J. A. Humphrey (Eds.), *Wrongly convicted: Perspectives on failed justice* (pp. 55–76). New Brunswick, NJ: Rutgers University Press.

Index

About the Authors

Helen Taylor Greene is Professor of Administration of Justice in the Barbara Jordan–Mickey Leland School of Public Affairs (SPA) at Texas Southern University (TSU) and currently serves as Interim Associate Dean in the SPA. Earlier, she served as chair and graduate program director of the Department of Administration of Justice at TSU. She completed her BS in Sociology at Howard University, her MS in the Administration of Justice at American University, and both her MA in Political Science and PhD in Criminology at the University of Maryland, College Park. Areas of interest include race and crime, juvenile justice, and policing. She has authored, co-authored, and edited peer-reviewed articles and books and, most recently, served as lead editor for the *Encyclopedia of Race and Crime* (2009). In 2010, she received the Lifetime Achievement Award from the American Society of Criminology's Division on People of Color and Crime. Dr. Greene can be contacted at greeneht@tsu.edu.

Shaun L. Gabbidon is Distinguished Professor of Criminal Justice in the School of Public Affairs at Penn State Harrisburg. He earned his PhD in Criminology at Indiana University of Pennsylvania. Dr. Gabbidon has served as a fellow at Harvard University's W. E. B. Du Bois Institute for Afro-American Research and as an adjunct faculty member in the Center for Africana Studies at the University of Pennsylvania. His areas of interest include race and crime, private security, and criminology and criminal justice pedagogy. Professor Gabbidon is the author of more than 100 scholarly publications, including 12 books and more than 50 peer-reviewed articles. His most recent books include *Race, Ethnicity, Crime and Justice: An International Dilemma* (2009), *Criminological Perspectives on Race and Crime* (2nd edition) (2010), and *A Theory of African American Offending* (with James Unnever) (2011). He currently serves as the inaugural editor of the new Sage journal *Race and Justice: An International Journal.* Dr. Gabbidon can be contacted at slg13@psu.edu.